CHILDREN'S SOCIAL BEHAVIOR
Development, Assessment, and Modification

Children's Social Behavior
Development, Assessment, and Modification

Edited by

Phillip S. Strain
Mellon Evaluation Center for Children and Adolescents
Western Psychiatric Institute and Clinic
Pittsburgh, Pennsylvania

Michael J. Guralnick
The Nisonger Center
Ohio State University
Columbus, Ohio

Hill M. Walker
College of Education
University of Oregon
Eugene, Oregon

1986

ACADEMIC PRESS, INC.
Harcourt Brace Jovanovich, Publishers
Orlando   San Diego   New York   Austin
London   Montreal   Sydney   Tokyo   Toronto

ACADEMIC PRESS, INC.
Orlando, Florida 32887

United Kingdom Edition published by
ACADEMIC PRESS INC. (LONDON) LTD.
24–28 Oval Road, London NW1 7DX

LIBRARY OF CONGRESS CATALOGING-IN-PUBLICATION DATA
Main entry under title:

Children's social behavior.

    Includes index.
    1. Social skills in children.   2. Behavioral
assessment of children.   3. Social skills in children
—Therapeutic use.   I. Strain, Phillip S.   II. Guralnick,
Michael J.   III. Walker, Hill M.
BF723.S62C45   1986   155.4′18   85-26691
ISBN 0-12-673455-0 (alk. paper)

PRINTED IN THE UNITED STATES OF AMERICA

86 87 88 89   9 8 7 6 5 4 3 2 1

CONTENTS

PART II   ASSESSMENT OF CHILDREN'S SOCIAL BEHAVIOR

PART III   MODIFICATION OF CHILDREN'S SOCIAL BEHAVIOR

CONTRIBUTORS

Numbers in parentheses indicate the pages on which the authors' contributions begin.

Edward J. Barton[1] (331), Department of Psychology, Northern Michigan University, Marquette, Michigan 49855

Robert B. Cairns (3), Department of Psychology, The University of North Carolina at Chapel Hill, Chapel Hill, North Carolina 27514

Jean E. Dumas (49), Child Behavior Institute, University of Tennessee, Knoxville, Tennessee 37996

Frank M. Gresham (143), Department of Psychology, Louisiana State University, Baton Rouge, Louisiana 70803

Michael J. Guralnick (93), The Nisonger Center, Ohio State University, Columbus, Ohio 43210

Annette M. La Greca (181), Department of Psychology, University of Miami, Coral Gables, Florida 33124

Anthony Mannarino (373), Child Psychiatric Treatment Service, Western Psychiatric Institute and Clinic, Pittsburgh, Pennsylvania 15213

Scott R. McConnell (215), Early Childhood Research Institute, Western Psychiatric Institute and Clinic, Pittsburgh, Pennsylvania 15213

Larry Michelson (373), Child Psychiatric Treatment Service, Western Psychiatric Institute and Clinic, Pittsburgh, Pennsylvania 15213

Samuel L. Odom (215), Developmental Training Center, Indiana University, Bloomington, Indiana 47405

Pamela G. Osnes[2] (407), Department of Psychology, West Virginia University, Morgantown, West Virginia 26506

Patricia Stark (181), Department of Psychology, University of Miami, Coral Gables, Florida 33124

[1] Present address: ECLECON, Lakewood, Colorado 80228.

[2] Present address: The Florida Mental Health Institute, University of South Florida, Tampa, Florida 33612.

Trevor F. Stokes[3] (407), Department of Psychology, West Virginia University, Morgantown, West Virginia 26506

Phillip S. Strain (287), Mellon Evaluation Center for Children and Adolescents, Western Psychiatric Institute and Clinic, Pittsburgh, Pennsylvania 15213

Joseph M. Strayhorn (287), Mellon Evaluation Center for Children and Adolescents, Western Psychiatric Institute and Clinic, Pittsburgh, Pennsylvania 15213

Robert G. Wahler (49), Child Behavior Institute, University of Tennessee, Knoxville, Tennessee 37996

[3] Present address: The Florida Mental Health Institute, University of South Florida, Tampa, Florida 33612.

PREFACE

The increasingly complex nature of the developing child's social behavior has been the topic of theoretical formulations and empirical research for decades. Indeed the development of children's social behavior has drawn the interests of psychologists, educators, ethologists, anthropologists, psychiatrists, and sociologists alike.

In essence, the developmental study of children's social behavior has centered around three global themes, each of which is represented in the chapters on Development of Children's Social Behavior. The first theme represents what may be described as a search (both theoretically and empirically) for causal variables. The major question is, to what do we attribute the seeming universality of social behavior patterns and processes of influence? In the lead chapter by Dr. Robert Cairns we are provided with a comprehensive portrayal of biological and social variables that account for the very phenomena of concern in this volume. Additionally, Cairns offers the reader a careful analysis of the interdependence and interplay between biological and social forces on the child's developing social repertoire.

The second theme to dominate the developmental study of children's social behavior is the search for explanations for the remarkable stability of behavior across time and persons. Probably the most significant form of stability is that represented by intergenerational similarities in social behavior patterns. In the specific example of coercive interaction between parent and child, Wahler and Dumas provide a broad array of social learning mechanisms that may promote behavioral stability across generations.

A third area of intensive study has focused on variation in social behavior produced when children display general developmental deficits. Guralnick's chapter begins with a thorough account of the normal course of social development in the early years. Next, the reader is provided with an analysis of causative factors that influence peer interaction deficits in handicapped children. Guralnick also considers interactions between handicapped and nonhandicapped children in mainstreamed settings and the assessment and treatment implications that arise from such a context.

The assessment of children's social behavior is a multidimensional area of study that incorporates naturalistic or descriptive aims, efforts to discriminate those who may need some skill training, and evaluations of specific interventions. These broad aims of assessment are treated in each chapter in the Assessment of Children's Social Behavior section.

The combination of varying assessment goals and the practice of social behavior assessment by diverse disciplines has led to considerable controversy regarding the merits of specific assessment techniques. The range of methodology available to the social behavior researcher is summarized in the chapter by Gresham, who also suggests the principal uses for checklists, role plays, sociometric ratings, and direct observation.

By far the two most widely used methods of assessment are sociometric procedures and direct observation. La Greca and Stark provide the reader with a comprehensive review of the intricacies and issues surrounding the direct observation of children's social behavior. Their chapter examines the uses, advantages, and weaknesses of rate measures, qualitative measures, and sequential observation codes. The authors also address the influence of settings, development, and sex of interactors on naturalistic data.

In the chapter by McConnell and Odom we see that sociometric methods are quite diverse, often yielding data that bear minimal correspondence. These authors highlight the importance of multiple informants to accurate sociometric assessment and further argue for a multidimensional approach to assessment in which sociometric and nonsociometric indices are used collaboratively.

It has been approximately two decades since systematic attempts were begun to improve children's positive social interactions. Across this time span, many changes have taken place in the behavioral targets of intervention and in the nature of interventions. The chapters in the section on the Modification of Children's Social Behavior attempt to capture the spirit of these changes.

Early efforts to improve the social interactions of children largely ignored issues of target behavior selection. By and large, children's specific deficits dictated the focus of interaction. That is, if children did not greet others they were taught greeting skills, if they did not smile they were taught to smile, and so on. In this section's initial chapter, Strayhorn and Strain focus on the myriad issues associated with target behavior selection and the selection of intervention tactics. Specifically, these authors highlight the importance of (1) beginning intervention early, (2) selecting skills that are functional for children in designated settings, (3) selecting powerful interventions, and (4) utilizing indigenous treatment agents (e.g., parents and other children).

As interventions on specific social skills have proliferated, highly specialized literatures have emerged. Arguably the most active area of research within a specific skill domain concerns efforts to enhance sharing and cooperation between children. The relative emphasis on sharing and cooperation can likely be traced to developmental and long-term social goals that are mediated by the ability to engage in such behavior. The chapter by Barton describes both laboratory and applied interventions that have resulted in increased sharing among children.

The breadth of social behavior targets that have been treated successfully is evidenced well in the chapter by Michelson and Mannarino. These authors provide a broad panorama of the many target populations and specific social skills that have been studied. The contribution by Barton and that of Michelson and Mannarino highlight several recurrent trends within the social interaction arena. These trends include (1) the development of comprehensive, multicomponent intervention strategies; (2) the extension of social skill training efforts to more disabled groups of children; (3) the use of intervention procedures in increasingly complex naturalistic settings; and (4) the use of systematic procedures to enhance skill maintenance across time and generalization to new persons and settings.

The issues surrounding the where, when, and how of maintenance and generalization are elaborated more fully in the chapter by Stokes and Osnes. These authors provide both a historical perspective on this topic as well as new and promising tactics to promote maintenance and generalization of children's newly acquired social skills.

PHILLIP S. STRAIN

PART I

DEVELOPMENT OF CHILDREN'S SOCIAL BEHAVIOR

CHAPTER 1

A Contemporary Perspective on Social Development

Robert B. Cairns

INTRODUCTION

A distinguished attorney and his wife, now in their mid-50s and living in the Northeast, have puzzled for years on what they should have done differently in raising their children. The four offspring are now young adults who have encountered problems at every turn since adolescence. At one time or another, one or more have been suspended from high school, flunked out of college, court-martialed by the armed services, arrested for felonies, and spent most of their adult lives unemployed and without direction. Looking back, neither parent anticipated this outcome, and for good reason. The family was close-knit, and both parents were loving and caring. As infants and elementary school students, the children were healthy, competent, and happy. The parents, well-read and well-intended, followed the then-current psychological thinking in rearing their children. When problems arose, they sought and followed the advice of qualified clinical practitioners. Despite these advantages, the offspring, as young adults, have found it difficult to cope with the basic problems of living. The parents, still loving and caring, are nonetheless worried about what the future holds for themselves and their children.

Give or take a few details, this depiction could fit a large number of American families nowadays. It seems reasonable to expect that a developmental theory should be a pragmatically useful one. But it is at this

critical point that traditional models have failed. At a practical level, we
have few reliable guides on precisely what parents might do when their
children are 5 and 10 years of age in order to enhance their adjustment at
20 and 30 years of age.

In this chapter, some features of the contemporary perspective on
social development relevant to assessment and prediction are outlined.
Our problem here is to be faithful to the logic of the perspective without
getting lost in its abstractions. Accordingly I first highlight the seminal
ideas and theoretical assumptions, then raise some questions about their
implications.

First, it might help if I were to make some remarks on what the
perspective is all about, and why it emerged. It came about because the
empirical findings since the mid-1960's seem to have leaped ahead of the
theoretical ideas that inspired the study in the first place. Although
some support can be claimed for traditional social learning and psychoanalytic theories of social development, key assumptions of these
models of human behavior have been consistently contradicted by empirical data. A major overhaul of these approaches seemed needed,
moving toward a perspective that is more firmly grounded in scientific
research.

The contemporary perspective begins with the observation that human personality and social development reflect the operation of ongoing, dynamic processes from gestation to senescence. Accordingly, biological and social networks converge to form identifiable stages of social
development. In all stages, there is a strong, pervasive bias to form
social relations even though the support for this bias differs as a function
of the person's developmental stage. Precisely how the individual's social relations are organized within each stage depends on an integration
of social network and internal factors. Within this framework, the assumption that early experiences are necessarily fundamental to later
personality and social dispositions is rejected. Even though there are
strong supports for maintaining continuity in patterns of interchange,
developmental accommodations can occur at every developmental
stage.

In this chapter, I do not dwell in depth on the practical implications of
this approach for assessment, prediction, and change, although some
implications for psychopathology are noted. Further, this revised view
of social development suggests that much of the continuity in social
behavior, including the prediction of individual differences, arises in the
course of living. Hence the attention of the clinician and parent must be
given to the conditions in which development is likely to occur, including the expected trajectory of biological changes, the social network, and

the cognitive status of the child. By the same token, if enduring changes are to be produced, they must be concerned not only with early experiences but with later ones as well, including those that occur within the individual and within the social system beyond the family.

SOME COMMENTS ON HISTORY

The new perspective is something of a misnomer; the approach has been in the making since the 1930's, and its roots extend even further back. Over that period, the concerns of social and personality development extended beyond the boundaries of psychology in sociology, psychiatry, evolutionary biology, education, and criminology, among other disciplines. This diversification of interest and talent paid off. When a particular line of thinking or research in developmental or social psychology was abandoned, the exploration continued in other disciplines.

A couple of historical examples should illustrate the nature of the progress in the study of social ontogeny. For one, consider the fate of James Mark Baldwin's (1897) concepts of self organization and interactional dynamics. When his ideas on the social "dialectics of personal growth" proved too rich for Baldwin's contemporaries in psychology, they were taken up in sociology. This provided the impetus for the "symbolic interactionist" positions of Mead (1934), Cottrell (1942), and others. The concepts were assimilated into neo-Freudian approaches, including the interaction theory of Sullivan (1940) and Jackson (1968). The essential ideas re-entered developmental psychology, due in large measure to the work of Kohlberg (1969), Sears (1951), and their colleagues. The interactionist ideas now constitute one of the foundations for modern views of social–cognitive development (Damin & Hart, 1982).

Another illustration comes from attempts to resolve the relations between biology and social behavior, beginning with F. Galton's identification of the nature–nurture issue. The problems of the relations between bodily states and their genetic roots were temporarily shelved in experimental psychology in the 1930s and 1940s. Rather than being abandoned, the questions were taken up on other disciplines and other areas of psychology. On the one hand, the work of ethologists and population biologists extended evolutionary thinking of the determinants of social behavior. On the other hand, investigators in comparative–developmental psychology pursued the linkages between internal states, experience, and social behavior. These issues re-entered the mainstream of developmental psychology in the 1960s, and they now constitute a major concern for developmental writers.

These two examples do not exhaust the possibilities, of course. Over the recent past, there has been a migration of ideas and interest across seemingly disparate developmental areas. When enthusiasm for psychoanalytic theory waned in developmental psychology, some of the essential ideas were given new life by a wedding with ethological approaches by psychoanalyst John Bowlby (1958, 1969). The return of this model to developmental psychology in the form of "attachment theory" has been of great significance in guiding socialization research since the mid-1970s.

One outcome of this division of labor and synthesis of interests has been a rich yield in productive ideas. It has also created a new set of puzzles on how to link these approaches and ideas together. The task of finding common ground is no simple matter. Conceptual development in this area has diverged as often as it has converged, and each orientation has tended to generate its own distinctive model of social behavior and personality.

By the mid-1970s, five different approaches to social development vied for hegemony. Each approach took for its primary emphasis a different critical component of social behavior control (Cairns, 1979, Chapters 18–21). Which approach is most adequate? Therein lies a dilemma because each model may claim support, more or less. That is to say, each of the views may be seen as winning some measure of empirical confirmation in the available findings. This curious paradox follows from the fact that social behavior patterns in development are determined by a confederation of influences, not single factors taken alone. The collaboration among multiple internal and external factors—which is at the core of individual adaptation—permits multiple opportunities for statistically significant findings. Hence, empirical research on social development is embarrassed by riches, and some evidence may be marshalled in support of virtually every rational view of development.

But comprehensive explanations of social development have been as elusive as partial accounts have been abundant. It has become increasingly clear that the major problem of developmental research is not merely to identify whether or not a given factor has an effect, but to figure out *how* the factors are integrated with other ones in determining the quality of the child's social accommodations. Moreover, in the course of development, it seems reasonable to expect that the nature of the integration would change over time. For the neonate, the contributions of biological factors to close social relations would likely be different from those in the child or the adult. Similarly, the contributions of one's thoughts of oneself (i.e., the *self-system*) would differ across the person's life span in function as well as in content. Even the social network—that matrix of relationships in which persons are embedded—would likely wax and wane in the nature and strength of its influence from infancy to maturity to senescence. The problem of integration is a fundamental one for the science. Even if it were possible to accurately measure the separate components of social interchanges, they must somehow be fitted together to account for how particular persons deal with each other. Humpty Dumpty has to be put back together again.

The consideration brings us to the point of this chapter. A worthy goal for students of social development will be to achieve a better understanding of interpersonal integration, as it occurs in the several stages of human development and in the lives of individual children. The essential task turns out to be as much theoretical as it is empirical. Taking the wrong turn could lead to continued murkiness.

On this score, the American psychologist Cattell proposed in 1890 that the best way to assess intelligence was to identify the individual's status on several elementary functions (including perceptual discriminations, sensory tests, and the like). But Frenchmen Binet and Henri (1895) demurred. They pointed out that Cattell's strategy was based on the dubious assumption that one could recombine the elements of cognition so as to reconstruct the complex configurations of human intelligence. Binet and Henri suggested another alternative. Rather than tease apart the simple components and put them back together again, why not assess complex intelligence directly, even if the measures might appear at first blush to be less precise than those used for elementary sensory assessments? The Binet–Henri (1895) idea proved of course to be vastly superior to the Cattell–Galton method. But the French solution begged the theoretical question of how intellectual integration in development occurred, creating a conceptual vacuum that persists to the present (e.g., in controversies on the essential innate and environmental contributions to intelligence, and on the relative weight that they should be given).

The historical lessons for social development are both prescriptive and proscriptive. The prescription is methodological, concerning how the area should proceed in formulating techniques for predicting, assessing, and intervening in the social lives of children. Following the cognitive solution, it would seem that our best bet would be to aspire to assess the "whole child" in the interpersonal and contextual surrounds in which development occurs. The second, proscriptive, lesson concerns a theoretical step that could have been taken in the study of intelligence but was not. The unhappy legacy for students of cognitive development has been a near-century of controversy on the nature of intelligence test scores, how they are determined, and how stabilities and changes arise. To avoid a parallel problem in understanding the social accommodations of children, it seems important to focus conceptual attention on the processes of developmental integration, and how particular patterns are organized in the several stages of life. To this end, I outline in the remainder of this chapter some thoughts on the development of social interactions.

HOW INTERACTIONS DEVELOP AND FUNCTION

In tackling complex issues, it is sometimes helpful to clear the air by outlining one's assumptions. If the list is not too long and the assumptions are not too complex, they can be useful in re-examining old ideas and generating new ones. Given the fact that our traditional models of social development were generated mostly on clinical and personal insight, or were fanciful generalizations from studies of animal learning, it may seem surprising that they have proved so durable. Their survival seems to be due in part to the genius of the original theorists, and in part to the aforementioned multiplicity of personality and social behavior determinants. In any case, it is altogether fitting and proper for an area to use research findings generatively; to ask what the accumulated empirical findings of the past half-century have to tell us about the nature of interactional development that was not foreseen by the original theorists. The outcomes should permit us to revise or reject the ideas that have not held up in empirical studies. Moreover, those outcomes that are novel and unanticipated may be the most important of all, leading to fresh generalizations about the essential nature of developmental change and integration.

It is in the spirit of the last possibility that I present five assumptions that capture contemporary findings on how interactions develop, how interactions are organized, and how they function. I first "zoom out" for an overview, then "zoom in" to examine each assumption individually.

1. **The social acts of the person, the social network, and the ecology in which they occur reflect the outcomes of continuously developing processes.** All persons experience inevitable biological changes in structure and function over development. Depending on how thinly or thickly one slices the span of life, five major biophysical stages (or 15 substages) can be identified. They are predictable, systematic, and sequential in ontogeny. These stages are also roughly correlated with nor-

mative cognitive changes, ecological circumstances, and social themes. The correspondence across persons and across domains is strongest early in life, in accord with von Baer's Law (de Beer, 1958). However, social patterns are inevitably more open to outside influences than biological and cognitive ones, more variable in succession, and more likely to be reversed or extended in the course of living.

2. **Social patterns are appropriately viewed as one feature of an organized, biosocial system comprising biophysical, cognitive, social network, and ecological components. Hence, the social patterns of individuals reflect the operation and interplay of internal and external sources of influence.** For each person, every component subsystem must first be organized within itself, then with respect to the other components. In some functions, the component may be semi-autonomous (e.g., the special phenomena of unconsciousness in behavior reflect the necessary disengagement of cognitive self-systems from activities in everyday life). The bidirectional interplay among component systems varies as a function of the individual's developmental stage and the type of interchange activity. A corollary of the organizational proposal is that interchange patterns should not be divorced from the system and stage in which they are embedded.

3. **Human beings are biased to enter social interchanges at all stages of social development.** Persons are biased to form relationships; which is to say, to synchronize their responses with those of others and to reciprocally respond in interchanges. (The phenomena called "imitation," "modeling," and "social facilitation" represent these biases.) It is not assumed, however, that a single mechanism supports these biases across species and ontogenetic stages. There are developmental realignments of the processes by which this outcome is achieved. The corollary of this assumption is that children need not learn to be social. Rather, one problem of social development is to establish techniques to escape from synchronies of interchanges, especially coercive and destructive ones.

4. **Social patterns, once organized, become increasingly resistant to change with each uninterrupted recurrence.** There is an integrity to social behavior, and a conservatism in its organization. Paradoxically, the tendency for interchanges to be conserved is one of the reasons why they are changed in social settings, and why conflicts escalate.

5. **The direction that any given interchange will take—who gives in to whom—depends on the interplay between the activities involved, the developmental status of the participants, the roles of the participants, and the context in which the interchange occurs.** In general, the eventual direction that an interchange will take depends on which activ-

ity is the most persistent, unyielding, and readily meshed with the acts of the "other."

In skeletal form, the proposals hardly seem revolutionary. Taken singly, they are not. But in combination, the assumptions suggest an exceedingly powerful alternative to the traditional views of normal and deviant personality and social development. To illustrate the potential of the ideas requires some explication, a task to which I now turn.

DEVELOPMENT AND CHANGE

The first assumption is that *the social acts of a person and the social network in which they occur reflect the outcome of a continuously changing, developing process.* Over their life span, persons undergo predictable and inevitable biological changes: from conception and birth to childhood and adolescence; from adulthood and middle age to senescence and death. Major changes in their interactive behaviors are also inevitable, to the extent that social patterns parallel changes in morphological–developmental conditions. The shifts are not merely biological and behavioral. Persons also change in the ways that they think of themselves, think of other persons, and interpret the interactions in which they are jointly involved. Similarly, others with whom the person interacts themselves undergo inevitable biological and cognitive changes, as do the social networks in which they together participate. This is true of nuclear social units (such as the family, the mother–infant bond, and the husband–wife dyad) as well as of other, not-so-close relationships. Given the transformational nature of development, whatever stability is achieved must necessarily be of a dynamic sort. That is, continuity emerges *despite* the ongoing realignment of processes within and without the person. To explore this central point further, it should be noted that the issues of continuity and change are embedded in three of the controversies that confront the area. These include (1) whether there are stages of social development that parallel cognitive and biological stages, (2) whether it will be possible to accurately predict social patterns at maturity on the basis of early assessments, and (3) whether the effects of early experience are primary in determining the character and quality of later social adaptation. A brief comment on the implications of the developmental assumption for these three matters seems in order.

Are There Stages in Social Development?

Consider first the problem of stages in social interactions. Within a developmental framework, changes need not be willy-nilly. To the contrary, some of the most basic ontogenetic changes that affect human personality and social development are systematic, predictable, and sequential in nature. This point has been emphasized in the context of the stage-progressive nature of cognitive development (Piaget, 1952), the stages in the development of ideas of the self (Baldwin, 1897; Lewis & Brooks-Gunn, 1979), and stages in moral development (Kohlberg, 1969). For social behavior, it may be feasible not only to describe some universal stages of interaction but also to explore directly the biological mechanisms that seem implicated in their formation and transition. (The biological structures that underlie cognitive and moral changes have been more elusive.) By way of example, Rosenblatt and Lehrman (1963) have neatly tracked infant-produced changes in the biophysiology of the mother that predispose mothers toward maternal behaviors. In humans, changes in morphology associated with early and late maturation provide a convenient index for social classification and the resultant changes in interactional responding. Later in life, the changes associated with menopause in women and the sensorimotor capabilities of men provide another species-typical change in biophysical status and potential for behavior.

Given the universality of biological–cognitive changes and the interactional patterns that they support, it seems reasonable to expect that there should be some common behavior problems, some common interpersonal strategies, and some common social solutions that appear as a function of age. Moreover, these commonalities, if they exist, should transcend the interests and techniques of developmental psychology. Anything so basic to the human condition should have become a focal theme in literature and philosophy. So it has. The "ages of humans" have been defined in one way or another since the 16th century (see Reinert, 1979). Perhaps the best known description of social stages is that of William Shakespeare. His familiar account of human "exits" and "entrances" on the stage of life in As You Like It demonstrate both the pitfalls and the advantages of characterizing a person's social behavior solely on the basis of age. Most of us can resonate with the Shakesperian descriptions of the "mewling infant"; the "whining school-boy"; the "lover, sighing like a furnace"; the soldier "quick in quarrel"; the "justice, in fair round belly"; the "pantaloon, with spectacles on nose and pouch on side"; and finally, the "second childishness, and mere oblivion, sans teeth, sans eyes, sans taste, sans everything." Aging, in the 16th century, had little to offer.

Beyond poetry, one finds in the full span of life in human beings evidence for different capabilities, different tasks, and different outcomes of living. One finds also a clear progression in the kinds of biological conditions that obtain. They range from infantile dependence to pubescent sexuality to debilities in old age. The problems arise, however, when it is assumed that the interpersonal responses to these biological changes and interpersonal conditions are somehow uniform. Lifted from the context of great literature, the stereotypic descriptions of stages break down. Soldiering may indeed be an activity designed by old men for young ones, but a youthful zest for fighting and dying hardly seems universal (regardless of the stringency of governmental policies on the military draft). Moreover, it does seem only modestly justified to depict all men in late middle age as lascivious pantaloons, and all school-age boys as whining truants. But Shakespeare was brilliant in capturing at least part of the truth in social development. And insofar as the biological substrate for behavior is concerned, the physical–developmental sequences of the 16th century seem valid as a broad outline of development in the 20th century. Further, the underlying stages will probably remain descriptive of the human biophysical development in the 24th century, genetic engineering permitting.

But can we now go beyond literary insight in describing the social development of men and women? Perhaps, but there is no guarantee. Developmental and cross-cultural study indicates that the social behaviors and personal attributes assigned to particular stages are highly relative. Among other things, there is a bidirectional relation between the biological–cognitive status of the child and the social controls–expectations of the society. How species-typical changes are assimilated into a given societal framework determines what is a normal behavior pattern for any given stage. Beyond raising questions about the universality of the social behavioral–attitudinal changes that have been described in stage frameworks, modern developmental studies have provided insights on how social patterns are organized within stages, and how transitions are made between them.

To illustrate, consider prenatal development. This initial stage of social life historically has been omitted by both lay writers and developmental psychologists. In the embryonic phase, young organisms are typically "prepared" for birth and interactional patterns by virtue of a bidirectional relation between self-produced stimuli and maternal states. In the case of some species, the outcomes specifically tailor the fetus for neonatal survival and the early establishment of social relations (see Gottlieb, 1976).

Later in this chapter, I comment on parallel processes that occur later on, including the ubiquitous attachment phase in infancy, the peer network–identification phase in childhood through adolescence, and the parent–offspring relations at maturity. Nor are the bidirectional relations limited to the onset of social life. At the other end of the life span, persons in senescence exercise cognitive interpersonal and cognitive processes that prepare them to cope with the inevitable changes of aging (Mills & Cairns, 1982). Shakespeare notwithstanding, aging per se does not shut the door to social accomodation (Baltes, Reese, & Nesselroade, 1977).

In addition to biological contributors to the stages of life, there are societal-determined transitions that are no less important. In the United States, these modern rites of passage include entering elementary school, leaving home for college or the military, getting a driver's license, securing a full-time job that pays real money, attaining the age of mandatory retirement. Each of these changes in status and life circumstance can bring about multiple changes in patterns of interactional style and relations to others. As it turns out, these societal stages are roughly consonant with the stages derived on cognitive and biological grounds. Ironically, the societal stages may be more rigidly defined than biological and cognitive ones. Institutions rarely consider the vast differences among persons who are the same chronological age but who differ markedly in developmental status.

In the light of these considerations, it would seem hazardous to attempt to depict any rigidly defined pattern of relations between age and social behavior. But it remains the case that there are certain near-universal stages of biological development. Further, these biological stages are roughly (and sometimes precisely) linked with recurrent social themes. Considerable information has accumulated from the empirical studies of social development since the mid-1930s among persons in the five major epochs of life: infancy, childhood, adolescence, maturity, and senescence. Each of these five major stages can be divided into three substages. A preliminary sketch of the social themes and salient outcomes found in these five stages is given in Table 1. Table 1 illustrates representative life events in the U.S. in the 1980s; it is clearly not exhaustive.

Three comments should be made on the table and how it was constructed. First, the basis for classification was biological, not psychological. That is, the stages and substages depicted are neutral with respect to other stage descriptions, whether by psychoanalytic (Freudian), neo-analytic (Erikson–Sullivanian), or cognitive–developmental (Baldwin–Piagetian) theory. Hence the convergence with any of these well-known models should be welcomed as support for them, not predetermination. Also, the biological origins of the chart account for the need, for example, to separate males and females in late childhood and beyond. Although the two sexes are generally synchronized in biological development, the more rapid onset of puberty in girls and the relatively abrupt cessation of reproductive potential in women demand separate consideration.

Table 1
Social Ontogeny

Biological periods	Major biological events	Major cognitive/learning events	Major ecological events	Major interactive/ social characteristics
I. Infancy A. Prenatal	Primary organization of tissues, organs, and peripheral structures including sensory, hormonal, and neural systems; rapid expansion of neural and morphological structures	Onset of sensorimotor capabilities, including somatosensory, proprioceptive, chemical, auditory, and visual organization; organized reflexive responding	In womb, insulated in part by the placental barrier, but susceptible to various blood-borne substances, severe mechanical stimulation, and self-produced stimuli; some auditory stimulation is possible and receptive capabilities of the fetus are high in the periods immediately prior to birth	Bidirectional feedback in structure–function relations in organismic establishment; host–embryo feedback in hormonal and behavioral systems
B. Postnatal	Rapid development of sensorimotor coordinations; maturation of internal regulatory systems, including	Early sensorimotor stages, including stages of circular reaction. Engagement of attention to salient	Restricted physical capabilities for movement, highly dependent on the schedule of the caretakers for feeding,	Maternal–infant behavioral synchrony in nutritive intake, reduction of arousal, and eliminative functions:

14

	endothermia; coordination of reflexive actions; continued rapid growth of central nervous system, including brain development presumably associated with peripheral sensorimotor coordinations	stimuli, including acts of others; productive organization of biological relevant adaptive patterns. Unstable conditioning	physical movement, and stimulation; self-stimulation restricted in some societies by infant swaddling and in most societies by placement in crib, babycarriage, or other confining apparatus	rapid learning of rudimentary lessons of interchange, including anticipation and circular responses
C. Transition	Locomotion capabilities (crawling, toddling, walking), ingestion of solid foods; extension in range of emotional expression, including sympathy and anger, decrease in rate of growth of central nervous system structures, though still rapid relative to subsequent developmental stages	Later stages of sensorimotor period, including onset of goal-directed actions; stable conditioning phenomena; short-term retention and directed attention; onset of receptive and productive language skills; classification of symbols and concepts	Some freedom of movement under protected circumstances permitted, depending on the society and surroundings; various social persons available for caretaking and stimulation, depending on the participation of the child in group care or in individual homes	Onset of strong preferences in social and contextual events, including stranger awareness; onset of mutuality in responding in dyadic "games" of infancy's rapid recognition and classification of familiar persons and settings; class- and person-specificity in general reactivity patterns

(*continued*)

Table 1 (*Continued*)

Biological periods	Major biological events	Major cognitive/learning events	Major ecological events	Major interactive/ social characteristics
II. Childhood A. Early	Proficiency in locomotor coordination in running and climbing; sensory systems and interrelations established; continued integration of sensorimotor patterns in catching, drawing; ability to feed self and onset of self-care in elimination	Rudimentary memory strategies; conditioning phenomena readily established but transient; concepts of numeration at transient stage, and conservation (of quantity, quality) at early stage of conceptual development; follows symbolic commands after brief period of retention; ability to perceive discrepancies in actions of others and gross absurdities; can define simple words satisfactorily in terms of concrete properties or usage	Movement within a restricted environment, usually a group of peers and mixed sex (siblings, peers, and supervisor); often within the immediate confines of the home area, but can be transported to a preschool or other groupcare setting; continued close supervision by others (parents, caretakers, adult relatives, older siblings)	Beginning of strong reciprocity in interchanges (in matching–fitting–coordinating social acts); rapid development in synchronizing interactions with peers and movement toward predominant relations with peers; balance of interruptive interchanges shifts to coordinated ones movement from sensorimotor, nonverbal signals and communication to verbal communicative patterns; dominant dyadic patterns, as opposed to small group; onset of self-classification (in terms of gender, age, race) and other- and

B. School age	Continued fine-tuning of intersensorimotor coordination in sports, play, and childhood tasks (writing, drawing, movement in space); development of strength and speed in coordinations; sexual monomorphism in basic potential, but some gender differences in performance emerge	Continued development of memory skills in strategy selection; increasing facility in employing concrete classifications and distinctions, with movement toward abstract thinking; concepts of number, quantity, conservation now firmly established; reading and abstract information from simple paragraphs; respond to informational questions; self-orientation in environment, with planned searches and directions for behavior; specify similarities among members of same conceptual class	Multiple and distinct settings, including the home, neighborhood, and the school when mixed-sex groups are permissible under supervised control; presence of one or both parents usually in the home, but a wide range of options available depending on the subcultural system and familial standards	situational classification; diminution of overt maternal attachment phenomena; High levels of mutuality in responding, and high suggestibility to others; respond simultaneously to more than a single peer, but tend to react to dyad, identification of same-sex structure and place in it; self-system concept reasonably stable and independent of evaluations that are contradictory; strategies available to recruit others to ongoing activity; engagement in group activities, with increasingly less physical and ecological structure; reliance on verbal as opposed to physical strategies in interpersonal control

(continued)

Table 1 (*Continued*)

Biological periods	Major biological events	Major cognitive/learning events	Major ecological events	Major interactive/ social characteristics
C. Late	Continued growth in external structure, with distinctive features of individual; continued sensorimotor coordination and perfection of skills, with same parallel between physical/reactive skills of males and females, but differences in performance; nervous system growth slower relative to the peripheral rate of development	Transitional stage in conceptual thinking, with movement toward symbolic thinking and transformations; planning in cognitive tasks, including maze solutions and other search tasks; ability to reproduce complex geometric discriminations, and identify relations among disparate parts; memory strategies begin to take advantage of abstract classes	Similar to the above, except the children are typically given increasing mobility and independence in the peer groups that are formed and the contexts–settings that are visited; transition from elementary school to middle school provides less adult structure and greater peer direction	Group formation and identification of role in it, with some skill in manipulating others; self-systems continue in levels of organization, with assimilation of congruent information from experience and communications with others; continued reliance upon authority in guiding one's behavior, but becoming increasingly peer directed in standards; continued reciprocity and integration with ongoing patterns of others, and they with the subject

II. Adolescence
A. Early

In females, onset of pubertal changes that occur, on the average, 2 years prior to males; in females, onset of changes in physical structure and adaptation to cyclical hormonal patterns, with divergence in growth patterns; in males, marked variations in rate of physical changes in structure and strength; sharp increase in romantic concern in females and sexual interest in both sexes; onset of sexual dimorphism

Continued movement toward abstract reasoning in all adolescents, with few differences that match the sexual dimorphism in physical structure: evidence in enhanced conceptual definitions, abstract reasoning, similarities on basis of higher order properties; specification of abstract moral principles and aesthetic judgments; failure to link abstractions to everyday affairs and commonsense problems

Within most societies, adolescents permitted opportunities for movement and for purchases of substances heretofore forbidden; increasing independence from home environment and participation in extrafamilial settings and relations; dual sexual standards in freedom, with girls' typically more restricted

Employment of social group to achieve particular social ends; employ one of several strategies to protect self-organization from jeopardy or change; continued reliance on reciprocal forms of control and integration; continued susceptibility to others, but now focusing on peers as a basic mechanism of norm establishment; continued autonomy of self-assimilation of ideas, with realignment only with the more public information; continued unconsciousness (unawareness) of some of most salient interpersonal characteristics

(continued)

19

Table 1 (Continued)

Biological periods	Major biological events	Major cognitive/learning events	Major ecological events	Major interactive/social characteristics
B. Puberty	Period of most rapid change in physical appearance characteristics, for both males and females; attainment of basic physical characteristics that will be foundational through maturity in size, vocal range, and appearance. Continued stabilization of sexual dimorphism and secondary characteristics, with potential fertility in males and females. Increase in strength and coordination in males	Basic potential for abstract thinking attained; continued identification of abstract classes and specification of similarities among and within them; changing content of conceptual classes, with increased facility in manipulation as skills become available. Hence, increased performance on assessments of cognitive (intelligence) tests as a function of continued experience	Continued independence and freedom for males, with females under greater restriction; multiple settings for behavior, including those provided by older peers who have availability to transportation and access to alternative settings; increase in part-time employment, with possible option of school drop-out	Sharp delineation between strategies for same-sex and opposite sex relations along with norms, behaviors, goals, and outcomes; continued skill in engagement of others, and use of group to achieve particular outcomes; rigidification of social structures, and evolution of sub-group norms for behavior and mores; self-system continues to serve integration function from internal and external sources; formation of transient cross-sex liaisons for mutual support and gratification; continued integration with same-sex groups and familial system, which may lead to conflicts

| C. Late | Modest changes in stature and internal neural–biological states; highest levels of coordination of physical action systems to be attained in this period and next, including sensorimotor integration; maximal capabilities for reproduction being reached in males and females; stabilization of growth | No significant changes in cognitive capabilities beyond last stage. Increments reflect continued operation of two factors: modest increases in abstract capabilities and increments in conceptual tools, including classification systems, knowledge, and the integration of the two | Greater mobility (e.g., attainment of or to driving age in US permits adult-level mobility throughout environment), along with freedom for action in particular contexts; dual standard remains, but the differential standards for male and female begins to diminish; greater range of social and economic options become available | Divergence of interactional styles as a function of the social groups in which the individuals engage, with maintenance of basic interactive skills (reciprocity, synchrony, disengagement) from childhood; tendency to form sexual pairs of more enduring sort, with increase in mutual and complementary actions and attitudes; sharpening of sexual stereotypes and actual behaviors as a function of complementarity and dimorphism; continued employment of cognitive capabilities to enhance relations with group and individuals, and continued use of skills to inhibit, remove, and control others; despite increased cognitive abilities, modest relation between cognitive achievement and social skills |

(continued)

Table 1 (*Continued*)

Biological periods	Major biological events	Major cognitive/learning events	Major ecological events	Major interactive/social characteristics
IV. Maturity A. Early	By end of period, attain optimal childrearing condition in females and optimal physical strength and coordination in males; attainment of fully mature physical status of strength, perception, and integration of capabilities	Parallel with biophysical attainment, by end of the period, attain maximal capabilities in forming conceptual categories. Increase in skills in abstraction due to achievement of knowledge and information about other concepts; continued vulnerability to change in status of concepts and meaning; although basic potential remains virtually unchanged, continued rise in intellectual performance due to expanded lexicon of concepts and ideas	Removal from the familial home in most societies, typically early in this substage of life; characteristics of new setting covers wide range of possibilities, from own independent household to military service, college, etc., by the end of the substage	Propensity to form enduring relations in terms of sexual–social goals, and increase in the contribution of partner to direction of social behavior; if children, new roles required and responsibilities for immediate care and constraint on life patterns; continued dissocation from earlier groups, including familial structure; commonality of behavior and reciprocity in action with newly formed social groups

B. Childrearing	Continued at asymptotic level in reproductive capabilities and physical skills–coordinations. Modest reduction in skill and vigor toward the end of the phase, with linearly increasing risk in reproduction, though basically safe; no significant reductions in perceptual–sensory capabilities	Same as the preceding period, with no immediate effect of slight diminution in sensory and perceptual skills. Intellectual performance paradoxically can continue to increase, with no change in the ability for the formation of abstract concepts; relatively independent of simple sensory skills	Multiple contexts, depending on the society and the role adopted by the person; economic responsibilities interact with job setting and quality of home environment along with number of dependents	Same as the preceding period, but with successive changes in lifestyle and responsibility if children present and growing; necessary accommodations within own behavior and family structure to deal with reactivities of young and continuously changing roles with respect to parents; if no family, continued performance of social patterns characteristic of late-adolescent/early adult phase, with maintenance of similar frames and social networks. In family structures, roles of male and female sharply defined consistent with social assignments

(continued)

Table 1 (*Continued*)

Biological periods	Major biological events	Major cognitive/learning events	Major ecological events	Major interactive/social characteristics
C. Late	Onset of irreversible changes in reproductive capabilities, psychobiological vigor, sensorimotor capabilities and coordination; by the end of subperiod, substantial decrements in vision, hearing, coordination, and physiological reactivity observed, with increasing risk in childbearing in females	Few changes in ability for abstract reasoning, and some modest increments despite sensorimotor unraveling; onset of short-term memory changes, along with a modest decrement in speed of computational thinking; continued capability for making changes in content of abstract categories, and reformulating ideas into new contexts and relations	Same as before, with only modest changes in basic circumstances depending on the society and the nature of the individual's performance	Shifts in social interchanges to accommodate biological–social–cognitive changes in offspring, and changes in own biological conditions (including reduction in vigor, sexual and otherwise, sensorimotor capabilities, etc.); self-systems continue to be generally responsive to changes, but insulated by own autonomy; roles of males and females beginning to converge, along with social and physical capabilities

V. Senescence A. Early	Beyond childbearing age in females; continued reduction in physical vigor, strength, and coordination in both sexes; irreversible onset can be lessened by compensatory activities and biochemical (hormonal) injections; biophysiological characteristics are undergoing permanent changes designed for a lower level of activity and interactive movement	Beginning onset of slower intellectual functions, although abstractive thinking remains at previous level; as in physical realm, compensatory activity can mask changes that occur, and keep level of performance at near asymptotic levels, despite demonstrative changes in rapidity and accuracy of immediate recall; continued changes in cognitive classificatory ability, although some indication for less flexibility in categorization and reassignment	Same as above, with living circumstances better or worse depending on the person's reliance on physical labor and skills in economy, and the societal responsibility for older persons; difficulty in job changes and relocation because of age discrimination	Significant change in status of familial relations with departure of young from home, with convergence of male and female roles; decrements in sexual and physical vigor lead to concomitant changes in social style and relations, with greater flexibility in social expression; social network becomes in most instances highly stable, with increasingly less mobility and activity; concepts of other-system and self-system are themselves increasingly difficult to change

(continued)

Table 1 (*Continued*)

Biological periods	Major biological events	Major cognitive/learning events	Major ecological events	Major interactive/ social characteristics
B. Retirement	Stabilization of sensorimotor changes of senescence, with slower rate of decrement in function in most systems (e.g., vision, hearing, activity); less likely to compensate for reduction through biochemical or functional activities; male and female aging rate now reversed, with males showing most rapid effects of aging process	Some decrement in abstraction skills, although the decrement in ability for sustained thought over short-term periods is relatively modest; intellectual performance can in the "crystallized" areas almost match that of earlier stages, but "fluid" performance shows a decrement that corresponds to biological changes; increasing rigidity of categorical thinking, with greater difficulty in making shifts across concepts and within categories	Restricted opportunities for movement, with removal from work force and the failure to the person to qualify for other alternative positions; fewer settings to adapt to, or to maintain different roles for; greater salience of informal clusters and groups of same-age peers	Stabilization of social patterns to the extent possible because of changes in social role and economic status; highly variable outcomes possible, due to dependence on nature of social system and reaction to the aged; male and female roles mostly a matter of form and society, with few psychobiological supports for differentiation of social function; self-concepts become increasingly rigid and increasingly removed from disconfirming information

| C. Late | Unraveling of key biological systems can account for severe dysfunctions in activity, although the decrements are not necessarily uniform, possible severe impairment of basic sensorimotor functions; some significant areas of strength and coordination remain in most persons though very aged | Though the sensory and perceptual capabilities become impaired, the connection to thinking and consciousness is not a direct one; though diminished in terms of fluidity of abstract thinking, the mental processes can remain accommodative and adaptive to the end of the life span; cognitive functions appear to be buffered from linear degeneration, save in cases of demonstrative brain disease | Typically constrained to severely limited conditions, dependent upon the activities of others, not unlike the severe restrictions on mobility and locomotion that prevailed in the early stages of life; however, vast individual differences in ability to maintain autonomy until death | Interactive styles directly reflect and affect other areas of organismic adaptation; role of the aged is highly dependent upon societal, cultural, and familial constraints; persistence of self- and other-concepts depends on the constraints of the surrounds, although there is a concomitant diminished flexibility in attributions to self and others; continued carryover of interactive styles remain, along with reciprocity and mutuality of responsiveness |

The second comment concerns the ordering of the stages. Again, the basis for Table 1 was clearly age-biological as opposed to psychological. Accordingly, it is expected that the age changes in biological structure are sequential in appearance, invariant in succession, and irreversible in structure. But not in social behavior patterns. Even though the social patterns (or the themes they depict) are gratifyingly predictable (i.e., the synchrony of early infancy, the attachment of mid-infancy, the reciprocity of early childhood, the sexual expressions of adolescence), they are more likely to be cumulative than successive. Social patterns are inevitably more open than organic ones in sequence, more variable in succession, and more likely to be reversed or modified in the course of living.

The third comment on Table 1 concerns the linkages between the salient interactive themes and processes and the biological-cognitive stages with which they are associated. In general, the younger the child (i.e., the earlier the stage), the more likely it is that the social process that is indicated will be found in the designated stage. The reason is that behavioral–biological linkages in the social behavior of human beings are most pervasive in young organisms. Some possible reasons for this linkage between age and social behavior–biology is discussed here later. Overall, the social processes are more likely to be cumulative than they are discrete, in that techniques and patterns that are established at an earlier age can typically be called on in subsequent stages of development.

Individual Difference Prediction

Now consider the problem of individual difference prediction, as opposed to the prediction of developmental stages. Within a dynamic, developmental framework, where intraindividual and social change is inevitable, how is it that individual difference predictability over time becomes possible? The problem is a nuclear one for developmental psychology. The idea that there are strong continuities in personality and social behavior from childhood to maturity has been widely accepted as axiomatic. For many investigators, individual difference continuity is a self-evident axiom that provides the essential foundation for developmental study. That is sufficient ground to be wary. There are also empirical grounds. Critical analyses of the continuity of significant interactional dispositions over the life span of humans have yielded mixed returns.

The stability of aggressiveness is a case in point. Depending on the review cited, one can conclude that there is considerable individual stability in aggressive patterns (Olweus, 1979), moderate stability in males but little in females (Moss & Susman, 1980), or that "we still know very little about the transition from criminal and noncriminal careers in adolescence and young adulthood to adult criminality" (Cline, 1980, p. 669). As it turns out, there is greater agreement on the matter than appears at first blush (Cairns & Hood, 1983).

One of the problems in achieving strong and consistent predictive relationships across studies is that much of the variance among individuals is not *in* the child at the time of the first test. Rather, significant determinants of interpersonal accommodation are in the child's social network, in the developmental context, and in the physical environment during development and at the time of the criterion assessment. Hence, the key to better individual difference prediction is not only better tests of the child's status at the time of the initial test, but better evaluations beyond the child and beyond the initial assessment.

Accordingly, for more powerful predictions, explicit attention should be given to the expected conditions in which developmental changes will be embedded: the likely social network, the likely social ecology, and the biophysiological changes that are likely to take place, and their likely impact on social interactions. Assessments of the child, divorced in space and time from the anticipated (or actual) social/ecological context of development, can only tell part of the story. It follows that competent childrearing should prepare the child not only for childhood but also for the conditions to which the child will subsequently adapt. On this score, the empirical literature of the past half-century indicates that much of the stuff out of which interpersonal consistencies arise comes about in the course of living.

But is there not a conflict between the two kinds of developmental continuities—the sequential invariance of interpersonal stages, on the one hand, and the variable levels of individual difference prediction, on the other? Not necessarily. The kinds of interactional competencies required at one stage of development may not necessarily be of import in subsequent stages. Elsewhere it has been pointed out that much of what the very young organism in the prenatal and postnatal stage absorbs from the social environment is transient and relevant primarily for the infant's immediate adaptation (Cairns, 1972, 1976; Sameroff, 1975). Indeed, if the social behaviors of infants and small children were fixed, profound difficulties would be encountered in later developmental stages.

Notwithstanding strongly held beliefs to the contrary, young infants are ill-equipped to retain the lessons of the early postnatal period, and for good reason. The infants' needs change rapidly and drastically, and so do the actions required of them. Given the delicate time-course of survival, adaptations in infancy should be rapid, ephemeral, and highly flexible within the limits of the biological equipment that is available. Hence the fickleness of very early social responsiveness, the rapidity of new attachment formation, and the reversibility of relationships. But as life proceeds and the patterns of internal and external conditions stabilize, there is great advantage to interpersonal and relational conservation.

Early Social Experience: Ephemeral or Enduring?

I turn now to a consideration of the idea that first in occurrence is first in importance in social development. The primacy hypothesis and the issues surrounding it have been discussed at length in the literature (see, for instance, Ainsworth, 1972; Brim & Kagan, 1980; Cairns, 1972, 1977, 1979; Clarke & Clarke, 1976; Klaus & Kennell, 1976; Sameroff, 1975). Suffice it to say that the primacy hypothesis remains the dominant hypothesis in the area, despite conflicting evidence with regard to its validity.

The developmental resolution permits both primacy and recency. Which outcome is expected depends on how the social response pattern is organized and the mechanisms by which it is supported. There is, for instance, irrefutable evidence that the effects of very early experience on song-learning in some species fits the primacy hypothesis rather neatly (Immelmann & Suomi, 1981). Further, the social and sexual preferences of some altricial birds (i.e., the zebra finch) are firmly set in the first 30 days of life, prior to the departure of the parental caretakers. Although the neural/biochemical mechanisms underlying these outcomes have yet to be identified, it seems likely that they are mediated by changes in the biophysiology of the organisms that transcend the usual association learning processes. Indeed, as Henderson (1980) documented in a masterful review of the early-experience literature, the effects of experience that are most likely to have enduring effects are those that produce identifiable biological changes. This would occur, for instance, in the early masculinizing effects of a female fetus being in contact with a male fetus (through testosterone transfer). Or the effects of early isolation or stress could produce enduring changes in ACTH production or inhibition.

Considerably less evidence is available on the enduring effects of social stimulation that is mediated by psychological (i.e., learning, memory) processes. Indeed, in the case of early interactional patterns, the preponderant evidence indicates that there are remarkable shifts among individuals and within individuals in intensity, focus, and form of the interchanges.

Another example may help clarify the point. Social attachment refers to the intense psychological bond (or bonds) that occur in the infancy of young mammals, including babies. (The bond typically involves the infant's mother, but it could be an aunt, father, sibling, caretaker, or an inanimate object, such as a favorite blanket or TV set.) Research on the matter shows that this phenomenon has a predictable time-course over ontogeny, regardless of the social structure of the society and of the family. The onset, maintenance, and diminution are correlated with biological conditions of the mother and of the infant. These conditions also show a predictable time-course and change over the course of ontogeny. As the biological subsystems change to give rise to the attachment bond, so do its manifestations. One important debate in the current literature concerns the next step: whether the attachment with the mother is somehow transformed to affect peer relations, or whether new relations arise.

Development is not simply a property of the embryo and neonate and child. As Baltes, Reese, and Nesselroade (1977) point out, there is development through the life span of human beings. On this count, developmental changes in senescence can produce differences in interchanges for precisely the same reasons that biological and cognitive changes in early life are effective in restructuring relationships. While this continuing accommodation of the person to changes in internal and external states is the hallmark of social adaptation, it generates obvious problems for those who aspire to "write biographies in advance" (James, 1890).

ORGANIZATION OF SOCIAL PATTERNS

It is proposed that *the social behaviors of each individual are organized simultaneously with respect to internal and external sources of influence*. This assumption, seemingly empty of content and controversy, has plenty of both. The key terms in the proposal are *organized*, and *internal and external sources of influence*. Some comment on these terms should help clarify its implications.

The concept of *organization* implies mutuality of influence, and some level of bidirectional control among the subsystems that make up the whole. Among other things, this means that changes in one part of the organismic system are likely to bring about changes in other parts, and vice versa. What are the subsystems? According to the preceding assumption, they are both under the skin and outside the organism. The several parts of the organism are organized within themselves and with respect to each other, a kind of balancing act requiring that some things are necessarily more fundamental than others. In general, the organizational assumption must hold that primary priority is for within-component organization, and in successive steps, integration with other components.

For convenience, it is useful to consider the internal influences to be of the two major sorts: biological patterns and cognitive patterns. But this breakdown is still a pretty crude one. Subsumed in the biloogical subsystem are such diverse factors as genetic control, hormonal secretions, rate of maturation, and acute and chronic states of emotion and arousal. These biological subsystems contribute in diverse ways to the direction and control of interchanges among persons. By the same token, the social system and the interchanges that it promotes feed back to influence the biological stages of the individual. The organizational assumption in this context implies a bidirectional influence between the biological states and the social interchanges that occur. Taken in conjunction with our earlier discussion of social stages, we might expect that this bidirectionality will take different forms—and be given different weight—as a function of the age-developmental status of the interactants. For instance, the neurological–hormonal supports for the mother-infant relationship are different in the early postnatal phase than they are in the late infancy phase. In childhood, it's a different story again.

For human social development, changes in the cognitive system must include thoughts of one's self (the self-system) as well as thoughts of others (the other-system). These cognitive constructions, like other internal systems, serve multiple functions. They are organized within themselves as well as with each other and across the broader picture of organismic adaptation. This wheels-within-wheels scheme, complicated in the abstract, is both necessary and quite workable at the individual level. The temptation in the past has been to prematurely simplify a truly elegant plan. Though the integration rules may be parsimonious, they are not intuitively obvious.

Consider, for instance, the popular and plausible concept of the "looking-glass self." In contrast with Cooley's formulation, recent empirical studies indicate that children's self-systems are not mere reflections of the views that others have of them. Nor should they be. The semi-autonomy of the self-system, whereby its functions within the organismic system are served, may transcend mere agreement with the consensual judgments of peers. One's thoughts of oneself need not be veridical in order to be serviceable. (Cairns & Cairns, 1981, 1986).

The highest priority should be given to internal balance, as has been argued by F. Heider, L. Festinger and others. Hence in some domains, one would expect an optimal discrepancy between one's self-thoughts and the objective circumstances of life. This was the case, for example, in the tendency of elderly black women to view themselves as happy and satisfied with their lives in center-city Washington, D.C. (Mills & Cairns, 1982).

For the self-system to serve multiple needs, it is not necessary for the attributions of others to determine concepts of the self. Indeed, it can be highly adaptive if the self-concepts include a buffer against disequilibrium and disorganization. This conclusion is of course not unlike that reached by S. Freud in the discussion of ego functions, and labeled by A. Freud as "defense mechanisms." In the present view, the discrepancies between the self-system and other features of the objective world, *if optimal*, would preserve the coherence of the self while providing a sufficiently valid picture of the social–ecological world to facilitate accommodations to it. Hence the processes might be better described as "constructive" or "generative" instead of defensive. This generation-assimilation is a productive activity, not a semipathological one.

While I am on the topic of the relations among subsystems, I should also point out that the same principle of semi-autonomy applies to the problem of acts that are *unconscious*, or outside the immediate awareness of the person. From the present perspective, *most* of one's behaviors (internal and external) are outside immediate cognitive supervision, and for good reason. As remarkable as the human brain may be, it has limits. These include restrictions on attention span, information channels available at any one instant in time, and memory storage.

Most important for the problem of unconscious processes are those of interpersonal significance. Embedded in my styles of action and counteraction in relationships are patterns that extend not only beyond my own awareness but also beyond the awareness of those with whom I deal most intimately. Unconsciousness is not only a property of the self. Others, too, respond unconsciously (i.e., with minimal awareness) to my acts. We all habituate our actions and attitudes, and may be unaware of them. But all unawareness is not mere happenstance. Many of society's courtesies and graces seem designed to conceal a direct expression of meaning or evaluation. This propensity—which serves to maintain relations and ongoing patterns—fits nicely with the tendency of persons to assimilate information that is consistent with the existing structure of the self-system. The social conspiracy in which we all participate is not necessarily a bad thing. To the extent that each of our self-systems is helped to come to terms with otherwise irreconcilable dilemmas by such unawareness, the purposes of everyday social deceptions will have been served. Not all the interpersonal games we play are without function or without productive returns. But some are, to be sure; a point that I comment on subsequently.

Turning now to the external sources of control, we might ask what kinds of outside influences contribute to the organization of the behavior of the individual. Again, we can for convenience dichotomize the patterns of influences into two components: interpersonal systems and ecological systems. Interpersonal influences include the dyadic actions of others as well as the social network in which they are embedded. This assumption captures the Baldwinian view that each child's behavior is embedded in a social matrix, and that each of us is in part someone else, even in our own thoughts of ourselves (Baldwin, 1897). Perhaps the most salient feature of social influences is the fact that others may also be characterized by organized social patterns. This brings us to the central problem of social adaptation: Who shall accommodate to whom? I return to the matter shortly.

The role of the physical environment in determining momentary and long-term social adaptations has concerned theories as diverse as Lewin's (1931) topographical psychology and Crook's (1970) social ecology. The supportive properties of the physical environment do bias which social responses can emerge, when they will emerge, and how social patterns will become assimilated into the broader social structure. This process may be seen as a kind of natural selection in ontogeny. This version of the Wallace–Darwin principle may prove to be as critical for understanding developmental accomodations as the original statement was in comprehending evolutionary adaptations. In any case, the ways in which the child's environment is arranged from infancy onward contribute significantly to the nature of the social patterns that are generated.

To sum up, the organizational assumption implies that there must be, first, coordination within component systems of the person, and second, coordination between them. One corollary of this assumption is that a social "act" or "pattern" cannot be divorced from the system in which it is embedded if one aspires to gain more than a superficial understanding of its determinants and likelihood for continuity.

INTERPERSONAL BIAS

Now it is time to discuss what may appear to be a more debatable assumption—that *human beings are biased to enter social interchanges at all stages of social development.* That is to say, *persons are biased to approach others: to form relationships, to synchronize responses with those of others, to reciprocally respond to others, and to elicit responses from them.* As it turns out, the statement is hardly speculative. It has been overwhelmingly supported by the empirical evidence in animals and humans of the past half-century.

For instance, the ubiquity of the empirical phenomenon of social attachment in infancy is one reflection of the species-typical bias. In all cultures studied, the attachment onset begins about the time that the infant is capable of locomotion, and it begins to diminish at roughly the developmental stage when the infant is capable of finding nonlactational forms of nourishment.

What is the source of this interpersonal bias? Consistent with our preceding discussion, we should expect that different mechanisms may be implicated as primary, dependent on the developmental stage in which the bias is observed. For instance, the early postnatal interchanges seem to be strongly supported by the biochemical states of the mother (or mother-surrogate) and neurological–sensorimotor capabilities of the infant. Accordingly, the synchrony is due in large measure to the mother's enchaining her actions to those of the infant, and the infant's programmatic responses being neatly coordinated with the capabilities of the mother. The momentary adjustments in the relationship are made by the more flexible and adaptive member of the dyad (who also happens to be the older and more capable one). In addition, the mother remains the one who arranges the caretaking environment, including schedules for feeding, binding in cribs, cradles, or swaddling clothes, and the nature and quantity of the infant's nourishment. If these environmental constraints and supports are maintained, they become the conditions to which the child must eventually accommodate.

In the second half of the infant's first year of life, the mechanisms that support social responsiveness have shifted. With the maturation of the sensory systems involved in the infant's distal perception, including vision and hearing, the more salient, reactive, and reciprocally dependent stimuli in the setting become the bases for its attention engagement. Hence "others" become for the infant a source of attention, attraction, and fear. They also provide the manipulanda and discrimination, along with self-produced stimuli, around which most of its activities become organized. Some time ago, I proposed that these events provided the bases for the onset of social attachment (Cairns, 1966). As some of the strong biological supports for interpersonal bias diminish, cognitive, motor, and attentional supports (i.e., psychological processes) take over.

With the onset of the informational processing abilities required for the coordination of one's self actions to those of others, the familiar phenomena of reciprocity and imitation emerge. Hence, the development of the games of peek-a-boo, pat-a-cake, and other ritualized interchanges of infancy and early childhood that prove a delight to the mother and infant. Delight? Obviously any statement of interactional development that omits the integration of ongoing emotional involvement would miss a significant component of the accommodation. In this instance, the preparatory bodily states are coordinated with the action, in an emerging circular reaction of organization.

Beyond the interpersonal bias in infancy, there is strong evidence for the propensity to form relationships of all sorts throughout the remaining stages of childhood, adolescence, adulthood, and senescence. These relationships extend from those of an ephemeral sort to the close relationships of life, whether with a spouse, child, pet, priest, or therapist. These relationships, too, are characterized by distinctive biological and/ or psychological mechanisms, some of which are shared across stages. On this matter, I must agree with the sociobiological theorists (e.g., Hamilton, 1964; Wilson, 1975) who have argued that there are evolutionary biases toward socialness, integration, and altruism. (Where we part company is the expectation that this bias may be reduced to a single process across the phyla and across the life span of the person.) As the organizational ground rules change over the course of development, there is in human beings a realignment of the processes by which the outcomes are achieved. In infancy, biological contributions dominate, but social processes contribute to what is learned. In childhood, interchange processes take the lead in providing the basis for organization of relationships. With the resurgence of biological–emotional salience at puberty, a new basis for alliances, attraction, and attachment comes to the fore, combined with the social interchange processes of the earlier stages.

One corollary of this assumption is that "others" may be a major force in the behavioral organization of individuals, no less basic than internal features. In this light, the actions of others and the social network should be viewed to be as primary as internal features in promoting response organization. The traditional distinction between internal primary drives and external secondary ones in the organization of behavior becomes meaningless. For behavior coherence, the social system is on the same footing as other internal biological systems.

A second corollary on the interrelations among action, thoughts, and emotions deserves comment. Combining the organizational assumption with that of interpersonal bias, one would expect some synchrony between the cognitive and emotional states of children and their behavior patterns at all stages. To the extent that interactions are mutually supportive as opposed to disruptive, the ideational states (and emotional tone) associated with the interaction should be also organized, and positive in tone. Propinquity and interchange does not require the individuals to like one another, but it should promote the emotion. Conversely, liking could bring about propinquity. In the more-intense activities, or ideas corresponding to those activities, the emotional states generated presumably would be consistent with the individual's acts or his/her perceptions of those acts. Passion, even lust, arises in the thoughts of anticipated action. Dissociations between thought, behavior, and emotions can occur when interactions are rebuffed, or when the thoughts that one has of another are not reciprocated or perceived as being reciprocated.

Finally, I should note that the bias to interact with others does not ensure that the interaction will be a happy one. Even when two persons are synchronized in their mutual behaviors, the synchrony can rapidly lead to mutual unhappiness and harm. This state of affairs occurs when a hurtful or punitive act is reciprocated by another hurtful, punitive act designed to inhibit the first one. If each successive attempt to inhibit is more intense than the immediately preceding one, there will be an escalation of aggressive behaviors. The angry words of the husband that produce a counterresponse in the wife would be an instance of reciprocity of a negative, escalatory sort. If the emotional states of the dyad become matched, the exchange can win additional internal supports. A mere shift in behavior strategy by one or the other person may be insufficient to extinguish the conflict. The forces supporting it may literally be out of the control of either member of the pair. Patterson (1979) has proposed that such recurrent coercive episodes underlie much of the unhappy acting out behavior in the families of aggressive children.

A consideration of the forces by which patterns of interchange are stabilized brings us to the fourth assumption, one concerned with the conservation of social behaviors.

SOCIAL INERTIA: THE CONSERVATION OF SOCIAL PATTERNS

Social patterns, once organized, become increasingly resistant to change with each uninterrupted recurrence. This assumption is consistent with the general proposition that the interrelations among parts of a system contribute to its stability, coherence, and direction. Depending on the action pattern, the resistance may arise from the consolidation of the biological substrate, from cognitive components (the self-system and the other-system), from social learning, or from social network factors. All this is to say that there is an integrity to behavior, and a conservatism in its organization. This propensity to endure and resist modification is onto-genetically useful on several counts. Among other things, it serves to ensure that adaptive patterns will be preserved over time. It also has interpersonal payoffs, in that it provides a basis for helping others to predict and respond appropriately to the child.

How is social inertia achieved? As might be expected by our discussion of the interactional–developmental perspective up to this point, the bases are multiple, not unitary. Consider, for instance, the role of the social interactive system. To the extent that each member of an interchange becomes proficient in an interactive script, the behaviors of the others are constrained. In recurrent relations, persons tend to fulfill their habitual assignments—to complete the theme— and thereby support and maintain the acts of others. (Another return to the Shakespearian stage of life, in which "all the men and women are players.") To a significant extent, the roles are self-generated. Once established, the force of the interchange, and the social system, may be compelling and unyielding. For instance, the social structure of a classroom in junior high school, once defined, has a permanence that transcends the identity of its individual members (Cairns & Cairns, 1986).

Other contributors to the social inertia are internal. For instance, the thoughts of onself or others can support choices and actions that serve to maintain continuity in relations. Similarly, the feelings and emotions of the person toward another person or place can contribute to the durability of the relations, despite a sharp disparity in actions. Over time, the loose coordination of actions with thought and feelings can provide a formidable obstacle to immediate change or variation. When these internal systems are combined with a reasonably stable social network and physical ecology, there should be ample grounds for the observed inertia in interchange pattern and style.

By the same token, shifts in these contributors to stability of behavior can bring about changes in the patterns themselves. Which subsystems and which interchange patterns? The answer requires the examination of the main supports for the particular behavior, which in turn depends on the stage of development of the interactants and on the primary contributors to the stability of the pattern. In the case of infantile attachment, for instance, changes in the sensorimotor capabilities of the child, in the stabilization of hormonal–biochemical states associated with emotional expression, and in the social network that prevails ensures that there will be a qualitative change in the intensity of the child's reaction to separation.

In adolescence, a different combination of inertial factors may prevail in, say, the involvement with others in a deviant subgroup. Here the supports may also be multiple. Depending on the group, they may include a shared alcohol dependence, an alienation from the acceptable groups in school, a tight social integration in the performance of night-time activities, and shared ideas about themselves, their parents, and their peers. Change in this instance may be considerably more difficult, in that there are fewer inevitable internal developmental shifts that might be expected. Nonetheless, marked changes in any of the primary supports for the behavior—or the entire combination of them—are likely to produce modifications in interactive patterns. The specific na-ture of the therapy would depend on the peculiar skills and capabilities of the adolescent, and the intractability of the adolescent's involvement with the now-extant system. The prescription for change thus depends on a careful analysis of the multiple levels of supports for the present pattern, and the alternative networks that are available. Under most conditions, change will not be easy to impose but it should always be possible.

Now let's return to the level of individual dyads, and what happens when one person interferes with the ongoing behavior of another. In the case of young children, disruption of one child's highly organized pat-tern by a peer, with no other activity to take its place, can lead to one of several outcomes. The child can leave the context, switch to some other activity, or join the enemy (i.e., fit into the behavior defined by the other person). In any case, the immediate effect of disruption is to produce some level of disorganization in both the response pattern and the sub-systems of the individual that are involved in its support. Among others things, as Mandler (1964) has argued, there is a concomitant emotional disorganization or arousal typically associated with the disruption. Selye (1974) has proposed that one function of such arousal is to prepare the individual to adapt to challenge, either through fighting or fleeing. At its core, the general adaptation syndrome presupposes an intimate relation between the behavioral and emotional subsystems in the organism.

But there are problems that social inertia produces. Ironically, the tendency for interchanges to be conserved is one of the reasons that they are changed, and that persons are disposed toward conflict, aggression, and hatred. Change of some sort inevitably arises when two highly organized but incompatible response patterns make contact. To the ex-tent that each resists reorganization, some level of interruption is likely to occur, all other factors equal. Given the opportunities for material disruption, and the skills persons have available to disrupt the behavior of others, it may seem remarkable that we experience so few interper-sonal conflicts. This outcome seems to follow because in most instances of potential conflict, all factors are *not* equal. Persons differ in roles, activities differ in integration, and most social settings and conventions are designed to curb disruptive conflicts. The delineation of roles in relationships, and the implicit acceptance of these roles, is one of the social devices that diminish conflict. Roles in this sense may be seen as socially established and mutually accepted interpretations as to whose patterns should be subordinated when mutually incompatible propensities arise. Persons who differ markedly in age, size, competence, status, or on some combination of these variables usually also differ in terms of the social position that they have to each other, or the social role that they fill in the interchange. This does not mean that power always prevails.

By way of example, the father of the young baby accommodates himself to the behaviors of the child, rather than vice versa. Most infants are more inflexible than their parents, most of the time. But when the infant becomes an adolescent 15 years later, the problem of whether father or son should yield to the other can create recurrent family conflicts. More generally, developmental shifts in capabilities and perceived areas of competence ensure that some behavioral readjustments must occur in the course of living. Further, changes in social contexts, from one context to another, from one group to another, from one relationship to another, can provide changes in social patterns. To the extent that individuals have a strong tendency to conserve their action patterns, resistance, emotional arousal, and interpersonal conflict are likely to follow.

The resistance of individuals to interpersonal change provides fresh light on one of the most ubiquitous social phenomena in animals and humans: the fear and rejection of strangers. Regardless of age or species, there is a near-universal propensity to insulate one's self and one's social network from intrusion. The phenomenon has been called, in various contexts, "stranger fear," "xenophobia," "neophobia," "newcomer rejection," and "intruder-directed aggression." It's not hard to find everyday parallels in human relations, extending from stranger anxiety in infancy to the unhappy problems that children have of fitting into a new school and its cliques and that their parents have of fitting into a new community of established families. The rejection seems born of the more basic tendency to maintain personal integrity and interpersonal organization. Conversely, rejection can be subverted by (1) the newcomer's reducing its threat or (2) productively contributing to the group or its members. The sorts of skills the newcomer brings are usually of great importance in achieving the second step.

On the surface, it would appear that the interpersonal bias assumption would contradict the tendency for individuals to reject others, including potential relations with them. Therein lies the tug-of-war between the propensity to be attracted to others, and the equally strong propensity to maintain one's own organismic coherence and integrity. This is the paradox that permits, in the same relationship, emotions of equal intensity but opposite content. One might love another, but experience intense anger when thwarted or jealous. The emotions, in turn, may promote seemingly contradictory behaviors.

This brings us to the problem of what determines which social pattern will be disrupted when two different ones come into direct conflict, and which pattern will be assimilated to the other.

DIRECTION AND CONTROL

The final interactional assumption concerns who—or what—calls the shots in an interpersonal exchange. Who determines whose behavior will be assimilated? The child who turns the other cheek or the child who smites it? The husband who rages and raves and rants or the wife who smiles and sits and knits? It is proposed here that *the direction that an interchange takes depends on the interplay between the activities involved, the developmental status of the interactants, the roles of the individuals involved, and the context in which the interchange occurs.* In general, the direction of the joint involvement will be determined by whose activity is the most persistent, unyielding, and readily meshed with the activities of the other.

This assumption on the nature of interpersonal control is derived from a more general proposal on how it is that direction arises in any organismic system. The answer, as discussed by von Bertalanffy (1962), is that the direction arises from properties of the system itself. Hence, directionality of interchanges is appropriately viewed in terms of the total pattern of events that surround the interchange, including the internal and external properties of each person and the setting in which the interaction occurs. The coercive influence of a persistent and recurring response pattern is such that the individual, against his or her will, may be drawn into it.

The phenomenon is not unlike the lesson learned by the political propagandists of the 1960s that repetition of a message or of an individual was an effective technique for recruiting interest in and sympathy for the person and the message. The Asch and the Milgram effects demonstrate the operation of a presumably similar process. Here, the messages were in direct conflict with the sensory abilities or moral sensitivities of the person, but they were nonetheless acted upon. The coercive effects of living within the confines of a persistent interchange are sufficient to produce, over time, the effects that have been attributed to the constructs of imitation, modeling, and social facilitation. But the effects may also be of a complementary sort. Each is folded into the essential interaction style of the other, to complete the mutually supported interaction chain.

In an earlier discussion of this problem, I suggested that it might be important to distinguish between the dominance of persons and the dominance of activities (Cairns, 1979). That is, it might not be so much a matter of who dominates as it is what activity is dominant in any given exchange among peers. This was then the basis for proposing that, in the short-run conflict between two response patterns, the more salient, intrusive, and readily enmeshed would be the one mutually adopted.

While this solution seems to be supported by studies of young children who are coequal in status, it should be noted that there is considerable age and situational relativity in the matter. For instance, it would make for a noisy household if the infant's violent cries served to trigger the mother's reciprocal responses. Even when we feel like it, we usually inhibit the temptation to scream back.

Other response strategies may be adopted by parents to modify the noxious behavior of infants (by changing the circumstance, including the diaper; by cuddling the child, and on.) In these instances, the caretaker *escapes from synchrony*, responding in ways that are likely to modify the trajectory of the behavior of the other. Hence the more-salient act does not always engage the other in a comparable activity. All this is to say that directionality is not merely an outcome of the acts of others, but of the organizing functions of the context, the individuals' internal states, and the alternative courses of action that are available.

As it turns out, the solution of interpersonal control in the short-run may be different from that in the long-run. To the extent that a response pattern perseveres, despite the counterresponses, it should eventually enchain the acts of the other into the response organization. In real life, it may not be feasible, practical, or possible to persist in the face of otherwise coercive challenges. In the face of physical punishment and injury, persistence may be tantamount to self-destruction. If not destroyed, one can become worn down, burned out, or otherwise overwhelmed by the persistent demands of others. The other may be an infant, an adolescent, a student, or another individual more energetic than oneself. Once a step is taken toward reorganization–by whatever means, whether by cajoling, coercing, or commanding—a shift in the direction of the interchange inevitably follows.

A comment should be made on the implications of this assumption on how it is that one might wisely deal with the exigencies of interpersonal direction. On the surface, there seems to be a sharp contraction between the principles of moral reciprocity that have been promoted in the so-cial–ethical guides of religion and the empirical reciprocity by which interchanges may be described. By moral reciprocity, I mean the exhor-tations for reciprocity found in the Book of Luke and the Confucian Analects ("Is there one word upon which the whole life may proceed?" The Master replied, "Is not reciprocity such a word?—What you do not yourself desire, do not put before others.")

But does putting before others what one desires for oneself—say, happiness and peace—bring about that state of affairs? Not in most experiments with children in early and mid childhood who act together. Instead of moral reciprocity, they become recruited by the most vigor-ous, commanding, and coercive acts of peers. Hence, in young children acting together, the more salient, active, gleeful patterns are likely to predominate over the quiet, inhibited, and studious ones (e.g., Sher-man, 1975). Similarly, expressions of anger tend, in subsequent ages, to have an edge over quieter expressions of sympathy. The problem is interpreting such observations—indeed, in interpreting interview re-ports and other episodic events—is that they are time-limited to rather short intervals. The essential message of moral reciprocity seems to be that over the long-term, others will become eventually enchained to a pattern whose tone, characteristics, and properties are determined by restraint and kindness. As it turns out, both empirical reciprocity and moral reciprocity are evolutionarily stable strategies (Maynard Smith, 1974).

CONCLUDING COMMENTS

The aim of this chapter has been to provide an introduction to a new way of viewing the development of social interactions and personality. The contemporary perspective does not reject traditional models of so-cial development so much as provide a general framework into which they may be fitted. The accumulated evidence over the past half-century has now clearly shown that a restricted focus on psychic causation and social learning is inadequate to account for the major features of social behavior, whether normal or deviant. Attempts to introduce a cognitive-constructivist perspective constitute a major step forward. But a fatal flaw remains. Failure to take into account the changing properties of the whole organism guarantees that one's view of social development will be incomplete, or severly limited. Rather than complicating the theoretical picture, the consideration of how biological, cognitive, social network, and ecological factors are organized helps clarify it. The mutual dependency of social development virtually demands attention to all of its primary contributors, and to their interplay at each ontogenetic stage.

Although I did not comment in detail on the implications for understanding psychopathology, it is in this realm that the perspective might find its most immediate application. For instance, research on autism since the mid-1950s was guided by the assumption that the essential roots of this psychotic disorder of early childhood were in the mother–infant relationship. The finding of contemporary investigators (e.g., Rutter & Schopler, 1978) that the psychogenic hypothesis has virtually no support has been seen as a negative finding for the psychoanalytic model. Worse, the psychoanalytic interpretation did not explicitly offer a new direction for research and thinking. In the present view, the stage of the very early onset of the disorder implicates the involvement of neural–physiological dysfunctions of the infant. These dysfunctions, in turn, should affect the nature of the social relations that are formed, and the social network in which the child would continue to participate.

For another, less pathological example, recall the offspring described at the beginning of this chapter. The implication was that they were social misfits and failures. But were they? Interviews with the children as adults indicate that they see themselves as being reasonably well adapted; they are satisfied with themselves and their circumstances. In their own self-systems, considerable weight is given to personal factors that are not included in the "objective" public evaluations. In terms of the children's own personal satisfaction, it would be misleading to label the earlier carerearing practices of their parents as incompetent. More generally, as the social systems beyond the family become increasingly influential—including the social networks of childhood and adolescence, the fraternity or sorority, the group at the diner or at work—parental control and responsibility become remote in time and in reality. To account for individual social patterns in adolescence and adulthood, one must look to the then-influential sources of social and sexual control.

What is new about the perspective is that it constitutes an explicit attempt to incorporate information about the nature of developmental changes to understand how social interactions are established, experienced, and modified. To the extent that it leads to a focus upon the integrated, adaptive properties of individuals within their constantly changing social worlds, the perspective will have served its purpose.

REFERENCES

Ainsworth, M. D. S. (1972). Attachment and dependency: A comparison. In J. L. Gewirtz (Ed.), *Attachment and dependency*. New York: Wiley.

Baldwin, J. M. (1897). *Social and ethical interpretations in mental development: A study in social psychology*. New York: Macmillan.

Baltes, P. B., Reese, H. W., & Nesselroade, J. R. (1977). *Life-span developmental psychology: Introduction to research methods*. Monterey, CA: Brooks/Cole.

Binet, A., & Henri, V. (1895). La psychologie individuelle. *L'Année Psychologique, 2*, 411–565.

Binet, A., & Simon, T. (1905). Sur la necessité d'établir un diagnostic scientifique des états inférieurs de l'intelligence. *L'Année Psychologique, 11*, 163–190.

Bowlby, J. (1958). The nature of the child's tie to his mother. *International Journal of Psychoanalysis, 39*, 350–373.

Bowlby, J. (1969). *Attachment and loss: Vol. 1. Attachment*. New York: Basic Books.

Brim, O. G., Jr., & Kagan, J. (Eds.). (1980). *Constancy and change in human development*. Cambridge: Harvard University Press.

Cairns, R. B. (1966). Attachment behavior of mammals. *Psychological Review, 73*, 409–426.

Cairns, R. B. (1972). Attachment and dependency: A psychobiological and social learning synthesis. In J. L. Gewirtz (Ed.), *Attachment and dependency*. New York: Wiley.

Cairns, R. B. (1976). The ontogeny and phylogeny of social interactions. In M. Hahn & E. C. Simmel (Eds.), *Evolution of communicative behaviors*. New York: Academic Press.

Cairns, R. B. (1977). Beyond social attachment: The dynamics of interactional development. In T. Alloway, P. Pliner, & L. Krames (Eds.), *Attachment behavior*. New York: Plenum Press.

Cairns, R. B. (1979). *Social development: The origins and plasticity of interchanges*. San Francisco: Freeman.

Cairns, R. B., & Cairns, B. D. (1981). Self-reflections: An essay and commentary on "Social cognition and acquisition of the self." *Developmental Review, 1*, 109–118.

Cairns, R. B., & Cairns, B. D. (1986). The developmental–interactional view of social behavior: Four issues of adolescent aggression. In D. Olwes, J. Block, & M. Radke-Yarrows (Eds.), *Development of antisocial and prosocial behavior*. New York: Academic Press.

Cairns, R. B., & Hood, K. E. (1983). Continuity in social development: A comparative perspective on individual difference prediction. In P. B. Baltes & O. G. Brim (Eds.), *Life-span development and behavior* (Vol. 5). New York: Academic Press.

Clarke, A. M., & Clarke, A. D. B. (1976). The formative years. In A. M. Clarke and A. D. B. Clarke (Eds.), *Early experience: Myth and evidence*. London: Open Books Publishing.

Cline, H. F. (1980). Criminal behavior over the life span. In O. G. Brim, Jr., and J. Kagan (Eds.), *Constancy and change in human development*. Cambridge: Harvard University Press.

Cottrell, L. S. (1942). The analysis of situational fields in social psychology. *American Sociological Review, 7*, 370–382.

Crook, J. H. (1970). Social organization and the environment: Aspects of contemporary social ethology. *Animal Behaviour, 18*, 197–209.

Damin, W., & Hart, D. (1982). The development of self-understanding from infancy through adolescence. *Child Development, 53*, 841–864.

de Beer, G. (1958). *Embryos and ancestors* (3rd ed.). London: Oxford University Press.

46

Robert B. Cairns

Gottlieb, G. (1976). Conceptions of prenatal development. *Psychological Review, 83*, 215–234.

Hamilton, W. E. (1964). The genetical theory of social behavior, I, II. *Journal of Theoretical Biology, 7*, 1–52.

Henderson, N. D. (1980). Effects of early experience upon the behavior of animals: The second twenty-five years of research. In E. C. Simmel (Ed.), *Early experiences and early behavior: Implications for social development.* New York: Academic Press.

Immelmann, K., & Suomi, S. (1981). Sensitive phases in development. In K. Immelmann, G. W. Barlow, L. Petrinovich, & M. Main (Eds.), *Behavioral development: The Bielefeld interdisciplinary project.* Cambridge: Cambridge University Press.

Jackson, D. D. (Ed.). (1968). *Communication, family, and marriage.* Palo Alto, CA: Science and Behavior Books.

James, W. (1890). *The principles of psychology* (Vol. 1). New York: Macmillan.

Klaus, M. H., & Kennell, J. H. (1976). *Maternal–infant bonding: The impact of early separation or loss on family development.* St. Louis: Mosby.

Kohlberg, L. (1969). Stage and sequence: The cognitive-developmental approach to socialization. In D. A. Goslin (Ed.), *Handbook of socialization theory and research.* Chicago: Rand McNally.

Lewin, K. (1931). Environmental forces in child behavior and development. In C. Murchison (Ed.), *A handbook of child psychology.* Worcester, MA: Clark University Press.

Lewis, M., & Brooks-Gunn, J. (1979). *Social cognition and the acquisition of self.* New York: Plenum.

Mandler, G. (1964). The interruption of behavior. In D. Levine (Ed.), *Nebraska Symposium on Motivation* (Vol. 12). Lincoln: University of Nebraska Press.

Maynard Smith, J. (1974). The theory of games and the evolution of animal conflict. *Journal of Theoretical Biology, 47*, 202–221.

Mead, G. H. (1934). *Mind, self, and society.* Chicago: University of Chicago Press.

Mills, L. A., & Cairns, R. B. (1982). *Life satisfaction in aged low-income widowed black women.* Unpublished manuscript.

Moss, H. A., & Susman, E. J. (1980). Longitudinal study of personality development. In O. G. Brim, Jr., & J. Kagan (Ed.), *Constancy and change in human development.* Cambridge: Harvard University Press.

Olweus, D. (1979). Stability of aggressive reaction patterns in males: A review. *Psychological Bulletin, 86*, 852–875.

Patterson, G. R. (1979). A performance theory for coercive family interaction. In R. B. Cairns (Ed.), *The analysis of social interactions: Methods, issues, and illustrations.* Hillsdale, NJ: Erlbaum.

Piaget, J. (1952). *The origins of intelligence in children.* New York: International Universities Press. (Original work published 1936).

Reinert, G. (1979). Prolegomena to a history of life-span developmental psychology. In P. B. Baltes & O. G. Brim, Jr. (Eds.), *Life-span development and behavior* (Vol. 2). New York: Academic Press.

Rosenblatt, J. S., & Lehrman, D. S. (1963). Maternal behavior of the laboratory rat. In H. L. Rheingold (Ed.), *Maternal behavior in mammals.* New York: Wiley.

Rutter, M., & Schopler, E. (1978). *Autism: A reappraisal of concepts and treatment.* New York: Plenum.

Sameroff, A. J. (1975). Early influences on development: Fact or fancy? *Merrill-Palmer Quaterly, 21*, 267–294.

Sears, R. R. (1951). A theoretical framework for personality and social behavior. *American Psychologist, 6,* 476–483.

Selye, H. (1974). *Stress without distress.* New York: Lippincott.

Sherman, L. W. (1975). An ecological study of glee in small groups of preschool children. *Child Development, 46,* 53–61.

Sullivan, H. S. (1940). Conceptions of modern psychiatry. *Psychiatry, 3,* 1–117.

von Bertalanffy, L. (1962). *Modern theories of development: An introduction to theoretical biology.* New York: Harper & Brothers.

Wilson, E. O. (1975). *Sociobiology: The new synthesis.* Cambridge: Harvard University Press.

CHAPTER 2

"A Chip off the Old Block": Some Interpersonal Characteristics of Coercive Children across Generations

Robert G. Wahler
Jean E. Dumas

INTRODUCTION

Popular wisdom commonly assumes that most children who exhibit undesirable behavior patterns will "grow out of it," if only given time to do so. While this may be true for many children presenting emotional complaints such as oversensitiveness, enuresis, fears, and speech difficulties (Rutter, 1976) it is certainly not true for the majority of children displaying coercive, antisocial disorders, such as agressiveness, noncompliance, and delinquency. In fact, the opposite would appear to be true in their case. A review of several follow-up studies of such children (Robins, 1979) indicates that, instead of outgrowing a generally coercive behavior pattern, they grow up to become coercive, antisocial adults, and that, once adult, they often rear coercive, antisocial children. In other words, these studies suggest that a behavioral continuity characterizes many antisocial disorders and that this continuity applies, not only within, but also across generations. Note that popular wisdom can easily handle this research finding: If it is true that little Johnny never grew out of being mean, it may be said of him later that he is just a chip off the old block!

This chapter focuses on cross-generational continuities in coercive, antisocial behaviors. These behaviors form a pattern corresponding to what Achenbach and Edelbrock (1978), in an extensive review of the literature, labeled "the broad-band undercontrolled syndrome." It is characterized by a person's repeated relationship problems with members of the social environment. These problems center on the use of considerable external pressure (e.g., temper tantrums, threats, physical aggression) to force others to behave in ways that are advantageous to the person exercising this pressure. This behavior pattern is generally the major characteristic of the specific activities summarized under labels such as noncompliance, aggressiveness, conduct disorder, and delinquency. It is not, therefore, limited to officially ascertained deviance. Following an overview of the literature pertaining to cross-generational continuities in coercive, antisocial behaviors at three developmental levels (early childhood, middle childhood, and adolescence), we discuss four possible processes that may account for the transmission of such behaviors from one generation to the next. These are (1) genetic transmission, (2) transmission via a process of shaping and negative reinforcement, (3) transmission via a process of modeling and vicarious reinforcement, and (4) transmission via a process of unpredictability training and inconsistent reinforcement. These four processes, which we do not consider to be mutually exclusive, are first outlined. Greatest emphasis is given to the process of unpredictability training and inconsistent reinforcement which, to our knowledge, is being presented here for the first time. Empirical findings that support or invalidate these processes are then discussed in detail, this within a developmental framework similar to the one within which the literature is reviewed. This discussion focuses on three broad areas of research: attachment and the development of coercive behaviors in early life, family organization and the acquisition of noncompliance and aggressiveness in middle childhood, and community organization and its impact on delinquency and aggression in adolescence.

CROSS-GENERATIONAL CONTINUITIES: AN OVERVIEW OF THE LITERATURE

It would appear that coercive, antisocial behavior patterns are passed on from one generation to the next at a rate well beyond chance. This has been shown in countless studies that have compared the proportion of antisocial adults who had antisocial parents or who have antisocial children (e.g., Jonsson, 1967; McCord, 1979; Osborn & West, 1979; Robins, West, & Herjanic, 1975; Wilson, 1975) after having controlled for confounding factors such as family size, area of residence, or rates of reported criminal behavior at different points in time. It is also the conclusion of detailed surveys of the literature on the relationship between parental and child behavior (e.g., Becker, 1964; Hetherington & Martin, 1979; Rollins & Thomas, 1979; Steinmetz, 1979). We review the literature on these cross-generational continuities at three developmental levels: early childhood, middle childhood, and adolescence.

Early Childhood: Abused and Abusive Children

Of the many personality attributes child-abusing parents have been reported to share, the most overriding one is probably a history of maltreatment in their own childhood (Altemeier, Vietze, Sherrod, Sandler, Falsey, & O'Connor, 1979; Curtis, 1974; Spinetta & Rigler, 1972; Steele & Pollock, 1974; Straus, Gelles, & Steinmetz, 1980). While this association is certainly not inevitable, its importance appears overwhelming.

Altemeier et al. (1979) constructed an interview schedule aimed at predicting, during pregnancy, mothers who would later be at risk of maltreating their children. Of the eight interview categories they isolated, a mother's history of abuse in her own childhood correlated most highly ($r = .52$) with her classification as a high-risk mother. A preliminary study showed that 75% of high-risk mothers were later officially reported for child abuse.

Straus et al. (1980), in a national survey of family violence in the United States, traced the incidence of violence across three generations. Their results showed that the more the grandparents made use of physical punishment to control their children and of physical violence to control each other, the more violent the parents in their study sample were toward each other and their children. The chances of becoming an abusive spouse and parent were greatest for those participants who had grown up in families where they were both abused and exposed to abusive parental conflict. Parents who grew up in homes in which both kinds of violence were exhibited were found to be approximately five times more likely to use violence toward one another than parents who grew up in nonviolent homes. Fathers who grew up in violent homes were twice as likely to become child abusers as fathers who did not, while mothers who grew up in similar homes were four times as likely to become child abusers as mothers who did not.

Considering parents as a group, the effect of growing up in a violent home was highly predictive of child abuse: One out of every four parents who grew up in such a home became violent enough to risk seriously injuring a child. Furthermore, the more violent the parents in the study sample, the more violent their children were toward them and their siblings. While less than 1 in 400 of the children whose parents did not hit them exhibited any violence toward them, half of the children who had been subjected to parental violence exhibited violence toward their parents that would be legally classified as aggravated assault had it not taken place in the privacy of the home. Similar findings were reported for sibling violence. While the authors insist that such findings do not imply that violent parents will necessarily have violent children, these results clearly indicate that abusive and coercive behavior patterns tend to be transmitted across generations. Similar results can be found in cross-generational case studies (Oliver & Taylor, 1971; Silver, Dublin, & Lourie, 1969).

Direct observational studies of abused children and their families indicate that these adverse cross-generational continuities manifest themselves very early in the behavior of abused children (Ainsworth, 1979; Blanchard & Main, 1979; George & Main, 1979). In this last study, the authors compared 10 abused children (aged 1–3 years) and 10 matched controls from families experiencing stress (not further defined). Direct observations of the social interactions of these children with caretakers and peers in a daycare environment indicated that the abused infants more often responded to the affiliative gestures of caregivers and peers with avoidance or combined approach–avoidance movements than the controls did. Moreover, the abused toddlers physically assaulted their peers over twice as often as the controls did. Similarly, five of the abused infants but none of the controls assaulted or threatened to assault their caregivers. When verbal and nonverbal aggressive behaviors were considered together, the abused group was found to aggress against caregivers over four times as often as the control group.

It thus appears that young victims of abuse tend to repeat in new relationships the patterns of interaction they have acquired with their parents. If they have learned to regard their parents as dangerous, they are more likely to aggress other adult caregivers as well as children of their own age. Note that such behavioral continuities across generations are not only found in extreme situations such as child abuse. Studies of compliance in normal children (Baumrind, 1975, 1978; Lytton, 1977, 1980; Lytton & Zwirner, 1975; Minton, Kagan, & Levine, 1971) indicate that parental use of inconsistent, harsh, or rejecting punishment is commonly associated with antisocial behavior in young children.

For example, Lytton (1980), in his observations of normal, 30-month-old children, found that mild suggestions were the most effective methods of verbal control used by parents. The probability of child compliance was highest following suggestion and then decreased progressively following command or prohibition. Physical control and other aversive actions (e.g., criticism) facilitated noncompliance more than compliance. Adding physical control or aversive actions to commands lessened their effectiveness in securing compliance, whereas joining positive actions (e.g., smiling, praise) to commands increased it. It would appear that such differences in parental behavior may affect compliance in infants even before the age of 1 (Stayton, Hogan, & Ainsworth, 1971).

The evidence just reviewed supports the contention that, from an early age, children tend to interact with members of their environment in a coercive fashion if they themselves are regularly coerced by their caregivers. In particular, abused children and children who are regularly exposed to family violence have been found to exhibit verbal and physical aggression in interpersonal situations (i.e., toward caregivers, siblings, and peers) and to grow up to abuse their own children and spouse, while normal children have been found to respond to physical coercion with noncompliance rather than compliance. If this is correct, it obviously perpetuates a coercive cycle in which the abused become abusers and the coerced become coercers.

Middle Childhood: Punishing Parents and Aggressive Children

Comparable findings have been reported in epidemiological and clinical studies of older populations. Langner, McCarthy, Gersten, Simcha-Fagan, and Eisenberg (1979) reported a study of two representative samples, each of approximately 1000 families with one child at least between the ages of 6 and 18. Both samples were taken from the same area of New York City, but were selected in different ways. One group comprised a socioeconomic cross-section of the population. The second group, however, was restricted to welfare families only. Both samples were administered a series of interview and questionnaire measures on two occasions. An interval of about 5 years separated each administration. The authors found that parental punitiveness measured at Year 1 forecasted fighting, conflict with parents, and delinquency 5 years later. Especially in the areas of aggression and antisocial behavior, punitiveness contributed more to behavior over time than any other of the several family variables measured. These results applied to boys and girls and to the cross-sectional and welfare samples. West and Farrington (1973), in a predictive study of delinquency, surveyed 411 boys living in a working-class neighborhood of London, first when the children were aged 8–9 years and regularly thereafter. They found that *poor parental behavior*—i.e., behavior characterized by emotional rejection, inconsistent, harsh, or very strict discipline, and parental conflict—was highly predictive of later delinquency. Boys who experienced the worst parental behavior became delinquent over twice as often as boys who did not. Similarly, Eron, Walder, and Lefkowitz (1971), in a survey of aggressive behavior among third-graders, found a consistent and significant increase in children's aggressiveness as the number of physical punishment items endorsed by their parents on a questionnaire increased. These findings suggest that, rather than having their intended effect, increases in parental punishment may lead to increases in child aggressive and antisocial behavior. Similar results have been reported in other epidemiological surveys (Cameron, 1977; Newson & Newson, 1980; Tonge, James, & Hillam, 1975; Wadsworth, 1979).

These findings are supported by more molecular analyses of both normal and clinical populations. Direct observations of family interactions in normal and coercive, antisocial families (Delfini, Bernal, & Rosen, 1976; Forehand, King, Peed, & Yoder, 1975; Johnson & Lobitz, 1974; Patterson, 1976; Snyder, 1977; Wahl, Johnson, Johansson, & Martin, 1974) have shown that a predictive relationship exists between parental aversiveness (generally measured in terms of commands) and child noncompliant and aversive behavior, with families of coercive children engaging in aversive interactions that (1) are more frequent, (2) are more intense, and (3) last longer, and in reduced rates of prosocial interactions than families of nonproblem children. Moreover, these families are more likely to be inconsistent and reinforce deviant and punish prosocial behavior. For example, Patterson (1976) found that the identified coercive children in his sample received approximately three times as much punishment as their nonproblem counterparts, and this often on a noncontingent basis. Furthermore, contrary to what happened in control families, such punishment had generally negative effects, leading to increases instead of decreases in child aggression. Similarly, Snyder (1977) reported that the rate of aversive behavior was higher in problem than in nonproblem families, whether the data were analyzed by family unit or specific family member. In other words, all family members were significantly more aversive toward one another in problem families. Moreover, while normal families generally responded to behavior contingently, there was an almost total lack of contingencies in problem families. And, when these families did respond to aversive behavior contingently, their use of punishment led to increases rather than decreases in such behavior.

It would appear, on the basis of the studies just reviewed, that coercive antisocial child behavior is found in a generally coercive, antisocial environment. In fact, studies (Burgess & Conger, 1978; Kent, 1976; Pfouts, Schopler, & Henley, 1981; Reid, Taplin, & Lorber, 1981; Timberlake, 1981) indicate that there may be a direct relationship between the amount of aversiveness a child is subjected to and the amount of aversiveness he/she exhibits. Burgess and Conger's (1978) observational study of abusive, neglectful, and normal families underlines this reciprocal nature of family interactions. These authors reported that mothers in abusive and neglectful homes displayed 40% less positive interaction (approval and support) and over 65% more aversive interaction (disapproval and rejection) than normal mothers. Children in abusive, but not neglectful, homes reciprocated in kind by displaying almost 50% more aversive interaction than normal children.

Comparable findings were obtained in two surveys by Pfouts et al. (1981) and Timberlake (1981). These authors reported that children directly involved in family violence were more likely to exhibit overt forms of aggression later in life than were neglected children or children who had witnessed family violence without actively participating in it. In another observational study, Reid et al. (1981) compared abusive, distressed but nonabusive, and normal families. They found that both mothers and children in abusive families scored significantly higher on most measures of aversive interactions than did their counterparts in the other two groups (as did the fathers, but not significantly so), while mothers and children in distressed but nonabusive families, in turn, scored generally higher than their normal counterparts. Specifically, parents in the two problem groups directed significantly more aggression toward their children and received more aggression from them than did normal parents. And parents in the abusive group directed significantly more aggression toward each other than did their counterparts in the other two groups.

The studies just presented support the existence of cross-generational continuities in aggressiveness manifested in childhood. Parents who exhibit high rates of coercive, physically aggressive behavior toward their children and/or each other are more likely to bring up coercive, antisocial children, thus perpetuating a cycle in which coercion begets coercion across generations.

Adolescence: Criminal Parents and Delinquent Adolescents

Moving along the developmental continuum, we find that, all other things being equal, antisocial parents tend to rear children that grow up to become antisocial adolescents. In a follow-up of their aforementioned 1973 study, West and Farrington (1977) found that the likelihood of a son acquiring a criminal record by age 18, and especially a recidivist one, was directly related to the presence or absence of a parental criminal record. Eight percent of sons of fathers free from any criminal convictions become recidivists, compared to 37% of sons of convicted fathers. The influence of a parental record became even more obvious when the participants and their brothers were considered together. Maternal criminality was found to be less common than paternal criminality but to have just as close an association with child behavior. The rate of delinquency in sons with criminal mothers was more than double (54%) that in sons with mothers free of convictions (23%), while that rate was highest in sons with two criminal parents (61%).

These results have since been confirmed by Osborn and West (1979) in an analysis of the criminal records of almost the same sample, but this time followed up until the participants' twenty-third birthdays. In a similar study, Robins et al. (1975) compared the criminal records of a normal group of 76 American black males from a large city with those of their children and their children's mothers. Results indicated that a juvenile delinquency record in the father, or a record of adult arrest, were both powerful predictors of juvenile delinquency in their sons. Forty-six percent of sons of fathers with a delinquency record were found to be delinquent, compared to 25% of sons of fathers without such record, while 44% of sons of fathers with a record of adult arrest were found to be delinquent, compared to 12% of sons of fathers without such record. Both comparisons were highly significant. Comparable results were obtained for maternal delinquency record and record of adult arrest.

Turning to the relationship between parental criminal records and delinquency in daughters, the authors found that both adult arrest in fathers and delinquency in mothers were significantly related to delinquency in daughters. Although female delinquency was rare in both generations, the association between mother and daughter delinquency was particularly strong. Forty-four percent of daughters of mothers with a delinquency record became delinquent, compared to 9% of daughters of mothers without such record.

Finally, having two criminal parents was the strongest predictor of delinquency for both sexes. Fifty percent of children with both parents arrested became delinquent. If, in addition, both parents had been delinquent, this figure rose to 67%. Comparable findings have been reported by McCord (1979), Offord, Allen, and Abrams (1978), and Wilson (1975).

While neither West and Farrington (1977) nor Robins et al. (1975) were able to account for these cross-generational continuities in any simple manner, the first study clearly showed that the boys who became delinquent in adolescence generally grew up in a dysfunctional family system in which they already exhibited serious behavioral problems as children. Farrington (1978), in a study of the most violent delinquents in the original sample, reported that harsh parental discipline at age 8 was the factor most closely related to violent delinquency (i.e., inflicting or threatening to inflict bodily harm) in adolescence, even after controlling for the child's degree of aggressiveness at age 8. Sixty-one percent of violent delinquents had experienced harsh discipline in comparison with 27% of nonviolent delinquents. However, violent delinquency was also significantly predicted by several other factors. Besides parental criminality, these included poor parental supervision and marital conflict or separation, suggesting that deviant parents may produce antisocial children in part through their harsh or inconsistent discipline, lack of social responsibility toward them, and/or personal disharmony.

Comparable evidence can be found in Alfaro (1981), Lewis, Shanok, Pincus, and Glaser (1979), and Welsh (1976). For example, Lewis et al. (1979), in a comparison of violent and nonviolent delinquent boys, reported that variables measuring the quality of family interactions best distinguished between the two groups. Participants who had witnessed extremely violent family incidents and/or had been victims of violent parental attacks were most likely to be classified as violent delinquents. In particular, a significant correlation ($r = .37$) was found between a boy's own level of violence as an adolescent and his having been abused.

Similarly, Alfaro (1981), in a study of officially ascertained child abuse and delinquency in New York state, reported that approximately 50% of abusive or neglectful families in his samples had one child or more who was later taken to court as delinquent or ungovernable and that delinquent children who had been reported as abused or neglected were generally more violent than other delinquents.

In keeping with findings pertaining to earlier developmental levels, the evidence reviewed here points to the existence of significant cross-generational continuities in antisocial behavior, with antisocial parents commonly rearing children who will become antisocial adolescents.

ACCOUNTING FOR CROSS-GENERATIONAL CONTINUITIES

Despite differences in populations, methodologies, and purposes, the studies just reviewed clearly indicate that coercive, antisocial behaviors tend to be passed across generations. Although, in our present state of

knowledge, this relationship is not predictive enough to warrant therapeutic or legal decisions in individual cases (e.g., Robins et al., 1975,
reported that, even with both parents convicted, five out of six children
did not become delinquent), it is both socially and statistically significant
and must be accounted for. We outline four theoretical models that may
all throw light on the processes underlying these cross-generational continuities.

Genetic Differences

The idea that humans may be genetically predisposed to act aggressively has a long and controversial history. Simplifying the issue somewhat, there are two broad conceptualizations of this process of genetic
influence. The first one assumes that human beings share a general
instinct for aggressive behavior with other animal species and that, if
this instinct is not regularly relieved in prosocial ways, it will express
itself in destructive actions. This view has been popularized by authors
like Lorenz (1966) and Morris (1967). The second conceptualization rejects the existence of a general aggressive instinct and assumes instead
that genetic influence refers to the probability that hereditary predispositions (such as the predisposition to behave aggressively) will manifest
themselves in a given environment. In this view, popularized by authors like Reynolds (1976) and Wilson (1975, 1978), aggressiveness is
seen not as a necessity, but as a possibility that depends on both hereditary predispositions and environmental influences.

Most of the evidence available on this issue supports a conceptualization based on a process of interaction between genetic predisposition
and learning. While the results of some studies of chromosomal abnor-
malities (e.g., Gardner & Neu, 1972; Jarvik, Klodin, & Matsuyama,
1973), twins and adopted offsprings (e.g. Christiansen, 1970; Crowe,
1972, 1974), and birth cohorts (e.g., Mednick, Kirkegaard-Sorensen,
Hutchings, Knop, Rosenberg, & Schulsinger, 1977) could be seen as
providing evidence for a radical instinctival view, most authors interpret
their findings in interactional terms. Specifically, research indicates that
genetic factors are likely to be most influential in cases of severe antisocial behaviors that develop in childhood or adolescence and persist into
adulthood (Shields, 1976) but that even in such cases they depend on
"favorable" environmental circumstances. We briefly consider how
such interplay between genetic and environmental influences might develop.

From birth, the young infant influences his/her environment. While
crying is the neonate's major means of influencing caretakers, the infant

soon acquires another means of social control: smiling. Unlike crying, smiling is not used to summon caretakers but rather to entice them to stay nearby and enables the young child to both initiate and modulate social interactions (Lamb, 1978a). While these two responses are used by most infants, there are considerable individual differences among them (Brazelton, 1973; Carey, 1970), which directly affect their social environment. These differences are commonly referred to as *temperamental differences*.

Consider the effects of crying upon caretakers. Frodi, Lamb, Leavitt, and Donovan (1978) reported both self-report and psychophysiological data supporting the commonsense notion that a crying infant acts as an arousing and aversive stimulus. While this type of stimulus commonly increases the likelihood that an aggressive response will follow, in most cases the arousal remains limited and the aversive situation is terminated by relieving the cause of the infant's discomfort. However, the situation is more complicated when one is dealing with a "difficult" infant. As reviews of temperamental differences indicate (Bates, 1980; Thomas, Chess, & Birch, 1970), these infants cry for longer periods and often seem inconsolable despite their caretakers' repeated efforts. As a result and through a process of conditioning, the child may become an aversive stimulus whether it is crying or not (Lamb, 1978b). This in turn may lead his/her parents to become less responsive and consistent in their caretaking behavior (Donovan, Leavitt, & Balling, 1978). In this respect, premature infants appear to run an increased risk of being negatively perceived by their parents, as their appearance is less attractive and their cry more aversive than that of full-term babies (Frodi, Lamb, Leavitt, Donovan, Neff, & Sherry, 1978).

The importance of temperamental differences can also be found in studies of older populations. The New York Longitudinal Study (Chess & Thomas, 1977; Thomas & Chess, 1976; Thomas, Chess, & Birch, 1968), a study of 136 middle-class children and their families, showed that mothers perceived temperamental differences such as differences in regularity, adaptability, and mood among their infants and that these remained relatively stable during the first 5 years of life.

Graham, Rutter, and George (1973), in a comparable survey conducted in London with a lower-socioeconomic-status sample of children aged 3 to 7 years, reported similar characteristics to be predictive of later behavioral and emotional disorders. Specifically, children who presented two or more adverse temperamental characteristics were three times more likely to present problems over a 4-year period than children without such characteristics. It would appear that temperamental adversity puts a child at increased risk at least partly because of its interactional effects with parental behavior.

Rutter (1979) reported that children exhibiting such adverse features were twice as likely to be the target of parental criticism and hence, presumably, of other aversive parental behaviors. If this is correct, even in disorganized and discordant homes, children of easier disposition may be able to avoid much of the aversive interchange, thereby creating for themselves a different, more harmonious, environment than that of their more difficult counterparts. This possibility appears to be supported by other studies of the effects of physical (e.g., Dion, 1974) and behavioral (e.g., Bell & Harper, 1977; Osofsky & O'Connell, 1972) characteristics of older children upon specific parental behaviors such as punitiveness and emotional support.

The genetic model just outlined suggests that, all other things being equal, infants and young children do not run an equal risk of acquiring antisocial behavior patterns. Rather, it would appear that, whenever present, adverse temperamental characteristics set the stage for increased vulnerability to adverse environmental circumstances, thus increasing the likelihood of such behavior patterns developing. The other three models offer alternative ways of accounting for the impact of environmental factors.

Modeling

Following the theoretical and experimental impetus provided by Bandura (1969, 1973), adult role modeling has emerged as a variable of major importance in child socialization. According to Bandura's social-learning theory, most behaviors are acquired through observational learning (imitation) and maintained mainly through direct reinforcement. Imitation may be deliberate or inadvertent and depends essentially upon the influence of examples or models. As the family provides a major source of models to the developing child, cross-generational continuities in coercive, antisocial behaviors could very plausibly be explained in terms of a modeling process.

Bandura's (1969) work initially relied on a series of laboratory experiments. Most of them were conducted with children and involved the measurement of imitative behavior following exposure to a live or filmed model as a function of a number of independent variables. From these experiments, it would appear that at least four principles govern the modeling of antisocial, and in particular aggressive, behavior: (1) Through association with past reinforcement, the modeled behaviors serve as prompts or informative cues that facilitate aggressive action in the observers (e.g., Bandura, 1962; Bandura, Ross, & Ross, 1961, 1963; Grusec, 1972). (2) When aggressors are reinforced or even treated indifferently for their aggression, the observers learn that such behavior is not only acceptable but also expected in certain circumstances, thus facilitating comparable action on their part (e.g., Hicks, 1968). (3) The observation of aggression in others tends to generate emotional arousal in the observers, again facilitating comparable action (e.g., Osborn & Endsley, 1971). (4) Aggressive models not only offer opportunities for learning new behaviors, but they also reduce the observer's inhibitions against performing aggressive actions that they have already learned (Bandura et al., 1963).

There is much evidence to support the heuristic usefulness of these principles, even from studies not conducted within a modeling approach. Most of the preceding findings on family violence and parental discipline are compatible with such principles. For example, the reader will recall that, in a comparison of violent and nonviolent delinquent boys, Lewis et al. (1979) reported that the two factors that best differentiated between the two groups were whether the child had witnessed extremely violent incidents in the family and/or had been the victim of violent parental attacks. Similarly, Straus et al. (1980), in their national study, demonstrated that, contrary to theories that see a certain amount of family conflict as necessary or cathartic, the use of physical violence by parents invariably increased the risk that children would use comparable behavior toward them or their siblings.

Clinical and laboratory studies involving direct observation of parent–child interactions also provide support for the importance of modeling influences by showing that aggressive, antisocial children are usually only a part of a larger dysfunctional family system in which most if not all members engage in frequent aversive interchanges (Patterson, 1976, 1980; Wahler, 1980; Wahler, Hughey, & Gordon, 1981).

For example, young children who at first may be repeatedly victimized generally appear to rapidly learn to adopt the very behaviors that are directed against them. Such learning, which at first enables them to defend themselves against attacks, eventually leads most of them to become instigators of attacks as a means of exercising control over their environment (Patterson, Littman, & Bricker, 1967). More precisely, certain types of family relationships appear to provide conditions favorable to child imitation.

Wahler and Nordquist (1973) found that imitation by young children was most likely to occur when parents were of high reinforcement value to the child and able to exercise immediate control (through reinforcement or punishment) on the child's behavior. In a comparable, laboratory study, Hetherington and Frankie (1967) assessed the effects of parental dominance, warmth, and conflict on child imitation of mother and father behavior in a game-playing situation. Children were found to imitate a dominant, hostile parent when the home was high in conflict and when both parents were low in warmth. Imitation of a hostile, dominant parent decreased, however if either interparental conflict was low or one parent was warm. While the responses imitated in the last two studies were not aggressive in nature, the results indicate conditions under which parents are likely to be imitated. Under such conditions, it is likely that exposure to aggressive parental behaviors will lead to child imitation.

Although modeling can account for a large number of experimental findings, there are some results that cannot be explained by this model. For example, West and Farrington (1977) reported that, more than the seriousness of a father's criminal record, the recency of his last conviction, or whether he was first convicted as a juvenile or an adult, it was the presence or absence of a paternal record that was most closely associated with a son's chances of becoming delinquent. Even among the fathers whose last offense occurred before their sons were born, more than 50% had a delinquent child. Comparable findings were reported by Mednick et al. (1977). Moreover, in their earlier report, West and Farrington (1973) found that, far from encouraging their sons to behave in coercive, antisocial ways, most criminal parents disapproved of such behavior. While this would not prevent all modeling to take place, it argues against a deliberate effort on the part of some parents to teach antisocial behaviors to their children.

Finally, while modeling principles have strong intuitive appeal, the processes through which a child comes to imitate a particular model remain poorly understood. Recent theoretical developments (Bandura, 1977) rely on hypothetical cognitive and symbolic variables which, at this stage at least, seem much too global to be able to account for cross-generational continuities in testable terms.

We now turn to an operant model that specifically attempts to account for the acquisition, maintenance, and performance of aggressive behaviors across generations.

Coercion Training

Following years of applied research with normal and deviant families, Patterson (1976, 1979, 1980) put forward the outline of a performance theory aimed at describing the determinants of the aggressive behaviors children often exhibit at home. This theory, which is remarkable in its specificity and, hence, in its testability, relies mainly on what is known as the *coercion hypothesis*. This hypothesis states that members of aggressive families generally tend to influence each other's behavior through the use of painful stimuli, that is, stimuli that are unpleasant for the recipient, to a greater extent than members of normal families. This process of control via pain assumes that performance variations in the behavior of one family member are, to a great extent, controlled by immediately impinging stimuli provided by other family members (Patterson, 1979).

There is considerable evidence in the literature to support this view of the aggressive child as a member of a generally dysfunctional family system. Work by Delfini et al. (1976) and Johnson and Lobitz (1974), Lobitz and Johnson (1975), Patterson (1976), Snyder (1977), and Wahler et al. (1981) shows that families of antisocial children engage in aversive interactions that are more frequent, more intense, and of longer duration than families of normal children. Moreover, these families also display reduced rates of prosocial interaction and differ in the ways in which they express their disapproval of child aversive behavior. Parents of aggressive children generally issue more commands (Forehand et al., 1975; Green, Forehand, & McMahon, 1979; Terdal, Jackson, & Garner, 1976) that are more often prescriptive rather than question-commands or suggestions (Green et al., 1979) and are often too vague to be complied with (Peed, Roberts, & Forehand, 1977). They also tend to aversively consequate behavior more frequently. Patterson (1976) found that the identified aggressive children in his sample received approximately three times as many aversive consequences as their nonproblem counterparts. Furthermore, such consequation generally has negative effects; parental aversive actions leading to increased disruption rather than quelling family conflict (Kopfstein, 1972; Patterson, 1976; Snyder, 1977).

While the literature broadly supports the coercion hypothesis, the processes through which environmental stimuli acquire their ability to control coercive performance must be identified if the hypothesis is to have any predictive value. Patterson (1979) assumes that environmental events acquire this ability through the mechanisms of positive and negative reinforcement. Specifically, he describes two different processes that may account for the maintenance of coercive family interactions.

The first process is assumed to depend on both positive and negative reinforcement. An example, borrowed from Patterson and Reid (1970), illustrates it. The child asks the mother for ice cream. The mother refuses. The child starts whining, crying, or screaming, generally intensifying such aversive behaviors with the passage of time. The mother gives in and allows her child to have ice cream. The child stops all aversive behaviors. As a diagram indicates (see Figure 1), the outcome of such an interaction provides positive reinforcement (ice cream) for child

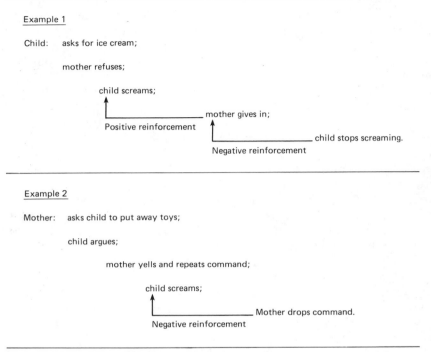

Figure 1 Diagrams of coercive parent–child interaction expressed in terms of positive and negative reinforcement or negative reinforcement only.

aversiveness (e.g., screaming) and negative reinforcement (child stops screaming) for maternal compliance (giving in), thus increasing the likelihood that the child will again initiate similar coercive interactions in the future and that the mother will respond to them by complying.

The second process is assumed to depend on negative reinforcement only. In this case, the child uses coercive behaviors, not to obtain a favorable outcome, but rather to bring an end to the aversive stimulus inputs of others. Consider the following example. The mother asks the child to put away some toys. The child does not comply but starts arguing with the mother. The mother repeats her command, this time yelling. The child screams and still refuses to comply. The mother drops her command. The child stops screaming. As a second diagram shows (see Figure 1), the outcome of such an interaction provides negative reinforcement (mother drops command) for child aversiveness (screaming) and negative reinforcement (child stops screaming) for maternal cessation of the command.

Although the first of the two processes just described clearly provides a parsimonious explanation for the performance of coercive behaviors in dyadic interchanges, it is unclear how the second process could account for such performance. Indeed, consider what is being reinforced when we assume that only negative reinforcement controls the interaction. The child's coercive behaviors are negatively reinforced as soon as the mother stops her manding behavior, thus increasing the likelihood that the child will exhibit similar behaviors when faced with a comparable situation in the future. However, the process appears to break down when we ask which parental behavior is negatively reinforced during the same exchange. The process suggests that maternal cessation of commanding is reinforced, i.e., that the mother is reinforced for not initiating commands to her child. If this is correct, we would expect that, over time, the mother would become less and less likely to initiate such manding behavior with her child, thereby effectively depriving the child of opportunities to respond to her coercively. However, this expectation runs contrary to the evidence (Patterson, 1979).

We acknowledge that Patterson (1979) describes his performance theory with great caution and never claims that it could account for all coercive family interchanges. In other words, he recognizes that aggressive child behaviors within the home are not solely under the control of immediate stimulus events provided by other family members. Unfortunately, however, the coercion model appears to be limited, at this stage at least, to immediate dyadic interactions and to be unable to account for the maintenance of some coercive interchanges solely in negative reinforcement terms.

We consider a fourth model that attempts to account for cross-generational continuities in aggressive child behavior by focusing not only on the immediate stimulus events exchanged by two parties in a dyadic interaction, but also on more distant environmental events that exercise an influence on each party's behavior at the time of the interaction.

Inconsistency Training

This last model, presented here for the first time, attempts to go beyond the narrow limits of immediate dyadic interactions by placing such interactions within a social *context* and using this context to account for their outcome. Given a child's aggressive behaviors at home, two classes of events are of interest here, namely, the immediate discriminative stimuli dispensed between child and parents and, further removed in time, the many stimulus–response contingencies that characterize these individuals' relationships with other members of the environment (i.e., context). We refer to the former class as *stimulus events* and to the latter as *setting events* (Wahler & Dumas, 1981; Wahler & Graves, 1982). Examples of stimulus events include child and parent behaviors such as complaints, commands, temper tantrums, and noncompliance. Examples of setting events include each family member's pattern of interaction with one another (i.e., parent–child interchanges; parent–parent interchanges), and the pattern of extrafamily (community) contacts that each individual experiences. In essence, the inconsistency model assumes that reinforcement functions of stimulus events are largely determined by setting events.

This model, similar to the uncertainty model proposed by D'Amato (1974) and more recently by Imada and Nageishi (1982), comprises two assumptions. First, the reinforcement generating power of any setting event context depends on its predictability. If the social context is inconsistent or unpredictable, that context serves an aversive function for the individuals who make up this context. Secondly, if an individual within this context produces a behavior that is followed by an increase in the predictability of stimulus events, that stimulus consequence will prove to be reinforcing. The critical feature of this consequence is its predictability compared to the surrounding social context: As long as the consequence exceeds its context in predictability, that consequence will serve a reinforcement function.

While the inconsistency model is also an operant model, it must be considered an expanded version of the latter because the reinforcement function of stimulus events lies solely in their relationship with the surrounding stimulus setting. The aversive or positive quality of the stimulus event is immaterial to the potential reinforcement function; it is the *relational* quality of that stimulus vis-á-vis the stimulus context that determines its reinforcement value. Thus, the common operant notion of cataloging stimuli in terms of their demonstrable aversive, positive, and neutral functions would not be applicable to the inconsistency model.

A good illustration of the inconsistency model and relational operations between setting events and stimulus events can be taken from studies we previously reviewed in the coercion training section. Patterson's "punishment acceleration" findings (Patterson, 1976) describe mother–child interchanges in which one party's use of aversive events (e.g., yell, hit, command) *increases* the likelihood that the other party will respond in kind. In other words, the aversive events appear to function as positive reinforcers. Now, when one also examines the overall mother–child social context for these punishment acceleration episodes, it is evident that the mothers are inconsistent in their use of positive and aversive responding to the children. Patterson (1976) and Snyder (1977) both discovered that home observation sessions were characterized by mother aversives and positives irrespective of the child's deviant and prosocial behavior. However, the punishment acceleration episodes occurring in this context were highly consistent or predictable, in that both parties traded aversives with one another. According to the inconsistency model, these sporadic exchanges of aversive behaviors are mutually reinforcing to mother and child—given that the surrounding context is unpredictable.

Our description of inconsistent setting-event context has thus far been restricted to that produced by mother and child. It is equally plausible to consider the contributions of siblings, spouse, and extra family members such as kinfolk, boyfriends, neighbors, and helping agents. As long as mother and/or child are either separately or simultaneously involved in inconsistent exchanges with these people, a stimulus context is created for the punishment acceleration episodes just described. Therefore, it is certainly possible to consider inconsistent exchanges between mother and adult as a setting-event context determining reinforcement functions of the mother's coercive exchanges with her child. Likewise, a child who participates in unpredictable exchanges with siblings or father is in a setting-event context relevant to future exchanges with these people or with mother.

In concluding our description of the inconsistency model, it is important to outline a type of pseudodiscrimination learning sometimes produced in experimental studies of inconsistent stimulus contingencies. When a child lives under environmental conditions marked by such contingencies, it is possible to generate what might be called "superstitious" control over that person's behavior. Under laboratory conditions, the following two steps are likely to produce the phenomenon: (1) A stimulus event must be established as a discriminative stimulus for a particular reinforced response; (2) the reinforcement contingencies for that response are then programmed to gradually become inconsistent or random. If the discriminative stimulus of Step 1 still functions in this capacity after Step 2, that stimulus might now be called a pseudodiscriminative stimulus because its power to set the occasion for that response is based on randomly arranged stimulus contingencies.

This sort of superstitious stimulus control has been demonstrated in the laboratory with animals (e.g., Hernnstein, 1966) and more recently in natural settings with children (Fowler & Baer, 1981). In the latter study, preschool children's sharing responses were brought under pseudodiscriminative stimulus control by use of the two previously described steps. First, the children were told that increased sharing with peers in a free play setting would be consequated by redeemable point reinforcers. When it was then shown that the instructions to share did in fact increase sharing in the setting, the children were then told that point deliveries had to be delayed until later in the day. In effect, these later deliveries were provided following a second free play setting. After this step, the children also increased their sharing in that second setting *even though the point reinforcers were only randomly associated with the increased sharing.* Thus, the instructions to share had become discriminative for reinforced sharing in the early setting, and pseudodiscriminative for sharing in the later setting.

At this point, it will be useful to familiarize the reader with a commonly seen, but puzzling, clinical example of superstitious control related to inconsistency training. Suppose we return to a previous description of an inconsistent setting context comprising mother, father, and child interchanges. In our example, all three parties are exchanging unpredictable patterns of positive, neutral, and aversive behaviors. Then, father hits mother and this exchange is followed by mother and child engaging in a punishment-acceleration episode when mother tries to get her child to leave the room. As we argued previously, the mother–child coercive episode should be mutually reinforcing to these individuals because the episode encompasses stimulus consequences of greater predictability than its setting context. In addition, because father hitting mother was a stimulus event just preceding the episode, this event could set the occasion for such episodes if this sequential arrangement happened repeatedly. In other words, father hitting mother might become a discriminative stimulus for mother–child coercion. Next, according to the principles of superstitious stimulus control, a discriminative stimulus established via inconsistency training can retain its behavior control function even though the original training conditions are no longer in effect. Thus, father hitting mother might continue to increase the likelihood of mother–child coercion in a variety of settings—although this stimulus event no longer predicts reinforcement. In effect, a clinical observer would find it difficult to comprehend such a sequential arrangement without benefit of appropriate historical information. Given that the observer comprehends the historical interchanges within this family triad, a peculiar discriminative function of the father–mother setting event becomes understandable. We return to this stimulus control process in all three of the following sections.

DEVELOPMENT OF THE MATCHING PROCESS

Early Childhood

Immediately upon birth, it is apparent that the infant has already developed a response style marking his or her individuality. For example, Bell (1960) was able to reliably distinguish up to 37 categories of infant behavior in the first week of life. Of even greater interest in these findings were the individual differences across infants; the newborns produced behavioral profiles of such variability that differences among infants were obvious. As noted earlier, this behavioral profile is commonly described as temperament (Brazelton, 1973; Carey, 1970) and is presumably the result of genetic factors and/or stimulus influences of the intrauterine environment (Spelt, 1948).

Given this rich repertoire of the neonate's action capabilities, one must consider the possibility of an immediately observable influence pattern in which parent and child have reciprocal effects on one another. The newborn is also capable of learning as defined in the principles of both classical and operant conditioning (see Lipsitt, 1969). Thus, it seems likely that infant development of normal or deviant interpersonal characteristics ought to become an observable process from the moment of birth. In reference to the development of antisocial children, one ought to witness the beginnings of a coercive process commonly seen in the interpersonal transactions of these children later in life (i.e., Patterson, 1976). That is, if children *learn* to deal with other people in antisocial ways, that learning could get underway at birth. The infant's mother might well set contingencies that nurture the development of her baby's coercive distress rather than affectionate behavior.

A tentative picture of such development can be derived from observational studies geared to the understanding of infant–mother attachment. These studies have examined the quality and quantity of mother–infant exchanges in a variety of common caretaking situations—some familiar to both parties and others involving unfamiliar environmental settings. The attachment studies are also relevant to our longitudinal questions about antisocial children. In some of these studies, efforts are made to predict infant social behavior in one time frame, based on the observed mother–infant attachment pattern in an earlier time frame. If the coercive process leading to a child's antisocial adjustment begins in the first year of life, these studies are surely relevant to an understanding of the process.

A look at the initial beginnings of mother-infant influence is clouded by a puzzling time-lag phenomenon. Bell and Ainsworth (1972) and Sander (1962) discovered that infant social behavior in the first 3 months of life had *no* relationship to the infant's later social interchanges. However, the mother's infant directed behaviors in this early time frame *did* predict the infant's later social behavior. For example, Bell and Ainsworth (1972) found that mother ignoring of infant crying in the first 3 months was positively correlated with infant crying during the second

3 months. In other words, mothers who tend to ignore crying in the first 3 months are apt to rear infants who cry more in the next 3 months. Not only is this finding difficult to understand within a reinforcement model of mother influence, but also the infant's role in these interchanges from 0 to 3 months is unclear. If the infant behavior profiles seen immediately after birth have little predictive value with respect to these infants' later interpersonal styles, it is difficult to specify the functional qualities of the early behavior profiles. Ainsworth (1979) has taken this phenomenon to mean that initial infant behavior cannot be considered as a constitutional basis for later social behavior. Rather, it appears to be mother behavior in these early months that sets the occasion for the infant's later development.

Just how the mother's ignoring could influence the infant crying-lag phenomenon is also addressed in the attachment studies. Stayton and Ainsworth (1973) provided a more complete description of ignoring in their factor analysis of observed mother–infant interchanges. Mothers who ignored infant crying were also insensitive to other infant social cues such as smiling, bouncing, and vocalizing. Although specific contingent relationships between these infant behaviors and mother attention were not reported, it would appear that "insensitive" mothers could also be described as "noncontingent" mothers. These mothers did initiate interactions with their infants, but in a manner described as "routine" (independent of infant response) and "abrupt" (likely to be terminated regardless of infant response). In Stayton, Hogan, and Ainsworth's (1971) words, "The insensitive mother is geared almost exclusively to her own wishes, moods and activity; her interventions tend to be prompted by signals within herself and therefore are rarely contingent upon the baby's signals" (p. 1061). On the other hand, mothers whose infants exhibited less crying later in Year 1 were apt to display caretaking actions involving prompt and consistent response to infant social cues as well as prolonged attention to these infant behaviors by "encouragement," "contingent pacing," and "playfulness."

It would appear, then, that a *contingent* or *predictable* social environment in the infant's early months is inversely related to the later emergence of one common form of infant coercive behavior—crying. Moreover, the mother's attention need not be selectively contingent on any particular infant behavior, such as smiling, bouncing or other noncoercive responses. As long as she offers her social actions contingent upon the full range of her infant's social actions, the infant's later repertoire is likely to become more prosocial. In other words, it may not be necessary for the mother to shape a prosocial repertoire through differential attention to those early beginnings of desirable infant behavior.

By the last quarter of Year 1, most infants display interpersonal patterns that are distinguishable on a prosocial–coercive dimension. Ainsworth (1979) has summarized these differentiating social clusters as well as the mothering styles related to the clusters. The coercive babies are described by Ainsworth as "insecurely attached" to their mothers. These babies are so grouped because of their relatively long-duration crying episodes and their greater likelihood of crying when separated from their mothers. In addition, these high-rate criers are more apt to be noncompliant with mother instructions and mother physical interventions aimed at enforcing instructions. The reader will recall from an earlier section of this chapter that distress-inducing behaviors such as crying, whining, hitting, et cetera, as well as noncompliance, are common signposts of the antisocial child later in life.

However, there is also another side to the coercive interpersonal behaviors of these babies—a side that we believe has equal relevance to the later emergence of antisocial behavior. Ainsworth and her colleagues found that the coercive babies were also deficient in affectionate behaviors. They were unlikely to greet their mothers' approaches with smiling and babbling and similarly unlikely to respond positively to being held by her. Ainsworth's descriptions showed that some of these unresponsive infants were particularly avoidant as marked by an absence of the commonly seen "sinking in" response to being held. This broad category of social avoidance is later in life inferred to reflect a lack of concern with others—another often-cited characteristic of antisocial children.

The mother's child care role in the later course of infant social development continues to resemble that seen in the time-lag phenomenon described earlier with respect to infant crying. The observations of Stayton and Ainsworth (1973) again revealed that mothers of the coercive, nonaffectionate 9- to 12-month old infants were essentially noncontingent in their caretaking activities. They tended to be "abrupt," "interfering with ongoing infant behavior," and "routine" in their overall manner of responding to the infant. As we understand the more fine-grained mother–infant interchanges summarized by these terms, it does appear that the coercive babies at the end of year one were still influenced by rather unpredictable maternal input.

As a good example of this mother–infant process, Stayton et al. (1971) conducted a correlational analysis of normal infants' compliance to maternal commands. The infants, all in the 9- to 12-month age range, were observed interacting with their mothers in free field home settings. The mothers' child-directed behaviors were coded into three classes: (1) a global rating that we interpret to reflect the degree of *contingent* response to infant behavior as well as the positive to aversive quality of this maternal response style; (2) verbal commands such as "No! No!" "Don't touch," "Come!" et cetera; (3) physical intervention such as dragging the baby away from a forbidden area, slapping the baby, pulling the baby into a sitting position, et cetera. Results indicated that frequency of mother commands and physical interventions were *unrelated* to infant compliance. However, the global rating of maternal contingent and affectionate response to infant behavior was positively correlated with the compliance measure, accounting for 44% of the variance in this measure. One must keep in mind that the global measure of mother contingent response was not an index of selective attention to infant compliance. Rather, maternal attention to *any and all* infant social actions could be considered in observer rating of this measure. Thus, in line with our previous discussion concerning the early months of infant development, a baby's coercive or prosocial interpersonal style does not appear related to differential shaping via mother attention. If the mother is affectionate and contingent in response to her infant's emerging social responses, that baby might well develop a compliant and affectionate style of response to mother.

We turn now to an oabious question concerning the two mothering patterns just described: Why would a mother begin the childrearing process with aversive and noncontingent interchanges with her infant? In our view, at least two avenues of stimulus influence are implicated: (1) The newborn infant might behave in ways that set the occasion for maternal inconsistency. (2) Other people in the mother's social network might function as setting events for this maladaptive mothering style.

The newborn's capability to influence maternal caretaking actions was pointed out some time ago (Bell, 1968). Since that contention was voiced, additional observational studies have added empirical support to the infant's stimulus role in promoting aversive maternal care. Butterfield, van Doornick, Dawson, and Alexander (1979) were able to predict aversive mothering patterns on the basis of neonate irritability and nonresponsiveness. In fact, several studies of maltreated infants have shown correlational relationships between maternal abuse and the infant's coercive temperament (Lamb, 1978; Parke & Collmer, 1975). The hypothesized process in these observed relationships has been described along the lines of either classical conditioning or operant discrimination learning (Lamb, 1978). That is, the neonate's aversive actions elicit avoidance responses in the mother, as well as increasing the likelihood that she will try a variety of other aversion-reducing responses (e.g., picking infant up, scolding infant, etc.). Given a sufficient number of these infant–mother experiences, the *infant's entire range of social actions* might become established as a class of conditioned stimuli—all functioning to elicit mother avoidance and to set the occasion for those aversion-reducing responses that worked for mother previously. If, in fact, *all* infant social behaviors function as an aversive class of stimuli for the mother, her inconsistent or noncontingent mode of caretaking would be understandable.

However, while mother's aversive responding to her irritable infant makes sense on the basis of the preceding assumptions, it is not clear why she would respond to *all* infant social behaviors as a single stimulus class. On the basis of discrimination learning, one would expect the mother to respond in avoidant–aversive ways following her infant's noxious actions, and in more affectionate ways following the baby's prosocial actions. Because even irritable infants will also smile, babble, and bounce, there ought to be numerous opportunities for the mother to discriminate and thus respond differently to this alternate set of infant stimuli.

The empirical literature indicates that inconsistent and aversive maternal caretaking may also be influenced by indirect or setting-event stimulus factors. These factors, outlined by Wahler and Fox (1981), describe a behavior influence process in which temporally distant stimuli may control behavior. The process can also be indirect in the sense that the controlling stimuli need not have a contingent relationship with the bahaviors in question. For example, a mother's aversive interchange with her husband might be shown to increase the likelihood of aversive exchanges with her infant—even though the two experiences are unrelated. While the specific operational characteristics of setting events are not well understood, there are correlational examples of the phenomenon in the literature. Wahler (1980) discovered that mothers of problem children were significantly more aversive with their children on days in which the mothers experienced coercive interchanges with their own kinfolk and helping agents. On such days, the coercive exchanges with adults appeared to operate as setting events for the mothers' child care interchanges. The coercive adult exchanges did not necessarily involve the mothers' child or child care routines. Nevertheless, occurrences of the exchanges functioned to increase the likelihood of mother aversiveness in relating to her child.

When attachment researchers describe the caretaking patterns of noncontingent mothers, they tend to assume that such maternal insensitivity is due to simulus factors *within* the mother. Thus, the insensitive mother is noncontingent in her response to the infant because this response style is prompted by "her own wishes, moods and activity" (Stayton et al., 1971, p. 1061); or, her poorly timed baby care may be related to "strong underlying depressive tendencies" (Ainsworth, 1979, p. 49). In our own work with older coercive children and their mothers, we too have been impressed with what appear to be internal cues influencing a mother's aversive child responses. However, while such a process might be operative, we are also convinced that these self-determined mother actions are in fact initiated by setting events. For example, a mother's unusually harsh response to her toddler's crying might be found to covary with her self-reports of depression—leading one to pick out depression as the determinant of her harsh response. But, it is also probable that mother's depression will covary with the sheer number of her daily or weekly coercive experiences—some of which have nothing to do with her toddler. One might correctly assume that depression is the immediate influence factor in this mother's child maltreatment; on the other hand, it would be equally reasonable to consider coercive setting events as the tangible, observable instigators of the maltreatment process.

Egeland and Sroufe (1981) addressed the setting-event issue in their longitudinal attachment study of mothers identified as abusing and/or neglecting their infants. These mother–infant pairs ($N = 31$) were compared with a sample of dyads ($N = 33$) in which maternal care was judged to be excellent. Mother–infant intercanges were observed in home settings when the infants were 12 months old and again 6 months later. As expected from the previous research we reviewed, the first comparison showed the maltreated infants more likely to respond in coercive and avoidant ways to their mothers than did the control sample. But, 6 months later, the maltreatment sample of infants did not differ from their counterparts. In essence, some infants in the maltreatment sample had changed their interpersonal styles, while the control sample remained the same. Now, while predictors of change in the maltreatment infants were based on interview data, all predictors could be classified as "life stress reductions in their mothers." If infants in the maltreatment group became more prosocial at 18 months of age, their mothers were likely to have altered their social network interchanges with adults: A grandmother might have entered the mother's home; a husband or boyfriend might have become more understanding; the mother might have made new friends. No doubt some of the reported changes could be described as direct influences on the infant care process; others appear to move along the lines of setting-event influences on the mother's quality of child care.

Certainly it seems probable that coercive and avoidant babies attain this style of action through their mothers' aversive and noncontingent child care strategies. The likelihood that such irritable and oppositional infant behaviors might continue into the early and middle childhood years also seems geared to the mother's continuation of her unfortunate strategy. Just *why* she reacts as she does to her infant is not well understood. We obviously are partial to a setting-event explanation for her behavior. Regardless of the theoretical notions concerning the whys of her child care practices, one outcome of the process will become obvious in the later years: The unchanged coercive–avoidant child will come to resemble his or her principal caretakers more and more in terms of behavior style.

Middle Childhood

Several follow-up studies of coercive and prosocial babies indicate some expected trends into the early and middle childhood years. Those infants who remain locked in the coercive and inconsistent mothering traps, up to 18 months of age, are apt to continue their own coercive actions into relationships with siblings, peers, and teachers (Arend, Gove, & Sroufe, 1979; Waters, Wippman, & Sroufe, 1979).

The previously described findings of George and Main (1979) are particularly impressive in this regard. This reader will recall that 10 toddlers in this observational study were confirmed child abuse victims earlier in life and thus were likely to have shown the previously described coercive–avoidant infancy patterns. Another 10 same-age toddlers with no abuse history served as a control group. Now, when all children were observed in a daycare environment with peers and caretakers, some striking differences emerged in the children's interpersonal behaviors. Following positive social approach gestures by peers and caretakers, children in the abuse sample were much less likely to respond in kind. Rather, they are apt to shy away from contact, display an approach–avoidance style, or to assault the other party. In fact, the rate of verbal and nonverbal assault on peers and caretakers was four times higher for the abuse sample! Clearly, this combination of toddler coercion and avoidance is reminiscent of that found in the infants reared by aversive and noncontingent mothers. However, instead of engaging only one partner in such entrapment (mother), these preschool children have likewise engaged their peers and teachers. From a social-network viewpoint, one must consider the entrapment of these older children to be more stringent and probably more difficult to change.

The coercive and avoidant preschoolers described by George and Main (1979) appear to continue their home-based lifestyles under give-and-take conditions much the same as those described in the infancy section of this chapter. Interestingly enough, the similarity of interpersonal style between child and parent is now quite obvious. For example, Burgess and Conger (1978) compared families known to have been guilty of child abuse or neglect with normal families. In the observational comparison, mothers in the clinic-referred families produced 40% fewer affectional approaches and 60% more aversive behavior—much of this directed to the abused child. Likewise, the children in these abuse–neglect families were much more likely (50%) to react aversively to the parents than were the children in the normal families. This mutually aversive interchange pattern between abused children and their mothers was also reported by Reid, Taplin, and Lorber (1981).

Another important characteristic of the preceding matching process has to do with a differential parenting factor. Mothers appear to be more directly involved in these deviance matchups than do fathers. For example, Patterson (1977) conducted baseline sequential analyses for mother–child, father–child, and sibling–child coercive interchanges in 27 clinic-referred families. Of all exchanges with the targeted problem child (ages 5 to 14 years), mothers were involved in about 50% of these episodes, siblings in most of the other half, and fathers seldom involved at all. In fact, only 2 of the 27 fathers took part in any of the coercive exchanges with their aggressive problem child.

In a similar vein, Burgess and Conger (1978) compared the differential involvement of mothers and fathers in coercive and positive interchanges with their elementary-school-age problem versus normal children. These investigators observed two groups of families: those in which one child had been abused or neglected and those in which no problems had been reported. Mothers in the abuse and neglect groups were significantly more aversive and less positive with their children than were mothers in the control group. However, the fathers in the abuse and control groups acted about the same toward their children. Fathers in the neglect group did display significantly less positive actions toward their children than did the control fathers. Reid et al. (1981) found similar differential parent interchanges in their comparison of abused and normal children. Once again, mothers in the abuse sample were much more likely to engage their children in coercive episodes than were mothers in the control sample. Fathers in the two samples, however, could not be differentiated in terms of their coercive interchanges with the children.

The preceding findings would suggest that those mothers who became coercively entrapped with their infants continue to be the child's partner of choice in future coercive encounters. Perhaps because fathers are not their infants' principal caretakers, they are simply less likely to become entrapped during that first year of childrearing. If so, then the absence of direct father involvement in the child's later problems would make some degree of sense. However, if one looks at longitudinal and retrospective studies of child coercive–antisocial behaviors, it is clear that both fathers and mothers contribute to such child behavior problems.

Robins, West, and Herjanic (1975) compared molar measures of parent and child antisocial behavior—namely, arrest records and other involvement with the criminal justice system. In this sample of 76 American black males, the fathers' as well as mothers' history of arrest and delinquency classification were correlated with the sons' delinquency. Of those fathers who had delinquency records, 46% of their sons were delinquent as opposed to 26% of the sons whose fathers had no history of criminality. Similar relationships were found in the mother–son dyads.

Likewise, the West and Farrington (1977) follow-up of 350 children examined parental criminal status as predictors of child delinquency adjudication by age 18. In this case, 37% of sons with criminal status fathers became delinquent, as opposed to 8% of the boys whose fathers had no such records. As far as mother–son communalities are concerned, twice as many boys with mother criminal status became delinquent. While a daughter's classification as delinquent was much less likely in this sample, parental criminal status (particularly with mothers) bore the same predictive relationships to the girls' delinquency likelihood.

Other follow-up studies of antisocial children (McCord, 1979; Tonge et al., 1975) add confirming support to the conclusion that fathers are indeed an important influence on their children's antisocial behavior. The difficulty we encounter at this point concerns a process explanation for such influence. Because the direct observational studies (e.g., Patterson, 1977) yield little evidence of father involvement in child development of coercive behavior, how is the eventual antisocial matchup produced? Even in the large-scale West and Farrington (1977) study, the correlational influence of criminal fathers on their children proved unrelated to other measures of father characteristics such as income and his typical actions toward the child.

However, this study did indicate that criminal-status fathers described themselves as "lax" in supervision of their children, suggesting perhaps that fathers' sins of omission might be an *indirect* factor in the development of child antisocial behavior. It may be, then, that mothers provide the direct teaching experiences involved in child antisocial development and fathers merely function to impede or permit the course of this development. Of course, it is equally reasonable to posit genetic contributions from the paternal side, as well as modeling influences based on father display of antisocial behaviors. While the available data shed little light on any one of these three speculations, it does seem reasonable to argue an *indirect* rather than direct impact of father influence.

The likelihood of indirect paternal influences on child antisocial behavior (as well as direct mother influence) is bolstered by some of the very studies that portray parent criminality as a precursor to this child outcome. The criminal-status factor is also associated with marital discord within the family (McCord & McCord, 1959; West & Farrington, 1973). In the former study, boys who came from homes in which mother–father conflict was high were twice as likely to become delinquent. It is also apparent from these studies that marital distress per se, not the separation of quarreling parents, is the critical predictor (McCord & McCord, 1959). Thus, Power, Ash, Schoenberg, and Sirey (1974) discovered that delinquent boys who repeated their criminal actions were more likely to have quarreling parents who remained together. Twenty-seven percent of the boys from divorced parents were recidivists, while 37% of the distressed but married parents had delinquent sons who were repeaters. When one then looks at childrearing factors associated with marital disharmony, we once again are presented with mother aversive exchanges with the child and father laxness in discipline. Farrington (1978) portrayed such parental inconsistency in finding that mothers in distressed marriages were apt to be the principal and hostile disciplinarians while the fathers were likely to sanction their children's coercive actions by doing nothing—again the paternal "sins of omission."

In a summary of the preceding differential parenting factors in delinquency, it does seem evident that some combination of direct maternal teaching–shaping and paternal modeling or contradiction of mother discipline will determine the course of child antisocial development. While we by no means intend to minimize genetic determinants, the current evidence simply gives a more complete picture of direct and indirect environmental influences. We believe that these influences can be usefully understood within our stimulus inconsistency model as follows: If a child's mother-taught coercive behavior is gradually brought under inconsistent social consequences, the maintenance and generalizability of that behavior can become a function of superstitious stimulus control.

As we have shown elsewhere (Wahler & Graves, 1982), it is possible to generate stimulus control over child behavior even when that behavior receives random reinforcement. For example, in Fowler and Baer (1980), this sort of superstitious control was readily produced over preschool children's sharing behavior. Following what amounts to an inconsistency model, the authors first placed sharing under discriminative instructional control by contingent reinforcement of that behavior after instructing the children to share. Then, by merely delaying the reinforcement deliveries, other nontargeted child sharing responses were adventitiously (inconsistently) reinforced as well. As expected from principles of superstition (Herrnstein, 1966), the nontargeted sharing responses were likewise brought under stable instructional control. The children acted *as if* their nontargeted sharing responses were contingently consequated. As discussed in the previous section, we refer to this type of instructional phenomenon as *setting-event* control (after Wahler & Fox, 1982).

If the fathers of coercive children are themselves models of antisocial behavior (criminal fathers) and they also model coercive behavior (marital disputes), one could readily see how these men could acquire setting-event control of their children's coercive and antisocial actions. It seems likely that paternal coercive behavior could occasionally precede mother–child coercive teaching exchanges. For example, father hitting mother is followed by mother screaming at her child's refusal to take a nap. These temporally close interchanges could establish father's deviant behavior as a setting event for his child's noncompliance. Despite the fact that father's behavior is only a random predictor of reinforcement for his child's mother's directed coercive behavior, the child acts *as if* a lawful relationship exists. Therefore, whenever father does something coercive–antisocial, the child is likely to act in a similar manner.

In a sense, then, mother and father might constitute a stimulus class for child coercive behavior. This stimulus class is faulty in its predictive value: Although mother's aversive behavior is a discriminative stimulus for child coercive behavior, the father component of this class has no such function. Nevertheless, both parents will set the occasion for their problem child's coercive actions. A parent–child similarity is therefore produced: The child matches parental output of coercion, with only the mother serving as a dependable consequence of that category of child behavior. We think that superstitious stimulus control will also account for the further generalization of a coercive child's antisocial actions. If the child responds (mistakenly) to paternal cues as if they were discriminative for maternal reinforcement, it stands to reason that people outside the nuclear family can serve a similar stimulus function.

Adolescence

Given the inconsistent parenting associated with antisocial–coercive children, one would expect an adolescent growing uninterrupted through such experiences to be unusual in several respects. We would expect the adolescent to display a full range of well-ingrained coercive behaviors unpredictably. That is, the youth's production of verbal and nonverbal harassment and noncompliance is apt to be situationally inappropriate. His or her acts of violence, stealing, and otherwise ignoring the rights of others will occur without the extensive provocation required for the nondelinquent youth. In essence, these characteristics describe an individual who is simply not influenced by those social cues that serve a cease-and-desist function for other adolescents. These latter youth, who have not been reared under the previously described coercive and inconsistent parenting contingencies, are less likely to be antisocial when presented with social signs of displeasure or stated rules and instructions.

Clinical observers have long noted the differential sensitivity of delinquent youth to social cues ahd have been inclined to attribute these characteristics to certain personal deficiencies. Thus, delinquents are apt to be described as lacking in "empathy," "morality," "love," "altruism," and other labels reflecting interpersonal deficiencies. In fact, the research literature does support the personal deficiency viewpoint, both with respect to the delinquent youth's social discrimination skills as well as social behavior skills. Chandler, Greenspan, and Barenboim (1974) and Kurtiness and Hogan (1972) assessed delinquent and normal youths' detection of various social cues (empathy). As expected, the delinquents proved significantly less sensitive than their normal counterparts. Also in line with the discrimination-deficiency notion, delinquents are apt to ignore the stated intentions of a rule-breaking model when judging the seriousness of these model actions (Hudgins & Prentice, 1973).

On the behavioral side, delinquent adolescents also demonstrate deficiencies in a variety of social skills such as eye contact, verbal acknowledgement of other peoples' directives to them, use of questions and appropriate head nods (Braukmann, Phillips, & Wolf, 1973). Compared to adolescents who have not followed the course of coercion and inconsistency leading to delinquent status, these deviant youth look to be quite deficient in social skills (Freedman, Rosenthal, Donahoe, Schlundt, & McFall, 1978). Small wonder, then, that these youth are judged unpopular by adults and by their nondelinquent peers (Winder & Rau, 1962). Undoubtedly, the combined impact of frequent and unpredictable coercion as well as a low-rate production of positive actions leads to the delinquent adolescent's isolate status in a community.

However, the skill-deficiency model of adolescent antisocial status has been found wanting in reference to situational factors, as well as the investigator's choice of what to measure. As Kazdin (1979) pointed out in his review of behavioral assessment, the measurement of one's behavior in a single environmental setting is hardly a trustworthy index of how that person will behave in other settings. Furthermore, that index changes when the assessment picture is broadened by additional measures.

Thus, Savitsky and Czyzewski (1978) discovered that the verbal skills of delinquent adolescents covaried with their discrimination of social cues. When the investigators measured youth discrimination of visually presented facial and body cues, delinquent adolescents differed from adult-derived norms to a significantly greater extent than nondelinquent adolescents. However, when measures of verbal intelligence were correlated with these outcomes, the supposed insensitivity of the delinquents failed to materialize. In fact, when all adolescents were presented with another social-cue task not requiring verbal responses, the delinquency status factor contributed nothing to performance. Likewise, in reference to the behavioral skill dimension, situational cues appear to contribute variance to the degree of social prowess demonstrated by delinquent youth.

Kazdin, Matson, & Esveldt-Dawson (1981) measured the social skills of severely disturbed preadolescents in a psychiatric hospital setting and compared the youths' performance to that of a matched sample of normal youth. Half of all youth were observed under routine assessment conditions while the other half were seen under "incentive" conditions, in which they were praised for performing. This latter condition virtually eliminated skill differences between the two groups. Only "appropriate motor activity" was more frequent in the normal group. Otherwise, all youth observed under the incentive conditions showed higher rates of eye contact, used more words in talking, were rated higher in appropriate intonations, and used more facial expressions. On a more molar level of performance, the youth observed under incentive conditions gave more compliments, offered more help, were more likely to respond calmly to negative provocation and more likely to show appropriate refusals to requests.

We agree with McFall (1982) in his interpretation of the skill-deficiency issue within a systems framework encompassing multiple levels of stimulus and response interaction. Our more strictly behavioral version of such a systems framework includes both stimulus-class and response-class concepts. The issue of personal deficiencies in adolescent delinquents becomes a question of understanding the faulty stimulus-class control described in the previous section of this chapter, as well as mapping out organizational features of the adolescents' response repertoire. Under certain stimulus conditions, these antisocial youth display the same social skills as do other adolescents. These problem youth will also demonstrate typical adolescent responsiveness to important social cues (displeasure, joy, fear) given that one assesses this responsiveness on more than a single response segment of their repertoires.

What, then, constitutes a complete picture of adolescents who have "run the gamut" of thorough teaching principles of coercion, parental inconsistency, and parental modeling of coercion? We suspect that these youth's skill deficits and coercive actions are under the stimulus control of environmental conditions unique to each youth. More importantly, this class of environmental stimuli may comprise events with little apparent interrelationship. According to our inconsistency model of stimulus control, not all stimuli composing a class need serve a common discriminative function with respect to behavior. As we suggested in the previous section, inconsistent environmental contingencies can lead to "superstitious" arrangements between stimuli and responses—arrangements that will, nevertheless, prove to be causal in function. Thus, a youth's chronic school truancy could be influenced by apparently irrelevant events (e.g., fight with sibling) as well as those bearing a more obvious connection (argument with teacher).

A further complication in understanding such faulty stimulus control concerns the response organization of each youth's behavior repertoire. Observational studies of children have repeatedly shown that some of a child's responses covary in predictable fashion (see Kazdin, 1982). In the case of coercive children, these classes appear to be quite stable, such that a single problem child may display the same response covariations in different environmental settings (Harris & Reid, 1981). More to the point of our present topic, Solnick, Braukmann, Bedlington, Kirigin, and Wolf (1981) were able to document an interesting response class held in common by delinquent adolescents. These youth's self reports of personal delinquent actions covaried inversely with their observed proximity to adult caretakers ("teaching-parents") ($-.81$) and their observed talking to these adults ($-.95$).

Such response-class phenomena are surely relevant in treatment plans for delinquent youth and these within-repertoire covariations also illustrate the potential difficulties in mapping out stimulus control of any single youth behavior. For example, if a delinquent act such as drug use covaries inversely with talking to a parent, the former behavior might be *indirectly* influenced by the latter response. This latter response (talking to parent) could be under direct stimulus control of an environmental class comprising multiple events, any one of which could affect the likelihood of its occurrence. Imagine, then, the puzzling array of functional arrangements in which a youth's delinquent actions are embedded.

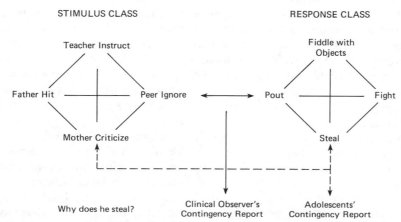

STIMULUS CLASS   RESPONSE CLASS

Figure 2 Hypothetical arrangements between a delinquent adolescent's response class and a stimulus class governing one of the responses (pouting). According to the functional connections, any one of four stimuli will affect the likelihood of the youth's pouting. That response is in a functional class comprising covarying delinquent and nondelinquent behaviors. When the youth and a clinician attempt to understand the boy's delinquent behavior (stealing), neither observer can derive a direct explanation.

Figure 2 presents a hypothetical picture of this puzzle in reference to one individual's problem behavior. If one were to "explain" why this youth engages in stealing and fighting, a variety of explanations are possible and each would have some degree of credibility. The youth attributes his stealing to mother criticism of him ("She's on my back all the time."). A clinical observer, on the other hand, can account only for the youth's tendency to pout, attributing this behavior to "poor peer relationships." In fact, both observers have sampled portions of the youth's ecosystem, but neither has derived a complete mapping of how that system functions.

In summary, it surely seems evident that delinquent adolescents have followed a fairly predictable course of development—possibly beginning in the first year of life. That course is marked by the child's use of coercion and avoidance of prosocial relationships, social characteristics also seen in his/her parents.

NEW DIRECTIONS

To conclude, our review of the literature indicates that children who are brought up in a generally coercive environment commonly grow up to become coercive, antisocial adults who, once adult, rear children likely to repeat the same behavioral pattern. Just how these cross-generational continuities develop is still a matter of speculation. Our bias in theorizing has centered on an expansion of basic principles of operant learning. This expansion generally assumes that the reinforcement function of immediate stimulus events lies solely in their relationship with surrounding setting events. In other words, it assumes that a person's behavior at any one point in time cannot solely be understood by making reference to its immediately preceding stimuli; these stimuli must also be related to the social context in which they are displayed.

Based on this assumption, we developed a model that attempts to account for cross-generational continuities in coercive, antisocial behavior by relying heavily on the role of inconsistent social contingencies in the development of stimulus control. Specifically, this model presupposes that inconsistent or unpredictable social contexts serve an aversive function for the individuals who are a part of them and predicts that, if an individual within such a context produces a behavior that generates an increase in the predictability of stimulus events, that consequence will prove reinforcing. Contrary to commonsense expectations, this will be the case even if this reinforced behavior (e.g., parental aversiveness) leads to increases in the aversive behavior of another party (e.g., child aversiveness), as appears to be the case in the transmission of antisocial behavior across generations.

We believe that, besides providing a better fit with the developmental data than other models, the inconsistency model also suggests relevant targets of change, for both clinical and preventive intervention, not previously specified in the behavioral literature. For example, it might prove reasonable to help distressed mothers increase their pattern of contingent response to *all* aspects of infant behavior—not simply the prosocial segments. In addition, if distressed mothers and their problem children are influenced by faulty, superstitiously constructed stimulus classes, a means of helping these individuals discriminate contingent from noncontingent stimulus–response associations might prove useful.

Our survey of the literature and our theoretical expansion of traditional formulation have attempted to put together some common threads in a developmental picture of child deviance. It may now be appropriate to consider new clinical means of unravelling these threads.

REFERENCES

Achenbach, T. M., & Edelbrock, C. S. (1978). The classification of child psychopathology: A review and analysis of empirical efforts. *Psychological Bulletin, 85,* 1275–1301.
Ainsworth, M. D. S. (1979). Attachment as related to mother–infant interaction. In J. S.

Rosenblatt, R. A. Hinde, C. Beer, & M. Busnel (Eds.), *Advances in the study of behavior* (Vol. 9). New York: Academic Press.

Alfaro, J. D. (1981). Report on the relationship between child abuse and neglect and later socially deviant behavior. In R. H. Hunner & Y. E. Walker (Eds.), *Exploring the relationship between child abuse and delinquency.* Montclair, NJ: Allanheld, Osmun & Co.

Altemeier, W. A., Vietze, P. M., Sherrod, K. B., Sandler, H. M., Falsey, S., & O'Connor, S. (1979). Prediction of child maltreatment during pregnancy. *Journal of the American Academy of Child Psychiatry, 18,* 2, 205–218.

Arend, R., Gove, F., & Sroufe, L. A. (1979). Continuity of individual adaptation from infancy to kindergarten: A predictive study of ego resiliency and curiosity in preschoolers. *Child Development, 50,* 950–959.

Bandura, A. (1962). Social learning through imitation. In M. R. Jones (Ed.), *Nebraska symposium on motivation, 1962.* Lincoln: University of Nebraska. Pp. 211–269.

Bandura, A. (1969). *Principles of behavior modification.* New York: Holt, Rinehart and Winston.

Bandura, A. (1973). *Aggression: A social learning analysis.* Englewood Cliffs, NJ: Prentice-Hall.

Bandura, A. (1977). *Social learning theory.* Englewood Cliffs, NJ: Prentice-Hall.

Bandura, A., Ross, D., & Ross, S. A. (1961). Transmission of aggression through imitation of aggressive models. *Journal of Abnormal and Social Psychology, 63,* 575–582.

Bandura, A., Ross, D., & Ross, S. A. (1963). Imitation of film-mediated agressive models. *Journal of Abnormal and Social Psychology, 66,* 3–11.

Bates, J. E. (1980). The concept of difficult temperament. *Merrill-Palmer Quarterly, 26*(4), 299–319.

Baumrind, D. (1975). *Early socialization and the discipline controversy.* Morristown, NJ: General Learning Press.

Baumrind, D. (1978). Parental disciplinary patterns and social competence in children. *Youth and Society, 9*(3), 239–276.

Becker, W. C. (1964). Consequences of different kinds of parental discipline. In M. L. Hoffman and L. W. Hoffman (Eds.), *Review of child development research* (Vol. 1). New York: Russell Sage Foundation.

Bell, R. Q. (1960). Relations between behavior manifestations in the human neonate. *Child Development, 31,* 463–477.

Bell, R. Q. (1968). A reinterpretation of the direction of effects studies of socialization. *Psychological Review, 75,* 81–95.

Bell, R. Q., & Harper, L. V. (1977). *Child effects on adults.* Hillsdale, NJ: Erlbaum.

Bell, S. M., & Ainsworth, M. D. S. (1972). Infant crying and maternal responsiveness. *Child Development, 43,* 1171–1190.

Blanchard, M., & Main, M. (1979). Avoidance of the attachment figure and social–emotional adjustment in day-care infants. *Developmental Psychology, 15,* 445–446.

Braukmann, C. J., Phillips, E. L., & Wolf, M. M. (1973). *The measurement and modification of heterosexual interaction skills of pre-delinquents at Achievement Place.* Unpublished manuscript, University of Kansas, Department of Human Development.

Brazelton, T. B. (1973). *The Neonatal Behavioral Assessment Scale.* Philadelphia: Lippincott.

Burgess, R. L., & Conger, R. D. (1978). Family interaction in abusive, neglectful and normal families. *Child Development, 49,* 1163–1173.

Butterfield, P., Van Doornick, W., Dawson, P., & Alexander, H. (1979, March). *Early identification of dysparenting.* Paper presented at the meeting of the Society for Research in Child Development, San Francisco.

Cameron, J. R. (1977). Parental treatment, children's temperament, and the risk of childhood behavioral problems: Relationships between parental characteristics and changes in children's temperament over time. *American Journal of Orthopsychiatry, 47,* 568–576.

Carey, W. B. (1970). A simplified method of measuring infant temperament. *Journal of Pediatrics, 77,* 188–194.

Chandler, M. J., Greenspan, S., & Barenboim, C. (1974). Assessment and training of role-taking and referential skills in institutionalized emotionally disturbed children. *Developmental Psychology, 10,* 546–553.

Chess, S., & Thomas, A. (1977). Temperamental individuality from childhood to adolescence. *Journal of the American Academy of Child Psychiatry, 16,* 218–226.

Christiansen, K. O. (1970). Crime in a Danish twin population. *Acta Geneticae Medicae et Gemellologicae, 19,* 323–326.

Crowe, R. R. (1972). The adopted offspring of women criminal offenders. *Archives of General Psychiatry, 27,* 600–603.

Crowe, R. R. (1974). An adoption study of antisocial personality. *Archives of General Psychiatry, 31,* 785–791.

Curtis, L. (1974). *Criminal violence: National patterns and behavior.* Lexington, MA: Lexington Books.

D'Amato, M. R. (1974). Derived motives. *Annual Review of Psychology, 25,* 83–106.

Delfini, L. F., Bernal, M. E., & Rosen, P. M. (1976). Comparison of deviant and normal boys in home settings. In E. J. Mash, L. A. Hamerlynck, & L. C. Handy (Eds.), *Behavior modification and families.* New York: Bruner/Mazel.

Dion, K. K. (1974). Children's physical attractiveness and sex as determinants of adult punitiveness. *Developmental Psychology, 10,* 772–778.

Donovan, W. L., Leavitt, L. A., & Balling, J. D. (1978). Maternal physiological response to infant signals. *Psychophysiology, 15,* 68–74.

Egeland, B., & Sroufe, L. A. (1981). Attachment and early maltreatment. *Child Development, 52,* 44–52.

Eron, L. D., Walder, L. O., & Lefkowitz, M. M. (1971). *Learning of aggression in children.* Boston: Little, Brown, & Co.

Farrington, D. P. (1978). The family backgrounds of aggressive youths. In L. A. Hersov, M. Berger, & D. Shaffer (Eds.), *Aggression and antisocial behaviour in childhood and adolescence.* Oxford: Pergamon Press.

Forehand, R., King, H., Peed, S., & Yoder, P. (1975). Mother–child interactions: Comparison of a non-compliant clinic group and a non-clinic group. *Behavior Research and Therapy, 13,* 79–84.

Fowler, S. A., & Baer, D. M. (1981). "Do I have to be good all day?" The timing of delayed reinforcement as a factor in generalization. *Journal of Applied Behavior Analysis, 14,* 13–24.

Freedman, B. J., Rosenthal, L., Donahoe, C. P., Jr., Schlundt, D. G., & McFall, R. M. (1978). A social–behavioral analysis of skill deficits in delinquent and nondelinquent adolescent boys. *Journal of Consulting and Clinical Psychology, 46,* 1448–1462.

Frodi, A. M., Lamb, M. E., Leavitt, L. A., & Donovan, W. L. (1978). Fathers' and mothers' responses to infant smiles and cries. *Infant Behavior and Development, 1,* 187–198.

Frodi, A. M., Lamb, M. E., Leavitt, L. A., Donovan, W. L., Neff, C., & Sherry, D. (1978). Fathers' and mothers' responses to the faces and cries of normal and premature infants. *Developmental Psychology, 14(5),* 490–498.

Gardner, L. I., & Neu, R. L. (1972). Evidence linking an extra Y chromosome to sociopathic behavior. *Archives of General Psychiatry, 26,* 220–222.

George, C., & Main, M. (1979). Social interactions of young abused children: Approach, avoidance, and aggression. *Child Development, 50,* 306–318.

Graham, P., Rutter, M., & George, S. (1973). Temperamental characteristics as predictors of behavior disorders in children. *American Journal of Orthopsychiatry, 43,* 328–339.

Green, K. D., Forehand, R., & McMahon, R. J. (1979). Parental manipulation of compliance and noncompliance in normal and deviant children. *Behavior Modification, 3,* 245–266.

Grusec, J. E. (1972). Demand characteristics of the modeling experiment: Altruism as a function of age, and aggression. *Journal of Personality and Social Psychology, 22,* 139–148.

Harris, A., & Reid, J. B. (1981). The consistency of a class of coercive child behaviors across school settings for individual subjects. *Journal of Abnormal Child Psychology, 9,* 219–227.

Herrnstein, R. J. (1966). Superstition: A corollary of the principles of operant conditioning. In W. K. Horrig (Ed.), *Operant behavior: Area of research and application* (pp. 35–51). New York: Appleton-Century-Crofts.

Hetherington, E. M., & Frankie, G. (1967). Effects of parental dominance, warmth, and conflict on imitation in children. *Journal of Personality and Social Psychology, 6*(2), 119–125.

Hetherington, E. M., & Martin, B. (1979). Family interaction. In H. C. Quay & J. S. Werry (Eds.), *Psychopathological disorders in childhood* (2nd ed.). New York: Wiley.

Hicks, D. J. (1968). Effects of co-observer's sanctions and adult presence on imitative aggression. *Child Development, 39,* 303–309.

Hudgins, W., & Prentice, N. M. (1973). Moral judgements in delinquent and nondelinquent adolescents and their mothers. *Journal of Abnormal Psychology, 82,* 145–152.

Imada, H., & Nageishi, Y. (1982). The concept of uncertainty in animal experiments using aversive stimulation. *Psychological Bulletin, 91,* 573–588.

Jarvik, L. F., Klodin, V., & Matsuyama, S. S. (1973). Human aggression and the extra Y chromosome. *American Psychologist, 28,* 674–682.

Johnson, S. M., & Lobitz, C. K. (1974). The personal and marital adjustment of parents as related to observed child deviance and parenting behavior. *Journal of Abnormal Child Psychology, 2,* 193–207.

Jonsson, G. (1967). *Delinquent boys, their parents and grandparents,* Copenhagen: Munksgaard.

Kazdin, A. E. (1979). Situational specificity: The two-edged swords of behavioral assessment. *Behavioral Assessment, 1,* 57–75.

Kazdin, A. E. (1982). Symptom substitution, generalization, and response covariation: Implications for psychotherapy outcome. *Psychological Bulletin, 91,* 349–365.

Kazdin, A. E., Matson, J. L., & Esveldt-Dawson, K. (1981). Social skill performance among normal and psychiatric inpatient children as a function of assessment conditions. *Behavior Research & Therapy, 19,* 145–152.

Kent, J. T. (1976). A follow-up study of abused children. *Journal of Pediatric Psychology, 1,* 25–31.

Kopfstein, D. (1972). The effects of accelerating and decelerating consequences on the social behavior of trainable retarded children. *Child Development, 43,* 800–809.

Kurtiness, W., & Hogan, R. (1972). Sources of conformity in unsocialized college students. *Journal of Abnormal Psychology, 80,* 49–51.

Lamb, M. E. (1978a). Influence of the child on marital quality and family interaction during the prenatal, perinatal, and infancy periods. In R. M. Lerner & G. B. Spanier (Eds.), *Child influences on marital and family interaction: A life-span perspective.* New York: Academic Press.

Lamb, M. E. (1978b). Social interaction in infancy and the development of personality. In M. E. Lamb (Ed.), *Social & personality development.* New York: Holt, Rinehart, & Winston.

88   Robert G. Wahler and Jean E. Dumas

Langner, T. S., McCarthy, E. D., Gersten, J. C., Simcha-Fagan, O., & Eisenberg, J. G. (1979). Factors in children's behavior and mental health over time: The Family Research Project. *Research in Community and Mental Health, 1,* 127–181.

Lewis, D. O., Shanok, S. S., Pincus, J. H., & Glaser, G. H. (1979). Violent juvenile delinquents. Psychiatric, neurological, psychological, and abuse factors. *Journal of the American Academy of Child Psychiatry, 18*(2), 307–319.

Lipsitt, L. P. (1969). Learning capacities in the human infant. In R. J. Robinson (Ed.), *Brain & early behavior.* New York: Academic Press.

Lobitz, W. C., & Johnson, S. M. (1975). Parental manipulation of the behavior of normal and deviant children. *Child Development, 46,* 719–726.

Lorenz, K. (1966). *On aggression.* London: Methuen.

Lytton, H. (1977). Correlates of compliance and the rudiments of conscience in two-year-old boys. *Canadian Journal of Behavioural Science, 9,* 242–251.

Lytton, H. (1980). *Parent–child interacting: The socialization process observed in twin and singleton families.* New York: Plenum.

Lytton, H., & Zwirner, W. (1975). Compliance and its controlling stimuli observed in a natural setting. *Developmental Psychology, 11,* 769–779.

McCord, J. (1979). Some child-rearing antecedents of criminal behavior in adult men. *Journal of Personality and Social Psychology, 37*(9), 1477–1486.

McCord, W., & McCord, J. (1959). *Origins of crime: A new evaluation of the Cambridge–Somerville Youth Study.* Columbia University Press.

McFall, R. M. (1982). A review and reformulation of the concept of social skills. *Behavioral Assessment, 4,* 1–33.

Mednick, S. A., Kirkegaard-Sorensen, L., Hutchings, R., Knop, J., Rosenberg, R., & Schulsinger, F. (1977). An example of biosocial interaction research: The interplay of socioenvironmental and individual factors in the etiology of criminal behavior. In S. A. Mednick & K. O. Christiansen (Eds.), *Biosocial bases of criminal behavior.* New York: Gardner Press.

Minton, C., Kagan, J., & Levine, J. (1971). Maternal control and obedience in the two-year-old. *Child Development, 42,* 1873–1894.

Morris, D. (1967). *The naked ape.* London: Cape.

Newson, J., & Newson, E. (1980). Parental punishment strategies with eleven-year-old children. In N. Frude (Ed.), *Psychological approaches to child abuse.* London: Batsford.

Offord, D. R., Allen, N., & Abrams, N. (1978). Parental psychiatric illness, broken homes, and delinquency. *Journal of the American Academy of Child Psychiatry, 17*(2), 224–238.

Oliver, J. E., & Taylor, A. (1971). Five generations of ill-treated children in one family pedigree. *British Journal of Psychiatry, 119,* 473–480.

Osborn, D. K., & Endsley, R. C. (1971). Emotional reactions of young children to TV violence. *Child Development, 42,* 321–331.

Osborn, S. G., & West, D. J. (1979). Conviction records of fathers and sons compared. *British Journal of Criminology, 19,* 120–133.

Osofsky, J. D., & O'Connell, E. J. (1972). Parent–child interaction: Daughters' effects upon mothers' and fathers' behaviors. *Developmental Psychology, 7,* 157–168.

Parke, R. D., & Collmer, C. N. (1975). Child abuse: An interdisciplinary analysis. In B. M. Caldwell & H. N. Ricciuti (Eds.), *Review of child development research* (Vol 5). Chicago: University of Chicago Press.

Patterson, G. R. (1976). The aggressive child: Victim and architect of a coercive system. In E. J. Mash, L. A. Hamerlynck, & L. C. Handy (Eds.) *Behavior modification and families: Vol. 1. Theory and research.* New York: Brunner/Mazel.

Patterson, G. R. (1977). Accelerating stimuli for two classes of coercive behaviors. *Journal of Abnormal Child Psychology, 5,* 335–350.

Patterson, G. R. (1979). A performance theory for coercive family interaction. In R. B. Cairns (Ed.), *The analysis of social interactions: Methods, issues, and illustrations*. Hillsdale, NJ: Erlbaum.

Patterson, G. R. (1980). Mothers: The unacknowledged victims. *Monographs of the Society for Research in Child Development, 45*(5, Serial No. 186).

Patterson, G. R., Littman, R. A., & Bricker, W. (1967). Assertive behavior in children: A step toward a theory of aggression. *Monographs of the Society for Research in Child Development, 32*(5, Serial No. 113).

Patterson, G. R., & Reid, J. B. (1970). Reciprocity and coercion: Two facets of social systems. In C. Neuringer & J. L. Michael (Eds.), *Behavior modification in clinical psychology*. New York: Appleton-Century-Crofts.

Peed, S., Roberts, M., & Forehand, R. (1977). Evaluation of the effectiveness of a standardized parent training program in altering the interaction of mothers and their noncompliant children. *Behavior Modification, 1*(3), 323–349.

Pfouts, J. H., Schopler, J. H., & Henley, H. C. (1981). Deviant behaviors of child victims and bystanders in violent families. In R. J. Hunner & Y. E. Walker (Eds.), *Exploring the relationship between child abuse and delinquency*. Montclair, NJ: Allanheld, Osmun & Co.

Power, M. J., Ash, P. M., Schoenberg, E., & Sirey, E. C. (1974). Delinquency and the family. *British Journal of Social Work, 4*, 13–38.

Reid, J. B., Taplin, P. S., & Lorber, R. (1981). A social interactional approach to the treatment of abusive families. In R. B. Stuart (Ed.), *Violent behavior: Social learning approaches to prediction, management, and treatment*. New York: Brunner/Mazel.

Reynolds, V. (1976). *The biology of human action*. San Francisco: W. H. Freeman.

Robins, L. N. (1979). Follow-up studies. In H. C. Quay & J. S. Werry (Eds.), *Psychopathological disorders of childhood* (2nd ed). New York: Wiley.

Robins, L. N., West, P. A., & Herjanic, B. L. (1975). Arrests and delinquency in two generations: A study of black urban families and their children. *Journal of Child Psychology and Psychiatry, 16*, 125–140.

Rollins, B. C., & Thomas, D. L. (1979). Parental support, power, and control techniques in the socialization of children. In W. R. Burr, R. Hill, F. I. Nye, & I. L. Reiss (Eds.), *Contemporary theories about the family: Research-based theories* (Vol. 1). New York: The Free Press.

Rutter, M. (1976). *Helping troubled children*. New York: Plenum.

Rutter, M. (1979). Protective factors in children's responses to stress and disadvantage. In M. W. Kent & J. E. Rolf (Eds.), *Primary prevention of psychopathology: Vol. 3. Social competence in children*. Hanover, NH: University of New England Press.

Sander, L. W. (1962). Issues in early mother–child interactions. *Journal of the American Academy of Child Psychiatry, 1*, 141–166.

Savitsky, J. C., & Czyzewski, D. (1978). The reaction of adolescent offenders and non-offenders to nonverbal emotion displays. *Journal of Abnormal Child Psychology, 6*, 89–96.

Shields, J. (1976). Polygenic influences in child psychiatry. In M. Rutter & L. Hersov (Eds.), *Child psychiatry: Modern approaches*. London: Blackwell.

Silver, L. B., Dublin, C. C., & Lourie, R. S. (1969). Does violence breed violence? Contributions from a study of the child abuse syndrome. *American Journal of Psychiatry, 126*, 152–153.

Snyder, J. J. (1977). A reinforcement analysis of intervention in problem and nonproblem children. *Journal of Abnormal Psychology, 86*(5), 528–535.

Solnick, J. V., Braukmann, C. J., Bedlington, M. M., Kirigin, K. A., & Wolf, M. M. (1981). The relationship between parent–youth interactions and delinquency in group homes. *Journal of Abnormal Child Psychology, 9*, 107–119.

Spelt, D. K. (1948). The conditioning of the human fetus in utero. *Journal of Experimental Psychology, 38,* 338–346.

Spinetta, J. J., & Rigler, D. (1972). The child-abusing parent: A psychological review. *Psychological Bulletin, 77,* 296–304.

Stayton, D. J., & Ainsworth, M. D. S. (1973). Individual differences in infant responses to brief everyday separations as related to other infant and maternal behaviors. *Developmental Psychology, 9,* 226–235.

Stayton, D. J., Hogan, R., & Ainsworth, M. D. S. (1971). Infant obedience and maternal behavior: The origin of socialization reconsidered. *Child Development, 42,* 1057–1069.

Steele, B. F., & Pollock, C. B. (1974). A psychiatric study of parents who abuse infants and small children. In R. E. Helfer & C. H. Kempe (Eds.), *The battered child.* Chicago: University of Chicago Press.

Steinmetz, S. K. (1979). Disciplinary techniques and their relationship to aggressiveness, dependency, and conscience. In W. R. Burr, R. Hill, F. I. Nye, & I. L. Reiss (Eds.), *Contemporary theories about the family: Vol. 1. Research-based theories.* New York: The Free Press.

Straus, M. A., Gelles, R. J., & Steinmetz, S. K. (1980). *Behind closed doors: Violence in the American family.* Garden City, NY: Anchor Press/Doubleday.

Terdal, L. G., Jackson, R. J., & Garner, A. M. (1976). Mother–child interactions: A comparison between normal and developmentally delayed groups. In E. J. Mash, L. A. Hamerlynck, & L. C. Handy (Eds.), *Behavior modification and families.* New York: Burner/Mazel.

Thomas, A., & Chess, S. (1976). Evolution of behavior disorders into adolescence. *American Journal of Psychiatry, 133,* 539–542.

Thomas, A., Chess, S., & Birch, H. G. (1968). *Temperament and behavior disorders in children.* New York: New York University Press.

Thomas, A., Chess, S., & Birch, H. G. (1970). The origin of personality. *Scientific American, 223*(2), 102–109.

Timberlake, E. M. (1981). Child abuse and externalized aggression: Preventing a delinquent life style. In R. J. Hunner & Y. E. Walker (Eds.), *Exploring the relationship between child abuse and delinquency.* Montclair, NJ: Allanheld, Osmun & Co.

Tonge, W. L., James, D. S., & Hillam, S. M. (1975). Families without hope: A controlled study of 33 problem families. *British Journal of Psychiatry* (Special publication No. 11).

Wadsworth, M. (1979). *Roots of delinquency.* Oxford: Martin Robertson.

Wahl, G., Johnson, S. M., Johansson, S., & Martin, S. (1974). An operant analysis of child–family interaction. *Behavior Therapy, 5,* 64–78.

Wahler, R. G. (1980). The insular mother: Her problems in parent–child treatment. *Journal of Applied Behavior Analysis, 13,* 207–219.

Wahler, R. G., & Dumas, J. E. (1981, September). Changing the observational coding styles of insular and noninsular mothers: A step toward maintenance of parent training effects. *Paper presented at the National Conference on Parent Training,* Dallas.

Wahler, R. G., & Fox, J. J. (1981). Setting events in applied behavior analysis: Toward a conceptual and methodological expansion. *Journal of Applied Behavior Analysis, 14,* 327–338.

Wahler, R. G., & Fox, J. J. (1982). Response structure in deviant child–parent relationships: Implications for family therapy. In D. J. Bernstein (Ed.), *Response structure and organization* (Pp. 1–46). Lincoln/London: University of Nebraska Press.

Wahler, R. G., & Graves, M. (1983). Setting events in social networks: Ally or enemy in child behavior therapy. *Behavior Therapy, 14,* 19–36.

Wahler, R. G., Hughey, J. B., & Gordon, J. S. (1981). Chronic patterns of mother–child coercion: Some differences between insular and noninsular families. *Analysis and Intervention in Development Disabilities, 1*(2), 145–156.

Wahler, R. G., & Nordquist, V. M. (1973). Adult discipline as a factor in childhood imitation. *Journal of Abnormal Child Psychology, 1*(1), 40–56.

Waters, E., Wippman, J., & Sroufe, L. A. (1979). Attachment, positive affect and competence in the peer group: Two studies in construct validation. *Child Development, 50,* 821–829.

Welsh, R. S. (1976). Severe parental punishment and delinquency: A developmental theory. *Journal of Clinical Child Psychology, 5,* 17–21.

West, D. J., & Farrington, D. P. (1973). *Who becomes delinquent?* London: Heinemann.

West, D. J., & Farrington, D. P. (1977). *The delinquent way of life.* London: Heinemann.

Wilson, E. O. (1975). *Sociobiology: The new synthesis.* Cambridge, MA: Harvard University Press.

Wilson, E. O. (1978). *On human nature.* Cambridge, MA: Harvard University Press.

Wilson, H. (1975). Juvenile delinquency, parental criminality, and social handicap. *British Journal of Criminology, 15,* 241–250.

Winder, C., & Rau, L. (1962). Parental attitudes associated with social deviance in preadolescent boys. *Journal of Abnormal & Social Psychology, 64,* 418–424.

CHAPTER 3

The Peer Relations of Young Handicapped and Nonhandicapped Children

Michael J. Guralnick

INTRODUCTION

Establishing successful relationships with one's peers is one of the most important accomplishments of early childhood. Despite the battles that rage around the possession of toys, the frustration surrounding social bids that are ignored or rejected, the accommodations children must make in relation to their own self interest, and the ephemeral nature of many early relationships, the process proceeds in a rather remarkably positive and predictable manner. Ultimately a set of shared experiences builds, rules are adopted, children become more proficient in resolving conflict and in gaining their own ends, and peer interactions eventually become a major influence in the lives of most children.

Interest in the study of peer relations and a recognition of its developmental significance is, however, a relatively recent phenomenon. Although detailed descriptions of peer relations were carried out in the 1930s (e.g., Bridges, 1933; Maudry & Nekula, 1939; Parten, 1932, 1933), a long period of inactivity followed. During this time, developmental research centered on adult–child relationships, viewing other aspects of social development as by-products of this more fundamental relationship. As noted by Lewis and Rosenblum (1975b), this narrow focus may have been due to the dominance of psychoanalytic thought, the fact that early characterizations of peer interactions were viewed as primarily negative, and interpretations of Piagetian theory that young children were too egocentric to engage in meaningful peer relations.

It almost seemed as if pressure were building beneath the surface during this period, for once the limitations of many of these views became evident, literally hundreds of studies materialized. Many factors contributed to this renaissance. The changing structure of the family resulted in the creation of a group care system for serving younger and younger children. Observers in these settings could hardly deny the emergence of a rich array of satisfying encounters with peers. These observations were supported by research demonstrating that even young children were not nearly as egocentric nor as negative in their peer relations as first thought (Garvey & Hogan, 1973; Lewis & Rosenblum, 1975a; Shatz & Gelman, 1973). Similarly, programs for disadvantaged and handicapped children beginning in the 1960s and extending to the more-recent efforts toward mainstreaming forced developmentalists to confront issues directly related to children's social behavior with their peers (Guralnick, 1978; Tjossem, 1976; Zigler & Trickett, 1978). In fact, peer relations not only became an object of study, but eventually were seen as a valuable outcome measure for assessing the impact of other factors, such as day care (Belsky & Steinberg, 1978), child abuse (George & Main, 1979), or divorce (Hetherington, Cox, & Cox, 1979).

Reflecting on the changes that have occurred, Hartup (1976, 1979) points to the now-considerable evidence suggesting that one's peers contribute significantly and uniquely to the development of children's social and communicative competencies. Although the exact processes through which these skills and abilities are acquired are not well understood, they appear to be linked to the coequal qualities of child–child social exchanges. The contrasts between typical adult–child and child–child interactions are particularly noteworthy. For example, adults typically provide a highly responsive and often anticipatory social environment in which they tend to be the initiators. Child–child exchanges, in contrast, rely on the effective participation and balanced contributions of both partners. At the same time, however, these exchanges are more unpredictable and are relatively impoverished from linguistic and communicative perspectives. Moreover, child–child and adult–child exchanges tend to occur in different situations, focus on different themes, and take on different forms.

These differential patterns allow the possibility that each type of interaction can serve a different function (Hartup, 1978; Lewis & Feiring, 1979; Lewis, Young, Brooks, & Michalson, 1975). In fact, some researchers have even suggested that autonomous systems of adult–child and child–child relationships can be identified (Mueller, 1979). Although concepts based on an understanding of interlocking systems will probably provide the most accurate representation of these relationships, the separate system conceptualization does highlight the dramatic turn of events that has occurred in the field of peer relations.

Unfortunately, despite its importance, not all children achieve an adequate level of social competence with their peers. A relatively small but significant subset of otherwise normally developing children fail, for a variety of reasons, to acquire the requisite skills or interests, becoming isolated from their peers and at risk for future adjustment problems (Conger & Keane, 1981; Wanlass & Prinz, 1982). Less is known about children with cognitive, motor, sensory, or language delays or dysfunctions, but it is reasonable to anticipate that the problems in establishing peer relations are likely to be even more widespread for these youngsters. In fact, handicapped children experience an entire range of difficulties in virtually every phase of the socialization process (Battle, 1974; Robinson & Robinson, 1976); difficulties that may have a profound effect on their social interactions with other children.

Any understanding of the early peer relations of handicapped children must occur within the framework and concepts drawn from the study of the peer relations of normally developing children. Descriptions of the developmental course of peer relations, its structure and organization, must be available as a means of gauging the existence and significance of delays or deviations from typical developmental patterns. Similarly, knowledge of factors that influence its quantitative and qualitative characteristics, both historical and contemporary, including environmental variables, family interrelationships, sibling interactions, and direct peer experiences provide important insights into the interplay of forces that govern the effectiveness of peer relations and may even suggest possible routes for intervention, should difficulties be evident. Beyond these factors, a detailed understanding of the specific social and communicative skills that constitute effective peer relations as well as their cognitive prerequisites and corequisites are necessary to identify particular processes that may require special attention. The skills and strategies children employ to enter, maintain, and terminate social interactions with their peers compose an area of inquiry that lends itself directly to the design of intervention techniques.

Accordingly, in this chapter, a summary of the current knowledge and issues of the early peer relations of normally developing children is presented here next, not only as an independent area of interest but also to provide a basis for subsequent discussions of the peer interactions of young handicapped children. Following an examination of the peer relations of handicapped children, the social interactions of handicapped and nonhandicapped preschool children enrolled in the same educational setting are considered. This discussion focuses not only on the potential value of these mainstreamed or integrated settings in promoting the peer relations of handicapped children, but also serves to further our understanding of the formation of social groupings in early childhood–early intervention programs. It is important to note that, because thorough reviews of children manifesting primary behavior disorders (Campbell & Cluss, 1982), as well as children considered socially withdrawn (e.g., Hops & Greenwood, 1981) are available elsewhere, discussion is limited in this chapter to other groups of children considered handicapped, especially those with cognitive and sensory impairments. Finally, information on the developmental patterns and characteristics of handicapped children are integrated with corresponding research for nonhandicapped children to form a framework for the design of much-needed assessment instruments and to suggest a system to guide the treatment of children having difficulties interacting with their peers.

DEVELOPMENT OF PEER INTERACTIONS OF NONHANDICAPPED CHILDREN

During the first year of life, most of the component behaviors of peer-directed social interactions become apparent when opportunities to interact regularly with peers are provided (Mueller & Vandell, 1979; Vandell, 1980). Smiling, vocalizing, gesturing, looking, touching, and approaching other children are common occurrences even at 6 months of age (Vandell, Wilson, & Buchanan, 1980). Later on, social interactions involving objects in the form of offering, sharing, and taking toys mediate these exchanges. Even some rudimentary forms of imitation and turn-taking can occur during this time (Vincze, 1971). However, although peer interactions can be fostered through regular playgroup experiences in familiar settings (Becker, 1977), the frequencies of initiations to peers do not change dramatically, the success rate infants have in eliciting responses from peers remains stable at about 50%, and social interactions rarely extend beyond simple initiation–response sequences (Vandell et al., 1980).

The child's second year marks the beginning of a relatively rapid period of increasing peer interactions, which extends throughout the preschool period. As revealed by a number of studies in both laboratory and naturalistic settings, the frequencies of socially directed behaviors, both initiations to peers and responses to social bids, increase steadily, socially directed behaviors become more complex (involving more than one action as part of a social behavior, e.g., vocalizing and gesturing), and social exchanges become longer and more varied (Eckerman, Whatley, & Kutz, 1975; Holmberg, 1980; Mueller & Brenner, 1977). As Eckerman et al. (1975) point out, a major achievement by the end of the second year is the ability to reliably coordinate actions and objects with social exchanges to yield a common activity or task. Offering, accepting, or showing toys, as well as turn-taking and imitating, become integrated into more elaborate play events with companions. In fact, most toddlers are capable of engaging in a variety of social games with one another (Ross, 1982). Negative behaviors such as struggling over toys increase between 12 and 24 months of age, but overall conflict and negative interactions are highly variable and soon give way to more positive relationships (Bronson, 1981; Eckerman et al., 1975; Holmberg, 1980; Rubenstein & Howes, 1976).

As significant as these accomplishments in relation to peers may be during the second year, the more advanced forms of cooperative or coordinated interactions are still highly fragile and occur with a relatively low frequency (see Bronson, 1981, for a critical discussion of this issue). By around $2\frac{1}{2}$ years of age, however, more-extended forms of interacting emerge and become a stable component of the child's social repertoire. In the Holmberg (1980) cross-sectional study, for example, in which children were observed during indoor play in their day care settings, elaborated interchanges (four or more exchanges) between children were infrequent until about 30 months. These extended social exchanges increased steadily from that point on, and by 3 years of age came to exceed the frequency of elaborated interchanges between children and adults.

A different perspective, one providing a sense of the qualitative nature of these changes, can be obtained by analyzing changes that occur across Parten's (1932) categories of social participation. Parten conceptualized social participation with peers as a progression from independent to group play. The definitions and categories she constructed, consisting of unoccupied, solitary, onlooker, parallel, associative, and organized supplementary or cooperative play, while not free from problems (see following discussion), did provide important distinctions among the qualitative characteristics of children's social play.

A crucial feature of the scale is in fact its emphasis on qualitative shifts in social participation and its hierarchical organization. Although Parten's (1932) definitions should be consulted directly, the nature of the distinctions she makes can be seen in her discussion of the differences among parallel, associative, and cooperative (organized supplementary) play as it might occur when children are playing at a sandbox.

> *Parallel activity*—Several children are engaged in filling cups in the sandbox. Each child has his [or her] own cup and fills it without reference to what the other children are doing with their cups. There is very little conversation about what they are making. No one attempts to tell who may or may not come to the sandbox, so children are coming and going all the time. Occasionally, one finds a child who remains at the sandbox during the entire period. The children play *beside* rather than *with* one another.
>
> *Associative play*—The children begin to borrow one another's cups, they explain why they need two cups; they advise and offer sand to one another. They call a child to the sandbox, and ask those present to make room for [her or] him. The others may or may not move over, depending upon their own wishes. No child or children dictate what the various children shall make, but each makes what he [or she] pleases. Someone may suggest that they all make a road, but in that case each child makes his [or her] own road, or none at all, as he [or she] chooses, and the other children do not censor [her or] him. There is much conversation about their common activity.
>
> *Organized supplementary play* (cooperative)—One child suggests that they are all making supper. Soon the various family roles are assigned or adopted and the children speak about their shares in preparing the meal. Domination by one or more of the children occurs, one child being informed that he [or she] can't cook because he's [or she's] the baby. The group becomes closed to some children and open to others, depending upon the wishes of the leaders. The children are criticized by one another when they do not play their roles correctly. They are not permitted to leave the sandbox unless it is known what they are going to do next. (pp. 251–252)

Interestingly, Parten (1932) observed that substantial amounts of cooperative play did not occur until around 3 years of age, generally corresponding to the emergence of Holmberg's (1980) elaborated interchanges. Associative play, although increasing throughout the preschool years, was evident even for the 2 to 2½ year old group, the youngest in Parten's sample. Both parallel and solitary play decreased over time, but parallel interactions were much more variable. Unoccupied play was only observed for the youngest children.

Social Competence and Social Play with Peers

The construct of social competence has become one of the most elusive in the field of child development (Anderson & Messick, 1974; Greenspan, 1981; O'Malley, 1977; Wine & Smye, 1981), yet it remains appealing perhaps because of its potential for establishing a framework for integrating the many and varied manifestations of social behavior. In the area of peer relations, not all the developmental changes just described are necessarily predictive of later social functioning, nor do they correspond to what has typically been considered as aspects of socially competent behavior with one's peers. For example, one of the most common approaches to assessing developmental changes has been to measure children's total rates of peer-related social interactions. This strategy is presumably based on the reasonable assumption that the absence of significant social activity reflects either an existing lack of competence in interacting with peers or that such incompetence will become manifest at a later time as a result of this failure to participate in social activities. Yet, as Asher, Markell, and Hymel (1981) have shown, interaction rate is in fact not predictive of future difficulties, nor does it correspond well with other measures presumed to tap various aspects of social competence. The failure of interaction rate to correlate with peer's ratings of their classmates' acceptance, referred to as sociometric status, is especially damaging because sociometric status appears to be one of the few measures predictive of later adjustment problems (Cowen, Pederson, Bibigian, Izzo, & Trost, 1973; Roff, Sells, & Golden, 1972).

In contrast, certain qualitative aspects of children's social interactions with their peers seem more closely related to social competence. It is not just children's positive style of relating with others and the extent to which they initiate and respond to social bids that are important (Hartup, Glazer, & Charlesworth, 1967). Of equal significance is their ability to use peers as resources, to take the lead in activities, and to show affection appropriately (Doyle, Connolly, & Rivest, 1980; White & Watts, 1973). In addition, an ability to meet antagonistic encounters (typically initiated by others) with reasonable resolution strategies seems essential (Vaughn & Waters, 1981). Taken together, these different skills all appear to reflect useful and interrelated indices of social competence. Not only do children who exhibit these competencies receive more-positive sociometric ratings but, from a more behavioral perspective, they also tend to be those children who are watched by their classmates (Vaughn & Waters, 1981) and imitated (Abramovitch & Grusec, 1978).

Interestingly, perhaps the most important index of children's social competence with peers is their ability to participate with others in sustained social play. After all, to engage in productive play activities, young children must successfully integrate those skills and abilities that allow them to enter and maintain interactions and to resolve conflicts as they occur. Indeed, the assessment of children's social participation based on Parten's (1932) classic work still retains an important role in our understanding of the development of social play with others. As noted earlier, this scale requires raters to evaluate children's ongoing peer interactions, usually during specified time intervals, and then to classify them into the social participation categories of unoccupied, solitary,

onlooker, parallel, associative, or cooperative play. As might be expected, more-advanced forms of social participation do correlate generally with measures related to the construct of social competence (Rubin,
Daniels-Bierness, & Hayvren, 1982).

Nevertheless, despite the descriptive utility of the scale for both normally developing (see Barnes, 1971) and handicapped populations
(Guralnick, 1981a; Wintre & Webster, 1974), some of the scale's initial
developmental assumptions have required modification by research;
modifications that have significantly advanced our understanding of the
relationship between social competence and social play in peer relations.
In particular, an absolute stage-like characterization, in which transitions from one level of social participation to another rigidly hold, has
not been supported by research (e.g., Bakeman & Brownlee, 1980).
Parallel play, however, does seem to be a springboard to group play for
many children. Moreover, although the movement from playing alone
to parallel to forms of group play seems reasonable for younger or inex-
perienced children, solitary play itself seems to constitute a separate
dimension (Smith, 1978). In fact, factor analytic work by Smith (1978)
has clearly distinguished between a social participation dimension and
an independent dimension consisting of how much children play independently of others. This important conclusion, that playing with others
and playing alone are not part of a continuum of group involvement, is
consistent with related research suggesting that solitary play is not necessarily a more "immature" form than parallel play (Moore, Evertson, &
Brophy, 1974), nor that playing alone (perhaps except in excessive
amounts) constitutes cause for concern from a clinical perspective (Rubin, 1982).

In view of this, and in order to obtain a more powerful, comprehensive, and accurate description of a child's social interaction abilities and
social competence, Rubin (Rubin, 1981; Rubin, Maioni, & Hornung,
1976) has developed an assessment approach that integrates measures
of cognitive play and social participation. In particular, Smilansky's
(1968) categories of functional, constructive, and dramatic play as well as
the category of games with rules are nested within Parten's play classifications of solitary, parallel, and group (associative and cooperative)
play. An example of the value of this combined scale in improving our
understanding of social competence with one's peers can be found in
Rubin's (1982) investigation. In this study, various forms of the nonsocial play of 4-year-olds were correlated with assessments of teacher-
rated social competence and peer-rated sociometric status, as well as a
variety of social–cognitive and cognitive measures. Of most interest to
this discussion was the finding that only certain forms of solitary play

correlated with social competence measures. In particular, the solitary–functional and solitary–dramatic-play activities were negatively related to indices of social competence. Solitary activity that was constructive did not correlate at all with the measures of competence, suggesting that this type of play, in the absence of information to the contrary, is not indicative of future concerns. In a related study, Rubin et al. (1982) demonstrated that although group play that was dramatic in form correlated with positive sociometric ratings, group play that was functional did not.

Clearly, then, social participation remains an important means for characterizing the peer-related social behavior of young children. By combining it with assessments of more-cognitive aspects of children's play, it is possible not only to obtain a more comprehensive profile of child–child social interactions but also to determine how patterns associated with certain profiles relate to aspects of social competence with one's peers.

Environmental Influences

The general and consistent developmental patterns of peer-related social interactions that have been found should not imply that these behaviors are not highly susceptible to variations in environmental factors. On the contrary, it is well known that these so-called programmatic or ecological variables (Guralnick, 1981d; Rogers-Warren & Wedel, 1980) have a major influence on moment-to-moment expressions of peer-related social behavior. The type of play area and the corresponding toys and equipment that are available in that area are especially influential. In an early effort, Shure (1963) observed 4-year-old nursery school children's play occurring in indoor areas designed for art, books, dolls, games, and blocks, finding that the level of social participation varied considerably. In particular, the most complex forms of social participation appeared in the doll area, although the book and art areas were most popular. Similarly, Rubin (1977) noted that most associative and cooperative play occurred during houseplay, vehicle play, and reading activities during which the teacher encouraged conversation. Nonsocial solitary and parallel play were more frequently observed when children were focused on more specific tasks such as painting and crayoning, working with puzzles, and during sand and water play. More-detailed comparisons between two separate environments, one containing gross-motor-type equipment such as jungle gyms and slides, and the other containing more table-type manipulative materials such as pencils, paste, crayons, and scissors, have also revealed an impact on children's social play (Vandenberg, 1981). In the latter study, associative play occurred more often in the gross-motor area, whereas more solitary and parallel play were found in the setting containing more manipulable fine-motor type materials.

It is very difficult in naturalistic studies such as the preceding to isolate the effects of specific variables. For example, the play areas differed not only in the type of equipment available but also varied in physical size and the numbers of children attracted to each area. Factors such as group size and both social and spatial density have been shown to alter peer-related social behavior (Hutt & Vaizey, 1966; Loo, 1972; McGrew, 1970). Increases in spatial density in particular are associated with lower levels of social interaction (Loo, 1972). Moreover, at least for younger children, small social groups tend to encourage social exchanges (Vandell & Mueller, 1980).

In a similar fashion, the availability of teachers changes with different settings, a factor that has considerable influence on peer-related social interactions. Perhaps by competing with child–child interactions, high teacher–child ratios tend to inhibit child–child interactions (O'Connor, 1975; Shores, Hester, & Strain, 1976). In fact, the generalized approaches teachers take in relating with children can have a significant impact. For example, preschools characterized by a tendency toward high teacher direction result in less peer-related social behavior (Huston-Stein, Friedrich-Cofer, & Susman, 1977; Miller & Dyer, 1975).

Child–child social behavior is of course likely to be influenced strongly by the characteristics of one's companions. Familiarity is one important dimension and is treated separately in a later section. Apart from familiarity, it should be noted that any potential effects created by children with varying characteristics tend to be mitigated both by self-selection factors and by the stratification across age or social class common to most nursery schools and day care settings. A number of recent efforts have attempted, however, to clarify the impact of interactions occurring among children at different chronological ages through laboratory studies. Despite these efforts, observations of pairs of same-age and mixed-age, primarily 3- and 5-year-olds, have produced inconsistent results. In some instances the older children seem to have a suppressive effect on younger playmates (Langlois, Gottfried, Barnes, & Hendricks, 1978); in others, mixed-age interactions tend to reduce the peer-related social behaviors for older children but increase interactions for younger ones (Lougee, Grueneich, & Hartup, 1977). Even in the latter instance, however, wide individual differences were noted. Moreover, observations comparing social interactions occurring during free play in mixed-age and same-age classrooms add further complexity. In particular, Goldman (1981) noted that 3- and 4-year-old children do differ in terms of social participation, with mixed-age groups engaging in more mature play than same-age classes. Taken together, all that can be said at this point is that mixed-age interactions appear to force accommodations and create interaction patterns that differ from same-age encounters, but their functions and developmental consequences are largely unknown.

Although the effects for some environmental variables seem robust, it is difficult to draw many firm conclusions because so many factors tend to covary with one another. Systematic data are lacking with regard to interactions that may exist among the important variables. Moreover, many of the studies of environmental variables have only evaluated their impact over a short time period. It may be important to know whether and how children eventually accommodate to environments with certain characteristics over prolonged periods of time and whether significant developmental consequences follow.

Corresponding Social–Communicative Skills

The development of peer interactions is, of course, paralleled and supported by changes occurring in related developmental domains. Emergence from the sensorimotor period provides the cognitive basis that enables young children to see relationships and understand interactions and contingencies that are necessary for improving their social interactions with peers. Although the research remains inconclusive, it is likely that corresponding changes in social-cognitive development, such as role- and perspective-taking skills (see Shantz, 1975) are associated with the development of successful peer interactions (Rubin et al., 1982; Rubin & Pepler, 1980). In fact, related skills such as turn-taking, imitating, and role complementarity figure prominently in accounts of processes characterizing early peer-related social development (Mueller & Lucas, 1975).

Young children learn quite rapidly which specific social skills are capable of eliciting responses from playmates. For example, Tremblay, Strain, Hendrickson, and Shores (1981) observed that, for socially interactive preschool children, bids to engage in rough-and-tumble play were successful 92% of the time and that offering an object to a playmate or exchanging one also is associated with a high probability of achieving a positive result (79%). Even though there are some increases across the preschool period, the ability to use objects and physical contact to successfully initiate interactions is established early on.

As important as these skills may be, more complex and extended forms of social exchanges with peers require that children develop less proximal and less object-dependent forms of interaction. Gradually, language and discourse skills become the primary means of social exchange. In fact, the emergence of child–child verbal exchanges can be seen even when 19-month-old toddlers interact, as over one-fourth of their time is spent talking to one another (Rubenstein & Howes, 1976). It is not the case that gestural forms of communication become insignificant as this occurs. On the contrary, motor and/or gestural patterns are supplemented by verbal ones (Finkelstein, Dent, Gallacher, & Ramey, 1978).

Skills such as adjusting the content of speech so that it is relevant to that of one's companion, clearly attending to the listener when speaking, moving closer to the target of one's social interactions, using attention-getting devices, and waiting until the listener is attending are all aspects of the communicative process that are predictive of successful social exchanges (Mueller, Bleir, Krakow, Hegedus, & Cournoyer, 1977). In addition, the clarity of one's speech as well as its form (commands or questions are more effective than declarative statements) are correlated with different outcomes (Mueller, 1972). Interestingly, around 2 years of age, the period when language begins to become more important in peer-peer exchanges, the power of most of these variables (e.g., clarity, attending) to elicit a response remains constant, but developmental changes are related to the fact that young children learn to use these techniques more effectively.

Mueller et al. (1977), for example, analyzed the utterances of children attending a playgroup on two occasions, first at 22 months of age and again at 30 months. Focusing only on those utterances that met with either a verbal response or none at all (intermediate types of responding such as nonverbal acknowledgements were not included), it was found that only 27% received a verbal response at 22 months, but by late in the year that figure rose to 64%. This increase appeared to be linked to the fact that children tended to utilize a greater percentage of those communicative behaviors that were predictive of successful outcomes. Specifically, for the two variables that had the greatest predictive power, selecting content relevant to the listener's activity and listener attention to speaker, the percentage of actually using those strategies (as opposed to the converse forms of the strategies, such as *not* having the listener's attention) more than doubled for each variable across the 8-month period.

Beyond selecting content that is appropriate to the listener and timing one's communication to maximize listener attention, children also learn to use linguistic devices and verbal routines to initiate and help sustain conversational interactions with peers. For example, Garvey and Hogan (1973) commented that the summons–answer routines described by Schegloff (1968) were effective strategies for producing mutual engagement in young children. Variations that occurred within an interchange, referred to as the rhetorical gambit, also provided a structured series of verbal routines that could be invoked to maintain interactions in a variety of contexts and circumstances.

The identification of isolated social or communicative strategies that are closely associated with the success of social exchanges is important, but provides only a limited perspective of the social skills necessary to effectively interact with peers. How these strategies are sequenced, the extent to which participants share a knowledge of the rules of communication, and the degree to which they understand their roles and recognize when to invoke behaviors associated with those roles constitute much of the essence of peer-related social competence. Moreover, the relationships between status factors and discourse functions and the sharing of common understandings and themes all must be appropriately attended to before social/communicative exchanges are likely to have their desired effects.

Clearly, this perspective serves to underscore the relevance of diverse fields to the area of peer relations. Rules of language use and communicative strategies that consider situational factors and listener characteristics are represented by the fields of developmental pragmatics (Ochs & Schieffelin, 1979) and child sociolinguistics (Ervin-Tripp & Mitchell-Kernan, 1977), as well as being linked to work on social–communicative competence (Schiefelbusch, 1981). The integration of these approaches is essential before a complete understanding of peer-related social development can be obtained.

One of the most revealing ways of seeing how these factors interrelate is to examine social episodes that may bring these underlying assumptions and perspectives to the surface. One important situation in which this can occur is when children request others to carry out some action or behavior. Analyzing spontaneous behavior request sequences in dyads of preschool-age children, Garvey (1975) observed that in fact a variety of *meaning factors* characterized the patterns of requests and responses. Evidence was obtained suggesting that young children considered many factors in their social exchanges, including willingness of participants to carry out an act, the reasonableness of the response, the ability and obligation of the companion to do what was asked, and the appropriateness of requesting that companion to carry out the request. For such sequences to have their intended effects, and most did, an understanding of these factors must be shared between participants.

Gaining entry into already established playgroups poses an equally important but very different task for many young children (Asher & Taylor, 1981; Putallaz & Gottman, 1981), and it is another situation that highlights the integrative processes necessary to achieve a successful outcome when relating with one's peers. The use of generally accepted and easily utilized formalized routines is certainly of value in gaining entry to a playgroup, but numerous other strategies, properly sequenced and timed, must be available in order to achieve a consistently favorable outcome. These *access strategies* were examined in a field study by Corsaro (1979). He observed the strategies to be wide ranging, including producing a variant of ongoing behavior, encirclement, direct requests for access, and offering an object. Interestingly, Corsaro found that nearly two-thirds of initial attempts by children did not achieve success. The main exception to this was "producing a variant of ongoing behavior" that achieved its end nearly two-thirds of the time.

Yet most preschool children remain undaunted by repeated failure to gain entry to playgroups. In fact, in most instances they do eventually succeed, a process that is accomplished typically by using strategies that are progressively more direct. For example, a sequence that Corsaro (1979) found to yield 90% success was as follows: Interaction 1—nonverbal entry⟶no response; Interaction 2—produce variant⟶accept. In a manner similar to Garvey's (1975) analyses of behavior-request episodes, the many patterns described by Corsaro strongly suggest that young children are aware of and respect possession rules and dominance structures. In particular, the use of more-direct strategies are deferred until a latter point in the sequence, as it is likely that the direct approach would have failed if attempted during the first try to gain access.

The importance of the concept of shared meaning to the effectiveness of social and communicative exchanges can even be seen in the absence of well-developed language during the toddler period. Brenner and Mueller (1982) constructed a taxonomy of shared themes or meanings obtained from observations of the social interactions of a group of 12-month-old and a group of 16-month-old toddlers over a 7-month period. Twelve such shared meaning themes were reliably identified, including "object exchange," "object possession struggle," "shared reference," and "rough and tumble." Overall, both the diversity and frequency of occurrence of shared-meaning themes increased from 12 to 19 months of age, with nearly two-thirds of all social interactions occurring within the context of these themes by 22 months of age. Perhaps most significant, however, was the finding that the episodes of shared meaning were associated with longer interaction episodes. Failure to agree on a theme frequently resulted in shorter and often abrupt social exchanges.

The development of peer social exchanges is also facilitated by the reciprocal relationships that characterize social–communicative interactions. In a manner analogous to verbal routines and the organization provided by the aforementioned shared themes, companions tend to achieve a level and a balance in their exchanges enabling them to interact more effectively. The balance that characterizes social–communicative interactions can be described along many dimensions. First and foremost is the fact that it is typically an alternating, turn-taking process. Second, it contains elements of both similarity and complementarity. Positive initiations are met with positive replies, questions with answers, demanding initiations with coercive or negative replies; moreover, a question–answer synchrony often arises in conversation, and the frequency with which children initiate social interactions is strongly correlated with the frequency with which they receive similar social bids (Berninger & Garvey, 1981; Charlesworth & Hartup, 1967; Kohn, 1966; Leiter, 1977).

This balance occurs in situations where children are free to choose partners, as well as in situations in which partner selection is constrained (see Cairns, 1979, for discussion). In fact, the quantitative balance can even be observed in certain structural features of language, including the correlation between the number of utterances in exchanges between same-age children (Garvey & Ben Debba, 1974) and in rhythmic aspects of speech, such as pauses (Welkowitz, Cariffe, & Feldstein, 1976). Furthermore, imitative behavior, although decreasing over the preschool years, occurs frequently (Abramovitch & Grusec, 1978; Grusec & Abramovitch, 1982), and various forms of verbal repetition of others' speech serve highly useful functions in balancing and sustaining conversational interactions (Keenan, 1977). A key element common to many of these reciprocity dimensions that may facilitate social interactions is that these processes increase the predictability of the forms and content of social exchanges.

The balance that is achieved through reciprocity should not of course imply that relationships are inevitably equal or harmonious. Although coequal interactions seem to be the rule for most children, many dyadic exchanges are characterized by dominance by one member of the pair. A child's developmental status and/or chronological age (Guralnick & Paul-Brown, 1977; Lougee et al., 1977) are two of the factors which govern the extent of this asymmetry. In fact, the selection of specific linguistic forms, especially imperative forms, is highly sensitive to a host of status relationships. The use of polite speech, the frequency of directives, the extent to which children qualify their comments or justify their requests have been observed consistently in preschool age children to vary with status related characteristics of one's companions (Gelman &

Shatz, 1977; Guralnick & Paul-Brown, 1980, 1984; James, 1978; Rubin & Borwick, 1984).

Taken together, young children integrate those strategies and techniques that are successful in achieving their social and communicative goals into their repertoires and mark the circumstances in which certain configurations or individual strategies have been most successful. By testing various combinations of strategies in an emerging rule structure, extending and modifying them to fit different problem situations, a gradually developing but effective repertoire of skills, applicable to varying listeners and contexts, develops. This shared set of rules and expectations, strengthened by a developing pattern of reciprocal interacting, adds further structure and predictability to the social exchange process.

Family Relations and Sociability with Peers

Individual differences in orienting to and approaching peers are apparent even in early infancy. Activity level, temperament, and other constitutional factors account in part for these early differences (Chess, 1979). However, a more complete understanding of the origins of a young child's initial interest and willingness to venture into the more unpredictable and often antagonistic domain of peer interactions must be sought in an analysis of interaction styles that emerge in the broad context of parent–child and family relationships.

Perhaps one of the most widely investigated areas of child development has been the formation of attachments between parents and children and the relationship of the quality of this bond to other developmental processes. Lieberman (1977) was one of the first to examine the relationship between security of attachment and competence with one's peers. In a short-term longitudinal study with 3-year-olds about to enter a preschool program, Lieberman found that security of attachment was related to one specific aspect of peer competence; namely, nonverbal social behaviors that typically reflect a positive or negative orientation toward other children. Specifically, giving, sharing, showing, and pointing were associated positively with peer competence, whereas physical aggressiveness, crying, and similar measures were negatively related. As Lieberman points out, these social gestures not only formed the basis for early communications but also "remain a powerful means of conveying positive or negative orientation to the social environment. If, as it seems likely, secure attachment fosters confident exploration of the social as well as the physical surroundings, securely attached children may be expected to show a positive orientation to others" (p. 1285).

This hypothesis has been confirmed generally by more-recent studies,

which have also provided additional insight into the nature of the continuity and stability of social competence. For example, Pastor (1981)
found that 20- to 23-month-old toddlers classified as securely attached at
18 months of age were considerably more sociable and socially competent than groups classified as either anxious avoidant or anxious resistant, although the anxious avoidant group often appeared similar to the
securely attached children. Generally, however, both qualitative ratings
of overall sociability and orientation toward peers, as well as quantitative measures of actual peer exchanges, supported the relationship between differences in attachment and children's initial interactions with
peers. Moreover, mothers of securely attached children appeared more
responsive and supportive of their child's behavior and were more sensitive to the situations that required their assistance. As expected, securely attached children were also more cooperative and positively oriented toward their mothers. In fact, these differences in attachment can
even discriminate among different subgroups comprised exclusively of
children classified as securely attached in relation to competence in initial encounters with peers as well as with familiar and unfamiliar adults
(Easterbrooks & Lamb, 1979). Accordingly, early differences in security
of attachment have developmental correlates for both peer relations and
social interactions with mothers and other adults, suggesting the existence of stable underlying developmental processes.

The stability and consistency among behavioral systems and the consistency across different situations and time, have led a number of developmentalists, particularly Sroufe and his colleagues (Matas et al.,
1978; Sroufe, 1979) to suggest that higher-order constructs, such as the
quality of adaptation, are essential for understanding the continuity of
social behavior, problem-solving styles, and other aspects of competence. Secure attachments, it is argued, form the fundamental basis for
an orientation to the world and a style of interacting that affects the
realms of social, emotional, and cognitive behavior.

Long-term continuities have also been obtained between early attachment patterns and more global measures of competence (Waters, Wippman, & Sroufe, 1979). Observing children interacting with one another
in preschool classes for a 5-week period, competence with peers was
assessed through a Q-sort procedure involving items focusing on children's abilities to initiate interactions and to engage peers in social exchanges as well as items relating to the extent of their social skills.
Overall, children observed to be securely attached at 15 months were
judged to be more competent with peers in the preschool at $3\frac{1}{2}$ years of
age than anxiously attached groups. These findings and those of other
studies (Matas, Arend, & Sroufe, 1978) were not related to measures of
cognitive level.

The stability and consistency among behavioral systems and the consistency across different situations and time, have led a number of developmentalists, particularly Sroufe and his colleagues (Matas et al.,
1978; Sroufe, 1979) to suggest that higher-order constructs, such as the
quality of adaptation, are essential for understanding the continuity of
social behavior, problem-solving styles, and other aspects of competence. Secure attachments, it is argued, form the fundamental basis for
an orientation to the world and a style of interacting that affects the
realms of social, emotional, and cognitive behavior.

Peer Experience and Peer Familiarity

This correspondence between parent–child interactions and later competence with peers appears to be a significant and well-established relationship. Whether a positive orientation to the social world that emerges from secure and effective parent–child relations ultimately results in successful and skillful peer relations, however, will depend on the adequacy of opportunities for relating with age mates and the quality of those interactions. In a short-term longitudinal study, Mueller and Brenner (1977) have in fact demonstrated this correspondence. Comparing the social interactions of toddler-age children who had participated in regular playgroup activities with age mates to children with only limited peer experience, these investigators obtained a number of interesting results. In particular, peer experience did not differentiate between the groups on the less-sophisticated forms of social behavior such as the frequency of socially directed behaviors or short initiation–response sequences. Significant differences did emerge, however, for long social interactions (more than two social exchanges) and for coordinated social interactions (those in which a child used more than one mode of communicating simultaneously, e.g., while looking at a playmate, the child not only vocalized but gestured as well). Specifically, the experienced group exhibited more of these sustained and complex forms of social interaction.

Familiarity with a peer, which almost inevitably covaries with peer experience, has nevertheless been shown to be an independent and important contributor to the development of social skills. Doyle et al. (1980) observed 36- to 46-month-old children enrolled in two day care centers in dyadic play sessions; one with a familiar playmate (same day care center) and another with an unfamiliar playmate (different day care center). During each play session, the extent of social participation, the cognitive level of play, the affective tone, and specific child–child behaviors based on the White and Watts (1973) scale were coded. Differences between children in the familiar and unfamiliar dyads occurred across many of these measures. Children with a history of experience with one another played in a more socially interactive manner (more associative and complex interactions and less onlooker and solitary play), engaged in more-complex object play when socially interacting, and were more successful and positive in their social exchanges.

Although a detailed understanding of the processes that can account for these and related findings must await future investigations, it is likely that the enhanced social skills of familiar playmates is based on their previously existing network of shared experiences and reciprocal activities (see Brenner & Mueller, 1982). In fact, rudimentary forms of this process that are associated with experiences with familiar peers can be seen even in very young children (Becker, 1977; Lewis et al., 1975).

Interrelation between Adult–Child and Peer–Peer Systems

As discussed earlier, conceptions of adult–child and peer–peer systems as having different characteristics, courses of development, and functions must also recognize the mutual influences and interdependencies that exist between these domains. There is little question that early socioemotional relationships established between parents and children affect the child's orientation to and styles of approaching new social experiences. Yet these influences can be felt in other more subtle ways, affecting processes thought to be more directly associated with peer experiences themselves.

Perhaps the clearest example of this point is Lieberman's (1977) analysis of the intercorrelations among secure attachment, peer experience, and measures of peer competence. Both secure attachment and peer experience were, as might be expected, positively correlated with social competence with one's peers. However, by statistically separating out the effects for each relationship, Lieberman noted that peer experience and secure attachment were in fact related to different aspects of peer competence. As noted earlier, secure attachment was directly related to nonverbal behaviors associated with reciprocal interactions such as sharing and giving, and inversely with negative behaviors—a pattern interpreted as reflecting a positive orientation to others. In contrast, peer experience was positively related to verbal exchanges between playmates. This latter finding corresponds with earlier discussions in this chapter, which had emphasized the uniqueness of the language and communicative skills that accompany more complex forms of peer interaction skills and the need for those skills to develop in the context of actual child–child exchanges.

The picture that emerges is one in which parents who have established secure attachments with their children not only promote a positive orientation toward social experiences but provide as well extensive opportunities for their children to interact with age mates. This dual influence enables us to understand more clearly the continuity that is found between early caregiver–child relations and later child–child social interactions, perhaps even the continuity evident between the early preschool and early elementary years (e.g., Waldrop & Halverson,

1975). Certainly, these interrelationships are even more likely to account for the short-term temporal and cross-situational consistencies that exist in peer-related social interactions. Moment-to-moment variations in peer interactions notwithstanding (see earlier discussion on environmental influences), considerable short-term stability in peer interactions and competence across different play settings have been found (Roper & Hinde, 1978; Vaughn & Waters, 1981). Children's social-play behaviors may vary substantially, but their skills and competence relative to their companions tend to remain stable.

Despite the pressures toward continuity and stability, there are ample opportunities for discontinuities to occur. First, although for some groups the stability of the patterns of attachment is high (e.g., Waters, 1978), much lower stability is obtained for socioeconomically disadvantaged families (Vaughn, Egeland, Sroufe, & Waters, 1979). These changes for the disadvantaged sample do appear predictable, however. In particular, many of the changes were associated with stressful life events, especially when classification shifted from securely attached at 12 months to anxiously attached at 18 months. In middle-class samples, instability in attachment classification also reflected environmental circumstances, such as maternal employment, although the direction of the change in relation to these life events is not well understood (Thompson, Lamb, & Estes, 1982).

Second, even favorable caregiver–child relations and a corresponding positive orientation are likely to be undermined by repeated contact with unresponsive or abusive peers. If this is the case, the clinical implications are clear: Involve other children in a therapeutic program of intervention. More recent approaches have in fact made extensive use of peers as agents of change, especially for children considered socially withdrawn (see Strain & Fox, 1981). Finally, for those youngsters who experience difficult early caregiver–child relations, it may be possible to overcome these early effects during the preschool years. In this instance the problems of social motivation are likely to be paramount, and an array of adult- and peer-related strategies will be required if discontinuity is to be achieved.

THE PEER RELATIONS OF YOUNG HANDICAPPED CHILDREN

Fortunately, for most children a favorable and coherent pattern of social relationships with peers does develop. There is, however, a large and often overlooked group of children who appear to be substantially at risk for developing difficulties in establishing peer relations. Handicapped children, particularly those with developmental delays, sensory or motor impairments, or some combination of problems, appear to be especially vulnerable in this regard.[1] For example, parental stress associated with coping with a child who is handicapped coupled with the often reduced, delayed, or inconsistent social signals emitted by many handicapped children (e.g., Cicchetti & Sroufe, 1976) may well serve to subvert the formation of positive caregiver–child relations. In addition to these disturbances in socialization (Battle, 1974), handicapped children often find their encounters with agemates in group care settings limited to children highly similar to themselves. Specialized settings for handicapped children often consist of an environment containing relatively homogeneous groups of children, many of whom are themselves struggling to find the keys to establishing positive relationships. Repeated failures to build peer relationships and the absence of appropriate models for establishing productive patterns of social exchange with other children may well damage both social motivation and social skill development.

That young handicapped children are indeed more vulnerable to deficits in peer interactions has been confirmed by a limited number of investigations. For example, preliminary comparisons between a group of delayed 4- and 5-year-olds equivalent in developmental age to 3- to 4-year-old normally developing children suggested that the delayed children had a less-extensive repertoire of peer-related social behaviors (Field, 1980). In a short-term longitudinal study of developmentally delayed preschool children, Guralnick and Weinhouse (1984) sought to describe the organization, characteristics, and developmental progression of a range of peer-related behaviors. As part of a larger study, 52 developmentally delayed children (mean chronological age 54.4 months) enrolled in specialized community programs were observed during free play at the beginning and end of the school year. Most of the children were mildly delayed (65%), with 27% categorized as moderately delayed, and only 8% (primarily older) as severely impaired. The primary etiological classifications for children were highly varied and were as follows: chromosomal disorders (19%); prenatal infections and intoxications, congenital anomalies and disorders of unknown origin, and inborn errors of metabolism (21%); perinatal disorders and trauma (2%); congenital neuromotor dysfunction (10%); postnatal trauma and

---

[1] Children considered handicapped who are classified as having serious behavioral and emotional problems also experience, of course, substantial problems in peer relations. In certain instances, as with some withdrawn children, it is the primary presenting problem. The focus in this chapter, however, is on those children with other primary handicaps.

other environmental causes (21%); and unknown (27%). Approximately 85% of the children were 3 years of age and older, and all were ambulatory.

To obtain a wide-ranging profile of peer-related interactions, sequential interactive measures of individual episodes of social exchanges occurring between children, ratings of social participation (using the Parten, 1932, scale), and constructiveness of play (nested within social participation similar to Rubin, 1981,) were coded. For the sequential measures, following Mueller and Brenner (1977), the socially directed behavior was used as the fundamental unit for analysis. From this unit, data regarding the frequency, quality (positive or negative), mode (motor–gestural or vocal–verbal), content (e.g., give–offer–show objects, physical contact), length, complexity (simple or coordinated), reciprocity (correspondence between initiations and responses), and contingencies (related responses to initiations or other socially directed behaviors within a social exchange) could be derived.

At first glance, analyses of social participation, constructiveness of play, and sequential interactive measures across a 1-year period suggested that developmentally delayed children displayed many of the features, organization, and developmental changes similar to those found for normally developing children. In particular, associative play increased and unoccupied play decreased across the year. Similarly, virtually all of the sequential interactive measures increased significantly over time. In addition, vocal and verbal interactions came to supplant motor and gestural forms of social communication; interactions became more positive; and exchanges were organized in a reciprocal fashion (correlations between giving and receiving socially directed behaviors were extremely high).

Yet despite these characteristics, closer inspection revealed what appear to be unusual and marked deficits in the peer related social interactions of these children. Not only did solitary and parallel play remain the dominant forms of social participation throughout the year, but also children often were not able to turn simple two-unit initiation–response sequences into longer, more elaborate social exchanges. In fact, the majority of the limited amount of associative play that did occur was the result of interactions by a very small subset (20%) of more highly interactive children. As a consequence, the large majority of delayed children rarely engaged in sustained social exchanges with their peers.

Two additional analyses further confirmed the nature of these deficits. First, when roughly matching the delayed children in terms of developmental age with normally developing children, there was a strong indication that the peer-related social interactions of the delayed children lagged substantially behind their cognitive development (using data from Barnes, 1971, Parten, 1932, and others for comparative purposes). For example, it would be expected that at least 25% of children's interactions at 3- to 3½-year-old developmental ages would involve some form of group play (associative or cooperative). However, at the end of the year, the delayed preschool children in the sample at that average developmental age engaged in associative play only 10% of the time, with no instance of cooperative play being observed whatsoever.

Second, and perhaps most remarkable, was the finding that when subjects were regrouped to carry out a cross-sectional analysis across chronological age (3 to 5½ years), no changes in the level of peer-related social development occurred with increasing age. As noted, delayed children became more socially interactive with their peers as the school year progressed. However, the data suggest that each new year disrupts this apparently highly fragile repertoire of peer-related social interaction skills.

These results must, of course, be confirmed through more long-term developmental studies. Certainly, not all moderately and mildly delayed children are likely to display deficits of this magnitude, and many, perhaps the highly interactive subset, may not show deficits at all. At the same time, however, the evidence strongly suggests that the peer-related social behaviors for a significant proportion of young delayed children lag substantially behind their level of cognitive development.

It should be noted that these data were probed in various ways to determine if (1) sampling bias, (2) other demographic characteristics of the population studied, or (3) the quality of the community programs could be responsible for these outcomes. Although alternative explanations cannot be ruled out entirely, explanations related to developmental issues seem most plausible. These possibilities will be discussed in detail in the following section.

Hearing-impaired children, specifically those youngsters with at least severe impairments, constitute the only other disability group for whom systematic research on peer-related social development has been carried out. For the most part, results for this population have been compatible with those obtained for developmentally delayed preschool children. Overall, severely and profoundly hearing-impaired preschool children frequently engage in noncommunicative and immature patterns of play (Darbyshire, 1977). Although hearing-impaired children often attempt to be socially interactive, their attempts are more likely to fail than those of normally hearing children. Moreover, hearing-impaired children spend considerably less time interacting with peers both in dyadic and in free-play settings; when they do interact socially, those interactions tend to be shorter and less developmentally complex (Higgenbotham & Baker, 1981; Vandell & George, 1981).

Extended forms of social interaction in particular appear to be most affected, resulting in an ever-increasing discrepancy over time between hearing-impaired children's levels of peer-related interaction in comparison to their normally hearing counterparts. In fact, Higgenbotham and Baker (1981) have demonstrated that by 5 years of age, solitary play is the dominant form of social participation for hearing-impaired children. While developmental data (e.g., Parten, 1932; Rubin et al., 1976) indicate that normally developing children prefer to spend most of their time in group activities and far less time in solitary and parallel play as they proceed through the preschool years, this pattern is reversed for hearing-impaired children. Moreover, the observation that hearing-impaired children spend a significant portion of their time in solitary-dramatic activities is of special concern in view of Rubin's (1982) research indicating that this pattern is correlated with overall social isolation, social maladjustment, as well as lower sociometric status and less sophisticated cognitive role-taking skills.

Taken together, although the development and characteristics of the peer interactions of handicapped children exhibit similarities to those of normally developing children, it is the differences that are most striking. These conclusions, however, must be placed in perspective. It is important to recognize that the differences that have emerged (1) were based on only a small number of studies, (2) used only a limited number of outcome measures, (3) observed social interactions for only brief periods of time, and (4) have been restricted primarily to two general groupings of handicapped children (developmentally delayed and severely or profoundly hearing-impaired children). In addition, comparisons with normally developing children have often been indirect; judged through normative expectations of populations that cannot be equated exactly to the environmental conditions existing for the handicapped groups. When more direct comparisons have been made, intact groups in different classroom settings have been employed, leaving researchers unsure of both the representativeness of the samples and the equivalence of the comparison groups in relation to factors not associated with a child's handicap (see Bailey, Clifford, & Harms, 1982). Moreover, no research has probed deeply the organizational features of the peer interactions of handicapped children, particularly whether their play interactions are affected by factors such as familiarity, types of toys available, teacher behavior, and other ecological–environmental variables known to alter the social interactions of normally developing children. Nevertheless, the consistency of findings and their compatibility with developmental

theory is in many ways compelling, suggesting that discrepancies between a handicapped child's cognitive and peer-related social development may well be confirmed by subsequent research.

Possible Causes of Peer Interaction Deficits

Assuming that such confirmation does in fact occur, it is worthwhile
speculating as to the possible causes of these deficits. At one level, it is
of course not surprising that the many disruptions and dislocations of
life's activities that commonly confront handicapped children and their
families would not also affect a child's peer relations. After all, abuse,
divorce, and other traumatic events eventually find their way through a
child's system of interlocking social relationships and alter the quality of
their peer relations (George & Main, 1979; Hetherington, Cox, & Cox,
1979).

In a similar fashion, the existence of a handicap, or even the threat of a
handicap, alters virtually every aspect of a child's social system, particularly parent–child relationships (Farber, 1975). There are no studies on
attachment relationships between handicapped children and their families in relation to subsequent peer interactions similar to those described
earlier for normally developing children (e.g., Lieberman, 1977). However, there is ample evidence that the formation of secure attachments is
lessened by the presence of a handicap (Solnit & Provence, 1979; Stone
& Chesney, 1978; Ulrey, 1981), a condition that would likely adversely
affect future peer relations. In fact, there is some suggestion that the
anxiety-provoking experience of children born "at risk" can create maladaptive parenting practices that are capable of substantially interferring
with growth and development. Misinterpretations of a child's behavior
and the holding of radically incorrect expectations, combined with a
shaken emotional state, are apparently powerful enough in certain instances to produce parent–child interaction patterns that create the
symptoms of significant delay in children whose cognitive potentials are
considerably higher (Kearsley, 1979).

Investigations of parent–child interactions for both developmentally
delayed and hearing-impaired children confirm the possibility that deficits in peer interactions may be part of a more general deficit in social
relations. Wedell-Monnig and Lumley (1980) compared the mother–
child interactions of hearing-impaired and normally hearing toddlers,
finding that mothers of hearing-impaired children were invariably dominant in their interactions, with their children initiating a very small
percentage of the social exchanges. Moreover, fewer social interactions
occurred for older than younger hearing-impaired children. Both of

these patterns are, of course, inconsistent with normal parent–child interactions, leading Wedell-Monnig and Lumley to suggest that hearing-impaired children may be learning that their social–communicative attempts are inadequate and ineffective. Moreover, this sense of "learned helplessness" (Seligman, 1975) may set the occasion for a future absence of an orientation toward social relationships.[2]

Parental dominance and reduced quality of social interactions also seem to characterize the behavior of many parents of developmentally delayed children as well. For example, Terdal, Jackson, and Garner (1976) found that, in contrast to groups of normal children similar in developmental levels, mothers of delayed children were more directive, and the delayed children less responsive to maternal social behavior such as questions. Similarly, Cunningham, Reuler, Blackwell, and Deck (1981) found that mothers of delayed children initiated fewer interactions than mothers of normally developing children, even though both groups of children were matched in terms of developmental level. In addition, although the delayed children complied equally well to mothers' requests, mothers of delayed children provided many more commands, but were not as likely to reinforce or attend to cooperative behavior when it occurred.

Whether these interactive difficulties contribute to future behavioral or emotional problems is not known. It does appear, however, that handicapped children, especially those with general cognitive delays and those with serious hearing impairments, are much more susceptible to difficulties in this area in later life (Meadow & Trybus, 1979; Reiss, Levitan, & McNally, 1982). Although we know little of the processes that are associated with these patterns, their impact on the formation and maintenance of peer relations is likely to be profound.

An additional factor that can contribute to the peer interaction deficit is the corresponding deficit in expressive language that is characteristic of most developmentally delayed children (Mahoney, Glover, & Finger, 1981; Miller, Chapman, & Bedrosian, 1977), and of course children with many other handicaps as well (Meadow, 1980). This discrepancy between cognitive and expressive language development tends to increase as children grow older and parallels the cognitive-level peer-interaction discrepancy described earlier. Language, of course, plays an ever-increasing role in regulating social play interactions (Garvey, 1977), and an

[2] This pattern appears to be primarily characteristic of children with highly limited communicative competence. It should also be noted that these findings cannot be extended to dyads when both parents and children are deaf. In this instance, social and communicative interactions closely resemble those of normally hearing dyads (Meadow, Greenberg, Erting, & Carmichael, 1981).

inability to engage in dialogue during play severely undermines the development of complex associative and cooperative social participation. Accordingly, the relative absence of more-sophisticated forms of social exchange during play that is found in hearing-impaired children may be less a function of deficiencies in symbolic functioning and more related to the absence of a context (verbal) for establishing group play.

Any or all of these likely contributors to a deficit in peer interactions are potentially capable of setting into motion a sequence of events in which handicapped children will show greater and greater lags over the course of time. For example, deficits in expressive language limit the development of higher forms of group play; in turn, handicapped children have fewer opportunities to learn the social, play, and communicative skills that are unique to and emerge from child–child social exchanges. Further complicating the picture are factors in parent–child social relationships that may serve to depress the expressive language development of handicapped children. As noted, many parents are highly directive, less socially interactive, and less responsive to their handicapped children—a pattern which is of course not conducive to expressive language development (Gleason & Weintraub, 1978; Mahoney & Seely, 1976; Moerk, 1977). In fact, Cunningham et al. (1981), who assessed speech complexity of both children and mothers in their study of delayed children in addition to social measures, suggested that child responsiveness was the key factor regulating the complexity of speech to handicapped children. The absence of responsiveness in many instances apparently produced a mismatch between what the children were capable of comprehending and the complexity of speech addressed to them by their mothers. Under these circumstances, the press toward higher levels of speech may be absent (see also Lasky & Klopp, 1982, for related findings for language-disordered children).

A final possibility that must be considered is the contribution to this deficit that may result from difficulties encountered in relating with peers in preschool programs designed for handicapped children. As noted earlier, most handicapped children find themselves grouped in highly specialized educational settings serving children with problems similar to their own. As a consequence, encounters with their peers are not as likely to be productive, nor are models available to stimulate advanced forms of social and communicative development.

One practice that has been adopted to provide a more responsive environment has been that of mainstreaming, or integration, in which handicapped and nonhandicapped preschool children are enrolled in the same educational setting (Guralnick, 1978). Although the rationale for mainstreaming includes humanistic and legal issues, there is little question that there is the expectation that involvement with nonhandicapped children will benefit handicapped classmates and result in more appropriate and more mature forms of social interactions with their peers (Guralnick, 1982). These issued are examined in detail in the following section.

PEER INTERACTIONS IN MAINSTREAMED SETTINGS

There is ample evidence that nonhandicapped preschool children can function as important educational and therapeutic resources in mainstreamed settings. Through specialized arrangements in the classroom and the structuring of events by teachers or clinicians, nonhandicapped children have been able to increase handicapped children's proper use of syntactical forms (Guralnick, 1976), promote the frequency of social initiations (Strain, 1977), establish imitative repertoires (Apolloni & Cooke, 1978; Nordquist, 1978), and improve discrimination learning (Egel, Richman, & Koegel, 1981), as a few key examples. In some instances, nonhandicapped peers accomplish this by taking a directive or tutorial role, while in others the children assist by setting the occasion for certain interaction patterns. In all instances, however, nonhandicapped peers are functioning as agents of change in an assigned role—a role that is often carried out in highly structured and specially arranged situations.

Despite problems associated with the durability and generalizability of some of the procedures (see Strain, 1981, as well as other chapters in this volume for a more detailed discussion), these techniques have proved to be extremely valuable additions to educational and therapeutic practice. Certainly the availability of nonhandicapped children in mainstreamed programs facilitates the use of these strategies. Yet apart from these structured, often contrived situations, proponents of mainstreaming contend that it is through the more natural processes of observational learning and through the ongoing social interaction patterns of day-to-day contact that the more significant and lasting benefits for handicapped children will be acquired. After all, substantial evidence exists suggesting that young children do indeed observe and imitate other more competent children (Abramovitch & Grusec, 1978; Akamatsu & Thelen, 1974; Grusec & Abramovitch, 1982; Peterson, Peterson, & Scriven, 1977; Strichart, 1974; Vaughn & Waters, 1981). Moreover, the reciprocity principle suggests that one's companions can be a major factor influencing important aspects of peer-related social interactions

(Cairns, 1979). Similarly, if the research on social interactions between children at different chronological ages (Goldman, 1981; Lougee et al., 1977) is applicable to interactions between children at different developmental levels, there are likely to be many circumstances in mainstreamed settings in which less developmentally advanced children would be encouraged to increase the frequency and quality of their social exchanges.

The difficulty in evaluating whether these observational and social learning processes operate as anticipated in mainstreamed programs has probably been responsible for the fact that only two experimental studies have been conducted to date. Moreover, both of these studies were only able to examine whether any immediate changes in child–child social interactions occurred as a result of including developmentally more-advanced children in playgroups. In one investigation (Guralnick, 1981e), the social and play interactions of developmentally delayed and nonhandicapped children were evaluated when playing in groups homogeneous with respect to developmental level in contrast to a heterogeneous grouping. The homogeneous groupings consisted of a severely and moderately delayed group as well as a group of mildly delayed and nonhandicapped children. The heterogeneous groupings consisted of children representing all four developmental levels. The results indicated that although the severely delayed children in the sample played less inappropriately when their playgroup included mildly delayed and normally developing children, neither the level of social participation nor the frequency of social and communicative interactions varied as a function of the composition of the playgroup.

Focusing on a mixed group of mildly handicapped children including those with developmental delays, cerebral palsy, and speech and hearing impairments, Field, Roseman, DeStefano, and Koewler (1981) observed that the social interactions of handicapped children increased when a group of nonhandicapped children was introduced into the play setting (outdoor playground). Not only did handicapped children tend to relate more to peers during the integrated play sessions, but nonhandicapped children appeared to be more socially interactive as well. Nevertheless, despite these differences, the relative magnitude of the changes was very small, especially when the additional numbers of children available in the integrated setting are taken into consideration.

In conjunction with other, primarily nonexperimentally based, reports (Cooke, Ruskus, Apolloni, & Peck, 1981; Devoney, Guralnick, & Rubin, 1974; Novak, Olley, & Kearney, 1980; see Guralnick, 1981b, 1982, for reviews), the limited data available suggest that, at best, involvement with nonhandicapped children produces modest improvements in social and play interactions of handicapped children, but no adverse effects seem to occur. Of course, it is quite possible that more dramatic, widespread effects did exist but were not detected during observational periods. Indeed, evidence does suggest that imitation is often deferred in this situation, manifesting itself only when the more developmentally advanced groups are no longer participating in the play session (Devoney et al., 1974; Feitelson, Weintraub, & Michaeli, 1972). Similarly, long-term positive outcomes cannot be ruled out, especially if more appropriate experimental designs involving comparable but independent groups of children could be employed, and cumulative effects of even relatively small gains in social interactions may have significant developmental consequences over extended periods of time. Moreover, more substantial positive outcomes may yet result if educational programs attend more closely to the array of programmatic factors and subtle teaching strategies that can alter the frequency and quality of peer relations (Guralnick, 1981d).

Alternatively, perhaps it is naive to believe that the involvement of nonhandicapped peers could substantially override a history of generalized social deficits that characterize many handicapped children, especially when these deficits are compounded by language and communication difficulties. In fact, under certain conditions the involvement of nonhandicapped children may be counterproductive. As noted earlier, when normally developing children interact in mixed-age situations, older children may actually suppress certain forms of social and communicative behaviors of their younger companions if the age discrepancy becomes too great (Langlois et al., 1978). It is possible that the discrepancies in developmental level, even where children were similar in chronological age, counteracted any tendencies toward increased social activity.

Perhaps the limited effects of mainstreaming on social behavior reflect the absence of substantial and productive interactions occurring between handicapped and nonhandicapped children. The tendency to form socially separate subgroups in preschool settings is in fact a very powerful one. Such groupings normally form on the basis of many dimensions, including age and sex (Goldman, 1981), physical characteristics (Langlois & Downs, 1979), socioeconomic status (Feitelson et al., 1972), and popularity (Putallaz & Gottman, 1981). Any tendencies toward social separation between handicapped and nonhandicapped children may result from many factors, with the absence of shared experiences and shared expectations being perhaps the most significant (Feitelson et al., 1972; see also Brenner & Mueller, 1982). A further contributor may be difficulties that occur when handicapped and nonhandicapped children attempt to communicate with one another. From the perspective of the nonhandicapped children, where discrepancies in sensory abilities or developmental levels exist, effective communication and social exchange require adjustments and accommodations not typically necessary when interacting with other nonhandicapped companions.

Social Integration

Direct observations of the social and communicative interactions that occur in mainstreamed programs can help identify those alternative explanations that seem most plausible. As suggested, it is possible that initial differences between handicapped and nonhandicapped children (be they differences in cognitive ability, social play levels, motor or sensory skills, or any other factors) are creating segregated subgroups of handicapped and nonhandicapped children. Clearly, if any immediate or long-term benefits are to result from mainstreaming, a minimal level of social integration must exist to allow opportunities for observational learning to occur as well as providing for direct social exchanges between handicapped and nonhandicapped children.

Fortunately, the extent to which social integration occurs in mainstreamed classrooms has received considerable attention (Arnold & Tremblay, 1979; Brackett & Henniges, 1976; Cavallaro & Porter, 1980; Dunlop, Stoneman, & Cantrell, 1980; Guralnick, 1980; Ispa, 1981; Ispa & Matz, 1978; Peterson & Haralick, 1977; Porter, Ramsey, Tremblay, Iaccobo, & Crawley, 1978; Sinson & Wetherick, 1981; White, 1980). Although the studies are diverse in terms of the samples of children observed, the measures employed, and the type and quality of program evaluated, a general and not unexpected pattern has emerged. Overall, mildly handicapped and nonhandicapped children were not distinguishable from each other on the basis of the measures used. Not only did mildly handicapped and nonhandicapped children interact with each other frequently, but proximity and parallel play measures suggested that numerous opportunities were available for observational learning to occur. It is important to note, however, particularly when developmentally delayed children were subjects, that the handicapped children were generally 1 year older than their nonhandicapped classmates.

In contrast to mildly handicapped children, moderately and severely handicapped youngsters apparently receive very little attention from normally developing classmates. Although numerous opportunities for observational learning appear to be available, the research clearly indicates that frequent social exchanges are not common. When considering the perspective of the handicapped children, virtually all of the studies have reported that their social interactions are distributed equally across handicapped and nonhandicapped classmates. This holds not only for the most seriously delayed children, where their ability to distinguish among peers may be questioned, but also for mildly delayed and hearing-impaired children, as well as children with a range of other disabilities.

Although this general pattern of outcomes is likely to be substantiated in future research, it is perhaps somewhat optimistic with regard to the extent to which mildly delayed children are socially integrated. It should be pointed out that many studies observed children in university-based laboratory preschools, and many of the mildly handicapped children in the programs were either at the upper end of the spectrum for this classification or exhibited unusually well-developed social play skills prior to participating in the mainstreamed setting. Clearly, additional research focusing on individual child characteristics such as interpersonal skills and observational learning abilities, as related to the social integration process, is needed.

Social–Communicative Interactions

Direct examination of the nature of social and communicative interactions when they do occur complements analyses of the extent to which handicapped and nonhandicapped children interact with one another. It is possible that the minimal effects of mainstreaming result from the fact that interactions are generally aversive. However, numerous studies clearly indicate that this is not the case (e.g., Guralnick, 1980). Another possibility is that communicative adjustments by nonhandicapped children to handicapped children are inadequate, yielding numerous instances of communicative failure. This possibility was examined in a series of studies focusing on developmentally delayed children by Guralnick and Paul-Brown (1977, 1980, 1984). By analyzing a wide range of syntactic, semantic, functional, and discourse aspects of speech of nonhandicapped children as addressed to mildly, moderately, and severely handicapped companions, as well as to other nonhandicapped children in both structured and unstructured settings, a pattern suggesting that appropriate adjustments do in fact occur was obtained. In general, the speech of nonhandicapped children was syntactically simpler, less diverse, and contained a variety of discourse devices such as repetition, prompting, and demonstrating used to facilitate communication when addressing less cognitively advanced children. Moreover, nonhandicapped children were extremely persistent, creative, and successful in achieving their interpersonal goals whether or not their partner was handicapped. For example, not only were many different adaptive communicative strategies used to gain compliance to a behavior request, but multiple strategies were used simultaneously more often in the same communication to severely delayed children, apparently in an effort to maximize their communicative effectiveness.

The pattern of these communicative adjustments clearly suggests that nonhandicapped children are not only more likely to be understood, but also that the nature of their communicative exchanges may have important developmental consequences. In particular, research on typical parent–child communicative interactions, as well as investigations focusing on interactions occurring between normally developing children at different ages, have clearly described the nature of selective input that is provided and its possible contributions to the acquisition of the listener's communicative skills (Broen, 1972; Gleason & Weintraub, 1978; Shatz & Gelman, 1973; Snow, 1972; Snow & Ferguson, 1977; Wilkinson, Hiebert, & Rembold, 1981). Although there are some important discrepancies, many features of the communicative input of nonhandicapped children to developmentally delayed children are highly similar to the adjustments of parents as identified in this literature, suggesting that conditions exist that can facilitate the development of the handicapped child's communicative skills (Guralnick, 1981c).

In contrast, nonhandicapped children do not do nearly as well when interacting with children with significant hearing impairments. Both Arnold and Tremblay (1979) and Vandell and George (1981) have shown that appropriate adjustments to children with these deficits do not seem to occur. Vandell and George in particular have noted that hearing children do not modify their use of gestures, touches, and vocalizations to accommodate to the different hearing abilities of their play partners.

Relatively little is known with regard to the style of interactions that occur between handicapped and nonhandicapped children. It does appear, however, that when nonhandicapped children interact with more moderately and severely handicapped children, they tend to become more directive than when interacting with mildly or nonhandicapped classmates (Guralnick & Paul-Brown, 1980). Moreover, even when interacting with mildly delayed children, their style of interacting differs from that which exists when interacting with other normally developing classmates. Of most relevance is the fact that nonhandicapped children tend to mitigate or justify their requests less often to mildly delayed than to other nonhandicapped children (Guralnick & Paul-Brown, 1984). Although these children interact freely and frequently with one another, these subtle differences in speech usage may well reflect different status relationships (Ervin-Tripp, 1977).

Taken together, these varying patterns of interaction between non-handicapped and handicapped children highlight differences in both *form* and *function*, differences that govern the possible developmental consequences that might arise from participation in mainstreamed settings. Especially when relating with children with significant handicaps, the available research suggests that nonhandicapped children (1) tend to initiate and control interactions with handicapped playmates, (2) are generally highly responsive companions if involved in a play sequence, and (3) often assume an instructional mode when communicating. Moreover, in the course of the interactions, they adjust the syntactic, semantic, functional, and discourse characteristics of their social–communicative exchanges in a manner that appears to facilitate communication and may even be organized in a way that can promote the handicapped child's communicative competence. The degree of reciprocity, sensitivity, and control tend to be less pronounced in these nonhandicapped child–handicapped child interactions in comparison to when adults interact with young normally developing children at comparable developmental levels. As a consequence, the nonhandicapped child–handicapped child interactions are likely to exhibit characteristics similar to more typical child–child exchanges. Yet it is clear that the preceding style is primarily more adult-like than peer-like in form and probably in function as well. Accordingly, even if children appear to be well integrated along some dimensions of social behavior, gains in peer-related social interactions that depend on specific, usually coequal experiences with peers could not be expected to occur.

As anticipated from the social integration findings, for developmentally delayed children the severity of a child's handicap appears to be the crucial factor regulating whether adult-like or peer-like characteristics predominate. As the discrepancy between developmental levels of children at similar chronological ages diminishes, interactions between participants become more peer-like. That is, relationships with peers become more balanced, reciprocity increases, and social interactions generally become more coequal. The question remains as to whether primarily peer-like experiences emerge when chronologically younger but normally developing children interact with older delayed children at similar developmental levels. The evidence for peer interaction deficits described earlier suggests that even for mildly delayed children, coequal interactions may be difficult to achieve for many of these children. Additional information is needed with regard to the styles of interaction that occur between children with sensory and motor impairments, especially any variations along the severity dimension. Whatever the case may be, the developmental consequences of adult-like and peer-like interactions do differ, and both the expectations of the effects of mainstreaming and the planning of the composition of groups in mainstreamed classes must recognize these differences.

A FRAMEWORK FOR ASSESSMENT AND TREATMENT

The possible factors contributing to deficits in peer-related social development described earlier underscore the interdependencies that exist among different behavioral systems. Yet, there remains no systematic or comprehensive approach to the assessment and treatment of peer-related social deficits that explicitly recognizes these interdependencies nor that takes these factors into account. In fact, an extensive analysis of assessment instruments in the field of child–child social interactions (see Guralnick & Weinhouse, 1983) revealed that tests have essentially taken a developmental milestone approach, emphasizing the content domains of social participation (usually the Parten categories), and cooperation (including sharing, turn-taking, borrowing, and returning). As such, virtually no attention has been given to corequisites, prerequisites, or other processes related to peer interactions, clearly limiting the usefulness of these instruments with regard to designing appropriate intervention strategies. Moreover, this review revealed that test items were few in number and probed only a limited number of content domains. Of equal concern was the fact that most tests were lacking in psychometric soundness and items were often ambiguous in their intent and method of scoring.

Although it is beyond the scope of this chapter to provide a detailed description of an intervention-oriented assessment instrument in this area, some general suggestions can be made. Of course, conventional assessments of the extent to which children participate in social interactions with others are needed. However, such an instrument must go well beyond traditional domains in order to be sufficiently comprehensive to be capable of evaluating the possible contributions of factors known to influence peer interactions. Included in this analysis, for example, should be an assessment of the use of established social routines, access strategies, the deployment of attention, content matches, turn-taking, and related characteristics of those communicative exchanges that have been correlated with successful peer interactions. Because the ability to play constructively with toys and objects is a factor that limits the nature of social interactions with peers, an evaluation of this primarily cognitive measure is in order. Of course, results from cognitive assessments and even language and communication evaluations provide important information needed to establish both the existence of a deficit and to plan intervention programs. Similarly, an assessment of sensory or motor impairments that can limit social interaction should also be carried out. Even the existence of relatively minor physical anomalies and clearly unattractive features should be recorded, because these have been implicated as contributors to the development of overly active or inappropriate social interactions (Halverson & Waldrop, 1976; Langlois & Downs, 1979). Moreover, because we know that social play can vary considerably from one situation to another, an assessment of the child's responsivity to different play partners, the influence of different play settings, and note of special play interests should be obtained. Information of this sort may be extremely helpful in establishing those conditions most favorable to later intervention efforts.

Finally, an examination of a child's motivational–interpersonal characteristics is necessary to identify any interpersonal style factors or behavioral disturbances that might interfere with initiating or maintaining social relations. If aggressive styles to achieving interpersonal goals predominate, or excessive anxiety is present, not only does this information help to identify problem areas but also aids in the interpretation of other aspects of a peer-interaction assessment. Included here as well could be assessments of parent–child interactions, in an effort to gain some understanding of possible links to peer interactions in terms of a child's orientation to the social world. Eliciting information with regard to the child's prior involvement in playgroups, sibling interactions, or other relevant early child–child experiences from the parents constitutes additional background data that may be useful in establishing various initial hypotheses regarding both the origins of any problem and which treatment paths to follow.

The question that immediately arises is how to develop and organize an assessment approach that can capture this complexity in a reasonably efficient manner, as well as lend itself to the design of intervention strategies. The approach recommended here is to first use more broad-based instruments to establish whether or not a deficit exists, as well as to obtain relevant background information regarding related developmental domains, historical information, and environmental characteristics. For this level, many useful rating scales are available, including variations of Parten's (1932) scale, in which constructive play is nested within (1) the social participation categories (see Rubin, 1981), (2) teacher assessments of social competence and interpersonal behavior

(Behar & Stringfield, 1974; Kohn, Parnes, & Rosman, 1979), and (3) peer sociometric ratings when appropriate (Asher et al., 1981). By combining this information with data on the child's cognitive development and language and communication results from conventional measures of receptive and expressive language and inventories of the child's tendencies to use language in social contexts and the functions of those communicative efforts (see Coggins & Carpenter, 1981; McLean & Snyder-McLean, 1978), a fairly comprehensive initial picture can be obtained.

Once the probable existence of a deficit has been established, more fine-grained approaches are in order. Unfortunately, observational instruments capable of those assessments, which require both the evaluation and integration of peer-interaction processes and social and communicative exchanges, need to be developed. An assessment of this type might best be organized around a series of *social tasks*. Such tasks might include gaining entry into a playgroup, resolving conflict, maintaining conversations, and terminating a social exchange. These broad tasks can be further classified into *situations*. For example, conflict can arise over possession of objects or leadership roles. Finally, a series of *contexts* can be identified, with each context consisting of specific participants (varying in age, familiarity, status, etc.) and a physical setting (snack, floor play, use of outdoor equipment). It is these tasks, situations, and contexts that interact to create *episodes* that can be marked and identified to elicit social and communicative strategies children use. Through an analysis of the behaviors of each child in a variety of episodes, it is possible to construct a profile providing a sense of a child's strengths and weaknesses in peer interactions. Both naturalistic and contrived or analogue situations may be necessary in order to establish this profile, especially for those episodes that have a naturally low frequency of occurrence.

The task before the clinician is to separate out and analyze these different areas of functioning and then to establish the most probable course of action. Treatment strategies may be developed for one or many domains, recognizing however that intervention techniques constitute in essence a means of testing hypotheses related to earlier assessments. A system for continual probes and revisions of strategies must be included in any approach that seeks to promote the development of peer interactions.

A technology of promoting social behavior has been empirically developed over the years (see Part III of this volume). The use of peers as agents of change, techniques for promoting interpersonal problem solving (see Urbain & Kendall, 1980), and methods for enhancing social–

communicative skills are all available. General principles for promoting
development that include building on the child's strengths, removing
barriers (e.g., physical ones or those related to appearance), and establishing conditions that can maximize the success of social encounters by
attending to a child's interests, the types and characteristics of playmates, and setting factors, can all be invoked. The use of nonhandicapped children may be a particularly powerful strategy, and the previous discussion of adult-like and peer-like interactions is especially
relevant in this context. When this technology is linked to a framework
capable of identifying developmentally and clinically useful goals for
treatment, perhaps an assessment system similar to the preceding one, a
highly generalizable, durable, and satisfying set of processes for promoting peer relations may well emerge.

SUMMARY AND CONCLUSIONS

The peer relations of young children has become a rich and rewarding
field of study. In-depth analyses of child–child interactions have not
only been recognized as sensitive indicators of a child's general social
functioning but have helped enlarge our understanding of the intricate
patterns and interrelationships that contribute to a young child's social
development. In a relatively short period of time, a comprehensive and
surprisingly consistent picture of the development and characteristics of
peer relations has emerged. Descriptive accounts have probed the early
development of peer relations, its rate, content, quality, structure, and
organization as well as traced the events that influence its expression,
both historical and contemporary. The relationship to other developmental processes such as social cognition and communicative development have also been clarified. Moreover, the unique contributions of
peer relations to a child's social functioning are becoming more firmly
understood and established. Although much remains to be accomplished, interest and advances in this field are striking.

In contrast to our knowledge of normally developing children, we
have only a limited understanding of the peer relations of young handicapped children. What is known suggests that these children may well
be unusually vulnerable to significant deficits with regard to their social
interactions with other children; deficits well beyond those expected on
the basis of their level of cognitive development. Although our knowledge of the peer relations of normally developing children has helped us
to understand the extent and nature of these deficits, the development
of a comprehensive diagnostic–assessment–intervention system in the

area of peer interactions for young handicapped children may well be one of the most important tasks for the next decade.

REFERENCES

Abramovitch, R., & Grusec, J. (1978). Peer imitation in a natural setting. *Child Development*, 49, 60–65.

Akamatsu, T., & Thelen, M. (1974). A review of the literature on observer characteristics and imitation. *Developmental Psychology, 10*, 38–47.

Anderson, S., & Messick, S. (1974). Social competency in young children. *Developmental Psychology, 10*, 282–293.

Apolloni, T., & Cooke, T. P. (1978). Integrated programming at the infant, toddler, and preschool levels. In M. J. Guralnick (Ed.), *Early intervention and the integration of handicapped and nonhandicapped children* (pp. 147–165). Baltimore: University Park Press.

Arnold, W., & Tremblay, A. (1979). Interaction of deaf and hearing preschool children. *Journal of Communication Disorders, 12*, 245–251.

Asher, S. R., Markell, R. A., & Hymel, S. (1981). Identifying children at risk in peer relations: A critique of the rate-of-interaction approach to assessment. *Child Development, 52*, 1239–1245.

Asher, S. R., & Taylor, A. R. (1981). Social outcomes of mainstreaming: Sociometric assessment and beyond. *Exceptional Education Quarterly, 1*(4), 13–30.

Bakeman, R., & Brownlee, J. R. (1980). The strategic use of parallel play: A sequential analysis. *Child Development, 51*, 873–878.

Bailey, D. B., Jr., Clifford, R. M., & Harms, T. (1982). Comparison of preschool environments for handicapped and nonhandicapped children. *Topics in Early Childhood Special Education, 2*(1), 9–20.

Barnes, K. E. (1971). Preschool play norms: A replication. *Developmental Psychology, 5*, 99–103.

Battle, C. U. (1974). Disruptions in the socialization of a young, severely handicapped child. *Rehabilitation Literature, 35*, 130–140.

Becker, J. M. T. (1977). A learning analysis of the development of peer-oriented behavior in nine-month-old infants. *Developmental Psychology, 13*, 481–491.

Behar, L., & Stringfield, S. (1974). A behavior rating scale for the preschool child. *Developmental Psychology, 10*, 601–610.

Belsky, J., & Steinberg, L. D. (1978). The effects of day care: A critical review. *Child Development, 49*, 929–949.

Berninger, G., & Garvey. C. (1981). Complementary balance in the use of the interrogative form by nursery school dyads. *Journal of Child Language, 8*, 297–311.

Brackett, D., & Henniges, M. (1976). Communicative interaction of preschool hearing impaired children in an integrated setting. *The Volta Review, 78*, 276–285.

Brenner, J., & Mueller, E. (1982). Shared meaning in boy toddlers' peer relations. *Child Development, 53*, 380–391.

Bridges, K. M. B. (1933). A study of social development in early infancy. *Child Development, 4*, 36–49.

Broen, P. A. (1972). The verbal environment of the language-learning child. *American Speech and Hearing Association Monograph, 17*.

Bronson, W. C. (1981). *Toddlers' behaviors with agemates: Issues of interaction, cognition, and affect*. Norwood, NJ: Ablex.

Cairns, R. B. (1979). *Social development: The origins and plasticity of interchanges.* San Francisco: W. H. Freeman.

Campbell, S. B., & Cluss, P. (1982). Peer relationships of young children with behavior problems. In K. H. Rubin & H. S. Ross (Eds.), *Peer relationships and social skills in childhood* (pp. 323–351). New York: Springer-Verlag.

Cavallaro, S. A., & Porter, R. H. (1980). Peer preferences of at-risk and normally developing children in preschool mainstream classrooms. *American Journal of Mental Deficiency, 84,* 357–366.

Charlesworth, R., & Hartup, W. W. (1967). Positive social reinforcement in the nursery school peer group. *Child Development, 38,* 993–1002.

Chess, S. (1979). Developmental theory revisited: Findings of longitudinal study. *Canadian Journal of Psychiatry, 24,* 101–112.

Cicchetti, D., & Sroufe, L. A. (1976). The relationship between affective and cognitive development in Down's syndrome infants. *Child Development, 47,* 920–929.

Coggins, T. E., & Carpenter, R. L. (1981). The communicative intention inventory: A system for observing and coding children's early intentional communication. *Applied Psycholinguistics, 2,* 235–251.

Conger, J. C., & Keane, S. P. (1981). Social skills intervention in the treatment of isolated or withdrawn children. *Psychological Bulletin, 3,* 478–495.

Cooke, T. P., Ruskus, J. A., Apolloni, T., & Peck, C. A. (1981). Handicapped preschool children in the mainstream: Background, outcomes, and clinical suggestions. *Topics in Early Childhood Special Education, 1*(1), 73–83.

Corsaro, W. A. (1979). "We're friends, right?": Children's use of access rituals in a nursery school. *Language in Society, 8,* 315–336.

Cowen, E. L., Pederson, A., Bibigian, H., Izzo, L. D., & Trost, M. A. (1973). Long-term follow-up of early detected vulnerable children. *Journal of Consulting and Clinical Psychology, 41,* 438–446.

Cunningham, C. E., Reuler, E., Blackwell, J., & Deck, J. (1981). Behavioral and linguistic developments in the interactions of normal and retarded children with their mothers. *Child Development, 52,* 62–70.

Darbyshire, J. O. (1977). Play patterns in young children with impaired hearing. *The Volta Review, 79,* 19–26.

Devoney, C., Guralnick, M. J., & Rubin, H. (1974). Integrating handicapped and nonhandicapped preschool children: Effects on social play. *Childhood Education, 50,* 360–364.

Doyle, A., Connolly, J., & Rivest, L. (1980). The effect of playmate familiarity on the social interactions of young children. *Child Development, 51,* 217–223.

Dunlop, K. H., Stoneman, Z., & Cantrell, M. L. (1980). Social interaction of exceptional and other children in a mainstreamed preschool classroom. *Exceptional Children, 47,* 132–141.

Easterbrooks, M. A., & Lamb, M. E. (1979). The relationship between quality of infant–mother attachment and infant competence in initial encounters with peers. *Child Development, 50,* 380–387.

Eckerman, C. O., Whatley, J. L., & Kutz, S. L. (1975). Growth of social play with peers during the second year of life. *Developmental Psychology, 11,* 42–49.

Egel, A. L., Richman, G. S., & Koegel, R. L. (1981). Normal peer models and autistic children's learning. *Journal of Applied Behavior Analysis, 14,* 3–12.

Ervin-Tripp, S. (1977). Wait for me, roller skate! In S. Ervin-Tripp & C. Mitchell-Kernan (Eds.), *Child discourse* (pp. 165–168). New York: Academic Press.

Ervin-Tripp, S., & Mitchell-Kernan, C. (Eds.). (1977). *Child discourse.* New York: Academic Press.

Farber, B. (1975). Family adaptations to severely mentally retarded children. In M. J. Begab

& S. A. Richardson (Eds.), *The mentally retarded and society: A social science perspective* (pp. 247–266). Baltimore: University Park Press.

Feitelson, D., Weintraub, S., & Michaeli, O. (1972). Social interaction in heterogeneous preschools. *Child Development, 43,* 1249–1259.

Field, T. M. (1980). Self, teacher, toy, and peer-directed behaviors of handicapped pre-school children. In T. M. Field, S. Goldberg, D. Stern, & A. M. Sostek (Eds.), *High-risk infants and children: Adult and peer interactions* (pp. 313–326). New York: Academic Press.

Field, T., Roseman, S., DeStefano, L., & Koewler, J. H., III. (1981). Play behaviors of handicapped preschool children in the presence and absence of nonhandicapped peers. *Journal of Applied Developmental Psychology, 2,* 49–58.

Finkelstein, N. W., Dent, C., Gallacher, K., & Ramey, C. T. (1978). Social behavior of infants and toddlers in a day-care environment. *Developmental Psychology, 14,* 257–262.

Garvey, C. (1975). Requests and responses in children's speech. *Journal of Child Language, 2,* 41–63.

Garvey, C. (1977). The contingent query: A dependent act in conversation. In M. Lewis & L. A. Rosenblum (Eds.), *Interaction, conversation, and the development of language* (pp. 63–93). New York: Wiley.

Garvey, C., & Ben Debba, M. (1974). Effects of age, sex, and partner on children's dyadic speech. *Child Development, 45,* 1159–1161.

Garvey, C., & Hogan, R. (1973). Social speech and social interaction: Egocentrism revisited. *Child Development, 44,* 562–568.

Gelman, R., & Shatz, M. (1977). Appropriate speech adjustments: The operation of conversational constraints on talk to two-year-olds. In M. Lewis & L. A. Rosenblum (Eds.), *Interaction, conversation, and the development of language* (pp. 27–61). New York: Wiley.

George, C., & Main, M. (1979). Social interactions of young abused children: Approach, avoidance, and aggression. *Child Development, 50,* 306–318.

Gleason, J. B., & Weintraub, S. (1978). Input language and the acquisition of communicative competence. In K. Nelson (Ed.), *Children's language* (Vol. 1, pp. 171–222). New York: Gardner Press.

Goldman, J. A. (1981). Social participation of preschool children in same- versus mixed-age groups. *Child Development, 52,* 644–650.

Greenspan, S. (1981). Defining childhood social competence: A proposed working model. In B. K. Keogh (Ed.), *Advances in special education: Vol. 3. Social influences on exceptionality* (pp. 1–39). Greenwich, CT: JAI Press.

Grusec, J. E., & Abramovitch, R. (1982). Imitation of peers and adults in a natural setting: A functional analysis. *Child Development, 53,* 636–642.

Guralnick, M. J. (1976). The value of integrating handicapped and nonhandicapped pre-school children. *American Journal of Orthopsychiatry, 46,* 236–245.

Guralnick, M. J. (Ed.). (1978). *Early intervention and the integration of handicapped and nonhandicapped children.* Baltimore: University Park Press.

Guralnick, M. J. (1980). Social interactions among preschool children. *Exceptional Children, 46,* 248–253.

Guralnick, M. J. (1981a). The development and role of child–child social interactions. In N. Anastasiow (Ed.), *New directions for exceptional children: Socioemotional development* (pp. 53–80). San Francisco: Jossey-Bass.

Guralnick, M. J. (1981b). The efficacy of integrating handicapped children in early education settings: Research implications. *Topics in Early Childhood Special Education, 1*(1), 57–71.

Guralnick, M. J. (1981c). Peer influences on the development of communicative competence. In P. Strain (Ed.), *The utilization of classroom peers as behavior change agents* (pp. 31–68). New York: Plenum.

Guralnick, M. J. (1981d). Programmatic factors affecting child–child social interactions in mainstreamed preschool programs. *Exceptional Education Quarterly, 1*(4), 71–91.

Guralnick, M. J. (1981e). The social behavior of preschool children at different developmental levels: Effects of group composition. *Journal of Experimental Child Psychology, 31*, 115–130.

Guralnick, M. J. (1982). Mainstreaming young handicapped children: A public policy and ecological systems analysis. In B. Spodek (Ed.), *Handbook of research on early childhood education* (pp. 456–500). New York: The Free Press/MacMillan.

Guralnick, M. J., & Paul-Brown, D. (1977). The nature of verbal interactions among handicapped and nonhandicapped preschool children. *Child Development, 48*, 254–260.

Guralnick, M. J., & Paul-Brown, D. (1980). Functional and discourse analyses of nonhandicapped preschool children's speech to handicapped children. *American Journal of Mental Deficiency, 84*, 444–454.

Guralnick, M. J., & Paul-Brown, D. (1984). Communicative adjustments during behavior request episodes among children at different developmental levels. *Child Development, 55*, 911–919.

Guralnick, M. J., & Weinhouse, E. (1983). Child–child social interactions: An analysis of assessment instruments for young children. *Exceptional Children, 50*, 268–271.

Guralnick, M. J., & Weinhouse, E. (1984). Peer related social interactions of developmentally delayed young children: Development and characteristics. *Developmental Psychology, 20*, 815–827.

Halverson, C. F., Jr., & Waldrop, M. F. (1976). Relations between preschool activity and aspects of intellectual and social behavior at age 7½. *Developmental Psychology, 12*, 107–112.

Hartup, W. W. (1976). Peer interaction and the behavioral development of the individual child. In E. Schopler & R. J. Reichler (Eds.), *Psychopathology and child development: Research and treatment* (pp. 203–218). New York: Plenum.

Hartup, W. W. (1978). Peer interaction and the process of socialization. In M. J. Guralnick (Ed.), *Early intervention and the integration of handicapped and nonhandicapped children* (pp. 27–51). Baltimore: University Park Press.

Hartup, W. W. (1979). Peer relations and the growth of social competence. In M. W. Kent & J. E. Rolf (Eds.), *Primary prevention of psychopathology* (Vol. 3, pp. 150–170). Hanover, NH: University Press of New England.

Hartup, W. W., Glazer, J., & Charlesworth, R. (1967). Peer reinforcement and sociometric status. *Child Development, 38*, 1017–1024.

Hetherington, E. M., Cox, M., & Cox, R. (1979). Play and social interaction in children following divorce. *Journal of Social Issues, 35*(4), 26–49.

Higginbotham, J., & Baker, B. M. (1981). Social participation and cognitive play differences in hearing-impaired and normally hearing preschoolers. *The Volta Review, 83*, 135–149.

Holmberg, M. C. (1980). The development of social interchange patterns from 12 to 42 months. *Child Development, 51*, 448–456.

Hops, H., & Greenwood, C. R. (1981). Social skills deficits. In E. J. Mash & L. G. Terdal (Eds.), *Behavioral assessment of childhood disorders* (pp. 347–394). New York: The Guilford Press.

Huston-Stein, A., Friedrich-Cofer, L., & Susman, E. J. (1977). The relation of classroom structure to social behavior, imaginative play, and self-regulation of economically disadvantaged children. *Child Development, 48*, 908–916.

Hutt, C., & Vaizey, M. J. (1966). Differential effects of group density on social behavior. *Nature, 209*, 1371–1372.

Ispa, J. (1981). Social interactions among teachers, handicapped children, and nonhandicapped children in a mainstreamed preschool. *Journal of Applied Developmental Psychology, 1,*, 231–250.

Ispa, J., & Matz, R. D. (1978). Integrating handicapped preschool children within a cognitively oriented program. In M. J. Guralnick (Ed.), *Early intervention and the integration of handicapped and nonhandicapped children* (pp. 167–190). Baltimore: University Park Press.

James, S. L. (1978). Effect of listener age and situation on the politeness of children's directives. *Journal of Psycholinguistic Research, 7,* 307–317.

Kearsley, R. B. (1979). Iatrogenic retardation: A syndrome of learned incompetence. In R. Kearsley & I. E. Sigel (Eds.), *Infants at risk: Assessment of cognitive functioning* (pp. 153–180). Hillsdale, NJ: Erlbaum.

Keenan, E. O. (1977). Making it last: Repetition in children's discourse. In S. Ervin-Tripp & C. Mitchell-Kernan (Eds.), *Child discourse* (pp. 125–138). New York: Academic Press.

Kohn, M. (1966). The child as a determinant of his peers' approach to him. *The Journal of Genetic Psychology, 109,* 91–100.

Kohn, M., Parnes, B., & Rosman, B. L. (1979). *A rating and scoring manual for the Kohn Problem Checklist and Kohn Social Competence Scale.* New York: The William Alanson White Institute of Psychiatry, Psychoanalysis, & Psychology.

Langlois, J. H., & Downs, C. A. (1979). Peer relations as a function of physical attractiveness: The eye of the beholder or behavioral reality? *Child Development, 50,* 409–418.

Langlois, J. H., Gottfried, N. W., Barnes, B. M., & Hendricks, D. E. (1978). The effect of peer age on the social behavior of preschool children. *The Journal of Genetic Psychology, 132,* 11–19.

Lasky, E. Z., & Klopp, K. (1982). Parent–child interactions in normal and language-disordered children. *Journal of Speech and Hearing Disorders, 47,* 7–18.

Leiter, M. P. (1977). A study of reciprocity in preschool play groups. *Child Development, 48,* 1288–1295.

Lewis, M., & Feiring, C. (1979). The child's social network: Social object, social functions, and their relationship. In M. Lewis & L. A. Rosenblum (Eds.), *The child and its family* (pp. 9–27). New York: Plenum.

Lewis, M., & Rosenblum, L. A. (Eds.). (1975a). *The origins of behavior: Vol. 4. Friendship and peer relations.* New York: Wiley.

Lewis, M., & Rosenblum, L. A. (1975b). Introduction. In M. Lewis & L. A. Rosenblum (Eds.), *The origins of behavior: Vol. 4. Friendship and peer relations* (pp. 1–9). New York: Wiley.

Lewis, M., Young, G., Brooks, J., & Michalson, L. (1975). The beginning of friendship. In M. Lewis & L. A. Rosenblum (Eds.), *The origins of behavior: Vol. 4. Friendship and peer relations* (pp. 27–66). New York: Wiley.

Lieberman, A. F. (1977). Preschoolers' competence with a peer: Relations with attachment and peer experience. *Child Development, 48,* 1277–1287.

Loo, C. M. (1972). The effects of spatial density on the social behavior of children. *Journal of Applied Social Psychology, 2,* 372–381.

Lougee, M. D., Grueneich, R., & Hartup, W. W. (1977). Social interaction in same- and mixed-age dyads of preschool children. *Child Development, 48,* 1353–1361.

Mahoney, G., Glover, A., & Finger, I. (1981). Relationship between language and sensorimotor development of Down syndrome and nonretarded children. *American Journal of Mental Deficiency, 86,* 21–27.

Mahoney, G. J., & Seely, P. B. (1976). The role of the social agent in language acquisition:

Implications for language intervention. In N. R. Ellis (Ed.), *International review of research in mental retardation* (Vol. 8, pp. 57–103). New York: Academic Press.

Matas, L., Arend, R. A., & Sroufe, L. A. (1978). Continuity of adaptation in the second year: The relationship between quality of attachment and later competence. *Child Development, 49,* 547–556.

Maudry, M., & Nekula, M. (1939). Social relations between children of the same age during the first two years of life. *The Journal of Genetic Psychology, 54,* 193–215.

McGrew, P. L. (1970). Social and spatial density effects on spacing behaviour in preschool children. *Journal of Child Psychology and Psychiatry, 11,* 197–205.

McLean, J. E., & Snyder-McLean, L. K. (1978). *A transactional approach to early language training.* Columbus, OH: Charles E. Merrill.

Meadow, K. P. (1980). *Deafness and child development.* Berkeley, CA: University of California Press.

Meadow, K. P., Greenberg, M. T., Erting, C., & Carmichael, H. (1981). Interactions of deaf mothers and deaf preschool children: Comparisons with three other groups of deaf and hearing dyads. *American Association for the Deaf, 126,* 454–468.

Meadow, K. P., & Trybus, R. J. (1979). Behavioral and emotional problems of deaf children: An overview. In L. J. Bradford & W. G. Hardy (Eds.), *Hearing and hearing impairment* (pp. 395–403). New York: Grune & Stratton.

Miller, J. F., Chapman, R. S., & Bedrosian, J. L. (1977). *Defining developmentally disabled subjects for research: The relationship between etiology, cognitive development, and language and communicative performance.* Unpublished manuscript, University of Wisconsin—Madison.

Miller, L. B., & Dyer, J. L. (1975). Four preschool programs: Their dimensions and effects. *Monographs of the Society for Research in Child Development, 40*(5–6 Serial No. 162).

Moerk, E. L. (1977). *Pragmatic and semantic aspects of early language development.* Baltimore: University Park Press.

Moore, N. V., Evertson, C. M., & Brophy, J. E. (1974). Solitary play: Some functional reconsiderations. *Developmental Psychology, 10,* 830–834.

Mueller, E. (1972). The maintenance of verbal exchanges between young children. *Child Development, 43,* 930–938.

Mueller, E. (1979). (Toddlers + toys) = (An autonomous social system). In M. Lewis & L. A. Rosenblum (Eds.), *The child and its family* (pp. 169–194). New York: Plenum.

Mueller, E., Bleir, M., Krakow, J., Hegedus, K., & Cournoyer, P. (1977). The development of peer verbal interactions among two-year-old boys. *Child Development, 48,* 284–287.

Mueller, E., & Brenner, J. (1977). The origins of social skills and interaction among playgroup toddlers. *Child Development, 48,* 854–861.

Mueller, E., & Lucas, T. (1975). A developmental analysis of peer interaction among toddlers. In M. Lewis & L. A. Rosenblum (Eds.), *The origins of behavior: Vol. 4. Friendship and peer relations* (pp. 223–257). New York: Wiley.

Mueller, E. C., & Vandell, D. (1979). Infant–infant interaction. In J. D. Osofsky (Ed.), *Handbook of infant development* (pp. 591–622). New York: Wiley.

Nordquist, V. M. (1978). A behavioral approach to the analysis of peer interactions. In M. J. Guralnick (Ed.), *Early intervention and the integration of handicapped and nonhandicapped children* (pp. 53–84). Baltimore: University Park Press.

Novak, M. A., Olley, J. G., & Kearney, D. S. (1980). Social skills of children with special needs in integrated and separate preschools. In T. M. Field, S. Goldberg, D. Stern, & A. M. Sostek (Eds.), *High-risk infants and children: Adult and peer interactions* (pp. 327–346). New York: Academic Press.

Ochs, E., & Schieffelin, B. B. (Eds.). (1979). *Developmental pragmatics.* New York: Academic Press.

O'Connor, R. D. (1975). The nursery school environment. *Developmental Psychology, 11,* 556–561.

O'Malley, J. M. (1977). Research perspective on social competence. *Merrill-Palmer Quarterly, 23,* 29–44.

Parten, M. B. (1932). Social participation among preschool children. *Journal of Abnormal Social Psychology, 27,* 243–269.

Parten, M. B. (1933). Social play among preschool children. *Journal of Abnormal Social Psychology, 28,* 136–147.

Pastor, D. L. (1981). The quality of mother–infant attachment and its relationship to toddlers' initial sociability with peers. *Developmental Psychology, 17,* 326–335.

Peterson, C., Peterson, J., & Scriven, G. (1977). Peer imitation by nonhandicapped and handicapped preschoolers. *Exceptional Children, 43,* 223–224.

Peterson, N. L., & Haralick, J. G. (1977). Integration of handicapped and nonhandicapped preschoolers: An analysis of play behavior and social interaction. *Education and Training of the Mentally Retarded, 12,* 235–245.

Porter, R. H., Ramsey, B., Tremblay, A., Iaccobo, M., & Crawley, S. (1978). Social interactions in heterogeneous groups of retarded and normally developing children: An observational study. In G. P. Sackett (Ed.), *Observing behavior: Vol. 1. Theory and applications in mental retardation* (pp. 311–328). Baltimore: University Park Press.

Putallaz, M., & Gottman, J. M. (1981). Social skills and group acceptance. In S. R. Asher & J. M. Gottman (Eds.), *The development of children's friendships* (pp. 116–149). Cambridge: Cambridge University Press.

Reiss, S., Levitan, G. W., & McNally, R. J. (1982). Emotionally disturbed mentally retarded people: An underserved population. *American Psychologist, 37,* 361–367.

Robinson, N. M., & Robinson, H. B. (1976). *The mentally retarded child: A psychological approach.* New York: McGraw-Hill.

Roff, M., Sells, B., & Golden, M. M. (1972). *Social adjustment and personality development in children.* Minneapolis: University of Minnesota Press.

Rogers-Warren, A., & Wedel, J. W. (1980). The ecology of preschool classrooms for the handicapped. In J. J. Gallagher (Ed.), *New directions for exceptional children: Ecology of exceptional children* (pp. 1–24). San Francisco: Jossey-Bass.

Roper, R., & Hinde, R. A. (1978). Social behavior in a play group: Consistency and complexity. *Child Development, 49,* 570–579.

Ross, H. S. (1982). Establishment of social games among toddlers. *Developmental Psychology, 18,* 509–518.

Rubenstein, J., & Howes, C. (1976). The effects of peers on toddler interaction with mother and toys. *Child Development, 47,* 597–605.

Rubin, K. H. (1977). The social and cognitive value of preschool toys and activities. *Canadian Journal of Behavioral Sciences, 9,* 382–385.

Rubin, K. H. (1981). *Manual for coding free play behaviors of young children.* Waterloo, Ontario: University of Waterloo.

Rubin, K. H. (1982). Nonsocial play in preschoolers: Necessary evil? *Child Development, 53,* 651–657.

Rubin, K. H., & Borwick, D. (1984). Communicative skills and sociability. In H. E. Sypher & J. L. Applegate (Eds.), *Communication by children and adults: Social, cognitive, and strategic processes* (pp. 152–170). Beverly Hills, CA: Sage.

Rubin, K. H., Daniels-Bierness, T., & Hayvren, M. (1982). Social and social-cognitive correlates of sociometric status in preschool and kindergarten children. *Canadian Journal of Behavioral Science, 14,* 338–349.

Rubin, K. H., Maioni, T. L., & Hornung, M. (1976). Free play behaviors in middle- and lower-class preschoolers: Parten and Piaget revisited. *Child Development, 47,* 414–419.

Rubin, K. H., & Pepler, D. J. (1980). The relationship of child's play to social–cognitive growth and development. In H. C. Foot, A. J. Chapman, & J. R. Smith (Eds.), *Friendship and social relations in children* (pp. 209–233). New York: Wiley.

Schegloff, E. A. (1968). Sequencing in conversational openings. *American Anthropologist, 70*, 1075–1095.

Schiefelbusch, R. L. (1981). Development of social competence and incompetence. In M. J. Begab, H. C. Haywood, & H. L. Garber (Eds.), *Psychosocial influences in retarded performance: Vol. 1. Issues and theories in development* (pp. 179–195). Baltimore: University Park Press.

Seligman, M. E. P. (1975). *Helplessness: On depression, development, and death.* San Francisco: W. H. Freeman.

Shantz, C. U. (1975). The development of social cognition. In E. M. Hetherington, J. W. Hagen, R. Kron, & A. H. Stein (Eds.), *Review of child development research* (Vol. 5, pp. 257–323). Chicago: University of Chicago Press.

Shatz, M., & Gelman, R. (1973). The development of communication skills: Modifications in the speech of young children as a function of listener. *Monographs of the Society for Research in Child Development, 38*, No. 5.

Shores, R. E., Hester, P., & Strain, P. S. (1976). The effects of amount and type of teacher–child interaction on child–child interaction. *Psychology in the Schools, 13*, 171–175.

Shure, M. B. (1963). Psychological ecology of a nursery school. *Child Development, 34*, 979–992.

Sinson, J. C., & Wetherick, N. E. (1981). The behaviour of children with Down syndrome in normal playgroups. *Journal of Mental Deficiency Research, 25*, 113–120.

Smilansky, S. (1968). *The effects of sociodramatic play on disadvantaged preschool children.* New York: Wiley.

Smith, P. K. (1978). A longitudinal study of social participation in preschool children: Solitary and parallel play reexamined. *Developmental Psychology, 14*, 517–523.

Snow, C. E. (1972). Mothers' speech to children learning language. *Child Development, 43*, 549–565.

Snow, C. E., & Ferguson, C. A. (Eds.). (1977). *Talking to children: Language input and acquisition.* Cambridge: Cambridge University Press.

Solnit, A. J., & Provence, S. (1979). Vulnerability and risk in early childhood. In J. D. Osofsky (Ed.), *Handbook of infant development* (pp. 799–808). New York: Wiley.

Sroufe, L. A. (1979). Socioemotional development. In J. D. Osofsky (Ed.), *Handbook of infant development* (pp. 462–516). New York: Wiley.

Stone, N. W., & Chesney, B. H. (1978). Attachment behaviors in handicapped infants. *Mental Retardation, 16*, 8–12.

Strain, P. S. (1977). An experimental analysis of peer social initiations on the behavior of withdrawn preschool children. Some training and generalization effects. *Journal of Abnormal Child Psychology, 5*, 445–455.

Strain, P. S. (Ed.). (1981). *The utilization of classroom peers as behavior change agents.* New York: Plenum.

Strain, P. S., & Fox, J. J. (1981). Peers as behavior change agents for withdrawn classmates. In B. B. Lahey & A. E. Kazdin (Eds.), *Advances in clinical child psychology* (Vol. 4, pp. 167–198). New York: Plenum.

Strichart, S. (1974). Effects of competence and nurturance on imitation of nonretarded peers by retarded adolescents. *American Journal of Mental Deficiency, 78*, 665–673.

Terdal, L., Jackson, R. H., & Garner, A. M. (1976). Mother–child interactions: A comparison between normal and developmentally delayed groups. In E. J. Mash, L. A. Hamerlynck, & L. C. Handy (Eds.), *Behavior modification and families* (pp. 249–264). New York: Brunner/Mazel.

Thompson, R. A., Lamb, M. E., & Estes, D. (1982). Stability of infant–mother attachment and its relationship to changing life circumstances in an unselected middle-class sample. *Child Development, 53,* 144–148.

Tjossem, T. D. (Ed.). (1976). *Intervention strategies for high risk infants and young children.* Baltimore: University Park Press.

Tremblay, A., Strain, P. S., Hendrickson, J. M., & Shores, R. E. (1981). Social interactions of normally developing preschool children: Using normative data for subject and target behavior selection. *Behavior Modification, 5,* 237–253.

Ulrey, G. (1981). Emotional development of the young handicapped child. In N. Anastasiow (Ed.), *New directions for exceptional children: Socioemotional development* (pp. 33–51). San Francisco: Jossey-Bass.

Urbain, E. S., & Kendall, P. C. (1980). Review of social–cognitive problem-solving interventions with children. *Psychological Bulletin, 88,* 109–143.

Vandell, D. L. (1980). Sociability with peer and mother during the first year. *Developmental Psychology, 16,* 355–361.

Vandell, D. L., & George, L. B. (1981). Social interaction in hearing and deaf preschoolers: Successes and failures in initiations. *Child Development, 52,* 627–635.

Vandell, D. L., & Mueller, E. C. (1980). Peer play and friendships during the first two years. In H. C. Foot, A. J. Chapman, & J. R. Smith (Eds.), *Friendship and social relations in children* (pp. 181–208). New York: Wiley.

Vandell, D. L., Wilson, K. S., & Buchanan, N. R. (1980). Peer interaction in the first year of life: An examination of its structure, content, and sensitivity to toys. *Child Development, 51,* 481–488.

Vandenberg, B. (1981). Environmental and cognitive factors in social play. *Journal of Experimental Child Psychology, 31,* 169–175.

Vaughn, B., Egeland, B., Sroufe, L. A., & Waters, E. (1979). Individual differences in infant–mother attachment at twelve and eighteen months: Stability and change in families under stress. *Child Development, 50,* 971–975.

Vaughn, B. E., & Waters, E. (1981). Attention structure, sociometric status, and dominance: Interrelations, behavioral correlates, and relationships to social competence. *Developmental Psychology, 17,* 275–288.

Vincze, M. (1971). The social contacts of infants and young children reared together. *Early Child Development and Care, 1,* 99–109.

Waldrop, M. F., & Halverson, C. F., Jr. (1975). Intensive and extensive peer behavior: Longitudinal and cross-sectional analyses. *Child Development, 46,* 19–26.

Wanlass, R. L., & Prinz, R. J. (1982). Methodological issues in conceptualizing and treating childhood social isolation. *Psychological Bulletin, 92,* 39–55.

Waters, E. (1978). The reliability and stability of individual differences in infant–mother attachment. *Child Development, 49,* 483–494.

Waters, E., Wippman, J., & Sroufe, L. A. (1979). Attachment, positive affect, and competence in the peer group: Two studies in construct validation. *Child Development, 50,* 821–829.

Wedell-Monnig, J., & Lumley, J. M. (1980). Child deafness and mother–child interaction. *Child Development, 51,* 766–774.

Welkowitz, J., Cariffe, G., & Feldstein, S. (1976). Conversational congruence as a criterion of socialization in children. *Child Development, 47,* 269–272.

White, B. L., & Watts, J. C. (1973). *Experience and environment* (Vol. 1). Englewood Cliffs, NJ: Prentice-Hall.

White, B. N. (1980). Mainstreaming in grade school and preschool: How the child with special needs interacts with peers. In T. M. Field, S. Goldberg, D. Stern, & A. M. Sostek (Eds.), *High-risk infants and children: Adult and peer interactions* (pp. 347–371). New York: Academic Press.

Wilkinson, L. C., Hiebert, E., & Rembold, K. (1981). Parents' and peers' communication to toddlers. *Journal of Speech and Hearing Research, 24,* 383–388.

Wine, J. D., & Smye, M. D. (1981). *Social competence.* New York: The Guilford Press.

Wintre, M. G., & Webster, C. D. (1974). A brief report on using a traditional social behavior scale with disturbed children. *Journal of Applied Behavior Analysis, 7,* 345–348.

Zigler, E., & Trickett, P. K. (1978). IQ, social competence, and evaluation of early childhood intervention programs. *American Psychologist, 33,* 789–798.

PART II

ASSESSMENT OF CHILDREN'S SOCIAL BEHAVIOR

CHAPTER 4

Conceptual Issues in the Assessment of Social Competence in Children

Frank M. Gresham

INTRODUCTION

Researchers operating out of a social learning theory perspective have demonstrated in the past several years that behavioral principles can be used to teach social behaviors to children (see Cartledge & Milburn, 1978; Combs & Slaby, 1977; Gresham, 1981a; Hops, 1983; Van Hasselt, Hersen, Whitehill, & Bellack, 1979 for reviews). Although we can demonstrate that social learning principles (e.g., modeling, coaching, reinforcement) can effect changes in children's *social behavior,* this does not ensure that these behaviors are in fact *social skills.* As Hops and Greenwood (1981) point out, researchers have been more concerned with developing treatments than establishing psychometrically sound assessment strategies.

It seems premature to develop rather elaborate treatment strategies for behavioral deficits without knowing at a conceptual level the deficits we are trying to remediate or how to assess these deficits reliably or validly. Investigators in this area have not done an adequate job in conceptualizing, defining, or providing an assessment technology for children's social skills. Social skill is a concept that begs for clarification in the behavioral literature. It appears that social skill is in need of a theoretical conceptualization that would assist researchers and practitioners in developing an adequate assessment technology.

The purpose of the present chapter is to discuss several conceptual issues in the assessment of social competence in children. These issues include (1) the conceptualization of social skill as a behavioral construct, (2) social competence versus social skill, (3) definitions of social skills, (4) conceptualization of children's social skill deficits, (5) methods of social skill assessment, (6) social validation of social skill assessment methods, (7) an assessment model for children's social skills, and (8) future research needs. It is hoped that the conceptual issues identified and discussed in this chapter will guide researchers toward well-designed research that may lead to theoretical refinement of children's social skills and assist in the establishment of an adequate assessment technology.

SOCIAL SKILL AS A BEHAVIORAL CONSTRUCT

Social skill can be conceptualized as a behavioral construct in the sense that specific categories of social behavior are often summarized into a global entity and are labeled "social skill." For example, researchers often measure rather molecular behaviors in videotaped role-played social interactions (e.g., eye contact, rates of verbalization, ratio of eye contact to speech duration, facial expression) and obtain a summary score based on judges' impressionistic ratings of overall level of social skill (Bellack, 1979).

It is important to distinguish between behavioral constructs and the more trait-oriented approaches to social skills. Behavioral constructs (e.g., social skill) are tied to observable behavior, which have clear behavioral referents within specific situations (Linehan, 1980). Trait-like conceptualizations of social behavior view social skillfulness as a hypothetical construct referring to a global, underlying personality characteristic or response predisposition (McFall, 1982) that is *not* situation specific but generic in nature. This distinction between behavioral and trait-like constructs directly parallel the "sample" versus "sign" approaches in personality assessment (Goldfried & Kent, 1972).

In a seminal theoretical review of the concept of social skill, McFall (1982) identified two general approaches that have been taken in conceptualizing social skill: (1) the *trait model,* which views social skills as an underlying, cross-situational response predisposition and (2) a *molecular model,* which views social skills as discrete, situation-specific behaviors with no reference to an underlying personality characteristic or trait.

McFall (1982) takes both models to task in his review of the social skills concept. The trait model is amorphous, highly abstract, and has little empirical data to support its adequacy as a trait (Bellack, 1979; Curran,

1977; Hersen & Bellack, 1977). Moreover, various measures of the trait of social skill have typically shown little or no empirical relationship to behavior in naturalistic or simulated situations (Bellack, Hersen, & Lamparski, 1979; Bellack, Hersen, & Turner, 1978; Chandler, 1973; Urbain & Kendall, 1980).

The molecular model, on the other hand, tries to correct the abstract, unobservable nature of the trait approach by providing operationally defined responses in specific situations. While this may appear to be an improvement to the behaviorist, it creates perhaps even more confusion and ambiguity than the trait model. McFall (1982) specified several issues that the molecular model has not resolved, including (1) the selection of appropriate units of behavior (head nods, eye flinches, toe taps, etc.), (2) classification of social situations (i.e., by physical characteristics of the situation or by the participants in the situation), and (3) classification and evaluation of outcomes (e.g., short-term vs. long-term consequences, "success" vs. "failure"). In evaluating the molecular model of social skill, McFall (1982) states:

> the molecular model is of limited value to investigators who are interested in making behavioral predictions. The model states that the best predictor of a person's future behavior is that person's past behavior in the same situation. . . . To make such a prediction requires little or no special understanding either of human behavior generally, or of the individual subject. (p. 10)

There is obviously a need for a rapprochement between the trait and molecular models of social skill. Perhaps a conceptualization that is intermediately placed on the trait–molecular continuum would be the most useful. Unfortunately, such a model has to date not been forthcoming. As such, social skill remains a construct in need of further conceptualization and theoretical refinement.

The following section provides a distinction between social competence and social skill, from which a general conceptualization of social skill deficits is derived. The proposed model focuses on the *classification* of different types of social skill difficulties based on the child's behavior and on the *outcomes* of socially skilled versus socially unskilled behavior.

SOCIAL COMPETENCE VERSUS SOCIAL SKILL

Social competence and social skills are not identical constructs, as most writers make key distinctions between these two concepts. McFall (1982) has clearly articulated his conceptualization of social skill versus social competence. *Social skills* are the specific behaviors that an individual exhibits to perform competently on a task. In contrast, *social compe-tence* represents an evaluative term based on judgments (given certain criteria) that a person has performed a task adequately. These judg-ments may be based on opinions of significant others (e.g., parents teachers), comparisons to explicit criteria (e.g., number of social tasks correctly performed in relation to some criterion), or comparisons to some normative sample.

Competence does not imply exceptional performance; it only indicates that the performance was adequate (McFall, 1982). The issue of social competence can be recast in terms of *social validity:* the determination of the clinical, applied, and/or social importance of exhibiting certain social behaviors in particular situations (Kazdin, 1977; Van Houten, 1979; Wolf, 1978). In other words, behavior can be considered socially compe-tent if it predicts important social outcomes for individuals (Gresham, 1983a). The relationship between social competence and social validity is an important one and is discussed in a subsequent portion of this chapter.

Social competence has also been considered important in psychiatric diagnosis, treatment, and adjustment of psychiatric patients to commu-nity life. Kazdin (1979) indicates that social competence, which includes not only interpersonal behaviors, but also demographic factors (e.g., age, socioeconomic status, marital status), plays a crucial rule in the prognosis of severe forms of psychopathology such as schizophrenia. In an extensive study, Paul and Lentz (1977) present data to suggest that social competence is related to responsiveness to treatment in hospital settings and successful community adjustment after release.

In the field of mental retardation, social competence assumes primary importance in the diagnosis, treatment, and prognosis of the mentally retarded (Robinson & Robinson, 1976). The earliest conceptualization of mental retardation dating back to the Middle Ages emphasized the ab-sence of social competence (e.g., failure to care for self, failure to adapt socially) as the primary criterion for mental retardation (MacMillan, 1982). In the 1980s, the field of mental retardation has shifted back to using social competence rather than intellectual ability as being the ulti-mate criterion to be used in classifying an individual as mentally re-tarded (Greenspan, 1981).

Most current discussions of mental retardation, particularly those of the American Association on Mental Deficiency (AAMD), use the term *adaptive behavior* rather than social competence. Leland (1978) views adaptive behavior as comprising three domains: (1) *independent function-ing,* which refers to an individual's ability to accomplish critical survival skills expected by society as a function of chronological age (e.g., toileting, feeding, dressing), (2) *personal responsibility*, which reflects an individual's decision-making and choice ability and (3) *social responsibility*, which refers to an individual's levels of social conformity, social adjustment, and emotional maturity. It is clear from the preceding global descriptions that social competence (or adaptive behavior) is an extremely important construct in the field of mental retardation.

More recently, Reschly and Gresham (1981) have conceptualized social competence as comprising two components: (1) *adaptive behavior* and (2) *social skills*. Adaptive behavior for children would include independent functioning skills, physical development, language development, and academic competencies. Social skills, on the other hand, would include (1) *interpersonal behaviors* (e.g., accepting authority, conversation skills, cooperative behaviors, play behaviors), (2) *self-related behaviors* (e.g., expressing feelings, ethical behavior, positive attitude toward self), and (3) *task-related behaviors* (e.g., attending behavior, completing tasks, following directions, independent work). Details regarding these social skills are provided in subsequent portions of this chapter and can be found in publications (see Gresham, 1981b, 1983b; Stephens, 1978; Stumme, Gresham, & Scott, 1982).

The preceding conceptualizations of social competence represent rather diverse views of this construct, although all agree that social competence is a global judgment based on behavioral performance and/ or demographic characteristics. McFall (1982) sees social competence as an evaluative term based on judgments by others or comparisons to some criterion. Kazdin (1979) views social competence as including not only interpersonal behaviors, but also demographic variables such as age, socioeconomic status, marital status, and so forth. The AAMD and Leland (1978) equate social competence with adaptive behavior and emphasize independent functioning as well as personal and social responsibility in the diagnosis, treatment, and prognosis of mentally retarded individuals. Finally, Reschly and Gresham (1981) view social competence as being composed of adaptive behavior and social skills, with each emphasizing different aspects of social behavior.

The previously described notions of social competence are perhaps useful at a conceptual level, but require much more empirical validation and clarification. Greenspan (1981) has provided an interesting conceptualization of social competence based on three definitional approaches. This conceptualization differs from those described earlier, in that the focus is on the outcomes, contents, and processes of social competence rather than descriptive labels for socially competent behavior.

The first approach is termed the *outcome-oriented approach*, which focuses exclusively on the outcomes or results of exhibiting certain social behaviors in particular situations. Greenspan (1981) uses a golf analogy in describing this approach, whereby competence as a golfer is defined by the end result of golfing behavior (i.e., the final score). This approach certainly allows us to define competence but does not tell us what specific behaviors were emitted in what situations that resulted in competence.

The second approach can be termed the *content-oriented approach*, which focuses on the specific behaviors that are associated with successful outcomes. This conceptualization is similar to McFall's (1982) view of social competence–social skill as well as Gresham's (1983a) social validity definition of social skills. Continuing with the golf analogy, an individual's swing, stance, grip, and coordination are typically associated with golfing competence (i.e., a low [good] score). This approach has the distinct advantage of identifying specific behaviors that lead to golfing competence. This is discussed later as the competence-correlates approach to social skills (Asher & Markell, 1978; Gresham, 1981a, 1981b, 1982a).

The final definitional approach to social competence is termed the *skill-oriented approach*, which focuses on interpersonal processes (e.g., knowledge, attitudes, perceptions) that lead to socially competent outcomes. Using Greenspan's (1981) golfing analogy, knowledge of golf rules, club selection, etiquette, controlling one's temper, judgment, and familiarity with the golf courses would be associated with golfing competence. While this approach attempts to get at the "processes" underlying social competence, it tends to focus on somewhat intangible aspects of social behavior.

The three preceding approaches provide yet another view of social competence, which may have some utility at both conceptual and practical levels. The bottom line in golf (and the only one that really counts) is the outcome (i.e., the score). Similarly, the bottom line in the social skills area is the outcome or result of social behavior. Unfortunately, we do not know the score or even what score to use because optimum outcomes have not been established. It would seem that a combination of the outcome- and content-oriented approaches would be the most useful way of conceptualizing social competence because the focus would be on the selection of only those behavioral competencies or social skills that predict important social outcomes. Given some consensus on what these outcomes should be, this approach holds promise in defining the construct of social competence. Based upon extensive research in the social skills area (to be reviewed here later), the skill-oriented approach does not appear to be a fruitful route at this time because of its emphasis on private events and underlying psychological processes rather than observable behavior.

DEFINITIONS OF SOCIAL SKILL

As previously discussed, social skill may be viewed as part of a broader construct known as social competence (Gresham, 1981b; McFall, 1982; Kazdin, 1979). Past conceptualizations of children's behavior have highlighted deviant aspects of social behavior (Foster & Ritchey, 1979). More-recent interest in social skills has focused primarily on building positive behaviors into the repertoire, as well as eliminating negative behaviors (Asher & Hymel, 1981; Asher, Oden, & Gottman, 1977; Cartledge & Milburn, 1978, 1980; Greenwood, Walker, & Hops, 1977; Gresham, 1981a, 1981b, 1982a, 1982b; Hops, 1983).

Several definitions of children's social skills have arisen during the past several years. Combs and Slaby (1977), for example, define social skills as "the ability to interact with others in a given social context in specific ways that are societally acceptable or valued and at the same time are personally beneficial, mutually beneficial or beneficial primarily to others" (p. 162). Pursuing a more operant definition, Libet and Lewinsohn (1973) define social skills as "the complex ability both to emit behaviors that are positively or negatively reinforced and not to emit behaviors that are punished or extinguished by others" (p. 304). Finally, Foster and Ritchey (1979) have defined social skill as "those responses, which within a given situation, prove effective, or in other words, maximize the probability of producing, maintaining, or enhancing positive effects for the interactor" (p. 626).

All of the preceding definitions provide a "ballpark" notion of what social skills are; however, they remain somewhat vague and ambiguous. For example, it is unclear what such terms as "personally beneficial" "complex ability," "positive effects," and so forth mean in an operational sense. Clearly, the definition of social skill requires delineation, operationalization, and explanation in order to be conceptually and practically useful.

At least three general definitions can be distilled rom the accumulated literature on children's social skills. One definition can be termed the *peer-acceptance definition,* in that researchers primarily use indices of peer acceptance or popularity (e.g., peer sociometrics) to define social skill. Using a peer-acceptance definition, children and adolescents who are accepted by or who are popular with their peers in school and/or community settings can be said to be socially skilled. This definition has been implicit in the work of many prominent researchers in the social skills area (Asher & Hymel, 1981; Asher et al., 1977; Asher, Singleton, Tinsley, & Hymel, 1979; Gottman, 1977; Gottman, Gonso, & Rasmussen, 1975; Gottman, Gonso, & Schuler, 1976; Ladd, 1981; LaGreca & Santogrossi, 1980; Oden & Asher, 1977).

In spite of its relative objectivity, the major drawback of a peer-acceptance definition is that it cannot identify what specific behaviors lead to peer acceptance or popularity. As such, we are left with a group of children who are identified as poorly accepted or unpopular without any knowledge of what social behaviors (or absence thereof) lead to this state of affairs. Research on the specific behavioral correlates of high and low social status is urgently needed. The existing knowledge base on this question is reviewed in the McConnell and Odom chapter.

Some researchers have opted for a *behavioral definition* of social skills. This approach essentially defines social skills as those situation–specific responses that maximize the probability of maintaining reinforcement and decrease the probability of punishment contingent on one's social behavior. Measures used to define social skills in this manner typically consist of observations of behavior in naturalistic or role-play situations and settings. Researchers adhering to a strict behavioral definition of social skills almost never utilize peer acceptance (via sociometric measures) as part of their criteria for defining social skills.

Many well-known investigators have adopted primarily a behavioral view of children's social skills (Bellack & Hersen, 1979; Bornstein, Bellack, & Hersen, 1977; Combs & Slaby, 1977; Foster & Ritchey, 1979; Greenwood, Todd, Hops, & Walker, 1982; Greenwood, Walker, Todd, & Hops, 1981; O'Connor, 1969, 1972; Rogers-Warren & Baer, 1976; Strain, 1977; Strain, Cooke, & Appolloni, 1976; Strain & Shores, 1977; Warren, Rogers-Warren, & Baer, 1976). This definition has the advantage over the peer-acceptance definition, in that the antecedents and consequences of particular social behaviors can be identified, specified, and operationalized for assessment and remedial purposes. In spite of the advantages, this definition does not ensure that these social behaviors are in fact *socially skilled, socially significant,* or *socially important.* That is, merely increasing the frequency of certain behaviors that researchers define *a priori* as "social skills" may not have any impact on goals or outcomes valued by society at large.

A final and less-often discussed definition may be termed the *social validity definition.* According to this definition, social skills are those behaviors which, within a given situation, predict important social outcomes for children. These so-called important social outcomes may be (1) peer acceptance or popularity, (2) significant others' judgments of social skill (e.g., parents, teachers), and/or (3) other social behaviors known to consistently correlate with 1 and 2 above.

This definition uses naturalistic observations of behavior, sociometric indices, and ratings by significant others to assess and define social skill. It has the advantage of being able to not only specify behaviors in which a child is deficient, but also define these behaviors as socially skilled based on their relationships to socially important outcomes (e.g., peer acceptance, parental acceptance, teacher acceptance).

The *social validity definition* has received recent empirical support (Green, Forehand, Beck, & Vosk, 1980; Gresham, 1981c, 1982b, 1983a) as well as past indications of validity (Hartup, Glazer, & Charlesworth, 1967; Marshall & MaCandless, 1957; McCandless & Marshall, 1957; McGuire, 1973; Moore & Updegraff, 1964; Singleton & Asher, 1977). Specific criteria for and discussion of social validity are presented in a subsequent portion of this chapter.

The aforementioned definitions of children's social skills emphasize social competence. The peer-acceptance definition equates peer acceptance or popularity with social skill. Hence, a child who is poorly accepted, socially rejected, or unpopular is, by definition, socially unskilled. The behavioral definition considers deficits or excesses in behaviors to be indications of poor social skill. Thus, children exhibiting behaviors below or above certain levels specified a priori are considered socially unskilled. Finally, the social validity definition considers children socially unskilled if specific social behaviors predict standings on socially important outcomes. This definition is a hybrid of the peer acceptance and behavioral definitions and is the most socially valid in the sense of predicting important social outcomes for children. It seems reasonable to use a definition of social skill that is based on *criterion-related* and, hence, *social validity*. This should provide a basis for accumulating empirical evidence for the construct of children's social skills.

CONCEPTUALIZATION OF SOCIAL SKILL PROBLEMS

Most conceptualizations of social skill problems have revolved primarily around either the sociometric or behavioral definitions. These definitions may be useful at a descriptive level, but they are less relevant in targeting specific types of social skill deficits. Gresham (1981a, 1981b, 1982c) has categorized social skill problems into four general areas that should be useful from assessment, diagnostic, and intervention standpoints. This conceptualization represents a modification and extention of Bandura's (1969, 1977a) distinction between acquisition versus performance of behavior.

Social skill problems may be delineated into four types: (1) *skill deficits,* (2) *performance deficits,* (3) *self-control skill deficits,* and (4) *self-control performance deficits.* The bases for these distinctions rest on whether or not the child knows how to perform the skill in question and the existence of *emotional arousal responses* (e.g., anger, impulsivity, etc.). Although this conceptualization is primarily speculative at this point, there is some empirical support for the majority of social skills problems described (Camp, Blom, Herbert, & Van Doorninck, 1977; Gottman, 1977; Gresham, 1981a, 1981b; Meichenbaum, 1977; Van Hasselt et al., 1979). These studies have used self-instructional strategies to successfully inhibit aggressive behavior or to disinhibit anxiety responses so that socially skilled behaviors can be exhibited and reinforced.

Skill Deficits

Children with social skills deficits do not have the necessary social skills to interact appropriately with peers or they do not know a critical step in the performance of the skill. A social skill deficit is similar to what Bandura (1969, 1977) refers to as an *acquisition* or *learning deficit*. Social *skill deficits* can be clarified by using an academic example. A child who not knowing the "+" operation sign has a skill deficit in that he/she does not know what behavior to exhibit when seeing the operation sign for addition. This means that the child does not have this skill in the repertoire. Similarly, a child can know the "+" operation sign, but not know how to regroup when confronted with a problem (e.g., 32 + 19 = _____). This is a skill deficit in the sense that although the child knows what behavior to perform when seeing the "+" sign, he/she has left out a critical component in addition skills when responding to the problem 33 + 19 = 41 (a regrouping error).

Several examples can be cited to elucidate social skill deficits. For example, the child may not know how to carry on a conversation with peers, ask to be recognized in class appropriately, or give a compliment. The barometer to use in determining whether or not a child has a skill deficit is based on the child's *knowledge* or *past performance* of the skill. That is, if the child does not know how to perform the skill or has never been observed to perform the skill, it is probably a skills deficit. An example of a skills deficit in which a child leaves out a critical step in a chain of behaviors is giving a compliment. The child may be able to formulate a reason for giving a compliment, may know how to phrase a compliment, and may be able to discriminate the most appropriate time for giving a compliment, but may not know how to give the compliment in a clear and sincere voice. Given this assessment, an intervention would focus on teaching the child how to compliment clearly and sincerely. Most social *skill deficits* are remediated primarily through direct instruction, modeling, behavioral rehearsal, and/or coaching (Gresham, 1981b, 1982b, 1982c, 1982d).

Performance Deficits

A *social performance deficit* describes children who have the social skills in their repertoires, but do not perform them at acceptable levels. Performance deficits can be thought of as a deficiency in the number of times a social behavior is emitted and may be related to a lack of motivation (i.e., reinforcement contingencies) or an absence of opportunity to perform the behavior (i.e., stimulus control problem). It is important to realize that fear, anxiety, or other emotional arousal responses do *not* enter into a social performance deficit. The presence of emotional arousal responses that either prevent the acquisition or performance of social behaviors are termed *self-control skill* and *self-control performance deficits*, respectively.

The key in determining whether a social skills problem represents a performance deficit is whether or not the child can perform the behavior. Thus, if the child does not perform a behavior in a classroom situation, but can perform the behavior in a behavioral role-play situation, it is a *social performance deficit*. Also, if the child has been observed to perform the behavior in the past, it is probably a performance rather than a skill deficit. Given that difficulties either in stimulus control or reinforcement contingencies are functionally related to social performance deficits, training strategies should focus upon antecedent and consequent control techniques. These strategies may include peer initiations (Strain, Shores, & Timm, 1977), sociodramatic activities (Strain, 1975), contingent social reinforcement (Allen, Hart, Buell, Harris, & Wolf, 1964), token reinforcement programs (Iwata & Bailey, 1974), and group contingencies (Gamble & Strain, 1979).

Self-Control Skill Deficits

This type of social skill problem describes a child who has not learned a particular social skill because some type of emotional arousal response has prevented the *acquisition* of the skill. One emotional arousal response that interferes with learning is *anxiety*. Anxiety has been shown to prevent the acquisition of appropriate coping responses, particularly in the literature concerning fears and phobias (see Bandura, 1969, 1977a, 1977b for comprehensive reviews). Hence, children may not learn how to interact with peers because social anxiety or fear prevent social approach behavior. In turn, avoidance of or escape from social situations reduces anxiety, thereby negatively reinforcing social isolation behaviors.

Another emotional arousal response that may prevent the acquisition of social skills is *impulsivity* (i.e., the tendency toward short response

latencies in social situations). Children who exhibit impulsive social behavior fail to learn appropriate social interaction strategies because their
behavior often results in social rejection by peers. Thus, peers avoid the
impulsive child, which results in the target child not being exposed to
models of appropriate social behavior or being placed on an extinction
schedule for his/her social responses.

This behavioral formulation suggests that the target child emits aversive social behaviors (i.e., as a result of a socially impulsive response
style) which results in social rejection from peers, parents, teachers, and
so forth. As such, other individuals in the environment are under aversive contingencies, in that behaviors that lead to avoidance of or escape
from the target child are negatively reinforced. In turn, this results in the
target child's behavior being either punished (e.g., by verbal or physical
reprimands, loss of reinforcement) or extinguished (e.g., by ignoring).
The outcome of this sequence of events is that the target child does not
learn the social skills for appropriate interaction (i.e., a skill deficit).

Several studies in the literature have described this type of child
(Bryan, 1978; Camp et al., 1977; Meichenbaum & Goodman, 1971;
O'Leary & Dubey, 1979; Zahavi & Asher, 1978). Determination of a self-
control skill deficit rests on two criteria: (1) the presence of an *emotional
arousal response* (e.g., anxiety, fear, impulsivity, anger), and (2) the child
either *not knowing* or *never having performed* the skill in question. Teaching
strategies typically take the form of anxiety-reducing techniques (e.g.,
desensitization, flooding) coupled with modeling/coaching and *self-control strategies* (e.g., self-talk, self-monitoring, self-reinforcement) (see
Kendall & Braswell, 1982; Kendall & Wilcox, 1979; Meichenbaum, 1977;
Urbain & Kendall, 1980 for reviews).

Self-Control Performance Deficits

Children with self-control performance deficits have the specific social
skill in their repertoires, but do not perform the skill because of an
emotional arousal response and problems in antecedent and/or consequent control. That is, the person knows how to perform the skill, but
does so infrequently or inconsistently. The key difference between self-
control skill and performance deficits is whether or not the child has the
social skill in the repertoire. In the former case, the skill has never been
learned, in the latter case, the skill has been learned but is not exhibited
consistently. Two criteria are used to detemine a self-control performance deficit: (1) the presence of an emotional arousal response (e.g.,
anger, fear, etc.) and (2) the inconsistent performance of the skill in
question.

Table 1
Classification of Social Skill Problems

	Acquisition deficit	Performance deficit
Emotional arousal response absent[a]	Social skill deficit	Social performance deficit
Emotional arousal response present[a]	Self-control skill deficit	Self-control performance deficit

[a] Emotional arousal responses can be anxiety, fear, anger, impulsivity, and so forth that interfere with the acquisition or performance of appropriate social behaviors.

Interventions with this type of problem typically focus upon self-control strategies to teach the child how to inhibit inappropriate behavior, stimulus control training designed to teach discrimination of potentially, conflictful situations, and/or reinforcement contingencies for appropriate social behaviors (Blackwood, 1970; Bolstad & Johnson, 1972; Bornstein & Quevillon, 1976; Drabman, 1973; Drabman, Spilnalnik, & O'Leary, 1973; Robin, Schneider, & Dolnick, 1976; Rosenbaum & Drabman, 1979; Turkewitz, O'Leary, & Ironsmith, 1975).

The four types of social skill problems suggest slightly different types of interventions to teach social behavior. Although this classification system requires empirical validation, it does provide a useful heuristic for conceptualizing social difficulties from an intervention–training standpoint. Table 1 presents a four-fold table graphically depicting this classification model.

METHODS OF SOCIAL SKILL ASSESSMENT

A plethora of assessment methods have been used in social skills research with children, some of which provide more useful, reliable, and valid information than others. Recent reviews have identified the following social skill assessment methods: (1) sociometrics, (2) ranking methods, (3) ratings by others, (4) behavioral role-play tasks, (5) self-report, (6) naturalistic observations, and (7) self-monitoring (Asher & Hymel, 1981; Asher & Taylor, 1981; Foster & Ritchey, 1979; Green & Forehand, 1980; Greenwood et al., 1977; Gresham, 1981a, 1981b, 1981c, 1982a, 1982b; Gresham & Lemmanek, 1984; Hops, 1983; Hops & Greenwood, 1981; Stumme, Gresham, & Scott, 1982).

Assessment of social skills is typically a twofold process (1) for *selection–diagnostic* and (2) for *intervention–therapy*. Some assessment approaches (e.g., sociometrics, ratings by others, self-report, and behavioral role-play tasks) are more useful for selection–diagnostic purposes than in yielding information that is useful for intervention purposes. Other assessment techniques (e.g., behavioral interviews, naturalistic observations, and self-monitoring) are most useful for intervention purposes because they assist in deriving a functional analysis of behavior (i.e., the antecedent, sequential, and consequent conditions surrounding social behavior).

The following sections briefly overview social skills assessment procedures under the rubrics of *selection–diagnosis* and *intervention–therapy*. Specifics of these methods are not presented because they are dealt with in other chapters of this volume. The purpose of the following section is to present a conceptualization of various assessment measures with a concluding discussion of direct versus indirect assessment procedures, developmental considerations, psychometric issues, and cost-benefit analyses (i.e., practicality and time consumption).

Assessment for Selection–Diagnosis

Several assessment procedures generate information that allows for a determination of the existence of a social skills problem. The most frequently used assessment procedures of this type are sociometrics, rankings or ratings by others, self-report, and behavioral role play tasks. Hops and Greenwood (1981) consider sociometrics and rankings by others (e.g., teachers) to be selection measures, whereas they consider behavior ratings and checklists to be useful for intervention–therapy considerations. According to Hops and Greenwood (1981), the extent to which the assessment procedure yields information about specific behavioral excesses or deficits determines its utility as a screening versus an intervention assessment procedure.

I use a slightly different conceptualization and classification of the various assessment procedures, based on the extent to which the assessment yields information for a *functional analysis of behavior*. In this view, the extent to which the assessment procedure provides data concerning the antecedent, sequential, and consequent conditions surrounding social behavior determines its classification as a screening or intervention device. As such, behavior ratings would *not* be an intervention assessment procedure because they do not provide data for functional analyses. Behavioral interviews, on the other hand, (e.g., with teachers, parents, etc.) would be considered an intervention assessment procedure because they yield information concerning the antecedents and consequences of behavioral excesses or deficits. Similarly, naturalistic behavioral observations and self-monitoring would be considered intervention assessment procedures because of the potential for a functional analysis these methods possess. The following section will review the various assessment methods used to identify or diagnose social skill difficulties in children.

Sociometric Techniques

Sociometric assessment procedures were initially developed by Moreno (1934), who used peer nomination methods to evaluate children's friendship patterns. Although sociometrics have a rather long history in psychology, particularly in the child development literature, they have only recently been utilized in the behavioral literature in the assessment of children's social skills. Two basic types of sociometric procedures are used (1) *peer nominations* and (2) *peer ratings,* each of which measure different aspects of sociometric status (Gresham, 1981c; Hymel & Asher, 1977).

The basic procedure in using peer nominations is to have children nominate peers according to certain *nonbehavioral* criteria (e.g., best friends, preferred play partners, work partners, physical attributes, etc.). These criteria are termed *nonbehavioral* because they are based upon activities (e.g., play or work) or attributes (friend, physical characteristics, etc.) rather than specific behaviors. As such, nomination measures are tapping children's attitudes or preferences for engaging in certain activities with certain peers rather than specific behaviors of target children.

Peer nominations can also be keyed to *negative criteria* such as least-liked peers, least-preferred play or work partners, and so forth. Research using peer nominations indicates that positive and negative nominations are measuring two dimensions of sociometric status (Asher et al., 1977; Asher & Hymel, 1981; Asher, Singleton, Tinsley, & Hymel, 1979; Ballard, Corman, Gottlieb, & Kaufman, 1977; Hartup, 1970, 1979). According to this literature, positive peer nominations are measuring *acceptance* in the peer group and negative nominations are measuring *rejection* in the peer group. Correlational analysis indicate relatively weak relationships between positive and negative nominations, suggesting that acceptance and rejection are not on opposite ends of a continuum, but rather two dimensions of sociometric status. Also, there is evidence to suggest that positive peer nominations are not measuring peer acceptance, but instead are assessing *popularity* (Gresham, 1981c; Hymel & Asher, 1977).

These distinctions between acceptance and rejection, as well as acceptance versus friendship, have definite conceptual implications for not only selecting children for social skills training, but also evaluating the outcomes of social skill training programs. That is, should we consider children socially unskilled if they receive few positive nominations (i.e., if they are not popular)? Should acceptance or popularity be the goal of social skills training? Just because children are not rejected, does this mean they do not need social skills training? Should the goal of social skills training be making children more tolerable, popular, less rejected, or accepted? These issues are addressed in a subsequent portion of this chapter, under the heading, *Social Validation of Social Skill Assessment Methods.*

Ranking Methods

Rankings of children, especially by teachers, have been frequently used to select children for social skills training programs. In this approach, teachers rank order children in their class according to some criteria. These criteria can either be *behavioral* (talks the least, interacts the least, most aggressive, etc.) or *nonbehavioral* (best liked, fewest friends, etc.). Several studies have demonstrated that teacher rankings correspond fairly well to naturalistically observed behaviors such as frequency of peer interaction, rates of disruptive behavior, and on-task behavior (Bolstad & Johnson, 1977; Greenwood et al., 1977; Greenwood, Walker, Todd, & Hops, 1979).

Teacher rankings are cost and time efficient in selecting children for social skills training. However, they may fail to identify socially withdrawn children because these behaviors are not usually perceived as being problematic for teachers (Evans & Nelson, 1977; Hops & Greenwood, 1981). Also, there is little evidence to suggest that teachers and peers agree in terms of their rank ordering of children on behavioral or nonbehavioral criteria. Also, little research has been directed toward how well parents and teachers agree in the ranking of children on various criteria.

Teacher rankings, like sociometrics, are useful for identification, but not for intervention purposes, in that they do not provide for a functional analysis of behavior. Their primary utility lies in their ability to identify children at the extremes of a criterion and for social validation purposes.

Ratings by Others

Teacher and peer ratings of social skills have become a popular method of social skills assessment, partly because of the relative ease of using these procedures. The key distinction between teacher ranking or sociometrics and behavior ratings is that the latter focuses on *specific behaviors* rather than global perceptions of the child. As such, behavior ratings yield information that is useful in identifying target behaviors that may be correlates of important social outcomes (e.g., peer acceptance, peer rejection, popularity).

Several teacher rating scales have been developed specifically to assess children's social skills. One of the most comprehensive rating scales is the Social Behavior Assessment (SBA) developed by Stephens (1978, 1979, 1980). Teachers rate children on 136 social skills, according to the degree to which they exhibit these social skills (i.e., acceptable level, less than acceptable level, or never). These 136 social skills are grouped into 30 subcategories, which in turn are grouped into four broad behavioral categories (environmental behaviors, interpersonal behaviors, self-related behaviors, and task-related behaviors).

The SBA has rather impressive evidence for reliability (interrater, internal consistency, and stability) and validity (content, criterion-related, and construct) (see Stephens, 1980 for a review). Stumme et al. (1982) performed discriminant and stepwise multiple regression analyses in order to determine the SBA's discriminative efficiency. Results demonstrated that the 30 SBA subcategories correctly classified 83% of the subjects into emotionally disturbed and nondisturbed categories. Preliminary evidence suggests that the SBA has reasonable psychometric properties and is useful in selection and classification of children for social skills training.

Another teacher rating scale that has received empirical validation is the *Guess Who Scale* (teacher version) developed by Gottlieb, Semmel, and Veldman (1978). Factor analytic work with this instrument suggests the presence of three factors: (1) *disruptive*, (2) *bright*, and (3) *dull*. Specific items loading on each of the three factors are (1) *disruptive* (Who is always bothering others? Who always wants their own way? Who disrupts the class? etc.), (2) *bright* (Who gets good grades? Who is the smartest in the class? etc.), and (3) *dull* (Who never knows the answers in class? Who never gets their work done on time? etc.).

Gottlieb et al. (1978) found that the *bright* and *dull* factors correlated moderately with peer acceptance, but not with peer rejection, suggesting that academic-related behaviors are a significant component of social acceptance. In contrast, the *disruptive* factor correlated with peer rejection, but not with peer acceptance. Research by MacMillan, Morrison, and Silverstein (1980) supports the convergent and discriminant validity of the *Guess Who Scale*. These investigators found that teacher and peer ratings of the three factors agreed with one another (disruptive = .65, bright = .50, and dull = .44) offering convergent–discriminant validity evidence.

These findings suggest that teachers and peers generally agree with one another on certain behavioral factors with each method source having similar factorial (i.e., discriminant) validity. Similar findings were reported by La Greca (1981) using teacher and peer ratings of *withdrawn* and *aggressive* behaviors. The bulk of the literature would suggest that teachers and peers rate certain social behaviors similarly; however, these ratings may not be interchangeable (Asher & Hymel, 1981; Gresham, 1981a, 1981b, 1983a; Matson, Esveldt-Dawson, & Kazdin, 1983; Vosk, Forehand, Parker, & Rickard, 1982).

Walker and his colleagues have developed a teacher rating scale to interface with the *Walker Social Skills Curriculum* or *Accepts Program* (Walker, McConnell, Holmes, Todis, Walker, & Golden, 1983). The Walker scale is a 28-item measure that requires teachers to rate children on a 1 to 5 Likert scale according to whether the statements are *not descriptive, moderately descriptive,* or *very descriptive* of target children. Although this instrument appears valid, there are currently no data regarding its reliability or empirical validity. Future research should address the psychometric characteristics of the Walker scale.

Peer ratings of social behavior have also been used in assessing children's social skills. The previously mentioned *Guess Who Scale* is perhaps the most commonly used peer assessment method (Asher & Hymel, 1981). Several variations of this basic technique have shown to be reliable and valid indicators of children's social behavior (Gottlieb et al., 1978; MacMillan & Morrison, 1980; MacMillan et al., 1980; Pekarik, Prinz, Liebert, Weintraub, & Neale, 1976; Winder & Wiggins, 1964). It is important to distinguish, as do Asher and Hymel (1981) and McConnell and Odom in this volume, between *sociometric* and *peer* assessment methods. Sociometrics are procedures for studying interpersonal attraction, likability, and friendship, whereas peer assessment methods that assess children's ratings of specific behaviors have been shown to correlate with sociometric status.

In summary, teacher and peer ratings have been shown to be reliable, valid, and useful methods for assessing children's social behavior. While these methods should not be used as the sole assessment technique, they are useful for targeting specific behaviors for observation, functional analysis, and discovering potential behavioral correlates of social acceptance and rejection.

Behavioral Role Play

Behavioral role play tests (BRP) or performances in analogue situations have essentially become the hallmark of assessment in social skills research (Bellack, 1979). Researchers have used BRPs because of several advantages they offer over sociometrics, ratings, and naturalistic observation. (1) BRPs can assess important social behaviors that occur at low frequencies in the natural environment. (2) BRPs represent actual behavioral enactment of a skill rather than a rating or perception of that skill. (3) Simulated settings can be more tightly controlled to assess a child's response to selected social stimuli (Hops & Greenwood, 1981). (4) BRPs can be constructed to simulate environments in which it is difficult to observe a child's naturalistic social behavior (e.g., home community). Finally, (5) BRPs are much less expensive than collecting data via naturalistic observation.

Given these advantages of role-play assessment, it is not surprising that it remains the most popular means of social skill assessment. However, what do the data suggest about the criterion-related (ecological) validity of BRPs in terms of predicting behavior in naturalistic settings as well as sociometric status?

A number of studies have demonstrated that performance on BRPs show little or no correspondence with the same behaviors assessed in naturalistic settings, nor do they predict sociometric status (Bellack, Hersen, & Lampmarski, 1979; Bellack, Hersen, & Turner, 1978; Berler, Gross, & Drabman, 1982; Gresham, 1983a; LaGreca & Santogrossi, 1980; Matson et al. 1983; Van Hasselt, Hersen, & Bellack, 1981).

In one of the more comprehensive studies to date concerning the validity of BRPs for children, Van Hasselt et al. (1981) found low and nonsignificant relationships between role-play measures and sociometric status (i.e., positive nominations, negative nominations, and peer ratings) and teacher ratings of social skills. Matson et al. (1983) found that role-play performance was not consistently related to sociometric status, self-report, or teacher ratings of social skills. Similar results were reported by Berler et al. (1982) in an attempt to predict naturalistic social interaction and sociometric status from performance on a 20-item behavioral role play test.

The previous studies prompt serious questions regarding the validity of BRPs in predicting naturalistically occurring social behavior and sociometric status. Empirically, it would appear that role-play measures are useful in predicting neither the degree to which a child will perform similar behaviors in different settings nor the extent to which a child will be accepted or rejected by peers. Behaviorally, this might be expected because behaviors are considered to be situation specific (Mischel, 1968). However, the value of using role-play measures to discern levels of social skills in naturalistic environments is dubious. Practically speaking, it is of little value to know the level of a child's social skills in a contrived environment if the intent of training is to have the child perform these same skills in a natural setting.

Conceptually, BRPs may be considered a means of discriminating *social skill* from *social performance* deficits. That is, if the child cannot enact the requisite behaviors on a role-play measure, the deficiency is most likely a *skill deficit*. In contrast, if the child performs the skill on a BRP but not in other settings, the problem is likely a *social-performance deficit*. Role-play measures perhaps are better considered diagnostic measures of social skill difficulty than assessment measures for intervention or evaluation of outcomes of social skills training programs.

Self-Report Measures

Self-report measures of children's social skills are not as frequently used as other assessment techniques (e.g., sociometrics, behavioral role play, ratings). The subjectivity and lack of criterion-related validity of these measures has resulted in rather limited development and use by behavioral investigators (Michaelson & Wood, 1980).

Most self-report inventories for children have been modifications of assertion scales developed for adult populations (e.g., the Rathus Assertiveness Scale). Reardon, Hersen, Bellack, and Foley (1979) developed a multiple-choice test designed to measure positive and negative assertion in elementary age boys. Empirical evaluation of this instrument revealed that the measure did not discriminate previously classified high or low assertive subjects, did not predict performance on a role-play measure, and had no evidence for reliability.

Pursuing a similar approach, Michelson and Wood (1980) developed the Children's Assertive Behavior Scale (CABS), a 27-item multiple-choice self-report instrument designed for elementary school children. Preliminary investigation of the instrument suggests that it is homogeneous, internally consistent (KR_{20} = .77 to .80), and relatively stable over a 4-week time span (.66 to .86). As one might expect, the criterion-related validity of this instrument is questionable, as there are little convincing data supporting its ability to predict sociometric status, teacher ratings of assertion, or naturalistically observed assertive behaviors.

Matson et al. (1983) developed a 92-item self-report rating scale called the Matson Evaluation of Social Skills with Youngsters (MESSY). This scale differs in two respects from the previously described instruments. (1) It assesses a much broader domain of social behavior (e.g., appropriate social interaction, negative interaction, expression of hostility, social isolation, conversation skills). The Reardon et al. (1979) scale and the CABS ostensibly measure childhood assertion. (2) The MESSY requires children to rate each of the 92 items on a 1 to 5 Likert scale rather than using a multiple-choice format.

Matson et al. (1983) found that the MESSY was not correlated with performance on a behavioral role play measure and demonstrated low (.27) but significant correlation with a structured child interview. The MESSY did not relate to sociometric status, teacher estimates of child popularity, teacher ratings of social skills, or global ratings of social adjustment.

It is not difficult to summarize the current status of self-report measures of social skills with children. In short, children's self-report measures have not shown to be useful in predicting peer acceptance, peer popularity, teacher ratings of social skills, role-play performance, or social behavior in naturalistic settings. Given this abysmal validity evidence, self-report measures should not be used as either selection or outcome measures in social-skills training research until and unless more convincing data can be accumulated to support their use.

ASSESSMENT FOR INTERVENTION-THERAPY

Some assessment techniques are better suited for obtaining information that is useful in designing social skills training programs. The extent to which an assessment technique allows for a *functional analysis* of behavior determines its utility as a behavioral assessment method that yields information for intervention–therapy. Two techniques that allow for such a functional analysis are discussed: (1) *behavioral interviews* and (2) *naturalistic observations*. Each of these assessment techniques are briefly discussed in the following sections.

Behavioral Interviews

Behavioral interviews have been used infrequently in the assessment of children's social skills. Other than sparsely reported cases studies, behavioral interviews have not received systematic research attention from social skills investigators. Using Cone's (1978) continuum of direct verses indirect behavioral assessment methods, interviews are classified as an indirect assessment method because they are a verbal construction of representation of behavior removed in time and place from its actual occurence. In contrast, naturalistic observations would represent the most direct form of behavioral assessment because they measure behavior at the time and place of its actual occurrence.

Behavioral interviews are extremely useful in conducting a functional analysis of social behavior. Research demonstrates that behavioral interviews are effective in defining behaviors in observable terms, identifying the antecedent, sequential, and consequent conditions surrounding target behaviors, and designing observational systems to measure target behaviors (Bergan, 1977; Bergan & Tombari, 1975, 1976; Haynes & Jensen, 1979; Tombari & Bergan, 1978).

Gresham (1983b) reviewed 21 studies investigating the psychometric characteristics of behavioral interviews and concluded that they have a reasonably strong nucleus of research supporting their reliability and validity. No systematic empirical investigation, however, has been conducted using the behavioral interview as an assessment method for children's social skills. This is obviously an area in need of much research because children are referred for social skills problems by sources (e.g., teachers or parents) who are likely to be interviewed before rating and observational data are collected. It would be interesting to know the convergent validity of behavioral interviews with other social skills assessment methods (e.g., teacher ratings, peer ratings, behavioral observations).

Naturalistic Observations

Assessment of children's behavior in natural settings (e.g., classroom, playground) is the most face-valid method of assessing children's social skills (Asher & Hymel, 1981). Naturalistic observations allow for a functional analysis of behavior in the setting and at the time that the behavior occurs. As such, they are more accurate in a functional analysis sense than behavioral interviews because they are more direct. Observations have been used to assess social withdrawal (Allen et al., 1964), sharing (Rogers-Warren & Baer, 1976), cooperation (Oden & Asher, 1977), initiating and receiving positive social interaction (Gresham, 1981c, 1982b), dispensing positive social reinforcement (Hartup et al., 1967), positive physical contact (Cooke & Apolloni, 1976), social initiations (Ragland, Kerr, & Strain, 1978), and many other social behaviors (see Asher & Hymel, 1981; Gresham, 1981a, 1981b; Hops & Greenwood, 1981; Michelson & Wood, 1980, for extensive reviews). An in-depth review of naturalistic observations is not presented, as the procedure is reviewed in a subsequent chapter (see LaGreca & Stark, this volume).

As previously stated, it would seem important to target those natural-istically occurring social behaviors that show empirical relationships to important social outcomes such as sociometric status. A number of stud-ies have shown significant relationships between naturalistically ob-served social behaviors and sociometric status (Bonney & Powell, 1953; Gresham, 1981c, 1982b; Hartup et al., 1967; Marshall & McCandless, 1957; Putallaz & Gottman, 1981; Singleton & Asher, 1977). This compe-tence-correlates definition of children's social skills ensures that one is identifying those behaviors that are functionally related to important social outcomes such as acceptance in the peer group or acceptance by significant adults.

Gottman, Gonso, and Schuler (1976) have previously recognized the importance of social validation of social skills by stating; "Social skills training programs need to demonstrate two things: that they teach the target social skills, and that these skills make a difference on criterion variables such as social position" (p. 195).

While naturalistic observations are a face-valid assessment method, this is no guarantee that the behaviors being assessed are in fact *social skills*. It seems unwise to target social behaviors for remediation that may not have any bearing on children's social development or acceptance by others. Further elaboration of this issue is found in a subsequent part of this chapter under the rubric of social validity.

SOCIAL VALIDITY: CONCEPTUAL ISSUES

Social validity has become an important concept in the behavioral literature over the past several years (Kazdin, 1977; Kazdin & Matson, 1981; Van Houten, 1979; Wolf, 1978). Gresham (1983a) presented a con-ceptualization for socially validating children's social skills using a crite-rion-related validity approach. These writings indicate that behavioral researchers are extremely interested in the social validity issue, as it appears to be crucial that society considers our goals of behavior change to be socially significant, our treatment procedures to be socially accept-able, and the effects we produce to be socially important.

The issues of *social significance* and *social importance* are most germane to the assessment of children's social skills and to the evaluation of outcomes produced by social skills training. The issue of *social acceptabil-ity* is most relevant to training of children's social skills. Because this chapter focuses on assessment considerations, the issue of social accept-ability is not discussed.

Social Significance

One aspect of social validity is the *social significance* of the goals specified for behavioral interventions. That is, are the goals for behavior change what society wants (Wolf, 1978)? For example, an investigator may target increases in the number of thank you verbalizations emitted by a child. Although this would appear to be an appropriate goal, significant others (e.g., parents, teachers) may not consider it a *socially significant goal*. A broader goal, such as increases in all positive verbalizations, might be considered more socially significant and hence, more socially valid by significant others in the child's environment.

It is important to recognize that the social significance of behavioral goals are typically based on subjective evaluation (Kazdin, 1977; Van Houten, 1979; Wolf, 1978). Subjective evaluations are judgments made by persons who interact with or who are in a special position to judge behavior (Kazdin, 1977). Parents, teachers, counselors, social workers, and other significant persons in an individual's environment are likely candidates for subjectively evaluating the goals of behavioral interventions.

Determining the social significance of the goals of a social-skills training program would seem to be vital. Obviously, we would not want to teach social behaviors that are not considered valuable or important. The likely result of teaching socially insignificant behaviors is extinction (i.e., the behaviors simply do not get reinforced). Some years ago Baer and Wolf (1978) stressed the importance of teaching only those behaviors that have a high probability of being "trapped" into natural communities of reinforcement.

Social significance has the most relevance for social-skills assessment during the *classification–diagnosis* phase. Here, we are trying to classify or diagnose the type of social skill problem and target the most important behaviors (i.e., the most socially significant) for remediation. The relationship between social significance of behavioral goals and the social importance of the effects of interventions are discussed in a subsequent portion of this section.

Social Importance

Evaluating the *social importance* of the effects produced by social skills training is crucial. The question here follows: Does the quantity and quality of behavior change make a difference in terms of an individual's functioning in society? In other words, do changes in targeted social behaviors predict an individual's standing on important social outcomes (Gresham, 1983a)?

It has been previously stated that social skills can be perhaps best defined in terms of their social validity. That is, to the extent that behaviors predict important social outcomes for individuals, they are (by definition) socially skilled behaviors. What are important social outcomes for children? A vast literature in the area of children's social development would suggest that acceptance in the peer group, acceptance by significant adults (e.g., parents and teachers), school adjustment, mental health functioning, and lack of contact with the juvenile court system are socially important and valued outcomes for children (see Asher et al., 1977; Cowen, Pederson, Babijian, Izzo, & Trost, 1973; Gilbert, 1957; Gresham, 1981a, 1981b; Hartup, 1970; Kohn & Clausen, 1955; Roff, 1970; Roff, Seels, & Golden, 1972; Strain, Cooke, & Apolloni, 1976 for reviews).

Sociometrics and teacher ratings have been the most frequently used measures to validate the outcomes of social skills training. These measures reflect socially important outcomes for children, based on the vast literature in the area of children's social development. For example, sociometric status has been shown to predict *juvenile delinquency* (Roff et al., 1972), *school maladjustment* (Gronlund & Anderson, 1963), *psychological functioning in adulthood* (Cowen et al., 1973; Garmezy, 1974; Kohn, 1977), *dropping out of school* (Ullman, 1957), *self-concept* (Cowen et al., 1973), and *vulnerability to psychopathology in childhood* (Weintraub, Prinz, & Neale, 1978). Peer acceptance is also a highly valued and desirable outcome in our society (Asher et al., 1977; Hartup, 1970; Oden, 1980).

Teacher ratings or judgments of children's social behavior also reflect an important social outcome for children. Teacher ratings tend to agree with sociometric status (Green, Forehand, Beck, & Vosk, 1980; Green, Vosk, Forehand, & Beck, 1981; LaGreca, 1981; MacMillan et al., 1980; Vosk et al., 1982). Teachers also prefer to interact with popular children and dispense more attention and praise statements toward popular than unpopular children (Brophy, 1981).

In summary, it would seem that the most effective and socially valid way to evaluate the outcomes of social skills training would be to track behavior changes that best predict an individual's standing on socially important outcomes (e.g., sociometric status, teacher or parent ratings). This would ensure that we are effecting changes in behavior that society considers important for children and youth.

Social Validation: Methodological Issues

Most social skills research focuses on changes in certain target behaviors without consideration of their social significance or social importance. One could socially validate these changes using norm-based comparisons by demonstrating that the frequencies of target behaviors are similar to the frequencies emitted by nonreferred or socially accepted children (Kazdin, 1977; Van Houten, 1979). Unfortunately, unless we can demonstrate that normative rates of certain social behaviors predict important social outcomes (e.g., sociometric status), then the intervention would not be socially valid in terms of the *social importance criterion*. A prime example of this was Gottman's (1977) finding, which showed that global rates of social interaction did not predict children's standing on sociometric measures. Thus, when social interaction rates were increased to normative levels, they did not have any impact on an extremely important social outcome (social acceptance). However, certain levels of performance or rates of social contact may be necessary to develop and refine key social skills that do predict status or important social outcomes such as peer acceptance and teacher ratings.

A second and related issue deals with the application of the norm-based approach to sociometric ratings, as opposed to behavioral observations. A number of studies have demonstrated social validity by using norm-based comparisons for observational data such as naturalistically observed social skills and role-play measures (see Foster & Ritchey, 1979; Gresham, 1981b; Van Hasselt et al., 1979 for reviews). I could find no social skills studies that have employed norm-based comparisons to evaluate the effects of SST (social skills training) on sociometric or teacher ratings. That is, what is a child's level of peer acceptance after training compared to children who are average and/or above average in peer acceptance? For an extremely disruptive or aggressive child who undergoes social skills training, what is his/her frequency of school suspensions compared to the base rate of school suspensions for his/her peer group?

Establishing appropriate norms for sociometrics has its own array of difficulties and ambiguities (Kazdin, 1977). One must be careful in deciding what is meant by normal or what is the most appropriate norm group for a particular child. Van Houten (1979) recommends that a single goal based on the performances of competent individuals be used as the standard for social validity. There are a number of potential problems with using a universal goal for social competence. Standards for social competence may vary as a function of age, setting, gender, race, cultural background, and socioeconomic status. For example, elementary-age children tend to show considerable sex bias in their sociometric choices (Asher & Hymel, 1981). Creating a universal standard of social competence based on cross-sex measures of peer acceptance in elementary-age children would yield an invalid estimate of social acceptance. Proper social validation of an SST program in this case would require comparisons of males to the average acceptance of males by males and comparisons of females to the average acceptance of females by females (i.e., separate norms by gender).

Another example of how standards of social competence may vary can be found in the literature concerning the social acceptance of mildly retarded children by nonretarded peers. A relatively large body of research suggests that mildly retarded children and adolescents are better accepted by nonretarded peers if they remain in self-contained classrooms rather than being integrated into regular education classrooms (Gottlieb, Semmel, & Veldman, 1978; MacMillan & Morrison, 1980; Morrison, 1981; Stager & Young, 1981). Thus, the social validation of a social skills training program with mildly retarded children using sociometrics as outcome measures will depend on whether the children are being educated primarily in self-contained or regular education classrooms. What is the appropriate norm to use? Do we want to move mildly retarded children to the average level of acceptance of mildly retarded children in special classes, in regular classes, or the average acceptance levels of nonretarded children? At this point, the social validity of such a program is probably best decided by the *subjective judgment* of the person primarily involved with educating the child (i.e., the special or regular education teacher) and standing on peer acceptance measures specific to the setting in which the child is placed.

Social validation of intervention programs for the mentally retarded has received increased attention (see Kazdin & Matson, 1981 for a review). Kazdin and Matson (1981) see a major problem with using subjective judgment as a method of social validation. They suggest that global ratings of behavior may improve dramatically, with little or no corresponding changes in objective measures of behavior rates. In this case, naturalistic rates of behavior would fail to predict subjective judgments or ratings by significant others. Using the *competence-correlates* definition of social validation, however this finding may call into question the validity of the observational data more so than the validity of the subjective judgments. It could be that nontarget behaviors changed as a result of the intervention (response covariation), which were reflected in the subjective judgments, but were not captured by the observation code. While extraneous variables (e.g., expectation biases, experimenter bias) can affect ratings or judgments, it cannot be assumed that increases in ratings without corresponding increases in certain observed behaviors automatically invalidates subjective judgments. As previously discussed, social behaviors are not socially valid in and of themselves, but rather they are socially validated by their ability to predict an individual's standing on important social outcomes.

A final issue regarding the social validation of social skills training programs using sociometrics and judgments relates to the *competence-*

correlates conceptualization of children's social skills (Asher & Markell, 1978; Gresham, 1981b, 1982a). Social skills are defined by McFall (1982) as the specific abilities that enable a person to perform competently at particular social tasks. This is another way of saying that behaviors can be considered socially skilled if they predict or correlate with important outcomes. By targeting those behaviors that best predict an individual's standing on important outcome measures, we should be able to effect socially valid changes in children's social behavior. To date, there is little research investigating those specific behaviors that best predict children's levels of peer acceptance, ratings of competence by parents and teachers, and mental health status in adulthood. Until we can demonstrate that certain social behaviors predict important social outcomes for children, the ultimate social validity of those behaviors will remain unknown.

There is an obvious need for multivariate research that would select various social behaviors and derive an optimum prediction of socially important measures. An initial, and somewhat restricted, attempt at this was done by Gresham (1982c) using stepwise multiple regression procedures and two different varieties of sociometric measures (i.e., peer nominations and peer ratings). Future research could be conducted using a much wider variety of outcome measures, taking into account such variables as age, gender, race, setting, and other demographics using sophisticated statistical procedures such as multiple regression, canonical correlation, stepwise discriminant analysis, factor analysis, and the like. Unless we can demonstrate that social skills training predicts important social outcomes for children, conclusions about the effectiveness of these training programs will be limited.

CONCLUSIONS AND FUTURE RESEARCH NEEDS

The assessment technology for children's social skills has made great strides over the past several years. However, the field is still in its infancy in terms of a general conceptual framework. As previously discussed, we still do not have an adequate definition of social skill, nor do we have sufficient empirical data to classify various types of social-skill problems. Moreover, assessment studies in the area use a variety of measures making cross-study comparisons a difficult, if not impossible, task. There is a surprising absence of a *developmental* approach to children's social skills. It seems strange that to date we do not know what specific social skills are most important at what age, how males and females differ in their social skills at various ages, or how social skills are modified by learning, maturation, or environmental influences. Finally, there appears to be an almost complete neglect of social validation procedures in selecting socially significant goals for social skills training and in evaluating the social importance of the outcomes of training programs.

Intense research effort should be directed toward deriving an adequate definition of social skill. Social skills are being researched by investigators who are either using their own idosyncratic definition of social skill or who are defining almost any behavior as a social skill. This is analogous to the proverbial "blind men and the elephant" problem, with each touching a part and guessing, but none basing their hypothesis on adequate data.

As previously discussed, three general definitions have been used in the social skills literature (peer acceptance, behavioral and social validity). The *peer acceptance definition* is advantageous in identifying poorly accepted, unpopular, or rejected children but not in targeting behaviors for remediation. The *behavioral definition* is useful for targeting specific social behaviors, but not for judging whether or not these behaviors are socially significant or lead to socially important outcomes. The *social validity definition* was proffered as perhaps the most useful and conceptually valid definition because it combines the advantages of the peer acceptance and behavioral approaches. Future research should be directed at assessing those specific behaviors that best predict an individual's standing on important social outcomes. This would necessitate a nomothetic approach to research using rather sophisticated statistical procedures such as multiple regression, stepwise discriminant analysis, canonical correlation, and other multivariate procedures.

Classification of various types of social skill problems is another area in need of empirical research. Four basic types of social skill difficulty were identified based in part upon Bandura's (1977a) distinction between learning and performance. These were labeled as (1) *skill deficits,* (2) *performance deficits,* (3) *self-control skill deficits,* and (4) *self-control performance deficits.* As previously mentioned, this classification is not based on empirical data, although it may be a useful heuristic for guiding future research efforts. Studies assessing children's knowledge and performance of social skills as well as the presence or absence of response-inhibiting emotional behaviors (e.g., anxiety, impulsivity, anger) should be conducted. Given a thorough assessment of these and perhaps other variables, a classification of various types of social skill difficulty should be possible using discriminant analyses or clustering procedures.

Assessment techniques used in social skills research have not been comparable from study to study. Some researchers use positive peer nominations as indices of peer acceptance, whereas others use nominations as reflections of popularity (see Asher & Hymel, 1981; Gresham, 1981c; Hops, 1983). Some investigators employ naturalistic observations, while others use behavioral role play tests, while still others use teacher ratings of social behavior. In short, we know little about how these various social skills assessment methods compare with one another in assessment of the same social skills.

Because it has been demonstrated that method variance can influence what is being measured (Campbell & Fiske, 1959; Cone, 1979), multitrait–multimethod (MTMM) studies should be designed to assess the unique contribution of various assessment methods. Gresham, Bruce, and Veitia (1983) conducted an MTMM study with adolescents using five assessment methods (peer ratings, parent ratings, teacher ratings, self ratings, and behavioral role play) assessing three behavioral response classes (traits). These investigators found significant method variance on several assessment methods, suggesting that what is being measured depends to a large degree on how it is being measured (multiple operationalism). Further research using the MTMM approach should be conducted to assess method and behavioral variance.

The failure to consider developmental factors in assessing children's social skills represents a major gap in our knowledge of children's social behavior. There are no normative data on large samples of socially skilled children at various age levels that could serve not only as a basis for selection, but also as a standard against which to compare the efficacy of social skills training. Foster and Ritchey (1979) cogently point out that socially competent behavior probably varies with age, gender, race, socioeconomic status, and geographic locale. The existence of such normative data would be a major conceptual advance in the technology of social skills assessment.

A final issue in need of further research is social validation. it is extremely important that we select socially significant goals for social skills training and that the outcomes make a difference in a child's societal functioning. The existence of social-skill norms would be a major contribution to the social validation enterprise. That is, if we could establish normative levels of social behavior, we could identify those children in most need of training (e.g., tenth percentile, fifth percentile). Social validation could occur by demonstrating that children moved into the normative range of social skills subsequent to intervention using age- and gender-appropriate norms.

These norms could be constructed for teacher and parent rating scales, a variety of sociometric measures, behavioral role-play tests, and even naturalistic observations. The social significance and social importance of specific social behaviors could be determined by their empirical relationships to important social outcomes (e.g., peer acceptance, teacher or parent judgments).

Attention given to the aforementioned areas of research should provide a useful conceptual and practical knowledge base with which to identify, select, train, and evaluate children who are experiencing social skill difficulties.

REFERENCES

Allen, K. E., Hart, B. M., Buell, J. S., Harris, F. R., & Wolf, M. M. (1964). Effects of social reinforcement on isolate behavior of a nursery school child. *Child Development, 35,* 511–518.

Asher, S. R., & Hymel, S. (1981). Children's social competence in peer relations: Sociometric and behavioral assessment. In J. D. Wine & M. D. Syme (Eds.), *Social competence.* New York: Guilford Press.

Asher, S. R., & Markell, R. S. (1978). *Peer relations and social interaction: Assessment and intervention.* Unpublished manuscript.

Asher, S. R., Oden, S. L., & Gottman, J. M. (1977). Children's friendships in school settings. In L. G. Katz (Ed.), *Current topics in early childhood education* (Vol. 1). Norwood, NJ: Ablex.

Asher, S. R., Singleton, L., Tinsley, B. R., & Hymel, S. A. (1979). A reliable sociometric measure for preschool children. *Developmental Psychology, 15,* 443–444.

Asher, S. R., & Taylor, A. R. (1981). The social outcomes of mainstreaming: Sociometric assessment and beyond. *Exceptional Education Quarterly, 1,* 13–30.

Baer, D. M., & Wolf, M. M. (1970). The entry into natural communities of reinforcement. In R. Ulrich, T. Stachnik, & J. Mabry (Eds.), *Control of human behavior* (Vol. 2). Glenwood, IL: Scott Foresman.

Ballard, M., Corman, L., Gottlieb, J., & Kaufman, M. J. (1977). Improving the social status of mainstreamed retarded children. *Journal of Educational Psychology, 69,* 605–611.

Bandura, A. (1969). *Principles of behavior modification.* New York: Holt, Rinehart, & Winston.

Bandura, A. (1977a). *Social learning theory.* Englewood Cliffs, NJ: Prentice-Hall.

Bandura, A. (1977b). Self-efficacy: Toward a unifying theory of behavior change. *Psychological Review, 84,* 191–215.

Bellack, A. S. (1979). A critical appraisal for strategies for assessing social skills. *Behavioral Assessment, 1,* 157–176.

Bellack, A. S., & Hersen, M. (Eds.). (1979). *Research and practice in social skills training.* New York: Plenum.

Bellack, A. S., Hersen, M., & Lampmarski, D. (1979). Role-play tests for assessing social skills: Are they valid? Are they useful? *Journal of Consulting and Clinical Psychology, 47,* 335–342.

Bellack, A. S., Hersen, M., & Turner, S. M. (1978). Role play tests for assessing social skills: Are they valid? *Behavior Therapy, 9,* 448–461.

Bergan, J. R. (1977). *Behavioral consultation.* Columbus, OH: Charles E. Merrill.

Bergan, J. R., & Tombari, M. L. (1975). The analysis of verbal interactions occurring during consultation. *Journal of School Psychology, 13,* 209–226.

Bergan, J. R., & Tombari, M. L. (1976). Consultant skill and efficiency and the implementation and outcomes of consultation. *Journal of School Psychology, 14,* 3–14.

Berler, E. S., Gross, A. M., & Drabman, R. S. (1982). Social skills training with children: Proceed with caution. *Journal of Applied Behavior Analysis, 15,* 41–53.

Blackwood, R. O. (1970). The operant conditioning of verbal mediated self-control in the classroom. *Journal of School Psychology, 8,* 251–258.

Bolstad, O. D., & Johnson, S. M. (1972). Self-regulation in the modification of disruptive classroom behavior. *Journal of Applied Behavior Analysis, 5,* 443–454.

Bolstad, O. D., & Johnson, S. M. (1977). The relationship between teacher's assessment of students and students' actual behavior in the classroom. *Child Development, 48,* 570–578.

Bonney, M. E., & Powell, J. (1953). Differences in social behavior between sociometrically high and sociometrically low children. *Journal of Educational Research, 46,* 481–496.

Borke, H. (1973). The development of empathy in Chinese and American children between three and six years of age: A cross-culture study. *Developmental Psychology, 9,* 102–108.

Bornstein, M. R., Bellack, A. S., & Hersen, M. (1977). Social skills training for unassertive children: A multiple baseline analysis. *Journal of Applied Behavior Analysis, 10,* 183–195.

Bornstein, P. H., & Quevillon, R. P. (1976). The effects of a self-instructional package on overactive preschool boys. *Journal of Applied Behavior Analysis, 9,* 179–188.

Brophy, J. (1981). Teacher praise: A functional analysis. *Review of Educational Research, 51,* 5–32.

Bryan, T. S. (1978). Social relationships and verbal interactions of learning disabled children. *Journal of Learning Disabilities, 11,* 107–115.

Camp, B. W., Blom, G. E., Herbert, F., & Van Doorninck, W. J. (1977). "Think Aloud": A program for developing self-control in young agressive boys. *Journal of Abnormal Child Psychology, 5,* 157–169.

Campbell, D. T., & Fiske, D. W. (1959). Convergent and discriminant validation by the multitrait–multimethod matrix. *Psychological Bulletin, 56,* 81–105.

Cartledge, G., & Milburn, J. (1978). The case for teaching social skills in the classroom: A review. *Review of Educational Research, 48,* 133–156.

Cartledge, G., & Milburn, J. (Eds.). (1980). *Teaching social skills to children: Innovative approaches.* New York: Pergamon.

Chandler, M. J. (1973). Egocentrism and antisocial behavior: The assessment and training of social perspective-taking skills. *Developmental Psychology, 9,* 326–332.

Combs, M. L., & Slaby, D. A. (1977). Social skills training with children. In B. B. Lahey & A. E. Kazdin (Eds.), *Advances in child clinical psychology* (Vol. 1). New York: Plenum.

Cone, J. D. (1978). The Behavioral Assessment Grid (BAG): A conceptual framework and a taxonomy. *Behavior Therapy, 9,* 882–888.

Cone, J. D. (1979). Confounded comparison in triple response mode assessment. *Behavioral Assessment, 1,* 85–96.

Cooke, T. P., & Apolloni, T. (1976). Developing positive social–emotional behavior: A study of training and generalization effects. *Journal of Applied Behavior Analysis, 9,* 65–78.

Cowen, E. L., Pedersen, A., Babigian, H., Izzo, L. D., & Trost, M. A. (1973). Long-term follow-up of early detected vulnerable children. *Journal of Consulting and Clinical Psychology, 41,* 438–446.

Curran, J. P. (1977). Skills training as an approach to the treatment of heterosexual-social anxiety: A review. *Psychological Bulletin, 84,* 140–157.

Drabman, R. S., Spitnalnick, R., & O'Leary, K. D. (1973). Teaching self-control to disruptive children. *Journal of Abnormal Psychology, 82,* 10–16.

Evans, J. M., & Nelson, R. O. (1977). Assessment of child behavior problems. In A. R. Ciminero, K. S. Calhoun, & H. E. Adams (Eds.), *Handbook of behavioral assessment.* New York: Wiley Interscience.

Foster, S. L., & Ritchey, W. L. (1979). Issues in the assessment of social competence in children. *Journal of Applied Behavior Analysis, 12,* 625–638.

Gamble, R., & Strain, R. S. (1979). The effects of dependent and interdependent group contingencies on socially appropriate responses in classes for emotionally handicapped children. *Psychology in the Schools, 16,* 253–260.

Garmezy, N. (1974). Children at risk: The search for antecedents of schizophrenia—Part I: Conceptual models and research methods. *Schizophrenia Bulletin, 8,* 14–90.

Gilbert, G. M. (1957). A survey of "referral problems" in metropolitan child guidance centers. *Journal of Clinical Psychology, 13,* 37–42.

Goldfried, M. R., & Kent, R. N. (1972). Traditional versus behavioral personality assessment: A comparison of methodological and theoretical assumptions. *Psychological Bulletin, 77,* 409–420.

Gottlieb, J., Semmel, M. I., & Veldman, D. J. (1978). Correlates of social status among mainstreamed mentally retarded children. *Journal of Educational Psychology, 70,* 396–405.

Gottman, J. M. (1977). The effects of a modeling film on social isolation in preschool children: A methodological investigation. *Journal of Abnormal Child Psychology, 5,* 69–78.

Gottman, J. M., Gonso, J., & Rasmussen, B. (1975). Social interaction, social competence, and friendship in children. *Child Development, 46,* 708–718.

Gottman, J. M., Gonso, J., & Schuler, P. (1976). Teaching social skills to isolated children. *Journal of Abnormal Child Psychology, 4,* 179–197.

Green, K. D., & Forehand, R. (1980). Assessment of children's social skills: A review of methods. *Journal of Behavioral Assessment, 2,* 143–159.

Green, K. D., Forehand, R., Beck, S. J., & Vosk, B. (1980). An assessment of the relationship among measures of children's social competence and children's academic achievement. *Child Development, 51,* 1149–1156.

Green, K. D., Vosk, B., Forehand, R., & Beck, S. (1981). An examination of differences among sociometrically identified accepted, rejected, and neglected children. *Child Study Journal, 11,* 117–124.

Greenspan, S. (1981). Social competence and handicapped individuals: Practical implications and a proposed model. *Advances in Special Education, 3,* 41–82.

Greenwood, C., Todd, N., Hops, H., & Walker, H. (1982). Behavior change targets in the assessment and treatment of socially withdrawn preschool children. *Behavioral Assessment, 4,* 237–297.

Greenwood, C. R., Walker, H. M., & Hops, H. (1977). Issues in social interaction/withdrawal assessment. *Exceptional Children, 43,* 490–499.

Greenwood, C. R., Walker, H. M., Todd, N., & Hops, H. (1979). Selecting a cost-effective screening measure for the assessment of preschool social withdrawal. *Journal of Applied Behavior Analysis, 12,* 639–652.

Greenwood, C. R., Walker, H. M., Todd, N., & Hops, H. (1981). Normative and descriptive analysis of preschool free play social interaction rates. *Journal of Pediatric Psychology, 6,* 343–367.

Gresham, F. M. (1981a). Assessment of children's social skills. *Journal of School Psychology, 19,* 120–133.

Gresham, F. M. (1981b). Social skills training with handicapped children: A review. *Review of Educational Research, 51,* 139–176.

Gresham, F. M. (1981c). Validity of social skills measures for assessing the social competence in low-status children: A multivariate investigation. *Developmental Psychology, 17,* 390–398.

Gresham, F. M. (1982a). Misguided mainstreaming: The case for social skills training with handicapped children. *Exceptional Children, 48,* 422–433.

Gresham, F. M. (1982b). Social interactions as predictors of children's likeability and friendship patterns: A multiple regression analysis. *Journal of Behavioral Assessment, 4,* 39–54.

Gresham, F. M. (1982c). Social skills instruction for exceptional children. *Theory into Practice, 20,* 129–133.

Gresham, F. M. (1982d). *Social skills: Principles, practices, and procedures.* Des Moines, IA: Iowa Department of Public Instruction.

Gresham, F. M. (1983a). Social validity in the assessment of children's social skills: Establishing standards for social competency. *Journal of Psychoeducational Assessment, 1,* 297–307.

Gresham, F. M. (1983b). Social skills assessment as a component of mainstreaming placement decisions. *Exceptional Children, 49,* 331–336.

Gresham, F. M., Bruce, B., & Veitia, M. (1983, December). *Convergent–discriminant validity in the assessment of adolescents' social skills.* Paper presented at the World Congress on Behavior Therapy, AABT 17th Annual Convention, Washington, DC.

Gresham, F. M., & Lemanek, K. L. (1984). Social skills: A review of cognitive-behavioral training procedures with children. *Journal of Applied Developmental Psychology, 4,* 439–461.

Gresham, F. M., & Nagle, R. J. (1980). Social skills training with children: Responsiveness to modeling and coaching as a function of peer orientation. *Journal of Consulting and Clinical Psychology, 48,* 718–729.

Gronlund, H., & Anderson, L. (1963). Personality characteristics of socially accepted, socially neglected, and socially rejected junior high school pupils. In J. Sederman (Ed.), *Educating for mental health.* New York: Crowell.

Hartup, W. W. (1970). Peer interaction in social organizations. In P. H. Mussen (Ed.), *Carmichael's manual of child psychology.* New York: Wiley.

Hartup, W. W., Glazer, J. A., & Charlesworth, R. (1967). Peer reinforcement and sociometric status. *Child Development, 38,* 1017–1024.

Haynes, S., & Jensen, B. (1979). The interview as a behavioral assessment instrument. *Behavioral Assessment, 1,* 97–106.

Hersen, M., & Bellack, A. S. (1977). Assessment of social skills. In A. R. Ciminero, K. S. Calhoun, & H. E. Adams (Eds.), *Handbook of behavioral assessment.* New York: Wiley.

Hops, H. (1983). Children's social competence and skill: Current research practices and future directions. *Behavior Therapy, 14,* 3–18.

Hops, H., & Greenwood, C. R. (1981). Social skills deficits. In E. J. Mash & L. G. Terdal (Eds.), *Behavioral assessment of childhood disorders.* New York: The Guilford Press.

Hymel, S., & Asher, S. R. (1977). *Assessment and training of isolated children's social skills.* Paper presented at the meeting of the Society for Research in Child Development, New Orleans. (ERIC Document Reproduction Service No. ED 136 930).

Iwata, B. A., & Bailey, J. S. (1974). Reward versus cost token systems: An analysis of the effects on students and teacher. *Journal of Applied Behavior Analysis, 7,* 567–576.

Kazdin, A. E. (1977). Assessing the clinical or applied importance of behavior change through social validation. *Behavior Modification, 1,* 427–451.

Kazdin, A. E. (1979). Situational specificity: The two-edged sword of behavioral assessment. *Behavioral Assessment, 1,* 57–75.

Kazdin, A. E., & Matson, J. L. (1981). Social validation in mental retardation. *Applied Research in Mental Retardation, 2,* 39–53.

Kendall, P. C., & Braswell, L. (1982). Assessment for cognitive behavioral interventions in the schools. *School Psychology Review, 11*, 21–31.

Kendall, P. C., & Wilcox, L. E. (1979). Self-control in children: Development of a rating scale. *Journal of Consulting and Clinical Psychology, 47*, 1020–1029.

Kohn, M. (1977). The Kohn Social Competence Scale and Kohn Symptom Checklist for the preschool child: A follow-up report. *Journal of Abnormal Child Psychology, 5*, 249–262.

Kohn, M., & Clausen, J. A. (1955). Social isolation and schizophrenia. *American Sociological Review, 20*, 265–273.

Ladd, G. W. (1981). Effectiveness of a social learning method for enhancing children's social interaction and peer acceptance. *Child Development, 52*, 171–178.

La Greca, A. M. (1981). Peer acceptance: The correspondence between children's sociometric scores and teacher's ratings of peer interactions. *Journal of Abnormal Child Psychology, 9*, 167–178.

La Greca, A. M., & Santogrossi, D. A. (1980). Social skills training with elementary school students: A behavioral group approach. *Journal of Consulting and Clinical Psychology, 48*, 220–227.

Leland, H. W. (1978). Theoretical considerations of adaptive behavior. In A. Coulter & H. Morrow (Eds.), *Adaptive behavior: Concepts and measurements.* New York: Grune & Stratton.

Libet, J. M., & Lewinsohn, P. M. (1973). Concept of social skills with special reference to the behavior of depressed persons. *Journal of Consulting and Clinical Psychology, 40*, 304–312.

Linehan, M. M. (1980). Content validity: Its relevance to behavioral assessment. *Behavioral Assessment, 2*, 147–160.

MacMillan, D. (1982). *Mental retardation in school and society* (2nd ed.). New York: Little Brown.

MacMillan, D. L., & Morrison, G. M. (1980). Correlates of social status among mildly handicapped learners in self-contained special classes. *Journal of Educational Psychology, 72*, 437–444.

MacMillan, D. L., Morrison, G. M., & Silverstein, A. B. (1980). Convergent and discriminant validity of Project PRIME's Guess Who? *American Journal of Mental Deficiency, 85*, 78–81.

Marshall, H. R., & McCandless, B. R. (1957). A study in the prediction of social behavior of preschool children. *Child Development, 28*, 149–159.

Matson, J., Esveldt-Dawson, K., & Kazdin, A. E. (1983). Validation of methods for assessing social skills in children. *Journal of Clinical Child Psychology, 12*, 174–180.

McCandless, B. R., & Marshall, H. R. (1957). Sex differences in social acceptance and participation of preschool children. *Child Development, 28*, 421–425.

McFall, R. M. (1982). A review and reformulation of the concept of social skills. *Behavioral Assessment, 4*, 1–33.

McGuire, J. M. (1973). Aggression and sociometric status with preschool children. *Sociometry, 36*, 542–549.

Meichenbaum, D. (1977). *Cognitive behavior modification.* New York: Plenum.

Meichenbaum, D., & Goodman, J. (1971). Training impulsive children to talk to themselves: A means of developing self-control. *Journal of Abnormal Psychology, 77*, 115–126.

Michelson, L., & Wood, R. R. (1980). A group assertive training program for elementary school children. *Child Behavior Therapy, 2*, 2–10.

Mischel, W. (1968). *Personality and assessment.* New York: Wiley.

Moore, S. G., & Updegraff, R. (1964). Sociometric status of preschool children related to age, sex, nurturance giving, and dependency. *Child Development, 35*, 519–524.

Morrison, G. M. (1981). Sociometric measurement: Methodological consideration of its use with mildly learning handicapped and nonhandicapped children. *Journal of Educational Psychology, 73,* 193–200.

O'Connor, R. D. (1969). Modification of social withdrawal through symbolic modeling. *Journal of Applied Behavior Analysis, 2,* 15–22.

O'Connor, R. D. (1972). Relative effects of modeling, shaping, and combined procedures for modification of social withdrawal. *Journal of Abnormal Psychology, 79,* 327–334.

Oden, S. (1980). A child's social isolation: Origins, prevention, intervention. In G. Cartledge & J. F. Milburn (Eds.), *Teaching social skills to children: Innovative approaches.* New York: Pergamon.

Oden, S. L., & Asher, S. R. (1977). Coaching children in social skills for friendship making. *Child Development, 48,* 496–506.

O'Leary, S. G., & Dubey, D. R. (1979). Applications of self-control procedures by children: A review. *Journal of Applied Behavior Analysis, 12,* 449–465.

Paul, G. L., Lentz, R. J. (1977). *Psychosocial treatment of chronic mental patients: Milieu versus social-learning programs.* Cambridge, MA: Harvard University Press.

Pekarik, E. C., Prinz, R. J., Liebert, D. E., Weintraub, S., & Neale, J. M. (1976). The Pupil Evaluation Inventory: A sociometric technique for assessing children's social behavior. *Journal of Abnormal Child Psychology, 4,* 85–97.

Putallaz, M., & Gottman, J. M. (1981). Social skills and group acceptance. In S. R. Asher & J. M. Gottman (Eds.), *The development of children's friendship.* New York: Cambridge University Press.

Ragland, E. V., Kerr, M., & Strain, P. S. (1978). Behavior of withdrawn autistic children: Effects of peer social initiations. *Behavior Modification, 2,* 565–578.

Reardon, R. C., Hersen, M., Bellack, A. S., & Foley, J. M. (1979). Measuring social skill in grade school boys. *Journal of Behavioral Assessment, 1,* 87–105.

Reschly, D. J., & Gresham, F. M. (1981). *Use of social competence measures to facilitate parent and teacher involvement and nonbiased assessment.* Unpublished manuscript, Iowa State University.

Robin, A., Schneider, M., & Dolnick, M. (1976). The turtle technique: An extended case study of self-control in the classroom. *Psychology in the Schools, 13,* 449–453.

Robinson, N., & Robinson, H. (1976). *The mentally retarded child.* New York: McGraw-Hill.

Roff, M. (1970). Some life history factors in relation to various types of adult maladjustment. In M. Roff & D. Ricks (Eds.), *Life history research in psychopathology.* Minneapolis: University of Minnesota Press.

Roff, M., Sells, S. B., & Golden, M. M. (1972). *Social adjustment and personality development in children.* Minneapolis: University of Minnesota Press.

Rogers-Warren, A., & Baer, D. M. (1976). Correspondence between saying and doing: Teaching children to share and praise. *Journal of Applied Behavior Analysis, 9,* 334–354.

Rosenbaum, M. S., & Drabman, R. S. (1979). Self-control training in the classroom: A review and critique. *Journal of Applied Behavior Analysis, 12,* 467–485.

Selman, R. L. (1980). *The growth of interpersonal understanding: Developmental and clinical analyses.* New York: Academic Press.

Singleton, L. C., & Asher, S. R. (1977). Peer preferences and social interaction among third-grade children in an integrated school district. *Journal of Educational Psychology, 69,* 330–336.

Spivack, G., Platt, J., & Shure, M. B. (1976). *The problem-solving approach to adjustment.* San Francisco: Jossey-Bass.

Stager, S. F., & Young, R. D. (1981). Intergroup contact and social outcomes for mainstreamed EMR adolescents. *American Journal of Mental Deficiency, 85,* 497–503.

Stephens, T. M. (1978). *Social skills in the classroom.* Columbus, OH: Cedars Press.

Stephens, T. M. (1979). *Social behavior assessment.* Columbus, OH: Cedars Press.

Stephens, T. M. (1980). *Technical information: Social behavior assessment*. Columbus, OH: Cedars Press.

Strain, P. S. (1977). An experimental analysis of peer social initiations on the behavior of withdrawn preschool children: Some training and generalization effects. *Journal of Abnormal Child Psychology, 5,* 445–455.

Strain, P. S., Cooke, R. P., & Apolloni, T. (1976). *Teaching exceptional children: Assessing and modifying social behavior*. New York: Academic Press.

Strain, P. S., & Shores, R. E. (1977). Social reciprocity: A review of research and educational implications. *Exceptional Children, 43,* 526–530.

Strain, P. S., Shores, R. E., & Timm, M. A. (1977). Effects of peer social initiations on the behavior of withdrawn preschool children. *Journal of Applied Behavior Analysis, 10,* 289–298.

Stumme, V. S., Gresham, F. M., & Scott, N. A. (1982). Validity of *Social Behavior Assessment* in discriminating emotionally disabled from nonhandicapped students. *Journal of Behavioral Assessment, 4,* 327–342.

Tombari, M., & Bergan, J. (1978). Consultant cues and teacher verbalizations, judgments, and expectancies concerning children's adjustment problems. *Journal of School Psychology, 16,* 217–219.

Turkewitz, H., O'Leary, K. D., & Ironsmith, M. (1975). Producing generalization of appropriate behavior through self-control. *Journal of Consulting and Clinical Psychology, 43,* 577–583.

Ullman, C. A. (1957). Teachers, peers, and tests as predictors of adjustment. *Journal of Educational Psychology, 48,* 257–267.

Urbain, E. S., & Kendall, P. C. (1980). Review of social-cognitive problem-solving interventions with children. *Psychological Bulletin, 88,* 109–143.

Van Hasselt, V. B., Hersen, M., & Bellack, A. S. (1981). The validity of role play tests for assessing social skills in children. *Behavior Therapy, 12,* 202–216.

Van Hasselt, V. B., Hersen, M., Whitehill, M. B., & Bellack, A. S. (1979). Social skill assessment and training for children: An evaluative review. *Behavior Research and Therapy, 17,* 413–437.

Van Houten, R. (1979). Social validation: The evolution of standards for competency for target behaviors. *Journal of Applied Behavior Analysis, 12,* 581–591.

Vosk, B., Forehand, R., Parker, J. B., & Rickard, K. (1982). A multimethod comparison of popular and unpopular children. *Developmental Psychology, 18,* 571–575.

Walker, H., McConnell, S., Holmes, D., Todis, B., Walker, J., & Golden, N. (1983). *The Walker Social Skills Curriculum*. Austin, TX: Pro-Ed.

Warren, S., Rogers-Warren, A., & Baer, D. M. (1976). The role of offer rates in controlling sharing by young children. *Journal of Applied Behavior Analysis, 9,* 491–497.

Weintraub, S., Neale, J. M., & Liebert, D. E. (1975). Teacher ratings of children vulnerable to psychopathology. *American Journal of Orthopsychiatry, 45,* 838–845.

Weintraub, S., Prinz, R. J., & Neale, J. M. (1978). Peer evaluations of the competence of children vulnerable to psychopathology. *Journal of Abnormal Child Psychology, 6,* 461–473.

Winder, C. L., & Wiggins, J. S. (1964). Social reputation and social behavior: A further validation of the peer nomination inventory. *Journal of Abnormal and Social Psychology, 68,* 681–684.

Wolf, M. M. (1978). Social validity: The case for subjective measurement or how applied behavior analysis is finding its heart. *Journal of Applied Behavior Analysis, 11,* 203–214.

Zahavi, S. L., Asher, S. R. (1978). The effect of verbal instruction on preschool children's aggressive behavior. *Journal of School Psychology, 16,* 146–153.

CHAPTER 5

Naturalistic Observations of Children's Social Behavior

Annette M. La Greca
Patricia Stark

INTRODUCTION

There has been a proliferation of research on the assessment and training of children's social and interpersonal skills (Combs & Slaby, 1977; Conger & Keane, 1981; Gresham, 1981a; Van Hasselt, Hersen, Whitehill, & Bellack, 1979; Wanlass & Prinz, 1982). The surge of interest in this area has been very rapid, and has drawn on a variety of sources, including clinical, behavioral, and developmental psychology.

One of the main methods employed for examining children's peer relationships has been naturalistic observation of social behavior. Naturalistic observations have been extensively employed for describing the developmental parameters of children's peer interactions and friendships (e.g., Dodge, Coie, & Brakke, 1982; Dodge, Schlundt, Schocken, & Delugach, 1983; Masters & Furman, 1981; Mueller, 1972; Mueller & Brenner, 1977), identifying children in need of social intervention (e.g., Furman, Rahe, & Hartup, 1979; Keller & Carlson, 1974; Walker & Hops, 1973), selecting appropriate goals for social behavioral interventions (Bierman & Furman, 1984), and assessing treatment outcome (e.g., Gresham & Nagle, 1980; La Greca & Santogrossi, 1980; Oden & Asher, 1977). Clearly, naturalistic observations of children's social behavior have been frequently and extensively employed as an assessment method and have played a critical role in our understanding of children's social relationships.

Behavioral observations offer a number of distinct advantages relative to other methods of assessing children's peer relationships. They are considered to be the most face-valid method available for assessing social competencies in children (Asher & Hymel, 1981; Foster & Ritchey 1979). They provide information on actual peer exchanges while minimizing some of the subjective bias inherent in more traditional assessment procedures, such as teacher and parent reports. Moreover, they have been demonstrated to be sensitive to intervention effects (Evers & Schwarz, 1973; Gresham & Nagle, 1980; La Greca & Santogrossi, 1980; O'Connor, 1969, 1972; Strain, 1977). Relative to other assessment methods, such as teacher and peer ratings, behavioral observations are more conducive to frequent repeated measures, making them ideally suited for evaluating treatment outcome in studies employing individual subject designs (Allen, Hart, Buell, Harris, & Wolf, 1964; Cooke & Apolloni, 1976; Kirby & Toler, 1970; Walker & Hops, 1973).

Despite these clear advantages, naturalistic observations have their limitations. Behavioral data are costly and time-consuming to obtain and analyze. The categories selected for study often do not provide sufficient information regarding the nature of the social difficulties, normative levels of behavior, or the differential importance of various social behaviors for successful interpersonal functioning. Perhaps of most concern is the relative paucity of data examining the predictive and social validity of commonly employed observation codes (Greenwood, Walker, & Hops, 1977; Kazdin, 1977a; Wolf, 1978). (For further discussion of the assets and limitations of behavioral observations of social interactions, see Asher & Hymel, 1981, Foster & Ritchey, 1979, and Gresham, 1981a.)

All factors considered, however, naturalistic observation of social behavior will continue to be an important assessment method in the future, and will retain its essential role in furthering our understanding of children's social relationships. In view of this vital role, the intent of the present chapter is to provide an overview of this important assessment method.

Several considerations guide the focus and content of this chapter, as the scope of available literature is sufficiently broad to preclude an exhaustive review. First, this chapter focuses exclusively on naturalistic observation methods for assessing peer interactions. Interactions with adults are not specifically included, nor are structured observation formats, such as role plays. Moreover, methodological issues, such as reliability and reactivity, that are applicable to observational assessments in general, are not covered. The reader is referred to several excellent sources for in-depth discussions of issues such as interrater reliability, observer drift and bias, reactivity of observation methods, and methods for calculating interrater agreement (Johnson & Bolstad, 1973; Kazdin, 1977b; Kent & Foster, 1977; Nelson, Kapust, & Dorsey, 1978; O'Leary & Kent, 1973).

Secondly, the chapter concentrates on methods that have been used with normal or nonhandicapped children. Although this volume is dedicated to social behavior in both handicapped and nonhandicapped populations, many of the observational codes selected for use with handicapped children have been adapted from existing methodologies employed with nonhandicapped children (e.g., Guralnick, 1980). For the most part, the methodologies described herein should be directly applicable to handicapped groups. Moreover, the broader conceptual issues to be addressed are relevant for all child populations.

It is recognized, however, that some special considerations may be important for observations of children with handicapping conditions. For instance, it may be desirable to assess additional areas of functioning, such as language skills or physical–motor skills (Hops, 1983). Evidence suggests that language–communication abilities and physical–motor skills appear to be important prerequisites for successful social interaction among preschool children (Hops & Finch, 1982). Considering that many young handicapped children evidence developmental delays in one or both of these areas, assessing these areas of functioning, in addition to social behavior, may be critically important for understanding the children's social capabilities.

Another guiding consideration for this chapter is the emphasis on observational codes that may have direct relevance for identifying and treating children with peer relationship difficulties. Most attention is accorded to observational codes that relate to other indices of social competence in children (e.g., teacher or peer ratings of acceptance) or that demonstrate some sensitivity to intervention effects.

Finally, it is noted that the current literature on children's social interactions spans a very broad age range—infancy (Mueller & Vandell, 1979) through adolescence (Grolund & Anderson, 1957). Yet, the predominant emphasis in the literature has been on children of preschool and elementary school ages, with the majority of studies concentrating on children free from other handicapping conditions. Consequently, the present chapter reflects this bias.

With these considerations in mind, the present chapter reviews commonly employed methods for observing children's social behavior. Several different types of observational methodologies have evolved; these are described herein, and their properties, strengths, and limitations are delineated. In addition, several conceptual issues affecting the use of naturalistic observations, as well as issues for further consideration, are discussed.

METHODS OF OBSERVATION

Rate of Interaction

Many of the initial investigations of children's social skills employed observations of the frequency of children's social interactions for identifying problem children and/or assessing treatment outcome (e.g. Allen et al., 1964; Evers & Schwarz, 1973; Furman et al., 1979; Keller & Carlson, 1974; O'Connor, 1969, 1972; Walker & Hops, 1973). The frequency of a child's social contacts, commonly referred to as the "rate of interaction," typically has been defined as "an act or behavior initiated by the target child and which is responded to in some manner by another child" (Keller & Carlson, 1974, p. 913). As a general index of sociability, the quality or form of the initiating behavior is not considered, nor is the kind of response obtained from peers.

Much of the rationale for employing the rate-of-interaction measure as an index of social competence stems from retrospective studies of psychotic and schizophrenic adults that reported these individuals to be socially withdrawn as children (see Strain, Cooke, & Apolloni, 1976, for a detailed review of this literature). Low-interacting individuals are thought to miss out on early and important social learning experiences that are critical to later emotional health and social development.

The main asset of the rate-of-interaction methodology is the simplicity and ease of recording and collecting data, relative to other observation codes. Excellent interrater agreement generally has been reported. However, in terms of identifying children in need of social intervention and evaluating treatment outcome, there has been considerable debate regarding the validity and clinical utility of the rate-of-interaction measure. (See Asher, Markell, & Hymel, 1981, for a detailed review.)

Concerns about the concurrent and predictive validity of the rate-of-interaction measure have called into question its utility for identifying children with social problems. This measure has been validated neither as an index of social maladjustment nor as a predictor of later life difficulties (Asher et al., 1981; Conger & Keane, 1981; Foster & Ritchey, 1979; Wanlass & Prinz, 1982). Studies of preschool and elementary school children provide little or no support for a relationship between a child's rate of social interaction and level of social competence, as assessed by

peer ratings of acceptance (Deutsch, 1974; Foster & Ritchy, 1983; Gottman, 1977a, 1977b; Gottman, Gonso, & Rasmussen, 1975; Hymel,
Tinsley, Geraci, & Asher, 1981; Jennings, 1975; Krantz, 1982). Thus, selecting a child based on low rates of social interaction does not guarantee
that the child is currently experiencing problems. Nor does it ensure that
the child is at risk for future difficulties. The few existing longitudinal
studies that have prospectively examined the relationship between social withdrawal and later psychiatric disturbance have found no evidence for such a relationship (Michael, Morris, & Soroker, 1957; Morris,
Soroker & Burruss, 1954; Robins, 1974).

To further complicate the picture, recent developmental investigations suggest that children's behavior while *not* interacting with peers
may also be an important consideration. Gottman (1977b) noted the
distinction between preschoolers who were alone and "tuned-out" versus those who were engaged in constructive activities. More recently,
Rubin (1982) examined the relationship between the quality of solitary
play and social competence in a group of preschoolers. *Immature solitary
play*, which consisted of repetitive motor movements and solitary dramatic play, was found to be negatively related to independent indices of
social competence. By contrast, *mature solitary play*, such as constructive
artwork, puzzle play, and block construction, was positively related to
social competence. In a similar vein, Dodge, Coie, and Brakke (1982)
examined the social behavior of middle elementary students, finding
that rejected children engaged in more solitary–inappropriate play and
less solitary–appropriate play than popular or average-accepted children. Thus, the kind of activities children engage in when not interacting with peers may contribute to their social status, yet are not addressed by rate-of-interaction measures.

Although based on peer reports, rather than behavioral observations,
other evidence suggests that children who are withdrawn *and* aggressive
are more rejected and less accepted by their peers (Milich & Landau,
1984) and are at greater risk for developing schizophrenia (Ledingham,
1981; Ledingham & Schwartzman, 1984) than those who are primarily
socially withdrawn. These data support the view that low peer interaction rates alone cannot be used to select children currently experiencing
or at risk for social problems. Additional information on children's so-
cial-behavioral functioning is necessary to identify problematic children.

Related to this issue is the concern that rate-of-interaction measures
do not provide sufficient information about children's peer interactions
to specify the precise nature of the problems or delineate areas in need
of remediation. Some have coped with this difficulty by gathering more-
detailed observations on the quality of children's social behavior after

they have been identified as possible intervention participants (e.g., Greenwood, Todd, Hops, & Walker, 1982), or by incorporating additional measures, such as teacher and peer ratings, into the assessment procedures (Greenwood, Todd, Walker, & Hops, 1978; Greenwood, Walker, Todd, & Hops, 1976; Hops, Fleischman, Guild, Paine, Street, Walker, & Greenwood, 1978; Hops & Greenwood, 1981; Hops, Walker, & Greenwood, 1979). Thus, assessments of a qualitative nature, as well as input from teachers and peers, will be necessary to further document the nature of children's social problems.

Although it appears that the rate-of-interaction measure, in conjunction with other assessments, can identify "socially unresponsive" or "neglected" children, one further concern arises. Such selection procedures undoubtedly will exclude children who are high interactors, but who are actively disliked or rejected by peers. Gottman (1977b) found that, among preschoolers, low-interacting children were *less rejected* by their peers than those who interacted more frequently. Considering that peer ratings of rejection and dislike have demonstrated good predictive validity for later social maladjustment (Cowen, Pederson Babijian, Izzo, & Trost, 1973; Roff, Sells, & Golden, 1972), disliked children may be in greatest need of intervention for improved social functioning. Yet, these children are largely excluded by rate-of-interaction measures.

In addition to difficulties as a selection tool, serious problems have been noted when using rate-of-interaction as an intervention goal or to evaluate treatment outcome. Improving the frequency of a child's social interactions does not necessarily improve the *quality* of the social exchanges (Asher et al., 1981) or level of peer acceptance (Gottman, 1977a). It may, in fact, produce undesirable results. For example, Kirby and Toler (1970) increased the frequency of peer contacts in a low-interacting child, finding that the target child displayed increases in the frequency of negative as well as positive behaviors.

In another study, Walker and colleagues (Walker, Greenwood, Hops, & Todd, 1979) noted that efforts aimed at increasing peer interactions alone produced awkward and superficial conversational exchanges among children. These studies suggest that other aspects of peer interactions, most notably the *quality* of the behavior and the *duration* of reciprocal exchanges (Strain & Shores, 1977), are preferable to rate-of-interaction as intervention goals and measures of treatment outcome. The importance of targeting socially important behaviors for intervention and assessing treatment outcome has been emphasized (Gresham, 1981a; Strain & Shores, 1977).

Despite these limitations, rate-of-interaction measures have received some support. Hops (1983) noted that rates of *negative* behaviors among low-interacting children appear to be negligible, suggesting that the rate-of-interaction measure primarily reflects positive social behavior. Positive social behavior, in turn, has been related to children's social status. One study that supports this view (Greenwood et al., 1982) compared low-interacting preschoolers to middle and high interactors, finding that the low interactors were deficient in initiating and receiving positive social interactions; they also initiated fewer negative interactions.

All factors considered, it appears that rate-of-interaction measures can be useful for the purpose of initially identifying withdrawn or socially unresponsive children for intervention programs, especially when other selection criteria are included to ensure that social problems do exist. Additional assessments of the qualitative aspects of children's behavior will be necessary to determine the nature of the interaction problems and to document treatment effects. However, reliance on rate-of-interaction as a treatment selection criterion will likely lead to the exclusion of children who are high interactors but who are actively disliked or rejected by peers (e.g., Gottman, 1977b). Thus, considerable caution would appear to be warranted when considering the rate-of-interaction measure as a tool for subject selection or treatment outcome.

Qualitative Measures of Social Interaction

In contrast to the rate-of-interaction measure, observations that assess the qualitative aspects of children's social behavior generally have obtained more favorable validating support (Bonney & Powell, 1953; Campbell & Yarrow, 1961; Clifford, 1963; Gottman, Gonso, & Rasmussen, 1975; Green, Forehand, Beck, & Vosk, 1980; Gresham, 1981b; Hartup et al., 1967; Hymel et al., 1981; Lippit, 1941; Marshall, 1957; Marshall & McCandless, 1957; Masters & Furman, 1981; McCandless & Marshall, 1957; Moore & Updegraff, 1964; Rubin & Hayvren, 1981; Rubin & Maioni, 1975; Vosk, Forehand, Parker, & Richard, 1982). Studies examining the relationships between positive and negative social behaviors and children's social competence, as assessed by peer ratings of acceptance and rejection, date back to the 1950s and 1960s and provide much of the basis for the observational codes employed today.

Generally speaking, assessments of qualitative aspects of peer interactions possess several distinct advantages relative to simple interaction measures. First, they provide more-specific information about the kinds of behaviors children display with peers, and thus, they may be more revealing in terms of the nature of children's social difficulties. Second, qualitative measures can be more informative regarding the specific impact of social interventions on children's peer contacts. Most importantly, there appears to be greater support for the validity of qualitative measures as indices of children's social competence. These issues are discussed, shortly, in greater detail.

Children's positive and negative social behaviors appear to be differentially related to indices of social competence. Evidence suggests that popular children engage in more friendly and positive interactions, whereas actively disliked and rejected children display more aggressive and aversive social behaviors than other children (Hartup, 1983). Accordingly, these qualitative aspects of peer interactions are discussed separately.

Positive Social Behavior

Definitions of positive or "socially approved" (Green & Forehand, 1980) behaviors have varied considerably across studies. However, many of the codes commonly employed by developmental and clinical researchers have been based on those originally developed by Hartup and colleagues to assess positive, "reinforcing" behaviors (Charlesworth & Hartup, 1967; Hartup, Glazer, & Charlesworth, 1967).

In these classic works with preschool children, positive reinforcement was defined as encompassing four major types of social behavior: (1) *giving positive attention and approval,* such as by attending, offering praise and approval, offering instrumental help, smiling and laughing, and general conversation; (2) *giving affection and personal acceptance,* both physical and verbal; (3) *submission,* which included passive acceptance, imitation, sharing, accepting another's idea or help, allowing another child to play, compromising, or following an order or request with pleasure and cooperation; and (4) *token giving,* which referred to spontaneously giving physical objects, such as toys or food (Charlesworth & Hartup, 1967, p. 995). This behavioral code was based on Skinner's (1953) writings on generalized social reinforcers. Since then, similar codes have been in widespread use with preschool (Furman & Masters, 1980; Greenwood et al., 1982; Hymel et al., 1981; Masters & Furman, 1981) and school-aged children (Gottman et al., 1975; Green et al., 1980; Gresham, 1981b; Vosk et al., 1982).

The main strength of this qualitative index of social behavior lies in its concurrent validity. Children who are well liked or highly accepted by peers consistently have been found to engage in higher rates of positive social behavior with peers (Hartup et al., 1967; Hymel et al., 1981; Masters & Furman, 1981; Green et al., 1980; Gottman et al., 1975; Milich & Landau, 1984). Moreover, several social intervention studies have obtained increases in children's positive social behavior as an outcome of treatment (Furman et al., 1979; Gresham & Nagle, 1980; Jakibchuk & Smeriglio, 1976; Keller & Carlson, 1974; Ladd, 1981; Ragland, Kerr, & Strain, 1981; Strain, Shores, & Kerr, 1976), though this has not been uniformly the case (e.g., Gottman, Gonso, & Schuler, 1976; Oden & Asher, 1977).

It is noteworthy, however, that positive behaviors generally do not relate to measures of peer rejection or dislike (Gottman et al., 1975; Green et al., 1980; Hartup et al., 1967; Hymel et al., 1981; Masters & Furman, 1981). Even children who are rejected by peers engage in positive interactions and social approach behaviors at a fairly high rate (Coie & Kupersmidt, 1983; Dodge, 1983; Dodge et al., 1982; Hartup et al., 1967). Apparently, other behavioral and nonbehavioral factors contribute to negative peer status.

The relationship between positive social behavior and peer acceptance must be qualified by the age of the children observed. Asher and Hymel (1981) noted that correlations between positive social initiations and peer acceptance have been most consistent for preschoolers and more equivocal for school-age children. Some recent work suggests that popular elementary school children may be the recipients of more positive behaviors from peers (Dodge, 1983; Foster & Ritchey, 1983; Gottman et al., 1975), though they may not initiate at higher rates than others. Differences across studies in the behavioral codes employed have obscured findings in this area. For instance, Gottman and colleagues (Gottman et al., 1975), using a modified version of the Hartup et al. code, examined behavioral differences between high- and low-status third- and fourth-grade children. The two social status groups did not differ significantly in positive interactions *initiated* toward peers, although the popular children were the *recipients* of more positive overtures from others.

Using similar behavioral categories with third-graders, Green and associates (Green et al., 1980) found that the rate of positive peer interactions was related to peer ratings of acceptance, though their coding did not permit a differentiation between initiating and receiving. It is possible that greater peer initiations toward the accepted children could have accounted for their results.

In a similar study with third- and fourth-graders (Vosk et al., 1982), peer acceptance was unrelated to the children's frequency of positive interactions. However, the behavioral code for positive interactions included contacts with both peers and teachers, rather than peer interactions alone. As a consequence, it is difficult to ascertain whether positive interactions relate differently to social status among older children or

whether variability in coding categories have contributed to the equivocal findings in this area.

Although positive social behavior, as a qualitative index of social interactions, represents a significant improvement over the rate-of-interaction measures, several important limitations remain. First of all, this
category of behavior is a very global one, encompassing a host of more
specific, though still fairly general, prosocial behaviors (e.g., smiling
and laughing, sharing, helping, cooperation). Specific behavioral
strengths and deficits, which could be translated into intervention goals,
are not possible to obtain from such a global behavioral measure.

Similarly, assessing treatment outcome with this measure is problematic, as little information is provided on the kinds of interactions that
were most affected by intervention. This lack of specificity has led behavioral researchers to examine more discrete observational categories
for assessing social deficits and evaluating treatment effects. Categories
such as conversation skills (Bierman & Furman, 1984), smiling, sharing,
compliments, and positive physical contact (Cooke & Apolloni, 1976), or
asking questions, leading, and offering support to peers (Ladd, 1981)
have been included in several intervention studies. Others have considered even more molecular behaviors, such as eye contact, speech duration, and number of requests, as components of assertiveness (Bornstein, Bellack, & Hersen, 1977) or questions, positive feedback, and
amount of time talked, as indicators of conversation skills (Minkin,
Braukmann, Minkin, Timbers, Timbers, Fixen, Phillips, & Wolf, 1976).

Considerable caution is essential with this more-specific observational
approach, however, as the more discrete behavioral categories do not
necessarily have the same validity and psychometric support as the
global measures of social reinforcement. Clearly, greater attention needs
to be devoted to empirically determining specific components of the
various social behaviors that contribute to positive peer interactions
(e.g., components of helping, sharing, conversation skills), and the
likely impact of component behaviors on peers. Many social skills intervention programs have derived their content from the literature on positive social behaviors (e.g., Gresham & Nagle, 1980; Ladd, 1981; La Greca
& Santogrossi, 1980; Oden & Asher, 1977), yet few specific, empirically
based skill components can be identified.

A second major shortcoming inherent in observing rates of positive
social behavior is that the skillfulness or appropriateness of the behavior
is not considered. Children may vary markedly in terms of how skillfully
they share or converse with others; such differences are not captured by
observational codes that concentrate on frequencies or rates of interactive behaviors. This poses a serious problem for evaluating treatment

outcome; children may become more skillful in their interactions as a result of intervention, but this will not be reflected in behavioral outcome measures focusing on interaction rates.

Work with adults stresses the importance of examining the timing and patterning of social behaviors, and not merely frequency (Fischetti, Curran, & Wessberg, 1977; Peterson, Fischetti, Curran, & Arland, 1981). Similar concerns apply to children. One means of determining skillfulness or effectiveness is by examining the impact of various social behaviors on peers, through sequential analyses of behavior—a topic we discuss shortly. Other methods, such as peer reports and subjective behavior ratings, may also be of merit.

A third major drawback of methodologies assessing frequency of positive behaviors is the monadic nature of the observational codes (Michelson, Foster, & Ritchey, 1981). Most often, only the behaviors of the target child (or children) are considered, and the impact of behavior on peers is largely ignored. Peer information can be tremendously useful for determining the importance of various behaviors for sustaining positive peer interactions. The particular social behaviors that tend to elicit positive and sustained interactive responses from peers are desirable skills to promote in children. However, even though coding methodologies have differentiated between behaviors that are initiated toward peers versus those that are responses to others' initiations, very few attempts have been made to examine behavioral sequences, as, for example, by coding and calculating the percentage of peer initiations that were responded to in various ways (e.g., positive, negative, or neutral responses). It is only very recently that behavioral sequences have begun to receive the attention they deserve (e.g., Dodge, 1983; Dodge et al., 1983; Putallaz, 1983; Putallaz & Gottman, 1981; Tremblay, Strain, Hendrickson, & Shores, 1981).

Finally, there is the issue of how to define positive interactions, or "what behavior belongs where?" Measures of positive social behavior have been criticized for including topographically different behaviors (e.g., sharing, conversation, affection) within the same category on an a priori basis (Michelson et al., 1981). Moreover, not all the behaviors included in positive interaction codes are necessarily positive (e.g., conversation); considerable variability across studies emerges in terms of the coding of potentially neutral behaviors. Some investigators code neutral behaviors separately (e.g., Furman & Masters, 1980; Gottman et al., 1975; Hymel et al., 1981), while many others have subsumed neutral behaviors within the positive interaction category (Foster & Ritchey, 1983; Gresham, 1981b; Vosk et al., 1982).

Furman and Masters (1080) addressed these two issues—a priori categorization of behaviors and the coding of neutral behaviors—by examining the correspondence between positive, negative, and neutral interactions categorized on the basis of an a priori classification (Hartup et al., 1967) versus on the effect the behaviors had on peers (i.e., produced a positive, negative, or neutral response). The neutral behavior category consisted primarily of behaviors that were not clearly positive or negative, such as visual attention and conversation. These authors obtained strong support for both types of coding classifications with preschoolers. Nevertheless, the authors point out that this does not validate the classification of all the specific behaviors within each category. It would be important to extend these findings by examining, on a more molecular level, the specific behaviors within each category and their impact on peers' responses. Clearly, more detailed investigations of specific categories of positive interactions (as well as negative and neutral interactions) are needed.

Another important finding in the Furman and Masters study was that neutral interactions comprised the majority of observed behaviors. The meaning of neutral interactions in children's peer relationships also warrants closer scrutiny; considerable variability is apparent in the treatment of neutral interactions across coding systems. While some studies found neutral and positive interactions to relate similarly to indices of social competence (e.g., Masters & Furman, 1981), this has not always been the case (Gottman et al., 1975; Hymel et al., 1981). Based on these results, investigators may be advised to consider the role of neutral interactions in children's peer relationships more carefully.

Negative Social Behavior

As was the case for positive social behavior, definitions of negative interactions have varied considerably across studies. The behavioral code employed by Hartup et al. (1967) has received the most attention. These authors defined negative interactions as "(a) *noncompliance* (refuse to submit or cooperate, withholding of positive reinforcement, ignoring overtures from 'other'), (b) *interference* (taking property, disrupting, or interfering with ongoing activities), (c) *derogation* (ridicule, disapproval, blaming, tattling, and (d) *attack* (aversive physical attacks, threats thereof, threatening demands)" (p. 1019, emphasis in original).

This behavioral category encompasses both verbally and physically aggressive behavior (e.g., hitting, fighting) as well as aversive, intrusive, and noncompliant acts. Numerous authors have used this broad category of negative interactions (e.g., Furman & Masters, 1980; Gresham, 1981b; Hymel et al., 1981; Vosk et al., 1982), although many have restricted their focus to the aggressive behavior component (e.g., Lesser, 1959; Olweus, 1979).

It is interesting to note that, to date, few intervention studies have monitored negative interactions (Furman et al., 1979; Greenwood et al., 1982; Gresham & Nagle, 1980; Pinkston, Reese, LeBlanc, & Baer, 1965), despite concerns that negative behavior change could result from intervention (Gottman, 1977a, 1977b; Kirby & Toler, 1970; Walker et al., 1979). In order to document treatment effectiveness, especially with rejected children who often display high rates of aggressive and aversive behaviors, it would seem essential to monitor changes in both negative and positive interactions.

The relationship between negative interaction and indices of children's social competence appears to be complex, though supportive of the concurrent validity of this observation code. When the general category of negative interaction is considered, it seems that children who engage in high rates of negative peer behaviors are more disliked or rejected by peers (Gottman, 1977b; Hartup et al., 1967; Hymel et al., 1981; Landau et al., 1984; Masters & Furman, 1981; Milich & Landau, 1984; Vosk et al., 1982), but are not necessarily less accepted (Bonney & Powell, 1953; Gottman et al., 1975; Green et al., 1980; Hartup et al., 1967; Landau et al., 1984). A generally similar pattern of relationships emerges for observation codes that specifically focus on physically aggressive behaviors, although there are some notable differences. Among preschoolers, the relationship between physical aggression and peer rejection has been supported (Dunnington, 1957; McGuire, 1973), however, more equivocal results have been obtained with elementary school children. Some authors found rejected children to be more physically aggressive (Dodge, 1983; Dodge et al., 1982) but others have not (Coie & Kupersmidt, 1983); still other investigators found aggressive behavior to be positively related to peer popularity (Campbell & Yarrow, 1961; Lesser, 1959).

One factor that may contribute to some of these equivocal findings concerns the lack of differentiation in the coding categories between appropriate and inappropriate forms of aggression. When distinctions between types of aggressive behavior have been made, it appears that well-liked children display more appropriate forms (Campbell & Yarrow, 1961; Lesser, 1959). For example, Lesser (1959) found that rejected children were more likely to display unprovoked aggressive behavior but, by contrast, provoked aggression (e.g., as in self-defense) was actually a correlate of popularity. Thus, aggressive behavior, per se, may have little implication for children's peer status unless more information about the form of the aggressive behavior is provided.

Viewing this issue from a slightly different perspective, Milich and Landau (1984) also distinguished between two different types of aggressive children: those who display more immature, disruptive, and poorly controlled behaviors versus those who may be disruptive, assertive, and controlling. The former group is consistent with descriptions of children who are rejected by peers, whereas the status of the latter group is more likely to be controversial—that is, the children are accepted by some and rejected by others (see Coie, Dodge, & Coppotelli, 1982; Coie & Kupersmidt, 1983). Again, this suggests that coding categories for negative behaviors may need to account for differences between these types of aggressive behaviors if they are to be sensitive to important social competence issues.

A developmental shift in the frequency and form of aggressive behavior may also explain the difficulty in obtaining a consistent relationship between physically aggressive behavior and social status in older children. It appears that base rates for aggressive behavior may increase during the early preschool years and then decline (Hartup, 1983). Rates of physically aggressive behavior have been reported to be very low among older children (Dodge et al., 1982; Foster & Ritchey, 1983). Moreover, when children's self-reports of strategies for handling peer conflict situations are considered, striking developmental changes emerge with a trend away from physical aggression in older children. Preschoolers and first graders typically report using physically aggressive behavior to resolve conflict, but older elementary school children report significantly fewer aggressive tactics and more assertive and verbal strategies (Wiley, 1983). (Also see Hartup, 1983, for a summary of developmental trends in aggressive behavior.) Thus, the frequency and form of aggressive behaviors may change, with perhaps more subtle, aversive, negative behaviors emerging at later ages—behaviors that may be very difficult to detect or code with existing naturalistic observation methodologies.

Unlike most of the literature described up to now, which has been correlational in focus, some recent evidence indicates that negative, aversive, and aggressive behaviors play a causative role in determining children's rejected peer status (Coie & Kupersmidt, 1983; Dodge, 1983; Dodge et al., 1983). For instance, Dodge (1983) observed unacquainted second grade males in small play groups for eight 1-hour sessions over a period of 2 weeks. At the completion of the study, children were interviewed about their feelings toward the other group members. Boys who came to be rejected by group members had displayed higher rates of aversive and physically aggressive behaviors than other boys. Thus, negative behaviors may be predictive of peer rejection, which in turn has demonstrated strong predictive validity for future mental health problems (Cowen et al., 1973; Roff et al., 1972). Moreover, an impressive and consistent finding in this area is that individual differences in aggressive and aversive behaviors appear to be very stable throughout middle childhood and adolescence (Cairns, 1983; Loeber, 1982; Olweus, 1979; Pulkkinen, 1982). Taken together, these studies provide some evidence for the predictive validity of observations of negative interactive behaviors.

Two general caveats pertain to negative peer interactions. First, as was the case with positive social behavior, the global category of negative interactions appears to have greater support for concurrent validity than the discrete components (other than perhaps aggression), yet the generality of this category masks a more detailed appreciation of which negative behaviors are most aversive to peers. Clearly, the impact of various negative behaviors needs to be examined. Negative behaviors may represent low frequency, but highly salient events in children's social interactions.

Secondly, the majority of studies, especially with children of school age and older, have focused exclusively on males (e.g., Coie & Kupersmidt, 1983; Dodge, 1983; Dodge et al., 1983; Milich & Landau, 1984; Olweus, 1979). Consequently, the obtained results are not generalizable to females. The glaring absence of females in research on negative social interactions among school-age children needs to be addressed in future endeavors.

Summary

In summary, qualitative measures of social behavior generally have received good support for their concurrent validity as measures of children's social competence. However, wide variation in the specific behavioral codes employed by investigators was noted. Major drawbacks to the qualitative measures have been the global nature of the observation codes and the absence of empirically based information on specific behavioral components of the interaction categories. These problems have limited the clinical utility of qualitative measures for pinpointing targets for intervention and, subsequently, documenting treatment outcome. Studies of naturalistic observations that examine the impact of various social behaviors on peers and that consider the patterning of behaviors, as may be possible with sequential data analyses, will be important directions for the future. Finally, research that validates components of qualitative categories, examines the role of "neutral" behaviors more carefully, and attends more closely to sex differences and developmental parameters, will be of major interest.

Sequential Observation Codes

Despite a long history of research emphasizing the reciprocal nature of children's social interactions (e.g., Charlesworth & Hartup, 1967; Hartup, 1970, 1983; Hartup et al., 1967; Leiter, 1977; Strain & Shores, 1977), as well as the noted importance of examining the differential impact of various social behaviors on peers (Furman & Masters, 1980; Strain & Shores, 1977), investigation of sequential aspects of children's peer interactions has just begun. One impetus for growth in this area has been the advent of sophisticated methodological and statistical approaches for studying sequential data (see Cairns, 1979; Castellan, 1979; Gottman & Notarius, 1978; Sackett, 1978; Yarrow & Waxler, 1979).

Although this is an important new avenue for exploration, it is a difficult one. Interactional data and behavioral sequences are much more difficult to observe and code than behavioral frequencies. Special difficulties and complexities arise in assessing the reliabilities of behaviors coded in sequential fashion. For example, agreement on the interaction sequence rather than on a simple behavioral occurrence must be assessed (see Gottman & Parkhurst, 1980). Complexities in data analyses also arise (Castellan, 1979). Moreover, detailed sequential analyses are difficult to code in naturalistic settings, often requiring that interactions be videotaped for later scoring (e.g., Dodge, 1983; Gottman, 1983; Putallaz, 1983; Putallaz & Gottman, 1981).

On the positive side, sequential analyses can reveal aspects of peer interactions that cannot be obtained from other observation methods. In particular, as previously discussed, this methodology can be employed to determine the general effectiveness of specific social behaviors or patterns of behavior. Such information may be invaluable for developing appropriate behavioral content for social intervention programs.

Efforts to examine children's social interactions in sequential fashion have included work on peer group entry strategies (Dodge, 1983; Dodge et al., 1983; Putallaz, 1983; Putallaz & Gottman, 1981), the process of acquaintanceship and friendship development (Gottman, 1983), and the effectiveness of various social behaviors for sustaining peer interactions (Tremblay, Strain, Hendrickson, & Shores, 1981). Little attention has been devoted, as yet, to including sequential analyses in treatment–outcome research, though this would be an important consideration for the future.

In order to illustrate the potential advantages of the sequential observation approach, two studies are described. Tremblay and colleagues (Tremblay et al., 1981) used sequential coding of behaviors to empirically identify socially effective target behaviors that could form the basis of a social intervention program for withdrawn preschoolers. Sixty preschool children were observed during free play activities for a total of 60 minutes per child. Each target child's behavior was coded for 12 behavioral categories: statements, commands, questions, play organizer, vocal attention, vocal imitation, attention seeking, imitation, sharing, assistance, affection, and rough-and-tumble play. In addition, the responses made by a second child (within 3 seconds) to any of these behaviors were recorded as either positive, negative, or no response; target behaviors that followed these responses were also coded. In order to simplify the recording of interactive behaviors within the natural setting, only behavioral sequences that were initiated by the target children were considered. Conditional probabilities were computed to assess the likelihood of each target behavior meeting with a specific peer response.

Of particular interest was the finding that the most frequently occurring behaviors were not the ones that were most likely to receive positive peer responses. This highlights the danger in examining behavioral frequencies alone, as it is tempting to view the most frequent behaviors as the most important even though, in fact, this may not be the case.

The authors also identified several socially effective behaviors, as determined by peers' responses. The behaviors that were associated with a greater than 50% chance of receiving a positive peer response were rough and tumble play (92%), sharing (79%), play organizer (67%), assistance (63%), affection (56%), and questions (51%). This information can be directly translated into appropriate goals for social intervention with preschool children.

An example of a more detailed and intensive approach to sequential interactions is the work by Dodge and colleagues (Dodge, 1983; Dodge et al., 1983). Dodge et al. (1983) described two studies that employed sequential analyses to determine patterns of social behavior leading to children's successful entry into a group of peers. In one of these, 7- and 8-year-old males were observed interacting with previously unacquainted peers in a play group for eight 1-hour sessions over a 2-week period; the free-play situation approximated that of a natural classroom setting. The particular behavioral situation of interest was that of joining peers or entering ongoing peer activities. Joining skills or peer-group entry behaviors have been included in several social intervention programs (e.g., La Greca & Santogrossi, 1980; O'Connor, 1972), though the specific components of an effective and developmentally appropriate entry strategy had not been previously delineated. Several specific entry behaviors or tactics were coded: group-oriented statements or questions, wait and hover, attention getting, self-referent statements, disruption, and mimicking the peer group. The peer groups' responses to each entry tactic were coded as positive, negative, or neutral. All play sessions were videotaped for later coding. At the end of the 2 weeks, sociometric interviews were conducted to determine the children's play-group peer status (rejected, neglected, popular, average, or controversial).

Analyses of frequencies of the six entry tactics did not reveal notable differences among the social status groups. However, sequential analyses disclosed that attention-getting and disruptive tactics were more likely to receive negative peer reactions than other behaviors, whereas group-oriented statements and mimicking the group had a high likelihood of receiving a positive response. Waiting and hovering tactics tended to receive neutral and ignoring responses. Further examination of three-step sequences, and the associated conditional probabilities of positive peer responses at each step, uncovered a particularly successful entry strategy. This sequence involved the tactics of waiting and hovering, followed by mimicking the peer groups' activity, and finally making a statement about the ongoing activity.

This kind of detailed information in the impact and patterning of social behavior can be of considerable benefit for determining developmentally appropriate behavioral strategies for improving children's social participation. Clearly, the use of sequential analyses for understanding social processes in children will be of continued interest and importance.

METHODOLOGICAL AND CONCEPTUAL ISSUES

Aside from the assets and limitations of particular observational methods, several broad issues germane to naturalistic observations are important to consider and merit careful thought. Attention is devoted to several such issues, including the validation of behavioral observations, situational specificity of children's social behavior, developmental concerns, and gender differences in children's peer interactions.

Validating Behavioral Observations

Throughout this chapter, mention has been made of peer ratings of acceptance and rejection (i.e., sociometric measures) as standards against which behavioral codes have been validated. The main reason for this emphasis, both within this chapter and in the literature in general, has been evidence that supports the predictive validity of peer ratings for children's future emotional functioning (e.g., Cowen et al.,

1973; Roff et al., 1972). (See chapter 6, this volume, for a detailed review of children's sociometrics.) While this is certainly an asset, several apparent limitations of sociometric measures will affect their utility as validation tools. Consequently, several difficulties associated with sociometric assessment are discussed briefly, as well as alternate validation strategies.

First, implicit in the use of peer ratings for validating behavioral measures is the assumption that the two measures are tapping the same underlying construct (Meehl, 1955). However, sociometric measures and observational assessments may be tapping different dimensions of social competence, as evidenced by the low-to-moderate level of correlations between them obtained in the vast majority of studies. Nor does it appear reasonable to expect higher correlations between the measures, as a host of different factors influence each of them. A wealth of data on sociometrics has indicated that multiple factors may determine a child's peer status, and social behavior is just one. Several excellent reviews (Asher, Oden, & Gottman, 1977; Hartup, 1970, 1983) noted the potential importance of physical attractiveness, children's names, academic achievement, athletic ability, and so on, for children's peer status. Social interactions, on the other hand, are known to be influenced by situational variables (e.g., Dodge et al., 1982; Rose, Blank, & Spalter, 1975) or the kinds of games and toys available for play (Quilitch & Risley, 1973). The extant literature does not provide clear indication that sociometrics and observational measures tap the same social construct. (Also see Gresham, 1981b, for a discussion of this point.)

When sociometrics assessments are employed for validation, a second issue emerges concerning their reliability and predictive validity with preschoolers. Many investigators (e.g., Greenwood, Walker, Todd, & Hops, 1977; Greenwood et al., 1982; Moore & Updegraff, 1964) have obtained low reliability estimates when using peer nomination methods (i.e., nominating three liked and three disliked peers) with preschoolers. This contrasts markedly with the observed stability of sociometric measures with older children (e.g., Busk, Ford, & Schulman, 1973; Coie & Dodge, 1983). Asher and colleagues (Asher, Singleton, Tinsley, & Hymel, 1979) demonstrated higher and more-acceptable reliability using a peer-rating sociometric (i.e., rating all peers on a Likert-type scale). Despite this psychometric advantage, investigators have just begun to use the rating scale sociometric with preschoolers (Hymel et al., 1981; Rubin & Clark, 1983). Even with this methodological improvement, acceptable reliability may be difficult to obtain with children under 4 years of age, and thus the utility of peer ratings for such young children has been seriously questioned (Hymel, 1983). Moreover, it still remains to be shown that preschool sociometrics are predictive of later social functioning. The current evidence for the predictive validity of peer ratings is based on children of school age; no studies have examined this important issue for preschool children (Hymel, 1983). In view of these difficulties, additional or alternative measures of social competence, such as teacher ratings, should be considered for validation studies with preschool children.

A third important concern, germane to validation, is the relative independence of children's ratings of peer acceptance and rejection (Goldman, Corsini, & de Urioste, 1980). Much of the literature on behavioral correlates of sociometric status has been muddled by the manner in which peer status was assessed. Oftentimes ratings of acceptance and rejection have been used interchangeably, even though measures of acceptance and rejection have very different behavioral correlates. Formulations of children's peer status have become refined to the point of identifying specific subgroups of children that differ in meaningful ways (Dodge et al., 1982; Gottman, 1977b). (Even this work has been conducted almost exclusively with school-age children.) The implication is that difficulties in previous attempts to validate behavioral coding methodologies must be tempered to some extent by the limitations inherent in prior methods for assessing children's social status. By neglecting to simultaneously account for children's acceptance and rejection status, many behavioral studies may have limited or confused their findings.

While peer sociometric measures will undoubtedly continue to serve as an important index of social competence for validating behavioral observation codes, these aforementioned difficulties should also lead investigators to consider other validation sources. With preschoolers, in particular, evidence suggests that teacher ratings may be reliable and valid indicators of social functioning; their correspondence to behavioral observations, and other social competence indicators, has been quite good (Connolly & Doyle, 1981; Greenwood, Walker, Todd, & Hops, 1976; Milich, Landau, Kilby, & Whitten, 1982; Rubin & Clark, 1983; Walker et al., 1979).

Evidence for the validity of teacher ratings of social competence has been more equivocal with older children (see Green et al., 1980; La Greca, 1981). Some problems with teacher ratings of children's likeability have been noted (La Greca, 1981); it is possible that, for school-age children, teachers may be better judges of noxious, aversive behaviors than of positive peer interactions. One study with third-graders found that peer ratings predicted positive peer interactions better than teacher ratings, but that teacher ratings were better predictors of negative interactions (Green et al., 1980). Because teachers continue to serve as a major referral source for children's social and emotional problems, the utility of teacher ratings as an index of social competence should be investigated further.

Other methods of validation need be considered as well. It is perhaps fair to say that the developmental and behavioral literatures have taken divergent paths to examining the utility of naturalistic observations of children's social behavior. The developmental area has focused on comparisons between behavioral observations and other general indices of social competence, most notably peer sociometrics. In contrast, the behavioral literature has concentrated on normative analyses (e.g., Greenwood, Walker, Todd, & Hops, 1981) and the functional utility of behavioral categories. An approach that incorporates both types of strategies may be very desirable. (See Furman, 1980, for a further discussion of this issue.)

Situation and Context Effects

The situational specificity of social behavior has been widely recognized (e.g., Foster & Ritchey, 1979; Hersen & Bellack, 1977; McFall, 1982), yet few investigators have systematically examined situation and context effects on children's peer interactions. For the most part, behavioral observations of preschoolers have been conducted during unstructured free-play situations, whereas observations of older children are commonly summed across a variety of classroom and playground situations, including seatwork, small group work, and recess (e.g., Gottman et al., 1975). As a consequence, little is known about preschool children's interactions in more-structured situations, and the situational specificity of older children's behavior is totally masked.

Attempts to examine context effects on children's social behavior have been very informative. Rose, Blank, and Spalter (1975) rated preschoolers' behavior in several situations over a 4-month period: children playing alone but in the presence of peers; children playing with others; teacher-led group activities; and a test-taking situation. Behavior ratings covered areas such as cooperation, the quality and quantity of interaction, energy level, and relatedness to others. The authors found that behaviors within situations were stable after 4 months, but cross-situational variability was very high. Another study (Redman & La Greca, 1983) obtained marked differences in the social and play behaviors of preschool children depending on whether they were observed during unstructured free play, or a more structured table-play period.

With older children, Dodge et al. (1982) obtained significant setting effects for playground versus classroom observations, with greater frequencies of social approaches occurring on the playground and more task-appropriate solitary activity in the classroom. It was especially interesting to note that children who were rejected by peers made *more* prosocial approaches to peers in the classroom than average or popular children, but *fewer* on the playground. This points to the likely inappropriateness of the rejected children's positive approach behaviors—a finding that would have been masked by observations summed across playground and classroom settings.

Although situation and setting effects merit more attention in studies of children's social behavior, there is some debate over the degree to which situational parameters need be specified (Hops, 1983). Situational variability cannot be ignored, yet an exhaustive listing of children's social situations with accompanying analyses of effective social behaviors would be an enormous task. Perhaps a reasonable compromise is to concentrate on common social situations that contribute to initiating and maintaining positive peer interactions, or that may be helpful in resolving conflict situations (e.g., Asher & Renshaw, 1981). An example of this approach is the work of Putallaz and Dodge (e.g., Dodge et al., 1983; Putallaz & Gottman, 1981) on the identification of specific behavioral strategies that children use to enter dyads or small groups of peers. Further work of this kind area would be of considerable interest and utility.

Developmental Issues

Although all would agree that children's social behaviors undergo developmental change, there has not been sufficient emphasis on the developmental parameters that are important to peer relationships. By and large, studies have focused on relatively narrow age groups (e.g., preschoolers and third- and fourth-graders), rarely spanning more than a 2-year age range and, consequently, leaving certain gaps in our knowledge. Furthermore, broader developmental shifts in the quality, form, and importance of various social behaviors are masked by this narrow focus.

Hartup (1983) cogently summarizes age-related changes in children's social behavior, noting the preponderance of studies at the preschool level, and the paucity of observational research with preadolescents. During the preschool through adolescent years, a general increase is observed in children's positive peer interactions, and a decline in aggressive and negative interactions. However, changes in these global categories belie the growing sophistication in children's social skills.

Several points can be made, consonant with the need for a developmental perspective, that have implications for the kinds of behavior we observe in children and the importance of further refinements in our observation methodologies. First, children's social behavior becomes more complex over the preschool through middle childhood years (Hartup, 1983). Other sources of developmental data, such as children's self reports, suggest that the parameters of peer interactions become less obvious and more subtle and complex. Developmental trends in children's perceptions of others and ideas about friendship (Barenboim, 1981; Bigelow, 1977; Bigelow & La Gaipa, 1975; Livesley & Bromley, 1973; Peevers & Secord, 1972; Scarlett, Press, & Crocket, 1971) indicate a shift away from a focus on physical characteristics and observable behavior during the late preschool and early school years, to a focus on more-subtle, psychologically oriented characteristics in middle childhood through adolescence. Others have noticed increasing sophistication in children's strategies for handling peer conflict (Wiley, 1983) or gaining entry into peer groups (Lubin & Forbes, 1981). If the parameters of children's peer relationships change so dramatically, we should reflect this in observation codes as well. Asher and Hymel (1981) point out that behavioral codes developed for preschoolers (e.g., Hartup et al., 1967) have been commonly used with much older children. This being the case, it will be difficult to capture some of the complex and subtle aspects of older children's peer relationships. A closer examination of the developmental appropriateness of the behavioral categories now in use appears in order.

Second, there is likely to be a developmental shift in the importance of certain social behaviors, suggesting that different types of behavioral categories should be emphasized at different ages. For instance, concomitant with increasing verbal abilities and behavioral self-control, children's peer interactions may reflect a growing emphasis on verbal communication and other verbally oriented social skills. This should be reflected in a greater emphasis of such skills in our observation codes. One consequence, however, is that verbal skills may be much more difficult to observe in detail in natural settings than other kinds of behaviors (e.g., hitting), and may require more sophisticated observation codes and observation methods (e.g., audiotaping conversations).

Third, throughout this chapter we have underscored the importance of examining more specific behavioral components of global social behavior categories. Such a task requires a developmental framework. The specific components of behavioral categories will vary considerably across the preschool to elementary school years. Children's ideas about peer conflict resolution (Wiley, 1983) or how to help peers (Ladd & Oden, 1979) undergo change; tactics that are appropriate for a first-grader will not be suitable for an older child. (Hartup, 1983, notes other developmental shifts in aggression and altruism.) Thus, the components of qualitative indices of social behavior are likely to have strong developmental ties that need to be considered in our future research endeavors.

Sex Differences

Sex differences in children's social behavior, as they relate to peer relationships and interaction problems, also are an important avenue for further study (Hops, 1983). Little is known about the differential importance of various social behaviors for male-oriented versus female-oriented peer interactions. Yet, prior to adolescence, males and females prefer same-sex playmates (Hartup, 1983) and display notable differences in their social behavior and activity level (Rubin, Maioni, & Hornung, 1976).

Waldrop and Halverson (1975) studied patterns of social behavior among 7-year-old males and females. When playing with peers, boys tended to be more active than girls and engaged in more *extensive* peer contacts involving groups of boys. Girls, on the other hand, were observed to prefer quiet, *intensive* interactions that involved just one or two other peers. These differential patterns of peer interactions may have implications for the kinds of social skills that are important for males and females.

Based on these findings, one might speculate that group-oriented play skills and cooperative behavior may be more important for males, whereas conversation skills may be more critical for females. Another possible implication is that the parameters of children's peer-group entry behavior (e.g., Dodge, 1983) may be sex-related, although this has not been examined systematically. Entry strategies appropriate to large peer groups (as boys are inclined to participate in) may differ from those involved in joining a single peer or dyad (as girls may prefer).

Aside from positive social behaviors, sex differences in the frequency and form of aggressive and aversive behaviors have not been fully explored. In fact, as previously noted, females are seriously underrepresented in studies of negative interactions among school-age children. Further investigation of sex differences in children's positive and negative social behavior is clearly desirable.

CONCLUSIONS

In the present chapter we have reviewed major issues and procedures in the observational assessment of children's social behavior. By necessity, our coverage of the topic has been more illustrative than exhaustive or comprehensive. The reader is referred to several additional sources for discussions of other points of interest. For instance, there is some debate about the appropriate *level* of behavioral assessment, molar versus molecular (see Bellack, 1983), which we have alluded to in earlier discussions. Our own bias is that, at the present time, both levels of assessment are necessary. The molar or global behavioral measures relate well to other indices of social competence, yet the detailed, molecular assessments are important for targeting specific intervention goals. Both are essential for assessing intervention effects.

We have resisted the temptation to define children's social skills in this chapter. However, discussions of this topic can be found in McFall (1982), Foster and Ritchey (1979), and Putallaz and Gottman (in press). In addition, Furman (1980) presents an excellent discussion of the assets and limitations of normative approaches and methods of social validation, as they relate to observations of children's social behavior.

Looking back on the literature reviewed in this chapter, several general observations are in order. First, it is apparent that correlational approaches predominantly have been used to study children's social behavior. This, of course, limits the causal statements that can be made about children's social behavior and peer relationships. Alternate research strategies, particularly longitudinal or short-term longitudinal designs (e.g., Dodge et al., 1983), are necessary to supplement and extend existing findings.

Second, although we have discussed observations of children's social behavior in very general terms, individual differences in social functioning are also very important. Each child has his or her own unique strengths and limitations. General information on children's social behavior can provide very useful guidelines for behavioral assessment and intervention. However, each child's skills must be evaluated individually. We cannot assume, for example, that a particular rejected child is physically aggressive, just because peer rejection and physical aggression have been related.

Finally, observational assessment has played a critical role in our understanding of children's social functioning, and will continue to do so in the future. Yet we must not lose sight of the importance of a comprehensive approach to assessing children's social competence—comprehensive both in terms of the breadth of behaviors that are observed as well as the variety of assessment methods that are employed. A comprehensive approach is essential, if we are to better understand and appreciate the complexities of children's social behavior and peer relationships.

REFERENCES

Allen, K. E., Hart, B., Buell, J. S., Harris, F. R., & Wolf, M. M. (1964). Effects of social reinforcement of isolate behavior of a nursery school child. *Child Development, 35,* 511–518.

Asher, S. R., & Hymel, S. (1981). Children's social competence in peer relations: Sociometric and behavioral assessment. In J. D. Wine & M. D. Smye (Eds.), *Social competence.* New York: Guilford.

Asher, S. R., Markell, R. A., & Hymel, S. (1981). Identifying children at risk in peer relations: A critique of the rate-of-interaction approach to assessment. *Child Development, 52,* 1239–1245.

Asher, S. R., Oden, S. L., & Gottman, J. M. (1977). Children's friendships in school settings. In L. G. Katz (Ed.), *Current topics in early childhood education* (Vol. 1). Norwood, NJ: Ablex.

Asher, S. R., & Renshaw, P. D. (1981). Children without friends: Social knowledge and social skill training. In S. R. Asher & J. M. Gottman (Eds.), *The development of children's friendships.* New York: Cambridge University Press.

Asher, S. R., Singleton, L. C., Tinsley, B. R., & Hymel, S. (1979). A reliable sociometric measure for preschool children. *Developmental Psychology, 15,* 443–444.

Barenboim, C. (1981). The development of person perception in childhood and adolescence: From behavioral comparisons to psychological constructs to psychological comparisons. *Child Development, 52,* 129–144.

Bellack, A. S. (1983). Recurrent problems in the behavioral assessment of social skill. *Behavior Research and Therapy, 21,* 29–41.

Bierman, K. L. & Furman, W. (1984). The effects of social skills training and peer involvement on the social adjustment of preadolescents. *Child Development, 55,* 151–162.

Bigelow, B. J. (1977). Children's friendship expectations: A cognitive-developmental study. *Child Development, 48,* 246–253.

Bigelow, B. J., & LaGaipa, J. J. (1975). Children's written descriptions of friendship: A multidimensional analysis. *Developmental Psychology, 11,* 857–858.

Bonney, M. E., & Powell, J. (1953). Differences in social behavior between sociometrically high and sociometrically low children. *Journal of Educational Research, 46,* 481–496.

Bornstein, M., Bellack, A. S., & Hersen, M. (1977). Social skills training for unassertive children. *Journal of Applied Behavior Analysis, 10,* 183–195.

Busk, P. L., Ford, R. C., & Schulman, J. L. (1973). Stability of sociometric responses in classrooms. *Journal of Genetic Psychology, 123,* 69–84.

Cairns, R. B. (1979). Toward guidelines for interactional research. In R. B. Cairns (Ed.), *The analysis of social interactions: Methods, issues, and illustrations.* Hillsdale, NJ: Erlbaum.

Cairns, R. B. (1983). Sociometry, psychometry, and social structure: A commentary on six recent studies of popular, rejected, and neglected children. *Merril-Palmer Quarterly, 29,* 429–438.

Campbell, J. D., & Yarrow, M. R. (1961). Perceptual and behavioral correlates of social effectiveness. *Sociometry, 24,* 1–20.

Castellan, N. J. Jr. (1979). The analysis of behavior sequences. In R. B. Cairns (Ed.), *The analysis of social interactions: Methods, issues, and illustrations*. Hillsdale, NJ: Erlbaum.

Charlesworth, R., & Hartup, W. (1967). Positive social reinforcement in the nursery school peer group. *Child Development, 38,* 993–1002.

Clifford, E. (1963). Social visibility. *Child Development, 34,* 799–808.

Coie, J. D., & Dodge, K. A. (1983). Continuities and changes in children's social status: A five-year longitudinal study. *Merrill-Palmer Quarterly, 29,* 261–282.

Coie, J. D., Dodge, K. A., & Coppotelli, H. (1982). Dimensions and types of social status: A cross-age perspective. *Developmental Psychology, 18,* 557–570.

Coie, J. D., & Kupersmidt, J. B. (1983). A behavioral analysis of emerging social status in boy's groups. *Child Development, 54,* 1400–1416.

Combs, S. L., & Slaby, D. A. (1977). Social skills training with children. In B. B. Lahey & A. E. Kazdin (Eds.), *Advances in clinical child psychology* (Vol. 1). New York: Plenum.

Conger, J. C., & Keane, S. P. (1981). Social skills intervention in the treatment of isolated or withdrawn children. *Psychological Bulletin, 50,* 478–495.

Connolly, J., & Doyle, A. (1981). Assessment of social competence in preschoolers: Teachers versus peers. *Developmental Psychology, 17,* 454–462.

Cooke, T. P., & Apolloni, T. (1976). Developing positive social–emotional behaviors: A study of training and generalization effects. *Journal of Applied Behavior Analysis, 9,* 65–78.

Cowen, E. L., Pederson, A., Babigian, H., Izzo, L. D., & Trost, M. A. (1973). Long-term follow-up of early detected vulnerable children. *Journal of Consulting and Clinical Psychology, 41,* 438–446.

Deutsch, F. (1974). Observational and sociometric measures of peer popularity and their relationship to egocentric communication in female pre-schoolers. *Developmental Psychology, 10,* 745–747.

Dodge, K. A. (1983). Behavioral antecedents of peer social status. *Child Development, 54,* 1386–1399.

Dodge, K. A., Coie, J. D., & Brakke, N. P. (1982). Behavior patterns of socially rejected and neglected preadolescents: The roles of social approach and aggression. *Journal of Abnormal Child Psychology, 10,* 389–410.

Dodge, K. A., Schlundt, D. C., Schocken, I., & Delugach, J. D. (1983). Social competence and children's sociometric status: The role of peer group entry strategies. *Merrill-Palmer Quarterly, 29,* 309–336.

Dunnington, M. J. (1957). Behavioral differences of sociometric status groups in a nursery school. *Child Development, 28,* 103–111.

Evers, W. L., & Schwarz, J. C. (1973). Modifying social withdrawal in preschoolers: The effects of filmed modeling and teacher praise. *Journal of Abnormal Child Psychology, 1,* 248–256.

Fischetti, M., Curran, J. P., & Wessberg, H. W. (1977). Sense of timing: A skill deficit in heterosexually–socially anxious males. *Behavior Modification, 1,* 179–195.

Foster, S. L., & Ritchey, W. L. (1979). Issues in the assessment of social competence in children. *Journal of Applied Behavior Analysis, 12,* 625–638.

Foster, S. L., & Ritchey, W. L. (1983). *Behavioral correlates of sociometric status of fourth, fifth, and sixth-grade children in two classroom situations*. Manuscript submitted for publication.

Furman, W. (1980). Promoting social development: Developmental implications for treatment. In B. B. Lahey & A. E. Kazdin (Eds.), *Advances in clinical child psychology* (Vol. 3). New York: Plenum.

Furman, W., & Masters, J. C. (1980). Affective consequences of social reinforcement, punishment, and neutral behavior. *Developmental Psychology, 16,* 100–104.

Furman, W., Rahe, D. F., & Hartup, W. W. (1979). Rehabilitation of socially-withdrawn preschool children through mixed-age and same-age socialization. *Child Development, 50,* 915–922.

Goldman, J. A., Corsini, D. A., & de Urioste, R. (1980). Implications of positive and negative sociometric status for assessing the social competence of young children. *Journal of Applied Developmental Psychology, 1,* 209–220.

Gottman, J. M. (1977a). The effects of a modeling film on social isolation in preschool children: A methodological investigation. *Journal of Abnormal Child Psychology, 5,* 69–78.

Gottman, J. M. (1977b). Toward a definition of social isolation in children. *Child Development, 48,* 513–517.

Gottman, J. M. (1983). How children become friends. *Monographs of the Society for Research in Child Development, 48,* Serial No. 201.

Gottman, J. M., Gonso, J., & Rasmussen, B. (1975). Social interaction, social competence, and friendship in children. *Child Development, 46,* 709–718.

Gottman, J. M., Gonso, J., & Schuler, P. (1976). Teaching social skills to isolated children. *Journal of Abnormal Child Psychology, 4,* 179–198.

Gottman, J. M. & Notarius, C. (1978). Sequential analysis of observational data using Markov chains. In T. Kratochwill (Ed.), *Strategies to evaluate change in single subject research.* New York: Academic Press.

Gottman, J. M. & Parkhurst, J. (1980). The development of friendship and acquaintance-ship processes. In A. Collins (Ed.), *Minnesota symposium on child psychology* (Vol. 13). Hillsdale, NJ: Erlbaum.

Green, K. D., & Forehand, R. (1980). Assessment of children's social skills: A review of methods. *Journal of Behavioral Assessment, 2,* 143–159.

Green, K. D., Forehand, R., Beck, S. J., & Vosk, B. (1980). An assessment of the relationship among measures of children's social competence and children's academic achievement. *Child Development, 51,* 1149–1156.

Greenwood, C. R., Todd, N. M., Hops, H., & Walker, H. M. (1982). Behavior change targets in the assessment and treatment of socially withdrawn preschool children. *Behavioral Assessment, 4,* 273–297.

Greenwood, C. R., Todd, N. M., Walker, H. M., & Hops, H. (1978). *Social assessment manual for preschool level (SAMPLE).* Eugene: University of Oregon, Center at Oregon for Research in the Behavioral Education of the Handicapped.

Greenwood, C. R., Walker, H. M., & Hops, H. (1977). Some issues in social interaction/withdrawal assessment. *Exceptional Children, 43,* 490–499.

Greenwood, C. R., Walker, H. M., Todd, N. M., & Hops, H. (1976). *Preschool teachers' assessments of student social interaction: Predictive success and normative data* (Report No. 26). Eugene: Center at Oregon for Research in The Behavioral Education of the Handi-capped.

Greenwood, C. R., Walker, H. M., Todd, N. M., & Hops, H. (1977). *The utility of the peer nomination sociometric as a predictive variable in preschool social withdrawal* (Report No. 30). Eugene: Center at Oregon for Research in the Behavioral Education of the Handi-capped.

Greenwood, C. R., Walker, H. M., Todd, N. M., & Hops, H. (1981). Normative and descriptive analysis of preschool free play social interaction rates. *Journal of Pediatric Psychology, 6,* 343–367.

Gresham, F. M. (1981a). Social skills training with handicapped children: A review. *Review of Educational Research, 51,* 139–176.

Gresham, F. M. (1981b). Validity of social skills measures for assessing social competence in low-status children: A multivariate investigation. *Developmental Psychology, 17*, 390–398.

Gresham, F. M., & Nagle, R. J. (1980). Social skills training with children: Responsiveness to modeling and coaching as a function of peer orientation. *Journal of Consulting and Clinical Psychology, 48*, 718–729.

Gronlund, N. E., & Anderson, L. (1957). Personality characteristics of socially accepted, socially neglected, and socially rejected junior high school pupils. *Educational Administration and Supervision, 43*, 329–338.

Guralnick, M. J. (1980). Social interactions among preschool children. *Exceptional Children, 46*, 248–253.

Hartup, W. W. (1970). Peer interaction and social organization. In P. H. Mussen (Ed.), *Carmichael's manual of child psychology* (Vol. 2). New York: Wiley.

Hartup, W. W. (1983). Peer relations. In P. H. Mussen (Ed.), *Handbook of child psychology* (Vol. 4). New York: Wiley.

Hartup, W. W., Glazer, J. A., & Charlesworth, R. (1967). Peer reinforcement and sociometric status. *Child Development, 38*, 1017–1024.

Hersen, M., & Bellack, A. S. (1977). Assessment of social skills. In A. R. Ciminero, K. R. Calhoun, & H. E. Adams (Eds.), *Handbook of behavioral assessment*. New York: Wiley.

Hops, H. (1983). Children's social competence and skill: Current research practices and future directions. *Behavior Therapy, 14*, 3–18.

Hops, H., & Finch, M. A. (1982, May). *A skill deficit view of social competence in preschoolers*. Invited address to the 8th Annual Convention of the Association for Behavior Analysis, Milwaukee.

Hops, H., Fleischman, D. H., Guild, J., Paine, S., Street, H., Walker, H. M., & Greenwood, C. R. (1978). *Program for establishing effective relationships skills (PEERS): Consultant manual*. Eugene: University of Oregon, Center at Oregon for Research in the Behavioral Education of the Handicapped.

Hops, H., & Greenwood, C. R. (1981). Social skills deficits. In E. J. Mash & L. G. Terdal (Eds.), *Behavioral assessment of childhood disorders*. New York: Guilford.

Hops, H., Walker, H. M., & Greenwood, C. R. (1979). PEERS: A program for remediating social withdrawal in the school setting: Aspects of a research and development process. In L. A. Hamerlynck (Ed.), *The history and future of the developmentally disabled: Problematic and methodological issues*. New York: Brunner/Mazel.

Hymel, S. (1983). Preschool children's peer relations: Issues in sociometric assessment. *Merrill-Palmer Quarterly, 29*, 237–259.

Hymel, S., Tinsley, B. R., Geraci, R., & Asher, S. R. (1981). *Sociometric status and social skills: The initiating style of preschool children*, Unpublished manuscript, University of Illinois.

Jakibchuk, Z., & Smeriglio, V. (1976). Influence of symbolic modeling on social behavior of preschool children with low levels of social responsiveness. *Child Development, 47*, 838–841.

Jennings, K. D. (1975). People versus object orientation, social behavior, and intellectual abilities in children. *Developmental Psychology, 11*, 511–519.

Johnson, S. M., & Bolstad, O. D. (1973). Methodological issues in naturalistic observation: Some problems and solutions for field research. In L. A. Hamerlynck, L. C. Handy, & E. J. Mash (Eds.), *Behavior change: Methodology, concepts, and practice*. Champaign, IL: Research Press.

Kazdin, A. E. (1977a). Assessing the clinical or applied importance of behavior change through social validation. *Behavior Modification, 1*, 427–452.

Kazdin, A. E. (1977b). Artifact, bias and complexity of assessment: The ABC's of reliability. *Journal of Applied Behavior Analysis, 10*, 141–150.

Keller, M. F., & Carlson, P. M. (1974). The use of symbolic modeling to promote social skills in children with low levels of social responsiveness. *Child Development, 45,* 912–919.

Kent, R. N., & Foster, S. L. (1977). Direct observational procedures: Methodological issues in naturalistic settings. In A. R. Ciminero, K. S. Calhoun, & H. E. Adams (Eds.), *Handbook of behavioral assessment.* New York: Wiley.

Kirby, F. D., & Toler, Jr., H. C. (1970). Modification of preschool isolate behavior: A case study. *Journal of Applied Behavior Analysis, 3,* 309–314.

Krantz, M. (1982). Sociometric awareness, social participation, and perceived popularity in preschool children. *Child Development, 53,* 376–379.

Ladd, G. W. (1981). Effectiveness of a social learning method for enhancing children's social interaction and peer acceptance. *Child Development, 52,* 171–178.

Ladd, G. W., & Oden, S. (1979). The relationship between peer acceptance and children's ideas about helpfulness. *Child Development, 50,* 402–408.

La Greca, A. M. (1981). Peer acceptance: The correspondence between children's sociometric scores and teachers' ratings of peer interaction. *Journal of Abnormal Child Psychology, 9,* 167–178.

La Greca, A. M., & Santogrossi, D. A. (1980). Social skills training with elementary school students: A behavioral group approach. *Journal of Consulting and Clinical Psychology, 48,* 220–228.

Landau, S., Milich, R., & Whitten, P. (1984). A comparison of teacher and peer assessment of social status. *Journal of Clinical Child Psychology, 13,* 44–49.

Ledingham, J. E. (1981). Developmental patterns of aggressive and withdrawn behavior in childhood: A possible method for identifying preschizophrenics. *Journal of Abnormal Child Psychology, 9,* 1–22.

Ledingham, J. E., & Schwartzman, A. E. (1984). A 3-year follow-up of aggressive and withdrawn behavior in childhood: Preliminary findings. *Journal of Abnormal Child Psychology, 12,* 157–168.

Leiter, M. P. (1977). A study of reciprocity in preschool play groups. *Child Development, 48,* 1288–1295.

Lesser, G. S. (1959). The relationship between various forms of aggression and popularity among lower-class children. *Journal of Educational Psychology, 50,* 20–25.

Lippitt, R. (1941). Popularity among preschool children. *Child Development, 12,* 305–332.

Livesley, W. J., & Bromley, D. B. (1973). *Person perception in childhood and adolescence.* London: John Wiley.

Loeber, R. (1982). The stability of antisocial and delinquent child behavior: A review. *Child Development, 53,* 1431–1446.

Lubin, D., & Forbes, D. (1981, April). *Motivational and peer culture issues in reasoning–behavioral relations.* Presented at a symposium at the biennial meeting of the Society for Research in Child Development, Boston.

Marshall, H. R. (1957). An evaluation of sociometric-social behavior research with preschool children. *Child Development, 28,* 131–137.

Marshall, H. R., & McCandless, B. R. (1957). A study in prediction of social behavior of preschool children. *Child Development, 28,* 149–159.

Masters, J. C., & Furman, W. (1981). Popularity, individual friendship selection, and specific peer interaction among children. *Developmental Psychology, 17,* 344–350.

McCandless, B. R., & Marshall, H. R. (1957). A picture sociometric technique for preschool children and its relation to teacher judgments of friendship. *Child Development, 28,* 139–148.

McFall, R. M. (1982). A review and reformulation of the concept of social skills. *Behavioral Assessment, 4,* 1–33.

McGuire, J. M. (1973). Aggression and sociometric status with preschool children. *Sociometry, 36,* 542–549.

Meehl, P. (1955). Construct validity in psychological tests. *Psychological Bulletin, 52.*

Michael, C. M., Morris, D. P., & Soroker, E. (1957). Follow-up studies of shy, withdrawn children II: Relative incidence of schizophrenia. *American Journal of Orthopsychiatry, 27,* 331–337.

Michelson, L., Foster, S. L., & Ritchey, W. L. (1981). Social-skills assessment of children. In B. B. Lahey & A. E. Kazdin (Eds.), *Advances in clinical child psychology* (Vol. 4). New York: Plenum.

Milich, R., & Landau, S. (1984). A comparison of the social status and social behavior of aggressive and aggressive/withdrawn boys. *Journal of Abnormal Child Psychology, 12,* 277–288.

Milich, R., Landau, S., Kilby, G., & Whitten, P. (1982). Preschool peer perceptions of the behavior of hyperactive and aggressive children. *Journal of Abnormal Child Psychology, 10,* 497–510.

Minkin, N., Braukmann, C., Minkin, B., Timbers, G., Timbers, B., Fixsen, D., Phillips, E. L., & Wolf, M. M. (1976). The social validation and training of conversational skills. *Journal of Applied Behavior Analysis, 9,* 127–139.

Moore, S. G., & Updegraff, R. (1964). Sociometric status of preschool children related to age, sex, nurturance-giving, and dependence. *Child Development, 35,* 519–524.

Morris, D. P., Soroker, E., & Burruss, G. (1954). Follow-up studies of shy, withdrawn children: Evaluation of later adjustment. *American Journal of Orthopsychiatry, 24,* 743–755.

Mueller, E. (1972). The maintenance of verbal exchanges between young children. *Child Development, 43,* 930–938.

Mueller, E., & Brenner, J. (1977). The origins of social skills and interaction among play group toddlers. *Child Development, 48,* 854–861.

Mueller, E., & Vandell, D. (1979). Infant–infant interaction. In Osofsky, J. (Ed.), *Handbook of infant development.* New York: Wiley/Interscience.

Nelson, R. O., Kapust, J. A., & Dorsey, B. L. (1978). Minimal reactivity of overt classroom observations on student and teacher behaviors. *Behavior Therapy, 9,* 695–702.

O'Connor, R. D. (1969). Modification of social withdrawal through symbolic modeling. *Journal of Applied Behavior Analysis, 2,* 15–22.

O'Connor, R. D. (1972). Relative efficacy of modeling, shaping, and the combined procedures for modification of social withdrawal. *Journal of Abnormal Psychology, 79,* 327–334.

Oden, S., & Asher, S. R. (1977). Coaching children in social skills for friendship making. *Child Development, 48,* 495–506.

O'Leary, K. D., & Kent, R. (1973). Behavior modification for social action: Research tactics and problems. In L. A. Hamerlynck, L. C. Handy, & E. J. Mash (Eds.), *Behavior change: Methodology, concepts, and practice.* Champaign, IL: Research Press.

Olweus, D. (1979). Stability of aggressive reaction patterns in males: A review. *Psychological Bulletin, 86,* 852–875.

Peevers, B. H., & Secord, P. F. (1972). Developmental changes in attribution of descriptive concepts to persons. *Journal of Personality and Social Psychology, 27,* 120–128.

Peterson, J., Fischetti, M., Curran, J. P., & Arland, S. (1981). Sense of timing: A skills deficit in heterosocially anxious women. *Behavior Therapy, 12,* 195–201.

Pinkston, E. M., Reese, N. M., LeBlanc, J. M., & Baer, D. M. (1965). Independent control of a preschool child's aggression and peer interaction by contingent teacher attention. *Journal of Applied Behavior Analysis, 6,* 115–124.

Pulkkinen, L. (1982). Self-control and continuity from childhood to late adolescence. In P.

B. Baltes & O. G. Brim, Jr. (Eds.), *Life-span development and behavior* (Vol. 4). New York: Academic Press.

Putallaz, M. (1983). Predicting children's sociometric status from their behavior. *Child Development, 54*, 1417–1426.

Putallaz, M., & Gottman, J. M. (1981). An interactional model of children's entry into peer groups. *Child Development, 52*, 986–994.

Putallaz, M., & Gottman, J. M. (in press). Conceptualizing social competence in children. In P. Karoly & J. J. Steffen (Eds.), *Advances in child behavior analysis and therapy* (Vol. 2). New York: Gardner Press.

Quilitch, H. R., & Risley, T. R. (1973). The effects of play materials on social play. *Journal of Applied Behavior Analysis, 6*, 573–578.

Ragland, E. U., Kerr, M. M., & Strain, P. S. (1981). Social play of withdrawn children. *Behavior Modification, 5*, 347–359.

Redman, T. A., & La Greca, A. M. (1983). *Sex differences in children's social and play behavior: The effects of play settings.* Unpublished manuscript, University of Miami.

Robins, L. N. (1974). *Deviant children grow up.* Huntington, NY: Robert E. Krieger.

Roff, M., Sells, S. B., & Golden, M. M. (1972). *Social adjustment and personality development in children.* Minneapolis: University of Minnesota Press.

Rose, S. A., Blank, M., Spalter, I. (1975). Situational specificity of behavior in young children. *Child Development, 46*, 464–469.

Rubin, K. H. (1982). Nonsocial play in preschoolers: Necessary evil? *Child Development, 53*, 651–657.

Rubin, K. H., & Clark, M. L. (1983). Preschool teachers' ratings of behavioral problems: Observational, sociometric, and social–cognitive correlates. *Journal of Abnormal Child Psychology, 11*, 273–286.

Rubin, K. H., & Hayvren, M. (1981). The social and cognitive play of preschool-aged children in an integrated school district. *Journal of Research and Development in Education, 14*, 116–122.

Rubin, K. H., & Maioni, T. L. (1975). Play preference and its relationship to egocentrism, popularity, and classification skills in preschoolers. *Merrill-Palmer Quarterly, 21*, 171–179.

Rubin, K. H., Maioni, T. L., & Hornung, M. (1976). Free-play behaviors in middle and lower class preschoolers: Parten and Piaget revisited. *Child Development, 47*, 414–419.

Sackett, G. P. (Ed.). (1978). *Observing behavior: Data collection and analysis.* Baltimore: University Park Press.

Scarlett, H. H., Press, A. N., & Crockett, W. H. (1971). Children's descriptions of peers: A Wernerian developmental analysis. *Child Development, 42*, 439–453.

Skinner, B. F. (1953). *Science and human behavior.* New York: Macmillan.

Strain, P. S. (1977). An experimental analysis of peer social initiations on the behavior of withdrawn preschool children: Some training and generalization effects. *Journal of Abnormal Child Psychology, 5*, 445–455.

Strain, P. S., Cooke, T. P., & Apolloni, T. (1976). *Teaching exceptional children: Assessing and modifying social behavior.* New York: Academic Press.

Strain, P. S., & Shores, R. E. (1977). Social reciprocity: Review of research and educational implications. *Exceptional Children, 43*, 526–531.

Strain, P. S., Shores, R. E., & Kerr, M. M. (1976). Experimental analysis of spillover effects on social interaction of behaviorally handicapped preschool children. *Journal of Applied Behavior Analysis, 9*, 31–40.

Tremblay, A., Strain, P. S., Hendrickson, J. M., & Shores, R. E. (1981). Social interactions of normal preschool children. *Behavior Modification, 5*, 237–253.

Van Hasselt, V. B., Hersen, M., Whitehill, M. B., & Bellack, A. S. (1979). Social skill assessment and training: An evaluative review. *Behavior Research and Therapy, 17,* 413–437.

Vosk, B., Forehand, R., Parker, J. B., & Rickard, K. (1982). A multimethod comparison of popular and unpopular children. *Developmental Psychology, 18,* 571–575.

Waldrop, M. F., & Halverson, C. F., Jr. (1975). Intensive and extensive peer behavior: Longitudinal and cross-sectional analyses. *Child Development, 46,* 19–26.

Walker, H. M., Greenwood, C. R., Hops, H., & Todd, N. M. (1979). Differential effects of reinforcing topographic components of social interaction: Analysis and direct replication. *Behavior Modification, 3,* 291–321.

Walker, H. M., & Hops, H. (1973). The use of group and individual reinforcement contingencies in the modification of social withdrawal. In L. A. Hamerlynck, L. C. Hardy, & E. J. Mash (Eds.), *Behavior change: Methodology, concepts, and practice.* Champaign, IL: Research Press.

Wanlass, R. L. & Prinz, R. J. (1982). Methodological issues in conceptualizing and treating childhood social isolation. *Psychological Review, 92,* 39–55.

Wiley, P. D. (1983, May). Development of strategies for coping with peer conflict in children from first through fifth grade. In R. K. Ullmann (Chair), *Assessment of children's social knowledge and attitudes: Coping with peer conflict.* Paper presented at the Annual Meeting of the Association for Behavior Analysis, Milwaukee.

Wolf, M. M. (1978). Social validity: The case for subjective measurement or how applied behavior analysis is finding its heart. *Journal of Applied Behavior Analysis, 11,* 203–214.

Yarrow, M. R., & Waxler, C. Z. (1979). Observing interaction: A confrontation with methodology. In R. B. Cairns (Ed.), *The analysis of social interactions: Methods, issues, and illustrations.* Hillsdale, NJ: Erlbaum.

CHAPTER 6

Sociometrics: Peer-Referenced Measures and the Assessment of Social Competence*

Scott R. McConnell
Samuel L. Odom

INTRODUCTION

Scientific interest in the processes underlying social development in children has come to the forefront of scholarly activity in psychology and education since the mid-1970s. Contemporary social scientists are rapidly extending the research literature and knowledge base regarding children's social development. Spurred on by findings suggesting that social skills deficits in early childhood are stable over time and may be predictive of social adjustment problems in later years, researchers have developed social skills training programs reflecting a variety of theoretical perspectives for teaching socially skillful behavior to children (see Michelson & Mannarino, this volume).

With increased attention to the identification, measurement, and treatment of social skills deficits has come a need for thorough evalua-

* This manuscript was prepared with the assistance of Department of Education Grant Number G00-82-00051 and Contract Number 300-82-0368. However, the opinions expressed herein do not necessarily reflect the positions or policy of the U.S. Department of Education, and no official endorsement should be inferred. The authors also gratefully acknowledge the assistance of Jamey Pentek, Jacqueline Molinaro, Michelle Bourgeois, and Kathleen Edwards in the preparation of the manuscript.

tion of the success of social skills training programs. Sociometric assessment has been proposed as one of several outcome or criterion measures that should be used in gauging the effects of interventions that promote children's socially competent behavior (Foster & Ritchey, 1979; Gresham, 1981a). Other researchers have suggested that sociometric assessments may be the *best* available measure of social competence in children (Asher, Markell, & Hymel, 1981; Gresham, 1983b) and the criterion measure against which other measures of social behavior should be compared (Gresham, this volume).

At least two problems arise when sociometric assessment is used as *the* criterion measure of social competence and/or the primary dependent measure of social skills training. First, sociometrics, though implicitly categorized as a uniform methodology, actually encompasses a number of differing methodologies. Even when similar assessment methods are used, differing test criteria (i.e., test items) make direct comparison among sociometric studies difficult. Similarly, data from different studies using identical methods and criteria are often analyzed in markedly different manners. Thus, when referring to sociometric status and social competence in synonymous terms, one must acknowledge that the definition of social competence will vary greatly depending on the type of sociometric measure employed.

A second problem relates to the multidetermined nature of sociometric status. In addition to the actual skills used in social interchanges with peers, a variety of other child-specific factors or characteristics that are not necessarily social in nature (e.g., gender, race, physical attractiveness) may affect status measures. These personal characteristics may affect social behavior among peers to some degree, but the existence of a direct relationship between these variables and social competence is tenuous at best.

Given these concerns, the frequent use of sociometric assessment as *the* primary measure of social competence and as an outcome variable for social skills training programs requires critical evaluation. The purposes of this chapter are (1) to examine critically the commonly employed rationales for using sociometrics as measures of social competence, (2) to describe the multiple methodologies employed in the assessment of sociometric status and to delineate the various forms of data analysis used for these methodologies, (3) to review the social and nonsocial variables associated with sociometric status, (4) to discuss the relationship of sociometric measurement to other forms of social skills assessment, and (5) to propose a model for including sociometrics as one component in the overall assessment of social competence.

SOCIOMETRICS AND SOCIAL COMPETENCE: DEFINITIONS AND COMMONLY EMPLOYED RATIONALES

Definitional and Historical Issues

Specific definitions for sociometric methodology have varied widely since the mid-1930s. The sociometric and social skills training literatures have been plagued by ambiguous terminology and loosely conceptualized rationales. In this section, we define, for our use, such common terms as *sociometrics, peer assessment, pure* versus *applied sociometry, social skills,* and *social competence*. In addition, we examine those rationales that have been proposed for using sociometrics as a measure of social competence.

Originally, Moreno (1934) specified two criteria for sociometric tests: (1) the subject had to make an emotional response, and (2) the referent had to be a real-life situation. In such tests, the raters had to make choices in reference to a situation in which they had been involved with the ratee. "Name three children you like" would not be acceptable according to Moreno's criteria because it does not have a real-world referent, whereas "Name a child with whom you like to play" would.

Troubled by the definitional ambiguity of sociometrics, Bjerstedt (1956) reviewed the literature and found 13 different definitions of sociometry. He asked prominent scientists in the fields of psychology and sociology to identify which of the 13 definitions was closest to their conception of sociometry. However, the 131 responses to his questionnaire were distributed across all 13 definitions. From these data, Bjerstedt generated a broad definition that referred to *preferential sociometry* as the "measurement of interhuman relations . . . with the primary focus at this time on research into human preferential situations by means of more or less specific subject report methods" (p. 28).

Following the lead of these two researchers, we define sociometric assessments as tests in which children make preferential responses to statements about peers in their social group. *Social status* is operationally defined as the score received from a sociometric test. The many ways in which social status is computed are discussed in the methodology section of this chapter.

Peer Assessment

Peer assessment is often confused with sociometric assessment and suffers also from definitional ambiguity. At times, the two methodologies have been combined in single instruments. *Peer assessment* is "the process of having members of a group judge the extent to which each fellow member has exhibited specific traits, behaviors, or achievements" (Kane & Lawler, 1978, p. 555). Peer assessment differs from sociometric assessment in that the rater is requested to make relatively objective judgements about peers on specified criteria, rather than preferential selections. Theoretically, peer assessments would lack the "emotional quality" of which Moreno spoke. An example may help clarify the distinction. On a peer assessment scale, a child in a third grade class might be asked to "choose a classmate with whom you play the most;" whereas, in a sociometric assessment the same child would be asked to "choose a classmate with whom you like to play the most." Though differences between the two assessments are sometimes subtle, they are designed to tap qualitatively different responses. A further discussion of these two types of assessments follows in the methodology section.

Pure versus Applied Sociometry

Though the roots of sociometrics can be traced directly to the early work of Moreno (1934) and Koch (1933), the methodology has separated into two fairly distinct subdomains that have been described as pure and applied sociometry (Bjerstedt, 1956). *Pure*, or *classical*, *sociometry* is the more descriptive and theoretical of the two. Topics of interest in pure sociometry are the analysis of group members' interrelationships and the mathematical modeling of group structure (Hallinan, 1974; Holland & Leinhardt, 1979). Pure sociometry appears to be the primary domain of social psychologists and sociologists and is often academic in nature.

In contrast, *applied sociometry* is more individually oriented, with sociometrics more often used as tools for identifying specific types of children in groups, examining behavioral correlates of social status, or evaluating the outcomes of social skills training procedures. Applied sociometry is practiced primarily by clinical and educational psychologists and educators. This chapter deals mainly with applied sociometry, but references to the findings of the "purists" are incorporated at times, to provide a broader perspective of social status and group structural processes.

Other Definitions

A number of terms associated with sociometric assessment have been vaguely defined and used in a variety of ways in the research literature. Terms such as social acceptance, popularity, and friendship relate specifically to sociometric methodological variations and are operationally defined in a later section. Our definition of *social skills* falls most directly into the "behavioral definition" classification offered by Gresham (this volume). For us, social skills are behaviors directed toward others that result in positive reciprocal responses (Strain, Odom, & McConnell, 1984). These social behaviors may begin a social interchange or maintain an ongoing social exchange. Our conceptualization of social competence is aligned more closely with Gresham's *social validity* definition of social skills and draws on Hops's (1983) conceptualization. *Social competence* is a summative measure of a child's social performance with peers and across situations, as evaluated by significant social agents (e.g., teachers, peers, parents). Suggestions for assessing social competence are offered in a later section.

Rationale for Sociometrics as a Measure of Social Competence

Face Validity

A variety of rationales have been proposed for using sociometrics as a criterion measure of children's social competence. These rationales are based on three forms of validity. Perhaps the most compelling rationale is that of *face validity*. In a discussion of peer assessment that is equally relevant for sociometrics, Kane and Lawler (1978) argued that peer ratings of classmates are particularly useful when (1) peers are given a unique view of each other's social behaviors (e.g., as in the context of social interchanges), (2) peers are capable of understanding, reporting, or interpreting the characteristics of the peer group being assessed, and (3) current measures of a behavior or skill to be rated are inadequate and improved assessment procedures are needed. Because classmates are the individuals most in contact with children, one would expect their attitudes or preferences to be most directly affected by the social behavior of their peers. Children's reports of whom they like to work or play with can provide important information about how their peers' social behavior affects social attitudes. Though this rationale makes good common sense, there is much evidence to indicate that peer preferences are multidetermined and are mediated by a variety of nonsocial factors (Foster & Ritchey, 1979).

Social Validity

Sociometrics are often recommended as outcome variables for social skills training programs because of their social validity. The inclusion of social validity measures is important in evaluating treatment outcomes

and providing evaluation of socially significant effects of treatment, independent of the experimenter's outcome measures (Kazdin, 1977;
Wolf, 1978). Because peers are the individuals who interact with children referred for social skills training, they are in a unique position for
viewing the effects of changes in the referred child's behavior. In a very
real sense, peers are the primary consumers of the social skills training.
Success in social skills training should be reflected in a positive change
in peer attitudes toward the target child (Gresham, 1981b).

Traditionally, target behaviors have been selected by adults on an a
priori basis (i.e., adults assume the target behaviors they select are important). It is possible—and indeed quite probable—that adults' views
of socially competent behavior may differ substantially from those of
children in a peer group. By identifying the most popular children in a
peer group and contrasting their social behavior with that of children of
low social status, it would be possible to determine which behaviors are
related to high sociometric status. These behaviors could then be targeted for behavioral interventions (Gottman, Gonso, & Rasmussen,
1975; Strain, 1983). Although this approach appears to be a socially valid
procedure for identifying target behaviors for social skills training, there
is a possibility that the behaviors observed of high status children are
only spuriously related to high social status (e.g., they could be more
directly related to language development which, in turn, is highly related to social status). Such a procedure for selecting behavioral targets
would require the additional social validation step of training the behaviors and experimentally assessing the subsequent change in social status, as Ladd (1981) did in his study of a social coaching approach to
social skills training.

Predictive Validity

The most commonly used rationale for employing sociometric assessment as a measure of children's social competence is that early social
deficits, especially deficits in peer relationships, are predictive of a variety of measures of social adjustment later in life. In introductions to
published manuscripts and reviews of social skills training procedures, a
litany of studies are typically cited to document the long-term and stable
nature of peer relationship skills deficits. From this array of studies, the
predictive validity of sociometric assessment is often inferred.

An examination of these studies provides insight into methodological
problems inherent in this research and highlights problems associated
with our ability to establish the predictive validity of sociometrics. Table
1 contains descriptions of 20 studies frequently cited as evidence of the

predictive validity of sociometric measures. As can be seen, three types of experimental designs are noted. In *retrospective* designs, adults manifesting aberrant social adjustment are identified, and data from their childhood are collected in a retrospective manner (e.g., teachers are asked to recall information about students). For example, Bower, Shellhamer, and Daily (1960) had the high school teachers of adult male schizophrenics rate the behavior of these individuals as they remembered them from high school. In comparison with a control group, the schizophrenic adults were, as adolescents, less interested in girls, less well liked by teachers and peers, and more anxious. In a second retrospective study, Kohn and Clausen (1955) interviewed adult schizophrenics about their peer relations as adolescents and found little support for the assertion that the schizophrenics were socially isolated as adolescents.

Studies using ex post facto designs appear most often in Table 1. In these designs, researchers have used archival records of both child and adult behavior to demonstrate a direct relationship between the two. In two studies, Roff (1961, 1963) examined the armed services records of adults, as well as individual records from school and child guidance clinics. He found significant positive relationships between poor peer relations as children and both bad conduct discharges from the army and incidences of psychotic episodes as adults. Case records of children who were diagnosed as antisocial at a child guidance clinic were examined by Robins (1966) and his colleagues in a third ex post facto study. In comparison to a control group selected randomly from local public school records, the antisocial children were significantly more likely to exhibit a variety of severe social adjustment problems (e.g., alcoholism, poor job histories, psychiatric hospitalization) as adults. Ullman (1957) used school records to examine predictors of success upon graduation from high school. Teacher ratings and sociometric scores taken during the ninth grade were the best predictors of appearance on the honor roll at graduation or withdrawal from school before graduation.

Longitudinal designs were used in a third group of studies. In these designs, researchers tested children at an early age with the intention of following their performance over an extended time period. Roff, Sells, and Golden (1972) conducted the most extensive longitudinal study, collecting sociometric scores and teacher ratings of 40,000 children in two states. These investigators found that children rated as least liked by their peers were significantly more likely to appear on juvenile delinquency registers than were children rated as most liked, if they were from high- or middle-income families. The relationship did not hold for children from low-income families. In a widely cited study, Cowen,

Table 1

Studies Cited to Document the Predictive Validity of Sociometrics

	Design	Sample	Informants and method	Results
Bower, Shelhamer, & Daily (1960)	Retrospective	88 males hospitalized as adult schizophrenics	High school staff; interview	Schizophrenic males, as adolescents, were less interested in girls, less well liked than peers, and less well liked by teachers than control group
Cowen, Pederson, Babigian, Izzo, & Trost (1973) Cowen, Zax, Izzo, & Trost (1966)[a] Zax, Cowen, Rappaport, Beach, & Laird (1968)[a]	Longitudinal	537 children tested in three cohorts at the first or third grade; 494 control children; roughly equal numbers of males and females (Cowen et al., 1973)	Peers; Class Play peer assessment procedure	Children nominated for negative roles more frequently appeared on register of psychiatric services
Janes & Hesselbrock (1978)	Longitudinal	187 males and females seen at Washington University's Child Guidance Clinic	Teacher ratings of classroom behavior at childhood. Structured interview of subject and mother 12 years later	Referred children who were rated as "failing to get along with other children" were most likely to exhibit poor social adjustment as adults
Janes, Hesselbrock, Myers, & Penniman (1979)	Longitudinal	149 males seen at Washington University's Child Guidance Clinic; X̄ age = 9.3 years.	Teacher rating of classroom behavior	Re-analysis of data from previous study, including only boys
Kohn (1977)	Longitudinal	1232 children enrolled in day care; tested in three cohorts	Teacher ratings at preschool and upper grades	Social behavior ratings in preschool predicted emotional impairment at fourth grade

Kohn & Clausen (1955)	Retrospective	45 schizophrenics; 13 manic-depressive individuals, and control group matched for age and sex	Subjects and controls were interviewed about peer relations as adolescents	Data did not support the hypothesis that social isolation in adolescence was associated with schizophrenia as adults
Kohn & Rosman (1972)	Longitudinal	323 male and female preschool aged children	Teacher ratings at preschool; achievement measures at upper grades	Social behavior at preschool age was related to academic achievement at fourth grade
O'Neal & Robins (1958)[a] Robins (1966)	Prospective	524 male and female children referred to a child guidance clinic; control group of 100 children selected from St. Louis public school	Case records at childhood; adult psychiatric records	Children referred to clinic as adults were more likely to exhibit psychosis, sociopathic reactions, or alcoholism as adults, as compared to a control group
Pritchard & Graham (1966)	Prospective	75 males and females seen as patients in psychiatric hospital as children and adults	Case records from psychiatric hospital	Children seen at psychiatric hospital were highly likely to be seen as adults; childhood diagnosis related to adult diagnosis
Roff (1961)	Prospective	164 male children referred to child guidance clinic who later served in military service; half received bad conduct discharges	Case histories as children; armed services records as adults	Children with reportedly poor peer adjustment were more likely to receive bad conduct discharges than children with good peer relations

(continued)

Table 1 (Continued)

	Design	Sample	Informants and method	Results
Roff (1963)	Prospective	166 male children referred to child guidance clinics, who later served in military service, half were later diagnosed as psychotic	Case histories as children; records from selective services	Adults who reportedly exhibited psychotic episodes were significantly more likely to have had poor peer relations as children, compared to controls
Roff & Sells (1968)[a] Roff, Sells, & Golden (1972)	Longitudinal	40,000 male and female children enrolled in third to sixth grades in public schools in Texas and Minnesota	Peer nominations; teacher ratings at third to sixth grade; records of juvenile delinquency 4 years later	Low rated children in upper and middle SES likely to appear on juvenile delinquency rosters; relationship was not found for low-rated children from low-SES families
Ullmann (1957)	Prospective	All students enrolled in 11 ninth-grade classes in three junior high schools	Peer ratings and teacher ratings at ninth grade; high school records at graduation	Both ratings by peers and teachers predicted appearance of a child on honor roll at graduation or withdrawal from school prior to graduation

Victor & Halverson (1976)	Longitudinal	10 males and 10 females in the third, fourth, and fifth grades; rated by teachers as extreme behavior problem	Teacher ratings and peer assessment	At 2-year follow-up, early ratings of mean–noisy and quiet related to conduct problems for boys, and academic achievement
West & Farrington (1973)	Longitudinal	411 boys from working class families originally tested when they were 8 years old	Teacher ratings of 8-year-olds; peer assessment by 10 year olds	Children rated as most troublesome, most daring, and least honest by peers were more likely to become juvenile delinquents than children not in those categories
Westman, Rice, & Bermann (1967)	Prospective	130 children attending nursery school between 1945–1950	Nursery school teacher records; records from high school	Factors at nursery school most related to adult social adjustment were relations with peers, signs of behavioral eccentricity, and pathological family reactions

[a] Studies describing the same research at different phases of the project are grouped together.

Pederson, Babigian, Izzo, and Trost (1973) administered the Class Play peer assessment to children referred to a child guidance clinic. Children who were nominated for negative roles on the Class Play assessment were significantly more likely to appear on psychiatric registers as adults. In two other longitudinal studies, peer ratings or nominations of classmates as mean–noisy or quiet (Victor & Halverson, 1976), and troublesome or least honest (West & Farrington, 1973) were significantly related to predictors of conduct problems and juvenile delinquency, respectively, at an older age.

Methodological problems exist for each of these types of research designs. Retrospective designs are the most suspect because they rely on the memories of the informants, which may not be accurate if the elapsed time between behavior occurrence and data collection is substantial. The ex post facto designs are restricted by the data that are available. Because random assignment or selection only occurs with a control group, there is no control for the effects of extraneous variables with these types of studies. Also, in a number of the ex post facto studies listed in Table 1, the subjects sampled were originally referred to child guidance clinics. The generalization of data from such a selective sample to the general population is questionable. Longitudinal designs, which are certainly the most robust of the three designs mentioned here, may be susceptible to cohort and/or historical threats to internal validity (Baltes, Reese, & Nesselroade, 1977).

Despite methodological flaws, support for the long-term developmental significance of early social skills deficits lies in the convergence of findings across these various investigations. Tentative evidence provided by the ex post facto studies has been supported and replicated by longitudinal investigations. For example, Roff's early ex post facto work has been extended and supported in part by his longitudinal study (Roff et al., 1972) and by those of other researchers (West & Farrington, 1973). Similarly, the large-scale ex post facto work by Robins (1966) and his colleagues has been supported by the longitudinal work of Cowen and his co-workers (1973). The more carefully controlled longitudinal studies provide replicative evidence that children who exhibit difficulties in establishing peer relationships are at greater risk for poor social adjustment later in life.

Given the apparent link between peer relations at an early age and later social functioning, sociometrics would appear to be an outcome measure of choice in studies of social development. A perusal of Table 1 reveals that longitudinal studies tended to use peer judgements more often than other studies (Cowen et al., 1973; Roff et al., 1972; Victor & Halverson, 1976; West & Farrington, 1973). However, for the 20 studies in Table 1, the teacher or individuals writing child guidance psychological reports (e.g., social workers, therapists) were more often the informants of peer relationship difficulties than were peers.

Though the predictive validity rationale for employing sociometric assessment is the most commonly cited, it is also the weakest of the three rationales herein stated. A rationale more directly supported by the data reported in these studies would be that peer relationship difficulties in childhood, assessed by a variety of methods, are associated with social adjustment problems as adults. Sociometric assessment, as a measure of children's social relationships with peers, may help identify children who could be at risk for adjustment problems as adults.

METHODOLOGY

Sociometrics contain three distinct methodological types. In this section, we discuss the variety of methodologies employed, data analysis procedures used, reliability information about each type, and cross-method comparisons. Peer assessments are also described because they have been frequently used in cross-method comparison studies.

Methodological Variations

Peer Nominations

Moreno (1934) originally developed the peer nomination procedure, which has become the most commonly applied sociometric assessment. Typically, children are asked to select one or more classmates with whom they would, or would not, like to engage in a common activity. For example, the child may be asked to tell whom he/she would like to sit next to, play with, or work with. Social status measures of this type are usually tabulated by adding the number of choices a child receives, although more complex forms of data analysis do occur. Though peer nomination assessments appear to be rather straightforward, a number of variations have occurred across studies, which markedly affect the final social status measure derived.

The number of nominated classmates has varied across peer nomination procedures as revealed in Table 2. In *fixed choice* procedures, a specific number of classmate choices are requested by the tester; conversely, *unlimited choice* procedures allow children to nominate as many peers as they would like. By fixing the number of choices to be made, the tester may inadvertently bias the test results because children may

Table 2

Examples of Sociometric and Peer Assessments

Author	Name	Description of methodology	Reliability
Peer nomination			
Busk, Ford, & Schulman (1973)		Child nominated peers they liked the most; unlimited choice	Test–retest (8 week interval) r = .76 to .84
Coie, Dodge, & Coppotelli (1982)		Child nominated three peers for one negative and one positive criteria, unweighted scores	Test–retest (3 month interval) r = .46 to .88 median = .65
McCandless and Marshall (1957)		Pictures shown to each child from kindergarten; child made three positive nominations on one criteria; weighted scores	Test–retest (10 days) .66 to .71
Moreno (1934)		Child nominated two classmates on one positive criterion; unweighted scores	
Northway (1942)	Social acceptability test	Child made three choices across four criteria; weighted scores; also allows child to nominate a peer from outside the class	
Peer ratings:			
Agard, Veldman, Kaufman, & Semmell	How I feel toward others	Child rated each peer on a three-point scale with additional question mark response	Test–retest: r = .71 to .80 for smiles, .56 to .81 for frowns, .33 to .56 for ? and neutral
Asher, Singleton, Tinsley, & Hymel (1979)		Picture rating task; child rated by sorting pictures into preferred, neutral, or reject boxes; one criteria	Test–retest (1 month) r = .80 and .75
Bruininks, Rynders, & Gross (1974)	Peer acceptance scale	Child rated each peer on a three-point continuum indicated by picture of stick figures; one criterion	

Reference	Description	Reliability
Dunnington (1957)	Three positive and three negative nominations made on one criterion; child nominated three peers for positive and negative criteria first, then rated everyone else in the class	Test–retest (2 months) $r = .86$
Hallinan (1974)	Each member of class classified each peer as best friend, friend, or everyone else	
Moore & Updegraff (1964)	Child nominated four peers on one positive and one negative criterion, then rated the rest of the class as liked or disliked	Test–retest (1 to 2 weeks) $r = .52$ to .78
Odom & DuBose (1981)	Two-point picture rating scale for one criterion	Test–retest (1 to 5 months) r's = .10 to .80 $\bar{X} = .50$
Roistacher (1974)	Child rated classmates on two-point rating for how well they knew peer being rated; seven-point continuum for one criterion	
Paired comparison		
Bjerstedt (1956)	Method of triplets All combinations of three classmates presented; rater indicated which most preferred and which least preferred	
Cohen & Van Tassell (1978)	All combinations of paired photographs presented for peer selection; also, 60% of the total number of possible pairs presented in second session	Test–retest, $r = .90$'s
Hops & Finch (1983)	Photographs of all possible dyads presented; raters chose which they preferred on one criteria	

(continued)

Table 2 (*Continued*)

Author	Name	Description of methodology	Reliability
Vaughn & Waters (1981)		Photographs of all possible dyads presented; raters chose which they preferred on one criterion	Test–retest (3 to 7 months) $r = .90$ to $.92$
Burns (1974)		Rater chose from paired photographs which peer was liked for two administrations and which was not liked during a third	Test–retest, $r = .96$ to $.98$
Peer assessment			
Agard, Veldman, Kaufman, & Semmel	Guess Who?	Children are read descriptive items and asked to guess which classmate(s) the items describe; items clustered into four factors: bright, dull, disruptive, and quiet/good	Internal consistency, .62 to .85; alphas for factors, .70 for disruptive and dull, below .70 for bright and quiet
Bower (1960)	Class Play	Child nominates children who fit the description of roles in a hypothetical class play; positive and negative roles assigned	
Bower (1960)	Class picture test	Child shown pictures of both positive and negative hypothetical social situations and ask to nominate the classmate(s) who the picture could represent	

Hartshorne, May, & Maller (1929)	Guess Who?	List of "picture–word" descriptions given to child who is asked to guess who they describe in the class	Split-half, .88
Shapiro & Sobel (1981)	Shapiro sociometric role assignment test	Descriptors generated by children in a class are read to child; rater nominates one classmate for each descriptor; positive and negative items included	
Mixed assessments			
Bailey & Pierce (1973)	Friendship Rating Scale	Adapted roster and rating scale, ratings range from one to five, included both peer assessment and sociometric items	Test–retest (1 week) $r = .56$ to $.92$
Milich, Landau, Kilby, & Whitten (1982)	Pupil Perception Inventory	Nomination of classmates on items measuring aggression, hyperactivity, and sociability	Internal consistency, .56 to .92
Pekarik, Prinz, Liebert, Weintraub, & Neale (1976)	Pupil Evaluation Inventory	Nomination of classmates on items from two assessment factors (i.e., aggression and withdrawal) and one preferential factor (i.e., likeability)	Test–retest, r greater than .80; Internal consistency for factors, .58 to .70
Winder & Wiggins (1964)	Peer Nomination Inventory	Modified Guess Who procedure: Children nominated on items from four assessment factors (i.e., aggression, dependency, withdrawal, and depression) and one preferential factor (likeability)	

actually wish to nominate more or fewer peers than the fixed number (Hallinan, 1974). Although with unlimited choices a tacit selection norm may occur in which the children feel that they should not pick more than two or three choices (Leinhardt, 1972), the unlimited choice procedure appears to introduce less measurement error, albeit there may also be less experimental control (i.e., unequal numbers of choices per child).

A weighting can be given to peer nominations by assigning a higher value to children nominated first relative to the children chosen later. The purpose for weighting the choices is to provide a finer discrimination of the choice made (e.g., first choice may be a very best friend, second a second-best friend). Weighting procedures also allow a more precise identification of reciprocal choices (e.g., children who choose each other as best friends). Weighting nominations, in effect, introduces a ranking quality into the peer nominations, resulting in a partial rank-order measure (Thompson & Powell, 1951). When using weighted choices, it is important for the children to know that the order in which they nominated their classmates is important. Without precise instructions, a child may name a number of friends without regard to preferential gradations, introducing measurement error into the assessment.

Either a single criterion or a variety of criteria may be used in nominations assessment. To gain a broader perspective of social status in a peer group, Moreno (1934) recommended that multiple criteria be used. For example, Northway (1942) used four criteria in her Social Acceptability Test (i.e., play at recess, move to another class with, like best in school, like best out of school). Multiple criteria undoubtedly increase the strength of the assessment as long as the criterion items are measuring the same general attribute. However, items that differ markedly from one another may obscure the total social status score if summed together. For example, children may well nominate different peers with whom they prefer to work as opposed to play (Hymel & Asher, 1977).

Possibly the most controversial aspect of sociometric assessment is the use of negative criteria. Peer nomination assessments may require the children to identify peers they do not like. The purpose for including negative nominations is to measure patterns of rejection in the social group. Hartup, Glazer, and Charlesworth (1967) were among the first to observe that negative choices were not simply at the opposite end of a positive–negative continuum. In their study, the number of positive and negative choices received by preschool children were not significantly correlated.

When only positive choices are used in peer nominations, it is impossible to discriminate between group members who are neglected (i.e., not picked as friends) and children who are actively rejected. In a study that compared the use of positive and positive plus negative criteria on an adapted peer nomination assessment, Dunnington (1957) found that membership in high or low social-status groups changed markedly when the rejection criteria were omitted. In addition, test–retest reliability was higher when negative nominations were used.

The prospect of eliciting negative choices from children is often disturbing to classroom teachers, parents, and members of research review committees. Opponents of negative nominations often argue that stating rejections leads to overt social rejection in the classroom, as well as other reactive effects (e.g., lower self image of the ratee). Fifty years of sociometric research with little, if any, evidence of such reactive effects does not assuage the concern voiced by these individuals. Systematic investigation of the reactive effects of positive and negative nominations has been repeatedly recommended (Asher & Hymel, 1981; Hops & Lewin, in press), but such investigations have yet to be conducted. Until systematic research does conclusively demonstrate that negative nominations are innocuous, researchers should be especially attentive to the possibility of increased incidences of overt rejection occurring among peers in the class.

However, because the efficiency of peer nomination assessments will decrease markedly when negative nominations are not used, it is imperative that they be included in the assessment process. Bjerstedt (1956) suggested several strategies for decreasing resistance to negative nominations. First, the privacy and confidentiality of child's sociometric scores must be maintained. Results can be presented as grouped data to avoid reference to individuals, and when results are communicated to parents and teachers, the importance of confidentiality should be emphasized. Second, the choices of the rater should remain anonymous. Individual assessments should be given outside of the classroom or out of earshot of classmates, and group administrations should be monitored closely by the tester. Third, by avoiding a forced-choice method, raters may not be forced to nominate a child who they might not ordinarily reject (e.g., fill in three negative choices even though they may only wish to nominate one child) and artificial patterns of rejection may be minimized. In addition, the possibility of not choosing anyone should be left open. Fourth, by selecting multiple criteria that are activity-based or classroom-based (i.e., play with, work with, sit by) rather than comprehensive (e.g., best friend, do not like at all), the children may minimize their stated rejection to a single, specific activity.

Peer Ratings

In peer rating sociometric assessments, also called roster and rating scales (Roistacher, 1974), each class member is rated along a continuum of attraction–rejection. Typically, raters are either given a class roster, read each classmate's name, or shown a picture of each classmate and are asked to rate the classmate according to how much they like or dislike the child. For example, a three-item continuum might include a first item indicating "likes to play with a lot," a second indicating "just kind of likes to play with," and a third item indicating "does not like to play with" (Asher, Singleton, Tinsley, & Hymel, 1979). Each rating is assigned a weighted value, in this case one (for "not liked") to three (for liked). The ratings received from classmates are then summed for each child to give an overall social status score. Scores may be ranked to reveal the relative social standing of each child in the class.

Studies described in Table 2 exemplify the variations in the peer rating procedure. Two-point (Odom & DuBose, 1981), three-point (Bruininks, Rynders, & Gross, 1974), five-point (Hymel & Asher, 1977) and seven-point (Roistacher, 1974) rating scales have been employed. With elementary-aged and younger children, the points on the continuum have been indicated by a happy face for the most positive end, a neutral face for the middle criteria and a sad face for the least-liked position (Asher et al., 1979), or by stick figure pictures indicating similar affective states (Bruininks et al., 1974). The How I Feel About Others assessment (Agard, Veldman, Kaufman, & Semmel, undated) included a question mark as the fourth point on the scale, which the raters circled if they did not know or could not rate a child on the roster.

While giving the appearance of being a peer nomination scale, some scales actually should be classified as peer rating scales because everyone in the reference group is rated according to a specified number of criteria. Hallinan (1974) used a scale in which every peer was classified as a best friend, friend, or everyone else. Dunnington (1957) requested that children nominate three classmates with whom they liked to play and did not like to play, gave progressive weighting values to each choice, and then had the children rate as liked or disliked all the remaining classmates who had not been previously chosen.

The importance of specifying items in "real world" concrete criteria, as noted for peer nominations, is more complicated for rating scales. Not only must the item criteria be clear (e.g., like to play with or work with), but also the different points on the scale continuum must be behaviorally anchored, with a definition for each point. Thus, a happy face may mean that a child likes to work with a specific classmate very much and a neutral face may mean that a child likes somewhat to work with the ratee. During the development of a rating scale, it is possible to let the raters themselves identify behavioral terms that may be associated with each scale point. Smith and Kendall (1963) found that such a procedure could make the scale clearer for raters and increase its reliability.

The advantage of using a peer rating scale is that every child in the class is rated, as contrasted with the peer nomination scale in which only a few children are chosen. The procedure prompts raters to make a qualitative judgement about each class member rather than relying on their memory when nominating classmates. Because ratings are obtained for a large number of subjects, a change of one or two choices across time will not greatly affect the reliability of the total rating scores (Asher et al., 1979). In addition, peer rating scales appear to be sensitive to subtle changes in the criteria used. Asher's research has revealed that children will rate their peers differently depending on whether the scaling criteria was "play with" or "work with" (Oden & Asher, 1977; Singleton & Asher, 1979).

Several disadvantages may also occur when using peer rating scales. Even when the scales are behaviorally anchored, there may be a tendency to rate most classmates in the middle of the scale. When rating scales are used with very young children, or children of low cognitive abilities, there may be a tendency to rate classmates stereotypically (i.e., give everyone in the class the same rating) or, when sorting classmates' pictures into categories, to exhibit a position preference (i.e., give every child the right-most scale item) (Odom & DuBose, 1981).

Paired Comparisons

Paired comparison sociometrics are probably the most homogeneous in terms of methodology, but also the most labor intensive. In this procedure, photographs are taken of all the children in a class. Photographs of each possible classmate dyad are paired, resulting in $(n-1)$ $(n-2)/2$ choices (n = number of students in the class). The rater is instructed to choose one of the two children in each dyad in reference to a specific criterion. The number of choices each child receives from his or her classmates is computed and used as a social status measure. In past studies, positive criteria have been used exclusively, though Burns (1974) did use one negative criterion that he converted to positive for comparison purposes. In a variation of the paired comparison methodology, Bjerstedt (1956) described a method of triplets in which all combinations of triads in a classroom are paired and the rater indicates which child is most preferred and which is least preferred. However, this technique has not appeared in more-recent sociometric literature.

The primary advantage of the paired comparison methodology is its excellent test–retest reliability with preschool-aged as well as older children (Hops & Lewin, in press). A second desirable feature is that negative criteria need not be used. By choosing one child, it may be assumed that the rater, in effect, rejects the other child. Though it is possible that a different pattern of results could occur if the rater was asked to pick the child with whom he would not like to associate, Burns (1974) found moderate to high correlations between positive paired comparison and inverted negative paired comparison scores for trainable mentally retarded and nonhandicapped adolescents.

A major disadvantage of the paired comparison technique is the time required for administration. For a class of 20 students, each child will have to make 171 selections. Because of the time required, assessments with young children are often completed in several installments. For instance, in the first use of paired comparisons to appear in the literature, Koch (1933) took 3 months to complete all assessments with a class of preschool children.

Peer Assessment

Peer assessment differs from sociometric assessment, in that the former requires children to make judgements about their peers' behavior whereas the latter requires children to make judgements about their feelings or sentiments toward peers. The two forms of assessment originated at about the same time but from differing sources (Asher & Hymel, 1981). Sociometrics grew out of the psychotherapeutic tradition of Moreno and his colleagues (see Moreno, 1953, for an interesting if not unbiased history of sociometry in the United States during the first half of this century). Hartshorne and his colleagues developed peer assessment as part of their study of "character" in children, with the intention of measuring a child's reputation in a social group (Hartshorne, May, & Maller, 1929). The purposes for including a discussion of peer assessment in this chapter are three-fold: (1) previous reviews of both assessment literatures (Asher & Hymel, 1981; Kane & Lawler, 1978) acknowledged the differences between the two methodologies, but did not discuss the overlap between the two (i.e., the development of mixed measures); (2) considerable confusion still exists about differences between the two measures, as indicated by the frequent reference to a series of longitudinal studies that purportedly supports the long-term predictive validity of sociometrics, but which in fact used a peer assessment as the major dependent variable (Cowen et al., 1973); and (3) when used in unison, peer assessment may provide information from a peer's perspective about child characteristics that relate to sociometric assessment.

With peer assessments, children are asked to nominate or rate other according to a variety of behavioral criteria and in a variety of manners. The Guess Who? test (Agard, Veldman, Kaufman, Semmel, & Walters, undated; Hartshorne et al., 1929) is a frequently used peer assessment in which the tester reads a number of descriptions of children (e.g., athlete, leader, bully) and the child "guesses" who in the class fits the criteria. There is an unlimited choice option and the children may nominate no one if they wish. The number of nominations for positive and negative measures are totalled to compute a final score. The "Guess Who?" test developed for Project Prime represents the most sophisticated version of the procedure to date. Principal-components analysis of the 29-item questionnaire revealed that four factors, clustering around two academic constructs (i.e., academic competence and misbehavior), are represented on the current version (Veldman & Sheffield, 1979).

The Shapiro Sociometric Role Assignment Test (SSRAT) is a second type of peer assessment (Shapiro & Sobel, 1981). As with the "Guess Who?" assessment, children are read descriptions of classmates and are asked to choose one classmate who fits the description. Shapiro and Sobel's assessment differed from others in that the classmates themselves originally generated classmates' description and then a "representative" group of class members assigned them to positive, neutral, and negative categories. As with sociometrics, using members of the class to select items for an instrument is one way of ensuring that the items are meaningful to children, thus building the content validity of the assessment.

A third peer assessment used with elementary school children is the Class Play (Bower, 1960). In this procedure, children are told that they are to choose children in their class to fill roles in a class play. The child nominates peers for positive (e.g., class president, teacher) and negative (e.g., afraid, stuck-up, mean) roles. Positive and negative items are summed separately for each peer.

"Mixed" Assessments

A variety of assessment instruments and studies have combined the sociometric and peer assessment methodologies. Items from these assessments tend to load on different factors, with at least one being a preferential factor (i.e., the sociometric component) and the other(s) being peer behavioral factors (i.e., the peer assessment component). The Pupil Evaluation Inventory (PEI) (Pekarik, Prinz, Liebert, Weintraub, & Neale, 1976), although described as a sociometric technique, is one example of a mixed assessment. On the 35-item questionnaire, children were instructed to make a checkmark by the name of each classmate described by each item. The three factors emerging from a principal-components analysis, conducted with 4000 raters, were popularity (a sociometric factor), aggression, and peer withdrawal (both peer assessment factors). An abbreviated form of the PEI, the Peer Perception Inventory (PPI), was developed by Milich, Landau, Kilby, and Whitten (1982) for use with preschool children. The PPI contains 13 items that assess popularity, rejection, aggression, hyperactivity, and sociability.

A somewhat different mixed assessment called the Friendship Rating Scale (Bailey & Pierce, 1975) requires children to rate each classmate, in a roster and rating-scale fashion, on a five-point continuum across five criteria. The scale includes friendship, leadership, positive mood, talkative, and greeting criteria. Another mixed assessment adapted from the Guess Who? procedure is the Peer Nomination Inventory (Wiggins & Winder, 1961). This test consists of 62 items, which load on four peer assessment factors (i.e., social isolation, hostility, crying, and attention getting) and one preferential factor (i.e., likability). Observations of children in group tasks have revealed that the Peer Nomination Inventory factor scores predict certain patterns of social behaviors among peers (Winder & Wiggins, 1964). An advantage in using these mixed scales is that information about social status and peer reputation can be gathered on one instrument in one administration.

Interpreting Sociometric Scores

The interpretation of social status is confused not only by the varying methodologies employed (Morrison, 1981), but also by the diverse manner in which the sociometric data are analyzed. The most traditional analyses of sociometric data have been to total the positive and/or negative nominations received by a child, to sum the total ratings received from peers on rating scales, or to add all the choices received from paired-comparisons and compare one child's score with the rest of the class. Such analyses provide global measures of social status relative to other classmates, but they do not give specific information about the nature of children's social relations with peers. A number of procedures have been developed to provide a more fine-grained, descriptive interpretation of scores received on sociometric assessments.

Identifying Child Types

By considering the number of positive and negative nominations received from peers, a child may be classified into one of several typologies. Children who receive a large number of positive nominations and few or no negative nominations have often been described as "stars" in a social group (Gronlund, 1959). Children who receive few positive or negative nominations have been classified as "neglected" (Green, Vosk, Forehand, & Beck, 1981). Children who receive a large number of negative nominations and a small number of positive nominations have been classified as "rejected" (Peery, 1979). Moreno (1953) identified the socially isolated child as one who neither nominates other children on positive criteria nor receives nominations from others.

Negative criteria must be included in a sociometric assessment procedure when identifying types of children. As noted, it is impossible to discriminate between neglected and rejected children without negative criteria. Similarly, peer ratings that yield summative global scores do not allow a discrimination between these two status types, although ratings may be combined with peer nominations to provide a more reliable and finer discrimination of unpopular and popular children. Vosk, Forehand, Parker, and Rickard (1982) used just such a multilevel assessment to identify popular (i.e., high positive nominations and high peer ratings) and unpopular (i.e., few positive nominations and low peer ratings) children in their study of the correlates of popularity in elementary school children.

A child's social impact on his or her peer group, as determined through sociometric assessment, is a dimension of social functioning that may aid in the more-precise discrimination of child types. Peery (1979) computed social-impact scores by summing positive and negative nominations and social preference scores and then subtracting positive nominations from negatives. In his conceptualization of social status classifications, social impact and social preference represented two orthogonal dimensions on which children were classified. From these two dimensions, Perry delineated four types of social status: *rejected* (i.e., low preference, high impact), *isolated* (i.e., low preference, low impact), *amiable* (i.e., high preference, low impact), and *popular* (i.e., high preference, high impact).

Using Peery's dimensions of social impact and social preference, Coie, Dodge, and Coppotelli (1982) identified a group of children who they described as *controversial*. These children exhibited a high measure of social impact and high frequencies of both positive and negative nominations.

Identifying child types is an important addition to the analysis of sociometric data. It allows the experimenter to cull more information from the data than does the traditional, summative sociometric score, and it provides a basis for choosing candidates for social skills instruction and behavior management programs. The next step in the development of this methodology is to identify behavioral correlates that discriminate among the various typologies; some important steps have been taken in this direction (see Dodge, 1983; Gottman, 1977; Peretti, Lane, & Floyd, 1981).

Reciprocal Choices

Interest in sociometric scores has advanced beyond the analysis of total nominations received from groups to the examination of (1) the scores given by individual children, (2) mutual positive nomination or ratings of peers, and (3) structure of mutual choices within a group (Hallinan, 1981). In a study using sociometrics as an outcome variable for a social skill training procedure, Conoley and Conoley (1983) analyzed not only the positive nominations received, but also the patterns of nominations given to other children. They computed a friendliness measure based on the status of the child giving the nomination and noted changes in the specific children chosen as friends.

Computing mutual positive nominations, ratings, or choices by peers (e.g., child A nominates child B, and child B nominates child A) appears to be an effective way of determining friendships between individual peers. Masters and Furman (1981) found that playing with a specific peer in the classroom was unrelated to overall social status but rather was related to the reciprocal choices given on a peer nomination measure. Similar results have been reported by Hops and Finch (1983) with reciprocal choices obtained by paired comparison assessments.

Using a peer rating measure, Roistacher (1974) found that the most well-liked children were the most efficient in their friendship choices; they gave the highest ratings to only slightly more peers than the class norm, but they participated in substantially more reciprocal ratings (i.e., giving and receiving the highest rating). In examining the stability of peer nominations across age groups, Busk, Ford, and Schulman (1943) found reciprocal choice to be less affected by time and age factors than were total nominations received or given.

Researchers in pure sociometry have been intensely interested in the use of reciprocated choices to determine the structure of social groups. By identifying reciprocal choice among peers, social networks may be discerned (Hallinan, 1981; Holland & Leinhardt, 1979). These friendship structures have been described as *transitive* (i.e., all members of a group are chosen by at least one member as friends), or *intransitive* (i.e., only a portion of the members of the group are chosen by any of the members as friends) and have been studied in triads or cliques. One theory is that groups are composed of cliques aligned in hierarchical fashions, in terms of popularity and power (Leinhardt, 1972).

Though group structure is rarely attended to in applied sociometry, it may be productive to ascertain the reciprocal nature of sociometric relations of rejected, isolated, or controversial children in comparison with the average or popular children in the class. By observing the social structure of a reference group, changes resulting from social skills training programs could be determined by the child's entrance into a specific triad or clique. Similarly, because certain groups, such as social isolates (Hallinan & Fermlee, 1975) and certain handicapped individuals (Burns, 1974) tend to be involved in intransitive cliques, increased transivity could be seen as a positive outcome for social skills training procedures.

Computer Analysis

One of the factors that may prevent individuals who use sociometrics in an applied setting from conducting sophisticated analyses of group structure is the complexity and considerable labor involved in such analyses. With the increasing accessibility of computer analysis, software could be developed to assist the applied sociometrist in conducting sophisticated analyses of group structure. Several such computer programs now exist.

To analyze child choices on peer nomination measures and the differential patterns across subgroups, Remington, Wall, Pickert, and Foltz (1982) developed a program that can analyze data from single or multiple classes. A similar software package has been developed by Langeheine (1978) for pure sociometric analyses (e.g., clique analysis, index analysis, and sociometric perception analysis), but it could be readily translated into analyses of a more-applied nature. Levin (1976) developed an interactive software package that will map sociometric choices for classes and identify mutual, asymmetric, and null dyadic relationships, as well as cliques. For analyzing the social structure of mainstreamed classes, Markus (1980) designed a package that graphically portrays the structure in a social "map" of the class. He proposed this method of portraying social relationships as a more-direct measure of social integration than the more traditional forms of sociometric analysis.

Popularity versus Acceptance

When sociometric scores are computed by totaling nominations, ratings, or paired comparison choices received (i.e., without regard to the reciprocal nature of the nominations, etc.) the three sociometric procedures appear to measure different dimensions of social status. A number of researchers (Asher & Taylor, 1981; Gresham, 1981a; Hops & Lewin, in press; Taylor, 1982) propose that peer ratings and paired comparisons measure a child's acceptability in the peer group, while peer nominations assess popularity, friendship, or high-priority playmates. In a large-scale study of low sociometric status children, which used both peer nominations and peer ratings, Hymel and Asher (1977) found that children who received no positive nominations were often rates as well accepted by their peers. Similarly, after administering a social skills training treatment to children who were rated as rejected, Oden and Asher (1977) found that subjects received higher ratings but did not receive more friendship nominations.

To investigate the different dimensions represented by peer nominations, peer ratings, and observational measures of social behavior, Gresham (1981b) administered all measures to a group of low social-status elementary school children and their classmates. A factor analysis of the scores revealed that ratings and nominations loaded highly on two different factors, which he called friendship and likability. In a large-scale study comparing two types of peer-rating scales, peer rankings, paired comparisons, and peer nominations, Bjerstedt (1956) reported that paired comparisons, peer ratings, and peer rankings were more similar to each other than they were to peer nominations, suggesting that the two groups of assessments (i.e., ratings and nominations) might be measuring different types of social preferences. Thus, we recommend, along with Asher and Taylor (1981), that *social acceptance* be operationally defined as the total score received on peer-rating scales and *popularity* be operationally defined as the total number of positive nominations received on peer-nomination assessments. While further research is necessary to partial out the effects of method variance on the relationship of sociometric scores, some tentative guidelines can be offered. When using single measures and total scores, the specific sociometric instrument chosen should be determined by whether the researcher or practitioner is interested in social acceptance or popularity.

Reliability of Sociometric Assessments

Peer Nomination

Peer nomination, the most commonly used sociometric assessment, has been shown to be adequately reliable with elementary-aged children and older individuals. Stable peer nominations have been reported by Bonney (1943) for a 1-year period (r's = .67 & .84), Roff and colleagues (1972) for a 1- to 2-year period (r's = .52 and .42), and Northway (1969a) for a 4-year period (r = .89). In looking at more than 2000 sociometric assessments for children from kindergarten to the fifth grades,

Northway (1969a) also found that reliability coefficients of peer nominations decreased as the interval between tests increased, and increased
with the age at which the children were tested. However, not all studies
have found high reliability or stability coefficients. In Gresham's (1981b)
study, test–retest correlations across a 6-week period varied from .19 to
.62 with a mean coefficient of .39.

With preschool children, the peer-nomination task has often been
restructured to include photographs of classmates. The photographs
may be posted on a large board or placed on a table, and the child is
usually asked to name the classmate in each photograph before nominating any of the classmates. McCandless and Marshall (1957), who
originated the procedure because of the low reliabilities often found on
peer-nomination assessments with young children (Marshall, 1957) obtained 10-day test–retest coefficients of .66 to .71. Other researchers
using the picture nomination procedure have obtained reliability coefficients ranging from the .30s (Asher et al., 1979; Greenwood, Walker,
Todd, & Hops, 1979; Hartup et al., 1967) to the .50s (Hartup et al., 1967,
for acceptance).

Peer Ratings

In contrast to peer nominations, peer ratings tend to yield higher
reliability and stability coefficients. Using the How I Feel About Others
rating scale with elementary-aged children, Agard and her colleagues
(undated) obtained coefficients of .70 to .80 for smiles, .56 to .81 for
frowns, and .33 to .56 for the neutral criteria. A similar measure, the
Peer Acceptance Scale, used with mentally retarded, learning disabled,
and nonhandicapped children, has also yielded test–retest coefficients
of .75 and above (Sainato, Zigmond, & Strain, 1983). Dunnington's
(1957) translation of a peer nomination technique into a peer rating
yielded a stability coefficient of .86 after a 60-day period.

To examine the differing reliabilities of peer ratings and nominations,
Thompson and Powell (1951) administered both scales to school-aged
children across three time-periods (i.e., on consecutive days, a week
later, and 5 weeks later). The rating-scale scores were more stable than
nominations, resulting in coefficients greater than .90 in all but one
instance, but the stability coefficient for the peer nomination assessment
was a respectable .84 at the 5-week assessment.

As with peer nominations, investigations have also employed pictures
when adapting peer rating scales for use with preschool children. Asher
and his colleagues (1979), using a three-point scale with two classes of
preschool children, obtained stability measures of .81 and .75 after 1

month. In an adaptation of a picture peer nomination procedure similar
to Dunnington's (1957), Moore and Updegraff (1964) reported reliability
coefficients of .62, .52, and .78 for groups of 3-, 4-, and 5-year-old children, respectively, after a 1- to 2-week retest.

To examine the use of peer ratings with handicapped preschool children, Odom and DuBose (1981) simplified the Asher et al. (1979) procedure to a two-point scale and obtained a stability coefficient of .61 after a
1-month period. In a follow-up study using the same assessment in
eight preschool and kindergarten special education classes, stability coefficients ranged from .10 to .80 ($\bar{X} = .49$) for 1- to 5-month time periods.
Thus, for preschool children and some young handicapped children,
peer-rating scales appear to be fairly stable across relatively short time
periods.

Paired Comparisons

The most reliable sociometric measure appears to be paired comparisons. In Burns's (1974) study of paired comparisons with mentally retarded and nonhandicapped adolescents, test–retest correlations ranged
from .96 to .98. With preschool children, Vaughn and Waters (1981)
obtained stability coefficients across a semester's time period of .92 and
.90 across the entire year. In two studies that examined the relative
stability of paired comparisons in relation to other sociometric measures,
Witryol and Thompson (1953a, 1953b) found that paired comparisons
were more stable than peer nominations. The former yielded coefficients
in the .90s, while stability coefficients for the latter ranged from .59 to
.96. Interestingly, the intercorrelations between the two measures
ranged from .36 to .89 (Witryol & Thompson, 1953a).

To alleviate the time-consuming nature of the paired comparisons
assessment, Cohen and Van Tassel (1978) developed a procedure in
which only 60% of the assessment was given to each child. Results of
this abbreviated form were then compared with a full paired comparison
assessment and a picture peer nomination assessment. The abbreviated
assessment was nearly as stable as the full assessment at a 3-month
retest and more stable than the picture nomination assessment.

Peer Assessment

Reliability analyses of peer-assessment instruments have often addressed the internal consistency of the test as well as the test–retest
reliability. In the original "Guess Who?" test, Hartshorne et al. (1929)
reported a split-half reliability of .88 for a subset of the total test items.
Evaluations of Project Prime's revision of the "Guess Who?" (Agard,

Veldman, Kaufman, Semmel, & Walters, undated) reported internal consistency coefficients ranging from .62 to .85. When examining the test–retest reliability for the Peer Perception Inventory with preschool children, Milich et al. (1982) found coefficients ranging from .56 to .92, with a mean of .78. Similarly, Pekarik et al. (1976) reported internal consistency coefficients in the .70s and test–retest coefficients of .80 or higher for the Pupil Evaluation Inventory. In all, most peer-assessment procedures adequately document both internal consistency and test–retest forms of reliability.

Conclusions

Substantial variability was present in the preceding reliability figures. As noted by Hops and Lewin (in press) and highlighted by this review, the temporal stability of an assessment is influenced by (1) the specific method employed, (2) the age of the child assessed, (3) the criteria or number of criteria used, (4) the length of time between assessments, and (5) the manner in which sociometric choices are analyzed (e.g., number received, number given, social impact score, number of reciprocal choices). In addition, some groups of children, although similar in appearance and demographic features, may be more volatile or unstable than others. Northway (1969b) identified cohort effects in two groups of children whom she followed in her study. Such differences highlight the need for determining the reliability of a sociometric measure each time it is used in research. Simply citing reliability figures established in other earlier studies does not appear to be an acceptable alternative, given the variety of factors that exert an influence on the final measure. As can be seen from Table 2, careful documentation of reliability is not a procedure that has been consistently followed in the past.

Cross-Method Studies

A number of studies have used peer assessments as a means of examining variables that affect or contribute to sociometric status. Moreno's (1934) early studies set a precedent for such investigations; he proposed that sociometric assessments should be followed by "a spontaneous test" in which the investigator asked the children why they nominated a peer for a certain criterion item. His anecdotal descriptions of children's spontaneous responses documented the changing nature of contributing factors across the elementary school years, particularly with regard to sex cleavage within groups (i.e., preference for same-sex peers).

Systematic investigations have followed Moreno's approach by having peers identify personality or behavioral characteristics of the children they nominate as preferred peers. Young and Cooper (1944) administered a peer nomination and "Guess Who?" assessment to a large number of elementary-aged children, chose five children with the highest and lowest scores in each class, and examined the groups' ratings on individual items. The items that discriminated between the groups were extroversion, sense of personal worth, feeling of belonging, social standards, school relations, and physical appearance. In a similar study with high school students, Brown (1954) had students nominate peers as companions in a joint activity and then complete a checklist containing reasons for choosing or not choosing those friends. Among the reasons for choosing freinds were "interests in common," "understands me," and "has good manners"; reasons for rejection were "bad conduct," "is insincere," and "has low ideals."

Studies have used peer assessments to more closely investigate the nature of sociometric typologies. Peretti et al. (1981) asked sixth-graders to nominate three peers by whom they would like to sit and three by whom they would not like to sit. Next, they asked the children to state why they chose peers for each criterion. From the responses, the authors identified four types of isolate children: passive-detached (i.e., shy, timid); passive-independent (i.e., self-centered, arrogant); active-detached (i.e., fearful); and active-independent (i.e., aggressive, bullying). In two studies Coie et al. (1982) administered peer nominations with positive and negative criteria to third-, fifth-, and eighth-graders and also asked the children to complete a peer assessment containing 24 behavioral descriptions. In their first study, social preference was positively related to cooperativeness, physical attractiveness, and supportiveness, and inversely related to disruptiveness and aggression. In the second study, the peer assessment provided information on controversial children, a previously unidentified group. These children were perceived ambivalently as disruptive and aggressive, and at the same time, as social leaders.

A further use of the joint sociometric–peer-assessment analysis of children's social relations is in the determination of possible target behaviors for social skills training and the evaluation of training procedures. Hoier and Cone (1980) used peer-nomination sociometrics to select rejected children and then identified children nominated by the rejected children as hopeful playmates. A jointly administered peer assessment revealed the behaviors that the hopeful playmates most liked about peers whom they had, in turn, chosen as friends. Following the logic that these behaviors would make the rejected children more attractive to their hopeful playmates, this behavioral template was proposed as the ideal set of target behaviors for the rejected children's social skills training interventions. Such a procedure could also be used to develop "local norms" of desirable social behaviors for a class as a whole or subgroups within a class (e.g., all the girls in the class).

As an outcome measure of a social skills training program, Lefevre, West, and Ledingham (1983) administered the Pupil Evaluation Inventory (PEI), a mixed assessment, to the class of a 7-year-old male subject who was experiencing severe difficulties in establishing peer relationships. The PEI, given before and after the program, revealed changes in the aggression and peer-withdrawal factor scores but little change on the likability score. In this case, peers perceived a behavior change in the targeted child but still did not choose him more often as someone they liked.

Used jointly, sociometrics and peer assessments provide complementary information about children's relationships with peers. The peer assessment offers relatively objective information about classmates from a peer's perspective, and sociometrics reveals preferential relationships. One procedure may supply information about the other, or both may be used to investigate a third issue.

One problem with using sociometric and peer assessments together is the possible presence of a friendship-bias effect. A high correlation between positive items on a peer assessment and sociometric status could occur if children assigned all predetermined positive items to friends regardless of their actual behavior. Though Kane and Lawler (1978) de-emphasize the friendship bias by inferring that individuals choose friends based on their good behavior or performance and reject peers based on undesirable behavior or performance, such an argument quickly becomes circular. A friendship bias undoubtedly influences peer assessment of interpersonal behavior and could, in fact, be bidirectional in nature. For example, a child could nominate peers as desired companions because they are cooperative, as noted on a peer assessment item, and at the same time rate the peers as "good sports" because they are friends. When interpreting the results of sociometric–peer-assessment studies, the reader should be aware of the influence of friendship biases. As Kane and Lawler (1978) accurately noted, such biases may be countered by validity evidence offered by developers of peer-assessment instruments.

CORRELATES OF SOCIOMETRIC MEASURES

Since the mid-1950s, considerable effort has been devoted to the identification of correlates of sociometric status. Some of these correlates (e.g., social-cognitive skills, specific social behaviors) seem intuitively obvious and increase our confidence in the validity of sociometric measures. Others (e.g., race differences, sex differences, handicapping conditions) may seem less obvious (or desired), and may have implications for social-service delivery systems (see Gresham, 1981a).

Examination of the correlates of sociometric status has important implications for the validation of these measures in the assessment of social competence. To establish validity, we would expect sociometric scores to be (1) significantly correlated with other measures that are construed as estimates of social behavioral competence, and (2) *not* significantly correlated with measures that we assume are unrelated to such competence. These patterns of correlations would suggest degrees of *convergent* and *discriminant* validity, respectively (Campbell & Fiske, 1959).

The identified correlates of sociometric measures can be arbitrarily divided into stable and manipulable features of the child or environment. *Stable features* are those that are the result of genetic or subtle environmental influences and are distinguished by their relative resistance or unavailability to change through direct intervention (e.g., sex, race, name of child, size of classroom, or play group). Manipulable characteristics, on the other hand, are under the more direct control of discriminable environmental variables, and are thus generally amenable to direct intervention (e.g., social behavior or skills, knowledge, social cognition, language).

Stable Features of the Child and Environment

The physical characteristics of individual children can greatly influence the sociometric evaluations they receive from their peers. Sex, race, and physical attractiveness have all been shown to contribute in varying degrees to observed measures of sociometric status.

Sex of Child

The presence of sex biases in children's friendship selections is consistent not only with cultural lore, which holds that children are most likely to have same-sex friends, but also with observational data that demonstrate specific differences between boys and girls in social behaviors and freeplay activities (Asher & Hymel, 1981; Hops, 1983). Sex differences do not occur in measures of overall social status for boys and girls; across equally proportioned groups, mean sociometric scores for boys and girls are equivalent (Moore & Updegraff, 1964). Rather, biases emerge only when cross-sex evaluations (i.e., boys' evaluations of girls or girls' evaluations of boys) are considered. Thus, while both boys and girls receive similar total scores on sociometric assessments, differences occur in the ratings received from same- and opposite-sex peers for both groups.

One of the most complete evaluations of cross-sex rating biases was offered by Asher and Hymel (1981). In a reanalysis of sociometric data from 205 elementary children, same-sex, opposite-sex, and all-classmate scores were compared for positive and negative nominations and a rating of play preference. The authors' analyses demonstrated that: (1) children received more positive nominations from same-sex peers than from opposite-sex peers, (2) more negative nominations were given by opposite-sex peers than by same-sex peers, and (3) ratings from same-sex peers were higher than those for opposite-sex peers. While Asher and Hymel (1981) did not report significance tests for these differences, they did report correlations between boys' and girls' evaluations. Interestingly, scores given by same- and opposite-sex classmates on each of the three measures were significantly correlated, but the relationships were only moderate in magnitude. As the authors note, one possible explanation for these results is that boys and girls use somewhat different standards or norms in their nominations and ratings of classmates. Cross-sex scores on two of the three measures, however, had relatively small standard deviations; this, too, may have restricted the magnitude of obtained correlations.

The results of Asher and Hymel (1981) are not without generalizability. Cross-sex rating biases have been noted across a broad range of populations and measures (e.g., Hops, 1983; Hops & Finch, 1983; Moore & Updegraff, 1964; Moreno, 1934; Oden & Asher, 1977; Singleton & Asher, 1979).

Race of Child

Similar findings have been reported for sociometric evaluations among children of different races. Sociometric measures have been used for a number of years to study friendship patterns in racially integrated settings (see Moreno, 1934), and are frequently employed in the study of outcomes of desegregation (Hallinan, 1981; Singleton & Asher, 1979).

The extent of cross-race bias in sociometric ratings is partially a function of the measure used. Singleton and Asher (1979) noted that a number of studies employing nomination procedures have detected high levels of same-race preference among elementary school children in integrated settings. These authors suggested that nomination procedures, with restricted numbers of nominations from each child, may establish overly stringent tests of cross-race acceptance and friendship. Singleton and Asher (1979) presented both longitudinal and cross-sectional analyses of rating data collected in racially integrated schools. The results indicated that significant preferences for same-race peers did exist, and that same-race preferences tended to increase with age, particularly for black children. However, the biases due to race in these ratings were considerably less extreme than those obtained in studies employing peer nominations procedures and relatively small when compared to the effects of gender differences on children's ratings.

Physical Attractiveness

Physical attractiveness has also been related to the sociometric evaluations children receive from their peers; however, this relationship is not always straightforward. Two investigators have compared children's social status to adults' ratings of their physical attractiveness (Dion & Berscheid, 1974; Vaughn & Langlois, 1983). In general, the results of these studies indicate that when significant relationships do occur, physical attractiveness is more closely associated with the social status of girls than of boys. Dion and Berscheid (1974) reported significant two- and three-way interactions among attractiveness, gender, and age in their analysis of sociometric scores. Post hoc tests indicated that most of these interactions were due to differences in various groupings of girls' peer popularity. Similarly, Vaughn and Langlois (1983) reported significant correlations for physical attractiveness with paired comparison sociometrics, but not with positive nomination picture sociometrics. Examination of the correlations between attractiveness and paired comparisons by sex indicated that the overall relationship was largely due to a substantial relationship among girls' scores. The correlation for boys' scores was not statistically significant.

Names

Children's names may also be related to sociometric status in peer groups. McDavid and Harari (1966) found that the social desirability of individuals' names, whether rated by playmates or unacquainted children, was significantly correlated with status on a combined positive and negative nomination sociometric measure. Based upon a review of similar studies, Foster (1983) suggested that unusual or infrequently encountered names may be uniquely associated with lower scores on peer sociometrics. This is supported by McDavid and Harari's (1966) data, in which children with relatively unusual names consistently received low social desirability ratings across multiple groups of children.

Handicapping Condition

Handicapped (special education) children are less often named as friends and more often rejected than their nonhandicapped peers. In two studies, Bryan (1974, 1976) demonstrated that (1) learning disabled students in the intermediate grades received significantly fewer positive nominations and significantly more negative nominations than matched nonhandicapped classmates, and (2) low popularity and high rejection scores are stable over 1 year's time, even when substantial changes in peer groups occurred. Findings of lower social status for handicapped students have been replicated across settings (Bryan, 1978; Bruininks et al., 1974; Gottlieb & Budoff, 1973), measures (Bryan & Wheeler, 1972; Sipperstein, Bopp, & Bak, 1978), and handicapping conditions (Bryan, 1974; Goodman, Gottlieb, & Harrison, 1972; Gottlieb, Semmel, & Veldman, 1978).

Ecological Variables

Structural aspects of a classroom or other social settings may significantly affect sociometric scores of individuals within groups. Class size appears to be one variable that exerts a significant influence on children's friendship choices. In a study of group formation, Hallinan (1979) found that the number of peers chosen and nominations received from peers increased with the size of the class and that there were fewer social isolates in large classes as compared with small classes.

In addition to class size, the structure of the classroom appears to influence sociometric status scores. In her study of open and traditional classroom structures, Hallinan (1976) found fewer social isolates in open classes than in traditional classes, perhaps because greater opportunity to engage in social interaction exists among all class members in open classrooms. Similarly, structuring a class so that children receive instructions in small groups or work on joint tasks together appears to determine the specific children nominated as friends on sociometric assessments (Hallinan & Tuma, 1978).

In a study of learning-disabled children enrolled in mainstreamed classes, Deno, Mirkin, Robinson, and Evans (1980) found that the reliabilities of sociometric scores and their correlations with observational measures varied across classes. The authors attributed this variance to differing classroom structures.

Finally, in an interesting retrospective study, Caulfield (1980) interviewed children who had been classified as neglected or isolated in the fifth grade but were ranked in the upper 50% of their class in the twelfth grade. These children attributed the change in their sociometric status to the availability of a wider range of activities in junior high (i.e., less-rigid class structure) than in the elementary classes.

Manipulable Characteristics of the Child

Like the stable features of individuals and environments, manipulable characteristics of children can influence the sociometric evaluations received from peers. These manipulable characteristics cover a wide variety of behaviors, including social, language, and motor skills, classroom performance, and social knowledge or cognition. Because of their availability to direct intervention, the correlational and functional relationships of these manipulable characteristics to sociometric measures have been frequently investigated.

Social Behaviors and Skills

Identification of social behavioral correlates of sociometric status, via naturalistic observation or analogue situation studies, has been a major focus of social-skills research (for complete reviews, see Asher & Hymel, 1981; Hops, 1982; Putallaz & Gottman, 1981b). This research is of central importance to the development of maximally effective intervention programs for socially rejected, neglected, or at-risk children.

Initial investigations of social behavioral correlates of sociometric status focused on somewhat general measures of children's interactions. In a seminal study, Hartup et al. (1967) found significant positive relationships (1) between rates of positive or appropriate social interaction and positive peer nominations, and (2) between rates of negative or inappropriate interaction and negative peer nominations. Similarly, Marshall and McCandless (1957) found positive correlations between two categories of appropriate interaction (i.e., Friendly Approach and Associative Play) and best-friend positive nomination scores. While the relationship between general measures of social interaction and sociometric status has been replicated (e.g., Gottman et al., 1975; Greenwood et al., 1979), the magnitude of this relationship is not great. In some cases, particularly with elementary school children, obtained correlations are not statistically significant (e.g., Asher et al., 1981; McConnell, 1983). As a result, some have suggested that interactive rate measures may have little utility for the identification of socially at-risk children (Asher et al., 1981; Gresham, 1983).

Researchers in this area have begun to focus their attention on the identification of more-specific topographic or functional correlates of sociometric status. Through a variety of unique, carefully executed, contrasted-groups designs, these investigators have explored (1) social initiations or bids that are characteristic of high- or low-status children (e.g., Strain, 1984), (2) strategies or tactics exhibited by high-status children for entry into established peer groups (e.g., Dodge, Schlundt, Delugach, & Schocken, 1982; Putallaz & Gottman, 1981a), and (3) the relationship of sociometric status to visual attention or regard received during freeplay (Vaughn & Waters, 1981). These investigations have typically obtained stronger, more stable relationships than the studies using general behavioral measures. To date, however, this research has been largely descriptive. Experimental manipulations are necessary to demonstrate the causal relationship between these behaviors and sociometric status.

The empirical identification of social behavioral correlates of sociometric status is a difficult process. To date, findings have been somewhat inconsistent, particularly for older children (Asher & Hymel, 1981). Stable, generalizable results require an extensive program of research, moving from broad-band naturalistic observation studies to intensive, carefully controlled experimental manipulations (McConnell, Strain, Kerr, Stagg, Lenkner, & Lambert, 1984). Rather than arguing from nonrejected null hypotheses (i.e., that because few stable relationships have been found, we can assume that few exist), investigators must meet the challenge of designing more complex studies and using more sophisticated procedures to identify important and necessary relationships.

Motor and Athletic Skills

Cultural lore suggests that one's strength, speed, agility, or athletic prowess might be a significant predictor of peer popularity. Such stereotypes are, in fact, borne out by empirical investigations.

Hops and his colleagues (Hops & Finch, 1983; Steigleman & Hops, 1983) have examined the relationship between sociometric status and various motor skills (e.g., timed runs, throwing form and distance) for preschool children. Factor analyses of children's performance on 14 different motor skills yielded four factors: Coordination, Arm Strength, Speed, and Throw-form. Each of these factors was significantly correlated with status on a paired-comparison sociometric. In addition, Speed and Arm Strength factor scores each made significant contributions to the prediction of a composite social-competence score, of which sociometric status was one part.

Among older children, athletic skills are also associated with sociometric status. Gross and Johnson (in press) correlated roster and rating sociometric scores with 12 motor and athletic skill measures for 108 children at a summer sports camp. For both boys and girls, at least half of the motor and athletic skill measures were correlated with social status. These results replicated the earlier work of Broekhoff (1977).

Active play is one important element of children's social interactions (McHale & Olley, 1982; Odom, Jenkins, Speltz, & DeKlyen, 1982). As Hops (1983) noted, children with limited motor or athletic abilities may have more difficulty finding playmates or successfully participating in active games. As such, ensuring adequate motor development may be a necessary condition for achieving social acceptance.

Language Skills

Language plays a significant role in children's interactions with peers. Children as young as 3 years of age tend to speak in clear, grammatically correct utterances that are highly successful at eliciting responses from peers (Mueller, 1972). Normative data indicate that rates of verbal interaction tend to increase throughout the elementary years (Walker, McConnell, & Clarke, in press).

To date, efforts to describe the relationship of language skills and sociometric status have failed to obtain consistent results. For instance, children's performance on a measure of egocentric communication (i.e., relative ability to take the other's point of view) has been shown to be significantly related to social status in kindergarten and second grade (Rubin, 1972), but not in preschool (Deutsch, 1974) or fourth and sixth grade (Rubin, 1972). Similarly, Gottman et al. (1975) did not find differences between high- and low-popularity children on perspective-taking or "blindfold listener" tasks, but did obtain one significant difference for the two groups' performance on a referential communications task.

Hops and Finch (1983) collected receptive vocabulary (i.e., the Peabody Picture Vocabulary Test) and basic concept (i.e., the Englemann Basic Concepts Inventory) measures for the preschool children in their sample. Both of these measures yielded significant but low correlations with peer popularity. In reviewing these and other findings, Hops (1983) suggested that well-developed language skills are not sufficient for attaining high levels of social status, but are necessary prerequisites of effective social communication, and thus make important contributions to children's social competence.

Classroom Performance and Academic Achievement

As noted earlier, children with educational handicaps tend to be less accepted and more rejected than nonhandicapped peers. More generally, children's classroom performance and academic achievement are also predictive of one's social status.

In one of the most comprehensive studies of its type, Green, Fore-hand, Beck, and Vosk (1980) collected data on the academic achieve-ment, peer ratings, teacher ratings, directly observed behavior, and child self-reports for 116 third-grade children. Academic achievement was significantly related to all three peer-referenced measures, with higher levels of achievement associated with (1) greater numbers of positive (i.e., best friend) peer nominations, (2) fewer negative peer nominations, and (3) lower mean ratings on a "dislike" peer rating. Rotated factor analyses indicated, however, that peer ratings and aca-demic achievement were somewhat distinct. The three sociometric mea-sures loaded significantly, along with several teacher ratings, on a single factor. Academic achievement loaded on another factor, along with di-rect observation measures of time on task and time spent in positive peer interaction.

The findings of Green et al. (1980), with consistent correlations be-tween academic achievement and acceptance or rejection sociometrics, are at variance with those of Gottlieb et al. (1978). To identify correlates of social status for mentally retarded students placed in regular educa-tion classrooms, Gottlieb et al. compared peer acceptance and rejection nominations with peers' and teachers' perceptions of academic–cogni-tive performance and disruptive behavior. Their results indicated that social acceptance was related only to teachers' and peers' evaluations of cognitive–academic performance, and social rejection was related most strongly to teachers' and peers' evaluations of misbehavior, with some contribution from teachers' academic performance ratings. It should be noted that Gottlieb et al. (1978) were correlating social acceptance with peers' and teachers' *perceptions* of handicapped students' cognitive–aca-demic and behavioral competence, whereas Green et al. (1980) em-ployed more behavior-specific rating scales and direct observation mea-sures. In addition, peers' and teachers' perceptions of child behavior in the Gottlieb et al. study accounted for relatively small proportions of variance in social competence and rejection (15.7 and 18.1%, respec-tively). It may be that more-direct measures of cognitive–academic and behavioral competence would yield more robust results.

A number of investigators have employed academic or cognitive refer-ents in sociometric measures (e.g., "How much do you like to work with _____ ?" or "Name three children with whom you most like to work"). These peer evaluations appear to be consistently related to other sociometric measures (e.g., Green et al., 1980; Gresham, 1981b; Haack & McConnell, 1983), but to also tap slightly different domains than "play with" or "best friend" ratings (Haack & McConnell, 1983; Oden & Asher, 1977). The importance of performance in academic settings for the development of social competence is highlighted by descriptive research (Hersh & Walker, 1983). To date, however, this research has been exclusively correlational. Given the development of academic training programs since the late 1970s (e.g., Becker & Carnine, 1980; Strain & Kerr, 1981), further research regarding the effects of academic intervention on children's social status may be a useful avenue of inquiry.

Social Knowledge and Social Cognition

Some investigators have sought to identify social knowledge or social cognition correlates of sociometric status. As Renshaw and Asher (1982) noted, "the investigation of popular and unpopular children's social knowledge has been guided by the hypothesis that children's behavior is regulated by the ideas they have about what to do in various situations" (p. 383). While these mediational characteristics of social knowledge have not yet been directly demonstrated, some differences between high- and low-status groups have been detected.

Most studies of social knowledge correlates of sociometric status have employed hypothetical-situations methodology (Renshaw & Asher, 1982), in which children are presented verbal and/or pictorial descriptions of social situations and are asked to describe how they might respond. Gottman et al. (1975) asked popular and unpopular children, grouped by a median split, to "pretend that the experimenter was a new child in school with whom [the subject] wanted to make friends" (Gottman et al., 1975, p. 712). Subjects' responses were scored for the inclusion of greetings, requests for information, efforts to include the new peer in an activity, and offers of information. The analyses presented by Gottman et al. indicated that high-status children scored significantly higher on this task than did low-status children.

The study of social cognition has also been extended to children's ideas about helpfulness. Ladd and Oden (1979) interviewed high- and low-status third and fifth grade students regarding how they might help peers in three different situations. Although children tended to offer similar responses to the helping situations, Ladd and Oden found a significant relationship between the number of unique or idiosyncratic responses given and sociometric status, with low-status children tending to give more unique responses.

Asher and Renshaw (1981) have extended the work of both Gottman et al. (1975) and Ladd and Oden (1979), eliciting kindergarten students' responses to three different examples of each of three social situations (i.e., initiating relationships, maintaining relationships, and coping with conflict). In this study, unpopular children provided more vague or negative–aggressive responses to these situations than did popular children. Additionally, judges blind to children's status rated popular students' responses as more effective and relationship-enhancing than unpopular children's responses.

The fact that popular and unpopular peers differ in their knowledge of how to make friends and behave appropriately has considerable face and empirical validity. However, the mediational link between social knowledge and social behavior is still tenuous. To date, we have little or no evidence of causal relationships, in either direction, between sociometric status and social knowledge. Renshaw and Asher (1982) note several potentially useful directions for future research, including the examination of social goals. Such research may more clearly highlight the relationship among these measures.

Summary

Differences in a wide variety of child social and other behaviors are moderately associated with children's sociometric status. These relationships increase our confidence in the validity of sociometric measures, and they form the basis for many treatment programs. However, differences in sex, race, physical attractiveness, or other stable features also have weak-to-moderate effects on the sociometric status of children. These latter findings are largely consistent with existing theories of interpersonal attraction (Lott & Lott, 1960). Unfortunately, these relationships may moderate the utility of sociometric measures in the assessment of children's social competence. To the degree that differences in sex, race, or physical appearance *do not* contribute to differences in children's social effectiveness or development, these variables contribute error to the measurement of competence. As we mention later, such error can only be detected through careful design and analysis of multirater–multibehavior evaluations.

RELATIONSHIP OF SOCIOMETRIC MEASURES TO OTHER MEASURES OF SOCIAL COMPETENCE

Mental health professionals have been unable to develop a precise, commonly agreed upon definition of social competence for children (Anderson & Messick, 1974; Zigler & Trickett, 1978). As a result, efforts to develop and validate measures for use in the identification and treatment of socially at-risk children have been severely hampered (Hops, 1983).

Since 1974, the framework for an operational definition of social competence has become available. Anderson and Messick (1974) identified 29 components of social competence, highlighting the range of domains that must be considered. Foster and Ritchey (1979) focused more closely on a functional definition of competence, suggesting that measures must reflect the situational specificity and interactive nature of social behavior. Drawing on these and other literatures, Hops (1983) has provided a useful distinction between social competence and social skill. From Hops's perspective, "competence is a summary term which reflects social judgement about the general quality of an individual's performance in a given situation" (Hops, 1983, p.3). Thus, the measurement of social competence is distinguished by its emphasis on general evaluations of children in specific social situations.

Who provides these general evaluations? As noted in this review, children can provide reliable social judgements about the general quality of their peers' performance. Measures have also been developed and validated for recording the social judgments of parents, teachers, and others.

Thus, we can accept as a working model that social competence is most directly assessed via general ratings of a child's social functioning, as completed by various social agents (e.g., parents, teachers, peers) in the child's environment. Two assumptions regarding this model can be made. First, it is assumed that different social agents' ratings will be based to some degree on observations and evaluations of the child's social performance in different social settings. For instance, whereas parents have an opportunity to most frequently observe the child in home and community settings, teachers most often observe the child in the classroom. Similarly, a child's peers have opportunities to observe social performance in settings that may not be available to adults. Second, it is assumed that social agents' ratings may differ as a function of their opportunities to observe the child's performance in these different settings. Such differences may be due to the situational specificity of behavior (Mischel, 1968), as well as the differing evaluative standards of raters (Hersh & Walker, 1983; Van Houten, 1979). We would expect, however, some convergence in different social agents' ratings. As Hops (1983) has noted, there is much to suggest that some behavioral competencies are critical for success across a wide range of settings and social situations. To the extent that these cross-situational competencies contribute to different raters' evaluations, we would expect ratings to converge.

As reviewed, sociometric measures have been shown to be related to other peer-referenced measures of social competence, as well as to both stable and manipulable characteristics of the child and setting. In addition, previous research has demonstrated the relationship of sociometric measures to other general ratings of children's social behavior. While these relationships have not always been of a large magnitude, they do have significance for understanding the role of sociometric measures in the assessment of social competence. For this reason, we next review available research on the relationship of sociometric measures to teacher ratings, as well as the convergence of peers' and adults' ratings with direct observation measures of children's social behavior.

Teacher Judgments and Sociometric Status

To date, almost all sociometric research has been conducted in preschool and elementary classrooms. This is partly due to our renewed interest in the social relations of young children with their peers Hops, 1982; Lewis & Rosenblum, 1975). However, it is also true that sociometric assessment typically requires an intact group of children; as a result, school settings provide natural laboratories for such research. Because of this focus on school settings, a great amount is known of the relationships between sociometric measures and teachers' judgments.

Two basic measurement procedures have been developed and validated for collecting teachers' judgments of children's social behavior and competence. These are *rankings* of intact groups of children, where an individual's performance is evaluated relative to that of others in the group, and *ratings* of specific behaviors or response classes, where an individual's performance is evaluated against a behavioral description or standard. The relationship of scores from each of these measurement strategies to sociometric status is discussed in turn.

Teacher Rankings

Teacher rankings of children's social acceptance and interactive rate were first developed as components of cost-effective screening procedures for identifying socially withdrawn children in preschool and elementary classrooms as developed by Greenwood, Todd, Walker, and Hops (1978). Two ranking procedures were evaluated. In one, teachers were asked to rank-order children in their classroom according to their relative rates of positive verbal interaction with peers. In the other, teachers rank-ordered their students according to the degree to which peers liked to play with each child (i.e., peer popularity). These rank-ordering procedures contribute to the identification of low-rate interactors in preschool classrooms. When compared to direct observation measures of social participation, 23% of the participating teachers placed the least interactive child in the lowest ranking for frequency of verbal interaction; 77% of the teachers identified this least interactive child in the lowest five ranks (Greenwood, Walker, Todd, & Hops, 1979).

Greenwood and his colleagues (1979) also examined the relationship of teacher rankings to direct, peer-referenced assessments of children's sociometic status. As part of a larger study, these investigators compared teacher rankings of interactive frequency and peer popularity with peer-referenced sociometric measures. Twenty teachers and 299 children participated. Teacher rankings and positive nomination picture sociometrics were collected concurrently on two occasions 1 month apart. The results indicated that teacher rankings were quite stable over the test–retest period, but that the sociometric scores were not. In addition, both teacher ranking procedures were significantly correlated with students' sociometric status. Teacher rankings of interactive frequency were moderately correlated with the number of nominations received ($r = .27$ and $.41$ for Time 1 and Time 2 assessments, respectively). Teachers' rankings of peer popularity were more highly and consistently correlated to sociometric status ($r = .57$ for both assessment occasions). It is interesting to note that, while teachers' rankings of popularity were more closely associated with sociometric status, the rankings of interactive frequency tended to be more highly correlated with observed rates of social interaction. These patterns of correlations may reflect differences in the method–behavior confound (Cone, 1979); that is, greater convergence would be expected when two groups of raters (i.e., teachers and peers or observers) are evaluating similar characteristics (i.e., peer popularity or social participation) for individual children.

Connolly and Doyle (1981) adapted the interactive frequency ranking procedure from Greenwood et al. (1979) to compare the predictive validity of teacher rankings and peer sociometrics for assessing the social competence of preschool children. In two studies, a total of nine preschool teachers ranked their children in order of frequency and extensiveness of interactions with peers. In addition, children in each class completed positive nomination picture sociometrics. The level of association between measures replicated the results of Greenwood et al. (1979). Although Connolly and Doyle's findings were somewhat inconsistent, teacher rankings were significantly correlated, in the expected direction, with peer sociometrics ($r = .35$ and $.55$, absolute value, for Studies 1 and 2 respectively).

The studies presented by Greenwood et al. (1979) and Connolly and

Doyle (1981) suggest that teacher rankings of interactive frequency and peer popularity tap, to some degree, the same domains as peer sociometrics. Correlations presented by these investigators indicate that teacher rankings and peer-referenced sociometrics share between 7 and 33% common variance. While this relationship across raters and methods is not especially strong, it is of sufficient magnitude to suggest that *both* measures may be of interest in the assessment of social competence.

Teacher Ratings

A number of investigators have also examined the relationship between peer sociometrics and child behavior rating scales completed by teachers. As noted, rating scales require teachers to evaluate each individual child's social behavioral competence with reference to standard descriptions or criteria (e.g., "The child engages in conversations longer than 30 seconds"). While the specific measures and methods used in different studies have varied, several common findings emerge.

In one of the earliest cross-rater comparisons, McCandless and Marshall (1957) evaluated the correspondence between teacher and peer measures of children's popularity. Teachers in three preschool classrooms were asked to identify the four best friends for each of their students. In addition, the 48 students in these classrooms each completed positive-nomination picture sociometrics, selecting their three best friends from photographs of their classmates. Best-friend scores were calculated from both teachers' and peers' nominations by summing the number of nominations, weighted for order of selection, each child received. Repeated assessments were completed at approximately 10-day intervals to assess the temporal stability of these best-friend scores. Three administrations of the teacher and peer assessments were completed in two of the participating classrooms; four administrations were completed in the remaining classroom.

Relationships between teacher-referenced and peer-referenced best-friend scores within each classroom for the three or four repeated assessments were inconsistent. In only one class were teachers' and peers' ratings significantly correlated (rs from .47 to .68) on all three occasions. Correlations of teacher- and peer-referenced scores for the total sample were all of low to moderate levels of magnitude (r's of .19, .63, and .40 for Time 1, Time 2, and Time 3 assessments, respectively), and only the latter two correlations differed significantly from zero.

Greenwood et al. (1979) compared peer popularity scores with two rating scales completed by teachers for the 299 preschoolers in their study. Both scales contained behavior-specific items that teachers rated on a seven-point bipolar differential (i.e., "false description" to "true description"). The two scales assessed problem behaviors (9 items) and positive social behaviors (12 items), respectively. Teacher ratings were collected concurrent with positive nomination sociometrics; all teachers and students completed retest assessments 1 month after the initial evaluation. Correlations between teacher ratings and sociometrics were all significant and in the predicted direction. As with the findings of McCandless and Marshall (1957), however, the obtained correlation coefficients were in the low- to low-moderate range (*Rho* for concurrent measures ranged from .23 to .43, absolute magnitude).

In addition to the work of Marshall and McCandless (1957) and Greenwood et al. (1979) with preschool samples, three other investigations have examined the relationship between peer sociometrics and teacher ratings in elementary populations. LaGreca (1981) asked teachers to complete the Pupil Evaluation Inventory (PEI) (Pekarik et al., 1976) for 92 children in Grades 3 through 5. The PEI yields three factor scores: likability, withdrawal, and aggression. In addition to the teacher ratings, LaGreca collected "play with" and "work with" roster and rating sociometrics for each of the participating children.

La Greca's (1981), examination of the correlations between teacher and peer ratings suggested that, in general, children receiving high ratings on either the "play with" or "work with" sociometrics also tended to receive (1) higher teacher ratings on the likability scale (i.e., rated as more likable), and (2) lower teacher ratings on the withdrawn and aggressive scales (i.e., rated as less aggressive and withdrawn). Stepwise regression analyses, with each peer rating independently regressed on the three teacher ratings (controlling for age), were also conducted. For both the total sample and the boys only, each of the teacher rating scales was found to contribute significantly to the prediction of sociometrics. For girls in the sample, only teacher ratings of withdrawn behavior contributed significantly to the regression. Again, both simple and multiple correlations between teacher ratings and sociometrics were in the low to moderate range. Coefficients for correlations between single teacher rating and sociometric scores ranged from .33 to .53, absolute magnitude, for the entire sample. Multiple correlation coefficients, drawn from the most complete equations for the six different regressions, were slightly higher (*R* from .61 to .67). Patterns of correlations for the different teacher rating scales with either "play with" or "work with" sociometrics were highly similar, most likely due to the substantial method variance present in the sociometric measures.

Similar results have been obtained for other teacher rating scales.

McConnell (1983) compared teacher responses on the Social Interaction Rating Scale (Hops, Guild, Fleischman, Paine, Street, Walker, & Greenwood, 1978) to "play with" rating sociometrics for 43 boys in Grades 1 through 4. The Social Interaction Rating Scale is an eight-item, seven-point Likert-type scale designed to identify elementary children who interact with peers at especially low rates. In 13 classrooms, teachers provided ratings for one male student who had been referred by his special education teacher for social skills training, as well as for two randomly selected male classmates. Sociometric scores were drawn from roster and rating scales completed by the boys' male and female classmates. Both teacher and peer ratings successfully discriminated referred and nonreferred groups. The correlation between the two ratings was significant ($r = .32$) but only of low-moderate magnitude.

A final comparison of peer sociometrics and teacher ratings can be drawn from the elaborate study presented by Green et al. (1980). As part of their investigation of the relationships among measures of social competence and school success, these authors collected general ratings from both teachers and peers for 116 third grade children. Teachers completed the Conners Teacher Rating Scale (Conners, 1969), from which two scores were computed: a Total Deviant score (the sum of conduct problem, inattentive–passive, tension–anxiety, and hyperactivity scale scores), and the Sociability scale score. Teachers were also asked to estimate (1) the average peer rating each child would receive, (2) the extent to which the child exhibited conduct disorders, and (3) the extent to which each child was socially withdrawn. From participating children, the authors collected three sociometric measures: positive-nominations, negative-nominations, and roster "dislike" ratings. Correlational analyses indicated that all of the peer sociometric measures were significantly associated, in the expected direction, with teachers' estimates of peer status (r's from .44 to .58) and withdrawn behavior (r's from .26 to .27), as well as with the Conners Total Deviance score (r's from $-.37$ to $-.46$). In addition, the Conners Sociability Scale was significantly related to the negative nomination and roster dislike rating (r's of $-.35$ and $-.30$, respectively). The correlational results were partially confirmed by a factor analysis, in which the Conners Total Score and the teachers' estimates of peer status loaded on the same factor as the three sociometric measures.

These comparisons of peer sociometrics and teacher ratings generally replicate the comparisons with teacher rankings. Again, correlations between peers' and teachers' judgments tend to be significant, but share only moderate amounts of common variance. As noted, this suggests some overlap in the domains assessed by the two types of measures. Again, we have some evidence that both measures are of interest in the assessment of social competence.

Summary

The findings reviewed in this section indicate that teachers' judgments, whether collected as rankings or ratings of individual students, have considerable face and empirical validity for the evaluation of children's performance in social situations. However, the magnitude of the relationships of teacher judgments to other measures of child performance appear to be mediated by several factors. First, as noted, cross-method relationships will vary as a function of teachers' opportunity to observe children's behavior in various settings. For instance, McConnell (1983) obtained markedly lower correlations between teacher ratings on the Social Interaction Rating Scale and observed rates of social interaction than did Hops et al. (1978), who originally developed this scale. McConnell (1983) suggested that this finding may have been due to the restricted opportunity teachers in his sample had to observe subjects' social interactions. Similar relationships might be obtained when teachers are asked to rate other situations to which they have little direct access (e.g., social behavior at home or during private interactions with peers).

Second, the magnitude of these relationships might be mediated by the degree of overlap in the content or domains sampled by the compared measures. As noted, teacher rankings of peer popularity and verbal interaction frequency were most closely associated with peer-referenced or direct observation measures that were most similar in content (Greenwood et al., 1979). Similarly, one would expect children's sociometric status to be more closely associated with teachers' ratings of students' estimated sociometric status than with teachers' ratings of sociability or social withdrawal, as Green et al. (1980) found.

In summary, the relationship of teachers' judgments to other measures of social performance appears to depend on the questions teachers are asked. Given appropriate questions and opportunities to observe relevant child behaviors, teachers can provide useful and highly accurate evaluations of child performance. Ultimately, the utility of teachers' social judgments for the assessment of social competence rests, as with other measures, on the effort given to the development or selection of appropriate ranking and rating tasks.

Sociometrics, Teacher Judgments, and
Direct Observation

Several of the studies reviewed in this section have also presented analyses of the relationships among sociometrics, teacher rankings and ratings, and direct observation measures of children's social behavior. While there is considerable debate regarding what the ultimate criterion for validating measures of social competence should be (e.g., Asher et al., 1981; Gottman, 1977; Gresham, 1983; Hops, 1983; Hops, Finch, & McConnell, in press), an examination of these relationships may have heuristic value in our understanding of how children differ and how we might best assess these differences.

Convergence among Measures

At least three groups of investigators have examined the degree to which sociometrics and teacher rankings or ratings are associated with direct observation measures of social interaction. In general, these analyses have produced results similar to the comparisons of peer- and teacher-referenced measures; that is, correlations across settings, measures, and populations tend to be in the low to low-moderate range. Some differences emerge, however, in the strength of the different relationships.

The most complete comparison of peer, teacher, and direct observation measures was offered by Greenwood et al. (1979). In addition to the positive peer-nomination sociometric, the teacher rankings of interactive frequency and peer popularity, and the teacher ratings of problem behaviors and social assets, Greenwood and his colleagues completed 10 15-minute observations for each of the 299 preschool subjects in both free-play and assigned (academic) task settings. Direct observation measures included (1) the rate of interaction with peers, (2) the proportion of shared interactions, (3) the proportion of peers' interactions initiated to each child, and (4) the number of different peers with whom each child interacted. Scores from the peer- and teacher-referenced assessments were then correlated with each of the direct observation measures. While sociometric and teacher ranking and rating measures all tended to correlate with the observational measures, coefficients between sociometric and direct observation measures were generally quite low (r's ranging from .06 to .39). Coefficients for the relationships of teacher ranking scores and observational measures were of greater consistency and magnitude (r's ranging from .28 to .63, absolute magnitude), as were correlations between observed behaviors and teacher ratings (r's from .18 to .53, with a median coefficient of .35).

In an extension of their earlier study, Marshall and McCandless (1957) correlated peer- and teacher-referenced best-friend scores with several scores derived from direct observation. Thirty-six preschool children were observed in free-play interactions with peers. Four categories of social interaction rate (i.e., Friendly Approach, Associate Play, Conversation, and Hostile) were recorded. In addition, observational best-friend scores were calculated, using the three peers with whom each child most frequently interacted as analogues to sociometric nominations. Rates of interaction in each of the behavioral categories and observational best-friend scores all tended to be correlated with scores derived from teachers' and peers' nominations. The patterns of correlations with direct observations were similar for peers' and teachers' scores, with most coefficients ranging from .30 to .70. There was a tendency, however, for correlations between teacher judgments and direct observation measures to be more consistent and of greater magnitude.

Direct comparison of the relative strengths of these types of relationships, as well as the degree to which teachers' and peers' ratings overlap in the prediction of direct observation measures, is difficult to ascertain from the analyses presented by Greenwood et al. (1979) and Marshall and McCandless (1957). For these types of comparisons, appropriate analyses employing multiple regression procedures would yield information regarding (1) the multiple correlation of teacher and peer ratings to direct observation measures (i.e., combined predictive variance), and (2) the comparative strength of teachers' and peers' ratings in predicting other measures of social competence. One such investigation is available.

Connolly and Doyle (1981) compared the relative efficiency of teacher rankings and sociometrics for the prediction of independent measures of social competence among their two preschool samples. Teacher ranking and sociometric scores were evaluated against children's scores on the Kohn Social Competence Scale (Kohn & Rosman, 1972), and one of two sets of factor-derived direct observation scores. By using stepwise regression techniques, Connolly and Doyle demonstrated that (1) in 8 out of 11 analyses, teacher rankings significantly predicted social competence measures (partialed for the effects of age), and (2) in none of these analyses did peer sociometrics contribute further to the prediction of social competence. When sociometric scores were forced into regression equations before teacher rankings, few significant relations were found; in every instance, however, the addition of teacher ranking scores to the equation significantly increased the prediction of social competence measures. Connolly and Doyle (1981) suggest that teacher rankings and sociometric scores in these two samples were assessing similar dimensions of social competence. While the overlap with respect to the criterion measures was great, the authors noted the potential for each measure to contribute uniquely to a general measure of social competence.

Summary

In this section, we have reviewed several studies that demonstrate the correspondence between sociometric measures and other social agents' ratings of social competence. In addition, we have examined the extent to which these various measures converge with direct observation measures of children's social behavior. From the findings of these studies, several conclusions can be drawn.

First, sociometrics are to some significant degree related to many other ratings of social behavior and performance completed by parents and teachers. Across investigators, populations, sociometric methods, and adult rating measures, there is a general tendency for different raters' scores for the same set of children to converge.

Second, the level of correspondence between peer and adult raters appears to vary, at least in part, as a function of the similarity of the two groups' rating tasks. In several of the aforementioned studies teachers have been asked to nominate children using the same standards as those used by peers (i.e., McCandless & Marshall, 1957), or to implicitly or explicitly estimate children's ratings from peers (i.e., the estimated peer rating of Green et al., 1980; the popularity ranking of Greenwood et al., 1979). Correlations between sociometrics and these highly similar teacher evaluations tend to be more consistent and of greater magnitude than correlations between sociometrics and dissimilar rating scales. These latter ratings have included the Conners Scale (i.e., Green et al., 1980), ratings of social problems and social skills (i.e., Greenwood et al., 1979), or the Pupil Evaluation Inventory (i.e., LaGreca, 1981).

Third, while there is general convergence between sociometrics and various teacher ratings, and while ratings of each group tend to converge with general observation measures of children's social behavior, the peer-, teacher-, and observation-referenced measures appear to be sampling slightly different domains. Sociometrics share as little as 5%, and never more than 46%, common variance with ratings or rankings completed by teachers. Even multiple teacher ratings, combined through multiple regression procedures (i.e., LaGreca, 1981), share only moderate amounts of common variance with sociometric ratings. Given the reliabilities of peer and teacher ratings in identical samples (i.e., Greenwood et al., 1979; McCandless & Marshall, 1957), and the intragroup correlations of ratings by both peers (i.e., Green et al., 1980; LaGreca, 1981) and teachers (i.e., Green et al., 1980; Greenwood et al., 1979; LaGreca, 1981), we can assume that the remaining variance not shared by the two groups' ratings is not solely due to error. Rather, the uniqueness of different ratings may be due to dissimilar standards or experiences that contribute to different evaluations of the same child. Thus, we must assume that peers and teachers are contributing both similar and unique information to the measurement of social competence in children.

SOCIOMETRICS AND THE ASSESSMENT OF SOCIAL COMPETENCE

As we stated in the introduction to this chapter, peer sociometrics have been suggested as the ultimate criterion for identifying critical social behaviors, evaluating social skills interventions, and assessing social competence in children. The assessment of friendship, popularity, or social status among children has considerable face validity for these applications. If children can provide reliable evaluations of others' social performance we can assume that, at least to some degree, these evaluations will covary with social competence. In addition, the predictive validity of sociometric measures has been documented through both longitudinal and ex post facto investigations. Although sociometric measures used in social skills assessment and treatment studies often differ from those used to measure peer relations in the aforementioned predictive validity studies, general support exists for the convergence of early measures of social, or sociometric, status and later measures of social adjustment. Finally, there is some evidence of the treatment validity (Nelson & Hayes, 1979), or sensitivity to intervention, of sociometric measures. In several instances, groups of children receiving social skills training have demonstrated significant increases in sociometric status (Gresham & Nagle, 1980; Ladd, 1981; Oden & Asher, 1977).

Given other evidence we have reviewed in this chapter, however, a singular reliance on sociometric measures for the assessment of social competence may be ill-advised. First, sociometric status is not a unitary phenomenon or construct. Not only are relationships among different sociometric measures highly variable, but also social status is frequently associated with a wide variety of nonsocial variables (e.g., race, sex, physical attractiveness). Second, the reliability of certain types of sociometric measures (e.g., peer nominations) among some populations, particularly preschool children, is frequently quite low. Finally, measures of sociometric status are, at best, only moderately associated with other measures of children's social performance or competence. As we noted in the previous section, these relationships suggest both commonality and divergence among the various measures.

Thus, sociometric measures have desirable characteristics that strongly support their use in the assessment of social competence among children. However, other characteristics of these measures suggest a need for caution in interpreting the results of sociometric assessments. Taken together, we cannot conclude that sociometric status is the only, or necessarily the best, criterion for evaluating social competence in children. Rather, we conclude that sociometric measures are necessary but not sufficient components of a multiple measure model for the assessment of social competence.

Assessing Social Competence: A Multiple-Measure Model

As we have noted, researchers and clinicians who work with children have been unable to agree on an operational definition of social competence. To date, most attempts to develop a common definition have relied on the methods of theoretical analysis or logical discourse.

In contrast, the fields of behavior analysis and behavior therapy are distinguished by a reliance on the empirical analysis of psychological problems (Biglan & Kass, 1977). Rather than defining social competence via expert opinion or convergent agreement indices, this empirical approach should attempt to (1) identify relationships among relevant, socially valid measures of social performance and (2) describe functional relationships that exist between these variables and other aspects of an individual's behavior. Such an empirical analysis may lead to a more complete, meaningful, and functional definition of social competence.

The authors have adopted a working assumption that social competence can be broadly conceptualized as the union of various social agents' evaluations of an individual child's performance in social settings. As Hops (1983, p. 4) suggests, "with the global impressions obtained from these agents, we can evaluate an individual's ability to function adequately and extract the most useful set of criteria currently available for defining social competence." Thus, the social impact of an individual's behavior, assessed across multiple measures, becomes the metric for evaluating competence.

Two examples of the potential power of this multiple-measure assessment model are available. In the first, Ladd (1981) combined sociometric and direct observation measures to select third-grade students for participation in a social skills training program. Students were selected in each of six classrooms if they (1) scored in the lowest third on a peer rating "like to play with" scale, and (2) were one of the three lowest-ranked males or females on direct observation measures of the four target social skills. Trained students made significant gains, both across time and compared to attention and nontreatment controls, on both sociometric and observational measures. In his discussion of these results, Ladd suggested that the use of two types of measures (i.e., sociometrics and direct observations) increased the specification with which children were selected for treatment, and increased the utility of information available for assessing the effects of the treatment.

Multiple measures have also been employed in the development of a social-competence criterion for the selection of critical social (and related) skills. Hops and his colleagues at the Oregon Research Institute (Hops & Finch, 1983) have collected measures of children's social performance from peers, parents, teachers, and direct observation procedures. A factor analysis of these measures yielded three primary factors, with significant loadings from peer ratings on the first, parent ratings on the second, and teacher rankings and ratings along with two free-play observation measures on the third. By combining children's scores on all three of these factors, an "index of social competence" was computed. This index has been shown to be stable, with replicated relationships to a variety of motor, language, and social behavior variables.

The work of Ladd (1981) and of Hops and Finch (1983) is particularly noteworthy for the thorough descriptions of children's social performance. In both cases, assessment of children's social performance was sampled across multiple general evaluations of individuals' social behavior. In psychometric terms, each of the general measures provided by various social agents (e.g., peers, parents, teachers, observers) contributed both shared and unique variance to the assessment of social competence.

In this sense, *shared* variance is represented by the convergence of general evaluations. This shared variance indicates that, to some degree, evaluations collected by different measurement methods are sampling a common domain, class of behaviors and characteristics, or set of phenomena. *Unique* variance is information that is not due to measurement error, but is sampled and represented by only one measure (or subset of measures) in the assessment model. Unique variance indicates that, to some degree, evaluations offered by a given class of social agents are sampling a domain or class of behaviors and characteristics available *only* to that group of raters. As we have noted, general evaluations of children's social performance can be expected to vary as a function of (1) the frequency and type of opportunities to observe the child; (2) the child's social behavior in the presence of the social agent(s) completing the evaluation; and (3) the norms and standards a given social agent holds for the child in the observed situations. Thus, both shared and unique sources of variance are necessary elements of a multiple-measure assessment model. Shared variance indicates that various groups are evaluating a common domain (i.e., social performance), whereas unique variance offers important information that can only be captured by sampling across measurement sources.

Future Directions

While the work of Ladd (1981) and of Hops and Finch (1983) offers support for the importance of a multiple-measure model, to date we know little about the factors that may affect the utility of this type of assessment. The greatest, and perhaps most immediate, need is for further information regarding how, and against what criteria, different social agents' evaluations can be combined into a useful metric of social competence. As necessary steps in the development of this metric, however, we must first increase our analysis and understanding of (1) those factors that contribute to different raters' evaluations of a child's social performance, (2) how different social agents' evaluations of a child are interrelated, and (3) how these multiple evaluations can best be combined into a useful measure of social competence.

Contributing Factors

A clearer and more complete analysis is needed of variables that control the evaluations of a child's social performance by individual social agents. It has been commonly assumed that the general ratings of peers, parents, or teachers are based, to some extent, on (1) social behaviors exhibited by the child and observed by the rater in one or more social situations, and (2) the rater's evaluation of the social impact, quality, or importance of the observed behavior. Available research tentatively supports this assumption. For instance, in an elegantly designed study, Dodge (1983) demonstrated social behavioral differences between sociometric status groups (i.e., popular, neglected, rejected, controversial, average) in a manner that allowed for comprehensive assessment of behavioral antecedents for peer ratings. To control for prior history,

Dodge brought together play groups of previously unacquainted second grade boys. Behavioral assessment included event-based sampling of each child's interactions and coding of all instances of social approach and termination. Due to this experimental control, Dodge's (1983) results provide a significant replication and extension of earlier investigations into the behavioral correlates of sociometric status (e.g., Hartup et al., 1967; Puttallaz & Gottman, 1981a).

Another possibility that must be considered, however, is that initial evaluations of a child's social desirability or status may shape subsequent interactions with others[1]. As we noted, a number of nonsocial variables (e.g., physical appearance, name, race, handicapping condition) are often associated with sociometric evaluations. Other variables, including direct reinforcement of verbal evaluations, may shape differential ratings and subsequent interactions with individual children. Thus, observed behavioral "antecedents" of sociometric status may indeed be the result of earlier, and perhaps more informal, social judgments.

Fortunately, causal relationships between social behaviors and social judgments can be evaluated by empirical analyses. Future experimental research, based on available descriptive and correlational findings, might benefit from a more careful analysis of (1) the functional relationships between specific social behaviors and subsequent social evaluations, and (2) the identification of variables, including setting effects and social evaluations, that in turn control social behaviors and social evaluations.

Convergence of Evaluations

Secondly, future research must provide a more clear and complete understanding of those factors controlling the convergence of different social agents' evaluations of an individual child. Several avenues of inquiry are suggested by our earlier discussion. Perhaps most importantly, we must assess the extent to which opportunity-to-observe contributes to the convergence of different evaluations. If we assume that general evaluations are indeed largely based on observed performance, and that social behavior varies from situation to situation, then *where* and *how often* a child is observed will have direct impact on the degree to which ratings of that child's performance converge.

One method for studying the relationship among different raters' evaluations of a child's social competence is multirater–multibehavior

---

[1] The authors are indebted to Frank Kohler and Donald Baer for initially offering this distinction.

analysis (Cone, 1979). Based upon the multitrait–multimethod procedures detailed by Campbell and Fiske (1959), this analysis provides a
methodology for partitioning variance due to raters, behaviors, situations, or measurement methods. This multirater–multibehavior analysis
focuses the researcher's attention on the identification of nonrandom
error components (e.g., method variance), and provides one empirical,
behavior-specific method for assessing and improving convergence
among multiple measures.

In a multirater–multibehavior analysis of the assessment of social
competence, evaluations of children's social performance could be collected across *raters* (e.g., peers and teachers), *behaviors* (e.g., specific and
general evaluations), and *situations* (e.g., various academic and/or social
settings). Raters would be asked to complete identical evaluations following opportunities to observe in the same situation. In this manner,
investigators may be able to partial out variance due to measurement
(i.e., convergence), method (i.e., rater, behavior, or situation), and
error.

Similar methodology, based more closely on the work of Campbell
and Fiske (1959), has been successfully applied in the development of
models for assessing managerial performance and competence in the
workplace (Borman, 1974; Kavanagh, MacKinney, & Wolins, 1971;
Lawler, 1967). Similar to the model proposed here, researchers in this
area have suggested that ratings of manager performance will vary as a
function of a rater's relative position in the organization (i.e., subordinate, peer, superior), the settings in which the rater observes the ratee's
performance, and the standards for managerial performance held by the
rater (Borman, 1974). The multirater–multitrait analyses completed by
these researchers have led to greater specification of the unique information or variance each group of raters can contribute to the overall assessment process.

Assessing the effects of different raters' standards and expectations on
subsequent evaluations of children's social performance may be another
useful approach to understanding the convergence of ratings across
social agents. Recent work with teachers indicates significant differences
in teachers' self-reports of social behavior standards and expectations, as
well as significant correlations between these self-reports and direct observation measures of teacher behavior and teacher–child interaction
(Walker & Rankin, 1983). Future investigation, both correlational and
experimental, may further explicate the development of these standards
and expectations and their role in the evaluation of children's social
competence.

Multivariate statistical procedures can also be used to examine the relationships among different measures, as well as to develop composite measures of social competence. While multivariate analysis has been relatively rare within the field of behavioral assessment (Nelson & Hayes, 1979), these techniques may have unique power in the specification of significant components of social competence (Foster & Ritchey, 1979).

Gresham (1981b) employed factor analytic procedures to assess the commonality of peer ratings and nominations with direct observation measures of the social behavior of low-status elementary school children. The results of these analyses indicated that peer ratings, peer nominations, and direct observation measures each loaded on unique factors. These results highlighted differences in the patterns of evaluations obtained across raters and measurement methods, and offered important evidence of the unique contributions of various measures.

However, factor analysis can also be used to highlight *similarities* across different measures. For instance, Gresham (1981b) rotated principal components to a final varimax, or orthogonal solution. Varimax rotation procedures, with either high or low loadings for each variable on each factor, are specifically designed to emphasize differences among measures (Rummel, 1970). As Gottman et al. (1975) demonstrated, however, principal components solutions may provide more information on the convergence of measures. Certainly, these and other multivariate procedures must be carefully explored in future research.

Combining Multiple Measures

Future research must also address issues related to the development and evaluation of procedures for integrating information from multiple sources of measurement. Examples of two different approaches are already available. In the first, Ladd (1981) identified children that scored in the lowest ranks for their classroom on both sociometric and direct observation measures. In the second, scores from multiple measures were evaluated and/or combined via multivariate statistical procedures (Hops & Finch, 1983; Gresham, 1981b). While these approaches may on some occasions yield similar results (e.g., identifying the same children as candidates for treatment), it is also possible that important differences exist, such that one of the two procedures may be more appropriate in a given application. The multivariate statistical approach may yield a single score or metric that, if appropriately validated, is particularly useful for screening large numbers of children or for completing normative evaluations. However, this combinative approach may also lack sufficient focus for use in planning or evaluating individual treatment programs. Similarly, the multiple-criteria approach employed by Ladd (1981) appears to be particularly useful in situations where relatively homogeneous groups of children must be identified, as well as in instances where treatment-specific assessment is necessary. However, this multiple-criteria approach may be of limited generalizability or applicability across populations or treatment programs. In either procedure, measures included in the assessment set can be chosen with consideration for the specific components included in a particular treatment program, or for the social validity effects an investigator wants to assess. Systematic analysis of these two approaches is necessary to further describe the specific application for which either procedure is appropriate.

Utility of a Multiple-Measure Model

Finally, research attention must be devoted to evaluating the utility of a multiple-measure model for identifying children for treatment, selecting target behaviors, and evaluating treatment outcomes. Ultimately, the validation of this assessment model will rest on the development of a clear, rational, and empirically based conceptualization of social competence. Rather than focusing on a diffuse, general-factor measure of competence, this conceptualization must account for both general consistencies in social performance and the situational specificity of much of childrens' repertoires.

Perhaps the clearest validation of an assessment model like the one described here would come through prospective, longitudinal research. By evaluating children's social performance across multiple sources of measurement (e.g., peer- and teacher-referenced ratings and direct observations), and then by following children and assessing status on subsequent socially significant outcome variables (e.g., school placement, social adjustment, behavioral competence), investigators could identify the contributions of each measure, both singly and in combination, for the prediction of later status among selected groups or individual children.

Concluding Statement

In this chapter, we have reviewed some of the extensive body of research on children's ratings of their peers. Throughout this literature, we find clear evidence of the importance and utility of sociometric measures. At the same time, we find reason to further explore the role of sociometric measures in the assessment of social competence.

By combining sociometric measures with other general evaluations of children's social behavior, we have proposed that more complete and useful assessments of social competence can be obtained. We do not, however, want to prompt the development of another poorly defined psychological construct. Rather, we hope to prompt continued research toward a more complete and comprehensive empirical analysis of children's social competence. Ultimately, the worth of any conceptualization of social competence must be evaluated with respect to its utility in the analysis of children's social behavior and the development of more effective treatment programs (Foster & Ritchey, 1979). While the initial evidence is promising, much work remains to be done.

REFERENCES

Agard, J. A., Veldman, D. J., Kaufman, M. J., & Semmel, M. I. How I feel toward others: An instrument of the PRIME Instrument Battery. Project PRIME, Technical Report, undated.

Agard, J. A., Veldman, D. J., Kaufman, M. J., Semmel, M. I., & Walters, P. B. Guess Who: An instrument of the PRIME Instrument Battery. Project PRIME, Technical Report, undated.

Anderson, S., & Messick, S. (1974). Social competency in young children. *Developmental Psychology, 10*, 282–293.

Asher, S. R., & Hymel, S. (1981). Children's social competence in peer relations: Sociometric and behavioral assessment. In J. Wine & M. Smye (Eds.), *Social competence.* New York: Guilford Press.

Asher, S. R., Markell, R. A., & Hymel, S. (1981). Identifying children at risk in peer relations: A critique of the rate-of-interaction approach to assessment. *Child Development, 52*, 1239–1245.

Asher, S. R., & Renshaw, P. D. (1981). Children without friends: Social knowledge and social skills training. In S. Asher & J. Gottman (Eds), *The development of children's friendships.* New York: Cambridge University Press.

Asher, S. R., Singleton, L. C., Tinsley, B. R., & Hymel, S. (1979). A reliable sociometric measure for preschool children. *Developmental Psychology, 15*, 443–444.

Asher, S. R., & Taylor, A. R. (1981). Social outcomes of mainstreaming: Sociometric assessment and beyond. *Exceptional Education Quarterly, 1*, 13–30.

Bailey, J. A., & Pierce, K. A. (1975). The friendship rating scale: A sociometric instrument. *Elementary School Guidance and Counseling, 9*, 218–225.

Baltes, P. B., Reese, H. W., & Nesselroade, J. R. (1977). *Life-span developmental psychology: Introduction to research methods.* Monterey, CA: Brooks/Cole Publishing Co.

Becker, W., & Carnine D. (1980). Direct instruction: An effective approach to educational intervention with disadvantaged and low performers. In B. B. Lahey & A. E. Kazdin (Eds.), *Advances in clinical child psychology* (Vol. 3). New York: Plenum.

Biglan, A., & Kass, D. J. (1977). The empirical nature of behavior therapies. *Behaviorism, 5*, 1–15.

Bjerstedt, A. (1956). *Interpretations of sociometric choice status.* Lund, Sweden: Hakan Hakan Ohlssons Boktryckeri.

Bonney, M. E. (1943). The relative stability of social, intellectual, and academic status in grades II to IV, and the interrelationships between various forms of growth. *Journal of Educational Psychology, 34,* 88–102.

Borman, W. C. (1974). The ratings of individuals in organizations: An alternate approach. *Organizational Behavior and Human Performance, 12,* 105–124.

Bower, E. M. (1960). *Early identification of emotionally handicapped children in school.* Springfield, IL: Charles C. Thomas.

Bower, E. M., Shelhamer, T. A., & Daily J. M. (1960). School characteristics of male adolescents who later become schizophrenics. *American Journal of Orthopsychiatry, 30,* 712–729.

Broekhoff, J. (1977). A search for relationships: Sociological and social-psychological considerations. *The Academy Papers, 11,* 45–55.

Brown, D. (1954). Factors affecting social acceptance of high school students. *School Review, 62,* 151–155.

Bruininks, R. H., Rynders, J. E., & Gross, J. C. (1974). Social acceptance of mildly retarded pupils in resource rooms and regular classes. *American Journal of Mental Deficiency, 78,* 373–383.

Bryan, T. H. (1974). Peer popularity of learning disabled children. *Journal of Learning Disabilities, 7,* 621–625.

Bryan, T. H. (1976). Peer popularity of learning disabled children: A replication. *Journal of Learning Disabilities, 9,* 49–53.

Bryan, T. H. (1978). Social relations and verbal interactions of learning disabled children. *Journal of Learning Disabilities, 11,* 58–66.

Bryan, T. H., & Wheeler, R. (1972). Perception of learning disabled children: The eye of the beholder. *Journal of Learning Disabilities, 5,* 484–488.

Burns, E. (1974). Reliability and transitivity of pair-comparison sociometric responses of retarded and nonretarded subjects. *American Journal of Mental Deficiency, 78,* 482–485.

Busk, P. L., Ford, R. C., & Schulman, J. L. (1973). Stability of sociometric responses in classrooms. *The Journal of Genetic Psychology, 123,* 69–84.

Campbell, D. T., & Fiske, D. (1959). Convergent and discriminant validation by the multitrait–multimethod matrix. *Psychological Bulletin, 56,* 81–105.

Caulfield, T. J. (1980). The successful ones. *Personnel and Guidance Journal, 59,* 241–245.

Cohen, A. S., & Van Tassel, E. A. (1978). Comparison: Partial and complete paired comparisons in sociometric measurement of preschool groups. *Applied Psychological Measurement, 2,* 31–40.

Coie, J. D., Dodge, K. A., & Coppotelli, H. (1982). Dimensions and types of social status: A cross-age perspective. *Developmental Psychology, 18,* 557–570.

Cone, J. D. (1979). Confounded comparisons in triple response mode assessment research. *Behavioral Assessment, 1,* 85–96.

Conner, C. K. (1969). A teacher rating scale for use in drug studies with children. *American Journal of Psychiatry, 126,* 884–888.

Connolly, J., & Doyle, A. B. (1981). Assessment of social competence in preschoolers: Teachers versus peers. *Developmental Psychology, 17,* 454–462.

Conoley, J. C., & Conoley, C. W. (1983). A comparison of techniques to affect sociometric status: A small step toward primary prevention in the classroom? *Psychology in the Schools, 21,* 41–47.

Cowen, E. L., Pederson, A. Babigian, H., Izzo, L. D., & Trost, M. A. (1973). Long-term follow-up of early detected vulnerable children. *Journal of Consulting and Clinical Psychology, 41,* 438–446.

Cowen, E. L., Zax, M., Izzo, L. D., & Trost, M. A. (1966). Prevention of emotional disorders in the school setting. *Journal of Consulting Psychology, 30,* 381–387.

Deno, S. L., Mirkin, P. K., Robinson, S., & Evans, P. (1980). *Relationships among classroom observations of social adjustment and sociometric rating scales* (Research Report No. 24). Institute for Research on Learning Disabilities, University of Minnesota.

Deutsch, F. (1974). Observational and sociometric measures of peer popularity and their relationship to egocentric communication in female pre-schoolers. *Developmental Psychology, 10,* 745–747.

Dion, K. K., & Bersheid, E. (1974). Physical attractiveness and peer perception among children. *Sociometry, 37,* 1–12.

Dodge, K. A. (1983). Behavioral antecedents of peer social status. *Child Development, 54,* 1386–1399.

Dodge, K. A., Schlundt, D. G., Delugach, J. S., & Schocken, I. (1982, November). *Multivariate information theory analyses of children's peer group entry behavior.* Paper presented at the annual meeting of the Association for the Advancement of Behavior Therapy, Los Angeles.

Dunnington, M. J. (1957). Investigation of areas of disagreement in sociometric measurement of preschool children. *Child Development, 28,* 93–102.

Foster, S. L. (1983, May). *The nature and recognition of stimulus cues in social situations.* Paper presented at the ninth annual meeting of the Association for Behavior Analysis.

Foster, S. L., & Ritchey, W. L. (1979). Issues in the assessment of social competence in children. *Journal of Applied Behavior Analysis, 12,* 625–638.

Goodman, H., Gottlieb, J., & Harrison, R. H. (1972). Social acceptance of EMRs integrated into a nongraded elementary school. *American Journal of Mental Deficiency, 76,* 412–417.

Gottlieb, J., & Budoff, M. (1973). Social acceptability of retarded children in nongraded schools differing in architecture. *American Journal of Mental Deficiency, 78,* 15–19.

Gottlieb, J., Semmel, M. I., & Veldman, D. J., (1978). Correlates of social status among mainstreamed retarded children. *Journal of Educational Psychology, 70,* 396–405.

Gottman, J. M. (1977). Toward a definition of social isolation in children. *Child Development, 48,* 513–517.

Gottman, J., Gonso, J., & Rasmussen, B. (1975). Social interaction, social competence, and friendship in children. *Child Development, 46,* 709–718.

Green, K. D., Forehand, R., Beck, S. J., & Vosk, B. (1980). An assessment of the relationship among measures of children's social competence and children's academic achievement. *Child Development, 51,* 1149–1156.

Green, K. D., Vosk, B., Forehand, R., & Beck, S. (1981). An examination of differences among sociometrically identified accepted, rejected, and neglected children. *Child Study Journal, 11,* 117–124.

Greenwood, C. R., Todd, N. M., Walker, H. M., & Hops, H. (1978). *Social assessment manual for preschool level (SAMPLE).* Eugene, OR: Center at Oregon for Research in the Behavioral Education of the Handicapped.

Greenwood, C. R., Walker, H. M., Todd, N. M., & Hops, H. (1979). Selecting a cost-effective screening measure for the assessment of preschool social withdrawal. *Journal of Applied Behavior Analysis, 12,* 639–652.

Greenwood, C. R., Walker, H. M., Todd, N. M., & Hops, H. (1981). Normative and descriptive analysis of preschool free play interaction rates. *Journal of Pediatric Psychology, 6,* 343–367.

Gresham, F. M. (1981). Assessment of social skills. *Journal of School Psychology, 19,* 120–133.

Gresham, F. M. (1981b). Validity of social skills measures for assessing social competence in low-status children: A multivariate investigation. *Developmental Psychology, 17,* 390–398.

Gresham, F. M. (1983). Multitrait–multimethod approach to multifactored assessment: Theoretical rationale and practical applications. *School Psychology Review, 12,* 26–34.

Gresham, F. (1983b). *Social validity in the assessment of children's skills: Establishing standards for social competency.* Paper presented at the Association for Behavior Analysis Convention, Milwaukee, WI.

Gresham, F. M., & Nagle, R. J. (1980). Social skills training with children: Responsiveness to modeling and coaching as a function of peer orientation. *Journal of Consulting and Clinical Psychology, 18,* 718–729.

Gronlund, N. E. (1959). *Sociometry in the classroom.* New York: Harper.

Gross, A. M., & Johnson, T. C. (in press). Athletic skill and social status in children. *Journal of Social and Clinical Psychology.*

Haack, M. K., & McConnell, S. R. (1983). *Sociometric assessment of mildly handicapped children's social acceptance of peers.* Manuscript submitted for publication.

Hallinan, M. T. (1974). *The structure of positive sentiment.* New York: Elsevier.

Hallinan, M. T. (1976). Friendship patterns in open and traditional classrooms. *Sociology of Education, 49,* 254–265.

Hallinan, M. T. (1979). Structural effects of children's friendships and cliques. *Social Psychology, 42,* 43–54.

Hallinan, M. T. (1981). Recent advances in sociometry. In S. Asher & J. Gottman (Eds.), *The development of children's friendships.* Cambridge, England: Cambridge University Press.

Hallinan, M. T., & Fermlee, D. (1975). An analysis of intransitivity in sociometric data. *Sociometry, 38,* 195–212.

Hallinan, M. T., & Tuma, N. (1978). Race differences in children's friendliness. *Sociology of Education, 51,* 270–289.

Hartshorne, H., May, M. A., & Maller, J. B. (1929). *Studies in the nature of character: II, Studies in service and self control.* New York: Macmillan.

Hartup, W. W., Glazer, J., & Charlesworth, R. (1967). Peer reinforcement and sociometric status. *Child Development, 38,* 1017–1024.

Hersh, R. H., & Walker, H. M. (1983). Great expectations: Making schools effective for all students. *Policy Studies Review, 2*(1), 147–188.

Hoier, T. S., & Cone, J. D. (November, 1980). *Inductive idiographic assessment of social skills in children.* Paper presented at the Association for Advancement of Behavior Therapy Convention, New York.

Holland, P. W., & Leinhardt, S. (1979). The advanced research symposium on social networks. In P. Holland & S. Leinhardt (Eds.), *Perspectives on social networks.* New York: Academic Press.

Hops, H. (1982). Social skills training for socially withdrawn/isolated children. In P. Karoly & J. Steffen (Eds.), *Advances in child behavior analysis and therapy* (Vol. 1): *Improving children's competencies.* Lexington: Lexington Books.

Hops, H. (1983). *Skills training for childhood social withdrawal.* Unpublished manuscript, Oregon Research Institute.

Hops, H. (1983). Children's social competence and skill: Current research practices and future directions. *Behavior Therapy, 14,* 3–18.

Hops, H., & Finch, M. (1983, April). *The relationship between observed social behavior and reciprocated sociometric choices: A dyadic view of friendship.* Paper presented at the biennial meeting of the Society for Research in Child Development, Detroit.

Hops, H., Finch, M., & McConnell, S. (in press). Social skills deficits. In P. H. Bornstein & A. E. Kazdin (Eds.), *Handbook of child behavior therapy.* Dorsey.

Hops, H., Guild, J., Fleischman, D. H., Paine, S. C., Street, A., Walker, H. M., & Greenwood, C. R. (1978). *Procedures for establishing effective relationship skills (PEERS): Consultant manual.* Eugene, OR: University of Oregon, Center at Oregon for Research in Behavioral Education of the Handicapped.

Hops, H., & Lewin, L. (1984). Peer sociometric ratings. In T. Ollendick & M. Hersen (Eds.), *Child behavioral assessment: Principles and procedures.* New York: Pergamon.

Hymel, S., & Asher, S. R. (1977). *Assessment and training of isolated children's social skills.* Paper presented at the biennial meeting of the Society for Research in Child Development, New Orleans, LA.

Janes, C. L., & Hesselbrock, V. M. (1978). Problem children's adult adjustment predicted from teacher ratings. *American Journal of Orthopsychiatry, 48,* 300–309.

Janes, C. L., Hesselbrock, V. M., Myers, D. G., & Penniman, J. H.(1979). Problem boys in young adulthood: Teachers' ratings and twelve year follow-up. *Journal of Youth and Adolescence, 8,* 453–472.

Kane, J. S., & Lawler, E. E. (1978). Methods of peer assessment. *Psychological Bulletin, 85,* 555–586.

Kavanagh, M. J., MacKinney, A. C., & Wolins, L. (1971). Issues in managerial performance: Multitrait–multimethod analyses of ratings. *Psychological Bulletin, 75,* 34–49.

Kazdin, A. E. (1977). Assessing the clinical or applied importance of behavior change through social validation. *Behavior Modification, 1,* 427–452.

Koch, H. L. (1933). Popularity in preschool children: Some related factors and a technique for its measurement. *Child Development, 4,* 164–175.

Kohn, M. (1977). *Social competence, symptoms and underachievement in childhood: A longitudinal perspective.* Washington, DC: Winston.

Kohn, M. L., & Clausen, J. A. (1955). Social isolation and schizophrenia. *American Sociological Review, 20,* 265–273.

Kohn, M., & Rosman, B. L. (1972). Relationship of preschool social–emotional functioning to later intellectual achievement. *Developmental Psychology, 6,* 445–452.

Ladd, G. W. (1981). Effectiveness of a social learning method for enhancing children's social interaction and peer acceptance. *Child Development, 52,* 171–178.

Ladd, G. W., & Oden, S. L. (1979). The relationship between peer acceptance and children's ideas about helpfulness. *Child Development, 50,* 402–408.

LaGreca, A. M. (1981). Peer acceptance: The correspondence between children's sociometric scores and teachers' ratings of peer interactions. *Journal of Abnormal Child Psychology, 9,* 167–178.

Langeheine, R. (1978). Computer aided data analysis in sociometry. *Educational and Psychological Measurement, 38,* 189–191.

Lawler, E. E. (1967). A multitrait–multirater approach to measuring managerial job performance. *Journal of Applied Psychology, 51,* 369–381.

Lefevre, E. R., West, M. L., & Ledingham, J. E. (1983). The sensitivity of a peer-nomination technique in assessing changes in children's social behavior: A case study. *Journal of the American Academy of Child Psychiatry, 22,* 191–195.

Leinhardt, S. (1972). Developmental changes in the sentiment structure of children's groups. *American Sociological Review, 37,* 202–212.

Levin, M. L. (1976). Displaying sociometric structures: An application of interactive computer graphics for instruction and analysis. *Games and Simulation, 7,* 295–310.

Lewis, M., & Rosenblum, L. A. (1975). *Friendship and peer relations.* New York: Wiley.

Lott, B. E., & Lott, A. J. (1960). The formation of positive attitudes toward group members. *Journal of Abnormal and Social Psychology, 61,* 297–300.

Markus, E. J. (1980). Mapping the social structure of a class: A practical instrument for assessing some effects of mainstreaming. *The Journal of Special Education, 14,* 311–324.

Marshall, H. R. (1957). An evaluation of sociometric–social behavior research with preschool children. *Child Development, 28,* 131–137.

Marshall, H. R., & McCandless, B. R. (1957). A study in the prediction of social behavior of preschool children. *Child Development, 28,* 148–159.

Masters, J. C., & Furman, W. (1981). Popularity, individual friendship selection, and specific peer interaction among children. *Developmental Psychology, 17,* 344–350.

McCandless, B. R., & Marshall, H. R. (1957). A picture sociometric technique for preschool children and its relation to teacher judgements of friendship. *Child Development, 28,* 139–147.

McConnell, S. R. (1983). Identification of social skills for handicapped boys: Evaluation of teacher rating, peer sociometric, and direct observation measures. (Doctoral dissertation, University of Oregon, 1982) *Dissertation Abstracts International, 43,* 29262A.

McConnell, S. R., Strain, P. S., Kerr, M. M., Stagg, V., Lenkner, D. A., & Lambert, D. (1984). An empirical definition of social adjustment: Selection of target behaviors for a comprehensive treatment program. *Behavior Modification, 8,* 451–473.

McDavid, J. W., & Harari, H. (1966). Stereotyping of names and popularity in gradeschool children. *Child Development, 37,* 453–459.

McHale, S. M., & Olley, J. G. (1982). Using play to facilitate the social development of handicapped children. *Topics in Early Childhood Special Education, 2,* 76–86.

Milich, R., Landau, S., Kilby, G., & Whitten, P. (1982). Preschool peer perceptions of the behavior of hyperactive and aggressive children. *Journal of Abnormal Child Psychology, 10,* 497–510.

Mischel, W. (1968). *Personality and assessment.* New York: Wiley.

Moore, S., & Updegraff, R. (1964). Sociometric status of preschool children related to age, sex, nurturance-giving, and dependency. *Child Development, 35,* 519–524.

Moreno, J. L. (1934). *Who shall survive? A new approach to the problem of human interrelations.* Washington, DC: Nervous and Mental Disease Publishing Co.

Moreno, J. L. (1953). *Who shall survive? Foundations of sociometry, group psychotherapy, and sociodrama.* Beacon, NY: Beacon House.

Morrison, G. M. (1981). Sociometric measurement: Methodological considerations of its use with mildly learning handicapped and nonhandicapped children. *Journal of Educational Psychology, 73,* 193–201.

Mueller, E. (1972). The maintenance of verbal exchanges between young children. *Child Development, 43,* 930–958.

Nelson, R. O., & Hayes, S. C. (1979). Some current dimensions of behavioral assessment. *Behavioral Assessment, 1,* 1–16.

Northway, M. L. (1942). Social acceptability test. *Sociometry, 5,* 180–184.

Northway, M. L. (1969). The stability of young children's social relationships. *Educational Research, 11,* 54–57.

Northway, M. L. (1969). The changing patterns of young children's social relations. *Educational Research, 11,* 212–214.

Oden, S., & Asher, S. (1977). Coaching children in social skills for friendship making. *Child Development, 48,* 496–506.

Odom, S. L., & DuBose, R. F. (1981). *Peer rating assessments of integrated preschool classes: Stability and concurrent validity of the measures and efficacy of the peer model.* Paper presented at the National Convention for the Council for Exceptional Children, New York.

Odom, S. L., Jenkins, J. R., Speltz, M. L., & DeKlyen, M. (1982). Promoting social integration of young children at risk for learning disabilities. *Learning Disabilities Quarterly, 5,* 379–387.

O'Neal, P., & Robins, L. N. (1958). The relation of childhood behavior problems to adult psychiatric status: A 30 year follow up study of 150 subjects. *American Journal of Psychiatry, 114,* 961–969.

Peery, J. C. (1979). Popular, amiable, isolated, rejected: A reconceptualization of sociometric status in preschool children. *Child Development, 50,* 1231–1234.

Pekarik, E. G., Prinz, R. J., Liebert, D. E., Weintraub, S., & Neale, J. M. (1976). The Pupil Evaluation Inventory: A sociometric technique for assessing children's social behavior. *Journal of Abnormal Child Psychology, 4,* 83–97.

Peretti, P. O., Lane, L., & Floyd, E. (1981). Perceived personality impressions of the sociometric isolate by elementary school classmates. *Education, 101,* 359–365.

Pritchard, M., & Graham, P. (1966). An investigation of a group of patients who have attended both the child and adult departments of the same psychiatric hospital. *British Journal of Psychiatry, 112,* 603–612.

Putallaz, M., & Gottman, J. M. (1981a). An interactional model of children's entry into peer groups. *Child Development, 52,* 986–994.

Putallaz, M., & Gottman, J. M. (1981b). Social skills and group acceptance. In S. R. Asher & J. M. Gottman (Eds.), *The development of children's friendships.* Cambridge: Cambridge University Press.

Remington, D. O., Wall, S. M., Pickert, S. M., & Foltz, M. L. (1982). HIARC: A FORTRAN program for measurement of children's social perceptions through group hierarchy construction. *Educational and Psychological Measurement, 42,* 227–230.

Renshaw, P. D., & Asher, S. R. (1982). Social competence and peer status: The distinctions between goals and strategies. In K. H. Rubin & H. S. Ross (Eds.), *Peer relationships and social skills in childhood.* New York: Springer-Verlag.

Robins, L. N. (1966). *Deviant children grown up.* Baltimore: Williams & Wilkins.

Roff, M. (1961). Childhood social interactions and young adult bad conduct. *Journal of Abnormal Social Psychology, 63,* 333–337.

Roff, M. (1963). Childhood social interactions and young adult psychosis. *Journal of Clinical Psychology, 19,* 152–157.

Roff, M., & Sells, S. B. (1968). Juvenile delinquency in relation to peer acceptance, rejection, and socioeconomic status. *Psychology in the Schools, 5,* 3–18.

Roff, M., Sells, B., & Golden, M. M. (1972). *Social adjustment and personality development in children.* Minneapolis: University of Minnesota Press.

Roistacher, R. C. (1974). A microeconomic model of sociometric choice. *Sociometry, 37,* 219–238.

Rubin, K. H. (1972). Relationship between egocentric communication and popularity among peers. *Developmental Psychology, 7,* 364.

Rummel, R. J. (1970). *Applied factor analysis.* Evanston: Northwestern University Press.

Sainato, D. M., Zigmond, N., & Strain, P. S. (1983). Social status and initiations of interactions by learning disabled students in regular education settings. *Analysis and Intervention in Developmental Disabilities, 3,* 71–88.

Shapiro, S. B., & Sobel, M. (1981). Two multinominal random sociometric voting models. *Journal of Educational Statistics, 6,* 287–310.

Singleton, L. C., & Asher, S. R., (1979). Racial integration and children's peer preferences: An investigation of developmental and cohort differences. *Child Development, 50,* 936–941.

Sipperstein, G. R., Bopp, M., & Bak, J. (1978). Social status of learning disabled children. *Journal of Learning Disabilities, 11,* 49–53.

Smith, P. C., & Kendall, L. M. (1963). Retranslation of expectations: An approach to the construction of unambiguous anchors for rating scales. *Journal of Applied Psychology, 47,* 149–155.

Steigleman, G., & Hops, H. (1983). *The effect of age and motor performance on the social status of preschoolers.* Manuscript in preparation, Oregon Research Institute.

Strain, P. S. (1983). Identification of social skill curriculum targets for severely handicapped children in mainstreamed preschools. *Applied Research in Mental Retardation, 4,* 369–382.

Strain, P. S., & Kerr, M. M. (1981). *Mainstreaming of children in schools: Research and programmatic issues.* New York: Academic Press.

Strain, P. S., Odom, S. L., & McConnell, S. R. (1980). Promoting social reciprocity of exceptional children: Identification, target skill selection, and interventions. *Exceptional Education Quarterly, 5,* 21–28.

Taylor, A. R. (1982). Social competence and interpersonal relations between retarded and nonretarded children. In N. Ellis (Ed.), *International review of research in mental retardation* (Vol. 2) New York: Academic Press.

Thompson, G. G., & Powell, M. (1951). An investigation of the rating scale approach to the measurement of social status. *Educational and Psychological Measurement, 11,* 440–445.

Ullmann, C. A. (1957). Teachers, peers, and tests as predictors of adjustment. *Journal of Educational Psychology, 48,* 257–267.

Van Houten, R. (1979). Social validation: The evolution of standards of competency for target behaviors. *Journal of Applied Behavior Analysis, 12,* 581–591.

Vaughan, B. E., & Langlois, J. H. (1983). Physical attractiveness as a correlate of peer status and social competence in preschool children. *Developmental Psychology, 19,* 561–567.

Vaughan, B. E., & Waters, E. (1981). Attention structure, sociometric status, and dominance: Interrelations, behavioral correlates, and relationships to social competence. *Developmental Psychology, 17,* 275, 288.

Veldman, D. J., & Sheffield, J. R. (1979). The scaling of sociometric nominations. *Educational and Psychological Measurement, 39,* 99–106.

Victor, J. B., & Halverson, C. F. (1976). Behavior problems in elementary school children: A follow-up study. *Journal of Abnormal Child Psychology, 4,* 17–29.

Vosk, B., Forehand, R., Parker, J. B., & Rickard, K. (1982). A multimethod comparison of popular and unpopular children. *Developmental Psychology, 18,* 571–575.

Walker, H., McConnell, S., & Clarke, J. (1985). Social skills training in school settings: A model for the social integration of handicapped children into less restrictive settings. In R. J. MaMahon & R. D. Peters (Eds.), *Childhood disorders: Behavioral–developmental approaches.* New York: Bruner/Mazel.

Walker, H. M., & Rankin, R. R. (1983). Assessing the behavioral expectations and demands of less restrictive settings: Instruments, ecological assessment procedures, and outcomes. *School Psychology Review, 12,* 274–284.

West, D. J., & Farrington, D. P. (1973). *Who becomes delinquent?* London: Heineman Press.

Westman, J. C., Rice, D. L., & Bermann, E. (1967). Nursery school behavior and later school adjustment. *American Journal of Orthopsychiatry, 37,* 725–731.

Wiggins, J. S., & Winder, C. L. (1961). The Peer Nomination Inventory: An empirically derived sociometric measure of adjustment in preadolescent boys. *Psychological Reports, 9,* 643–677.

Winder, C. L., & Wiggins, J. S. (1964). Social reputation and social behavior: A further validation of the peer nomination inventory. *Journal of Abnormal and Social Psychology, 68,* 681–684.

Witryol, S. L., & Thompson, G. G. (1953). An experimental comparison of the partial-rank-order and paired comparison approaches to social acceptability. *Journal of Educational Psychology, 44,* 20–30.

Witryol, S. L., & Thompson, G. G. (1953). A critical review of the stability of social acceptability scores obtained with the partial-rank-order and the paired comparison scales. *Genetic Psychology Monographs, 48,* 221–260.

Wolf, M. M. (1978). Social validity: The case for subjective measurement or how behavior analysis is finding its heart. *Journal of Applied Behavior Analysis, 11,* 203–214.

Young, L. L., & Cooper, D. H. (1944). Some factors associated with popularity. *Journal of Educational Psychology, 35,* 513–535.

Zac, M., Cowen, E. L., Rappaport, J., Beach, D., & Laird, J. (1968). Follow-up study of children identified early as emotionally disturbed. *Journal of Consulting Psychology, 32,* 369–373.

Zigler, E., & Trickett, P. K. (1978). IQ, social competence, and evaluation of early childhood intervention programs. *American Psychologist, 33,* 789–798.

PART III

MODIFICATION OF CHILDREN'S SOCIAL BEHAVIOR

Social and Language Skills for Preventive Mental Health: What, How, Who, and When

Joseph M. Strayhorn
*Phillip S. Strain**

INTRODUCTION

This review is written with one overriding question in mind: How should we best design interventions for children that both promote the growth of mental health competencies and prevent the appearance of mental symptoms?

We may divide this question into four subquestions:

1. **What** should be the goals of preventive intervention programs? What targets provide the best way stations toward the ultimate goal of promoting mental health?

2. **How** should we promote these goals? What are the most useful methods of promoting mental health competencies?

3. **Who** should be the change agents who implement these methods in the service of these goals?

4. **When** in the life span, at what age, should persons begin to receive such positive influences?

* This work was supported in part by grant number MH39461-02 to Dr. Strayhorn from the National Institute of Mental Health.

QUESTION 1: WHAT GOALS SHOULD
TAKE PRIORITY?

In considering the goals for preventive interventions, let us restrict the scope of our inquiry somewhat. Strayhorn (1983) mentioned three general preventive intervention strategies: those aimed at preserving the integrity of the brain (e.g., the prevention of lead toxicity), which we may call *biologically based prevention;* those aimed at softening or easing the situations with which people have to deal (e.g., improving employment opportunities), which we may call *situationally based prevention;* and finally, those strategies aimed at improving people's learned competencies in dealing with situations (e.g. teaching interpersonal skills), which we may call *learning-based prevention.* This review restricts itself to the third set of strategies. Thus, the preceding question is reduced to the following: "What competencies, what skills, should be promoted with highest priority if one wishes to prevent psychological symptoms?"

As a second restriction, in answering this question, we can look for many "narrow-band," specific competencies, or we can search for a few "broad-band" competencies. Strayhorn (1983) took the former approach in a paper that derived from a review of the psychotherapy and mental health literature nine groups of competencies, comprising some 59 competencies in all. Such a large list is unquestionably needed if one is to capture with some accuracy the complexity of learning to live in the world. But for the present purposes, such a list is too cumbersome, and this review arbitrarily restricts itself to a search for a few broad-band competencies that can be used as outcome variables in preventive interventions.

The literature reviewed in the following paragraphs leads to the conclusion that among the broad-band competencies, the following three are paramount.

1. The ability to be kind, cooperative, and appropriately compliant, as opposed to having a prevailing habit of being hostile and defiant.
2. The ability to show interest in people and things, to be appropriately outgoing, to socialize actively, as opposed to being withdrawn, fearful, and shy.
3. The ability to use language well, to have a command of a wide range of vocabulary and syntax such that ideas may be both comprehended and expressed with facility.

The first two competencies are among those commonly referred to as "social skills"; the third is, as we discuss later, intimately related to the first two. Let us now review the evidence leading to a selection of these three abilities.

The first two skills represent the main factors derived from a large number of factor analyses of varying assessments of children's problems. These two factors usually have been referred to by their negative poles; terms to describe the first one include undercontrol syndrome, externalizing syndrome, anger–defiance, hostile–aggressive, conduct problems, and antisocial disorders.

Terms to describe the second include overcontrol syndrome, internalizing syndrome, apathy–withdrawl, anxious–fearful, personality problems, emotional disorders, neurosis, and shyness. In 1961, Peterson stated that "the generality of these factors appears to be enormous" (1961, p. 206). Since that time, many studies have confirmed this statement (see reviews by Achenbach & Edelbrock, 1978; Behar & Stringfield, 1974; Kohn & Rosman, 1973). Studies have factor analyzed items from mental health workers' reports, teachers' reports, and parents' reports; the two major factors are evident in all three sources of data (Achenbach & Edelbrock, 1978). Rutter (1967) called the distinction between these two factors "perhaps the most universal . . . of all the diagnostic distinctions made in child psychiatry" (p. 164).

These two factors have not been limited to measures of problem behavior, but have also been found in a questionnaire assessing positive competencies, as well as problem behaviors, namely the Kohn Social Competence Scale (Kohn & Rosman, 1972a). Kohn's two factors were named so as to include positive poles: Interest–Participation versus Apathy–Withdrawal, and Cooperation–Compliance versus Anger–Defiance. An example of an item loading on Interest–Participation is "Child displays enthusiasm about work or play;" an item leading on Cooperation–Compliance is "Child cooperates with rules and regulations."

To summarize so far, if we may conceive of interest–participation and cooperation–compliance as skills, then teaching those skills thoroughly and successfully would be expected to remove problems accounting for most of the variance in problem behavior checklists.

However, the fact that skill deficiencies in these areas account for a great portion of the variance in behavior checklists is only one argument for devising intervention programs to teach the skills. A second argument has to do with how persistent and disabling these social relationship problems are if unchecked.

The longitudinal persistence of conduct problems over time, even into adulthood, has been documented by several studies. Robins (1978) summarized results of studies of four cohorts of males. Of children with a high level of antisocial behavior, from 36% to 41% showed high levels of antisocial behavior in adulthood. All types of antisocial behavior in childhood predicted a high level of antisocial behavior in adulthood, and each kind of adult antisocial behavior was predicted by the number of childhood antisocial behaviors. Adult antisocial behavior virtually *required* childhood antisocial behavior, which is another way of saying that prevention of childhood conduct disorders should effectively prevent adult antisocial disorders.

Conger and Miller (1966), in a retrospective study, found that even during kindergarten and early school years, future delinquents showed more antisocial conduct than matched controls, and were less well liked and accepted by their peers.

The longitudinal persistence of the trait of anger–defiance holds even when the sample is not restricted to extreme examples of pathology. In Kohn's 1977 report of children studied longitudinally from preschool years fourth grade, the preschool anger–defiance scores predicted fourth grade scores with $r = .36$; the two testing occasions involved different teachers, different instruments, and different schools or pre-schools. First grade scores predicted fourth grade scores with $r = .48$, and third grade scores predicted fourth grade scores with $r = .60$.

Eron (1980) summarizes results on a 10-year longitudinal study of aggressive behavior in a population of nonreferred school children. Aggression ratings at age 8 years predicted those at age 19 with $r = .38$ for boys and $r = .47$ for girls. Because of the skewness of the sample, Eron reports that actual coefficients underestimate the strength of the relationship, which he says is "comparable to the predictability of intelligence test scores over a similar period."

Kagan and Moss (1962) studied, among other variables, the incidence of "unprovoked nonphysical aggression toward same sex peers, for example, verbal threats or taunts, teasing, destruction or seizure of a peer's property." On this variable, correlations between measurements taken at 8 and 12 years of age were .71 for males and .60 for females. Tuddenham (1954) studied the stability of various traits from adolescence to adulthood; aggression was the most stable variable for men, with a stability coefficient of .68. This variable was far less stable for women.

What evidence do we have about the longitudinal persistence of the other factor, that of interest–participation versus apathy–withdrawal? In Kohn's 1977 report, preschool apathy–withdrawal scores predicted fourth-grade scores with $r = .28$; third-grade scores predicted fourth-grade scores with $r = .50$. Bronson (1966) studied the stability of the trait of expressiveness versus withdrawal. Over four 3-year intervals between ages 5 and 16 years, the mean stability coefficients were .73 for boys and .65 for girls.

How disabling is the factor of apathy–withdrawal, on the average? Here, the evidence is mixed. Hafner, Quast, and Shea (1975) found that when a group of adolescents who had been treated for internalized problems were followed into adult life, and compared to matched controls who in adolescence had been treated for externalized problems, the internalizers had performed better in school, completed more grades, had more friends, had better job stability, fewer divorces, and higher socioeconomic status. On the other hand, Kohn (1977) found that apathy–withdrawal in preschoolers predicted third-grade academic problems more strongly than did anger–defiance.

Cowen et al. (1973) reported on an 11- to 13-year follow-up of children first studied in first and third grade. Unpopularity with peers was, of all measures gathered, the most powerful predictor of later appearance on a community-wide register that recorded psychiatric treatment. Although this study has been cited by some other authors (e.g., Greenwood et al., 1977) as evidence of the seriousness of the problem of social withdrawal, the peer popularity rating probably reflected anger–defiance as much as, if not more than, social withdrawal, because the unpopular children were reported by Cowen et al. to have been more highly visible than other children in the study.

Although there is less compelling evidence for the necessity for prevention of apathy–withdrawal than that for anger–defiance, the evidence does suggest that good may be done by the prevention of this problem through the promotion of interest–participation.

Another argument for placing problems both of anger–defiance and of apathy–withdrawal at high priority for prevention programs is the fact that they are very common. In Rutter's Isle of Wight studies (Rutter et al., 1976), conduct disorders severe enough to provide a social handicap had a prevalence of 4%. In a London borough, the rates were much higher. Rutter's group found that the difference between the Isle of Wight and the London borough was accounted for by the greater prevalence of socioeconomic disadvantage in the London borough.

Kellam et al. (1975) reported on a study of four cohorts of first-graders in Chicago's Woodlawn Community, a socioeconomically disadvantaged neighborhood. The measures of maladaptation factored into the two familiar factors, which these investigators called shyness and aggressiveness. Approximately 20% of first-graders had significant problems from the "shy" cluster; 15% had significant problems from the "aggressive" cluster; and another 13% were classified as both shy and aggressive. Thus, approximately half of the children in this neighborhood were judged as having significant social impairment along one or both of the two familiar factors.

Now let us examine the third of the preceding skills, that of using language with facility. What evidence leads to a conclusion that this skill is of high priority for learning-based preventive interventions?

To quickly preview: language facility as measured by verbal IQ scores or various other measures is highly related to school success, which in turn is highly related to presence or absence of conduct problems; oral language ability is highly related to future reading ability, which in turn is highly related to both school success and presence or absence of conduct problems.

Certain studies find a direct relationship between ratings of language difficulty and the label of psychiatric disturbance. Behar and Stringfield (1974), in studying their preschool behavior questionnaire, report that the item that best discriminated between the normal and disturbed groups was "other speech difficulty." This supports Brown's (1960) finding that the most typical characteristic of disturbed preschoolers was the odd quality of their speech. Eisenberg et al. (1962) and Rutter (1967) have also found that items pertaining to language development discriminated well between deviant and normal populations.

Other studies imply more directly that giving disadvantaged preschoolers practice in language use is likely to prevent reading problems. Norman-Jackson (1982) visited the homes of low-income black families selected so as to have a second-grader and also a preschooler in the family. This author measured the language abilities of the preschoolers by calculating the mean length of utterance in their conversations. By this measure, the language of preschool siblings of successfully reading second-graders was significantly more mature than that of preschool siblings of unsuccessful readers. One way of explaining these findings is to posit that certain parents who are more encouraging of verbal interaction tend to produce preschoolers with more mature language development; when those children enter school, their increased language facility aids them in the task of learning to read. Further observations reported by the same author strengthened this notion. Five years after the first set of observations, the same families were again studied, when the Phase I preschoolers were now in primary grades. The successful readers among those children were more likely to be the ones who had participated in more verbal interactions with their families and who had produced language of greater maturity when they were studied as preschoolers. Furthermore, according to direct observations the researchers had carried out in the homes, the parents of the unsuccessful readers had responded in a discouraging manner to their children's attempts to start conversations more often than had the parents of the successful readers. This study supports the idea that encouraging preschoolers to practice talking should help them in reading later on.

Other evidence strengthens this notion. Loban (1963) collected and analyzed oral language productions of 237 students in a longitudinal study that began when these students were in kindergarten and continued until they were in sixth grade. Loban found that in oral language, a number of parameters covaried with one another: higher vocabulary; more verbal dexterity; longer utterances; more expressions of tentativeness through statements of supposition, condition, or concession; more subordinate and dependent clauses; and more analogies and generalizations. According to these measures, the children were ranked according to their oral language fluency. As one way of looking at the relation between oral fluency and reading ability, Loban compared the reading achievement scores of the students in the top 10% and the bottom 10% of the oral fluency rankings. As the children became older, the gap between the high-fluency children and the low-fluency children became wider and wider with respect to reading achievement; by the sixth grade, there was almost no overlap in the reading achievement scores of the two groups. *All* the high-fluency group were reading above grade expectation; virtually all of the low-fluency group were reading below grade expectation.

In Loban's study, oral fluency predicted listening comprehension, writing, and intelligence score as well as reading achievement. The highest correlation was between the Kuhlmann-Anderson group test of intelligence and the vocabulary size inferred from the samples of oral speech; the correlation coefficient was .84.

Receptive vocabulary as measured by the Peabody Picture Vocabulary Test has correlated with $r = .62$ and .66, respectively, with scores on two standard measures of reading achievement given on the same day as the vocabulary test (Robertson & Eisenberg, 1981). The fact that this vocabulary test correlates in the region of .6 with tests such as the Stanford-Binet and the Wechsler intelligence tests (Robertson & Eisenberg, 1981), a fact that justifies its being called a measure of intelligence, reminds us of the strong relation between vocabulary and IQ. The fact that reading attainment is predicted by other IQ measures with r in the region of .6 (Rutter & Yule, 1977), reminds us of the relation between IQ scores and academic success.

The listening comprehension portion of the Gates-MacGinnitie Readiness Test, given to kindergartners, predicts reading comprehension scores when the same children are tested near the end of first grade; r is reported to be .40. The entire score on this readiness test, which may be considered a test of oral language, correlates in the region of .6 with reading comprehension (Teachers College Press, 1969).

More evidence on the importance of speech and language skills for reading achievement was given by the Edinburgh follow-up of children with speech delay (Mason, 1967; Ingram et al., 1970). Two years after starting school, a third of the speech-retarded children were below grade level in reading and spelling, compared with some 5% of the controls. The reading difficulties occurred both in the children with a true delay in spoken language and also in those with just an articulation defect.

To summarize: The evidence suggests that facility in oral language, vocabulary size, IQ score, and reading achievement level are quite highly related variables. There is more than a little reason to believe that stimulating the fluency of preschoolers in oral language development would promote higher IQ scores and higher levels of reading achievement.

Why, in a review of preventive intervention strategies for mental health problems should there be such a concern with IQ and reading achievement? The answer is that these variables are related quite strongly to mental-health variables. Strayhorn (1984) found that in 11 classes of first- through fifth-grade children, reading achievement (as measured by the California Achievement Test) was significantly correlated with the following measures of adjustment: teachers' ratings of the children's psychological skills, Rosenberg self-esteem score, Nowicki-Strickland Locus of Control Scale, sociometric status, and ability to recognize the feelings portrayed in a series of tape-recorded statements.

Rutter and Yule (1977), in summarizing their epidemiological studies, mention that it has long been known that delinquency and other disorders are frequently accompanied by severe reading difficulties. In the Isle of Wight studies, a quarter of the children with specific reading retardation showed antisocial behavior—a rate several times that in the general population. Conversely, a third of the children with a disorder of conduct were retarded in reading, compared with only 4% in the general population they studied. The association was not just with delinquency; reading retardation was as common among antisocial and aggressive children who were not overtly delinquent as in those who had appeared in court. There was also reported some association between reading difficulties and emotional disturbance (i.e., the apathy–withdrawal–anxiety factor); however, much the stronger association was with disorder of conduct.

Rutter and Yule (1977) also summarize attempts to find out the direction of causality between reading problems and conduct problems. Both Rutter and his colleagues and Varlaam (1974) found that antisocial reading-disabled children were in several ways similar to purely reading-disabled children and rather unlike purely antisocial children. For example, in the Isle of Wight study, antisocial disorder in children who could read adequately was associated with broken homes; antisocial disorder in poor readers was not associated with broken homes, but was associated with large family size, a family history of reading difficulties, speech delay, and poor concentration. These latter variables were also found in those poor readers without conduct problems. These findings suggest that in some cases, educational failure causes antisocial problems to arise. Thus, if early language training were to improve the chances of disadvantaged children to learn to read, we might expect a lower incidence of conduct problems.

Other studies give evidence for another direction of causality: that is, behavioral problems' causing academic difficulties. Kohn (1977) reported that girls high in anger–defiance on the preschool rating scales began to show significant decrements in intellectual achievement beginning with the second grade of elementary school. Apathy–withdrawal in preschoolers was linked with low achievement for both boys and girls. Because the behavior problems preceded the academic problems, we might suppose that they interfered with learning. Such a supposition is intuitively appealing, because school learning requires both obedience and interest.

Of course, neither of the last two studies established direction of causality by manipulation of the independent variable. If such experiments could be carried out, we might find that the relationship between reading problems and behavior problems run in both directions, so as to make possible a vicious cycle: failure experiences lead to behavior problems, which interfere with learning and produce more academic failure experiences.

Of relevance to the issue of direction of causality is a study by Arnold (1977) in which first-graders screened as vulnerable to academic failure and behavioral decompensation were each assigned to one of three groups: two of the groups contrasted differing methods of teaching reading, and the third was a no-contact group. One of the groups was most successful in learning reading; this group also improved significantly on three behavioral scales, while the other two groups deteriorated on these measures. In this study, manipulating the reading achievement variable affected the behavior disorder variable.

IQ score has also been found to be related to presence or absence of social behavior problems. Miller (1972) studied the relationship between IQ and total disability on a rating scale measuring the adjustment of elementary school children; IQ and maladjustment were significantly correlated. Hirschi and Hindelang (1977), after a thorough review of the relation between IQ and delinquency, state that the "assertion that delinquents have lower IQs than nondelinquents is firmly established" (p. 584). Rutter and colleagues' (1976) Isle of Wight study also found a negative correlation between aggressive behavior and IQ, although the behavioral difficulties were substantially more associated with educational retardation (of which reading retardation was the index) than with IQ per se.

One quite simple explanation for the relationship between low language skill or reading skill and behavior disorders is simply that children find it difficult to pay attention to tasks that are over their heads, and most of the tasks of school involve reading and use of language. When given tasks that are above one's ability level, one tends to drift into deviant or off-task activities. Once this happens, there often starts a vicious cycle between teacher and pupil, with punishment's leading to more rebellion and rebellion's leading to more punishment. A study that suggests this explanation is one by Camp and Zimet (1975), which studied children's behavior during reading periods as a function of reading ability. Off-task behavior and deviant behavior were higher for poorer readers.

One other pocket of literature suggests another mechanism for the relationship between low language ability and aggression or impulsivity or other behavior problems: the skill of verbal mediation between situations and responses has been found deficient in impulsive children. Spivak and Shure (1974) and Camp and Bash (1981) have reported therapeutic methods that rely for their success upon the notion that sharpening the skills of verbal mediation of decisions and problem-solving will result in better performance in situations, especially social situations. Learning to think in words about the options available in a given situation and the consequences of each of those options represents a specific aspect of verbal skill. It is within such a conceptual framework that Camp (1977) interprets her results from a study of 49 aggressive and 46 normal boys aged 77–97 months. A number of measures of verbal ability, types of self-guiding speech, and ability to inhibit responses on finger-tapping tests were studied. Discriminant function analysis resulted in correct classification of 88% of the cases. One of the most discriminating variables was the degree of irrelevant or immature verbal production the child uttered during a task requiring inhibition of impulses. Camp hypothesized that both learning and behavior problems in aggressive boys may be symptomatic of an "ineffective linguistic control system" (p. 145).

This notion of the role of language in the autoregulation of behavior may be traced to the pioneering work of Vygotsky (1962). Luria (1964) gives an example of Vygotsky's notion in this way: "For example, the mother says to the child, 'You must take a spoon' and in this way she regulates his behavior. This verbal behavior then becomes interiorized. At the next stage, the child says to himself, 'I will take a spoon.' This is now autoregulation of behavior. . . . Therefore, development as a whole is a kind of interiorization of social conduct" (p. 392).

Although Spivack and Shure (1974), Meichenbaum (1977), and Camp and Bash (1981) have used very specific teaching strategies for their brands of verbal autoregulation, such learning requires a prerequisite level of general verbal ability. Because of this, Spivack and Shure's (1974) training program for disadvantaged children began with the teaching of prerequisite vocabulary, such as the meaning of *same* and *different*. It is not unreasonable to surmise that a teaching program producing a higher level of general verbal ability might facilitate verbal autoregulation in children.

In summary, there are at least two very plausible mechanisms whereby improved language functioning could lead to reduced social behavior problems. One is that improved language functioning leads to greater success in school activities, particularly reading, and thus conduces to the cycle of teacher approval and pupil obedience rather than the cycle of teacher disapproval and pupil rebellion. The second is that language, when used with more facility, permits superior autoregulation of behavior.

In arguing for placing a high priority on prevention of conduct problems, we cited the fact that such problems tend to persist over time, often into adulthood. The same argument can be made with respect to lack of facility in language, especially with regard to reading disabilities. Rutter et al. (1976) report on the longitudinal studies of reading retardation that were part of the Isle of Wight studies. Children who were tested at ages 9 to 11 years were retested at ages 14 to 15 years. Of the children who were $2\frac{1}{2}$ years behind in reading at the first testing, only 4% had come up to the mean score for their age by the time of the second testing. The majority still had a reading attainment score more than two standard deviations below the general population group mean.

Levels of language ability as measured by the Stanford-Binet Intelligence Test also tend to be persistent from middle childhood into adulthood. Honzik et al. (1984) report that Stanford-Beinet scores at age 7 years predict scores at age 18 years, with $r = .71$. As is discussed here later, the stability of these scores from preschool years to later years is not so high.

The final argument for placing language ability, and the reading problems with which it is highly related, high on the priority list for primary prevention is that these problems are quite common, especially among disadvantaged children. Harris (1968) cites figures to the effect that the *average* child from a disadvantaged neighborhood is likely to be reading at 2 years behind grade level by the time he or she reaches seventh grade. As time passes, the difference between grade level and reading level increases.

To summarize: This section raised the question of what should be the high-priority goals of learning-based preventive interventions with children. The literature gives evidence that skills of being cooperative, kind, and appropriately compliant, of being active and interested in people and things, and of using language with facility are very high priority skills. The problems resulting from deficiencies in these skills are very common, are persistent, and are debilitating.

QUESTION 2: HOW MAY ONE MOST EFFECTIVELY PROMOTE THE AFOREMENTIONED SKILLS?

This section examines particularly those methods of skill promotion that are useful for young children, especially preschoolers. To preview: Symbolic play and fantasy are quite useful vehicles for communicating favorable influences to small children. For the child, simply to engage in symbolic play and to hear stories, according to certain evidence, are likely to have positive effects. If the stories and fantasy dramas the child is exposed to are of cooperative, kind, brave, actively socializing patterns (especially if communicated by adults who act in similar ways), then the child is likely to be influenced favorably by these models. If the child then constructs his or her own fantasies of characters enacting these patterns, there is evidence that the practice carried out in fantasy will be a favorable influence on the child. Contingent reinforcement of favorable patterns in the child, particularly by means of adult attention, has been shown repeatedly to be a powerful method of influence. The literature leads us to expect that programs combining these elements might be very effective in promoting the growth of the target skills in children.

Fantasy and Play: Preexperimental Observations from Psychoanalytically Oriented Therapists

If a young child is taken to a psychoanalyst or a Rogerian therapist for treatment of acting-out or withdrawal, an observer would describe most of the interactions of the subsequent therapy by saying that the therapist and child are engaging in play, often symbolic play. The analyst, of course, would be continually thinking about the meaning of the symbolic characters and actions, and might occasionally interpret these to the child. If the dream of the adult was to Freud the "royal road to the unconscious," the play of children is to analysts such as Erik Erikson "the royal road to the understanding of the infantile ego's efforts at synthesis" (Erikson, 1963, p. 209).

If we assume that play therapy sometimes helps children (controlled studies do not seem available), what aspects of it are helpful? One explanation based on a hydraulic model of human energy is that by enacting scenes of hostility or fear or other negative emotion, the child rids himself or herself of the ill effects of these by a catharsis. Bandura (1973) examines the evidence for and against the catharsis hypothesis, and makes a convincing case that performance of aggressive acts, either verbally, physically, or in fantasy, is more likely to be a rehearsal of aggression and to make aggression more likely rather than to make it less likely. This evidence would suggest that enacting aggressive or maladaptive patterns in child therapy may sometimes be more harmful than helpful.

However, another more sophisticated rationale is given by some for the salutary effect of play therapy. This rationale qualifies as a cognitive explanation: it is that the child who can symbolize through play the wishes, fears, preoccupations, and other mental phenomena that are troublesome is more able, by using that mental device, to process those mental phenomena in an adaptive way. That is, the symbol makes information processing more efficient. In the words of Erikson, "I propose the theory that the child's play is the infantile form of the human ability to deal with experience by creating model situations and to master reality by experiment and planning" (1963, p. 222). Bettelheim (1977) speaks of fairy tales allowing a child to embody his contradictory urges in the various characters of the fairy tales, and thus more easily sort them out, and be less "engulfed by unmanageable chaos" (p. 66). According to these ideas, fantasy play serves something of the same function as language: It facilitates the thinking process. There is some evidence, garnered by cognitively oriented psychologists, to support this notion; we soon review that evidence here.

Before leaving the psychoanalytic framework, however, mention must be made of the technique of Richard Gardner (1971, 1975, 1979), a pioneer in the use of stories in child psychotherapy. Gardner describes his technique as follows:

> When utilizing the technique, the therapist elicits a self-created story from the child, ascertains its psychodynamic meaning, and surmises the pathological elements in it. He then creates a story of his own, using the same characters in a similar setting, but introduces what he considers to be healthier adaptations and resolutions than those utilized in the child's story. One might view the method as an attempt to bypass conscious resistance to unacceptable interpretations and insights by communicating directly with the unconscious. (Gardner, 1979, p. 426)

Although controlled studies of the outcome of Gardner's technique have apparently never been conducted, Gardner cites cases wherein improvement occurred, seemingly related to the use of the technique (Gardner, 1971).

If Gardner's technique does indeed produce favorable results in child psychotherapy, as it seems to, it is interesting to ask by which mechanism it does so. The method gives the child practice in expressive and receptive language; it provides models of adaptive thought, feeling, and behavior patterns via the characters in the therapist's stories; if the child's stories gradually come to resemble the therapist's (as they do according to inspection of the transcripts recorded in Gardner, 1971), then the child gets a chance to practice adaptive patterns in fantasy when he or she constructs stories. The following sections examine empirical studies on the construction of fantasies by children.

Evidence That Skill in the Use of Fantasy and Symbolic Play Is an Asset for Children

In the previous section, we alluded to the notion that symbolic play might help children think. What evidence is there to support this notion?

Fein (1979) reports a correlational study that assessed, in $1\frac{1}{2}$- and 2-year-olds, the ability to comprehend language and the capacity for symbolic play. High comprehension scores were found to characterize children who engaged in more advanced forms of pretend play. Fein states, "These results are consistent with Vygotsky's position concerning the relation between language and play; the child's comprehension of relationships between words and objects is related to the occurrence of mature symbolic play forms" (p. 11).

The ability to conjure up stories is related to ability in pretend play. Story-making skill seems, according to some data, to be correlated with adjustment. Sutton-Smith (1979) cites a study in which teachers were asked to rate children aged 2 to 14 years on a 1–5 scale of adjustment. The children were asked by the investigators to tell stories. While conditions were unfortunately not conducive to blind ratings, the teachers rated the children with low or no proficiency in storytelling as significantly less well-adjusted than the other children. These two studies thus suggest that abilities to create fantasy (disregarding, for the time being, the content of the fantasy) are positively related to adjustment and language ability.

Singer (1973) summarizes a variety of studies in which children were assessed as being *high fantasy* (i.e., high in the ability to use imagination) or *low fantasy*. High-fantasy children were able to remain seated or standing quietly for significantly longer time periods before giving up than were the low-fantasy subjects. Generalizability is somewhat reduced by the fact that the children were directed to imagine themselves in a space-exploration situation in which they needed to be still; nevertheless, this study suggests that use of imagination as a mediational tool might enable children to defer gratification or suppress impulsivity more readily. Pulaski (1973) found that high-fantasy children became "more deeply absorbed in their play" than low-fantasy children, and gave more evidence of concentration on their play (p. 93). Yet, these high-fantasy children were able to respond more cooperatively when an adult interrupted their play and asked them to tell a story about a new toy. Biblow (1973) also measured fantasy predisposition, and studied the relationship of this characteristic to the child's response to frustration. The high-fantasy children showed less overt aggression than their low-fantasy counterparts. Biblow described the low-fantasy child as more "motorically oriented," less creative in his or her play, and more direct in her or his approach to play materials and in expression of aggression than the high-fantasy youngster.

Several investigators have noted that middle-class subjects were higher in fantasy ability than lower socioeconomic-status (SES) children (Korchin et al., 1950; Rosen, 1974; Smilansky, 1968).

All the studies cited so far in this section have been ex post facto studies. A study by Freyberg (1973) involved manipulation of the fantasy ability variable. The experimenter taught lower-SES 5-year-olds to play more imaginatively. Enhanced fantasy play ability outside the experimental setting did ensue from the procedure; this increase was reported to be associated with greater verbal communication, longer and more complex sentence usage, more-sensitive responding to the cues of other children, more-apparent spontaneity, increased attention span, and more-positive expressions of emotion. Freyberg's training procedure was one in which groups of four experimental children were taken to a separate room; the children were encouraged to adopt a role and play a character in a story, using pipecleaner people. At first, the investigator used much prompting and modeling; then she gradually excluded herself. A control group put together jigsaw puzzles. The entire intervention consisted of eight 20-minute sessions. The dependent variables were measured by independent raters, observing the children's free play outside the experimental setting.

Rosen (1974) carried out a similar experimental intervention with disadvantaged black kindergarten children. After finding that these children engaged in less sociodramatic play in their free-play activities than did either black or white middle-class children, the experimenter assigned the disadvantaged children to experimental or control groups. Instruction and guided participation of the experimental group in sociodramatic play extended over 40 1-hour sessions. The intervention was reported to increase the experimental children's productivity in working on tasks, their cooperative behavior in a game to test cooperation–competition, and their capacity to choose appropriate birthday presents for various people—mother, brother, sister, teacher.

To summarize this section, there is a fair amount of correlational evidence, and some experimental evidence, that the ability to fantasize is a useful skill for children. Fantasy ability is associated with improved social and cognitive performance, and it appears to be a teachable skill.

Evidence That Reading to Children Helps Develop Their Language and Reading Skills

The skill of comprehending oral language, like other skills, would be expected to improve with practice. And the skill of comprehending oral language, as pointed out in a previous section, has much in common with the skill of reading. We would expect, then, that reading to children would improve their language abilities and their reading abilities. In the education literature we find evidence for that proposition.

Cohen (1968) reported a study in which 20 classes of Harlem secondgraders were read to in school for 20 minutes a day for 1 school year. A control group did not receive this experience. The experimental group was reported to show significantly higher gains in vocabulary and reading comprehension than did the control group.

Durkin (1966) studied 79 *early readers:* children who apparently taught themselves to read, and arrived at first grade or kindergarten already knowing how to read. One of the variables studied was whether the child had been read to regularly at home. *Each one* of the 79 early readers had had this experience.

Harkness (1981) and McCormick (1981) have reviewed other literature on the effects of reading aloud to young children. Both reviews conclude that this activity has positive effects on the child's eventual reading achievements and on language development. Measures positively affected by adults' reading aloud to preschoolers included mean length of the sentences the child used, score on the Peabody Picture Vocabulary Test, frequency of the child's looking at books in an open classroom, score on several reading readiness tests, and scores on reading achievement in Grades 1 and 2.

The evidence reviewed so far suggests that reading to children and allowing children to construct their own fantasies is of benefit. So far, nothing about the content of the stories the child hears or the fantasies the child constructs has been mentioned. The next section examines evidence that stories or other models of adaptive patterns, and fantasy rehearsals of adaptive patterns, will be particularly useful.

Evidence That Providing Models of Adaptive Behavior Patterns Makes Their Performance in Real-Life Easier

Modeling has been used with children to overcome problems with anxiety and withdrawal. Bandura and Menlove (1968) used films of models interacting with dogs to help children who had been markedly fearful of dogs to reduce their fears; this technique was significantly more useful than a control film not involving animals. Modeling has been used to reduce children's fears of swimming (Lewis, 1974) and of dental procedures (see the six studies cited in a review by Kirkland & Thelan, 1977).

Modeling films have also been used with preschool children in the teaching of social skills. O'Connor (1969) selected a group of preschool children who had, according to the teacher's report, exhibited long-standing social withdrawal. These children were found to exhibit isolate behaviors, according to direct observation. Half of these isolate children were shown a 23-minute film in which an initially withdrawn child engaged in increasingly complex social interaction in a preschool setting. Participation in peer activities was followed by reinforcing consequences for the child model in the film. The other half of the group of isolate children were shown a neutral control film unrelated to peer interaction. Behavioral observations in the classroom immediately following the film viewing indicated that those children who had viewed the experimental modeling film showed a dramatic increase in the frequency and quality of their social interactions. Only one of the six children in this group continued to be rated as socially withdrawn by the teachers. The children who had viewed the control film continued to be withdrawn.

In a later study, O'Connor (1972) carried out a 2 × 2 factorial study. The two interventions were modeling, via the same film, and shaping of desirable social behavior through social reinforcement delivered by trained graduate students. Modeling in this experiment modified social withdrawal as it had in the first experiment; furthermore, it did so faster than shaping, and produced changes more stable than shaping. In follow-up assessments 3 weeks after termination of the intervention, the subject taught by modeling remained socially active, whereas those taught only by shaping returned to the isolate level. The combination of modeling and shaping was not significantly different from modeling alone in its effects. Evers and Schwarz (1973) used O'Connor's modeling film, and again produced increased social interactions in withdrawn preschoolers. Again, modeling was just as effective as modeling plus praise.

In discussing his results, O'Connor (1972) surmises that modeling may be particularly useful in introducing new patterns into a child's repertoire, and superior to shaping at that task, whereas reinforcement contingencies might have their most efficient effect on behaviors already within the repertoire of the individual. Thus, the distinction is drawn between learning and performance (in the words of Bandura) or, in other words, between knowing how to do something and doing it.

Keller and Carlson (1974) however, found that when they used modeling films with socially isolated children to teach imitating, smiling and laughing, token-giving, or affectionately touching other children, only those specific behaviors that had been highest in the children's pretreatment hierarchy of social skills increased in frequency after the modeling. The authors comment that the modeling effects fall into the category of facilitation effects. The study implies that one should not be too quick to make a rigid division of labor between modeling as a way of getting new responses into the repertoire and reinforcement as a way of increasing performance of responses already in the repertoire.

The studies reviewed so far have had to do with modeling as a treatment for children with internalizing or overcontrolled patterns, patterns of our apathy–withdrawal factor. What is the evidence for the effect of modeling in alleviating problems with the other major factor of child psychopathology, that is, problems of anger–defiance, or externalizing patterns? Staub (1978, 1979) has extensively reviewed research on the influence of modeling on positive behavior. Exposure to the behavioral example of other people does affect positive behavior immediately following the child's observation; this finding has been repeated many times. Fewer experiments have demonstrated the long-term or generalized effects of modeling procedures on prosocial behavior; however, those that have looked for such effects have usually found some. Rushton (1975) found that children who had been exposed to generous models were more willing to donate to needy people when tested 2 months after the modeling exposure. Midlarsky and Bryan (1972) found similar results.

Chittenden (1942) conducted a study designed to teach children non-aggressive reactions to frustration. She exposed children to a series of plays depicting aggressive, and then cooperative solutions to interpersonal problem situations; the experimenter facilitated discussion of the advantages of cooperation. The children who observed the modeling plays showed a decrease in domination and aggression in response to frustration at nursery school. Thomas (1974) used modeling via videotapes to improve the attending behavior of highly distractible first-graders. Meichenbaum and Goodman (1969, 1971) trained impulsive children to make slower, more reflective responses on cognitive tasks by training the children to talk to themselves and guide themselves verbally through the tasks; this training involved exposure to models.

Coates et al. (1976) found that exposing preschool children to segments of the television show, "Mister Rogers' Neighborhood," that contained a high frequency of positive reinforcement significantly increased the children's giving of positive reinforcement to other children and adults in the preschool. In summary, modeling seems to have had some success in helping children increase cooperation and compliance as well as to reduce anxiety and withdrawal. In a discussion of the power of modeling effects, we must mention the voluminous evidence on the negative effect that television has had on behaviors in the anger–defiance realm via repeated modeling of violent acts (Pearl et al., 1982; Liebert et al., 1973). Perhaps the most powerful pieces of evidence for a causal relationship between these variables come from cross-lagged correlational analyses (e.g., Eron, 1980). Eron reports findings from such a design in which the relation between viewing violent television at age 8 years and aggressive behavior at age 19 years is actually higher than the relation between watching violent television at age 8 and aggressive behavior at age 8.

Assuming that one wishes to use modeling to help children learn psychological skills, what particular parameters seem to most facilitate the effectiveness of the procedure? Kirkland and Thelan (1977) have reviewed the characteristics of clients, models, modeled consequences, and adjunctive instructions that seem to maximize the effects of the modeling. According to their survey, modeling works best with younger children, with more-dependent children, and with less-resistant children. Two studies they review (Gelfand, 1962; Kanareff & Lanzetta, 1960) suggest that children who have failure experiences prior to modeling treatment imitate more than do children with prior success experiences in the activity relevant to the modeling.

With respect to model characteristics, those models who seem nurturing, who express positive emotion, and who powerfully control resources of value to the child seem to elicit a high rate of imitation.

Yarrow and Scott (1972) found an interaction between the nurturant or nonnurturant style of the experimenter and the content of the modeled behavior that children choose to imitate. Adults were trained to supervise groups of children in either nurturant or nonnurturant ways.

All of these adults modeled both nurturant and nonnurturant behaviors toward animal play materials. The children who were supervised in a nurturant way imitated more of the nurturant activities toward the toys, and those supervised in a nonnurturant way imitated more of the non-nurturant activities toward the toys, despite the fact that both groups of children were exposed to the same models of behavior toward the toys. The conclusion is that children may selectively imitate the symbolic models of adults that are most consonant with the adults' real-life behavior.

Both adult-aged and peer-aged models have proven successful; Kirkland and Thelan (1977) found that the data permitted neither a definitive statement on which age of models are most potent, nor a statement as to whether same- or opposite-sex models are superior with small children. Multiple models seem more potent than a single model (Bandura & Menlove, 1968; Marburg et al., 1976). Meichenbaum (1971) found that models who initially showed some difficulty with the task, and then gradually mastered it, were more effective than models who demonstrated immediate mastery. Models who talked to themselves about their coping responses (i.e., who used self verbalization) were also more effective.

With respect to model consequences, models who are rewarded for their behavior elicit more imitation. Selective reward and punishment of models has been used to help the child discriminate which behaviors to imitate and which to avoid.

With respect to adjunctive instructions, asking the subject to verbally describe the actions of the model seems to elicit greater imitation (Bandura et al., 1966). In one study, giving subjects direct instructions to imitate also tended to increase imitation (Rennie & Thelan, 1976). According to Bandura (1973), conditions of observational learning combining repeated exposure with repeated opportunities for overt practice and symbolic rehearsal (another term for fantasy rehearsal, or covert modeling) ensure more-or-less permanent retention of modeled activities (p. 78).

In summary, modeling has been shown to be a powerful method of influence, both with problems of apathy–withdrawal and with those of anger–defiance. Certain findings give us clues as to how to arrange modeling experiences to be most effective.

Evidence That Rehearsal, in Fantasy, of Adaptive Patterns Makes Their Performance in Real-Life Easier

The technique of carrying out desirable patterns of thought, feeling, or behavior in the imagination, in order to facilitate their performance in real life, has been given several labels, among them goal rehearsal (Laza-rus, 1977), covert rehearsal (McFall & Twentyman, 1973), behavior re-hearsal (Suinn, 1972), and covert modeling (Cautela et al., 1974). Most of the studies of this technique have been with adults. Suinn (1972) found that with competitive skiers, the technique of skiing a course in the imagination was helpful in improving performance. Cautela et al. (1974) found that fantasy practice, or covert modeling, was just as effective as live modeling in reducing avoidance behavior in college students. Mc-Fall and Twentyman (1973) found covert rehearsal no different from overt rehearsal in promoting the ability to refuse unreasonable requests; both methods of practice improved the subjects' abilities in the target behavior. Kazdin (1974a, 1974b, 1974c, 1974d, 1976) found covert model-ing superior to no treatment in reducing avoidance of harmless snakes and in promoting assertive behavior.

Studies have also examined some of the parameters of fantasy re-hearsal that seem to make it more effective. If one's fantasy sequence has the protagonist rewarded for performing the desired behavior pat-terns, the fantasy rehearsal seems more effective (Kazdin, 1974a, 1974b). Imagining oneself performing the activity or imagining someone else doing so both produced improvement (Kazdin, 1974d). Imagining some-one of the same sex and similar age performing the desirable pattern improved the effectiveness of the procedure, as opposed to imagining someone much older and of opposite sex (Kazdin, 1974c). Imagining someone initially carrying out the desired pattern with some hesitation or difficulty (as might the subject herself or himself in initial trials) seemed to enhance the effectiveness of the procedure (Kazdin, 1974d).

All of the preceding studies have been done with adults. Meichen-baum (1972, cited in Singer, 1974) reported that imagery methods were helpful in teaching impulsive children to do more thinking before act-ing. A child for example, was taught to remind himself, "I will not go faster than a slow turtle, slow turtle." Imagining the turtle constitutes a form of fantasy practice. Role-playing, which might be conceived of as acted-out fantasy rehearsal, has been used with kindergarten children in the teaching of sharing behavior. Staub (1971) led kindergarten children to enact situations in which one child needed help and another provided help. This intervention tended to increase the children's tendency to help a child in distress, and also to share candy, in simulated real-life situations 1 week after the intervention.

To summarize, systematic studies have demonstrated the usefulness of fantasy practice in adults, and have begun to delineate some of the ways in which such practice should be carried out for maximum effec-tiveness. The use of fantasy practice with children has been far less widely studied.

How Can Contingent Reinforcement Be Best Used to
Increase the Psychological Skills of Preschool Children?

Because a positive reinforcer is defined as a consequence that tends to increase the rate of the response that precedes it, it is tautological to say that reinforcement contingent on a target behavior is effective in strengthening that behavior. What is not tautological, however, is to note that for children, adult attention tends to be reinforcing. This principle has been used in hundreds of studies. Harris et al. (1967), for example, used adult social reinforcement in a nursery school setting to promote the cessation of a variety of undesirable behaviors: excessive crying and whining, isolate play, and excessive passivity. These authors note that for each case, adult attention was a strong positive reinforcer. However, these authors noted the possibility that for some children, adult attention may not be reinforcing, or may even be aversive; with one child the teachers spent several weeks trying to make themselves positively reinforcing to the child before the study was begun.

There is some evidence that aggressive and cooperative behaviors in children may be incompatible in the sense that reinforcing behavior of either of these two types simultaneously weakens behavior of the other type (Combs & Slaby, 1977). In one study, a group of children whose cooperative behaviors were increased through contingent teacher attention to verbal cooperation simultaneously decreased their verbal and physical aggression; when the children's aggressive behaviors were increased through teachers' attention to verbal aggression, they simultaneously showed less peer cooperation (Slaby & Crowley, 1977).

Adult attention to the child's desirable social behavior sometimes has the disadvantageous effect of interrupting that behavior. Strain et al. (1979) studied a sample of abused and neglected children. The efficacy of the social reinforcement delivered by the teacher contingent upon the child's positive social behavior was evaluated by determining the percent[age] of intervals following the delivery of social reinforcement in which the child's positive social behavior was continued from the preceding interval. Of all the times social reinforcement was delivered by a teacher, it was followed by positive interaction only 12% of the time. Sixty-eight percent of such adult reinforcers were followed by no social behavior, and 10 percent were followed by negative social behavior. By contrast, positive social initiations by peers resulted in a .53 probability of a positive response. Similarly, Evers and Schwarz (1973), who found that teacher praise did not significantly add to the effects of a modeling film in increasing positive social behavior of preschool children, raised the possibility that "the use of an adult to reward peer interaction may in fact interfere with the subject's behavior. The adult's attention, even though given to the peer group, may either inhibit or redirect the child's activity" (p. 254).

However, some interesting studies by Becker and colleagues (Madsen et al., 1968; Thomas et al., 1968) demonstrate that attention can be reinforcing in the long run even when, in the short run, the behavior in question is interrupted or redirected. These investigators studied out-of-seat behavior in a classroom as a function of teachers' requests to sit down. When the teacher systematically attended to out-of-seat behavior with this request, the rate of out-of-seat behavior increased, despite the fact that the teacher's request was followed by the child's sitting down. In a second study, when the teacher criticized off-task behavior, off-task behavior increased. In both studies, when the attention to the negative behavior was eliminated and the teacher concentrated on praising the positive behavior, negative behavior decreased. These studies reinforce the idea that even though adult attention may interrupt a child's behavior, and even though conceivably some children do not find adult attention reinforcing, in general adult attention tends to reinforce, even when it is critical or negative in quality, and even when it consists of instructions counter to the behavior being attended to.

A difficult problem with the use of reinforcement contingencies is that when they are withdrawn, the behavior tends to revert to pretreatment levels; such an effect is readily evident in the classic ABAB single-case designs often used to demonstrate the effect of the reinforcement. In dealing with this problem, there are two strategies: one is to make an intermittent reinforcement schedule contain more and more sparse reinforcement so that resistance to extinction is gradually acquired. This procedure, called fading, has been reported on the basis of case studies to result in longer-lasting effects (Combs & Slaby, 1977).

The second strategy to maintain the effects of contingent reinforcement programs involves finding some arrangement wherein reinforcement for the desired behavior can be continued indefinitely. With respect to peer interactions, once a child learns to interact well enough to make friends and participate in normal peer activities, he or she presumably enters what might be called a "natural community of reinforcement" (Baer & Wolf, 1970) in which peers provide reinforcers for continued adaptive social interaction. On the more-pessimistic side, however, are the findings of Patterson et al. (1967) that 80% of the aggressive incidents observed in a preschool class were directly rewarded by such victim reactions as giving up objects, crying, or running away. Furthermore, aggression seemed contagious, in that formerly nonaggressive peers observed the aggression of other children, became victims themselves, and began to adopt defensive strategies. If defensive aggression was effective, they then began to imitate aggression. The maintenance of prosocial behavior when the natural community differentially reinforces aggression is a very difficult problem.

The literature provides other guidelines on how reinforcement may be most effectively used. The principle of the temporal gradient of reinforcement is a way of expressing the finding that reinforcement delivered immediately after the behavior in question is most effective (Bijou & Baer, 1961). The principle that the strength of an operant is proportional to the number of times it has been reinforced in the past (Bijou & Baer, 1961) implies that programs for children that are extended over time might produce a higher level of habit strength than those lasting only long enough to reinforce a few occurrences of the desired behavior. The findings that continuous reinforcement develops a response most quickly, and that intermittent reinforcement produces the most resistance to extinction (Bijou & Baer, 1961), should also be taken into account in programs designed to instill and strengthen the target skills of cooperation, interest, and language facility.

QUESTION 3: WHO SHOULD BE THE CHANGE AGENTS WHO IMPLEMENT THESE METHODS IN THE SERVICE OF THESE GOALS?

The evidence cited in this section supports the notion that the primary change agents who provide for young children the influences toward psychological, behavioral, and linguistic growth may be lay people: parents, lay volunteers, and children helping other children.

Parent Training Studies

Bronfenbrenner (1974) reviewed a number of effective and ineffective programs for early intervention with disadvantaged children. The data from this review led the author to conclude that "the family seems to be the most effective and economical system for fostering and sustaining the child's development. Without family involvement, intervention is likely to be unsuccessful, and what few effects are achieved are likely to disappear once the intervention is discontinued" (p. 300). Bronfenbrenner suggested that the reason parent involvement is so important is that when parents are involved, they can continue the favorable influences on their children when the program has officially terminated.

In addition, Bronfenbrenner states that all the effective parent strategies he examined focused attention on interaction between parent and child around a common activity, as contrasted with approaches that simply disseminated information to parents. An example of such activity is the mother–child interaction fostered in a project by Levenstein (1970). This project employed people called "toy demonstrators" who visited the homes of disadvantaged children aged 23 to 40 months. The task of the toy demonstrator was to enhance the relationship of the child to the mother by fostering communication between the two around a common activity. The toy demonstrator was to "treat the mother as a colleague in a joint endeavor in behalf of the child" (p. 429). The mother was encouraged to "play and read with the child between home sessions" (p. 429). After 7 months of this intervention, the experimental group of children demonstrated a mean gain of 17 points on the Catell or Stanford-Binet intelligence test, whereas the control groups made gains of only a point or 2.

Within the camp of behavior therapists, the field of parent training has enjoyed some documented success, beginning with a study by Wahler et al. (1965) on mothers as behavior therapists for their own children. This study used single-case design to demonstrate that mothers could control relevant behaviors in their children, ranging from dependent behaviors to commanding and uncooperative behavior, by varying reinforcement and/or punishment contingencies.

The most difficult question regarding behavioral training procedures is how to maintain treatment effects after treatment ceases. To date, some data have accumulated suggesting that parent training produces persistent effects. Patterson and Fleischman (1979) report a follow-up study on parent training for families of socially aggressive or stealing children between the ages of 3 and 12 years. There was a quite significant drop in deviant behavior from baseline to posttreatment; this effect was sustained at 6- and 12-month follow-up. At 12-month follow-up, 84% of the children had a score in the normal range, whereas only 42% had scored in that range at pretest. There was no control group for this study. Patterson and Fleischman cite a study by Alexander and Parsons (1973) in which juvenile offenders referred for treatment by the juvenile court were referred for either behaviorally oriented family treatment or one of several comparison groups. Follow-up after 6 to 18 months showed that the behaviorally trained group had one-third to one-half the recidivism rates of the comparison groups. Methodological problems vitiate the impact of this study.

Strain et al. (1982) report a follow-up of 40 children who as 3-, 4-, and 5-year-olds had exhibited severe and prolonged tantrums, continual opposition to adults' requests and commands, and physical aggression toward parents. Each child and mother had participated in a standard-ized intervention package, the main ingredient of which involved teach-ing the parent to attend to positive behaviors and ignore negative behav-iors. The treated children, when studied 3 to 9 years after graduation from the program, were found by direct observational measures to have, in general, positive relations with parents and a habit of compliance with adult requests. The parents' behavior was consistent with that taught in the program. The children did not differ, either by direct observational measures or by scores on a problem checklist, from ran-domly selected classmate controls.

Peer Tutoring Studies

Peer tutoring is not a recent invention. Joseph Lancaster, in the early nineteenth century, founded a school for working class children in Lon-don. Lancaster set up a *monitorial system* consisting of a hierarchy of children who, under the guidance of a single teacher, managed the learning of hundreds of students. The apparent success of this program has been attributed to behavior management principles and hierarchi-cally arranged skill-building curricula that have been formally described only since the 1960s (Gerber & Kauffman, 1981).

In the 1960s and 1970s in this country, more formal research on peer tutoring was begun. Duff and Swick (1974), Epstein (1978), and Jenkins et al. (1974) tried peer tutoring as a means of teaching reading, and found it superior to teacher-led control groups. Other studies have found no differences between peer-tutored and teacher-led instruction (Oakland and Williams, 1975; Stainback & Stainback, 1972).

Peers have been used as trainers in areas other than academic tutor-ing. Strain et al. (1977) trained two 4-year-old peers to engage handi-capped children in social play. The target children ranged in IQ from 30 to 58. The peers learned to initiate play by saying things like, "Come and play," or "Let's play ball." The peers were taught to initiate play physi-cally (e.g., by rolling a ball to the target child), as well as verbally. When the intervention was begun with the target children, their responses to social initiations immediately increased; their own positive initiations of social play also increased. In some ways, peer-mediated interventions proved superior to adult-mediated tactics. An interesting part of the training procedure was a training-to-expect-rejection procedure. The adult trainers of the peer tutors carried out a role play in which the adult ignored half the initiations by the peer trainer. After ignoring, the adult trainer would explain what he or she was doing and encourage the peer trainer to "keep trying, even when children don't play at first."

What parameters are important in obtaining success in peer tutoring programs? According to a review by Gerber and Kauffman (1981), the nature of the children being tutored and the children doing the tutoring has varied exceedingly widely in published accounts of successful programs. What appear to be crucial to success, according to these authors, are two factors: mutual reward between tutor and tutee, and a clear hierarchical and sequential arrangement of the material to be taught, such that the tutor could easily follow it. Regarding this second factor, the responses to be expected from the tutee were, in successful programs, consistently simple and unambiguous. This type of structure aided the tutors in discriminating correct responses that were to signal them to deliver reinforcement or correction.

Regarding the exchange of reinforcement between tutor and tutee; Hartup (1976) reviews data suggesting that both in free-play and in problem-solving situations, cross-aged pairs of children seem to exchange fewer social rewards than same-aged peers. However, the rewards given by older or younger children seem more potent than those given by same-aged peers. Feshbach (1976) found that middle-class white children administered much higher frequencies of positive reinforcement to their tutees than did either lower-class white or lower-class black children. The middle-class white children also issued lower frequencies of critical remarks or gestures. Conrad (1975) provided some tutors training in reinforcement and correction procedures; others were untrained. The performance of the tutees being taught by trained tutors was significantly better than that of tutees taught by untrained tutors.

College Students, High School Students, Housewives, and Other Lay Helpers

Cowen, in a 1973 review, mentions many studies in which college or high school students or housewives were pressed into mental health service; although most programs have not been rigorously evaluated, many seem to have the ring of success.

In a program carried out by Jason et al. (1973), college students worked three times a week for 5 months with children of average age 20.8 months. These children were from a disadvantaged neighborhood, and were selected because of slowed cognitive or social development. At the beginning of the intervention, it was striking how little the adults in the children's homes interacted verbally with the children. The student helpers, during their meetings with children, "continually modeled language use, read to the children, and encouraged them to label toys and objects and to use words . . . to communicate requests" (p. 53). During home sessions, which occurred after each session with the child, "parents were encouraged to interact with their children, and techniques that had proved effective in group sessions were modeled for them" (p. 53). The results were positive: "At the end of the program the children, initially 20% slowed down, were functioning within an average intellectual range and their behavior . . . was judged to be significantly more cooperative, content . . . and less distractible" (p. 58). On the Banham Intelligence test, the children improved nearly a standard deviation. The study lacked a control group; still, the results are impressive and the methods combine much that theoretically should be helpful.

A program pioneered by Cowen and his colleagues has paired maladapting school children with housewives trained as child aides." The aide's functions, under professional supervision, are varied, including educational, recreational, and conversational activities with the child" (Cowen et al., 1972, p. 236). During 7 consecutive years of outcome research on this program, this team (Weissberg et al., 1983) has found that the program children were rated by school mental health professionals as improving in adjustment from preintervention to immediately postintervention. When the intervention was implemented by school districts, in offshoots from the established program model, similar positive results were reported (Cowen et al., 1983).

Cowen et al. (1972) conducted follow-up interviews with parents of the children served in one wave of this program; these interviews indicated that the short-term gains of the program maintained themselves over 2 to 5 years. These program evaluations have lacked control groups. In them, as well as in the Jason et al. (1973) study, children were initially selected for low adjustment scores. Thus, the positive effects could have come partially from regression to the mean. Nevertheless, the services could be delivered by lay people in a way satisfying to the customers, and with some objective evidence of improvement, in problems not known for their tendency to remit spontaneously. These facts definitely spur further efforts.

To summarize this section, there is mounting evidence to support the notion that even maladapting children, and certainly normal children, can be encouraged to flourish even without the benefit of direct exposure to someone with an advanced degree in a mental-health discipline. The change agents who teach skills of cooperating, socializing, and using language well should most often, in a cost-effective world, by lay people, trained, if necessary, by mental-health professionals. Whenever parents can be trained to be those change agents, they should be selected with high priority.

QUESTION 4: WHEN SHOULD PREVENTIVE
INTERVENTION BEST BE BEGUN?

White (1975) articulates the frequently heard statement that very early influences on a child's personality are crucial: "The degree of flexibility that humans have, their capacity for fundamental change in their life style, in their intellectual capacity, and so forth, declines steadily with age. This has been the theme of any number of studies of child development, and I do not know of anybody who has studied human development in any serious way over the years who disagrees with it" (p. 257). White then makes a stronger statement, that the first priority with respect to helping children develop their maximum levels of competence is to do the best possible job of structuring their experiences in the first 3 years of life.

There is not such widespread agreement on this issue as the preceding statement would imply, however. Brim and Kagan (1980), Clarke and Clarke (1976), and Rutter (1980) published reviews concluding that the resiliency and flexibility of the human organism does not decrease so rapidly with age as theorists had previously held.

What sorts of evidence on this question do we have available? One sort of evidence has to do with increasing stability of traits as the child grows older, when stability is measured by the correlation between a child's scores on that trait in a certain year and the scores in future years, as assessed by longitudinal studies. If, under the natural set of influences children are subject to, their relative positions in groups with respect to the trait becomes more and more stable over time, that fact would suggest that they become less malleable or flexible with age and that change-directed interventions should be carried out early.

Honzik et al. (1948) used the aforementioned strategy to study the stability of performance on intelligence tests. These investigators started with a sample of 252 infants and followed them over 18 years with yearly intelligence tests; 153 of the original sample were still available at the end of 18 years. One way of analyzing these data involved the calculation of correlation coefficients that measured how well a child's score in 1 year predicted his or her score 3 years later, for the various possible 3-year intervals. According to Honzik et al. (1948, p. 311), "Comparison of the correlation coefficients for three-year intervals shows clearly the increase in mental test constancy with age":

$$2 \times 5 \text{ years} \qquad r = .32$$
$$3 \times 6 \text{ years} \qquad r = .57$$
$$4 \times 7 \text{ years} \qquad r = .59$$

$$5 \times 8 \text{ years} \qquad r = .70$$
$$7 \times 10 \text{ years} \qquad r = .78$$
$$9 \times 12 \text{ years} \qquad r = .85$$
$$14 \text{ or } 15 \times 18 \text{ years} \qquad r = .79$$

Wohlwill (1980) reviews three other longitudinal studies of intelligence test data, and affirms the finding that for a constant test–retest interval, test–retest correlations increase with age. Wohlwill considers and rules out the notion that such results could be a simple artifact of increasing test reliability with age. He questions, however, the interpretation of this finding as unequivocal evidence of reduced susceptibility to environmental influence over increasing age, partly because the crucial data on what is happening to the children's environment are not included in such studies.

The finding of increasing test–retest correlations with increasing age is not limited to intelligence scores, but has also been found with the two other major factors we have been examining, namely cooperation–compliance versus anger–defiance and interest–participation versus apathy–withdrawal. Kohn (1977) found this pattern in children studied longitudinally between preschool and fourth grade, using the Kohn instruments and the Schaefer and Petersen instruments, all of which, when factor-analyzed, produce these two major factors. For example, preschool to first-grade correlations were .37 for apathy–withdrawal, and .47 for anger–defiance; third- to fourth-grade correlations were .50 for apathy–withdrawal and .60 for anger–defiance. These results are somewhat confounded by a change in instruments and by the fact that the preschool-to-first-grade data may involve, on the average, a longer time lapse than the grade-to-grade data in elementary school.

Some longitudinal studies have given evidence of the stability of traits of aggressiveness and withdrawal from the middle childhood years to adolescence or even early adulthood. I have mentioned some of these studies in a previous section.

As mentioned, correlational data in which no intervention has taken place and no measure of environmental change is included can give us only limited evidence as to when preventive interventions should best be begun. The data do, however, tend to point to the importance of the preschool years as a time when stability of our three variables is least likely to have been crystallized.

Which studies provide us with situations where (1) major environmental change has taken place, and (2) the effect of that change can be studied as a function of the age at which it occurred? One sort of study involves children who have been in unfavorable environments and who have moved to more-favorable environments via adoption. From studies of this sort, it is clear that an environmental improvement that occurs only after age 6 or 7 years may still be of immerse benefit to the child. The most dramatic demonstrations of this fact are provided by reports of children rescued from severely deprived circumstances in a state of greatly retarded intellectual and social development, who after being rescued gradually achieved normal intelligence and at least close-to-normal social development (Koluchova, 1972, 1976; Davis, 1947). However, group studies of adopted children have revealed that the IQ scores of later-adopted children tend to be slightly lower than those adopted in infancy (Dennis, 1973; Goldfarb, 1943; Tizard & Hodges, 1978). It is not possible to rule out selection bias to explain these results, because adoption is of course not done by random assignment.

With respect to social development, the adoption study of Tizard and Hodges (1978) gives some evidence for a sensitive period in the pre-school years. Children studied were raised in an institution with many caregivers; some were adopted after age 4 years. The children adopted after age 4 usually developed deep relationships with their adoptive parents, and thus contradicted the notion that there is a critical period before age 4 years for the development of social bonds. However, these later-adopted children showed the same social and attentional problems in school as did those who remained in the institutions: they were more attention-seeking, restless, disobedient, and unpopular than the other children, when studied at age 8 years.

A cross-cultural study by Kagan and Klein (1973) gives evidence that stimulation of infants in the first 15 months of life is not crucial for the attainment of normal cognitive abilities by preadolescence. These investigators tested rural Guatemalan children who by cultural tradition were kept in nearly complete isolation for the first 15 months of life. They were behind on tests of cognitive development given in the first year of life, but by age 11 or 12 years, they had apparently completely caught up in their cognitive development, at least with respect to recall and recognition memory and perceptual tasks. Because these children received little schooling, it is impossible to say what the effect of those early experiences would have been on the intellectual skills relevant to success in modern urban culture, such as reading, writing, and articulate expression of ideas.

Another source of evidence that has been cited often with respect to the crucialness of early experience has to do with differing responses of human beings of different ages to brain injury, particularly to that which impairs language function. The fact that young children seem to recover language function more readily than adults (Denckla, 1979) is a piece of evidence for a biologically based greater plasticity of brain functioning in the younger organism. The evidence and the conclusion from it are immensely complex; difficulties have to do with differences in different types of brain lesions that occur at various ages (James-Roberts, 1979) and the great complexity of the phenomenon of recovery of brain functioning and the large number of variables that can affect it (Stein & Dawson, 1980).

Another way of approaching the hypothesis of a sensitive period for language learning in early childhood is by looking at the speed and facility with which people can learn a second language—when for example they move to a new country—as a function of what age they make this transition. Snow and Hoefnagel-Hohle (1978) studied in this fashion the learning of Dutch by English speakers of various ages. In the first few months, the adults and the 12- to 15-year-olds learned the fastest, and by the end of a year the 8- to 10- and the 12- to 15-year-olds had become the most fluent. The 3- to 5-year-olds scored lowest on all measures of learning used in the study. This finding, as well as previous research on second language learning (McLaughlin, 1977) fails to give evidence that younger children learn a second language more easily than older children, adolescents, or adults. This finding, of course, does not rule out the idea that there is a sensitive period for learning of one's first language.

Another source of evidence regarding plasticity as a function of age comes from early intervention studies. It should be immediately mentioned that the question, "Is early intervention effective?" is so general as to be meaningless. Early intervention can encompass a wide variety of procedures, performed in varied settings and with varied samples. A specification of the sample, the setting, and the procedure is the minimum requirement for linguistic clarity in speaking about the effects of early intervention.

Given this caveat, let us look at the effects of cognitively oriented preschool curricula, carried out in group settings, with socioeconomically disadvantaged preschool children. Lazar and Darlington (1982) present pooled data from long-term follow-up of 12 such studies. At follow-up, the children who had participated in these programs were in third to twelfth grade, with median seventh grade. The effects of the programs on intelligence scores were statistically significant after the programs had ended for from 2 to 4 years, depending on which statistical criteria were used. After that, the pooled groups did not differ significantly. However, even at the latest follow-up, fewer of the experimental children had been assigned to special education classes (14% vs. 29%), and fewer had had to repeat a school year (26% vs. 37%). The pooled data do tend to reject the idea that the entire job of "compensatory education" should be focused solely on the preschool years, and that nothing that comes later makes a difference in modifying or sustaining early gains. However, the fact that such a nondrastic environmental change as participation in preschool could effect a significant change in IQ lasting 2 to 4 years, and a significant change in school success evident in seventh grade argues in favor of such preschool experiences being provided widely. The pooled data should not even reject the notion that the effects of some programs might become more evident over time rather than diminish over time. Schweinhart and Weikart (1978), following up one of the groups contributing to the Lazar and Darlington pooled sample, found an effect size that increased over time rather than decreased. Looking at school achievement test scores and controlling for 10 covariates, they found the following two-tailed p values for program–control comparisons: Grade 1, $p = .16$; Grade 2, $p = .08$; Grade 3, $p = .06$; Grade 4, $p = .03$; Grade 5, $p = .04$; and Grade 8, $p = .008$.

In asking the question of at what age a certain sort of intervention should be carried out, the most direct answers are to be found by carrying out the same intervention with different-aged children and looking at the contribution of age to the intervention's effects. Strain et al. (1981) carried out such an analysis on the data generated by an oppositional-child treatment program mentioned earlier. Parents of oppositional and aggressive children were taught to use "differential social attention" to their children's behavior: that is, they learned to attend to the positive and ignore the negative as much as possible, using the principle that attention is a powerful reinforcer. The extent to which the child's behavior changed as a result of the intervention was studied as a function of 10 demographic variables: age of child at the time of treatment, sex of child, race of child, birth order, number of siblings, age of mother, income level of family, education level of mother, percentage attendance during treatment, and family intactness. These variables—age of child at the time of treatment, percentage attendance during treatment, and family intactness—were found to be significantly related to the demonstration of appropriate levels of cooperative behavior in the home. The younger the child was at the beginning of treatment, the more beneficial effect the treatment had. The children in this sample ranged from 17 to 70 months of age at the beginning of treatment.

Before leaving this topic, it is important to remind ourselves that there are several theoretical mechanisms whereby interventions may be more effective early in life, mechanisms other than a reduced capacity for learning with increasing age. One mechanism was labeled by Sameroff and Chandler (1975) as the "transaction hypothesis": that a behavior pattern can affect the child's environment, and that that environment can then in turn strengthen the tendency toward the original behavior, with the result that patterns become fixed not solely because of durable learning, but also because of durable environmental changes.

For example, an aggressive child might affect his or her environment in several ways: she or he might teach other children to give him or her what she or he wants contingent upon being aggressive; he or she might elicit retaliatory aggression from other children; and she or he might tend to become selected by an aggressive subgroup of peers. Any of these changes could help perpetuate the aggressive pattern, despite the fact that his or her learning mechanisms are plastic enough to unlearn the aggressive pattern.

A similar deviation-amplifying feedback loop may be set up, mediated not only by changes in the environment, but changes within the individual. For example, a child with language skills far below average is exposed to reading instruction, which he or she experiences as totally over her or his head. The child might gradually learn a response of confusion and frustration and wish to escape the situation, which becomes associated with exposure to reading instruction. Later attempts to teach the child to read then have to deal not only with the cognitive task of reading but also with the negative emotional conditioning. If such a task requires more individualized training, and if such training experiences are in short supply, the reading difficulties could become fixed despite an adequate capability of the child to learn.

Another theoretical mechanism whereby early experiences may be important has to do with continuous versus intermittent schedules of reinforcement. Habits are optimally developed for most behaviors via continuous reinforcement at first, progressing to intermittent reinforcement later on when the habit has become strong enough that intermittent reinforcement is sufficient to maintain it. The cognitive-behavioral complex of attending to *language,* that is, listening to a teacher, following verbal directions, listening to verbal instruction, reading, and so forth, is absolutely crucial for school success. Yet when one teacher directs 20 or more students, the teacher cannot provide each child with continuous reinforcement for attending to language.

On the other hand, when a preschooler and a parent converse or play with each other in a one-to-one interaction, the child may be reinforced continuously for attending to the parent's verbal output, for example, by being able to continue the plot of the symbolic play or continue the thread of the conversation, or receiving an attentive response from the parent. Similarly, the habit of compliance to an adult's requests is crucial for school success; the parent of a preschooler in the best of circumstances can provide nearly continuous reinforcement for compliance, whereas the school teacher is forced to rely on intermittent reinforcement. If there is a necessary stage where a high fraction of the child's responses are reinforced, and the child has not had such an experience by the time he or she has reached school, the child may already be in fixed and crystallized maladaptive patterns, despite the fact that learning capacity is fully present. This mechanism might explain the frequent remark heard by those who consult to schools: "When [s]he's in a one-on-one situation, [s]he's fine, but in a group, [s]he's terrible."

A final theoretical mechanism whereby intervention may need to occur early has to do with the decreasing dependency of the child over increasing age. For the preschool child, the attention of an adult is necessary for survival; this fact coexists with the clinical observation that adult attention rarely fails to be reinforcing for preschoolers. However, among children of the grade-school years, and more so among adolescents, it now becomes possible to survive without adult attention, and to accumulate enough negative experiences with adults that adult overtures toward benign intervention may be met with rejection.

Furthermore, as the child becomes older, the child's physical strength increases relative to that of the adult. If the power of the adult to set limits on the child's behavior, no matter how benignly and gently this power is used, relies at least partially on the knowledge that the adult could physically enforce commands if necessary, then this source of adult power obviously decreases as the child gets older. In other words, as the child grows older, he or she needs adults less and is more powerful in opposing their overtures if desired; as a result, the power of the adult as a change agent for many (not all) children diminishes greatly with increasing age. Strategies of differential attention effective with aggressive 3-year-olds may simply have no effect on an aggressive adolescent. Strategies of time-out techniques easily enforceable by the mother of a preschooler may be out of the question for the parent of the adolescent. Thus, even though the organism may have just as much capacity for learning in adolescence, the power of the adult to intervene and to influence that learning in a favorable direction may be far less.

Each of these three theories—the setting up of deviation-amplifying feedback loops, the necessity for continuous reinforcement at some stage of learning certain skills, and the decreasing power of adults as the child becomes stronger and less dependent—is compatible both with the data that suggest a continued capacity for new learning well into the life span, and with the data that suggest that maladaptive patterns may be very difficult to reverse, once learned. Each of these theories would suggest that if we want to prevent aggression and illiteracy and interpersonal difficulties, we should start early. None would imply that we can necessarily finish early.

CONCLUSIONS

This review asked four questions of the literature. With all the necessary hedging and qualifications, the following answers were obtained.

First: What Should Be the High-Priority Goals of Learning-Based Preventive Mental Health Interventions with Children?

The three goals most supported by the literature as relevant to vast numbers of children are the promotion of cooperation, compliance, and kindness, as opposed to hostility and defiance; the promotion of confident social interaction and interest in people and things, as opposed to anxiety, withdrawal, and apathy; and the promotion of facility in the use of language.

Second: How Should These Goals Be Promoted with Children?

The literature supports the basic general mechanisms of modeling of adaptive patterns, providing opportunities to practice these patterns, and providing reinforcement contingent on the performance of those patterns. Of the myriad specific ways for these basic mechanisms to be delivered, several are especially appropriate for young children. The literature suggests that for children to hear stories told or read, and to engage in symbolic play, are useful in their own right. When the stories model imitation-worthy examples of our three target skills and when the child's fantasies allow rehearsal of such adaptive patterns, a definite positive effect should be expected. For young children, an adult's attention is usually a strong reinforcer for adaptive (as well as maladaptive) patterns.

Third: Who Should Be the Direct Agents of Change Who Deliver These Influences to the Children?

The literature gave evidence that these people can be nonprofessionals, and that professional mental-health workers can train lay people to carry out useful interventions in a time involving weeks or months rather than years. Parents should come high on the priority list as potential agents of influence on their children.

Fourth: When Should Preventive Interventions Best Be Begun?

There is some evidence that the human organism retains the capacity for learning of new and better behavior patterns of behavior and language use throughout childhood and adolescence, and into adulthood. There is also some evidence that certain maladaptive patterns, for example, aggression and reading difficulties, tend to be somewhat difficult to change in older children, and that early interventions may be more useful than later interventions. There were advanced three hypotheses compatible both with the continued capacity of the organism to learn, and with the importance of early beginnings to preventive efforts: the existence of deviation-amplifying feedback loops, the necessity for more-continuous reinforcement in certain skills in the early stage of learning than is available in most schools, and the decreasing dependency of the child in advancing age, which (while not affecting the capacity for learning) affects the ability of adults to control the content of that learning. Nothing has contradicted the notion that favorable influences in the preschool years should be built upon by continued favorable influences throughout childhood and adolescence.

REFERENCES

Achenbach, T. M. & Edelbrock, C. S. (1978). The classification of child psychopathology: A review and analysis of empirical efforts. *Psychological Bulletin, 85,* 1275–1301.

Alexander, J. R., & Parsons, B. V. (1973). Short-term behavioral intervention with delinquent families: Impact on family process and recidivism. *Journal of Abnormal Psychology, 81,* 219–225.

Arnold, L. E. (1977). Prevention by specific perceptual remediation for vulnerable firstgraders: Controlled study and follow-up of lasting effects. *Archives of General Psychiatry, 34,* 1279–1294.

Baer, D. M., & Wolf, M. M. (1970). The entry into natural communities of reinforcement. In R. Ulrich, T. Stachnik, & J. Mabry, (Eds.), *Control of human behavior: From cure to prevention* (Vol. 2). Glenview, IL: Scott, Foresman.

Bandura, A. (1973). *Aggression: A social learning analysis.* Englewood Cliffs NJ: Prentice-Hall.

Bandura, A., Grusec, J. E., & Menlove, F. L. (1966). Observational learning as a function of symbolization and incentive set. *Child Development, 37,* 499–506.

Bandura, A., & Menlove, F. L. (1968). Factors determining vicarious extinction of avoidance behavior through symbolic modeling. *Journal of Personality and Social Psychology, 8,* 99–108.

Behar, L., & Stringfield, S. (1974). A behavior rating scale for the preschool child. *Developmental Psychology, 10,* 601–610.

Bettelheim, B. (1977). *The uses of enhancement: The meaning and importance of fairy tales.* New York: Vintage Books.

Biblow, E. (1973). Imaginative play and control of aggressive behavior. In J. L. Singer (Ed.), *The child's world of make-believe: Experimental studies of imaginative play.* New York: Academic Press.

Bijou, S. W., & Baer, D. M. (1961). *Child development: Vol. 1. A systematic and empirical theory.* New York: Appleton-Century-Crofts.

Brim, O. G., & Kagan, J. (1980). *Constancy and change in human development.* Cambridge: Harvard University Press.

Bronfenbrenner, U. (1974). Is early intervention effective? *Teacher's College Record, 76,* 279–303.

Bronson, W. C. (1966). Central orientations: A study of behavior organization from childhood to adolescence. *Child Development 37,* 125–155.

Brown, J. L. (1960). Prognosis from presenting symptoms of preschool children with atypical development. *American Journal of Orthopsychiatry, 30,* 382–390.

Camp, B. W., & Bash, M. A. S. (1981). *Think aloud: Increasing social and cognitive skills—a problem-solving program for children.* Champaign, IL: Research Press.

Camp, B. W. (1977). Verbal mediation in young aggressive boys. *Journal of Abnormal Psychology, 86,* 145–153.

Camp, B. W., & Zimet, S. G. (1975). Classroom behavior during reading instruction. *Exceptional Children, 42,* 109–110.

Cautela, J., Flannery, R., & Hanley, E. (1974). Covert modeling: An experimental test. *Behavior Therapy, 5,* 494–502.

Chittenden, G. E. (1942). An experimental study in measuring and modifying assertive behavior in young children. *Monographs of the Society for Research in Child Development, 7,* (1, Serial No. 31).

Clarke, A. M., & Clarke, A. D. B. (1976). *Early experience: Myth and evidence.* New York: Free Press.

Coates, B., Pusser, H. E., & Goodman, I. (1976). The influence of "Sesame Street" and "Mister Rogers' Neighborhood" on children's social behavior in the preschool. *Child Development, 47,* 138–144.

Cohen, D. (1968). The effect of literature on vocabulary and reading achievement. *Elementary English, 45,* 209–217.

Combs, M. L., & Slaby, D. A. (1977). Social-skills training with children. In B. B. Lahey & A. E. Kazdin (Eds.), *Advances in clinical child psychology* (Vol. 1). New York: Plenum.

Conger, J. J., & Miller, W. C. (1966). *Personality, social class, and delinquency.* New York: Wiley.

Conrad, E. E. (1975). *The effects of tutor achievement level, reinforcement training, and expectancy on peer tutoring.* Washington, DC: Department of Health, Education, and Welfare/ Office of Education.

Cowen, E. L. (1973). Social and community interventions. *Annual Review of Psychology, 24,* 423–472.

Cowen, E. L., Dorr, D. A., Trost, M. A., & Izzo, L. D. (1972). Follow-up study of maladapting school children seen by nonprofessionals. *Journal of Consulting and Clinical Psychology, 39,* 235–238.

Cowen, E. L., Pederson, A., Babigian, H., Izzo, L. D., & Trost, M. A. (1973). Long-term follow-up of early detected vulnerable children. *Journal of Consulting and Clinical Psychology, 41,* 438–446.

Cowen, E. L., Weissberg, R. P., Lotyczewski, B. S., Bromley, M. L., Gilliland-Mallo, G., DeMeis, J. L., Farago, J. P., Grassi, R. J., Haffey, W. G., Weiner, M. J., & Woods, A. (1983). Validity generalization of a school-based preventive mental health program. *Professional Psychology: Research and Practice,* 613–623.

Davis, K. (1947). Final note on a case of extreme isolation. *American Journal of Sociology, 52,* 432–437.

Denckla, M. B. (1979). Childhood learning disabilities. In K. M. Heilman & E. Valenstein (Eds.), *Clinical neuropsychology.* New York: Oxford University Press.

Dennis, W. (1973). *Children of the Creche.* New York: Appleton-Century-Crofts.

Duff, R. E., & Swick, K. (1974). Primary level tutors as an instructional resource. *Reading Improvement, 11,* 39–44.

Durkin, D. (1966). *Children who read early.* New York: Teachers College.

Eisenberg, L., Landowne, J., Wilmer, M., & Iamber, D. (1962). The use of teacher ratings in a mental health study: A method for measuring the effectiveness of a therapeutic nursery program. *American Journal of Public Health, 62,* 18–28.

Epstein, L. (1978). The effects of intraclass peer tutoring on the vocabulary development of learning disabled children. *Journal of Learning Disabilities, 11,* 518–521.

Erikson, E. H. (1963). *Childhood and society.* New York: W. W. Norton.

Eron, L. D. (1980). Prescription for reduction of aggression. *American Psychologist, 35,* 244–252.

Evers, W. L., & Schwarz, J. C. (1973). Modifying social withdrawal in preschoolers: The effects of filmed modeling and teacher praise. *Journal of Abnormal Child Psychology, 1,* 248–256.

Fein, G. G. (1979). Echoes for the nursery: Piaget, Vygotsky, and the relationship between language and play. In E. Winner et al. (Eds.), *New Directions for Child Development* (Vol. 6, pp. 1–14). San Francisco: Jossey-Bass.

Feshbach, N. D. (1976). Teaching styles in young children: Implications for peer tutoring. In V. L. Allen (Ed.), *Children as teachers: Theory and research on tutoring.* New York: Academic Press.

Freyberg, J. T. (1973). Increasing the imaginative play of urban disadvantaged kindergarten children through systematic training. In J. L. Singer (Ed.), *The child's world of make-believe: Experimental studies of imaginative play.* New York: Academic Press.

Gardner, R. A. (1971). *Therapeutic communication with children: A mutual storytelling technique.* New York: Science House.

Gardner, R. A. (1975). *Psychotherapeutic approaches to the resistant child.* New York: Jason Aronson.

Gardner, R. A. (1979). Helping children cooperate in therapy. In S. I. Harrison (Ed.), *Basic handbook of child psychiatry: Vol. 3. Therapeutic interventions.* New York: Basic Books.

Gelfand, D. M. (1962). the influence of self-esteem on rate of verbal conditioning and social matching behavior. *Journal of Abnormal and Social Psychology, 65,* 259–265.

Gerber, M., & Kauffman, J. M. (1981). Peer tutoring in academic settings. In P. S. Strain (Ed.), *The utilization of classroom peers as behavior change agents.* New York: Plenum.

Goldfarb, W. (1943). The effects of early institutional care on adolescent personality. *Journal of Experimental Education, 12,* 106–129.

Greenwood, C. R., Walker, H. M., & Hops, H. (1977). Issues in social interaction/withdrawal assessment. *Exceptional Children,* 490–499.

Hafner, A. J., Quast, W., & Shea, M. J. (1975). The adult adjustment of one thousand psychiatric and pediatric patients: Initial findings from a twenty-five year follow-up.

In R. D. Wirth, G. Winokur, & M. Roff (Eds.), *Life history research in psychopathology* (Vol. 4). Minneapolis: University of Minnesota Press.

Harkness, F. (1981). Reading to children as a reading readiness activity. *Viewpoints in Teaching and Learning, 57,* 39–48.

Harris, A. J. (1968). Beginning reading instruction for educationally disadvantaged children. In A. H. Passow (Ed.), *Developing programs for the educationally disadvantaged.* New York: Teachers College Press.

Harris, F. R., Wolf, M. M., & Baer, D. M. (1967). Effects of adult social reinforcement on child behavior. In S. W. Bijou & D. M. Baer (Eds.), *Child development: Readings in experimental analysis.* New York: Appleton-Century-Crofts.

Hartup, W. W. (1976). Cross-age versus same-age peer interaction: Ethological and cross-cultural perspective. In V. L. Allen (Ed.), *Children as teachers: Theory and research on tutoring.* New York: Academic Press.

Hirschi, T. & Hindelang, M. J. (1977). Intelligence and delinquency: A revisionist view. *American Sociological Review, 42,* 571–587.

Honzik, M. P., Macfarlane, J. W., & Allen, L. (1948). The stability of mental test performance between two and eighteen years. *Journal of Experimental Education, 17,* 309–323.

Ingram, T. T. S., Mason, A. W., & Blackburn, I. (1970). A retrospective study of 82 children with reading disability. *Developmental Medicine and Child Neurology, 12,* 271–281.

James-Roberts, I. (1979). Neurological plasticity, recovery from brain insult, and child development. In H. W. Reese, L. P. Lipsitt (Eds.), *Advances in child development and behavior* (Vol. 14). New York: Academic Press.

Jason, L., Clarfield, S., & Cowen, E. L. (1973). Preventive intervention with young disadvantaged children. *American Journal of Community Psychology, 1,* 50–61.

Jenkins, J. R., Mayhall, W. F., Peschka, C. N., & Jenkins, L. N. (1974). Comparing small group and tutorial instruction in resource rooms. *Exceptional Children, 40,* 245–250.

Kagan, J., & Klein, R. E. (1973). Cross-cultural perspectives on early development. *American Psychologist, 28,* 947–961.

Kagan, J., & Moss, H. (1962). *From birth to maturity.* New York: Wiley.

Kanareff, V. T., & Lanzetta, J. T. (1960). Effects of success–failure experiences and probability of reinforcement upon the acquisition and extinction of an imitative response. *Psychological Reports, 7,* 151–166.

Kazdin, A. E. (1974a). Comparative effects of some variations of covert modeling. *Journal of Behavior Therapy and Experimental Psychiatry, 5,* 225–231.

Kazdin, A. E. (1974b). Covert modeling, model similarity, and reduction of avoidance behavior. *Behavior Therapy, 5,* 325–340.

Kazdin, A. E. (1974c). The effect of model identity and fear-relevant similarity on covert modeling. *Behavior Therapy, 5,* 624–635.

Kazdin, A. E. (1974d). Effects of covert modeling and model reinforcement on assertive behavior. *Journal of Abnormal Psychology, 83,* 240–252.

Kazdin, A. E. (1976). Effects of covert modeling, multiple models, and model reinforcement on assertive behavior. *Behavior Therapy, 7,* 211–222.

Kellam, S. G., Branch, J. D., Agrawal, K. C., & Ensminger, M. E. (1975). *Mental health and going to school: The Woodlawn program of assessment, early intervention, and evaluation.* Chicago: The University of Chicago Press.

Keller, M. F., & Carlson, P. M. (1974). The use of symbolic modeling to promote social skills in preschool children with low levels of social responsiveness. *Child Development, 45,* 912–919.

Kirkland, K. D., & Thelen, M. H. (1977). Uses of modeling in child treatment. In B. B.

Lahey & A. E. Kazdin (Eds.). *Advances in clinical child psychology* (Vol. 1). New York: Plenum.

Kohn, M. (1977). *Social competence, symptoms, and underachievement in childhood: A longitudinal perspective.* Washington, DC: V. H. Winston & Sons.

Kohn, M., & Rosman, B. L. (1972). A social competence scale and symptom checklist for the preschool child: Factor dimensions, their cross-instrument generality, and longitudinal persistence. *Developmental Psychology, 6,* 430–444.

Kohn, M., & Rosman, B. L. (1973). A two-factor model of emotional disturbance in the young child: Validity and screening efficiency. *Journal of Child Psychology and Psychiatry, 14,* 31–56.

Koluchova, J. (1972). Severe deprivation in twins: A case study. *Journal of Child Psychology and Psychiatry, 13,* 107–114.

Koluchova, J. (1976). The further development of twins after severe and prolonged deprivation: A second report. *Journal of Child Psychology and Psychiatry, 17,* 181–188.

Korchin, S. J., Mitchell, H. E., & Meltzoff, J. (1950). A critical evaluation of the Thompson Thematic Apperception Test. *Journal of Projective Techniques, 14,* 445–452.

Lazar, I., & Darlington, R. B. (1982). Lasting effects of early education. *Monographs of the Society for Research in Child Development, 47,* (2–3, Serial No. 195).

Lazarus, A. (1977). *In the mind's eye: The power of imagery for personal enrichment.* New York: Rawson Associates.

Levenstein, P. (1970). Cognitive growth in preschoolers through verbal interaction with mothers. *American Journal of Orthopsychiatry, 40,* 426–432.

Lewis, S. (1974). A comparison of behavior therapy techniques in the reduction of fearful avoidance behavior. *Behavior Therapy, 5,* 648–655.

Liebert, R. M., Neale, J. M., & Davidson, E. S. (1973). *The early window: Effects of television on children and youth.* Elmsford, NY: Pergamon.

Loban, W. (1963). *The language of elementary school children.* Urbana, IL: National Council of Teachers of English.

Luria, A. R. (1964). Verbal regulation of behavior. In M. A. B. Brazier, (Ed.), *The central nervous system and behavior.* New York: Josiah Macy, Jr. Foundation, 1960. (Reprinted in Stendler, C. B. (Ed.), *Readings in Child Behavior and Development.* New York: Harcourt, Brace, and World, 1964.)

Madsen, C. H., Becker, W. C., Thomas, D. R., Koser, L., & Plager, E. (1968). An analysis of the reinforcing function of "sit-down" commands. In R. K. Parker (Ed.), *Readings in educational psychology.* Boston: Allyn and Bacon.

Marburg, C. C., Houston, B. K., & Holmes, D. S. (1976). Influence of multiple models on the behavior of institutionalized retarded children: Increased generalization to other models and other behaviors. *Journal of Consulting and Clinical Psychology, 44,* 514–519.

Mason, A. W. (1967). Specific (development) dyslexia. *Developmental Medicine and Child Neurology, 9,* 183–190.

McCormick, S. (1981). Reading aloud to preschoolers age 3–6: A review of the research. *Research in Education,* Accession number ED199657.

McFall, R. M., & Twentyman, C. T. (1973). Four experiments on the relative contributions of rehearsal, modeling, and coaching to assertion training. *Journal of Abnormal Psychology, 81,* 199–218.

McLaughlin, B. (1977). Second-language learning in children. *Psychological Bulletin, 84,* 438–459.

Meichenbaum, D. H. (1971). Examination of model characteristics in reducing avoidance behavior. *Journal of Personality and Social Psychology, 17,* 298–307.

Meichenbaum, D. (1972). *Clinical implications of modifying what clients say to themselves* (Research Report No. 42). University of Waterloo, Waterloo, Ontario.

Meichenbaum, D. (1977). *Cognitive-behavior modification: An integrative approach.* New York: Plenum.

Meichenbaum, D., & Goodman, J. (1969). Reflection–impulsivity and verbal control of motor behavior. *Child Development, 40,* 785–797.

Meichenbaum, D., & Goodman, J. (1971). Training impulsive children to talk to themselves: A means for developing self-control. *Journal of Abnormal Psychology, 77,* 115–126.

Midlarsky, E., & Bryan, J. H. (1972). Affect expressions and children's imitative altruism. *Journal of Experimental Research in Personality, 6,* 195–203.

Miller, L. C. (1972). School behavior check list: An inventory of deviant behavior for elementary school children. *Journal of Consulting and Clinical Psychology, 38,* 134–144.

Norman-Jackson, J. (1982). Family interactions, language development, and primary reading achievement of black children in families of low income. *Child Development, 53,* 349–358.

Oakland, T., & Williams, F. C. (1975). An evaluation of two methods of peer tutoring. *Psychology in the Schools, 12,* 166–171.

O'Connor, R. D. (1969). Modification of social withdrawal through symbolic modeling. *Journal of Applied Behavior Analysis, 2,* 15–22.

O'Connor, R. D. (1972). Relative efficacy of modeling, shaping, and the combined procedures for modification of social withdrawal. *Journal of Abnormal Psychology, 79,* 327–334.

Patterson, G. R., & Fleischman, M. J. (1979). Maintenance of treatment effects: Some considerations concerning family systems and follow-up data. *Behavior Therapy, 10,* 168–185.

Patterson, G. R., Littman, R. A., & Bricker, W. (1967). Assertive behavior in children: A step toward a theory of aggression. *Monographs of the Society for Research in Child Development, 32,* 1–43.

Pearl, D., Bouthilety, L., & Lazar, J. (1982). *Television and behavior: Ten years of scientific progress and implications for the eighties.* Rockville, MD: National Institute of Mental Health.

Peterson, D. R. (1961). Behavior problems of middle childhood. *Journal of Consulting Psychology, 25,* 205–209.

Pulaski, M. A. (1973). Toys and imaginative play. In J. L. Singer (Ed.), *The child's world of make believe.* New York: Academic Press.

Rennie, D. L., & Thelen, M. H. (1976). Generalized imitation as a function of instructional set and social reinforcement. *JSAS Catalog of Selected Documents in Psychology, 6,* 107–108.

Robertson, G. J., & Eisenberg, J. L. (1981). *Technical supplement, Peabody Picture Vocabulary Test—Revised.* Circle Pines, MN: American Guidance Service.

Robins, L. N. (1978). Sturdy childhood predictors of adult antisocial behavior: Replications from longitudinal studies. *Psychological Medicine, 8,* 611–622.

Rosen, C. E. (1974). The effects of sociodramatic play on problem-solving behavior among culturally disadvantaged preschool children. *Child Development, 45,* 920–927.

Rushton, J. P. (1975). Generosity in children: Immediate and long-term effects of modeling, preaching, and moral judgment. *Journal of Personality and Social Psychology, 31,* 459–466.

Rutter, M. (1967). Classification and categorization in child psychology. *International Journal of Psychiatry, 3,* 161–172.

Rutter, M. (1980). The long-term effects of early experience. *Developmental Medicine and Child Neurology, 22,* 800–815.

Rutter, M., Tizard, J., Yule, W., Graham, P., & Whitmore, K. (1976). Research report, Isle of Wight studies (1964–1974). *Psychological Medicine, 6,* 313–332.

Rutter, M., & Yule, W. (1977). Reading difficulties. In M. Rutter & L. Hersov (Eds.), *Child psychiatry: Modern approaches.* Oxford: Blackwell Scientific Publications.

Sameroff, A. J., & Chandler, M. J. (1975). Reproductive risk and the continuum of caretaking casualty. In F. D. Horowitz, M. Hetherington, S. Scarr-Salapatek, & G. Siegel (Eds.), *Review of child development research* (Vol. 4). Chicago: University of Chicago Press.

Schweinhart, L. J., & Weikart, D. P. (1978, July). *Perry Preschool effects nine years later: What do they mean?* Paper presented at the NICHD Conference on Prevention of Retarded Development in Psychosocially Disadvantaged Children, University of Wisconsin—Madison. (Summarized in Lazar & Darlington, 1982.)

Singer, J. L. (1973). *The child's world of make-believe: Experimental studies of imaginative play.* New York: Academic Press.

Singer, J. L. (1974). *Imagery and daydream methods in psychotherapy and behavior modification.* New York: Academic Press.

Slaby, R. G., & Crowley, C. G. (1977). Modification of cooperation and aggression through teacher attention to children's speech. *Journal of Experimental Child Psychology, 23,* 442–258.

Smilansky, S. (1968). The effects of sociodramatic play on disadvantaged preschool children. New York: Wiley.

Snow, C. E., & Hoefnagel-Hohle, M. (1978). The critical period for language acquisition: Evidence from second language learning. *Child Development, 49,* 1114–1128.

Spivack, G., & Shure, M. (1974). *Social adjustment of young children: A cognitive approach to solving real-life problems.* San Francisco: Jossey-Bass.

Stainback, W. C., & Stainback, S. B. (1972). Effects of student to student tutoring on arithmetic achievement and personal social adjustment of low achieving tutees and high achieving tutors. *Education and Training of the Mentally Retarded, 7,* 169–172.

Staub, E. (1971). The use of role playing and induction in children's learning of helping and sharing behavior. *Child Development, 42,* 805–816.

Staub, E. (1978). *Positive social behavior and morality: Vol. 1. Social and personal influences.* New York: Academic Press.

Staub, E. (1979). *Positive social behavior and morality: Vol. 2. Socialization and development.* New York: Academic Press.

Stein, D. G., & Dawson, R. G. (1980). The dynamics of growth, organization, and adaptibility in the central nervous system. In O. G. Brim & J. Kagan (Eds.), *Constancy and change in human development.* Cambridge: Harvard University Press.

Strain, P. S., Kerr, M. M., & Alpher, R. (1979). Child–child and adult–child interaction in a preschool for physically-abused and neglected children. *Reading Improvement, 16,* 163–168.

Strain, P. S., Shores, R. E., & Timm, M. A. (1977). Effects of peer initiations on the social behavior of withdrawn preschool children. *Journal of Applied Behavior Analysis, 10,* 289–298.

Strain, P. S., Steele, P., Ellis, T., & Timm, M. A. (1982). Long-term effects of oppositional child treatment with mothers as therapists and therapist trainers. *Journal of Applied Behavior Analysis, 15,* 163–169.

Strain, P. S., Young, C. C., & Horowitz, J. (1981). Generalized behavior change during oppositional child training: An examination of child and family demographic variables. *Behavior Modification, 5,* 15–26.

Strayhorn, J. M. (1983). A diagnostic axis relevant to psychotherapy and preventive mental health. *American Journal of Orthopsychiatry, 53,* 677–696.

Strayhorn, J. M. (1984). [Reading achievement and mental health in grade school students]. Unpublished raw data.

Suinn, R. M. (1972). Behavior rehearsal training for ski racers. *Behavior Therapy, 3,* 519–520.

Sutton-Smith, B. (1979). Presentation and representation in fictional narrative. In E. Winner & H. Gardner (Eds.), *Fact, fiction, and fantasy in childhood.* San Francisco: Jossey-Bass.

Teachers College Press. (1969). *Gates-MacGinitie Reading Tests Readiness Skills, technical supplement.* New York: Teachers College Press.

Thomas, D. R., Becker, W. C., & Armstrong, M. (1968). Production and elimination of disruptive classroom behavior by systematically varying teacher's behavior. *Journal of Applied Behavior Analysis, 1,* 35–45.

Thomas, G. M. (1974). Using videotaped modeling to increase attending behavior. *Elementary School Guidance and Counseling, 9,* 35–40.

Tizard, B., & Hodges, J. (1978). The effect of early institutional rearing on the development of eight-year-old children. *Journal of Child Psychology and Psychiatry, 19,* 99–118.

Tuddenham, R. D. (1959). The consistency of personality ratings over two decades. *Genetic Psychology Monographs, 60,* 3–29.

Varlaam, A. (1974). Educational attainment and behavior at school. *Greater London Council Intelligence Quarterly, 29,* 29–37.

Vygotsky, L. (1962). *Thought and language.* New York: Wiley.

Wahler, R. G., Winkel, G. H., Peterson, R. T., & Morrison, D. C. (1965). Mothers as behavior therapists for their own children. *Behavior Research and Therapy, 3,* 113–134.

Weissberg, R. P., Cowen, E. L., Lotyczewski, B. S., & Gesten, E. L. (1983). The primary mental health project: Seven consecutive years of program outcome research. *Journal of Consulting and Clinical Psychology, 51,* 100–107.

White, B. L. (1975). *The first three years of life.* Englewood Cliffs, NJ: Prentice-Hall.

Wohlwill, J. F. (1980). Cognitive development in childhood. In O. G. Brim & J. Kagan (Eds.), *Constancy and change in human development.* Cambridge: Harvard University Press.

Yarrow, M. R., & Scott, P. M. (1972). Imitation of nurturant and nonnurturant models. *Journal of Personality and Social Psychology, 8,* 240–261.

CHAPTER 8

Modification of Children's Prosocial Behavior*

Edward J. Barton

INTRODUCTION

"You won't go to heaven if you don't share" (Benson, Shigetomi, Skeen, Gelfand, & Hartmann, 1981). Although this statement may be presumptive, it does underscore the importance of sharing and other prosocial behaviors in our society.

Since the mid-1960s, there has been a proliferation of interest in the relationship of prosocial behavior to deviant and antisocial behavior. "Descriptive studies of normal preschool children have shown that sharing behavior is very likely to result in a reciprocal positive social response by peers. Conversely, children who do not share turn off opportunities for positive social responses by others" (Bryant & Budd, 1982). Thus, it is not surprising that children with social adjustment problems, such as being defiant or withdrawn, tend to emit fewer prosocial behaviors than their peers who display normal adjustment to school (Factor & Frankie, 1980). These socially incompetent children, as noted by Foster and Ritchey (1979), are more likely than their peers to underachieve academically, drop out of school early, and/or become juvenile delinquents. In addition, there is evidence to indicate that highly aggressive

* Preparation of this chapter was supported in part by a Faculty Research Grant (No. 9-90007) from Northern Michigan University. The author gratefully acknowledges the assistance and cooperation offered by many of his colleagues during the preparation of this manuscript, expecially Frank Ascione and Rick Sanok.

boys emit less prosocial behavior than their less aggressive peers (Barrett, 1979). Collectively, the literature suggests that the facilitation of prosocial behavior may be of paramount importance for the development of a society in which peace and harmony prevail.

Unfortunately, the American educational and legal systems have been loathe to encourage prosocial behavior (Kaplan, 1972; Michaelson & Wood, 1980). Educators compulsively monitor and promote our children's academic progress; however, they fail to do likewise for prosocial behavior. In the past, teachers monitored and assigned conduct grades; in some cases, they even noted areas in need of improvement! Thus, historically schools focused somewhat on prosocial behavior. Today, except for the "values clarification" movement, they leave the development of prosocial behavior to chance. This negligence on the part of our educational system has had pernicious results. For example, children who attend so-called "high quality" preschools for an extended period of time become more aggressive and less cooperative than their peers (Belsky & Steinberg, 1978).

Furthermore, "as a child grows older, the demands and skills required for successful social interactions become increasingly more complex, and the child who already encounters difficulty in the social realm is likely to fall progressively further behind his/her more socially competent peers" (LaGreca & Mesibov, 1979, p. 234). Likewise, the legal system continues to concentrate on the surveillance and punishment of overt antisocial conduct, rather than promoting prosocial behavior. Again, the results have been disheartening, as can be discerned by the extreme problems with juvenile-group gangs and summertime riots in cities such as Detroit and Miami. Thus, in general, our educational and legal systems have not been working systematically to enhance prosocial behavior in our society. Of course, there are some exceptions. For example, I recall in the summer of 1981, a city in Texas was having its police pull over people for being considerate prosocial drivers. The police were instructed then to reward the drivers with praise and a $10.00 municipal check!

"Prosocial behavior is affected by a variety of incentive conditions and social learning experiences" (Gelfand & Hartmann, 1982, p. 34). For example, it has been shown that the generosity of nursery school boys is directly related to children's reports of their fathers' nurturance and prosocial behavior (Rutherford & Mussen, 1968). Thus, children's prosocial behavior is influenced by the environment—even at an early age. Hay (1979) has reported that as early as 12 months, infants learn to engage in cooperative and sharing behavior. Therefore, it has been proposed by this author and others (e.g., Barton & Osborne, 1978; Eisenberg, Cameron, Tryon, & Dodez, 1982) that deficits in prosocial responding, if identified early, should be rectified via behavioral intervention. In this chapter, behavioral methods for facilitating children's prosocial behavior is discussed. The clinical utility of these behavioral approaches, as well as the scientific rigor of these researches, are evaluated. In addition, other behavioral alternatives for developing prosocial behavior are offered, as well as suggestions for methodological improvement.

The literature on prosocial behavior dates back to the 1930s, and as such, is overwhelming. However, in the hope of providing the reader with information that has ecological validity and pragmatic value, as well as in the spirit of avoiding redundancy, the content of this chapter is limited to studies conducted in naturalistic or quasi-naturalistic settings. Thus, the numerous laboratory investigations of prosocial behavior are not discussed (for an excellent review of these laboratory studies, refer to Rushton, 1976).

The focus of this chapter is consistent with Bronfenbrenner's (1977) assertion that the time has come for developmental psychologists to move their investigations out of the laboratory and into the real world to determine if, in fact, their work has ecological validity. Although some laboratory findings on prosocial behavior generalize to more naturalistic situations, other do not. For example, Hibbard, Barton, Dorcey, and Klamfoth (1980) verified empirically that children's donating in the laboratory is not correlated with their sharing in the classroom. Likewise, it has been reported repeatedly that modeling is not as effective for facilitating prosocial behavior in the classroom as in the laboratory (Barton, 1981; Geller & Scheirer, 1978; Rogers-Warren, Warren, & Baer, 1977).

Before proceeding, it is important to clarify the meaning of prosocial behavior. *Pro* is a Latin prefix that means, "on behalf of." Thus, prosocial behavior refers to those social responses emitted by an individual that benefit others. This definition excludes nonsocial behaviors that neither enhance nor harm another's condition (e.g., isolate play) and antisocial behaviors that are detrimental to another (e.g., stealing). There is a potpourri of behaviors that have been labeled prosocial, including aiding, altruism, comforting, complimenting, cooperation, defending, generosity, helping, other-centeredness, physical affection, positive contact, praising, rescuing, sharing, smiling, and sympathizing. Some of these behaviors are fairly distinct (e.g., rescuing and sharing) whereas others are quite similar (e.g., aiding and helping).

METHODS OF PROMOTING PROSOCIAL
BEHAVIOR

To date, there have been 52 reports of behavioral attempts to facilitate
prosocial behavior in naturalistic and quasi-naturalistic settings. In the
mid-1960s, it was discovered that aggression could be ameliorated by
increasing the frequency of cooperation (Brown & Elliott, 1965); however the occurrence of the latter behavior was not measured. The first
study, in which the frequency of prosocial behavior was actually both
measured and facilitated, did not appear in the literature until 3 years
later (Hart, Reynolds, Baer, Brawley, & Harris, 1968).

Figure 1 is a graphic summary of the growth of research interest and
study in behavioral methods for encouraging prosocial behavior. As can
be seen from this graphic representation, between 1965 and 1975 there
was slightly more than one publication or convention presentation per
year focusing on this topic. During the most recent 6.5 years, this average has increased dramatically to over six publications–presentations

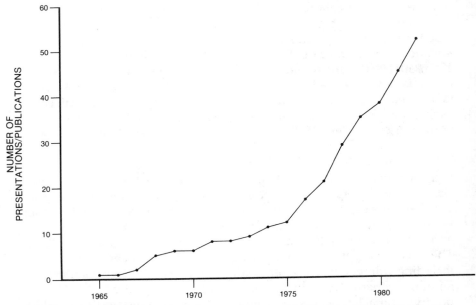

Figure 1 Cumulative number of presentations–publications on the use of behavioral
techniques to facilitate childrens' prosocial behavior from January 1, 1965 through June 30,
1982. Presentations that were subsequently published were not plotted on the graph. Note
the data point for 1982 is based on only 6 months of information.

per year. Thus, although this literature is somewhat sparse, it has begun to burgeon.

Most of the behavioral attempts at facilitating prosocial behavior have concentrated on cooperation (52%) and/or sharing (48%). In only 27% of the studies have other prosocial behaviors been investigated; in 64% of these latter studies, cooperation and/or sharing have been investigated as well! Thus, most of this section is concerned with cooperation and sharing. However, it appears that most of the naturalistic findings for one prosocial behavior are similar for most other prosocial behaviors.

Instruction

One of the simplest methods for fostering children's prosocial behavior would appear to be providing instructions. Even though many researchers (e.g., Rogers-Warren et al., 1977) have suggested that the sole use of instructions might suffice to advance prosocial behavior, this question has been addressed in only one investigation. Barton (1981) found that providing three groups of five preschool children with instructions on not only why it is important to share, but also on how to share, did not influence their sharing of toys during free play. Based on this limited information, it appears that solely instructing children to engage in prosocial behavior has little impact on their behavior. Although this finding could be interpreted to indicate that instructions are unnecessary and should not be used to teach prosocial behavior, such a conclusion is not warranted. Instructions have been used successfully in combination with other behavioral techniques to enhance prosocial behavior (e.g., Cooke & Apolloni, 1976). Whether or not instructions are a necessary prerequisite for the efficacy of these other behavioral techniques remains an empirical question.

Modeling

Research findings from the laboratory have suggested that modeling should be a potent means for encouraging prosocial behavior in naturalistic settings. Consistent with this assumption, many investigators (46%) systematically have incorporated modeling, to various degrees, in their approaches to promoting prosocial behavior. There have been seven attempts at determining whether or not modeling alone is functional in facilitating prosocial behavior in naturalistic settings.

On an affirmative note, Keller and Carlson (1974) used symbolic modeling with 19 isolate preschoolers. They discovered that showing audio–videotapes in which three prosocial behaviors were modeled and accompanied with narrative description, augmented some of these preschoolers' behaviors but not others. Specifically, smiling occurred more frequently, whereas physical affection and giving tokens did not. Their inconsistent results and unanswered questions about their methodology, make it difficult to interpret their findings.

In a somewhat similar investigation, Alvord (1978) found that symbolic modeling (in book and slide form) prior to four 15-minute free-play sessions produced an increase in preschool and kindergarten childrens' ($n = 24$) sharing behavior. To elevate the probability that modeling would be effective, Alvord (1) programmed the books and slides such that the models were praised for sharing, and (2) asked the children after each viewing, "What does sharing mean, how do you share, what bad things happen when you don't share, and what good things happen when you share?" (1978, p. 73). These additional techniques used by Alvord (1978) somewhat mask the effects of the sole use of modeling. In addition, the generality of his results is questionable, because of methodological limitations with respect to his observational system and experimental procedure.

Unlike the previous two investigations, the findings of the five remaining studies fail to support the laboratory findings concerning the enhancement of prosocial behavior solely through the use of modeling. Two of these investigations, like the previous two, utilized symbolic modeling. Geller and Scheirer (1978) showed two groups of seven preschool children, on 3 consecutive days, a film that contained four separate sequences of children engaged in cooperative play and included positive comments about this behavior. Subsequent observation of these children each day during a 20-minute free-play session revealed no increase in the children's cooperation. The short intervention (i.e., 3 days) makes the generality of their finding also questionable.

Using the same basic approach as the previous investigations but with a superior methodology, Freidrich-Cofer, Houston-Stein, Kipnis, Susman, and Clewett (1979) evaluated the use of symbolic modeling with 30 children in two Headstart classrooms. Twenty "Mr. Roger's Neighborhood" programs that stressed eight prosocial behaviors, were edited down in length to 14 to 20 minutes. For an 8-week period, the children viewed these 20 films. During all free-play and most instructional activities the children were observed for a baseline period of 3 months and an experimental period of 8 weeks. Through the use of two control classrooms ($n = 31$), it was discerned that modeling did not affect the children's rate of the eight prosocial behaviors.

In vivo models were used in the remaining three studies. In one of these, Rogers-Warren et al. (1977) tried unsuccessfully to enhance the sharing of two groups of four 4-year-old preschool children during five 8-minute art sessions by using adult modeling. In a subsequent evaluation of modeling, Barton (1981) attempted to increase the probability that modeling would be effective with an approach similar to Rogers-Warren et al. (1977). This was accomplished through the use of (1) detailed instructions prior to the modeling episode, (2) peer models as distinct from adult models, and (3) praising the model's sharing behavior.

According to laboratory literature, these additions should have strengthened the potency of the modeling effect. However, the use of modeling had no influence on the sharing of three groups of five preschool children during five 10-minute free-play sessions. Lacioni (1982) corroborated the results of these previous two studies by finding that use of peer models and subsequent praise of the models' behavior was ineffective in promoting the prosocial behavior of nine mentally retarded elementary school children.

Collectively, these investigations indicate that modeling by itself is not a sufficiently potent technique to facilitate prosocial behavior in naturalistic situations. In addition, it appears that supplemental use of instructions and peer models who are praised does not make modeling effective.

Behavior Rehearsal

Behavior rehearsal, as applied to prosocial behavior, is the structured practice of specific prosocial behavior. Typically, behavior rehearsal follows instructions and/or modeling and includes evaluative feedback and praise for satisfactory performance of the behavior. Behavior rehearsal was used in 33% of the studies reviewed for this section of the chapter. However, there have only been two reported attempts at determining the relative importance of behavioral rehearsal in promoting prosocial behavior.

In the Friedrich-Cofer et al. (1979) study, which was described in the subsection on modeling, four additional classrooms were evaluated. Besides viewing the prosocial films, students in two classes (Condition 3, $n = 32$) viewed, in their classrooms, film-related materials (e.g., pictures of Mr. Roger's characters). It was hypothesized that the relevant materials would serve as discriminative stimuli for prosocial behavior. Students in a fourth condition ($n = 48$) not only received the modeling and relevant material, but also engaged in teacher-directed behavior rehearsal. The addition of relevant materials in Condition 3 facilitated not only prosocial behavior but also aggression. However, the addition of behavior rehearsal in Condition 4 produced an increase only in prosocial behavior—not aggression. The authors concluded that Condition 4 helped the children to differentiate more effectually between prosocial and antisocial forms of behavior. Although these findings were very robust, Condition 4 was not designed exclusively to evaluate behavior rehearsal. The teachers also provided the children with more (1) opportunities to engage in prosocial behavior via their choice of games and stories, and (2) encouragement to be prosocial. As such, although it is well-conceived and rigorous research, the Friedrich-Cofer et al. (1979) study provides only a suggestive answer to the importance of behavior rehearsal.

The investigation by Barton (1981), which was described in the subsection on modeling, however, provides a more definitive answer to this question. After discovering that detailed instructions and peer modeling with praise were not potent enough to facilitate preschoolers' sharing, he provided the children with an opportunity to practice the model's behavior. The behavior rehearsal also included the trainer providing the children with feedback on the adequacy of their performances and praise for satisfactory rehearsal. The addition of the behavior rehearsal component produced dramatic and immediate increases in all three groups.

Accordingly, these studies suggest that behavior rehearsal is a technique that is functional in increasing the frequency of prosocial behavior. Whether or not behavior rehearsal would be similarly effective (1) in the absence of prior instructions and/or modeling, (2) without behavior rehearsal and/or praise, and (3) upon treatment termination has yet to be addressed. Nevertheless, it appears that in teaching prosocial behavior "children should be provided with the opportunity to practice" (Barton, 1981, p. 386).

Positive Reinforcement

Probably the most widely publicized technique in the field of behavior technology is positive reinforcement. It should not be surprising that in 75% of the studies reviewed for this section of the chapter, procedural reinforcement was utilized. In fact, in the first five published reports (1965–1968) on the enhancement of prosocial behavior, procedural reinforcement was the main technique used. Procedural reinforcers that have been used include praise, attention, public posting, high frequency activities, food, candy, drinks, tokens, and toys.

Procedural reinforcement frequently has been used in combination with extinction in this literature to alleviate common childhood problems such as aggression (Wahler, present volume) and isolation (Strain, present volume). When used in combination, these techniques often are referred to collectively as differential reinforcement because the behavior technologist differentially reinforces one behavior and extinguishes another. For example, Brown and Elliott (1965) had teachers in two preschool classrooms selectively attend to cooperation and ignore aggression. The intervention effectively reduced the aggression; no data were presented for cooperation.

In a somewhat similar approach, Wahler (1967) treated the aggression of five preschool boys by having their peers selectively praise the target boys' speech and ignore their aggression. As a consequence, aggression decreased, and speech and cooperation increased. In another investigation Slaby and Crowley (1977) used this same tactic to reduce the aggression of 23 third- and fourth-grade students. Teachers selectively attended to verbal offers to cooperate and ignored aggression. The intervention produced an increase in cooperation and a corresponding decrease in aggression.

Norquist and Bradley (1973) also used differential reinforcement to treat a childhood behavior problem. However, in this case, the presenting problem was the social isolation and elective mutism of a 5-year-old girl. Teacher attention was made contingent on cooperation, whereas isolation was put on extinction. The intervention produced not only the expected increase in cooperation and a decrease in social isolation, but also a decrease in elective mutism (i.e., an increase in the girl's conversation with peers). Although this strategy has been ineffective with electively mute children in subsequent investigations (e.g., Barton & Freeborn, 1979), the Norquist and Bradley (1973) study underscores the importance of cultivating prosocial behavior as a method for mitigating social isolation.

Whereas these four studies demonstrate the clinical utility of treating problematic social behavior of children via differential reinforcement of prosocial behavior, the two studies that tested for immediate posttreatment maintenance failed to find it. Whenever cooperation was no longer selectively reinforced in both the Wahler (1967) and the Norquist and Bradley (1973) studies, the frequency of these prosocial behaviors decreased.

This lack of treatment maintenance was also found in another study by Serbin, Tonick, and Sternglanz (1977). They had teachers in two classrooms praise their preschool children ($n = 33$) during a 45-minute free-play period for cross-sex cooperation. Their manipulation produced an immediate increase in cross-sex cooperation; yet, this behavior returned to its operant level during the subsequent reversal phase. Thus, although the sole use of reinforcement typically facilitates prosocial behavior, the effects do not maintain after treatment termination.

Another problem with the use of procedural reinforcement is, "What do you do if the prosocial behaviors do not occur?" Obviously, it is impossible to reinforce a behavior that does not occur. The typical solution is to use priming and/or shaping. *Priming* is the technique of making sure that the target child engages in the prosocial behavior so that she or he can experience the reinforcer. This typically involves prompting other children to initiate prosocial behavior with the target child. On the other hand, with shaping, the prosocial behavior is broken down into smaller units of behavior. Successive approximations to the target response are then reinforced until finally only the entire prosocial behavior is reinforced.

In three investigations, researchers have had to utilize priming and/or shaping to initiate prosocial behavior. Hart et al. (1968), in their classic study, encouraged a 5-year-old preschool girl to engage in some cooperative play by (1) prompting her peers to initiate cooperation with her (i.e., priming), and (2) initially reinforcing all verbalization in proximity to other children (shaping). Once this girl was engaging in a minimum amount of cooperation, the teachers made their praise and attention contingent on the girl emitting the target prosocial behavior. As predicted, cooperation increased in frequency.

In a similar and frequently cited study, Buell, Stoddard, Harris, and Baer (1968), during the initial part of the treatment phase, placed a 3-year-old girl on outdoor equipment (i.e., priming) to get her to use these resources at a minimum rate. As soon as this occurred, the teacher no longer placed the girl on the equipment and her attention was made contingent on the girl's use of the play equipment. This technique not only promoted equipment-use but also the girl's cooperation.

In a third study Ploutzain, Hasazi, Streifel, and Edgar (1971) used priming with 10 institutionalized severely retarded children to foster three prosocial behaviors (i.e., physical affection, pulling a peer in a wagon, and smiling). Even though the use of priming and/or shaping with procedural reinforcement consistently was successful in advancing prosocial behavior, the desired effect diminished during reversal phases instituted by Hart et al. (1968) and Buell et al. (1968).

In one of the more innovative studies in which positive reinforcement was used, Reisinger (1978) applied the Premack principle to three uncooperative preschool children. He made the opportunity for these children to engage in high-frequency behaviors contingent on emission of initially lower frequency cooperative behavior during an assembly task. This approach facilitated cooperation during the assembly task and the results generalized to free play. On a more negative note, when the Premack principle was not in effect, the children's cooperation regressed to its operant level.

A more-intrusive type of reinforcement approach that also has been evaluated for promoting prosocial behavior, is the *token economy system,* in which children are given tokens that can later be exchanged for back-up reinforcers (e.g., food, toys). Emshoff, Redd, and Davidson (1976) gave four delinquent adolescents praise and tokens (i.e., points) for each positive comment they made to a peer during seven 30-minute training sessions in a residential treatment center. These points were later re-deemable for 3 cents each. This token economy system produced an increment in the adolescents' comments, which generalized to their resi-dential homes, and which was maintained during a 3-week follow-up phase. The authors concluded that the results generalized across set-tings and time because they programmed for generalization. Specifi-cally, the activities, trainers, locations, and times had been varied for the two adolescents who showed generalized increases in positive com-ments during successive sessions.

Knapczyk and Yoppi (1975) also used a token economy with five educable mentally retarded children (8- to 10-years-old). The study was conducted every evening for 30 minutes following dinner in the chil-drens' cottage living room where all the toys were kept. During every 30-second interval in which they engaged in cooperation, they were given a point and praise by the house parent. Their points were dis-played publicly on a wall chart and could be exchanged for materials or activities (e.g., model cars, field trips, indoor basketball, board games) that were otherwise not available. The intervention enhanced coopera-tion; yet, during reversal phases, the results did not endure.

Collectively, the investigations on the efficacy of procedural reinforce-ment to facilitate prosocial behavior indicate that this technique is effec-tive. Functional control typically has been demonstrated through the use of the single-subject reversal design. In all but one study, however, the increases in prosocial behavior have not been maintained once treat-ment has been terminated. Thus, it appears that the sole use of positive reinforcement is contraindicated. Other techniques need to be used with positive reinforcement to program for generalization across time (e.g., Emshoff et al., 1976).

Prompting

Another obvious yet simplistic technique for prompting prosocial be-havior is prompting. The rationale for using this approach is to provide

children with supplementary discriminative stimuli that are functional
in controlling their behavior (e.g., adult instruction). This prompt is
then paired with the main discriminative stimulus (e.g., another child
needs help to move a heavy toy), which will hopefully become functional in setting the occasion for the child to engage in prosocial behavior. Once this is accomplished, the prompt is gradually faded out until it
is no longer used. Prompting is almost always used in combination with
reinforcement. Prompting–reinforcement was utilized in 42% of the
studies reviewed for this section of the chapter. Six studies have addressed the issue of whether the use of prompts with subsequent procedural reinforcement is enough to enhance children's prosocial behavior.

These techniques were used in a classic study by Hopkins (1968) to
develop and maintain the smiling of an 8-year-old retarded boy. Making
candy contingent on the boy's smiling did not affect his zero-baseline
rate. Therefore, the boy was prompted to smile via adult instruction
whenever 5 seconds elapsed since he had met an individual and had not
smiled. Initially, this procedure worked very well but as time passed it
became progressively less effective. As a consequence, the prompts
were discontinued and the candy contingency was reinstituted. As long
as smiling was followed by the delivery of candy, the target behavior
occurred. However, when smiling was subsequently no longer consequated with candy, the behavior returned to its operant level.

In an investigation by Redd and Birnbrauer (1969), an adult at a residential center carried about a cup of edible reinforcers during the free-
play period in which five severely retarded children had access to toys.
One of the boys in the group, whose social repertoire was extremely
limited, served as the subject. Whenever this boy engaged in cooperative play, he was given an edible and praise. The authors hypothesized
that the cup would function as a prompt for the boy, indicating free play
as a situation in which cooperation would be reinforced. A second adult
used the same approach with a second boy. In both cases, the use of
prompts and reinforcers facilitated cooperative play. In the absence of
the intervention, however, the boys' rate of cooperation repeatedly returned back to their respective operant levels.

Prompting was also used by Strain and Wiegerink (1976) to treat 12
behaviorally disordered preschool children. A classroom teacher read to
the children stories that focused on prosocial play such as sharing, taking turns, and holding hands. She then prompted her children to act out
at least two role behaviors of the characters in the story. During the
subsequent 25-minute free-play period, in which the adults did not interact with the children, the children's rate of prosocial behavior increased. When the treatment was terminated, however, the gains were
not sustained.

In two other studies (Kelley & Johnson, 1978; Whitehead, Cooper, Ruggles, Etzel, & LeBlanc, 1982), children were prompted to emit cooperative responses and were reinforced for doing so. Likewise, in yet another study, affection during group affection activities was prompted and praised by teachers and positively consequated by peers (Twardosz, Norquist, Simon, & Botkin, 1983). The intervention in these three studies produced the desired results, but again the effects were not enduring.

The findings of these six studies indicate that prompting in combination with procedural reinforcement is functional in facilitating prosocial behavior. However, these effects do not maintain after treatment termination.

Positive Practice

Another approach for producing increments in prosocial behavior is positive practice, which is a reeducative technique in which an individual, following the emission of an error or an undesirable response, is required to practice repeatedly the correct manner of behaving. Barton and Osborne (1978) received a referral from a kindergarten teacher, whose hearing-impaired children failed to share classroom materials, which consequentially was impeding their educational process. The teacher reported that he had tried instruction, preaching, and praise, but to no avail. Barton and Osborne (1978) had the teacher monitor his class during a 30-minute free-play period. Whenever he noticed a child not sharing, he required the child to practice successfully, three times, verbal offers to share or verbal acceptance of share-offers with another student. The teacher modeled verbal sharing and prompted its emission as needed during the children's practice. To separate the positive practice effects from potential procedural reinforcement, sharing was never praised. Positive practice produced an immediate and dramatic increase in sharing. The following school year, 15 weeks after treatment termination in the same class room but in the presence of a new teacher, three new students, and new toys, these children were still sharing four times their initial baseline rates. On a less enthusiastic note, in the absence of appropriate controls during the following school year, the apparent long-term maintenance results might have been produced by other uncontrolled variables (e.g., maturation). Regardless, these powerful results were replicated in a sequel study by Chandler (1977).

Given the paucity of research on the application of positive practice to prosocial behavior, more information is needed concerning its potential long-term effects. Nonetheless, the results have been very encouraging. The findings for positive practice need to be tempered with the knowledge of society's emphasis on the least-restrictive model of intervention. This model would suggest that more benign approaches be used before positive practice is implemented. "If such attempts fail and are verified through appropriate data collection and experimental design, then positive practice could be used." (Barton, 1982, p. 37).

Correspondence Training

Some investigators have attempted to facilitate prosocial behavior indirectly through *correspondence training*. This approach involves developing veracity between childrens' verbal reports of their behavior and their actual behavior. The desirability of correspondence training stems from its potential cost–benefit effectiveness. Without having to be present physically, an adult can modify overt prosocial behavior merely by reinforcing reports of the behavior. Therefore, a discernable savings in terms of training time should be realized. In addition, correspondence training would appear intuitively to be an excellent method for facilitating generalization across settings and time because it is difficult for children to discriminate when the intervention contingencies are not in effect, as trainer presence is not necessary for treatment.

In the first application of correspondence training to prosocial behavior, Rogers-Warren and Baer (1976) observed five groups of preschool children ($n = 32$) in a series of three experiments during a 10-minute art period and a subsequent 5-minute report period in which the children were asked what they had done during art. During the art sessions, the trainer and a model displayed sharing approximately five times. Then, during the report period, the model demonstrated how to report sharing and was reinforced by the experimenter with praise and food. Immediately following this episode, each child was given the opportunity to imitate the model's response. Regardless of veracity, all reports of sharing were reinforced (note, sharing was never directly reinforced during art). Once the children consistently reported sharing, true reports of sharing were reinforced. This training approach was also applied to the children's praising of peers.

In Experiment 1, correspondence training produced an increase in both reports of and actual sharing; the greatest gains were realized when only true reports were reinforced. Increases in sharing did not generalize to praising. The latter prosocial behavior also had to be treated with correspondence training. In the subsequent two experiments, Rogers-Warren and Baer (1976) discovered that these same effects could be realized without prior reinforcement of any report. As a test for setting generalization in Experiment 2, the children were observed about 1 hour before the art activity during free play. Sharing, but not praising, generalized to free play. The setting generalization of sharing, however, may have been confounded because reinforcing other social behaviors during free play may have encouraged more sharing.

The preceding findings for correspondence training were replicated by Rogers-Warren and her colleagues in a sequel (Rogers-Warren et al., 1977). Likewise, in a study by Fowler and Baer (1981), correspondence training á la Rogers-Warren was incorporated successfully into a multimethod training package for facilitating sharing, cooperation, and three other social behaviors.

Although the results of these three studies are encouraging, one other attempt at replication of the Rogers-Warren findings failed to enhance sharing. Barton, Madsen, and Olszewski (1978) modified the correspondence training method to exclude modeling of sharing because the latter was really a form of direct training that is antithetical to the rationale for the use of correspondence training. The failure of Barton et al. (1978) to facilitate sharing via correspondence training is difficult to interpret, however, because they used a different training setting (free play), observational system, and data analyses than Rogers-Warren and her colleagues. Thus, additional research is needed to clarify the potential efficacy of correspondence training for promoting prosocial behavior.

Strategic Placement

Another indirect method for encouraging prosocial behavior is strategic placement. This procedure involves coplacement of target children with children who emit the desired prosocial behavior at a high frequency. The rationale for the use of strategic placement is that a peer can act as a discriminative stimulus, a model, or a person who promotes and reinforces the desired prosocial behavior.

Strategic placement has been used as the sole treatment approach for facilitating prosocial behavior in three studies. In its first reported application, Levison (1971), during a 15-minute free-play period, paired preschool children who dispensed social rewards at a high rate with isolate peers. She found that isolate children cooperated more frequently as a result of strategic placement. One of the four isolate children maintained his gains in cooperation during a 1.5-month follow-up phase. Although these findings are promising, limitations in the experimental design prevent a conclusion that the author demonstrated functional control.

In a similar study, Jason, Robson, and Lipshutz (1980) assigned 27 first- and third-grade children to one of seven triads during a 5-minute art activity. Seven triads were formed by placing one child who shared at a low rate with two peers who shared at a high rate. Two additional triads were formed by placing two high-sharing children with four low-sharing children. Strategic placement facilitated sharing, but during a subsequent reversal phase, the children's sharing returned to its pretreatment level. Jason, Soucy, and Ferone (1980) in a sequel investigation, replicated these findings. In addition to the lack of maintenance, these two studies also were afflicted with methodological problems that have been detailed elsewhere (Barton, 1982). Thus, one is left in a quandary as to the effectiveness of the sole use of strategic placement for promoting prosocial behavior.

Strategic placement also has been used in combination with other behavioral techniques in attempts at enhancing prosocial behavior. For example, Morris and Dolker (1974) incorporated strategic placement into a multimethod training package for facilitating cooperative play in dyads. Six severely retarded children (4 to 12 years old) who were socially withdrawn were paired with a highly interactive peer who used numerous behavioral techniques to encourage cooperation. As predicted, the isolate children showed an increase in cooperation, and these positive effects were sustained throughout a 3-week follow-up phase. Using a similar strategy with two preschool children, Whitehead et al. (1982) replicated Morris and Dolker's (1974) findings and found the treatment gains generalized across settings. On the other hand, Peck, Apolloni, and Raver (1978, Experiment 1) and Barton and Freeborn (1979) have reported that their use of strategic placement, combined with other behavioral techniques, failed to facilitate cooperative social interaction. Thus, at present, the studies concerning the use of strategic placement to encourage prosocial behavior are inconclusive.

Picture-Cue Training

An exciting new development in the field, initiated by Curl (1981), is the use of play-activity picture-cue cards as language mediators for promoting prosocial interaction among socially deficient, language-delayed children and their peers. Curl (1981) generated sets of picture-cue cards for four types of preschool activity: small motor, gross motor, art, and role playing. "The picture cues were used to indicate activity choice to another child and to indicate or maintain interaction with that child" (Curl, 1981, p. 17). During 15-minute free-play sessions, preschool teachers prompted picture-cue card use and social interaction eight times per session. The subject or peer chose and showed a card to the other child as an indication of activity and peer choice. After the activity began, the children were given verbal procedural reinforcement; in addition, they received stickers and/or a special outdoor activity.

The picture cues were used successfully by Curl (1981) with all three of her subjects: a 4-year-old deaf girl, a 4-year-old aggressive boy with poor speech, and a 6-year-old electively mute girl. Picture cuing produced an increment in cooperation, giving–showing, and physical affection, as well as a decrement in aggression. No data were gathered with respect to setting and time generalization. Regardless, her findings suggest that picture cuing might be a very potent means for facilitating the prosocial behavior of language-handicapped children. On the other hand, critics have argued that picture cuing is an unnatural way of producing prosocial behavior, and therefore lacks pragmatic clinical value (Sanok, personal communication, July 12, 1982).

Multimethod Training Packages

Probably most of the approaches that have been evaluated for facilitating prosocial behavior have involved multimethods. However, by fiat, I have limited this subsection to reviewing those articles in which four or more behavioral methods were used. Moreover, studies that meet this criterion, but in which the author cited a main technique (e.g., Barton & Osborne, 1978—positive practice; Rogers-Warren et al., 1977—correspondence training), are not included in this classification.

Multimethod training packages that meet the preceding criteria have been used in 43% of the studies reviewed for this section of the chapter. Since the dramatic increase in these investigations (since 1976), this percentage has increased to 55%. The heavy reliance on training packages reflects the fact that to facilitate an increment in prosocial behavior that generalizes across settings, time, responses, and/or individuals, several behavioral techniques are needed.

The first study reported in the literature using a multimethod training package for promoting prosocial behavior was conducted by Morris and Dolker (1974). In addition to strategic placement (as discussed previously), they had an adult (1) instruct the children how to roll a ball cooperatively, (2) model the behavior, (3) initially guide the children through the response, and (4) procedurally reinforce their behavior with praise and candy. As noted earlier, their training package results in an increment in cooperation that maintained through a 3-week follow-up phase. Given the very limited and specific nature of the cooperative response (i.e., rolling a ball), the response generality of their findings is questionable.

In a more methodologically sophisticated investigation conducted 2 years later, Cooke and Apolloni (1976) developed a multimethod training package that involved instructions, adult modeling, prompting, and praise. Four learning-disabled children were taught to be prosocial during a 16-minute free-play period. Prior to this period, an adult instructed the children on why they should engage in one of four prosocial behaviors (i.e., smiling, sharing, positive physical contact, or praise), and subsequently modeled the behavior. During free play, the adult prompted and praised the children for emitting the prosocial behavior. Once the target behavior increased in frequency, a second behavior was trained and so on, until all four behaviors increased in frequency. The effects for smiling and sharing generalized to three untrained children who joined the group for a second 16-minute free-play period after the training session had ended. In addition, gains in smiling, sharing, and positive physical contact maintained across 4 weeks of follow-up observation.

In a subsequent study, Barton and Ascione (1979) attempted to (1) develop a multimethod training package that would be more potent for facilitating prosocial behavior (i.e., sharing) than Cooke and Apolloni's (1976) and (2) resolve some of the questions not addressed by the prior study. The training package included not only instructions that provided a rationale for the importance of sharing but also detailed instructions on how to share. The modeling component also was expanded. Rather than having an adult model with another adult, during each treatment session, the adult selected a child to help her model sharing. Five scenarios were used in which both the position of the materials and who initiated the sharing were varied systematically. The model was praised for each sharing response. Based on previous findings of the importance of practicing prosocial behavior (Barton & Osborne, 1978), a behavioral rehearsal component was added. After the children indicated that they understood how to share, the children were requested to rehearse the model's prosocial behavior. Immediately following each practice, the children were given feedback on the quality of their sharing behavior and were praised. Following this presession training, sharing was prompted and praised during the free-play session. However, fewer in-session prompts and praises were used than in the Cooke and Apolloni (1976) study, in an attempt to foster greater generalization.

The multimethod training package of Barton and Ascione (1979) was used during 16-minute free-play periods with eight groups of four preschool children. The intervention produced a dramatic increase in sharing, which was sustained 4 weeks after treatment termination. The gains in sharing also generalized to another setting (a different room), another activity period (art), a different adult supervisor, and different observers.

Barton and Ascione's (1979) training package, which was developed in Utah, has been studied systematically by more researchers throughout the United States than any other approach for enhancing prosocial behavior. Sequential thematic research has been conducted in Marquette, Michigan (e.g., Barton, 1981; Barton & Bevirt, 1981; Barton et al., 1978; Barton et al., 1979), in Talahassee, Florida (e.g., Partington, 1980), Morgantown, West Virginia (e.g., Partington & Barton, 1983), Birmingham, Alabama (e.g., Campbell-Olszewski, Sappington, & Barton, 1982), and Omaha, Nebraska (e.g., Bryant & Budd, 1982; Gaillard, Carder-Smith, & Budd, 1983). This package, which was initially used with predominantly white middle-class average to bright preschool children (Barton & Ascione, 1979), has also been used with disadvantaged Head Start preschool children (Barton et al., 1978), inner-city black preschool children (Campbell-Olszewski et al., 1982), and behaviorally handicapped children in early elementary school (Bryant & Budd, 1982).

In their initial study, Barton and Ascione (1979) had undergraduate trainers in unused but fully equipped preschool classrooms work with groups of four children. Campbell-Olszewski et al. (1982) used the Barton and Ascione (1979) training package in its nonmodified form in three preschool classrooms with 60 children. The teachers ($n = 3$) and their aides ($n = 3$) in these classrooms were trained on a Saturday morning for approximately 2 hours in the use of Barton and Ascione's (1979) package via a script (Barton & Ascione, 1979), an audio-video training film (Olszewski & Barton, 1978), modeling, and behavior rehearsal with feedback. In addition, the teachers and aides were requested to practice the package at home with their own children. Although some minor problems emerged in getting teachers to use the package as systematically as hoped for, its application effectively produced a dramatic increment in the children's sharing behavior.

In another replication–extension of Barton and Ascione's (1979) multimethod training approach, Bryant and Budd (1982) made two slight modifications of the original package. First, the presession training package was not used with the entire class, as in Campbell-Olszewski et al. (1982). Instead, two children at a time received this training from the teacher in a separate area of the classroom. Second, the teachers not only modeled correct but also incorrect ways to share. Five of the six behaviorally handicapped children who received the training demonstrated large increases in sharing and concomitant decreases in negative interactions with their peers (e.g., physical aggression).

Four other studies have been reported in this literature (Haring, 1981; Peck et al., 1978; Sato, Zunio, & Claerhout, 1978; Warren, Baer, & Rogers-Warren, 1979), which were very similar to those previously described. In the spirit of conserving space and reducing redundancy, they are not reviewed here. However, it should be noted, that for a critique of the latter three studies, the reader should refer to Barton (1982).

In an interesting, innovative extension of the previous type of training package, Fowler and Baer (1981) incorporated correspondence training. During two brief (1- to 5-minute) training sessions in a quasi-naturalistic classroom four children were taught daily to emit peer-directed offers to share play materials and/or to play cooperatively; one additional children was taught to give praise. During the first training session, the child and experimenter briefly rehearsed the target behavior. In addition, the experimenter informed the child of a criterion number of times that she or he was to perform this behavior in the classroom during a 20-minute free-play period. Subsequently, in the second training session the children were given the opportunity to report whether or not they met the criterion. For reaching the criterion, they received stickers or points that were exchangeable for toys.

Fowler and Baer's (1981) package produced an increase in offers and praise in the training setting, but these gains did not generalize to the regular classroom. One would have expected that the incorporation of correspondence training into their package would have promoted more generalization of prosocial behavior than the packages previously described. Conceivably, this lack of generalization may have occurred because some important behavioral techniques were not included in their package (e.g., presession instruction, peer modeling, and model praise; in-session prompts and praise).

Another multimethod training package that differs radically from those previously reviewed was developed by LaGreca and Santogrossi (1980) to remediate the social deficiencies of 10 learning-disabled children. Their package was prescribed to treat eight behaviors, of which the following five were prosocial: sharing–cooperating, greeting others, extending invitations, smiling–laughing, and compliments. The students met as a group weekly after school for four 90-minute sessions. During each group session, two skills were trained. For each skill area, the children viewed a 4-minute videotape film of peer models. Subsequently, they discussed what the models were doing and how they might use the videotaped behavior with peers in their daily activities. The children then rehearsed the model's behavior with their peers and received coaching suggestions from the group leader. Before leaving the session, the children were given a homework assignment to practice the newly acquired behavior with peers during the week. At the start of the next session, this homework was discussed.

LaGreca and Santogrossi's (1980) package increased the children's skills during behavior rehearsal, produced a greater verbal knowledge of how to interact with peers, and resulted in more social interaction at school (e.g., during recess, physical education, and club meetings). Much to the investigators' chagrin, however, classroom prosocial behavior did not increase. Why LaGreca and Santogrossi's (1980) package failed to promote prosocial behavior is unknown. Three possible explanations can be offered. First, the weekly training sessions may have been too infrequent. Second, perhaps prosocial training needs to be conducted initially in target settings (e.g., Barton & Ascione, 1979). Third, symbolic modeling may not be potent enough to facilitate prosocial behavior.

Vliestra, Schannahan, and Tylka (1982) reported that they found live modeling was more effective in promoting sharing than symbolic modeling. Given the potential cost saving of LaGreca and Santogrossi's (1980) training approach, as well as its pragmatic value, it is hoped that additional research will be conducted to work out the bugs. Such efforts are strongly advocated because LaGreca and Santogrossi's (1980) multimethod package for promoting prosocial behavior has the potential to be applicable to both mental health and penal settings, unlike most of the other packages, which are suitable mainly for school and home settings.

An attempt at facilitating prosocial behavior, via a multimethod training package, involved peers as the change agents (Lacioni, 1982). Peer tutors instructed isolate children to watch the tutor model one of four behaviors, including cooperation and positive verbalizations (i.e., "That's good" and "Thank you"). A peer experimenter immediately reinforced the peer tutor. If the targeted isolate child imitated the model's behavior within a specified interval (5 to 15 seconds) she or he was reinforced by the peer experimenter. A variety of reinforcers were used, including social attention, edibles, children's books, and tokens.

In a series of three experiments, Lacioni (1982) demonstrated that fourth- and fifth-grade peers were able to apply his training package successfully with nine withdrawn mentally retarded children (8.5 to 12.3 years old). More importantly, the results generalized from the training room to probe play areas and maintained during a follow-up phase that was conducted immediately after termination of the intervention. Although naturalistic replications of Lacioni's (1982) findings are needed, his investigation underscores the potential therapeutic and cost-saving value of the use of peers in promoting prosocial behavior via multimethod training packages.

In summary, barring only a few exceptions, the multimethod training packages consistently have produced dramatic increases in prosocial behavior, which have generalized across time and settings. There even have been some reports of response generalization. Thus, the multimethod training approach appears to be a desirable method for facilitating prosocial behavior and is applicable to a wide range of types of children and settings.

Major Intervention Programs

The last two methods for facilitating prosocial behavior that are reviewed in this chapter are actually multimethod training packages. They were not included in the previous subsection because they are major programs that have been or will be implemented over a number of years. As such, they represent an application and integration of all the previously discussed interventions. In addition, they are programs that, if conducted in other locations throughout the United States, could help change our society into one in which peace and harmony prevail.

Goldstein and his associates modified a training package, which they had developed for psychiatric clients, to teach prosocial behavior to aggressive adolescents. In their approach (Goldstein, Sherman, Gershaw, Sprafkin, & Glick, 1978), modeling tapes are played to small groups of adolescent trainees who have common skill deficits. The traineers are then guided through behavior rehearsal and subsequently praised. The clients are then given homework assignments to perform the rehearsed behavior in their natural environment. At the start of the next session, the assignments are discussed. Goldstein et al. (1978) have reported that they and their colleagues have repeatedly trained cooperation, sharing, helping, other prosocial behaviors and relaxation, as alternatives for adolescents to cope with their aggression (they cite 12 unpublished dissertations by their graduate students; refer to their Table 1, p. 78). However, no documentation has been presented anywhere in the published literature to demonstrate that they can exert functional control over aggression and prosocial behavior through the use of their program. Nonetheless, their efforts have been exemplary and suggest that deficits in prosocial behavior may be remediated in clinical and penal settings.

Probably the most exciting development in this field, is Solomon, Watson, Battistich, Solomon, and Schaps's (1981) initiation of a 5-year early-intervention program to promote prosocial behavior. Their project involves approximately 700 children in three elementary schools in the San Francisco Bay area. In the fall of 1982, teachers of 3-year-old preschool children used Solomon et al.'s (1981) program in their classrooms. During the subsequent autumn, the program was instituted by teachers in kindergarten classes. The effects of early prosocial intervention will be followed through the second grade for the preschoolers and through fourth grade for the kindergarten children. This multimethod training package in its preliminary form includes (1) instructions, modeling, behavior rehearsal, and social approval for prosocial behavior, (2) extinction of antisocial behavior, and (3) a few nonbehavioral techniques. Although it is not known whether the program will be effective, it serves as an excellent model for the types of investigations that are needed. It would be extremely beneficial if Solomon et al. (1981) could obtain addition funding to extend their study another 5 or even 10 years! At present, there is no information available to determine what effect early prosocial intervention has on a child's later development (e.g., during adolescence).

Summary

As can be concluded from this section, most of the previously described techniques are potent enough to facilitate prosocial behavior. The sole use of instructions and/or modeling, however, does not appear to be effective. Likewise, the efficacy of using only strategic placement or correspondence training is questionable until further evaluations are conducted. By itself, behavior rehearsal appears to be functional in promoting prosocial behavior: Whether or not these increments are durable has not been tested. On the other hand, the sole use of prompting and/or positive reinforcement has been shown to produce increases in prosocial behavior that do not maintain in the absence of intervention. Using only positive practice facilitates dramatic increases in prosocial behavior that maintain after treatment termination; however, because this technique is somewhat aversive, more-benign approaches should be instituted first. Preliminary findings for picture cuing suggests its use for language-handicapped children, but no information is available as to whether the results generalize across time and/or settings. Dramatic increases in prosocial behavior that are durable and generalizable across settings, individuals, and occasionally responses have only been reported with the use of multimethod training packages. In addition, there have been numerous replications throughout the country of the efficacy of these packages with a wide variety of types of children. Thus, at this time, multimethod training packages appear to be the optimal treatment approach for facilitating prosocial behavior. Which package to select for use is dependent on the setting in which it will be introduced. Whereas a package like Barton and Ascione's (1979) would be an excellent choice for a school setting, one like Goldstein et al.'s (1978) would be a better choice for a clinical setting.

PRAGMATIC ASPECTS OF TRAINING

It has been my experience since the mid-1970s, while working within both clinical and academic environments, that it is not enough to have just a general working knowledge of the behavioral techniques that may foster prosocial behavior. For the novice, the first attempt at encouraging children to be prosocial is usually tedious, frustrating, and full of surprises. Optimally, the novice should receive extended concentrated training and on-site supervision, as suggested by Fleischman (1982). However, because such extensive training and supervision are currently unavailable to most individuals, practical issues related to implementation of prosocial intervention strategies and programming for generalization are discussed in this section. It is hoped that information contained in this section will make it both easier and more rewarding to facilitate prosocial behavior.

Activities and Materials

The materials that are chosen for training influence the frequency of prosocial behavior. As noted elsewhere (Barton, 1982), most prosocial studies have been conducted at school during either free-play or art periods. Perschoolers, however, emit differential rates of prosocial behavior during these two activities. Barton and Hart (1980) found, after observing 300 children in 18 preschools across a 4-month interval for approximately 8000 minutes, that both sharing and cooperation occur much more frequently during free play than art. Their findings suggest that it is probably much easier to teach prosocial behavior (especially sharing and cooperation) with toys rather than art materials.

Once the general type of material is selected, the next two questions to be resolved are (1) "what quantity of materials should be available", and (2) "should single piece (e.g., a wooden truck) or multiple-piece materials (e.g., Lincoln Logs) be provided?" Although intuitively one would predict that the number and type of materials available should affect prosocial behavior, the number of materials does not (Partington, 1980). On the other hand, it has been reported that preschool children share more multiple-piece than single-piece items (Deinzer, Feudo, & Shook, 1982; Partington, 1980) These results suggest that when encouraging prosocial behavior, the number of materials are not critical but multiple- versus single-piece materials are.

Numerous other variables related to materials and activities may affect the frequency of children's interactions. For example, it has been noted (Barton, 1982) that teacher structure of an activity (none vs. limited vs. high structure), material sociability (isolate vs. social vs. isolate–social), material novelty (familiar vs. novel), and material access (all day vs. in-session only, and every vs. some sessions) may affect children's operant level of prosocial behavior. Thus, considerable time and effort should be expended in selecting activities and materials, because as shown by

Twardosz et al. (1983), certain types of activities (e.g., group affectionate play) and materials (e.g., toys) may lend themselves more readily to promoting prosocial behavior than others.

Number of Children

How many children can or should be trained at once to be prosocial? Campbell-Olszewski et al. (1982) have provided empirical evidence that teachers in three classrooms were able to implement successfully Barton and Ascione's (1979) package with their entire classes (each $n = 20$). Nonetheless, even though the teachers received intensive training and continual encouragement throughout the implementation phase, problems did arise. Bryant and Budd (1982) took the opposite approach. They had the teachers implement Barton and Ascione's (1979) package sequentially with pairs of children in a separate part of the classroom until all the children were trained. As a consequence, their approach was easier to implement than Campbell-Olszewski et al. (1982). Barton and Bevirt (1981), based upon their empirical findings that the effect of training prosocial behavior generalizes across small groups of preschool children ($n = 4$), have suggested yet another approach. They proposed that "it may be possible to train a small sub-group, wait for a generalization to the larger group, and then give the non-trained children only a very brief training experience" (p. 520). However, if maximal treatment effectiveness is desired, it is this author's belief that probably all or most of the children should be trained as a group to exhibit prosocial responses.

Presence of Adult

How does the presence of adults affect children's prosocial behavior? Barton et al. (1979) experimentally manipulated, with three groups of preschool children ($n = 5$), the presence of adult observers and supervisors before, during, and after treatment in both intervention and generalization settings. Observers' presence suppressed sharing and smiling prior to, during, and after treatment. Thus, their results indicate that to maximize the potential effectiveness of treatment, observers should not be present. Barton et al. (1979) also found that the increases in sharing only maintained when an adult supervisor was physically present in the room. Therefore, to ensure the likelihood of posttreatment maintenance, it appears that one adult should be present to supervise children who have been trained previously to engage in prosocial behavior. "To kill two birds with one stone," the supervisor can also be trained to function as an observer (Hay, Nelson, & Hay, 1977), to decrease the problem of observer reactivity.

Change Agent Behavior

In most of the investigations reviewed for this chapter, the change agent, who has typically been a classroom teacher, has not been monitored to make sure she or he has carried out the treatment as prescribed. When not implementing a program, teachers typically prompt and reinforce prosocial behavior at an alarmingly low rate (Barton, 1980; Eisenberg et al., 1982). Thus, for teachers who are extremely busy, who have many children to supervise, and who have numerous teaching goals, it is critical to monitor their behavior because it is quite possible that they may fail to carry out the training as frequently and consistently as desired. Likewise, for parents who are often exhausted from a long day's work and for others who are less experienced at teaching children, this suggestion is equally crucial. Methods for monitoring the behavior of change agents are discussed elsewhere (Barton & Ascione, 1983).

In the absence of information concerning the monitoring of trainer behavior, one is left in a quandary. Were the independent variables consistently and adequately manipulated? If the independent variables were not manipulated as prescribed, the treatment may produce (1) even greater facilitation of prosocial behavior than obtained, (2) negative side effects that did not emerge when the treatment was applied less frequently, or (3) an absence of any effect. In addition, without monitoring the trainer's behavior, it is impossible to do a cost–benefit analysis of the potential efficacy of an intervention, because the amount of trainer time and effort required to conduct a treatment program is unknown. Besides making thorough evaluation of treatment programs impossible the failure to monitor the behavior of trainers also leaves potential change agents bewildered as to how much time and effort will be required of them to carry out the training. It is hoped in the future that investigators of prosocial behavior will provide this essential information on the change agent's behavior.

In addition to monitoring the change agent's behavior, she or he must also be given feedback and praise. For example, Parsonson, Baer, and Baer (1974) evaluated the effectiveness of two aides in reinforcing differentially cooperation and other desirable childhood behaviors. They found that the aides' effectiveness was enhanced through feedback and praise. Accordingly, it appears more likely that a prosocial intervention will be effective if the trainer's behavior is monitored and if she or he is provided with feedback and praise.

Verbal versus Physical Prosocial Behavior

Should children be taught to initiate prosocial behavior (e.g., offers to share), to engage in the actual prosocial behavior (e.g., physical sharing of a toy), or both? In an experiment designed to study this question, Barton and Ascione (1979) discovered that gains produced by training physical sharing were limited to physical sharing and were not durable. On the other hand, increases facilitated by training in verbal sharing were durable and generalized to physical sharing and to another setting. Training both response modes was slightly superior to training only verbal sharing. Bryant and Budd (1982) extended these findings when they detected that by facilitating offers to engage in prosocial behavior, negative peer interaction (e.g., aggression) decreased. Therefore, ostensibly when teaching prosocial behavior, at a minimum, children should be taught to initiate sharing verbally.

Prosocial Deficits

Because every child is unique, no training method for promoting prosocial behavior will work with all children. The intervention strategies discussed in this chapter should be viewed as a starting point. Each training method should be modified to meet individual needs. As succinctly highlighted by Bornstein, Bellack, and Hersen (1980, p. 185), "there can be no substitute for careful assessment and individualized treatment planning."

Just because a child has a prosocial deficit does not mean that the child has to be trained in all aspects of the response class. For example, careful evaluation of the nonsharing child may reveal that she or he engages in physical sharing satisfactorily but is incompetent at initiating sharing. As a consequence, training this child should be modified to be directed only at share offers—not at physical sharing. Thus, as a pragmatic and ethical tactic, children should receive prosocial training only in their deficit areas and use should be made of their strengths.

During the past couple of years, investigations have begun to appear in which both (1) the target behaviors have been selected, and (2) the training methods have been modified to meet the individual needs of children. For investigations that are exemplary in this respect, the reader should refer to Bryant and Budd (1982), and Curl (1981), and Fowler and Baer (1981).

Prompting Prosocial Behavior

As discussed earlier, prompting has been used frequently to facilitate prosocial behavior. In addition, it has been shown to enhance the effects of programs that include instructions, modeling, and behavior rehearsal (Barton, 1981). It is this author's subjective contention that the nature of the prompt is very important to the success of a treatment program. The change agent has to be very careful to prompt the correct aspect of the prosocial behavior (i.e., the child's deficit area) that he or she wants to encourage. For example, Barton and Osborne (1978) required their teacher to identify whether a nonsharing child was deficient in his or her ability to engage in share-offers or acceptance of share-offers, before the child was prompted to practice one of these two behaviors.

It is important to determine not only what aspect of the prosocial behavior to prompt, but also who should be prompted. For example, is it better to prompt an isolate child to engage in cooperative play with a peer, or to prompt the peer to engage in cooperative play with the isolate child? Haring (1981) recently studied this question with isolate preschool children. She found that prompting the isolate child to initiate cooperation with peers was more effective than prompting peers. In addition, she discovered that the gains produced by prompting the isolate child endured during a 5-month follow-up phase. Thus, there appear to be a number of parameters that affect the robustness of prompting prosocial behavior.

Delivery of Procedural Reinforcement

Procedural reinforcement has been used in most attempts at encouraging prosocial behavior. Even if the prosocial behavior is occurring fairly frequently, the addition of procedural reinforcement has been found to enhance the rate of this behavior (Barton, 1981).

When considering the use of social approval, it is important to remember that it is not a functional reinforcer for all children. With some handicapped children (e.g., some autistic and electively mute children) social attention functions as a punisher (Barton & Freeborn, 1979). To make praise and hugs, which have been ineffective or punishing, effective reinforcers, they need to be paired with known functional reinforcers. For example, Lacioni (1982) found that peer praise was ineffective in facilitating the prosocial behavior of his nine isolate mentally retarded children, whereas edibles were functional reinforcers. By pairing praise with the edibles, praise acquired reinforcing properties and the edibles were gradually withdrawn.

In using praise, it is important to include a description of what aspect of the children's behavior is being reinforced (Serbin et al., 1977). In the absence of descriptive feedback, young children as well as older individuals, often experience difficulties differentiating what it is they did to earn the praise. As a consequence, praise tends to lose its reinforcing properties.

Given the busy schedules of parents and teachers, change agents often ask, "Do prosocial behaviors have to be reinforced immediately and after every occurrence?" Fowler and Baer (1981) found that once children were taught to emit offers to share and/or cooperate via immediate reinforcement, the delivery of reinforcement could be delayed up to 2.5 hours without any negative side effects. More importantly, the use of delayed reinforcement facilitated generalization of treatment gains across settings. Likewise, consistent with the laboratory findings, Hopkins (1968) discovered that once a consistent rate of smiling was established via a continuous schedule of reinforcement, delivering reinforcers progressively more intermittently to an 8-year-old boy, produced an increase in his rate of smiling. In addition, his elevated rates of smiling were maintained once treatment was discontinued. Thus, it appears that initially children should be reinforced consistently and immediately for emitting prosocial behavior. Once the behavior is occurring at a consistent rate, it can be made more resistant to extinction by delaying reinforcement and/or by using a progressively more intermittent schedule of reinforcement.

UNTESTED INNOVATIONS

Although many innovative approaches to facilitating prosocial behavior in the natural environment have been developed and evaluated, many other possibilities exist. In this section, a few possibilities that have never or only minimally been tested, are suggested. These suggestions have arisen out of (1) laboratory investigations of prosocial behavior, (2) studies of neutral or negative social behavior, (3) recent technological advances, and (4) discussion with colleagues. Remember that these suggestions barely scrape the surface of the myriad possibilities that await scientific scrutiny. In addition, note that some individuals already may be using these suggestions, but to my knowledge, no reports exist in the literature.

Correspondence Training as a Maintenance Strategy

Although the efficacy of the sole use of correspondence training to facilitate prosocial behavior is equivocal, it would appear prima facie that this technique would be an effective maintenance strategy for multi-method training approaches. Fowler and Baer (1981) incorporated correspondence training into their multimethod approach, but they did not test for response maintenance. Moreover, they found that their treatment gains did not generalize across settings. As noted earlier, they did not include some behavioral techniques (e.g., presession instructions, peer modeling, and model praise; insession prompts and praise) that are typically incorporated into multimethod training packages for promoting prosocial behavior.

What is being proposed here is that prosocial behavior be taught first directly via a multimethod training package (e.g., Barton & Ascione, 1979). This is consistent with Barton et al.'s (1978) conclusion that prosocial behavior should be taught directly rather than indirectly (e.g., correspondence training). Once the behavior is well established, correspondence training then could be added. One hopes that the direct training approach could be gradually faded out with only correspondence training eventually being used. This sequence of direct training followed by correspondence training is suggested because: (1) multimethod training packages have consistently produced durable gains in prosocial behavior that frequently generalize across settings, (2) correspondence training is in essence a form of delayed and intermittent reinforcement, and should promote maintenance of a well-established response, and (3) correspondence training is much easier to implement and is more efficient than a training package.

Use of Peers

As discussed by Strain in an earlier chapter in this book, peers have used to treat social isolation. He reviewed a number of practical reasons for use of peers as change agents and discussed a series of studies by his colleagues and himself in which school children were taught to initiate, instruct, model, and/or reinforce social interaction by their isolate peers. Use of peers as change agents has been limited mainly to interactions of social isolates. Although, as aforementioned, there have been a few reports (e.g., Lacioni, 1982; Wahler, 1967) of the use of peers to instruct, model, and/or reinforce prosocial behavior, little is known about the limitations of their use with respect to types of settings, prosocial responses, and target children. Furthermore, whether the use of peers is superior (i.e., in terms of adult time and treatment potency) to the use of adults as change agents, awaits empirical verification. Thus, much research is needed on the efficacy of peers as change agents of prosocial behavior.

In the future, peers also might be taught to engage in behaviors that function as supplementary discriminative stimuli (i.e., prompts) for the target child to initiate prosocial behavior. For example, Camras (1980) has demonstrated that kindergarten children respond differentially to specific facial expressions. It may be the case that certain facial expressions, body postures, and/or voice qualities are associated with various situations in which prosocial behaviors are desirable and/or omitted. Once these prompts are identified, peers could be trained to use these behaviors (e.g., a facial expression) as a cue for the target child to emit the target prosocial behavior.

Peers also could be taught to provide feedback on how frequently target children emit prosocial behavior. Ragland, Kerr, and Strain (1981) produced an increase in social interaction among three 10-year-old isolate boys by using this approach. Each boy was given the goal, "play more with more friends during recess." Classmates provided feedback as to whether they met the goal. A similar approach could be used to promote prosocial behavior. This strategy would result in considerable savings for adults who, in most training approaches, must spend a considerable amount of time monitoring the children's prosocial behavior. In addition, this approach potentially could be used with correspondence training to facilitate maintenance of treatment gains. When used in this manner, peer feedback would help assure veracity of the children's reports of prosocial behavior.

Materials

The list of materials that potentially could promote prosocial behavior is probably longer than this chapter! Therefore, this subsection should be considered just a sample. Only three materials are discussed; however, I am convinced that each will play a role in the development of prosocial behavior in the future.

One apparatus that is frequently used in social skills training is audio–video equipment. In many clinical settings and even in some educational settings, audio-visual equipment is available. Although audio-visual tapes (films, slides, etc.) have been used to incorporate symbolic modeling into some prosocial training programs (e.g., LaGreca & Santogrossi, 1980), a more efficacious use of them is proposed here. Children's performance during their behavior rehearsals of prosocial behavior could be recorded via the audio–video equipment. Then the children could view and/or critique whether they successfully practiced the prosocial behavior and whether they erred. Use of audio-visual equipment in this manner, could enhance the efficacy of behavioral rehearsal.

Another type of material that could be useful in prompting prosocial behavior is children's books (especially comic books!). Alvord (1978) has written a children's book entitled *Learning to Share* that consists of 12 scenes illustrating sharing with subsequent positive consequences and nonsharing with subsequent negative consequences. She tested the use of her book using preschool and kindergarten children. Although her results are confounded by methodological problems, they suggest that prosocial books as part of a training package, may be effective in facilitating prosocial behavior.

One final type of material that is sometimes used in play therapy is puppets. Franzini, Litrownik, and McGuire (1978) used puppets to model prosocial behavior in short 9-minute taped vignettes. However, in a laboratory test of their symbolic modeling, no increases in candy donations occurred. What is being proposed here is the use of puppets during therapy á la recommendations by Kelly (1981) for social skills training. In order that a child may practice the deficient prosocial behavior in therapy and yet closely approximate his/her real-world troublesome situations, the therapist manipulates a number of puppets that represent peers (and are so named) who are present in the situation being simulated. In addition, the child manipulates a puppet that represents himself or herself. "Through the puppet, the child rehearses the verbal and nonverbal skills she or he should now use in that situation, and the therapist's puppet responds as actual peers might" (Kelly, 1981, pp. 62–63). Although no one has evaluated the potential efficacy of behavior rehearsal via puppets for facilitating prosocial behavior in the natural environment, it undoubtedly would hold a young child's attention. In fact, most of the components of the prosocial multimethod training packages (e.g., Barton & Ascione, 1979) could be conducted with young children via puppets.

FINAL CONSIDERATIONS

Extent of Training

One question that is frequently asked is "How much should prosocial behavior be increased?" Implicit in this question is the assumption that you can not only provide too little, but also too much training. There is no simple answer to this important question because it raises pragmatic, philosophical, as well as ethical issues.

One method for answering this momentous question is to "manipulate the behavior of interest over its entire range and determine at which values the behavior is maximally useful or effective" (Van Houten, 1979, p. 586). Warren, Rogers-Warren, and Baer (1976) used this tactic to answer the question with respect to offers to share. At the end of each 5-minute segment of a 10-minute art activity, every child who made a share-offer was given praise plus a piece of cereal or an M-&-M. This procedure produced an immediate increase in share-offers but as share-offer rates increased, the percentage of acceptance of share-offers decreased. Warren et al. (1976) interpreted their results as supporting the belief that you can train a child to offer to share too frequently. Barton (1982) has raised a number of methodological questions about this study, but the most pertinent one is that acceptance of share-offers was not trained. This potential confound is particularly important given Barton and Ascione's (1979) findings that when they trained both share-offers and acceptance of share-offers, refusals to share did not increase. Pursuing Barton's (1982) reservation about the Warren et al. (1976) conclusion, Bryant and Budd (1982) found, with concomitant training in acceptance of share-offers, that as the rate of share-offers increased, so did the absolute frequency of the children's acceptance of share-offers. "Thus, the increased rates of offers and requests to share [which were extremely elevated] did not adversely affect the children's likelihood of accepting sharing initiatives" (Bryant & Budd, 1982, p. 5).

It is my position that you cannot provide too much training in prosocial behavior, although you can certainly provide too little! This statement should be tempered by the following two points. First, it must be remembered that in certain situations it may be nonadvantageous to be prosocial. In fact, in certain situations prosocial behavior is inappropriate. For example, if my nephew, who is a preschooler, gave away my antique mantle clock, I definitely would not reinforce his sharing! Thus, researchers in the future need to (1) identify those situations in which prosocial behavior is appropriate and those in which it is inappropriate, and then (2) train children to make this discrimination. Once this occurs, the question of whether we can overtrain prosocial behavior will be a nonissue. The second point to consider is that both normative information (e.g., Barton & Hart, 1980; Eisenberg et al., 1982; Melahn & O'Donnell, 1978; Tremblay, Strain, Hendrickson, & Shores, 1981) and peer comparison data should be used to identify children who are in need of training and/or should continue to receive training.

Prosocial Behaviors Taught

Two more questions frequently asked are "Which prosocial behaviors should be taught, and how should they be defined?" The importance of these questions can be found in an unusual article by Nordyke, Baer, Etzel, and LeBlanc (1977), in which they questioned whether a behavior in another article, which was published by different researchers, should have ever been treated. Thus, this is a vital question that raises ethical concerns. Because society defines desirable and undesirable behavior, there never will be a ubiquitous answer to which prosocial behaviors should be taught. However, once the behavior has been selected, it concurrently should be defined operationally and socially validated. For detailed information on how to assure that the definitions are both operational and socially valid, refer to Barton and Ascione (1983).

Twardosz, Schwartz, Fox, and Cunningham (1979) have provided an excellent example of how a prosocial behavior, in this case affection, can be operationally defined and socially validated. First, operational definitions were prepared based on informal observation and past research. Second, 8 trained observers and 85 community volunteers used the definitions to score video tapes of child–caregiver interactions in daycare settings. Third, statistical techniques were used to determine the reliability and validity of the measurement system. A similar approach could be used with any prosocial behavior.

Assessment

Being in the part of this book concerned with modification, this chapter barely addressed the area of assessment of prosocial behavior. However, it should be remembered that outstanding training of prosocial behavior is meaningless in the absence of satisfactory assessment. Assessment should be used as the basis for determining (1) if treatment is warranted for a particular prosocial behavior of a particular child and (2) if the treatment produced a change in the child's prosocial behavior. Low assessment scores are generally considered to reflect deficient prosocial skills. However, a low score does not necessarily imply that the prosocial behavior is not in the child's repertoire. Thus, "assessment procedures need to be defined in such a way that they distinguish among persons who can perform the response, but for whatever reason do not, and those who cannot perform the response under a variety of conditions when inducements are offered. Presumably, the treatment needed for persons who can and cannot perform the desired types of behavior would be considerably different" (Kazdin, Matson, Esveldt-Dawson, 1981, p. 151). Thus, because assessment is so critical before, during, and after treatment, the reader is encouraged to examine closely the chapters in this book by Walker, LaGreca, and Oden, as well as the chapter elsewhere by Barton and Ascione (1983), before attempting to evaluate a program for promoting prosocial behavior.

Although the assessment procedures that have been used in the naturalistic prosocial literature, in general, have been excellent, researchers have been negligent in evaluating generalization. Most assessments of generalization have been over time, through the use of single subject ABA designs. Rarely have long-term follow-up phases been conducted. Even less frequently have treatment effects been assessed across settings, individuals, and/or responses. The paucity of generalization assessment has created a serious lacuna in the naturalistic prosocial literature. I feel strongly, as I have argued elsewhere (Barton, 1982; Barton & Ascione, 1983), that a treatment approach should be considered *clinically effective only if the gains are generalizable.*

Another sparsely addressed assessment area in the prosocial literature, is sociometric evaluation (refer to Oden, present volume). The few sociometric evaluations conducted to date, have been conflicting (e.g., LaGreca & Santogrossi, 1980; Oden & Asher, 1977). From what I can surmise from colleagues who have attempted pilot sociometric evaluations, they quit in frustration and hope that old sociometric techniques can be upgraded and adapted for prosocial behavior. Thus, much research is needed in this area.

Still, yet another assessment area where the research literature is lacking is social validation of programs for facilitating prosocial behavior. In part, this is an outgrowth of the previous two assessment deficits. Social validation of prosocial programs has been limited to the repeated findings that by enhancing prosocial behavior, social isolation (e.g., Norquist, 1973) and aggression decrease (e.g., Curl, 1981), and positive reciprocal social interactions increase (Hendrickson, Strain, Shores, & Tremblay, 1982).

In addition to researchers being lax in certain areas of prosocial assessment, so have educators. From the moment a child enters school until she or he leaves school (which typically takes one to two decades!), his/her intellectual growth is monitored via sundry tests. At regular intervals not only does she or he receive feedback on his or her intellectual development, but so do his or her parents (for obvious reasons). When a child is not performing up to academic "potential," she or he is often counseled and in some cases so are his or her parents. Do teachers in our educational system similarly work as arduously at monitoring prosocial behavior? Of course, the answer obviously is no. Systematic monitoring, feedback, and counseling of prosocial behavior that parallel intellectual behavior is nonexistent in our educational system. Given the fact that the majority of childhood and adolescence is spent in school, and given the surge of dual-career and single-parent families in which parents have little time to instruct prosocial behavior, it is not surprising to me that our society is plagued with antisocial behavior. It is clear that our schools must be held accountable for assessing our children's prosocial development. Teacher use of the prosocial training approaches described in this chapter would be prodigal without concomitant assessment. Such a tactic would be similar to teaching mathematics without monitoring a child's solutions to assigned problems! Thus, it is recommended that teachers systematically use some sort of student prosocial behavior record. For example Filipczak, Archer, and Friedman (1980) have developed a Student Activity Record (SAR) form which students carry to each of their classes, on which teachers indicate how well the student behaved socially. SAR is but one of many assessment systems that could be implemented with minimal cost.

Application to Adults

Ideally, the effects of training children to be prosocial would endure throughout their adulthood years. Obviously, whether this will occur is an empirical question. In addition, the techniques used to train children to be prosocial may be modified to be used with adults.

There have been a few naturalistic reports of systematic attempts at encouraging adults to be prosocial. Rushton and Campbell (1977) found that female trainee occupational therapists, who viewed a female volunteer donate blood, were more likely to agree and actually give their blood than those who did not view the model. In another intriguing study, Goldstein, Minkin, and Baer (1978) analyzed why people rarely place Found ads in the Lost and Found classified section of newspapers. They hypothesized that this prosocial behavior typically is punished in that finders have to pay for Found advertisements. Therefore, Goldstein et al. (1978) managed to entice three Kansas newspapers to offer free Found advertisements. As a result, not only were more Found ads placed, but more personal property was returned. In yet another interesting application of this literature to adults, Tidd and Lockard (1978) trained a 22-year-old cocktail waitress, who was working in a bar, to give her customers an affiliative smile. It was discovered that her broad smile resulted in more tips and more reciprocal smiles from customers than when she gave minimal smiles. These three investigations typify the multitudinous possibilities that exist for developing the prosocial behavior of adults.

Conclusion

The literature on the behavioral facilitation of prosocial behavior among young children in naturalistic settings is evolving rapidly. Although there remain many gaps in this literature and although the need for additional research is great, many answers have been provided since the mid-1960s on how to teach children to be prosocial. The social utility of this literature, however, probably will not be known for at least another 20 years. The bottom line will be what impact these prosocial programs (e.g., Solomon et al., 1981) have on society's problems (e.g., juvenile delinquency, theft rings, and gang violence). I hope that this literature will eventually add credence to Skinner's (1948) belief and dream that the use of behavioral technology can lead to a society in which cooperation and peace prevail.

REFERENCES

Alvord, M. K. (1978). The effects of non-motion symbolic modeling on the sharing behaviors of young children (Doctoral dissertation, University of Maryland, 1977). *Dissertation Abstracts International, 39*, 764–765A.

Barrett, D. E. (1979). Relations between aggressive and prosocial behaviors in children. *The Journal of Genetic Psychology, 134*, 317–318.

Barton, E. J. (1980, May). *An evaluation of how frequently teachers encourage preschool children to share classroom materials.* Paper presented at the 52nd annual meeting of the Midwestern Psychological Association, St. Louis.

Barton, E. J. (1981). Developing sharing: An analysis of modeling and other behavioral techniques. *Behavior Modification, 5*, 386–398.

Barton, E. J. (1982). Classroom sharing: A critical analysis of current assessment, facilitation, and generalization procedures. In M. Hersen, R. E. Eisler, & P. M. Miller (Eds.). *Progress in behavior modification* (Vol. 13). New York: Academic Press.

Barton, E. J., & Ascione, F. (1979). Sharing in preschool children: Facilitation, stimulus generalization, response generalization, and maintenance. *Journal of Applied Behavior Analysis, 12*, 417–430.

Barton, E. J., & Ascione, F. R. (1983). Direct observation. In T. H. Ollendick & M. Hersen (Eds.), *Child behavioral assessment: Principles and procedures.* New York: Pergamon.

Barton, E. J., & Bevirt, J. (1981). Generalization of sharing across groups: Assessment of group composition with preschool children. *Behavior Modification, 5*, 503–522.

Barton, E. J., & Freeborn, G. (1979, June). *Modification of elective mutism through the use of positive reinforcement within a peer group setting.* Paper presented at the 5th Annual Convention of the Association of Behavior Analysis, Dearborn, MI.

Barton, E. J., & Hart, R. J. (1980, May). *Big bird tells the new story about Dick and Jane's prosocial behavior in the preschool classroom.* Invited address given at the 6th Annual Convention of the Association for Behavioral Analysis, Dearborn, MI.

Barton, E. J., Madsen, J. J., & Olszewski, M. J. (1978, November). *Correspondence between reports of sharing and actual sharing: A further analysis.* Paper presented at the 12th Annual Convention of the Association for Advancement of Behavior Therapy, Chicago.

Barton, E. J., Olszewski, M. J., & Madsen, J. J. (1979). The effect of adult presence on prosocial behavior among preschool children. *Child Behavior Therapy, 1*, 271–286.

Barton, E. J., & Osborne, J. G. (1978). The development of classroom sharing by a teacher using positive practice. *Behavior Modification, 2.* 231–250.

Belsky, J., & Steinberg, L. D. (1978). The effects of day care: A critical review. *Child Development, 49*, 929–949.

Benson, N. C., Shigetomi, C., Skeen, J., Gelfand, D., & Hartmann, D. P. (1981, April). *Children's knowledge of prosocial behavior: "You won't go to heaven if you don't share."* Paper presented at the meeting of the Western Psychological Association, Los Angeles.

Bornstein, M., Bellack, A. S., & Hersen, M. (1980). Social skills training for highly aggressive children: Treatment in an inpatient psychiatric setting. *Behavior Modification, 4*, 173–186.

Bronfenbrenner, U. (1977). Toward an experimental ecology of human development. *American Psychologist, 32*, 513–531.

Brown, P., & Elliott, R. (1965). Control of aggression in a nursery school class. *Journal of Experimental Child Psychology, 2*, 103–107.

Bryant, L. E., & Budd, K. S. (1982, May). *Teaching behaviorally handicapped preschoolers to share.* Paper presented at the 8th Annual Convention of the Association for Behavior Analysis, Milwaukee.

Buell, J., Stoddard, P., Harris, F. R., & Baer, D. M. (1968). Collateral social development accompanying reinforcement of outdoor play in a preschool child. *Journal of Applied Behavior Analysis, 1*, 167–173.

Campbell-Olszewski, M. J., Sappington, A. A., & Barton, E. J. (1982, May). *Promotion of classroom sharing by teachers.* Paper presented at the 8th Annual Convention of the Association for Behavior Analysis, Milwaukee.

Camras, L. A. (1980). Children's understanding of facial expressions used during conflict encounters. *Child Development, 51*, 879–985.

Chandler, L. (1977). *The use of positive practice to facilitate physical sharing: A replication.* Unpublished manuscript, Utah State University.

Cooke, T. P., & Apolloni, T. (1976). Developing positive social–emotional behaviors: A study of training and generalization effects. *Journal of Applied Behavior Analysis, 9*, 65–78.

Curl, R. M. (1981). *The facilitation of children's social interaction by a picture-cue training program.* Unpublished doctoral dissertation, University of Kansas.

Deinzer, R., Feudo, V., & Shook, G. L. (1982, May). *The effects of multi-piece and single-piece toys on the sharing behavior of mentally retarded preschoolers.* Paper presented at the 8th Annual Convention of the Association for Behavior Analysis, Milwaukee.

Eisenberg, N., Cameron, R., Tryon, K., & Dodez, R. (1982). Socialization of prosocial behavior in the preschool classroom. *Developmental Psychology, 18*, in press.

Emshoff, J. G., Redd, W. H., & Davidson, W. S. (1976). Generalization training and the transfer of prosocial behavior in delinquent adolescents. *Journal of Behavior Therapy and Experimental Psychiatry, 7*, 141–144.

Factor, D. C., & Frankie, G. H. (1980). Free-play behaviors in socially maladjusted and normal preschool children: A naturalistic study. *Canadian Journal of Behavioral Science, 12*, 273–277.

Filipczak, J., Archer, M., & Friedman, R. M. (1980). In-school social skills training: Use with disruptive adolescents. *Behavior Modification, 4*, 243–263.

Fleischman, M. J. (1982). Social learning interventions for aggressive children: From the laboratory to the real world. *The Behavior Therapist, 5*, 55–58.

Foster, S. L., & Ritchey, W. L. (1979). Issued in the assessment of social competence in children. *Journal of Applied Behavior Analysis, 12*, 625–638.

Fowler, S. A., & Baer, D. M. (1981). "Do I have to be good all day?" The timing of delayed reinforcement as a factor in generalization. *Journal of Applied Behavior Analysis, 14*, 13–24.

Franzini, L. R., Litrownik, A. J., & McGuire, M. J. (1978, November). *Sex and social class differences in observational learning of prosocial behaviors (helping and sharing).* Paper presented at the meeting of the Association for the Advancement of Behavior Therapy, Chicago.

Friedrich-Cofer, L. K., Huston-Stein, A., Kipnis, D. M., Susman, E. J., & Clewett, A. S. (1979). Environmental enhancement of prosocial television content: Effects on interpersonal behavior, imaginative play, and self-regulation in a natural setting. *Developmental Psychology, 15,* 637–646.

Gaillard, J., Carder-Smith, L., & Budd, K. S. (1983). *Generalization of sharing in behaviorally handicapped preschool children through peer interaction.* Manuscript submitted for publication.

Gelfand, D. M., Hartmann, D. P. (1982). Response consequences and attributions: Two contributors to prosocial behavior. In N. Eisenberg-Berg (Ed.), *The development of prosocial behavior.* New York: Academic Press.

Geller, M. I., & Scheirer, C. J. (1978). The effect of filmed modeling on cooperative play in disadvantaged preschoolers. *Journal of Abnormal Child Psychology, 6,* 71–87.

Goldstein, R. S., Minkin, B. L., Minkin, N., & Baer, D. M. (1978). Finders keepers?: An analysis of validation of a free-found-ad policy. *Journal of Applied Behavior Analysis, 11,* 465–473.

Goldstein, A. P., Sherman, M., Gershaw, N. J., Sprafkin, R. P., & Glick, B. (1978). Training aggressive adolescents in prosocial behavior. *Journal of Youth and Adolescence, 7,* 73–90.

Haring, M. J. (1981, August). *Comparison of two procedures for increasing social interactions of isolated preschoolers.* Paper presented at the meeting of the American Psychological Association, Los Angeles.

Hart, B. M., Reynolds, N. J., Baer, D. M., Brawley, E. R., & Harris, F. R. (1968). Effect of contingent and noncontingent social reinforcement on the cooperative play of a preschool child. *Journal of Applied Behavior, 1,* 73–76.

Hay, D. F. (1979). Cooperative interactions and sharing between very young children and their parents. *Developmental Psychology, 15,* 647–653.

Hay, L. R., Nelson, R. O., & Hay, W. H. (1977). The use of teachers as behavioral observers. *Journal of Applied Behavior Analysis, 10,* 345–348.

Hendrickson, J. M., Strain, P. S., Shores, R. E., & Tremblay, A. *Functional effects of peer social initiations on the interactions of behaviorally handicapped children.*

Hibbard, T., Barton, E. J., Dorcey, T. C., & Klamfoth, E. (1980, November). *Behavioral assessment of the relationship between preschool children's donating in the laboratory and classroom sharing.* Paper presented at the 14th Annual Convention for the Association of Behavior Therapy, New York.

Hopkins, B. L. (1968). Effects of candy and social reinforcement, instructions, and reinforcement schedule learning on the modification and maintenance of smiling. *Journal of Applied Behavior Analysis, 1,* 121–129.

Jason, L. A., Robson, S. D., & Lipshutz, S. A. (1980). Enhancing sharing behaviors through the use of naturalistic contingencies. *Journal of Community Psychology, 8,* 237–244.

Jason, L. A., Soucy, G., & Ferone, L. (1980). Open field investigation in enhancing children's social skills. *Group, 4,* 56–62.

Kaplan, J. (1972). A legal look at prosocial behavior: What can happen for failing to help or trying to help someone. *Journal of Social Issues, 28,* 219–226.

Kazdin, A. E., Matson, J. L., Esveldt-Dawson, K. (1981). Social skill performances among normal and psychiatric in patient children as a function of assessment conditions. *Behaviour Research & Therapy, 19,* 145–152.

Keller, M. F., & Carlson, P. M. (1974). The use of symbolic modeling to promote social skills in preschool children with low levels of social responsiveness. *Child Development, 45*, 912–919.

Kelley, L., & Johnson, J. M. (1978). *Development of prosocial behavior through mutual reinforcement of severely retarded children.* Paper presented at the Annual Convention of the Midwestern Association of Behavior Analysis, Chicago.

Kelly, J. A. (1981). Using puppets for behavior rehearsal in social skills training sessions with young children. *Child Behavior Therapy, 3*, 61–64.

Knapczyk, D. R., & Yoppi, J. O. (1975). Development of cooperative and competitive play responses in developmentally disabled children. *American Journal of Mental Deficiency, 80*, 245–255.

Lacioni, G. E. (1982). Normal children as tutors to teach social responses to withdrawn mentally retarded schoolmates: Training, maintenance, and generalization. *Journal of Applied Behavior Analysis, 15*, 17–40.

LaGreca, A. M., & Mesibov, G. B. (1979). Social skills intervention with learning disabled children: Selecting skills and implementing training. *Journal of Clinical Child Psychology, 6*, 234–241.

LaGreca, A. M., & Santogrossi, D. A. (1980). Social skills training with elementary school students: A behavioral group approach. *Journal of Consulting and Clinical Psychology, 48*, 220–227.

Levison, C. A. (1971, April). *Use of the peer group in the socialization of the isolate child.* Paper presented at the meeting of the Society for Research in Child Development, Minneapolis.

Melahn, C. L., & O'Donnell, C. R. (1978). Norm-based behavioral consulting. *Behavior Modification, 2*, 309–338.

Michaelson, L., & Wood, R. (1980). *Behavioral assessment and training of children's social skills.* New York: Academic Press.

Morris, R. J., & Dolker, M. (1974). Developing cooperative play in socially withdrawn children. *Mental Retardation, 12*, 24–27.

Nordquist, V. M., & Bradley, B. (1973). Speech acquisition in a nonverbal isolate child. *Journal of Experimental Child Psychology, 15*, 149–160.

Nordyke, N. S., Baer, D. M., Etzel, B. C., & LeBlanc, J. M. (1977). Implications of the stereotyping and modification of sex roles. *Journal of Applied Behavior Analysis, 10*, 553–557.

Oden, S., & Asher, S. R. (1977). Coaching children in social skills for friendship making. *Child Development, 48*, 495–506.

Olszewski, M. J., & Barton, E. J. (1978). *Teaching kids to share: An audio–video training film.* Marquette.

Parsonson, B. S., Baer, A. M., & Baer, D. M. (1974). The application of generalized correct social contingencies: An evaluation of a training program. *Journal of Applied Behavior Analysis, 7*, 427–437.

Partington, J. W. (1980). *The effects of play materials on the sharing behavior of normal preschoolers.* Unpublished doctoral dissertation, Florida State University.

Partington, J., & Barton, E. J. (1983). *Social validation of prosocial training.* Manuscript submitted for publication.

Peck, C. A., Apolloni, T., & Raver, S. A. (1978). Teaching retarded preschoolers to imitate the free-play of nonretarded classmates: Trained and generalized effects. *The Journal of Special Education, 12*, 195–207.

Ploutzain, R. F., Hasazi, J., Streifel, J., & Edgar, C. L. (1971). Promotion of positive social interaction in severely retarded young children. *American Journal of Mental Deficiency, 75*, 519–524.

Ragland, E. U., Kerr, M. M., & Strain, P. S. (1981). Social play of withdrawn children: A study of teacher-mediated peer feedback. *Behavior Modification, 5,* 347–359.

Redd, W. H., & BirnBrauer, J. S. (1969). Adults as discriminative stimuli for different reinforcement contingencies with retarded children. *Journal of Experimental Child Psychology, 7,* 440–447.

Reisinger, J. J. (1978). Generalization of cooperative behavior across classroom situations. *The Journal of Special Education, 12,* 209–217.

Rogers-Warren, A., & Baer, D. M. (1976). Correspondence between saying and doing: Teaching children to share and praise. *Journal of Applied Behavior Analysis, 9,* 335–354.

Rogers-Warren, A., Warren, S. F., & Baer, D. M. (1977). A component analysis: Modeling, self-reporting, and reinforcement of self-reporting in the development of sharing. *Behavior Modification, 1,* 307–321.

Rushton, J. P. (1976). Socialization and the altruistic behavior of children. *Psychological Bulletin, 83,* 898–913.

Rushton, J. P., & Campbell, A. C. (1977). Modeling, vicarious reinforcement and extroversion on blood donating in adults: Immediate and long-term effects. *European Journal of Social Psychology, 7,* 297–306.

Rutherford, E., & Mussen, P. (1968). Generosity in nursery school boys. *Child Development, 39,* 737–754.

Sato, S. D., Zunio, C., & Claerhout, S. (1979). *The effects of instructions, modeling, and reinforcement on increasing altruistic behaviors in young children.* Paper presented at the Annual Convention of the Midwestern Association of Behavior Analysis, Chicago.

Serbin, L. A., Tonick, I. J., & Sternglanz, S. H. (1977). Shaping cooperative cross-sex play. *Child Development, 48,* 924–929.

Skinner, B. F. (1948). *Walden two.* New York: MacMillan.

Slaby, R. G., & Crowley, C. G. (1977). Modification of cooperation and aggression through teacher attention of children's speech. *Journal of Experimental Child Psychology, 23,* 442–458.

Solomon, D., Watson, M., Battistich, V., Solomon, J., & Schaps, E. (1981, August). *A program to promote interpersonal consideration and cooperation in children.* Paper presented at the meeting of the American Psychological Association.

Strain, P. S., & Wiegerink, R. (1976). The effects of sociodramatic activities on social interaction among behaviorally disordered preschool children. *The Journal of Special Education, 10,* 71–75.

Tidd, K. L., & Lockard, J. S. (1978). Monetary significance of the affiliative smile: A case for reciprocal altruism. *Bulletin of the Psychonomic Society, 11,* 344–346.

Tremblay, A., Strain, P. S., Hendrickson, J. M., & Shores, R. E. (1981). Social interactions of normal preschool children. *Behavior Modification, 5,* 237–253.

Twardosz, S., Norquist, V. M., Simon, R., & Botkin, D. (1983). *The effect of group affection activities on the interaction of socially isolate and non-isolate children.* Manuscript submitted for publication.

Twardosz, S., Schwartz, S., Fox, J., & Cunningham, J. L. (1979). Development and evaluation of a system to measure affectionate behavior. *Behavioral Assessment, 1,* 177–190.

Van Houten, R. (1979). Social validation: The evolution of standards of competency for target behaviors. *Journal of Applied Behavior Analysis, 12,* 581–591.

Vlietstra, A. G., Shannahan, P., & Tylka, L. (1982). *Preschool children's cooperative play: Effects of live-behavioral, pictorial, and verbal instruction in sharing concepts.* Manuscript submitted for publication.

Wahler, R. G. (1967). Child–child interactions in free field setting: Some experimental analyses. *Journal of Experimental Child Psychology, 5,* 278–293.

Warren, S. F., Baer, D. M., & Rogers-Warren, A. (1979). Teaching children to praise: A problem in stimulus and response generalization. *Child Behavior Therapy, 1*, 123–137.

Warren, S. F., Rogers-Warren, A., & Baer, D. M. (1976). The role of offer rates in controlling sharing by young children. *Journal of Applied Behavior Analysis, 9*, 491–497.

Whitehead, B. S., Cooper, A. Y., Ruggles, T. R., Etzel, B. C., & LeBlanc, J. M. (1982, May). *The use of teacher attention with primes and a special activity to increase cooperative play in two preschool children.* Paper presented at the 8th Annual Convention of the Association for Behavior Analysis, Milwaukee.

CHAPTER 9

Social Skills Training with Children: Research and Clinical Application*

Larry Michelson
Anthony Mannarino

INTRODUCTION

Since the mid-1960s, research has demonstrated that children who manifest social deficits also suffer other significant emotional, behavioral, and academic problems. For example, in a thorough review of the research on children's peer relations, Hartup (1970) concluded that social isolation and low popularity are highly correlated with poor academic achievement and low self-esteem. Furthermore, socially unskilled children are more likely to rate themselves as having an external locus of control (Nowicki & Strickland, 1971). Conversely, children who are socially skilled have been shown to demonstrate superior academic achievement (Laughlin, 1954; Muma, 1965, 1968; Porterfield & Schlichting, 1961); to receive greater social reinforcement from their interpersonal environment (Gottman, Gonso, & Rasmussen, 1975), teachers (Noble & Nolan, 1976) and from peers (Hartup, Glazer, & Charlesworth, 1967); and they are rated as more popular than their nonskilled counterparts.

* Preparation of this manuscript was supported in part by a grant (MH39642) from the National Institute of Mental Health to the first author.

Longitudinal retrospective research also suggests that childhood social abilities have significant implications in regard to subsequent adult adjustment. A number of investigators have reported that childhood social deficits are highly correlated with adult alcoholism, antisocial behavior, and subsequent psychiatric disturbances (Lovaas, Freitas, & Whalen, 1972; Morris, 1956). In addition, socially deficient children have a higher rate of adolescent delinquency (Roff, Sells, & Golden, 1972), more bad-conduct discharges from the military (Roff, 1961), and more frequent adult mental health problems (Cowen, Pederson, Babigian, Izzo, & Trost, 1973; Kohn, 1977) than socially skilled children. Conversely, Kohlberg, LaCrosse, and Ricks (1972), in a comprehensive review of studies examining childhood predictors of adult adjustment, concluded that good peer relations during childhood was a highly sensitive predictor of adequate adult outcome.

Thus, there is an expanding body of evidence documenting that social skills during childhood has significant short- and long-term consequences. Socially skilled children feel good about themselves, perform well at school, and are more likely to be socially adjusted as adults. On the other hand, socially deficient children receive little positive reinforcement, are subject to academic and behavioral difficulties, and may be more likely to experience a variety of poor adult outcomes, including alcoholism, antisocial behavior, and serious psychiatric disturbances (cf. Michelson, 1981).

Given these findings, many clinical researchers have begun to explore the impact of training programs designed to facilitate social skills in children. The major focus of these social skills training programs has largely been a function of how social skills and social deficits are defined and what methods of intervention are employed to ameliorate these deficiencies. Prior to reviewing the major social-skills training strategies, we present contemporary conceptualizations and definitions of the term *social skills*.

DEFINITIONS OF SOCIAL SKILLS

In an attempt to provide a basic understanding of the term *social skills*, various definitions and concepts of social behavior, assertiveness, and social competency must be considered. Recognizing that all interactive interpersonal behavior can be considered social, and given the breadth and complexity of the topic area, it is not surprising that numerous definitions have been advanced. Social skills are generally regarded as a set of complex interpersonal behaviors. The term *skill* is used to indicate that it is not a global personality trait, but rather a set of learned and acquired behaviors. For example, Rinn and Markle (1979) stated that social skills can be defined

> as a repertoire of verbal and nonverbal behaviors by which [we] affect the responses of other individuals. . . . This repertoire acts as a mechanism through which [individuals] influence their environment by obtaining, removing, or avoiding desirable and undesirable outcomes in the social sphere . . . the extent to which they are successful in obtaining desirable outcomes and avoiding or escaping undesirable ones without inflicting pain on others is the extent to which they are considered "socially skilled" (p. 108).

Libet and Lewensohn (1973) offered a more general definition of *social skills* as the ability to behave in a way in which we are rewarded and to avoid behaving in ways that lead to punishment or extinction by others. Combs and Slaby (1977) define social skills as "the ability to interact with others in a given social context in specific ways that are societally acceptable or valued and at the same time personally beneficial, mutually beneficial, or beneficial primarily to others" (p. 162). Trower (1979) defined *social skills* as "the individual having goals or targets which he seeks in order to obtain rewards. Goal attainment is dependent on skilled behavior which involves a continuous cycle of monitoring and modifying performance in light of feedback. Failure in skill is defined as a breakdown or impairment in some point in the cycle . . . leading to negative outcomes" (p. 4). Still another definition put forth by Foster and Ritchey (1979) defines *social skills* as "those responses which within a given situation prove effective, or, in other words, maximize the probability of maintaining or enhancing positive effects for the interactor" (p. 626). As can be seen from the preceding discussion, defining social skills has become an assessment issue in its own right. Definitions such as those just quoted can be highly useful as integrative constructs that summarize behavior sequences.

An equally important function is also to stimulate research by indicating relevant areas on which to focus investigation. Although these conceptualizations of social skills are by no means exhaustive, they are representative of the current social-skills literature. Despite differences in terminology, certain basic or core truths appear evident in regard to defining social skills. Recognizing this, Michelson, Sugai, Wood, and Kazdin (1983) advanced an integrated definition of *social skills*. The components of this definition include the following:

1. Social skills are primarily acquired through learning (e.g., observation, modeling, rehearsal, and feedback).
2. Social skills comprise specific and discrete verbal and nonverbal behaviors.

3. Social skills entail both effective and appropriate initiations and responses.
4. Social skills maximize social reinforcement (e.g., positive responses from one's social environment).
5. Social skills are interactive by nature and entail both effective and appropriate responses (e.g., reciprocity and timing of specific behaviors).
6. Social skill performance is influenced by the characteristics of the participants and environments in which it occurs (i.e., situational specificity). That is, factors such as age, sex, and prestige status of the recipient affects one's social performance.
7. Deficits and excesses in social performance can be specified and targeted for intervention.

In addition to these definitional components of social skills, the directionality of the social deficits need to be considered. This includes both social withdrawal and social aggression.

Social Withdrawal

Researchers describe the unassertive, socially withdrawn child as isolated, shy, passive, and lethargic. *Passive behavior leads to a violation of one's own rights* by failing to express one's needs and opinions, which results in other's not attending and/or responding to feelings. Likewise, passive social responses can evoke feelings of inadequacy, incompetence, and depression. Research suggests that unassertive children carry their social skill deficiencies into their adulthood. In a longitudinal study examining the stability of childhood characteristics, Kagan and Moss (1962) found that "passive withdrawal from stressful situations, dependency on the family, lack of anger or arousal and involvement in intellectual mastery and social interaction anxiety were strongly related to analogous behavior dispositions during later school years" (p. 277). Social withdrawal in children can also represent a potentially serious threat to both present and future functioning, in that it has been associated, in varying degrees, with childhood psychopathology (Cowen et al., 1973; Kohn, 1977).

Unassertive children may permit others to violate their basic desires, feelings, and thoughts, which results in an apologetic and self-effacing manner. The nonassertive child can also find social situations highly aversive due to the concomitant anxiety experienced when engaged in interpersonal interaction. Chittenden (1942) elaborated on the importance of assertiveness and social skills in children. She stated that "the little child enters into a social group unequipped with the repertoire of responses he [or she] needs to enable him [or her] to engage in successful social interchange. His [or her] attempts to influence the behavior of others and his [or her] responses to their attempts to influence him [or her] are crude. He [or she] must learn, largely by trial and error and with more or less incidental help from experienced persons, which of these attempts and responses are likely to result in his [or her] acceptance by his [or her] associates and which will meet with their disapproval. Such a learning period, if marked with many failures and only limited successes, may result in the child's loss of interèst in initiating social contacts accompanied by increased submission to other person's attempts to influence him [or her], or it may result in a more frequent use of force in an attempt to make himself [or herself] successful. Neither of these possible results, if extreme, contributes toward the integration of the child in[to] the social group. Consequently, the sooner that he [or she] builds up a fund of useable social knowledge and develops attitudes which indicate his [or her] increasing awareness of other individuals and their needs and desires, the sooner he [or she] will be in rapport with those individuals" (p. 1).

As previously mentioned, the relationship between social confidence and peer interaction can have serious implications for the passive child. Recognizing that peer interaction is reciprocal, withdrawn children elicit fewer positive social responses from peers, resulting in an overall diminished level of social contact. This hypothesis was supported by the research of Greenwood, Walker, Tood, and Hops (1977), who demonstrated that peer interaction of 457 preschoolers was reciprocal correlation of .97, showing a clear relationship between behaving and subsequently receiving positive social interaction. Additionally, Hartup, Glazer, and Charlesworth (1967), a decade earlier, reported that popular children were more socially reinforcing to their peers than their lesspopular counterparts. Thus, withdrawn children may experience decreased popularity in comparison to their socially skilled peers and may experience numerous social side effects from behaving in a socially withdrawn manner.

Recognizing the relationship between popularity and academic achievement (Hartup, 1970), and between cognitive and emotional development and social withdrawal in later years (Waldrop & Halverson, 1975), it is important that these children be identified for subsequent intervention. In summary, social withdrawal and passivity have been negatively correlated with a variety of adaptive developmental, interpersonal, and intellectual capacities, both concurrently and prospectively. Recognizing that important and perhaps critical social milestones may be thwarted or delayed, leading to even more pervasive dysfunctions, these children appear to be at risk for experiencing higher rates of adult psychopathology. Therefore, although socially withdrawn children may not be as readily perceived by adults in their environment as being problematic, is important that their social deficits be remediated.

Social Aggression

At the other end of the social deficit spectrum are children with behavioral excesses. These children are typically labeled as aggressive, uncooperative, and acting out. Generally, they fail to demonstrate the requisite social skills necessary to perform effectively and appropriately in social interactions. Socially aggressive children also tend to behave in a manner that is unpleasant to others in the child's social environment. Various researchers such as Quay (1972) and Patterson, Reid, Jones, and Congor (1975) have identified many of the commonalities within this socially deficient subtype. These include verbal and physical assaultiveness, teasing, provoking, quarreling, and fighting as a means of resolving conflicts, and violating and/or ignoring the rights of others. The aggressive child tends to behave in ways that deprecate others and lead to the recipient feeling humiliated and defensive. He/she may use tactics that are effective, but rarely appropriate. The aggressive behavior leads to the violation of other's rights and feelings by the use of physical, psychological, or emotional force. Not surprisingly, this type of social behavior generates many negative side effects. According to Patterson et al. (1975),

> the socialization process appears to be severely impeded for many aggressive children. Their behavioral adjustments are often immature and they do not seem to have learned the key social skills necessary for initiating and maintaining positive social relationships with others. Peer groups often reject, avoid, and/or punish aggressive children, thereby excluding them from positive learning experiences with others. Socially negative/aggressive children often have academic difficulties and they achieve at lower levels than their classmates (p. 4).

Thus, socially aggressive children not only acquire academic skills at greatly reduced rates compared to their nonaggressive peers, but their aggressive social interactions elicit counteraggression from their peers and social rejection from adults.

In the long run, the loss of friends, reduced interpersonal contact, feelings of guilt, and decreased opportunities for academic enrichment, as a result of alienating both peers and adults, far outweigh the possible short-term benefits of the aggressive behavior. In addition, left untreated, aggressive children appear to make unsatisfactory adjustments as adults (Robbins, 1976). Specifically, aggressive children manifest decreased popularity with their peers (Winder & Rau, 1962), a greater incidence of academic failure (Schindler, 1941), and adult alcoholism, antisocial behavior, psychiatric disturbances (see Michelson & Wood, 1980; Morris, 1956; Roff, 1961).

In summary, both the passive and the aggressive child exhibit behavioral dysfunctions related to their inability to act effectively and appropriately within their social environment. For these two types of children, their present and future adjustment may greatly depend on whether their social skill deficits are identified and remediated. (Kohlberg et al., 1972). The following sections describe a variety of strategies that have been effectively applied to developing social skills in children.

SOCIAL-SKILLS TRAINING METHODS

A wide variety of social-skills training procedures have been used with children. The skills that are trained vary as a function of the characteristics of the child, including their specific problems, age, and social situations. Social skills training has been effectively applied to children whose social-skill deficits run the gamut from social isolation to aggressive behavior. Although the reader is referred to Combs and Slaby (1977), Michelson and Wood (1980a,b), Michelson et al. (1983), and Van Hasselt, Hersen, Bellack, and Whitehill (1979) for more substantive reviews of the social skills training literature, an illustrative, if not exhaustive examination of this area is now provided. It is important to note that despite the presence of numerous strategies which have been developed to effectively teach children social skills, these techniques can be applied either individually or in combination. To clarify how these procedures are carried out, we first describe the specific method and subsequently examine strategies of combining techniques into social-skills training packages.

Modeling consists of exposing the child to live or film exemplars (models) who perform the desired prosocial behaviors. The use of models is referred to as observational or vicarious learning because the child learns by observing the model rather than actually engaging in the responses overtly. O'Connor (1969) was one of the first researchers to evaluate the effectiveness of modeling as a treatment for social withdrawal in preschool children. Six nursery school children were exposed to a film that depicted increasingly active social interactions between children, with positive consequences ensuing in each scene, while a soundtrack emphasized the appropriate behavior of the models. Seven control group children observed a film that presented no social interaction. Following exposure to the films, children returned to their regular classrooms where they were observed for social interaction.

Results suggested that the control children remained unchanged, whereas treated children who had been exposed to the modeling film evidenced significantly higher rates of social interaction. Indeed, these improved rates of interaction were equal to those of the normal preschoolers, who had been used as a norm for treatment goals. In addition, positive changes were observed across all subjects in the modeling group. The author also reported anecdotal follow-up conducted informally by a second set of teachers. The teachers, blind as to which children were in which group, rated only one of the six treated children as being isolative, whereas four of the seven control children were rated as being isolative at the end of the school year.

In a second study, O'Connor (1972) assigned 31 nursery school isolates to one of four experimental conditions consisting of (1) modeling and shaping, (2) modeling only, (3) shaping only, and (4) control group. Children in the modeling and modeling-plus-shaping condition were exposed to the film used in the original O'Connor study (1969). Children in the modeling-plus-shaping, and shaping-only conditions also received social reinforcement from trained graduate students who administered reinforcement contingent on positive peer interaction. The results of the pre- and postassessment supported the author's original findings by showing that children receiving modeling procedures evidenced the highest rates of positive peer interaction. Results of the 3- and 6-week follow-ups also showed continuation of treatment gains for both modeling groups.

In a similar study, Keller and Carlson (1974) used film modeling to increase social behavior among socially isolated preschool children. Children were exposed to videotape segments in which several socially appropriate behaviors such as displaying affections, smiling, and laughing were presented. The modeling film increased social behavior during the free-play period. Conversely, children exposed to a control film in which social behaviors were not displayed did not evidence any gains.

Although the modeling studies just reviewed reported significant treatment effects, these findings have not been universally observed. Indeed, Gottman (1977) subjected O'Connor's (1969, 1972) findings to a partial replication, with numerous methodological refinements added to original studies. The author reported no significant differences between control and experimental subjects in regard to behavioral improvements or sociometric measures of peer acceptance or rejection. In light of these findings, the author raises questions concerning the definition of social

withdrawal and the utility of modeling via films as a sole effective intervention strategy.

These findings suggest that modeling using filmed examplars may not
be potent enough to lead to observable modification in the social behaviors of withdrawn children. However, its utility as an integral component of a more comprehensive program is widely recognized.

Occasionally, live rather than filmed models have been used to develop social behavior. For example, Ross, Ross, and Evans (1971) administered a multifaceted treatment for a socially withdrawn 6-year-old boy
who exhibited extreme fear and avoidance of social situations. Several
procedures were used which involved having one of the trainers engage
in social interaction with the child's classmates, using symbolic models,
picture stories, and movies of social interaction, demonstrating social
interaction by two trainers and enlisting participation of a trainer with a
child in social interaction with peers. Modeling with participation, combined with other procedures, effectively increased the overall social interaction both immediately after treatment and at the 2-month follow-up
evaluation.

Overall, the modeling studies have demonstrated their potential effectiveness in regard to developing and promoting prosocial behaviors. In
addition, investigators have identified a number of variables that appear
to contribute to the effectiveness of modeling as a therapeutic procedure. Specifically, modeling effects can be enhanced by providing persons with multiple models who perform the desired behaviors rather
than with a single model. Moreover, a wide range of behaviors should
be displayed by the model to help facilitate a broad set of responses by
the observer. Also, perceived similarity of the observer to the model is
another variable that can influence modeling effects. When observers
perceive themselves to be similar to the model, modeling effects are
often greater than when they perceive themselves as dissimilar. The
effects of modeling can be further augmented by providing opportunities for children to practice the behaviors they observe the model perform. Observing one or more models followed by immediately rehears-
ing the observed behaviors produces greater improvement than does
exposure to modeling alone. Therefore, both modeling and behavioral
rehearsal typically are included as parts of a larger social-skills training
package.

Positive reinforcement refers to the process by which behaviors increase
in frequency because they are followed by a reward or a favorable event.
The goal of any social-skills training program is to increase the rate or
frequency of a variety of socially appropriate behaviors. If social behaviors are to be increased, they need to be followed by positively reinforc-

ing consequences. These rewarding consequences might be social attention or approval, or points or tokens that can be exchanged for other rewards, special privileges, or activities. Thus, it is not surprising that a wide variety of reinforcement techniques have been used to increase social skills.

For example, Pinkston, Reise, LeBlanc, and Baer (1972) used social reinforcement and extinction to develop appropriate social skills in a preschool child who displayed highly aggressive behavior and low rates of appropriate peer interaction. Initially, the target behavior of aggression was the focus of treatment. Training consisted of not attending to the aggressive classroom behavior except to remove the child from his contact with others. However, the aggressive child received attention subsequently for nonaggressive behavior. This training procedure effectively reduced the aggressive behavior, as demonstrated in several phases of a single-case experimental design in which attention was presented and withdrawn across phases. Subsequently, socially appropriate peer interaction was the target of a behavioral intervention program using positive reinforcement. The teacher provided prompts to peers to facilitate the child's interaction with his classmates. In addition, the teacher provided direct reinforcement to the child for appropriate social interaction. This procedure increased appropriate peer interaction.

Applications of reinforcement for social behavior have used peers as well as adults to help facilitate appropriate social behavior. In a programmatic series of studies employing peer confederates to facilitate social skills in withdrawn peers, Strain and his colleagues (Strain & Timm, 1974; Strain, Shores, & Timm, 1977; Strain et al., 1977) have trained socially adept preschool children to improve the social behaviors of peers who infrequently engaged in positive interaction with others. The peer trainers were first instructed in role playing on how to initiate interactions with the withdrawn children. Subsequently, peer trainers were praised for helping their withdrawn classmates to interact socially. The withdrawn children were not treated directly by adults. Peers who were trained and received reinforcement for prompting interaction were quite successful at altering the social behaviors of the withdrawn students.

Another application of contingencies has been that of token reinforcement. For example, Todd, Walker, Greenwood, and Hops (1976) systematically investigated the effects of token reinforcement on increasing positive social interaction of low-interacting children and the addition of cost contingency to decrease the hostile interactions of socially aggressive children. Thus, the authors examined the effectiveness of social reinforcement, token reinforcement, combined social and token reinforcement, differential reinforcement of other behavior, and cost contingency. The results indicated that social reinforcement plus token reinforcement contingencies were insufficient and did not affect occurrence of negative aggressive behavior. Conversely, the cost contingency was a critical requirement to affect behavior change of the aggressive children, which led to 100% positive interaction patterns. It is noteworthy that the follow-up of the aggressive children indicated continued improvement in the regular classroom. Moreover, for the socially unresponsive children, a reinforcing procedure that included positive consequences for starting, answering, and continuing interactions with peers was most effective in increasing the amount of time of peer interaction.

As can be seen from the previous review, there are a variety of effective reinforcement techniques that can be used to facilitate social skills in children. However, there are certain common requirements for all of the procedures. First, when attempting to develop new behaviors, it is important to provide reinforcement as soon as possible following the desired response. A delay, such as complimenting a child at the end of the day, risks having little or no effect on performance. Therefore, as a general rule, immediate reinforcement is best when establishing new social skills. Next, reinforcement should occur frequently, especially when the behaviors are just developing. The desired behaviors may occur relatively infrequently. Therefore, to increase their frequency, reinforcers should be provided initially for every or almost every instance of the behavior. As widely documented, behavior develops at a faster rate when reinforcement is delivered continuously than when it is delivered intermittently. However, once responding is at a high level, reinforcement can be delivered less frequently to maintain the behavior.

In addition, two of the most important ingredients in any effective reinforcement program are prompting and shaping. *Prompting* refers to antecedent stimuli that help evoke the behavior. Prompts can include instructions, coaching, modeling cues, et cetera, to help the child to see what is to be done before the behavior is performed. Prompts facilitate performance of the desired behavior. Once the behavior occurs, it can then be reinforced. Eventually prompts can be removed without resulting in decreases in the actual frequency of the behavior. *Shaping* refers to reinforcing approximations of the final behaviors that are to be developed. The goals of social-skills programs often consist of developing complex sequences of social behaviors such as how to begin a conversation, make requests of others, or stand up for one's rights. For severely withdrawn children, it may be difficult to reinforce the occurrence of these responses because they rarely, if ever, occur. Gradual steps toward these responses need to be reinforced so that behaviors can gradually move in the direction of the terminal goal.

As discussed subsequently in the generalization-programming section, to enhance the maintenance of the new social skills, once they are firmly established, fading procedures are often employed. *Fading* involves the gradual and systematic reduction in the frequency and increase between intervals of reinforcement until they approximate naturalistic contingencies, which are typically more random. This procedure enhances generalization across time, settings, and people.

An important caution in regard to using reinforcement strategies concerns the method in which responses are targeted for intervention. For example, Walker, Greenwood, Hopps, and Todd (1979) found that providing token reinforcement and praise to withdrawn children for such behaviors as "starting a conversation" and "answering others," actually suppressed overall interaction. In contrast, reinforcement of maintaining and continuing social interaction produced marked improvements in overall levels of interaction. At present, few comparisons exist evaluating the impact of reinforcement on different types of responses and their implications for successful social skills training. Therefore, the best recommendation, at present, is to provide reinforcing consequences for the individual responses that are deficient, as well as for including both the initiation and maintenance of social interaction.

A number of clinical and ethical issues regarding the use of operant and modeling approaches have been raised. For example, Combs and Slaby (1977) stated that "in both operant and modeling studies, there has been a heavy emphasis on increasing the frequency of peer interaction in social isolates. This training goal can be empirically justified, to some extent, by research indicating that social isolates may have considerable adjustment problems and that social participation is correlated with peer acceptance. However, exclusive emphasis on the quantity of pure interaction has serious limitations" (p. 186). Likewise, Michelson and Wood (1980b) stated that "operant procedures that direct treatment goals toward increasing positive peer interaction, may be reinforcing peer interaction per se, but not necessarily social skills or peer acceptance. Ignoring questions of qualitative deficits, most operant studies have focused almost entirely on increasing peer interaction rates." This has several limitations, including (1) overemphasis on the *rate* but not the *quality* of the social interaction and responses; (2) interaction rates may be increased with no corresponding increase in the amount of reinforcement the child emits or elicits because of lacking specific social skills requisite for generating social reinforcement; and (3) this approach does not necessarily instruct, teach, or model more appropriate means of social interaction. In a critique of rate-of-interaction research, Asher, Markle, and Hymel (1981) cogently concluded that quantitative indices of peer interaction, without qualitative assessment lacks concurrent, predictive and social validity. Thus, it is critical that social-skills trainers not only perform social validation on the targeted behaviors, but also that they incorporate into the training program methods for ensuring that the child's qualitative as well as quantitative dimensions of social behavior are improved.

Coaching and Practice

To evoke a desired behavior, a child can be coached or instructed on which behaviors to perform and how to perform them. Coaching may rely on several procedures aside from instructions. For example, the training may provide a model of the desired statements to explain how the child should speak to parents or teachers. The trainer may also provide feedback on how well the behaviors were performed by the child and what behaviors should be modified. Coaching is, therefore, a multifaceted intervention involving clear prompts for what to do, practice of the behavior, and feedback to reinforce correct elements of response and prompt improved performance. Practice or rehearsal is a critical component of coaching. It is also sometimes used by itself. Practice consists of enacting the desired behavior or sequence of behavior, such as role playing the desired response. Through repeated practice of the desired response, the child learns how to perform the new behaviors and the coaching sequence of instruction–practice–feedback is repeated until performance matches the desired objective.

An example is the study by Oden and Asher (1977), who evaluated a social-skills training program that utilized instructions and practice. Children were instructed to use the behaviors in a play situation with a nonisolate peer. Following practice, the interactions were reviewed with a trainer. Children who were coached showed increases in sociometric ratings relative to other conditions in which coaching was excluded. Although the gains were not evident on a behavioral measure, a 1-year follow-up showed that the sociometric ratings continued to reflect treatment effects.

Similarly, Ladd (1979) used a training program that emphasized coaching to facilitate development of social behaviors among withdrawn third grade children. Training was conducted with pairs of children during which they were coached on how to interact appropriately with others. Children who received the coaching procedure improved relative to children who received attention placebo or no-treatment control conditions. Improvements were reflected in social interaction during free play and on peer-acceptance measures. Treatment effects were maintained up to the 4-week follow-up.

Several other studies have examined the effectiveness of coaching in which children were given verbal instructions on how to perform, supplemented with opportunities to practice. Although some programs have been successful, others have not (e.g., Gottman et al., 1975; Hymel & Ascher, 1977). Therefore, while coaching and practice are important ingredients in social skills training, they should be used in conjunction with other strategies. Both coaching and practice emphasize aspects of training that need to be incorporated in social-skills training programs. *Coaching* emphasizes the importance of clear and detailed guidelines for the child. Prompts of all sorts and direct modeling experiences can greatly speed the acquisition of the desired behaviors. Finally, *practice* emphasizes the importance of actually performing the requisite behaviors. As noted earlier, each of the techniques of modeling contributes uniquely to developing the desired social behaviors. Thus, all these methods should be incorporated in training, as practice alone would ordinarily prove insufficient without further coaching and feedback to shape the components of social behaviors.

INTERPERSONAL COGNITIVE PROBLEM-SOLVING (ICPS)

Interpersonal cognitive problem-solving (ICPS) focuses on how children think about and approach interpersonal problems. In particular, ICPS programs teach children to identify interpersonal problems, generate alternative solutions to these problems, and evaluate the consequences of their actions. Although interpersonal problems cannot be avoided, it is hoped that by learning ICPS skills, children will become more effective future problem-solvers and will develop more confidence in their capacity to successfully face interpersonal conflict. Thus, ICPS programs deal directly with the issue of generalization of treatment effects. As noted by Urbain and Kendall (1980), "A major hypothesis based on the social-cognitive problem-solving model is that training at the level of the cognitive processes that presumably mediate behavioral change will build in generalization as an integral part of treatment" (p. 110).

ICPS in School Settings

The majority of ICPS programs have been conducted with elementary school children in the natural setting of their school (Gesten et al., 1979). In this regard, the pioneer theoretical work in this area was done by D'Zurilla and Goldfried (1971). After reviewing the research on problem solving, these authors concluded that the ability to solve social and interpersonal problems is a critical element in human adjustment. They further posted several guidelines as to the stages of interpersonal problem solving, and how the various abilities in these areas might be trained.

The most significant early research on the assessment and training of ICPS skills in school-aged children was conducted by Spivack and Shure and their colleagues at the Hahnemann Medical College (Shure & Spivack, 1978; Spivack, Platt, & Shure, 1976; Spivack & Shure, 1974). Building on the work of D'Zurilla and Goldfried (1971), they identified four major ICPS skills: (1) sensitivity to interpersonal problems, (2) ability to generate alternative solutions, (3) ability to understand means–ends relationships, and (4) awareness of the consequences of one's actions. Furthermore, Spivack and Shure have developed several ICPS curricula for preschoolers, kindergartners, and older children.

The training for kindergarten children (Spivack & Shure, 1974) largely consisted of a series of games designed to build prerequisite cognitive skills, followed by interpersonal problem situations that the children were taught to respond to with alternative solutions and awareness of consequences. Children participated in the program for 20 minutes a day for 3 months. The results of this training program demonstrated positive correlations between overt behavioral adjustment, as measured by teacher ratings, and the abilities to generate alternative solutions and anticipate consequences. Specifically, ICPS training resulted in significant increases in problem-solving ability and these newly acquired skills were found to mediate healthy behavioral functioning, independent of intelligence. Similar findings have been reported for preschool children and preadolescents (Spivack & Shure, 1974). Despite the consistency over time of Spivack and Shure's findings, the one major drawback on this and their other research is that they have repeatedly used no-treatment control groups. This type of methodology makes it difficult to ascertain whether ICPS training was responsible for the outcomes or whether gains were the result of such nonspecific treatment factors as therapist attention.

Allen, Chinsky, Larcen, Lochman, and Selinger (1976) have also developed a social problem-solving program for elementary school children. Like Spivack and Shure, these investigators used classroom activities and small-group exercises. In addition, they added videotapes that depicted children "modeling" problem-solving strategies. Unfortunately, their success with the ICPS model with elementary-age children has not been nearly as great as those reported by Spivack and Shure with preschool and kindergarten children. Whereas children made significant gains in their capacity to generate alternative solutions, there were no corresponding improvements in behavioral adjustment (Allen et al., 1976). Whether the latter finding was due to problems in the intervention or increased severity of behavior-problems in older children is not known. Future research needs to address these issues directly.

In a later study, McClure, Chinsky, and Larcen (1978) evaluated an expanded version of this same training program. Four experimental conditions were used (1) videotape modeling only, (2) videotape plus discussion, (3) videotape plus role-play exercises; and (4) a no-treatment control group. McClure et al. (1978) reported that children in all training conditions improved in their problem-solving ability and developed a more-internal locus of control compared with the children in the control group. However, because there was no assessment of overt behavioral adjustment, it was not possible to ascertain whether gains in problem-solving abilities had any impact on real-life behavior.

Other social skills programs can be similarly criticized for their failure to assess overt behavioral adjustment. For example, Stone, Hinds, and Schmidt (1975) developed a creative, short-term program designed to teach both social and nonsocial problem-sharing skills to third- and fifth-graders. In addition, Houtz and Feldhusen (1976) incorporated a reward component into their program whereby some children received only training, others received training plus a reward, and others served as a no-treatment control group. Unfortunately, in both of these studies, actual behavioral adjustment was not measured, thus limiting the significance of the reported gains in problem-solving abilities. Teaching children problem-solving skills is theoretically sound and intuitively appealing. However, ICPS needs to demonstrate efficacy in training skills that are related to actual adaptive behavioral functioning. Failure to include behavioral change measures remains a critical methodological limitation and concern in the evaluation of ICPS training programs.

Since then, ICPS programs have become more methodologically sophisticated and have included measures of both problem-solving abilities and behavioral adjustment. In this regard, Weissberg, Gesten, Rapkin, Cowen, Davidson, Flores de Apodaca, and McKim (1981) conducted a comprehensive ICPS program with third-graders, in which 52 highly structured 20–30 minute lessons were employed. The major ICPS skills taught were (1) recognizing feelings in ourselves and others, (2) problem sensing and identification, (3) generation of alternative solutions, (4) consideration of consequences, and (5) integration of problem-solving behavior, which instructed children to consider factors needed to carry out solutions effectively and provided opportunities for role-playing the entire problem-solving sequence. Lessons were presented four times a week for 13 weeks and were taught by classroom teachers. With regard to pre- and posttreatment assessments, four measures of cognitive problem-solving and a behavioral problem-solving test were used, as well as four measures of behavioral adjustment, namely, the Health Resources Inventory, a teacher rating scale, a measure of self-reported anxiety, and a self-concept scale.

The results of the Weissberg et al. (1981) study found that children receiving ICPS made significantly more gains in alternative-solution thinking, gave more effective solutions, and were better at identifying interpersonal problems and in anticipating consequences to solutions than untreated controls. Adjustment findings were more inconsistent. Specifically, ICPS training did not affect children's self-esteem, sociometric status, or self-report of anxiety, However, the intervention did result in improved behavioral adjustment, as rated by teachers, for the program children in suburban schools. In contrast, the training did not positively affect the behavioral adjustment of program children in urban schools. The latter finding conflicts with the earlier work of Elardo and Cladwell (1979) who reported teacher-rated adjustment gains in inner-city children who were taught both social-role-taking and ICPS skills.

Perhaps the most significant finding of the Weissberg et al. (1981) study was that ICPS skills and adjustment gains were unrelated. The authors noted that "the consistent failure of researchers, working with 7–11 year olds, to identify such relationships contrasts with Spivack and Shure's (1974) replicated demonstrations of ICPS-adjustment gain linkages for younger inner-city preschoolers" (p. 260). This failure to find relationships between ICPS and adjustment gains in this older age group may be due to more-advanced cognitive development or to the fact that behavioral problems at this age are more intractible. Future research needs to address whether these or alternative possibilities are responsible for the attenuated efficacy of ICPS with older children.

In an investigation, Mannarino, Durlak, Christy, and Magnussen (1982) implemented an ICPS program with 64 high-risk children in Grades 1 through 3. Children were identified as being high-risk, based on teachers' behavioral ratings. Training was conducted on a small-group basis for 14 weeks with weekly 1-hour meetings. This ICPS program differed from earlier strategies in that the first phase of training strongly emphasized feeling identification as an essential problem-solving skill. In this regard, during the initial 4 weeks, children engaged in a variety of exercises designed to enhance their capacity to recognize their own feelings and those of other children. To illustrate, in one exercise, program children were given pictures of people exhibiting a wide array of feelings. They were then asked to label the feeling for each picture and explain what features of the person (e.g., facial expression, gestures) helped them to identify the feeling. In a similar exercise, children were asked to pretend that they were feeling sad, happy, angry, et cetera, and the remaining group members were to guess the feeling based only on facial expressions and nonverbal gestures. The remainder of the program focused on standard ICPS skills such as generating alternative solutions and consequential thinking.

Mannarino et al. (1982) reported that program children made significantly greater gains in behavioral adjustment, as rated by teachers, than no-treatment controls. Furthermore, with respect to sociometric status, the level of social acceptance of the control group remained virtually unchanged while ICPS children manifested significant improvement in popularity. The latter finding is important for two reasons. First, previous ICPS programs report little or no impact on sociometric status (Allen et al., 1976; Weissberg et al., 1981). Secondly, considering the well-documented evidence on the stability of sociometric status over extended time periods (Bonney, 1943; Campbell & Yarrow, 1961; Hartup, 1970; Miller & Maruyama, 1976), the fact that gains were achieved in peer acceptance as a function of a brief intervention program is highly promising.

Unfortunately, two methodological shortcomings of the Mannarino et al. (1982) study temper the significance of their findings. First, there was no attempt to measure ICPS skills. It is, therefore, impossible to know whether gains in problem-solving abilities mediated the positive changes in behavioral adjustment. In addition, as with the Spivack and Shure (1974) work, there was a failure to include an attention-placebo control group, which could have ruled out the possibility that positive findings were the result of the added attention and time given to the ICPS children. Despite these limitations, the findings with respect to sociometric status gains in this study are noteworthy. In this regard, it is possible that the heavy emphasis on feeling identification as a basic problem-identification skill was responsible for this outcome. Finally, the fact that the Mannarino et al. study employed only high-risk children may have enhanced the probability of behavioral changes compared with previous investigators, who have used classroom children (Allen et al., 1976; McClure et al., 1978; Weisburg et al., 1981).

Although an impressive number of ICPS programs have evolved since the mid-1970s, none have systematically attempted to isolate which specific problem-solving skills accounts for corresponding behavioral improvements. A study by Richard and Dodge (1982) sheds some light on this matter. These authors selected three groups of boys who were identified as either aggressive, isolated, or popular, based on peer ratings. These children were presented with six hypothetical problem situations and asked to generate alternative solutions to the problems and to evaluate the effectiveness of the solutions presented to them by the experimenter. Richard and Dodge reported that the popular children generated more alternative solutions to problems than either the aggressive or isolated groups, which did not differ on this dimension. However, the initial solutions of all groups were generally rated as "effective," by independent raters. Interestingly, with respect to subsequent solutions, the popular children continued to generate effective solutions whereas both the aggressive and isolated boys evidenced increases in their proportion of aggressive and ineffective solutions. It is also worth mentioning that no differences were found among the subject groups in the evaluations of the effectiveness of given solutions. Richard and Dodge (1982) concluded that "this finding suggests that the adequacy of the problem-solving skills in aggressive and isolated boys may be limited to an initial solution. When further solutions are called for, aggressive and isolated boys are unable to generate as many effective solutions as do the popular boys. The solutions they do choose are often characteristic of their behavior (aggressive or ineffective)" (p. 231).

These findings suggest that the capacity to generate a wide range of effective solutions may account for some of the behavioral differences between socially adjusted and maladjusted children. The implication of these results is that ICPS programs should focus on helping children to generate *numerous* effective alternative solutions. Future research should also examine whether there are differences between normal and socially deficit children on other traditional ICPS skills such as problem identification and consequential thinking.

ICPS in Clinical Settings

There have been relatively few attempts to implement ICPS programs with clinical populations. In an early study Giebink, Stover, and Fahl (1968) taught six boys in a residential treatment setting to increase the number of alternative solutions given to four frustrating situations. Unfortunately, the small sample size precluded any meaningful analysis of the data, although there was a modest increase among the trained children in their use of adaptive solution in the residential setting. In a modified program with strong behavioral components (Ollendick & Hersen, 1979), an attempt was made to help 18 incarcerated juvenile delinquents generate alternative solutions to problems they were having with each other and with the staff. The results at posttesting found that those delinquents who participated in the social-skills training made significantly greater gains in eye contact and decreased their aggressiveness in role-play situations, compared to untreated controls. However, because the program incorporated many behavioral features in the training such as behavioral rehearsal, modeling, and feedback, it is entirely unclear what contribution, if any, the ICPS training component had on adjustment.

A comprehensive examination of ICPS training with emotionally disturbed children has been undertaken by Michelson, Mannarino, Marchione, Stern, Figueroa, and Beck (1982b). This study compared the relative effectiveness of ICPS training with behavioral social skills training and a control group with boys who were referred to a child guidance clinic for behavioral problems and social skills deficits. Michelson et al.'s (1982b) findings were rather discouraging with respect to ICPS training. Although both the behavioral and ICPS treatments resulted in some significant gains on parent, self-report, and teacher measures at posttreatment, only the behavioral treatment maintained its gains at the 1-year follow-up. In fact, children in the ICPS treatment manifested significant declines at the follow-up, as did the control group. These data suggest that although ICPS training may have some impact on the behavioral adjustment of normal children (Elardo & Caldwell, 1979; Weissberg et al., 1981) and high-risk children (Mannarino et al., 1982), it may not be a sufficiently potent therapeutic experience for children who already manifest significant behavioral and social problems.

SUMMARY

Although the results of ICPS training programs have been encouraging, there are a number of significant issues that must be addressed in future research. First, outcome studies examining the efficacy of ICPS training must include behavioral measures of adjustment. Likewise, sociometric data should be routinely collected as a means of demonstrating socially validated improvements in social functioning. As mentioned earlier, teaching children problem-solving skills is theoretically sound and intuitively appealing. However, it needs to be demonstrated that these skills are functionally related to adaptive social behavior in order to justify such training programs. Second, future ICPS programs need to routinely include problem-solving measures as part of their overall assessment to determine if change in behavioral adjustment are mediated by gains in problem-solving abilities. Third, a major flaw in many previous ICPS training programs has been the failure to include attention-placebo control groups. The inclusion of such groups in future outcome studies will ensure that treatment gains are not the result of nonspecific therapist factors such as attention.

Another major issue that needs to be examined is whether teaching ICPS skills to maladjusted children will enhance their long-term adaptation. Unfortunately, previous research with disturbed children has not been encouraging. Perhaps ICPS training will need to be combined with other intensive therapeutic experiences, like family therapy and parent training, in order to have a significant impact on children with serious emotional and/or behavioral problems. Finally, the issue of generalization has received scant attention in ICPS training programs. This issue is discussed at length later in the chapter and its importance cannot be overemphasized. Unless ICPS training programs can demonstrate that children use these skills across a variety of settings and with diverse groups of people, then training efforts will have fallen far short of their ultimate aims. We hope that closer consideration of the issue of generalization will aid ICPS programs in achieving the legitimacy and validity its proponents seek.

Social-Skills Training Packages

Although several programs have applied the individual techniques such as those just reviewed to alter social behaviors, a number of new programs have appeared, which offer multifaceted treatments or packages in which the aforementioned procedures and others are combined (e.g., Hops et al., 1979; Michelson et al., 1982a, 1982b; Michelson et al., 1983; Michelson & Wood, 1980a). Combining alternative techniques is assumed to maximize the *impact*, *durability* and *generality* of treatment effects.

Also, as increasingly severe clinical populations have been studied, the need for more intensive treatments has increased. Major ingredients frequently included in social-skills training packages include instructions, modeling, rehearsal and practice, feedback, social reinforcement, scripts, homework assignments, and procedures to enhance generalization.

For example, Michelson and Wood (1980a) trained 80 fourth-grade elementary school children in social skills. All training was conducted in the elementary school setting. The training program consisted of instructions, coaching, modeling, behavioral rehearsal, prepared scripts for assertive responses and reactions of others in the situation, discussion, and homework assignments. Multiple topic areas that were socially validated were covered including giving and receiving compliments; giving and receiving complaints; refusing unreasonable requests from others; requesting favors; asking why, expressing empathy; requesting behavior change from others; standing up for one's rights; initiating, maintaining, and terminating conversations; dealing with authority figures; dealing with people of the opposite sex; humor as a social skill; and related topic areas.

The 80 children were randomly assigned to one of four conditions: (1) 16 hours of social skills training (SST); (2) 8 hours of SST; (3) 16 hours of placebo-ecology discussions; and, (4) pre- and posttesting control groups. Statistically significant results were obtained at posttreatment with the 8 and 16 hours of SST groups being rated (by self-report and by teacher and parent's reports) superior to the control groups. The follow-up data collected at the 1-month posttreatment assessment, revealed similar findings. Moreover, the 16-hour SST children were rated significantly higher in social skills by teachers who were blind as to their specific experimental condition. In addition to the statistically significant treatment effects of the 8- and 16-hour SST programs, the children, teachers, and parents reported high levels of consumer satisfaction and clinical improvement, adding socially validated gains to the positive results obtained. Following these positive results, Michelson and his colleagues (Michelson et al., 1982a,b) examined the utility and long-term effectiveness of the social-skills training program with psychiatric inpatients, socially maladjusted outpatient children, at risk elementary school children, and normal children as a preventative measure. Although the reader is referred to these sources from more exhaustive reviews of the results, it is clear that the social-skills training program has much potential as both a remedial and a preventative intervention across the diverse populations to which it has been applied.

Michelson et al. (1982b) conducted an NIMH (National Institutes of Mental Health) investigation of the relative efficacy of this approach vis-à-vis interpersonal problem-solving and a Rogerian nondirective control group, the results of which are briefly described. The purpose of the study was to compare the short- and long-term efficacy of behavioral social-skills training and interpersonal problem-solving with a control condition (nondirective treatment) with a clinical population of 61 socially maladjusted outpatient boys. Treatment consisted of 12 weekly 1-hour sessions, with follow-up conducted at 12 months. A comprehensive assessment strategy was employed, which included direct behavioral observations; parent, teacher, peer, and self-reports (Michelson & Wood 1982); and academic performance measures. The results of this social-skills comparative outcome study indicated that the behavioral and interpersonal treatments resulted in significant changes on parent-, teacher-, and self-report, and on peer sociometric ratings at posttreatment. At the 1-year follow-up, the behavioral treatment maintained its gains and continued to show modest improvement. Conversely, the interpersonal treatment manifested significant declines, as did the control group.

As a result of this programmatic research, Michelson et al. (in press), developed a social-skills training program, consisting of 17 modules, each module covering a specific social skill that has been identified as being an important component of the daily repertoire of children's social behaviors. All themes pertain to the ability of the child to behave in a socially competent manner. Topics included a wide variety of socially validated content areas including compliments; complaints, empathy; refusing unreasonable requests; standing up for one's rights; dealing with authority figures; mixed-sex interactions; initiating, maintaining, and terminating conversations; and related interpersonal domains.

The training format for the 17 modules consists of a rationale for trainers, sample lecture for children, introduction to the topic, and modeling with and without scripts, first between trainers, then between trainers and children, and finally between two children in front of the class. Feedback from trainers is then given with reinforcement, followed by feedback from the class. Next, behavior rehearsal with and without scripts, class discussion, feedback from trainers, summary and review, followed by homework assignments.

The modules were designed in sequence, in a progressively more complex manner. Therefore, earlier modules focus on simpler social skills while subsequent modules describe more complex skills that are built upon these more basic ones. The modules follow a standard format, each comprising three main sections: a rationale, procedures, and class discussion. The first section, rationale, provides a trainer with a description and definition of the target behavior. This section describes why the behavior is of particular importance for children. The rationale section is followed by a lecture for the children and a listing both of the benefits children may gain by acquiring the particular skill and pitfalls they may encounter if deficient in those abilities. This section allows trainers to underscore the usefulness and practicality of learning and improving the children's social behaviors, which may help children understand the importance of acquiring these new and valuable skills and of participating in the program. The sample lecture includes the actual teaching component of the module and provides trainers with a sample introductory lecture on the topic, as well as suggested questions to stimulate class involvement. The lecture is intended to serve as an example of how the topic can be introduced, with classroom discussion encouraged.

In addition to the sample lecture, the procedure section also includes scripts to be used by trainers in modeling target behaviors as well as practice scripts for the children. These scripts, when used in conjunction with the training techniques previously described, provide children with both observational and experiential learning material. Specifically, the trainer's scripts detail situations and dialogue that illustrate the theme of the module. The trainer, working in conjunction with instructional aides, fellow teachers, student volunteers, et cetera, models how a person can respond to the scripted situation in either assertive, passive, or aggressive modes. Throughout training, trainers emphasize the importance of responding assertively.

The modules themselves consist only of appropriate responses which the children practice. Following the script rehearsal, spontaneous role-playing is encouraged, followed by group feedback and trainer reinforcement. Next, during the class discussion, the children regroup in order to discuss what they have been practicing. Trainers than ask students about any difficulties they may have encountered and point out any problem areas they might have observed. This is then followed by a general summary statement by the trainer that reiterates the important aspects of topic areas, including definition, rationale, and benefits.

Finally, suggested homework assignments are included at the end of each training module. Trainers encourage homework assignment tasks that have particular relevance for the population they are working with in order to enhance the use of these newly learned social skills outside the training session. Specifically, assignments typically involve in vivo observation and practice of social behaviors covered in the training modules. Children tend to enjoy homework assignments, as they are easy, nonthreatening, and generally require only a modest amount of time. These homework assignments are then reviewed at the beginning of the next session. Each module requires approximately 45–60 minutes to effectively complete. After having conducted training with several hundred children, with a wide variety of social deficits, it appears that the children not only enjoy but benefit from the intervention.

Social-skills training packages are becoming increasingly popular. Obviously, the package approach is designed to combine the advantages and to circumvent the limitations of any single technique. There are additional features that recommend the use of a multifaceted treatment package. The package provides an approach that uses antecedent events (instructions, models), direct performance of the desired responses (rehearsal and practice), and consequences (feedback and reinforcement). By including these different facets of the training, impact on the child is likely to be optimal. In addition, the procedure lends itself well to individualization for particular children. As a child enacts the responses, trainers can identify quickly and focus on these particular areas where additional prompting, practice, and feedback are needed. In addition, the use of packages facilitates and is conducive to wide-scale dissemination and application in educational settings as part of a social–affective curriculum.

CONCLUSION

Although numerous social-skills training procedures have proven their effectiveness, additional research is greatly needed. Specifically, research directed toward increasing generalization will be of paramount importance. Suggestions for accomplishing this endeavor were made by Michelson and Wood (1980) and include

> 1) utilizing both operant and modeling approaches; 2) fading out of operant contingencies as soon as the behavior is well established and at peer criterion level; 3) utilizing a wide variety of modeling procedures such as coaching, rehearsal, and role playing to facilitate treatment effects and reduce the effect of individual differences; 4) including self-monitoring, self-maintenance and self-coping procedures; and, 5) conducting regular and periodic follow-up assessments by blind, independent raters [moreover], . . . it is vital to both the success of training and the ethical reputation of behavior therapy that trainers give serious consideration to which skills are being trained, for whom, and how well the child's acquired skills will be responded to in his or her natural environment of peers, siblings, parents, and adults. Researchers and trainers need to involve these individuals in the treatment process, preferably before training has even begun. Reinforcement will need to be programmed if these fragile, but vital skills are to be maintained over time and generalized across settings, people and time. (Michelson & Wood, 1980, p. 281–282).

Future research in regard to examining the effects of booster sessions, engaging parents in training, social validation, and the long-term maintenance of a social-skills program is greatly needed. Moreover, future investigations need to examine individual differences, incorporate peers in training, and attempt to use combinations of both operant and modeling procedures as a means of enhancing both the short- and long-term effects of training, recognizing social validation as an important ingredient in the process. Likewise, a component analyses of these programs is needed to identify the most critical and salient ingredients. Finally, future efforts should be addressed to questions and issues of cost efficiency and methods of implementing of training on a large-scale basis as a form of *primary prevention.*

GENERALIZATION PROGRAMMING

A critical consideration when undertaking any social-skills training program is to ensure that these fragile but vital social skills will be applied in appropriate situations outside the original setting in which treatment occurred. This is usually termed generalization (Rodgers-Warren & Baer, 1976). As stated by Stokes and Baer (1977), the rationale for emphasizing generalization is that "a functional behavioral change, to be effective, must occur over time, other persons, and other settings, and the effects of the change sometime should spread to a variety of selected behaviors." Thus, it is clear that generalization programming is necessary in both remedial and preventative social-skills strategies.

Since the mid-1970s, there has been increasing evidence that generalization does not naturally occur for most educational training programs (Baer, Wolf, & Risley, 1968). For example, research has indicated that socially deficient children do not automatically acquire the necessary social skills through contact with regular students (Cooke & Apolloni, 1976). It has also been shown that behaviorally disordered children are often ignored by their peers, rather than becoming involved in actions that facilitate the development of more appropriate social behaviors (Strain & Timm, 1974). Thus, generalization cannot be regarded as a passive function where a skill, once taught, magically appears and continues to appear thereafter. Generalization requires an active stance by the trainer and must be programmed into any social skills intervention. Although the more common approach to generalization is to train and hope, this strategy is not likely to prove fruitful.

Stokes and Baer (1977) and Michelson et al. (1983) posited several strategies for promoting generalization beyond the training setting, including maintenance over time and transfer across other settings. The procedures to promote generalization include

1. **Teach behaviors that will be supported by the natural environment.** This is one of the most reliable and functional facilitation tech-

niques. Training is designed to ensure that the new repertoire of behaviors is supported and maintained by the natural contingencies currently operating in the child's environment (Baer & Wolf, 1970). Specifically, social skills that are taught should be supported by parents, teachers, and peers. For example, following the learning and practice of appropriate compliment responses, a youth will probably experience many positive consequence from others that will serve to maintain and strengthen the skill, thereby consolidating this response into his or her repertoire. Conversely, teaching and developing social skills that are not supported by the child's environment (e.g., if the particular compliment taught is not acceptable to peers and friends) would result in poor generalization.

2. **Teach a variety of responses.** Teaching children multiple examples and responses should be included in any training program. The more diversified responses that can be taught through behavioral rehearsal, role playing, and other procedures, the more capable the child will be in successfully meeting the challenges found within these diverse situations. By acquiring a variety of responses for each social skill the child will be more responsive to variations in cultural, religious, and ethnic backgrounds of others with whom they will interact.

3. **"Train loosely" under varied conditions.** Rather than controlling all dimensions of a training situation a variety of stimuli should be included. To increase generalized ability of the skills being taught, children should be allowed to develop some of their own specific situations and responses when developing particular social skills. For example, many training programs make use of practice scripts which detail specific situation and responses for a particular social skill. To use the "train loosely" approach, children should also be encouraged to eventually initiate some of their own situations and responses once they are able to demonstrate proficiency with the original material.

4. **Train across multiple persons and settings common to the natural environment.** Generalization can be facilitated by making the training situation as comparable to the natural environment as possible. For example, including peers from the home, neighborhood, or school environments in a social-skills class would provide relevant common stimuli for the child. Similarly, role playing should include many different combinations for partners: peer to adult, peer to peer, same-sex, opposite-sex, old–young, mixed-race, high–low status, et cetera, to approximate interactions in the real world. Through the use of common stimuli, children can learn to respond to persons they will encounter outside the classroom. This subsequently increases generalizability beyond that which would be obtained if children only role-played with the adult trainer as a partner.

5. **Fade training consequences to approximate natural contingencies.**
Although research clearly emphasizes the importance of immediate and
frequent reinforcement in regard to acquiring new skills, the generalization of these skills appears to rely on the fading of contingencies to
approximate those operating in the natural environment. An example of
a fading technique would be to move gradually from continuous reinforcement to intermittent schedules of delayed reinforcement. As contingencies are faded, children begin to respond similarly between training and natural situations. Hence, children begin to transfer skills into
naturalistic settings. According to Michelson et al. (1983), "This technique could be incorporated into a flexible school curriculum in the
following manner. A social skills class could provide special privileges
contingent on improvement in social skills. As the contingencies used in
the class are faded, they would then be applied at random times in other
classes, throughout the day. Under these conditions, the repertoires
learned in the social skills training class would generalize to other
classes. Gradually, all contingencies could be faded with the skills being
maintained by the natural social environment."

6. **Reinforce accurate self-reports of performance.** Verbal mediation,
such as the reinforcement of self-reports of on-task performance, have
been shown to increase children's ability to engage in a task for longer
periods of time without interruption (Israel & O'Leary, 1973; Rogers-
Warren & Baer, 1976). These research findings suggest that reinforcement of accurate self-reports may increase generalization of target behaviors (cf. Risley & Hait, 1976). For example, administering homework
assignments is a useful mediator in social-skills training. Thus, after a
skill is taught in class, students can be instructed to perform this skill
outside of class. Children can later report their successes and/or problems in applying the social skill outside the training situation. When
self-reports of performance are reinforced, additional efforts to use the
trained skills outside class will increase. Both homework assignments
and student self-reports of performance are considered mediators that
may enhance transfer of learning to the natural environment.

7. **Train the ability to generalize by reinforcing new appropriate
applications.** This procedure involves reinforcing generalization itself,
as if it were an explicit behavior. Role-play situations using social skills
training are usually specified by the trainer. However, children could
also be reinforced for suggesting responses other than those specified in
scripts or by the trainer. Such a procedure reinforces children for incorporating additional examples into the training situation, thus increasing
generalization. Children can be trained to generalize by exploring alternative responses that are potentially more effective in their particular
social environment.

8. **Use peers as change agents.** Peers may be especially useful in regard to developing and maintaining appropriate social behavior and to ensuring its transfer across various settings. Peers can be easily incorporated into training in different ways (e.g., group reinforcement contingencies that foster interaction of all participants, peers to initiate social interaction with target children, peer models to serve as role exemplars). Peers have been used as the primary behavioral change agents in classroom settings. For example, Strain et al. (1977) trained preschool children using rehearsal and modeling to interact with a withdrawn child and continue their interactions even if these efforts were not reciprocated. At the beginning of each day, the teacher prompted the peers to try to get the withdrawn child to play. Over a short period of time, the withdrawn child increased in overall social responsiveness. The use of peers to develop social behaviors has been reported in numerous investigations (see Strain & Fox, 1981). In some cases the use of peers has led to increased generalization beyond the training setting (Strain, 1977) and in other reports the use of peers has not led to sustained training effects (Hops et al., 1979). Although the parameters of which factors mediate the efficacy of peers in regard to promoting generalization have not been elucidated, it does appear that the use of peers can help to optimize maintenance and transfer effects.

In summary, generalization is an essential feature of all socioeducational programs such as social-skills training. Without generalization, newly established social skills will probably be employed only in the training setting, rarely the goal of a training program. Rather than assuming it will occur, generalization should be programmed into the training process. Therefore, the generalization facilitators previously described should be planned as an integral part of the social-skills training program because their inclusion will maximize the effectiveness and responsiveness of any training program. Michelson et al. (1983), summarizing the social-skills training literature with children, posit that the best strategy is to adopt a multifaceted approach to maximize the likelihood that behaviors will generalize after training. They recommend that training should be conducted until the individual consistently performs the target skill at a highly proficient level. In addition, the length of treatment may have to be extended in order to ensure that the skill levels reach competency criteria, especially when severe skilled deficits are present. (Michelson & Wood, 1980). Practice outside of the training sessions should also be included to increase the durability and generality of treatment effects. Moreover, individuals who might help support the child's newly acquired behaviors should be incorporated into the training program. Parents, teachers, and peers can be especially helpful because they have access to a wide variety of situations where the child's interpersonal skills may be problematic. Parents and teachers are both in an excellent position to provide modeling, prompts, and immediate feedback and reinforcement for appropriate behavior performance. Peers may also be helpful to incorporate into training. Direct incentives can be provided to peers for interacting with or providing support and reinforcement of the behavior of the target child. Group contingencies also may be useful to ensure that trained behaviors are reinforced outside the training situation. Finally, a broad range of persons in varying situations should be incorporated into training. To the extent that this is accomplished, maintenance and generalization training effects are likely to be increased.

REFERENCES

Allen, G., Chinsky, J. M., Larcen, S. W., Lochman, J. E., & Sellinger, H. V. (1976). *Community psychology in the schools: A behavioral oriented, multi-level preventive approach.* Hillsdale, NJ: Erlbaum.

Asher, S. R., Markle, R. A., & Hymel, S. (1981). Identifying children at risk in peer relations: A critique of the rate-of-interaction approach to assessment. *Child Development, 52,* 1239–1245.

Baer, D. M., & Wolf, M. M. (1970). Recent examples of behavior modification in preschool settings. In C. Neuringer and J. L. Michael (Eds.), *Behavior Modification in Clinical Psychology.* New York: Appleton Century Cross.

Baer, D. M., Wolf, M. M., & Risley, T. R. (1968). Some current dimensions of applied behavior analysis. *Journal of Applied Behavior Analysis, 1,* 91–97.

Bonney, M. E. (1943). Personality traits of socially successful and unsuccessful children. *Journal of Educational Psychology, 34,* 449–472.

Campbell, J. D., & Yarrow, M. R. (1961). Perceptual and behavioral correlates of social effectiveness. *Sociometry, 24,* 1–20.

Chittenden, G. F. (1942). An experimental study in measuring and modifying assertive behavior in young children. *Monograph of the Society for Research in Child Development, 7,* 1–87.

Combs, M. L., & Slaby, D. A. (1977). Social skills training with children. In B. B. Lahey, & A. E. Kazdin (Eds.), *Advances in child clinical psychology,* (Vol. 1). New York: Plenum.

Cooke, T. P., & Apolloni, T. (1976). Developing positive social–emotional behaviors: A study of training and generalization effects. *Journal of Applied Behavior Analysis, 9,* 65–78.

Cowen, E. L., Pederson, A., Babigian, H., Izzo, L. D., & Trost, M. A. (1973). Long-term follow-up of early detected vulnerable children. *Journal of Consulting and Clinical Psychology, 41,* 438–446.

D'Zurilla, T. J., & Goldfried, M. R. (1971). Problem solving and behavior modification. *Journal of Abnormal Psychology, 78,* 107–126.

Elardo, P. T., & Caldwell, B. M. (1977). The effects of an experimental social development program on children in the middle childhood period. *Psychology in the Schools 16,* 93–100.

Foster, S. L., & Ritchey, W. L. (1979). Issues in the assessment of social competence in children. *Journal of Applied Behavior Analysis, 12,* 625–638.

Gesten, E., Flores de Apodaca, R., Rains, M., Weissberg, R., & Cowen, E. (1979). Promoting peer-related social competence in schools. In M. W. Kent & J. Rolf (Eds.), *Social competence in children*. Hanover, NH: University Press of New England.

Giebink, G. W., Stover, D., & Fahl, M. (1968). Teaching adaptive responses to frustration to emotionally disturbed boys. *Journal of Consulting and Clinical Psychology, 32*, 366–368.

Gottman, J. (1977). The effects of a modeling film on social isolation in preschool children: A methodological investigation. *Journal of Abnormal Child Psychology, 5*, 69–78.

Gottman, J., Gonso, J., & Rasmussen, B. (1975). Social interaction, social competence and friendship in children. *Child Development, 46*, 709–718.

Gottman, J., Gonso, J., & Schuler, P. (1976). Teaching social skills to isolated children. *Journal of Abnormal Child Psychology, 4*, 179–197.

Greenwood, C. R., Walker, H. M., Todd, N. M., & Hops, H. (1977). *Normative and descriptive analysis of preschool free play social interactions* (Report No. 29). Eugene, OR: University of Oregon.

Hartup, W. W. (1970). Peer interaction and social organization. In P. H. Mussen (Ed.), *Carmichael's manual of child psychology* (Vol. 2). New York: Wiley.

Hartup, W. W., Glazer, J. A., & Charlesworth, R. (1967). Peer reinforcement and sociometric status. *Child Development, 38*, 1017–1024.

Hops, H., Walker, H. N., & Greenwood, C. R. (1979). Peers: A program for remediating social withdrawal in a school setting; Aspects for research and development process. In L. A. Hammerlink (Ed.), *The history and future of the developmentally disabled: Problematic and methodological issues*. New York: Bruner-Mazel.

Houtz, J., & Feldhusen, J. (1976). The modification of fourth graders' problem solving abilities. *Journal of Psychology, 93*, 229–237.

Hymel, S., & Asher, S. R. (1977, March). *Assessment and training of isolated children's social skills*. Paper presented at the biennial meeting of the Society for Research in Child Development, New Orleans, CA.

Israel, A. C., & O'Leary, K. D. (1973). Developing correspondence between children's words and deeds. *Child Development, 44*, 575–581.

Kagan, J., & Moss, H. A. (1962). *Birth to maturity: A study in psychological development*. New York: Wiley.

Keller, M., & Carlson, P. (1974). The use of symbolic modeling to promote social skills in preschool children with low levels of social responsiveness. *Child Development, 45*, 912–919.

Kirby, F. D., & Toler, H. C. (1970). Modification of preschool isolate behavior: A case study. *Journal of Applied Behavior Analysis, 3*, 309–314.

Kohlberg, L., LaCrosse, J., & Ricks, D. (1972). The predictability of adult mental health from childhood behavior. In B. Wolman (Ed.), *Manual of child psychopathology*. New York: McGraw-Hill.

Kohn, M. (1977). *Social competence, symptoms and underachievement in childhood: A longitudinal perspective*. New York: Winston.

Ladd, G. W. (1979). *Social skills and peer acceptance: The facts of social learning methods for training verbal social skills*. Paper presented at the biennial meeting of the Society of Research and Child Development, San Francisco.

Laughlin, F. (1954). *The peer status of sixth and seventh grade children*. Bureau of Publications, Teachers College, Columbia University.

Libet, J. M., & Lewinsohn, P. M. (1973). Concept of social skill with special reference to the behavior of depressed persons. *Journal of Consulting and Clinical Psychology, 40*, 304–312.

Lovaas, I., Freitas, K., & Whalen, C. (1972). The establishment of limitation and its use for the development of complex behavior in schizophrenic children. *Behaviour Research and Therapy, 5,* 171–181.

Mannarino, A. P., Durlak, J. A., Christy, M., & Magnussen, M. G. (1982). Evaluation of social competence training in the schools. *Journal of School Psychology, 20,* 11–19.

McClure, L. F., Chinsky, J. M., & Larcen, S. W. (1978). Enhancing social problem-solving performance in an elementary school setting. *Journal of Educational Psychology, 70,* 504–513.

Michelson, L. (1981). Behavioral approaches to prevention. In L. Michelson, M. Hersen, & S. Turner (Eds.), *Future perspectives in behavior therapy.* New York: Plenum.

Michelson, L., Foster, S., & Ritchey, W. (1981). Behavioral assessment of children's social skills. In B. Lahey & A. E. Kazdin (Eds.), *Advances in child clinical psychology* (Vol. 4). New York: Plenum.

Michelson, L., Mannarino, A. P., Marchione, K., & Martin, P. (1982a). *Relative and combined efficacy of behavioral and cognitive problem solving social skills programs with elementary school children.* Unpublished manuscript, University of Pittsburgh.

Michelson, L., Mannarino, A. P., Marchione, K., Stern, M., Figueroa, J., & Beck, S. (1982b). *A comparative outcome study of behavioral social skills training, cognitive-problem solving and Rogerian control treatment for psychiatric outpatient children.* Unpublished manuscript, University of Pittsburgh.

Michelson, L., Sugai, D., Wood, R., & Kazdin, A. E. (1983). *Social skills assessment and training with children: An empirical handbook.* New York, Plenum.

Michelson, L., & Wood, R. (1980a). A group assertive training program for elementary school children. *Child Behavior Therapy, 2,* 1–9.

Michelson, L., & Wood, R. (1980b). Behavioral assessment and training of children's social skills. In M. Hersen, P. Miller, & R. Eisler (Eds.), *Progress in behavior modification* (Vol. 9). New York: Academic Press.

Michelson, L., & Wood, R. (1982a). Development and psychometric properties of the children's assertive behavior scale. *Journal of Behavioral Assessment, 4,* 3–14.

Miller, N., & Maruyama, G. (1976). Ordinal position and peer popularity. *Journal of Personality and Social Psychology, 33,* 123–131.

Morris, H. H. (1956). Aggressive behavior disorders in children. A follow-up study. *American Journal of Psychiatry, 112,* 991–997.

Muma, J. R. (1965). Peer evaluation and academic performance. *Personnel and Guidance Journal, 44,* 405–409.

Muma, J. R. (1968). Peer evaluation and academic achievement in performance classes. *Personnel and Guidance Journal, 46,* 580–585.

Noble, C. G., & Nolan, J. D. (1976). Effect of student verbal behavior on classroom teacher behavior. *Journal of Educational Psychology, 68,* 342–346.

Nowicki, S., & Strickland, B. R. (1971). *A locus of control scale for children.* Paper presented at the Annual Meeting of the American Psychological Association, Washington, DC.

O'Connor, R. D. (1969). Modification of social withdrawal through symbolic modeling. *Journal of Applied Behavior Analysis, 2,* 15–22.

O'Connor, R. D. (1972). The relative efficacy of modeling, shaping and the combined procedures for the modification of social withdrawal. *Journal of Abnormal Psychology, 79,* 327–334.

Oden, S., & Asher, S. R. (1977). Coaching children in social skills for friendship making. *Child Development, 48,* 495–506.

Ollendick, T. H., & Hersen, M. (1979). Social skills training for juvenile delinquents. *Behaviour Research and Therapy, 17,* 547–554.

Patterson, G. R., Reid, J. G., Jones, R. R., & Conger, R. E. (1975). *A social learning approach to family intervention* (Vol. 1). Eugene, OR: Castilla.

Pinkston, E. M., Reise, N. M., LeBlanc, J. M., & Baer, D. M. (1972). Independent control of a preschool child's aggression and peer interaction by contingent teacher attention. *Journal of Applied Behavior Analysis, 6,* 115–124.

Platt, J. J., & Spivack, G. (1974). Means of solving real life problems: psychiatric patients vs. controls in cross cultural comparisons in normal females. *Journal of Community Psychology, 2,* 45–48.

Platt, J. J., Spivack, G., Altman, N., Altman, D., & Peizer, S. B. (1974). Adolescent problem solving thinking. *Journal of Consulting and Clinical Psychology, 42,* 787–793.

Porterfield, D. V., & Schlichting, G. F. (1961). Peer status and reading achievement. *Journal of Educational Research, 54,* 291–297.

Quay, H. (1972). Patterns of aggression, withdrawal and immaturity. In H. Quay & J. Werry (Eds.), *Psychopathological disorders of childhood.* New York: Wiley.

Richard, B. A., & Dodge, K. A. (1982). Social maladjustment and problem solving in school-aged children. *Journal of Consulting and Clinical Psychology, 50,* 226–233.

Rinn, R. C., & Markle, A. (1979). Modification of social skill deficits in children. In A. S. Bellack & M. Hersen (Eds.), *Research and practice in social skills training.* New York: Plenum.

Risley, T. R., & Hart, B. (1976). Developing correspondence between the nonverbal and verbal behavior of preschool children. *Journal of Applied Behavior Analysis, 9,* 335–354.

Robbins, L. N. (1966). *Deviant children grown up.* Baltimore: Williams and Wilkins.

Roff, M. (1961). Children's social interactions and young adult bad conduct. *Journal of Abnormal Social Psychology, 63,* 333–337.

Roff, M., Robins, L. N., & Pollock, M. (1972). *Life history research and psychopathology.* Minneapolis: University of Minnesota Press.

Roff, M., Sells, S. B., and Golden, M. M. (1972). *Social adjustment and personality development in children.* Minneapolis: University of Minnesota Press.

Rogers-Warren, A., & Baer, D. (1976). Correspondence between saying and doing: Teaching children to share and praise. *Journal of Applied Behavior Analysis, 9,* 335–354.

Ross, A. O. (1981). *Child behavior therapy.* New York: Wiley.

Ross, D. M., Ross, S. A., & Evans, T. A. (1971). The modification of extreme social withdrawal by modeling with guided participation. *Journal of Behavior Therapy and Experimental Psychiatry, 2,* 273–279.

Schindler, P. (1941). The psychogenesis of alocholism. *Quarterly Journal of the Study of Alcoholism, 2,* 277–292.

Shure, M. B., & Spivack, G. (1974). *Mental health program for kindergarten children: A cognitive approach to solving interpersonal problems.* Philadelphia: Department of Mental Health Services, Community Mental Health/Mental Retardation Center.

Shure, M. B., & Spivack, G. (1974). *Preschool interpersonal problem solving test manual.* Philadelphia: Department of Mental Health Serices, Community Mental Health/Mental Retardation Center.

Shure, M. B., & Spivack, G. (1975). *Training mothers to help their children solve real life problems.* Paper presented at the meeting for the Society for Research and Child Development, Denver.

Shure, M. B., & Spivack, G. (1978). *Problem solving techniques in child rearing.* San Francisco: Josie Bass.

Shure, M. B., & Spivack, G. (1979). Interpersonal cognitive problem solving in primary prevention: Programming for preschool and kindergarten children. *Journal of Clinical Child Psychology, 2,* 89–94.

Shure, M. B., & Spivack, G. (1980). Interpersonal problem solving as a mediator of behavioral adjustment in preschool and kindergarten children. *Journal of Applied Developmental Psychology, 1,* 29–44.

Stokes, T. F., & Baer, D. M. (1977). Am implicit technology of generalization. *Journal of Applied Behavior Analysis, 10,* 349–367.

Stone, G., Heinz, W., & Schmidt, G. (1975). Teaching mental health behavior to elementary school children. *Professional Psychology, 6,* 34–40.

Strain, P. S. (1977). An experimental analysis of peer social initiations on the behavior of withdrawn preschool children: Some training and generalization of facts. *Journal of Abnormal Child Psychology, 5,* 445–455.

Strain, P. S., Cook, T. P., & Appoloni, T. (1976). *Teaching exceptional children: Assessing and modifying social behavior.* New York: Academic Press.

Strain, P. S., & Fox, J. J. (1981). Peer as behavior change agents for withdrawing classmates. In B. B. Leahey & A. E. Kazdin (Eds.), *Advances in clinical child psychology,* (Vol. 4). New York: Plenum.

Strain, P. S., Shores, R. E., & Timm, M. A. (1977). Effects of peer social initiations on the behavior of withdrawn preschool children. *Journal of Applied Behavior Analysis, 10,* 289–298.

Strain, P. S., & Timm, M. A. (1974). An experimental analysis of social interaction between a behaviorally disordered preschool child and her classmate peer. *Journal of Applied Behavior Analysis, 7,* 583–592.

Sugai, D. P. *The implementation and evaluation of a social skills training program for preadolescents: A preventative approach.* (1978, November). Paper presented at the Annual Meeting of the Association for the Advancement of Behavior Therapy, Chicago.

Todd, N. M., Walker, H. M., Greenwood, C. R., & Hops, M. (1976, August). *Manipulating peer social interactions within an experimental classroom setting.* Paper presented at the 84th Annual Meeting of the American Psychological Association, Washington, DC.

Trower, P. M. (1979). Fundamentals of interpersonal behavior: A social-psychological perspective. In A. S. Bellack & M. Hersen (Eds.), *Research and practice in social skills training.* New York: Plenum.

Urbain, E. S., & Kendall, P. C. (1980). Review of social-cognitive problem-solving interventions with children. *Psychological Bulletin, 88,* 109–143.

Van Hasselt, V. B., Hersen, M., Bellack, A. S., & Whitehall, A. B. (1979). Social skill assessment and training for children. An evaluative review. *Behavior Research and Therapy, 17,* 413–438.

Waldrop, M. F., & Halverson, C. F. (1975). Intensive and extensive peer behaviors: Longitudinal and cross sectional analyses. *Child Development, 46,* 19–26.

Walker, H. M., Greenwood, C. R., Hops, H., & Todd, N. M. (1979). Differential effects of reinforcing topographic components of social interaction. *Behavior Modification, 3,* 291–321.

Weissberg, R. P., Cohen, E. L., Lotyczewski, B. S., & Gesten, E. L. (1983). The primary mental health project: Seven consecutive years of programmatic research. *Journal of Consulting and Clinical Psychology, 51,* 100–107.

Weissberg, R. P., Gesten, E. L., Cornike, C. L., Toro, P. A., Rapkin, B. D., Davidson, E., & Cohen, E. L. (1982). Social problem solving skills training: A competent building intervention with second-grade children. *American Journal of Community Psychology, 9,* 411–423.

Weissberg, R. P., Gesten, E. L., Rapkin, B. D., Cowen, E., Davidson, E., Flores de Apodaca, R., & McKim, B. J. (1981). The evaluation of a social problem-solving–training program for suburban and inner-city third-grade children. *Journal of Consulting and Clinical Psychology, 49,* 251–261.

Winder, C., & Rau, L. (1962). Parental attitudes associated with social deviance in preadolescent boys. *Journal of Abnormal Social Psychology, 69,* 418–424.

CHAPTER 10

Programming the Generalization of Children's Social Behavior

Trevor F. Stokes
Pamela G. Osnes

INTRODUCTION

Social behavior may be defined broadly as interactive responses within a social context, or they may be defined more strictly as interactive responses at least partially controlled by reciprocal reinforcement within the social behavior interaction. Hake and Olvera (1978), in an analysis of cooperation and social behavior, proposed that social and cooperative behavior should be more precisely defined as occurring only when they are maintained by reinforcers within the reciprocal contingencies of the social interaction rather than being maintained by another reinforcer that is external to the social interaction itself. Thus, each person's behavior functions as a discriminative stimulus for the other in a way that the social behaviors are under the control of social antecedent and consequent stimuli. Certainly, adherence to such a definition of social behavior in research will advance our understanding of social phenomena. Unfortunately, however, this sophisticated and appropriate definition of social behavior has not yet guided a large portion of research. Therefore, the content of this chapter is guided by a broad definition of social behavior, while acknowledging and recommending the more thorough and complete approach of Hake and Olvera (1978).

There are many behaviors that are part of the broad area of social behavior. By its name, *social behavior* suggests behavior(s) that can only

407

be exhibited in the presence of, and in the context of, possible interaction with other persons. Speaking is an important social behavior. Approaches to others, eye contact, and body orientation are prerequisites to socially appropriate speech. Responding to approaches of others is a behavior vital to the perpetuation of other social contacts. Sharing and cooperation are both integral components of social behavior, usually with cooperation viewed as a broader area than sharing. The skill of cooperating with others is one that involves sharing (e.g., toys, classroom notes at home, space at the office), compliance (e.g., with parents' instructions, with household responsibilities and rules, with employers' instructions), and verbal–nonverbal correspondence (i.e., a child telling his/her parents she/he will come home at a specific time and actually coming home at that time, or an individual telling a teacher–employer she/he will complete a task at a prearranged time and actually completing the task by the time).

The exhibition of polite behavior is a social behavior that occurs concurrently with other social behaviors. Polite verbal behavior includes the use of words and phrases such as "please," "thank you," and "excuse me"; helping others carry heavy materials or waiting at the school door to allow others to enter before you are examples of polite nonverbal behaviors. Other important social behaviors include affective behaviors such as smiling, touching, hugging, and handshaking.

Like any behavior, social behavior can be exhibited either in appropriate or inappropriate ways. Aggression, disruption, and withdrawal are examples of inappropriate social behaviors. The time when the behavior is exhibited, the frequency and duration of the behavior, and the intensity of the behavior all clarify the appropriateness of the behavior. A change in previously demonstrated skills also determines appropriateness.

With social behavior encompassing such a large range of behaviors, it is hardly surprising that the analysis of such behavior is often a detailed and tedious process. The following case illustrates the complexity of what at first glance may appear to be a straightforward deficit in the exhibition of appropriate social behavior.

A CASE STUDY IN GENERALIZATION

Assessment

Patricia was a 7-year-old girl who was brought to the local mental health center by her mother, Joni. The presenting problems were school phobia and social withdrawal. To the behavioral psychologist who began working with the family, Patricia appeared to be an attractive, intelligent second-grader. Her 30-year-old mother appeared to be concerned, tired, and somewhat tense, which the psychologist did not find surprising considering the presenting problem. Pat, as she was called by her family, had one sibling, John, an active, well-behaved 3-year-old. (All names are pseudonymes).

The psychologist's first task was to get a complete history of the problem behavior, Pat's skills in the area of social behavior, and of the family's environment. The family had moved only a month ago to the university town where Joni had accepted a nursing position at the medical center. Six months prior to moving, Joni had gone through a "messy divorce" from her 33-year-old spouse, Pat's father. Joni reported that this had been quite sudden and unexpected, and she was opposed to the divorce. Because of her husband's insistence, Joni obtained a divorce and began applying for nursing positions in her hometown, where her parents still reside. A position was obtained shortly thereafter, and the family moved to the town of 50,000 in a predominantly rural state.

Joni reported that the children had behaved well through the traumatic period around the divorce and the move, although she admitted she had been in "quite a daze," and it was possible she had overlooked behaviors in her children that may have indicated they were tense or anxious. Pat had completed the first grade, where she was reported to have been an average to above-average student. Her teacher told Joni that Pat got along well with the other children, seemed to be quite well-adjusted, and was a "joy to be around." A report written by the school psychologist before Pat was admitted to first grade verified the teacher's comments. Pat had performed well on all academic assessments administered prior to her placement in first grade.

The problem behaviors began the first day Pat was to attend her new school. She had begun second grade prior to moving; therefore, the academic year had been in progress 1 month when Pat was to begin attending her new school. According to Joni, Pat yelled, cried, and screamed when she got out of bed the first day she was to go. Joni explained to her that it was natural and all right to be a little scared, but that she would just have to go to find out that everything would be fine. When this strategy failed to calm Pat, Joni began to threaten her with losing the opportunity to go to play at the park after school "if she didn't straighten up." Eventually Joni forcefully dressed Pat, took her to the breakfast table, where Pat refused to eat, then took her to the car and drove her to school. When they got to the school, Joni described Pat's behavior as sullen—she failed to establish eye contact or smile but answered the questions the principal and teacher asked her. Talking to the teacher at the end of the day, Joni was told that Pat had done the tasks presented to her but had not attempted to speak to anyone all day. She had watched other children intently at recesses and lunch, but had avoided eye contact with them and did not respond to their invitations to play. The teacher assured Joni that this was not uncommon for a child in a new school, especially for a child whose parents had recently been divorced. She told Joni she would wait for Pat to "settle in" and would place no special demands on her other than those required by the academic tasks until Pat appeared to be more comfortable with her new surroundings.

Joni was somewhat reassured by the teacher's analysis of Pat's behavior and by Pat's behavior itself after school. She seemed to be her "old self" from the time she stepped into the car to the time she went to bed that night. Before going to bed, Joni made Pat promise "to be good for Grandma" the next day, because Joni's mother, Dorothy, would be responsible for sending Pat to school.

Unfortunately, the problem persisted. Pat refused to ride the bus, so Dorothy drove her to and from school daily. Joni was getting increasingly upset and angry at Pat's behavior, but Dorothy insisted all Pat needed was some love, understanding, and tender loving care to learn to be more comfortable in her new environment. This became the source of tension between Joni and Dorothy, who began to argue frequently about how to approach the problem. When a co-worker of Joni's suggested she go to a psychologist, Joni willingly went in spite of her mother's insinuation that "Joni should learn to handle these things herself."

When questioned by the psychologist about the presence of other problem behaviors, Joni responded that there was nothing problematic, just the "typical kid stuff." When she was asked what this meant, Joni revealed that Pat had always been aggressive toward her brother and never shared toys with him, that Pat frequently refused to eat the food prepared at mealtimes, and that Pat usually tantrummed when it was her bedtime. These problems were responded to in a variety of ways by Joni. When Pat behaved inappropriately with John, she sometimes ignored it, sometimes threatened to spank Pat, sometimes explained to Pat that it was not nice to "be mean" to her little brother, and sometimes spanked Pat. When Pat refused to eat her food, Joni sometimes would give her something different to eat, sometimes would ignore it and let Pat sit at the table until she ate it, sometimes would threaten her with a spanking or with losing the opportunity to watch TV, and sometimes would spank her or take away a privilege. The pattern of Joni's behavior was similar when Pat refused to go to bed. Sometimes Pat would go to bed at bedtime, sometimes she would go to bed and get up several times, sometimes she would fall asleep on the living room couch and Joni would carry her to bed later. Joni often would ignore these bedtime problems to try to avoid a confrontation with Pat, but sometimes she threatened Pat and sometimes spanked her and put her to bed.

After obtaining this information, the psychologist arranged to observe Pat interacting in a play setting with John, and to observe Pat in the classroom and during recess at school.

Functional Analysis

After compiling the information from these assessment techniques, the psychologist determined she had enough information to analyze the behaviors of Joni and Pat to determine the function of each. She analyzed the interactions of Pat and Joni, Pat and Dorothy, Pat and John, and Pat and her teacher–classmates, attending especially to the paradigms of positive and negative reinforcement. Pat's inappropriate social behaviors apparently resulted in avoidance of tasks both at home and at school and in accessibility to increased attention from her mother, grandmother, teacher, and, to some extent, from her classmates. By this time, Pat's behavior was the topic of many discussions by her peers concerning "why that girl doesn't talk." Dorothy's increased affectionate behaviors toward Pat resulted in a temporary decrease in Pat's early morning crying, as did her agreeing to drive Pat to school instead of riding the bus. This resulted in an additional benefit to Pat—she gained an extra 20 minutes of contact with her grandmother in addition to avoiding her peers on the bus for the same amount of time daily. The angry behaviors Joni exhibited toward Pat (i.e., threatening, spanking, explaining, pleading) also resulted in a temporary decrease in the duration and intensity of Pat's early morning crying. Likewise, the variety of strategies Joni used in response to Pat's other inappropriate social behaviors (i.e., aggressing toward John, failing to share with John, exhibiting demands at mealtime and bedtime) sometimes effectively reduced the duration and intensity of the inappropriate behaviors, albeit temporarily. Therefore, Joni's and Dorothy's behaviors to manage Pat were probably negatively reinforced. They effectively decreased Pat's inappropriate behavior temporarily. However, Pat's inappropriate social behaviors were being reinforced by the resulting avoidance of bus riding, peer contact, and demands from the teacher, the classmates, and Dorothy. Combined with the additional attention Pat was receiving from the adults in her environment and the intermittency of her contact with the various consequences of her behaviors, Pat's inappropriate social behaviors appeared to be on a powerful intermittent schedule of positive reinforcement which could have been maintaining them.

In addition to this, Pat's appropriate social behaviors were frequently ignored by the adults in her environment. Occasionally, she did initiate a short conversation with her peers at school, to which the teacher did not respond. She frequently played appropriately after school and occasionally sampled nonpreferred foods on her plate before refusing to eat them. These behaviors resulted in no attention from Joni.

Treatment and Intervention

Following this functional analysis (Stokes, 1985), the psychologist designed interventions in the home and school settings, which interrupted the negative reinforcement cycle and established positive consequences for Pat when she exhibited appropriate behaviors incompatible with the targeted problem behaviors. The interventions incorporated the use of a verbal mediation strategy involving the training of a reliable correspondence between verbalizations and peformance of the related behaviors. The psychologist hypothesized that these procedures would expose Pat to a naturally occurring community of reinforcement and pleasant attention from adults, which would be available to Pat in any setting in which she was present. After being consistently exposed to positive consequences for doing what she said she would (i.e., riding the bus to school, talking to her peers daily with changing and increasing criteria as the initiations increased, playing nicely and sharing toys with John, eating the designated portion of all the food on her plate, and going to bed at the predetermined time), the psychologist hypothesized that Pat's inappropriate social behaviors would decrease and her appropriate social behaviors would increase in frequency and duration and would maintain with only infrequent setbacks. Part of the program also included training Joni to manage her delivery of consequences, especially interpersonal and social consequences, so that she would better be able to modify Pat's behavior.

Given this summary of a functional assessment and treatment plan, how effective are these interventions likely to be for facilitating generalized behavior changes? Before analyzing this intervention from the generalization programming perspective, the concept of generalization and strategies for programming generalization are considered. A discussion of programming tactics used in Patricia's case are presented at the conclusion of the chapter.

THE CONCEPT OF GENERALIZATION

A successful outcome in any behavior modification project must be evaluated according to both the utility and the function of the directly targeted behavior change and the value of extant generalized behavior changes. Thus, in the preceding example, it is first important that Pat learn how to initiate and maintain positive interactions with her peers at school. It is also important, however, that she be able to develop similar positive interactions with peers at home and in her neighborhood. In addition, it is necessary that Pat's mother, Joni, learn new strategies to effectively manage Pat's behavior problem. The application of those techniques across time is also necessary so that Pat's behavior remains under the control of appropriate parental contingencies. Facilitating the development and refinement of Pat's appropriate social initiations can be accomplished by her peers. They also need to continue to facilitate the development and refinement of other interaction behaviors such as sharing and cooperation in play. That the behavior modification procedures initially accomplish appropriate behavior changes is essential. That those changes generalize across settings, children, behaviors, and time is critical to the broad clinical significance of the procedures for the child. Undoubtedly, the attainment of those generalized behavior changes is not accidental. It is usually insufficient to complete initial behavior changes and merely hope for the display of generalized changes (Stokes & Baer, 1977). Specific generalization programming tactics probably need to be implemented. That is, specific procedures may need to be implemented in addition to the original intervention procedures, in order to ensure that generalized behavior change is accomplished.

Definition of Generalization

Generalization has been defined in the applied literature as "the occurrence of relevant behavior under different non-training conditions (i.e., across subjects, settings, people, behaviors, and/or time) without the scheduling of the same events in those conditions as had been scheduled in the training conditions" (Stokes & Baer, 1977, p. 350). Essentially, this is a cost-effectiveness definition, emphasizing that generalization of behavior changes may be claimed whenever those relevant behaviors occur in circumstances different to the original behavior changes, and those changes are accomplished through the use of procedures less extensive or costly than that required of direct intervention in those different environmental conditions. This definition is descriptive and topographical in nature. It does not itself make clear the functional contingencies and environmental variables responsible for the occurrence of the observed generalization. It does, however, delineate some minimal conditions under which generalization of behavior changes may be said to have occurred.

Four types of generalization have been discussed by Forehand and Atkeson (1977). *Temporal generalization* concerns the durability or maintenance of behavior changes following the termination of the treatment interventions. *Generalization across settings* refers to the display of treatment changes in settings outside of the initial therapeutic setting. *Generalization across behaviors* is noted when changes are recorded in behaviors not specifically targeted for the treatment. *Sibling generalization* concerns changes in the behaviors of the targeted child's siblings, and is essentially the same as *generalization across subjects*.

In a similar classification system, Drabman, Hammer, and Rosenbaum (1979) described 16 possible categories that may be assessed in determining the occurrence or nonoccurrence of generalized behavior changes. Their generalization map proposed four major classes to describe possible generalization effects: across subjects, settings, behaviors, and time. *Generalization across subjects* was noted when there are changes in the behavior of a nontarget subject as a result of an intervention with a different subject, even though experimental contingency manipulations are not directed at that nontarget subject. *Generalization across settings* was noted when the subjects' behavior was displayed in settings that are different from the training environment. Major differences in settings, for example, school and home, as well as less comprehensive differences, for example, different teachers supervising play during recess, are considered. Drabman et al. (1979) define a setting change as a change in salient discriminative stimuli. Generalization across behaviors was noted when there are changes in behaviors of the subject even though those behaviors are not specifically targeted through contingency manipulations. This type of generalization is sometimes referred to as the demonstration of collateral or side-effects after intervention with a specific behavior or defined set of behaviors. *Generalization across time* was noted when behavior changes continue, maintain, or are durable following the withdrawal of specific contingency manipulations. The various combinations of these 4 major classes of generalization produced the 16 classes of generalization in the map described by Drabman et al. (1979).

These classification systems help to categorize and summarize the research literature according to the topographical types of generalization that have been documented. They do not focus attention on the functional relationships between certain therapeutic procedures and the demonstration of those resulting generalized behavior changes.

Some examples of the generalization of behavior across subjects, settings, people, behaviors, and time follow. An assessment of generalization across subjects was conducted in the study by Barton and Bevirt (1981). They examined the development and generalization of sharing among 4- and 5-year-old preschoolers enrolled in a Head Start program. Training of the sharing involved instructions, peer modeling, rehearsal, prompting, and praising during a structured session. During a subsequent free-play period, the children were prompted to share and praised for sharing behaviors, which included handing materials to another child and simultaneously manipulating materials with another child working on a common project. Barton and Bevirt then proceeded to examine the generalization of sharing to different small groups of children. They found that when trained and nontrained peers of children were present in the same group, sharing increased, although mostly as a function of the interactions among trained children. Nevertheless, there was also increased sharing by the nontrained children, among themselves and with the trained children.

An example of generalization across settings is the study by Altman (1971). Preschool children received edible reinforcers for task cooperation in a laboratory task. Generalization of interactive and cooperative behaviors during play in the preschool was assessed. Increased social interactions were observed during the play, both to partners who had participated in training and to other children present in play.

Stokes, Baer, and Jackson (1974) examined the generalization across staff members of retarded children's greetings. Initially, the children's greeting of staff members of their institutional dormitory were assessed. Subsequently, the generalization of greetings after training by one or by two trainers was examined. The results showed that training by one person was not usually sufficient to promote generalization of the greeting to other staff members who had not participated in the training of the greeting response. However, following training by two persons concurrently, the children reliably greeted more than 20 members of the institution staff, who probed for the generalization of trained greetings.

Elder, Edelstein, and Narick (1979) presented another example of generalization across behaviors. A social-skills training program, consisting of instructions, modeling, and feedback during role-playing was used to increase nonaggressive interactions by aggressive adolescent psychiatric patients. The adolescents received training on specific role-playing scenes relating to interruptions, responses to criticism, threats, and teasing, and the subjects' requests for others to change their behaviors. There was a prompt change during role-playing of treatment scenes, such that the adolescents consistently displayed more socially appropriate behaviors. Furthermore, the subjects showed generalization to non-treated role-playing scenes. In addition, there were concomitant decreases in fines within the ward's operating token economy point system, and in the amount of time spent by the subjects in seclusion timeout for inappropriate occurrences of the three targeted behaviors.

A comprehensive example of the analysis of generalization across time is provided in the study by Paine, Hops, Walker, Greenwood, Fleischman, and Guild (1982). Elementary school children who exhibited low rates of social interaction with their peers were trained to increase their social behaviors, which included initiations and responses to peer social initiations and continuing interactions with peers. These intervention procedures included two components: social tutoring sessions in which social behaviors were modeled, role-played, and praised, and a token reinforcement procedure operated during recess, which involved the target subjects and their peers. Intervention periods were repeated a number of times and were interspersed with baseline assessments to determine the maintenance of the improved social behavior. The results showed that after these repeated treatment periods, some of the children maintained their appropriate social interaction above their initial baseline levels and within the normative range of their grade peers.

Functional Control of Generalization

The generalization of behavior changes has long been recognized as a major issue in the development of significant behaviors in children by using behavior analysis and modification techniques (Baer, Wolf, & Risley, 1968). Although the technology relevant to the accomplishment of generalized behavior changes has lagged behind the important initial development of a technology to accomplish meaningful direct behavior change, that lagging technology has burgeoned. After a review of the literature, Stokes and Baer (1977) outlined a number of procedures that contributed to an implicit technology of generalization. These generalization-programming techniques included the introduction of newly trained behaviors to natural maintaining contingencies; the training of multiple and sufficient exemplars of behaviors and training environments; the use of loose training strategies that involve less tightly controlled training circumstances; the employment of indiscriminable contingencies such that the contingencies of reinforcement, punishment, and extinction are less predictable; the scheduling of salient common stimuli in both training and nontraining environments; the mediation of generalization, whereby the child's own behavior, such as language, may be transported to generalization environments and serve a discriminative function controlling behaviors in those environments; and, to occasionally reinforce generalization itself, as if it were an operant-response class.

Stokes and Baer's (1977) taxonomy of research on the assessment and programming of generalization focused on the processes by which generalized behavior changes are obtained. Working from a broad topographical definition of generalization, which allowed incorporation of most of the studies that applied researchers had proposed as relating in some way to generalization, some general tactics for programming generalization were inferred. The focus of the paper was to examine general techniques or classes of techniques that were functionally related to the display of generalized behavior changes. Specifically, the categories described some functional contingencies documented in the research literature that systematically related to the occurrence of generalization, which was itself broadly and topographically defined.

Unfortunately, not all studies fit easily into the generalization-promotion categories. Some studies apparently were examples of more than one general tactic, and there was some apparent overlap in the principles in different classes. Therefore, in order to further develop the classification system, and to emphasize the more general principles underlying the classification, a revision of the Stokes and Baer (1977) categories is proposed. Each of the original seven categories of generalization programming is included, some with expansion. There are 11 tactics that may be grouped into three general areas or principles of generalization programming, as follows:

1. Take advantage of natural communities of reinforcement
   a. Teach relevant behaviors
   b. Modify environments supporting maladaptive behaviors
   c. Recruit natural communities of reinforcement
2. Train diversely
   a. Use sufficient stimulus exemplars
   b. Use sufficient response exemplars
   c. Train loosely
   d. Use indiscriminable contingencies
   e. Reinforce unprompted generalization
3. Incorporate functional mediators
   a. Use common physical stimuli

b. Use common social stimuli
c. Use self-mediated stimuli

The following section of the chapter considers each of these categories in more detail as they relate to the generalization of children's social behavior.

GENERALIZATION OF CHILDREN'S
SOCIAL BEHAVIOR

Take Advantage of Natural Communities
of Reinforcement

Teach Relevant Behaviors

Social behavior is an eminently suitable target for entry into and successful capture by a natural community of reinforcement. A natural community of reinforcement is usually an existing contingency in a particular environment that apparently occurs without special programming and that functions to increase and maintain those behaviors that come within its operating environment. Most natural reinforcement communities are likely to provide social consequences as controlling reinforcers. For example, relatively skilled greetings by one person are likely to consistently evoke a pleasant reaction from other people in most settings. To the extent that such a greeting reliably captures a positive consequence and that consequence functions to increase greetings and probably some additional pleasant social interaction, that person has come under the control of a readily available natural community of reinforcement. Children's initiations and invitations to share may similarly come under the control of a peers' typical consequences, those of reciprocal sharing, interaction, and play. In this example, the consequences are both social and material, the sharing of toys and materials.

Hendrickson, Strain, Tremblay, and Shores (1982), for example, showed that social approach behaviors such as suggesting a play activity, offering to share, and providing assistance during play reliably evoked positive social behavior in withdrawn children. Apparently, the social initiations set up a reciprocal interaction likely to maintain further social interaction and play. In a similar fashion, Strain, Shores, and Timm (1977) showed that withdrawn children respond with positive social behavior to their peers' social approaches. The subjects also increased their own social initiations, which are likely to contact a similar natural community of reinforcement.

A natural community of reinforcement may exist, but a child's behavior might not come effectively within its control. Relevant there is the notion of *trapping*. In the study reported by Baer and Wolf (1970), a preschool child initially had a low rate of skilled interactions with peers. Apparently, the child was not skilled enough to consistently come into contact with the positive consequences of engaging in interaction and play with the peers. Therefore, the preschool teachers prompted other children to interact with the child and reinforced appropriate interactions. Over time, it was shown that the teachers' control over the interactions diminished and that the target child's interactions maintained, independent of the consequences provided by the teacher. Thus, the child needed only to be introduced effectively to the natural community of reinforcement. An effective introduction involved increasing the skill proficiency through the provision of artificial teacher consequences, which maintained the behaviors at a sufficient level to come into frequent contact with the positive consequences that occurred in the children's interaction and play. That is, the natural community of reinforcement only required effective entry; once the behavior was displayed within its environment with a suitable frequency, it was trapped.

In a similar fashion, the development of social behavior may occur as a collateral change when a nonsocial behavior change is accomplished which brings the child into more frequent social contact with peers. For example, Buell, Stoddard, Harris, and Baer (1968) reinforced the use of outdoor play equipment by a young girl. This modification, in turn, brought the child into natural social contact with peers. The data showed that in addition to the increased use of the play equipment, collateral positive changes were also noted in touching, verbalizing, and playing with other children.

Unfortunately, a natural community of reinforcement may not always exist for a particular behavior. A natural community of reinforcement is not documented until its effect on a particular behavior is demonstrated. By definition, the reinforcement must function to increase the behavior that the consequence follows. Therefore, the apparent existence of a natural community of reinforcement for one child's behavior does not guarantee that the same existing consequences will be a reinforcer for similar behavior by another child. This point is important in any intervention, for it should never be assumed that the same consequences, whether occurring reliably or naturally or not, will always function in the same way for each child. Of course, it is a good sign if similar consequences usually have similar effects on similar behaviors, but that is not a guarantee in any particular instance.

It should also be noted with caution that although there is a core of literature describing natural communities of reinforcement, experimental documentations of such contingencies and their effects are sparse and speculation is extensive. The recommended approach is therefore one that does not expect to regularly capitalize on natural communities of reinforcement. They may be few and their effects fleeting. Nevertheless, there are some tactics that may be proposed. For example, whenever possible, the behaviors taught should be those that frequently contact positive consequences (see Ayllon & Azrin, 1968). These are likely to be useful, high-rate behaviors the skilled performance of which is followed by a rich schedule of positive consequences. Greetings and other forms of positive social initiations are examples of such behaviors. Hopkins (1968), for example, examined smiling by two retarded children. He found that the children's smiling reliably came under the control of social consequences, such as people talking to them, after a more intrusive reinforcer (candy) was used to increase the rate of smiling. Apparently, there is a natural community of reinforcement for a high rate of smiling.

Effective language, communication, and interpersonal skills are also examples of behaviors likely to evoke positive consequences from people in a child's environment. For example, Rogers-Warren and Baer (1976) taught children to increase their sharing of play materials and praising of peer's art work. When the children reported correctly that they increased those behaviors when they had in fact done so, the researchers provided edibles and praise as reinforcers. In a test of the generalization of these behaviors across settings to a different classroom, it was found that sharing generalized, but praising did not. The authors hypothesized that this differential generalization was a function of the natural consequences that followed the performance of these behaviors. That is, sharing generalized because sharing and offers to share occasioned material exchange and interaction, but praising of peers facilitated less reciprocal interaction and payoff.

Modify Environments Supporting Maladaptive Behavior

Another potential concern with natural communities of reinforcement is that existing contingencies may function to increase and maintain behaviors that are considered maladaptive. For example, adolescent promiscuity is a status offense under our legal system and is, therefore, inappropriate. Nevertheless, sexual activity by adolescents often has positive consequences such as immediate gratification and peer acceptance. Such contingencies frequently are more potent than longer-term consequences such as pregnancy, delayed sanctions from parents such as losing privileges, or even intervention by juvenile authorities. Therefore, any researcher or practitioner who endeavors to employ natural communities of reinforcement should carefully assess the existent contingencies maintaining diverse behaviors. Many of these maintaining communities of reinforcement may be outside the control of an agent of behavior change, and may be supportive of maladaptive behavior. For example, the parents of an adolescent may want to recover more effective control over their child's behavior, for example, alcohol consumption. However, the natural contingencies of intoxication and peer support may be beyond ready influence by parents or any other adult.

A natural community of reinforcement might thus function to the disadvantage of the children whose behavior is under its control. For example, Solomon and Wahler (1973) showed that some peers of grade-school children provided consistent attention to classmates' disruptive behaviors. In a similar fashion, Sanson-Fisher and Jenkins (1978) and Buehler, Patterson, and Furniss (1966) found that adolescent delinquents attended positively to both the appropriate and inappropriate behaviors and conversation of their peers. Sanson-Fisher, Seymour, Montgomery, and Stokes (1978) documented similar effects, noting that the delinquents attended less frequently to their peers' prosocial conversations than they attended to their peers' antisocial comments. To establish the feasibility of using peers as part of an intervention, Sanson-Fisher et al. (1978) employed self-recording procedures to modify the content of conversation and to increase the attention given to prosocial comments during interactions. Thus, the authors attempted to accomplish a direct intervention in the naturally available reinforcement community. Similar reinforcement communities probably operate within many adolescent groups. It is likely that the most effective interventions will be those that can control the consequences provided by peers. Peer-mediated self-government systems are a promising technique for ensuring such intervention (Fixsen, Phillips, & Wolf, 1973). Fortunately, there are other examples of the positive use of peer consequences. Ragland, Kerr, and Strain (1981), for example, employed a peer-feedback procedure to increase positive social behaviors of withdrawn 10-year-old boys.

Another example of natural contingencies maintaining maladaptive behavior is when children who are capable of more sophisticated communication and social interaction, use gestures and mumbled words that are difficult to interpret. The function of these behaviors is that adults and other children tend to pause to try to determine the content of the communication. Such reactions might well have the effect of maintaining these behaviors because they are reinforcing consequences.

If these normal consequences can be prevented from occurring, the child may need to engage in clearer and more appropriate verbalizations, which also have natural consequences that may function as a natural reinforcement community. A documented example of this technique of modifying the natural consequences was provided by Horner (1971). A 5-year-old retarded boy usually walked on crutches in one setting and was taken in a wheelchair everywhere else. As an intervention procedure, staff refrained from assistance in other settings, whereupon the child soon walked using crutches in all of his environments.

Recruit Natural Communities of Reinforcement

A natural community of reinforcement for particular behaviors might not always be readily available and active, ready to entrap unsuspecting behaviors of suitable frequency that come within its operating environment. Sometimes that natural community may be dormant but ready to work if the right environmental manipulations are accomplished. In this case, an active recruitment of a natural community of reinforcement may be effective in setting it into motion and capturing its activity.

For example, a child might learn to actively solicit and evoke praise from others for appropriate social behaviors. If the praise is a reinforcer, this evoked praise may contribute to the maintenance of behavior changes. That children can effectively recruit positive attention following appropriate behaviors has been demonstrated by Seymour and Stokes (1976), Stokes, Fowler, and Baer (1978), and Hrydowy, Stokes, and Martin (1984). In these studies, juvenile delinquents, preschoolers, and elementary school children were taught to improve their academic and work activities, to evaluate their own performance and to draw adults' attention to their behavior when the quality was high. Under these circumstances, adults who were unaware of the manipulations consistently provided positive consequences for the children's improved behavior.

When considering the role of natural communities of reinforcement, it is true that the generalization of behavior change may not be the major issue. Strictly speaking, taking advantage of a natural community of reinforcement may just be a matter of coming under the control of certain direct, albeit naturally occurring contingencies of reinforcement. As such, searching for and/or trapping natural communities of reinforcement may be productive and effective, but might not be conceptually clear examples of the programming of generalized behavior change. Nevertheless, taking advantage of a natural community of reinforcement is an operation that efficiently facilitates generalization and maintenance without having to intervene in every relevant environment and time. Thus, it should be considered as a loose technique of facilitating generalization. In either case, whether or not it is considered a legitimate programming strategy, it is still an important technique to consider in the development and maintenance of children's social behavior.

Train Diversely

Use Sufficient Stimulus Exemplars

Employing a range of training conditions is the guideline in programming generalization by training sufficient stimulus exemplars. This tactic has intuitive appeal. The environment is diverse and therefore a productive tactic in any behavior modification program would be to sample that variety in training, that is, to conduct the training in more than one relevant setting or set of training circumstances, in an endeavor to facilitate generalization of changes across various settings and stimuli.

The successful application of this technique would require that the practitioner have at least a plan that specifies the extent of generalization that is to be targeted. That is, is generalization across people the target? Is it across adults and children? What of generalization across settings? Which settings? How diverse are the settings? Perhaps all of these types of generalization are important, such as when the target is teaching an adolescent to engage in skilled conversation with different people in diverse settings? Given a thorough plan, the tactic recommended is to teach multiple examples of the behaviors on each dimension, such as talking to different people, and the use of skilled conversation in different settings. Sufficient exemplars is noted post hoc—that is, the program has taught enough examplars of stimuli at that point in training at which generalization across untrained examplars is demonstrated. Fortunately, the threshold of sufficiency has frequently been reached before every possible examplar has been trained and the behavior change agent exhausted. For example, Stokes, Baer, and Jackson (1974) showed that greetings by retarded children generalized across more than 20 staff members after training was conducted by 2 staff members. Adequate generalization was not exhibited after training by just 1 staff member.

Another example relating to the social behavior of children is the teaching of appropriate interactions through reinforcement of initiations and continuing verbalizations of children (see Walker, Greenwood, Hops, & Todd, 1979). If the children's behaviors are reinforced in a particular setting such as a playroom when certain toys are available (e.g., balls, trucks, dolls,) and the training is conducted in the presence of the same peers and the same adult teacher, the effects may be appropriate to that setting and those persons. However, after initial control has been obtained, it would probably be advantageous to conduct training sessions in other rooms, outside, on the playground with different peers on a rotating basis, and with different adults dispensing the reinforcers.

As with many other tactics of generalization programming, it may be best at the outset of any intervention program to bring the targetted behavior under the control of relatively well-defined contingencies in a more restricted environment. Then, as the program advances successfully, to expand the scope of the intervention to include the diversity of the multiple exemplars of stimulus conditions. The training exemplars should reflect the diversity along the dimension(s) of generalization desired. A careful balance needs to be maintained between teaching a few exemplars that are too diverse and not sampling sufficient diversity to facilitate the targeted generalization. If an error in programming is to be made, it is probably better to err by training too many related exemplars than by training too few.

Use Sufficient Response Exemplars

Like the training of sufficient stimulus exemplars, the training of multiple responses is a tactic used to program generalization across responses. Targetted behaviors can vary considerably, given varying conditions even within one environment. Therefore, it is recommended that more than one example of the same (or similar) behavior be incorporated into training, for example, conducting an appropriate conversation with a peer, which includes different content areas, the diversity of which might be reflected in the training. Another example would be the training of multiple instances of interpersonal problem-solving with adolescents and parents (Kifer, Lewis, Green, & Phillips, 1974; Robin, Kent, O'Leary, Foster, & Prinz, 1977). In a similar manner, Horner, Sprague, and Wilcox (1982) have described a response exemplars approach in general case programming that in training samples the variety of behaviors that constitute complex skills.

There are few documented examples of the successful employment of the use of sufficient response exemplars to facilitate generalization of children's social behavior. There are, however, numerous examples of the successful use of this technique, with such targets as imitation (e.g., Baer, Peterson, & Sherman, 1967; Steinman, 1970) instruction-following (Craighead, O'Leary, & Allen, 1973; Whitman, Zakaras, & Chardos,

1971), and language development (Guess & Baer, 1973; Rubin & Stolz, 1974).

Train Loosely

Train loosely may be considered a variation of the training of sufficient stimulus and response exemplars. In essence, it proposes that a little controlled chaos is more advantageous than carefully controlled order. Training is conducted under conditions in which some latitude is allowed as to the acceptable training conditions and the acceptable responses. Training loosely is a concept that is the reverse of frequently recommended research and practice. Instead of training occurring in a special laboratory room devoid of all or most distractions, the training may be conducted in a regular classroom where other children and activities are present. These more loosely structured environments are more similar to the typical environment to which a child often returns after special training, and so generalization is likely enhanced. Loose training may also be incorporated into a program in which generalization across behaviors is sought. Thus behaviors that are more-or-less appropriate to the training but are slight variations of the correct targeted behavior may be reinforced, or multiple appropriate behaviors may be taught concurrently, rather than one at a time in a serial fashion (see Schroeder & Baer, 1972).

This tactic of training loosely may be employed from the outset of a program, or may be incorporated later, in much the same manner as schedules of reinforcement are made intermittent following the development of behaviors on a continuous schedule. Probably the choice of early or late loose training is dependent on the ease with which the behaviors can be readily established in the loose conditions. It is recommended, however, that the least tightly controlled yet effective training environment be used.

In the area of social behavior, language training may be a target. The training might be conducted in individual sessions on the same days, with a group of children on other days, sometimes in one room without distractions, sometimes in the same room with other activities going on, sometimes changing environments, or conducting training at different desks on a different part of the same room. For example, Campbell and Stremel-Campbell (1982) employed a loose training strategy to facilitate generalization of language training. Language training sessions were conducted within the context of other academic and self-help training programs and allowed the children to initiate responses and respond to a broad range of naturally occurring stimuli. This training, which was unlike the frequent systematic standardization of language sessions, resulted in both the development of correct language forms taught and a generalized increase in those verbalizations during play. Hart and Risley (1975) in a similar natural approach to language training, used "incidental teaching." Instead of conducting training in controlled settings, they took advantage of natural student–teacher setting interactions (e.g., requests for play materials) to teach more complex language. During these procedures, the children showed increased use of unprompted compound sentences.

Use Indiscriminable Contingencies

By definition, reinforcement, punishment, and extinction work to effect systematic changes in behavior. Typically, the effect of these consequences are true in the environments where they operate and on the behaviors targeted, yet the effects of those consequences are not evident in other environments or with other behaviors. That is, the function of consequences is usually well discriminated, as the consequences of behavior are carefully restricted and presented only following those behaviors in those settings. The tactic of using indiscriminable contingencies may be considered as the consequences-equivalent of training loosely. The procedure of training loosely recommends less rigid control over stimulus conditions and behavior; the procedure of using indiscriminable contingencies recommends similarly that there be less rigid control over behavior consequences.

The most obvious example of the use of this technique is with the effects of intermittent schedules of reinforcement. It has been established that behaviors reinforced on an intermittent schedule compared to those reinforced on a continuous schedule will prove to be more durable. This outcome was demonstrated by Kazdin and Polster (1973), who showed that social interactions by two retarded persons could be maintained by either continuous or intermittent schedules of token reinforcement, but interaction with peers during a subsequent extinction condition was maintained only following intermittent reinforcement. An important recommendation, therefore, is that the schedule of maintaining consequences for children's social behavior should be programmed to be intermittent and hopefully indiscriminable by the subject prior to the program termination. This tactic is implicit in a practitioner's recommendation to parents that after a successful intervention on their children's playing together and sharing, that the parents provide similar consequences (e.g. a colorful sticker) every now and then, in an unpredictable fashion, when their children display these appropriate behaviors.

Similar manipulations were employed by Koegel and Rincover (1977) to reduce the discriminability of reinforcement schedules in a therapy setting and an extratherapy setting. Their subjects were autistic children. The targeted behaviors were imitation and instruction following. They demonstrated that behaviors in the extratherapy environment maintained for a greater number of trials following intermittent schedules of reinforcement (FR 5) than following continuous reinforcement of praise and candy. Furthermore, they found that the occasional presentation of the previous reinforcer noncontingently in the extratherapy setting after formal training was concluded led to excellent durability of the behavior changes.

Apparently, the reinforcer acquired the properties of a discriminative stimulus, and the real contingency was not being adequately discriminated by the children. The application of similar procedures with children's social behavior is relatively straightforward. If the target of a procedure is to develop cooperation between children, and then to facilitate the generalization of those changes across settings and time, then the recommended procedure would be to occasionally present the reinforcer of the cooperative play in the other targeted settings and during the passage of some time after the initial training. This reinforcer may be presented either contingent on the targeted behavior or independent of the behavior, but always in an unpredictable manner.

The occurrence of vicarious reinforcement operations are another example of possible indiscriminable contingencies. Kazdin (1973, 1977) demonstrated the effect that when praise is delivered to one child for appropriate behavior, other children's behavior may show a similar improvement, as if the praise was reinforcing the behavior performed by the nontarget child as well as the child whose behavior was directly reinforced. Here also, it may be that praise to the target child functions as a discriminative stimulus for the behavior of the nontarget child. Within the confines of the experimental study, the nontarget child never received any direct reinforcers. It may be possible, however, that the delivery of an occasional reinforcer (as in Koegel & Rincover, 1977) may be necessary in order to maintain the potency of the vicarious reinforcement effect over a long period of time.

The tactic based on this research would be to present positive consequences in the presence of other children, contingent on some children's appropriate social behavior. Fortunately, social behavior is never possible in the absence of peers, so one is forced to maintain practice consistent to this tactic. The fact that afterward there is not generalization across subjects suggests that this may not prove to be a widespread and reliable procedure. This may be true of many procedures, however, and an effective practitioner may need to try a number of techniques with any child before discovering those that are both functional and useful for an individual child.

There are other techniques that may make a contingency of reinforcement less discriminable to a child. The use of delayed reinforcement is one tactic. Fowler and Baer (1981) have provided an example of the systematic application of delayed reinforcement to facilitate generalization of children's social behavior. Behaviors targeted in that study included sharing play materials, playing cooperatively, and conversation with peers. Two classroom observation times were assessed: one early and one later in the preschool day. The children rehearsed the target behavior(s) at the beginning of the day and the teacher asked the child to perform the behavior in the classroom, without specifying the time during which the behavior should occur. During initial interventions, the teacher provided feedback and reinforcers (stickers, toys) following the first observation time. The children's behavior during that time increased systematically. However, there were no generalized changes displayed in the later period. In a subsequent delayed reinforcement condition, the feedback and reinforcement concerning behavior during the first observation period was delayed so that it occurred some time after the second observation period. As a result of these procedures, the children showed high levels of sharing, cooperation, and conversation in both the early and later observation periods, even though the feedback and reinforcers were entirely dependent on performance during the early observation time. Thus, the children generalized their behavior change across classroom activity times, acting as though the contingency operated throughout the days (i.e., apparently coming under the control of an indiscriminable contingency).

Similar indiscriminable contingencies may operate when a number of behaviors occasionally occur together prior to the presentation of a reinforcer or punisher contingent only on one of those behaviors. Pendergrass (1972) decreased the destructive behavior of a retarded child using a time-out from the positive environment during classroom play. The brief period of time-out followed inappropriate banging of toys and tearing of clothing and rugs. In addition to a decrease in the target behaviors, the data showed decreased touching, speaking to, and, responding to other person's initiations during play, as well as increased aggression toward the experimenters. Concomitant decreases in self-abusive behavior were also observed. This latter behavior frequently occurred at the same time as the destructive behavior which was subjected to the timeout contingency. In this example, when the behaviors occurring close together in time were followed by the punishing consequence contingent on only one of them, both decreased as if the behav-

ior–consequence contingency was not discriminable. Many social behaviors similarly occur together and so the child could readily come
under the control of the consequences dispensed for only one of a few of
those behaviors.

Reinforce Unprompted Generalization

Reinforcement, by definition, increases the probability of the behavior
that precedes those consequences. The reinforced behavior may be simple (e.g., waving to a friend) or it may be more complex and socially
sophisticated (e.g., conducting a skilled conversation for 10 minutes). In
either case, the behavior will come under control if followed by suitable
reinforcing consequences. A similar logic applies in the tactic of reinforcing unprompted generalization. If generalization itself is considered to
be an operant response class, then generalization, whenever it occurs,
may be reinforced, thereby increasing its occurrence. In this way, "to
generalize" may be considered the operant response to be reinforced.

Using the tactic of reinforcing unprompted generalization, or training
to generalize, the practitioner might reinforce the display of skills in new
situations without prompting, or alternatively, reinforce the absence of
certain maladaptive behaviors across settings when there are no other
training contingencies operating there.

A variant of these procedures is to reinforce skills in novel situations
or to reinforce novel behavior in the same situation in which training
was conducted, whenever such generalized behavior changes are displayed.

Incorporate Functional Mediators

Use Common Physical Stimuli

Whenever a behavior is followed by certain controlling consequences
in a certain environment, that environment and the stimuli present in
that environment may acquire the function of reliably evoking the behavior that is typically followed by reinforcing or punishing consequences. This process is known as *discrimination,* and the antecedent
stimuli that have some control over the performance of the behavior are
called *discriminative stimuli.* The generalization programming technique
of employing common stimuli uses such discrimination as a means to
enhance generalization. In this tactic, the stimuli that reliably function as
discriminative stimuli are deliberately employed by ensuring their presence in different settings. The presence of these evoking stimuli across

environments might therefore function to facilitate the occurrence of the targeted behavior across the various environments.

The choice of stimuli to draft for such a purpose may be guided by some general recommendations. First, salience of the controlling stimuli is an important variable. There are many environmental stimuli present in both training and generalization settings, e.g., tables, chairs, lights, clocks, books, toys, adults, and peers. However, they may not all function as discriminative stimuli. The mere presence of the same stimulus in different environments is not a guarantee that the stimulus will function as a discriminative stimulus controlling behavior in both settings. Therefore, the best choices for functional common stimuli are those environmental events that are more obvious (e.g., some play materials, some peers).

To be maximally effective, the common controlling stimulus should be carefully integrated into the training procedures so that it can acquire a discriminative stimulus function. There are no guarantees that if a stimulus is present in a training and a generalization environment that it will therefore control responding in the generalization environment. The typical discrimination training procedures should operate—that is, reinforce the target behavior in the presence of that stimulus, but not in its absence. In fact, it might be best to test for a discriminative function in training prior to expecting generalization to be exhibited under that stimulus' control in the generalization environment. Unfortunately, if a stimulus functions as a discriminative stimulus in the training setting, that is not a guarantee that it will act as a controlling discriminative stimulus in a generalization environment, but it may. The successful use of controlling common stimuli is not well documented as a general effect, and examples of the control of social behavior are few.

One example of the use of common physical stimuli was described by Rincover and Koegel (1975). Working with autistic children learning to imitate a behavior modelled by an adult, they found that some children failed to generalize across settings. That is, behaviors reliably performed in training were not displayed during a transfer test with a stranger in a different setting. Generalized behavior changes occurred, however, when a controlling stimulus that was functional in training was added systematically to the generalization setting. These discriminative stimuli included the presence of the training table and chairs in the generalization setting and gestures by the stranger that were the same as those made by the original trainer.

Stimulus control over the display of generalization was also noted by Marholin and Steinman (1977) in their research with 10- to 12-year-old children in a special education classroom. In a teacher's presence, on-task behavior and the number of work problems completed increased using a token system with free time as reinforcer. When the teacher was absent from the room, performance varied according to the experimental condition. When the teacher had reinforced accuracy and rate of performance, on-task and number of correct problems was superior than when on-task behavior only was reinforced. In this study, reinforcement of work output enhanced the discriminative properties of the academic materials, which became salient, controlling generalization to improved performance to times when the teacher was not present in the classroom.

The stimuli present in training that develop discriminative stimulus function will vary. They may be an idiosyncratic movement in training or the presence of a table and chairs (e.g., Rincover & Koegel, 1975); they may be the presence of certain work materials (e.g., Marholin & Steinman, 1977); or they may be something associated with reinforcer delivery (e.g., Redd, 1970). Redd (1970) taught retarded boys to engage in cooperative play. He then tested to see whether the increased cooperative play generalized to a different playroom. The data showed that when the adult who had dispensed reinforcers (praise and candy) entered the generalization setting, there was an increase in cooperative play. This generalization occurred even if the training adult entered the room with an adult who had provided reinforcers noncontingently in the training setting. The properties of the controlling stimulus, however, were multifaceted. The training adult only controlled cooperative play if he was carrying a cup in which the reinforcer was held, even though he never dispensed the reinforcer in the generalization setting. For some subjects, the reinforcer cup by itself was not the discriminative stimulus, though, because when the cup was carried by the noncontingent adult, control over cooperative play was not demonstrated. With other subjects, any adult who entered the playroom carrying the cup served as a discriminative stimulus controlling cooperative play. Thus, the generalization of cooperative play was controlled by the salient common stimuli of the reinforcer cup.

A useful training tactic, therefore, would be to make physical stimuli in training closely associated with reinforcer delivery. The ideal stimuli would be those that are obvious, small, and readily transported across environments. These stimuli may be first presented in training and then transported as common stimuli (e.g., reinforcer cup) or they may be stimuli that are naturally occurring, prominent, or functional in generalization environments and may be readily incorporated into the training manipulations. A common stimulus does not need to be already present in both the training and generalization settings. Any stimulus may be introduced into training and generalization environments.

Use Common Social Stimuli

Common stimuli that control generalization because of their discriminative function may be social in nature. A most appropriate target for a common stimulus is any stimulus normally and frequently present in the many settings to which generalization is desired. Peers may be particularly suitable choices as common stimuli to control the generalization of children's social behavior because they are both the stimuli common to both settings and the subjects who are targeted for increased social interactions. Thus, if peers are not present and involved in an important fashion in training, they may be so introduced, thereby acquiring discriminative function.

An example of the use of peers as common stimuli controlling generalization across settings was the study by Johnston and Johnston (1972). Two 8-year-old girls were trained to monitor their peers' correct speech articulation. Articulation was then examined during an activity in which correct articulation was not reinforced. During this assessment of generalization, the peer involved in training was present on some occasions, and a new child previously uninvolved in the procedures was present on other occasions. Stimulus generalization was displayed. The subjects monitored the peers' sounds in the generalization activity period, even when they did not receive reinforcers for doing so. Furthermore, articulation by the monitored child also was controlled in this condition. These effects operated only for the children who had participated in training and not for the uninvolved peer. Thus, the peers functioned as common social stimuli who facilitated the generalization of correct articulation across activity periods. Speech articulation was also targeted for modification by Bailey, Timbers, Phillips, and Wolf (1971). Predelinquent youth provided consequences within a token economy for their peers' correct articulation of sounds that previously had been a problem. Articulation changes were maintained over a period of 2 months. This was probably a function of the continuing presence of the peers, who were discriminative for correct articulation. It may, however, be partly a function of consequences provided informally by the peers, an effect that may be classified under the rubric of natural communities of reinforcement. These results are similar to those of Stokes and Baer (1976) and Stokes, Doud, Rowbury, and Baer (1978), who showed that when preschoolers with academic and behavior problems acted as peer-tutors for each other, they developed discriminative functions such that academic behavior generalized across settings when the peer-tutors were common social stimuli.

Another example of the use of common social stimuli might be the study by Strain et al. (1977). They showed that withdrawn children's social behavior reliably comes under the control of social stimuli (initiations) presented by their peers. Thus, the children's social behavior was reliably coming under the control of antecedent social stimuli. If these social stimuli were transferred across settings, generalization is likely to be enhanced.

It is apparent that common social stimuli may be incorporated into programs to develop children's social behavior. Significant peers and adults present in the child's natural settings may participate actively in training, either early in the training sequence or after initial skill development has occurred. As with any generalization programming strategy, there is no guarantee that an adult or peer who assumes a discriminative function in training will control generalized responding as well, but it may prove fruitful to try. For example, if a child is observed to exhibit social interaction problems with certain children, then a program involving instruction, role-playing, and reinforcement may successfully intervene with those behaviors with the peers present and participating in the training. Then, in the generalization settings, the peers are present, and they and the target child may be discriminative for each other's performance of the modified behaviors.

Use Self-Mediated Stimuli

The tactic of using self-mediated stimuli to promote generalization is a variant of the use of common stimuli. In self-mediated generalization, however, the stimulus controlling the occurrence of generalization is itself under the control of and carried by the subject. In this way, its presence in the generalization environment is assured as long as the subject transports and produces that stimulus at the appropriate time. That stimulus is then common to both the training and any number of generalization settings. Of course, if the mediating stimulus is to work effectively, a practitioner may need to provide the subject with a relevant history of training so that the mediator will develop a controlling function and will also be produced by the child at an appropriate time and place.

A common example of self-managed mediated stimuli to control behaviors across remote places and times is the use of small, salient, and easily transported stimuli such as written instructions, prompts, reminders, or even a string on the finger. Even though they are obviously common stimuli, they are different from the use of the aforementioned common stimuli because the stimuli are self-mediated, that is, carried by and under the control of the child, rather than arranged to be present or naturally present in both the training and the generalization environment.

The choice of a mediating stimulus is important. Language is a logical target as an important mediating stimulus for a number of reasons. It is generally a well-developed skill already in a subject's repertoire and often has a history that has given it some controlling function; it may be readily transported by a subject across diverse environments; and it may be produced conveniently with little effort. Self-instructional training is one example of the use of language in this way. O'Leary and Dubey (1979) suggested that the instructional content of a self-verbalization may function as a discriminative cue that facilitates the probability of the instructed behavior. Most of the self-instruction work in applied research has examined academic performance.

Bryant and Budd (1982), for example, modified the independent work of preschoolers by employing a modified version of Meichenbaum and Goodman's (1971) self-instruction training. Specifically, three preschool children who had learning problems were taught to verbalize task requirements, including attending to the task, describing the task, describing answers and tactics for completing the task, and acknowledging their own completion of the task. In the beginning of the training, a teacher modeled the task and verbalized the self-instructional steps. Then the child completed the task while the teacher verbalized the instruction. Then the child performed the task while the child self-instructed aloud as the teacher whispered the steps. Then the child continued the task while progressively making the self-instructions quieter, making only lip movements, and then self-instructing inaudibly while doing the task. In this way, the use of the controlling verbalization was systematically faded from external and overt sources to a covert, self-managed verbalization that may be produced to control performance in different settings.

The children in this study reliably learned to use the self-instructional procedure and showed generalized improvements in their academic performance in a regular classroom that was different from the training setting. Similar procedures could be applied to children's social behavior. Once the child has been taught the specific components of the skill, the generalization-programming, verbal-regulation components can be taught. That is, the child can learn to describe the behavior, evaluate ongoing performance, and provide appropriate evaluations of that performance. After learning to produce the verbalizations overtly, the verbalizations can be faded sytematically so that they are produced covertly. An additional set of contingencies might also be included to control the child's use of the covert verbalizations across settings. The schedule of these additional consequences may be thinned after the child is reliably showing appropriate behavior changes.

Another example of the use of self-mediated stimuli would be bringing children's behavior under the reliable control of their verbalizations and then using that verbal control to program the performance of certain behaviors across more remote places and across time. This is the area of correspondence training and generalized verbal control (Israel, 1978; Karlin & Rusch, 1982). The controlling function of children's language is often assumed and is depended on.

For example, a child is asked if she is going to "behave" herself during a visit to the dentist. An answer in the affirmative supposedly is a reliable predictor of the appropriate behavior she will display at that not-too-distant event. Yet, the child's honor is not always as important as that of a gentleman. Frequently, the child's verbalization has no consistent relationship to actual behavior, no matter how much adults might wish it so. The verbalization might increase and maintain simply as a function of the contingencies that operate on it immediately, rather than the contingencies or absence thereof for the matching or correspondence between the verbalization and the occurrence of the related behavior (Baer, Williams, Osnes, & Stokes, 1985). In order to develop the controlling function of children's verbalizations, a number of researchers have provided reinforcers to children contingent on the correspondence of verbal and nonverbal behavior. Subsequent to this correspondence training, the children reliably came under the control of their verbalizations (e.g., Baer, Osnes, & Stokes, 1983; Israel & O'Leary, 1973; Risley & Hart, 1968). For example, Williams and Stokes (1982) provided preschoolers with praise and tokens exchangeable later for trinkets if they said they were going to play with certain toys and in fact played with those designated toys during a play period following the verbalizations. After the children had some exposure to the contingencies for correspondence, a generalized verbal control was displayed, such that the teacher needed only to reinforce a verbalization by the child concerning play with a particular material and the child reliably performed that targeted behavior. It was interesting to note that after generalized verbal control was developed with toy play, this control did not spread to a social behavior: invitations to peers to play with the target child. Specific contingencies for correspondence were required to bring such invitations under control. In another study, however, invitations to peers were brought under generalized verbal control after providing a history of reinforcement for correspondence with toy play (Baer, Williams, Osnes, & Stokes, 1984).

Correspondence training has focused on other social behaviors such as sharing and praising peers (Rogers-Warren & Baer, 1976), conversation directed at peers by bilingual and developmentally delayed children (Osnes, Guevremont, & Stokes, in press), and choice of playmate and invitations to play (Guevremont, Osnes, & Stokes, in press.) The necessity of providing an appropriate history of correspondence training was documented by Guevremont et al. (in press), who showed that prior to any correspondence training, preschoolers did not come under the control of their reinforced verbalizations. However, after correspondence training was systematically introduced across diverse settings more remote in time from the verbalization, the children showed, among other generalized verbal controlling effects, reliable control of their home behavior as a function of a verbalization at a preschool that was met only with minimal acknowledgment.

Various manipulations falling under the general rubric of self-management or self-control procedures may also be relevant as tactics to program generalization through the use of self-mediated stimuli (O'Leary & Dubey, 1979; Rosenbaum & Drabman, 1979). For example, the use of self-recording in training may facilitate generalized behavior change because it is a skill readily transported and used (covertly or overtly) in different settings after any other formal intervention procedures have been discontinued. The use of self-management procedures such as self-assessment, self-recording, self-determination of consequences, and self-administration of consequences, individually or together, may contribute to the generalization of behavior changes (Glynn, Thomas, & Shee, 1973). Much of the research in this area has related to children's academic performance. For example, Kelley and Stokes (1984) examined the role of student goal setting in the performance of academic tasks by disadvantaged high-school dropouts. Contracting between the teacher and the adolescents was sufficient to increase the academic productivity of the students. However, this productivity decreased rapidly during subsequent baseline conditions. In contrast, if the students were able to set their own work performance standards in a contingency contract, productivity maintained well above the baseline levels.

CONCLUSION

Let us return now to Patricia's case study to evaluate the probability of effectiveness of the interventions in programming the generalization of her social behavior. A correspondence training procedure was planned to be implemented in both home and school setting. The psychologist hoped to introduce Pat's behavior to, and bring it under the control of, natural communities of reinforcement. The target behaviors were: riding the bus to school, talking to peers, playing nicely with and sharing with her brother, eating the majority of food on her plate at mealtime, and going to bed appropriately. Pat was to exhibit these behaviors without instructions, prompts, or cues. Considering the information presented in this chapter, what is the probability of successful generalization of Pat's behaviors?

The first thing to be considered when trying to take advantage of natural communities of reinforcement is the relevance of the behaviors being taught. Do they typically result in naturally occurring, pleasant social consequences? Bus riding is an activity which thrusts the rider into an environment populated by peers. It could potentially provide pleasant social consequences, i.e., greetings and conversation. Playing nicely with and sharing with John and talking to peers at school both have obvious social value and consequences, the first by a family member whose attention may be a potent reinforcer and the second by an almost unlimited number of people, the reinforcing function of whose attention may vary considerably from person to person. Mealtime is frequently a time during which many social behaviors occur, including conversation, smiling, and polite behaviors. Its social value can be high. Perhaps the only target behavior whose social consequence may be limited is that of going to bed appropriately. The consequence of this behavior may be a mere "Good night" followed by the person's isolation from other family members.

In evaluating the social relevance of Pat's target behaviors, most appear to potentially have many social consequences that may trap Pat in a natural community of reinforcement. It is obvious that Pat's exhibition of inappropriate behaviors in the five areas has already been trapped in a natural community of reinforcement which, in this case, reinforces maladaptive behavior. The careful teaching of systematic attending to and ignoring of Pat's behaviors will be a crucial component of the intervention the psychologist must teach the school personnel and family members. This training will complement the correspondence training procedure and will be an essential aid in shutting down the natural community that is currently reinforcing Pat's maladaptive behaviors.

The correspondence training procedure itself will arrange opportunities for Pat to recruit a possible natural community of reinforcement, attention from adults and peers. Therefore, the possibility of the generalization of Pat's social behavior appears to be strong this far into our evaluation of critical predisposing variables.

Our analysis now comes to an evaluation of the "train diversely" recommendation. Has Pat's psychologist programmed for generalization by using a variety of stimulus and response examplars? If a thorough plan consists of teaching examples of the behaviors on several dimensions of settings and people, it would seem that the program is continuing in the direction of success. Appropriate talk is a critical component of all Pat's target behaviors. Talk is targeted across an endless number of people in a diversity of settings—on the school bus, at school, and at home. This satisfies both the recommendation to train sufficient stimulus examplars (various people in at least three different settings with many different subsettings, i.e., classroom, playground, cafeteria) and to train sufficient response examplars (different kinds of appropriate talk, e.g., conversation, polite talk, and absence of crying, whining, and tantrumming).

Another recommendation in the "train diversely" area is to train loosely. Because the contingencies of natural environments, including public schools and homes, are seldom tightly controlled and consistently managed with scientific precision, the possibility of successful generalization in this area is strong. Pat's psychologist has naturally occurring contingency inconsistencies working as an advantage for her to increase the possibility of generalization. The psychologist's task in natural environments frequently is to teach enough skills to enough people to ensure that the result is enough controlled chaos to be effective for the client.

What about the recommendation to reinforce unprompted generalization? The use of this tactic is frequently hidden in the strategy used to teach a client effective management skills: Appropriate contingency management includes reinforcing unprompted generalization. Pat's psychologist can increase the likelihood of this occurring by training Pat's teachers, mother, and grandparents to be keen observers of Pat's behavior. By being good observers, these crucial contingency managers in Pat's environments may notice and attend to appropriate generalized effects of the intervention on other behaviors in Pat's repertoire. Because in all likelihood they will not observe and dispense reinforcement for all the unprompted, generalized effects, they may put Pat's appropriate behaviors on a powerful, intermittent schedule of reinforcement, which may itself help to increase the durability of the behavior changes. The strong possibility of the existence of this intermittent schedule suggest that Pat's intervention will also be under the control of indiscriminable contingencies, another recommended strategy to program generalization of children's social behavior.

The final recommendation was to incorporate the use of functional mediators when planning a behavior change procedure. Three kinds of mediators were discussed: common physical stimuli, common social stimuli, and self-mediated stimuli. Pat's psychologist has not systematically incorporated the use of common physical stimuli into Pat's intervention. Of course, there are physical stimuli which are common to all targeted settings (e.g., jewelry, school books). However, the possibility that any of these will function as discriminative stimuli is remote unless that possibility is carefully integrated into the overall behavior change plan for Pat. This also applies to the use of common social stimuli.

Most of the social stimuli present in each targetted setting are exclusively present in that setting only. For example, teachers are present only in the school setting, as are peers. Family members are present only in the home setting. Efforts to ensure the presence of common social stimuli would require the introduction of stimuli into the school and home environments which normally are not present in these environments.

Such a strategy would be plausible, and would perhaps even be recommended in Pat's case if it were not for the opportunity to use the third type of mediator, self-mediated stimuli. The intervention arranged by Pat's psychologist, correspondence training, is a self-mediated strategy that can easily be used across diverse settings. By using it with each separate target behavior concurrently, Pat will be acquiring a successful history of correspondence between what she says she will do and what she actually does. After this, her self-mediated verbalizations will have a greater probability of functioning as discriminative stimuli. The arrangement of the correspondence training was planned by the psychologist to include a thorough initial assessment of consequences which might function as reinforcers for Pat's newly displayed, appropriate correspondence behaviors. Without this crucial preliminary step, the intervention may be no more functional than her mother's instructions have been.

After retracing the psychologist's steps through the planning and intervention stages with attention given to factors that may affect the generalization of Pat's social behavior, it is apparent that the planned procedure includes many of the strategies recommended to promote generalization. Pat's targeted behaviors are likely to increase, appropriate responses by her family, peers, and teacher are likely to increase, and the negative reinforcement paradigm that appeared to be controlling reactions to her inappropriate behaviors is likely to be severely disrupted. The probability of durable effects is strong, based on a program intervention plan that endeavors to take advantage of natural communities of reinforcement, trains diversely, and incorporates functional mediators. Of course, program outcomes need to be assessed continuously and appropriate program adjustments made if needed.

REFERENCES

Altman, K. (1971). Effects of cooperative response acquisition on social behavior during free-play. *Journal of Experimental Child Psychology, 12,* 387–395.

Ayllon, T., & Azrin, N. H. (1968). *The token economy: A motivational system for therapy and rehabilitation.* New York: Appleton-Century-Crofts.

Baer, D. M., Peterson, R. F., & Sherman, J. A. (1967). The development of imitation by reinforcing behavior similarity to a model. *Journal of Experimental Analysis of Behavior, 10,* 405–416.

Baer, D. M., & Wolf, M. M. (1970). The entry into natural communities of reinforcement. In R. Ulrich, T. Stachnik, & J. Mabry (Eds.) *Control of human behavior: Vol. 11. From cure to prevention* (pp. 319–324). Glenview, IL: Scott, Foresman, and Co.

Baer, D. M., Wolf, M. M., & Risley, T. R. (1968). Some current dimensions of applied behavior analysis. *Journal of Applied Behavior Analysis, 1,* 91–97.

Baer, R. A., Osnes, P. G., & Stokes, T. F. (1983). Programming across setting generalization using delayed reinforcement of verbalizations. *Education and Treatment of Children, 6,* 379–388.

Baer, R. A., Williams, J. A., Osnes, P. G., & Stokes, T. F. (1984). Delayed reinforcement as an indiscriminable contingency in verbal/nonverbal correspondence training. *Journal of Applied Behavior Analysis 17,* 429–440.

Baer, R. A., Williams, J. A., Osnes, P. G., and Stokes, T. F. (1985). Generalized verbal control and correspondence training. *Behavior Modification, 9,* 477–489.

Bailey, J. S., Timbers, G. D., Phillips, E. L., & Wolf, M. M. (1971). Modification of articulation errors of predelinquents by their peers. *Journal of Applied Behavior Analysis, 4,* 265–281.

Barton, E. J., & Bevirt, J. (1981). Generalization of sharing across groups: Assessment of group composition with preschool children. *Behavior Modification, 5,* 503–522.

Bryant, L. E., & Budd, K. S. (1982). Self-instructional training to increase independent work performance in preschoolers. *Journal of Applied Behavior Analysis, 15,* 259–271.

Buehler, R. E., Patterson, G. R., & Furniss, J. M. (1966). The reinforcement of behavior in institutional settings. *Behavior Research and Therapy, 4,* 157–167.

Buell, J., Stoddard, P., Harris, F. R., & Baer, D. M. (1968). Collateral social development accompanying reinforcement of outdoor play in a preschool child. *Journal of Applied Behavior Analysis, 1,* 167–173.

Campbell, C. R., & Stremel-Campbell, K. (1982). Programming "loose training" as a strategy to facilitate language generalization. *Journal of Applied Behavior Analysis, 15,* 295–301.

Craighead, W. E., O'Leary, K. D., & Allen, J. S. (1973). Teaching and generalization of instruction-following in an "autistic" child. *Journal of Behavior Therapy and Experimental Psychiatry, 4,* 171–176.

Drabman, R. S., Hammer, D., & Rosenbaum, M. S. (1979). Assessing generalization in behavior modification with children: The generalization map. *Behavioral Assessment, 1,* 203–219.

Elder, J. P., Edelstein, B. A., & Narick, M. M. (1979). Adolescent psychiatric patients: Modifying aggressive behavior with social skills training. *Behavior Modification, 3,* 161–178.

Fixsen, D. L., Phillips, E. L., & Wolf, M. M. (1973). Achievement Place: Experiments in self-government with pre-delinquents. *Journal of Applied Behavior Analysis, 6,* 31–47.

Forehand, R., & Atkeson, B. M. (1977). Generality of treatment effects with parents as therapists: A review of assessment and implementation procedures. *Behavior Therapy, 8,* 575–593.

Fowler, S. A., & Baer, D. M. (1981). "Do I have to be good all day?" The timing of delayed reinforcement as a factor in generalization. *Journal of Applied Behavior Analysis, 14,* 13–24.

Glynn, E. L., Thomas, J. D., & Shee, S. M. (1973). Behavioral self-control of on-task behavior in an elementary classroom. *Journal of Applied Behavior Analysis, 6,* 105–113.

Guess, D. & Baer, D. M. (1973). Analysis of individual differences in generalization between receptive and productive language in retarded children. *Journal of Applied Behavior Analysis, 6,* 311–329.

Guevremont, D. C., Osnes, P. G., & Stokes, T. F. (in press). Preparation for effective self-regulation: The development of generalized verbal control. *Journal of Applied Behavior Analysis.*

Hake, D. F., & Olvera, D. (1978). Cooperation, competition, and related social phenomena. In A. C. Catania & T. A. Brigham (Eds), *Handbook of applied behavior analysis: Social and instructional processes* (pp. 208–245). NY: Irvington.

Hart, B., & Risley, T. R. (1975). Incidental teaching of language in the preschool. *Journal of Applied Behavior Analysis, 8,* 411–420.

Hendrickson, J. M., Strain, P. S., Tremblay A., & Shores, R. E. (1982). Interactions of behaviorally handicapped children: Functional effects of peer social initiations. *Behavior Modification, 6,* 323–353.

Hopkins, B. L. (1968). Effects of candy and social reinforcement, instructions, and reinforcement schedule learning on the modification and maintenance of smiling. *Journal of Applied Behavior Analysis, 1,* 121–129.

Horner, R. D. (1971). Establishing use of crutches by a mentally retarded spina bifida child. *Journal of Applied Behavior Analysis, 4,* 183–189.

Horner, R. H., Sprague, J. & Wilcox, B. (1982). Constructing general case programs for community activities. In B. Wilcox and T. Bellamy (Eds). *Design of high school for severely handicapped students.* Baltimore: Brookes.

Hrydowy, E. R., Stokes, T. F., & Martin, G. L. (1984). Training elementary students to prompt teacher praise. *Education and Treatment of Children, 7,* 99–108.

Israel, A. (1978). Some thoughts on correspondence between saying and doing. *Journal of Applied Behavior Analysis, 11,* 271–276.

Israel, A. C., & O'Leary, K. D. (1973). Developing correspondence between children's words and deeds. *Child Development, 44,* 575–581.

Johnston, J. M., & Johnston, G. T. (1972). Modification of consonant speech-sound articulation in young children. *Journal of Applied Behavior Analysis, 5,* 233–246.

Karlan, G. R., & Rusch, F. R. (1982). Correspondence between saying and doing: Some thoughts on defining correspondence and future directions for application. *Journal of Applied Behavior Analysis, 15,* 151–162.

Kazdin, A. E. (1973). The effect of vicarious reinforcement on attentive behavior in the classroom. *Journal of Applied Behavior Analysis, 6,* 71–78.

Kazdin, A. E. (1977). Vicarious reinforcement and direction of behavior change in the classroom. *Behavior Therapy, 8,* 57–63.

Kazdin, A. E., & Polster, R. (1973). Intermittent token reinforcement and response maintenance in extinction. *Behavior Therapy, 4,* 386–391.
Kelley, M. L., & Stokes, T. F. (1984). Student–teacher contracting with goal-setting for
maintenance. *Behavior Modification, 8,* 223–244.
Kifer, R. E., Lewis, M. A., Green, D. R., & Phillips, E. L. (1974). Training predelinquent
youths and their parents to negotiate conflict situations. *Journal of Applied Behavior
Analysis, 7,* 357–364.
Koegel, R. L., & Rincover, A. (1977). Research on the difference between generalization
and maintenance in extra-therapy responding. *Journal of Applied Behavior Analysis, 10,*
1–12.
Marholin, D., & Steinman, W. M. (1977). Stimulus control in the classroom as a function of
the behavior reinforced. *Journal of Applied Behavior Analysis, 10,* 465–478.
Meichenbaum, D. J., & Goodman, J. (1971). Training impulsive children to talk to them-
selves: A means of developing self-control. *Journal of Abnormal Psychology, 77,* 115–126.
O'Leary, S. G., & Dubey, D. R. (1979). Applications of self-control procedures by children:
A review. *Journal of Applied Behavior Analysis, 12,* 449–464.
Osnes, P. G., Guevremont, D. C., and Stokes, T. F. (In press). "If I say I'll talk more, then I
will": Correspondence training to increase peer directed talk by socially withdrawn
children. *Behavior Modification.*
Paine, S. C., Hops, H., Walker, H. M., Greenwood, C. R., Fleischman, D. H., & Guild, J.
J. (1982). Repeated treatment effects: A study of maintaining behavior change in
socially withdrawn children. *Behavior Modification, 6,* 171–199.
Pendergrass, V. E. (1972). Timeout from positive reinforcement following persistent high-
rate behavior in retardates. *Journal of Applied Behavior Analysis, 5,* 85–91.
Ragland, E. V., Kerr, M. M., & Strain, P. S. (1981). Social play of withdrawn children.
Behavior Modification, 5, 347–359.
Redd, W. H. (1970). Generalization of adult's stimulus control of children's behavior.
Journal of Experimental Child Psychology, 9, 286–296.
Rincover, A., & Koegel, R. L. (1975). Setting generality and stimulus control in autistic
children. *Journal of Applied Behavior Analysis, 8,* 235–246.
Risley, T. R., & Hart, B. (1968). Developing correspondence between the nonverbal and
verbal behavior of preschool children. *Journal of Applied Behavior Analysis, 1,* 267–281.
Robin, A. L., Kent, R. N., O'Leary, K. D., Foster, S. L., & Prinz, R. J. (1977). An approach
to teaching parents and adolescents problem-solving communications skills: A preliminary report. *Behavior Therapy, 8,* 639–643.
Rogers-Warren, A., & Baer, D. M. (1976). Correspondence between saying and doing:
Teaching children to share and praise. *Journal of Applied Behavior Analysis, 9,* 335–354.
Rosenbaum, M. S., & Drabman, R. S. (1979). Self-control training in the classroom: A
review and critique. *Journal of Applied Behavior Analysis, 12,* 467–485.
Rubin, B. & Stolz, S. B. (1974). Generalization of self-referent speech established in a
retarded adolescent by operant procedures. *Behavior Therapy, 5,* 92–106.
Sanson-Fisher, B., & Jenkins, H. J. (1978). Interaction patterns between inmates and staff
in a maximum security institution for delinquents. *Behavior Therapy, 9,* 703–716.
Sanson-Fisher, B., Seymour, F. W., Montgomery, W., & Stokes, T. F. (1978). Modifying
delinquents' conversation using token reinforcement of self-recorded behavior. *Journal of Behavior Therapy and Experimental Psychiatry, 9,* 163–168.
Schroeder, G. L., & Baer, D. M. (1972). Effects of concurrent and serial training on generalized vocal imitation in retarded children. *Developmental Psychology, 6,* 293–301.
Seymour, F. W., & Stokes, T. F. (1976). Self-recording in training girls in increase work and

evoke staff praise in an institution for offenders. *Journal of Applied Behavior Analysis, 9*, 41–54.

Solomon, R. W., & Wahler, R. G. (1973). Peer reinforcement control of classroom problem behavior. *Journal of Applied Behavior Analysis, 6*, 49–56.

Steinman, W. M. (1970). Generalization and the discrimination hypothesis. *Journal of Experimental Child Psychology, 10*, 79–99a.

Stokes, T. F. (1985). Contingency Management. In A. S. Bellack and M. Hersen (Eds). *Dictionary of Behavior Therapy Techniques* (pp 74–78). Elmsford, N.Y.: Pergamon.

Stokes, T. F., & Baer, D. M. (1976). Preschool peers as mutual generalization–facilitation agents. *Behavior Therapy, 7*, 549–556.

Stokes, T. F., & Baer, D. M. (1977). An implicit technology of generalization. *Journal of Applied Behavior Analysis, 19*, 349–367.

Stokes, T. F., Baer, D. M., & Jackson, R. (1974). Programming the generalization of a greeting response in four retarded children. *Journal of Applied Behavior Analysis, 7*, 599–610.

Stokes, T. F., Doud, C. L., Rowbury, T. G., & Baer, D. M. (1978). Peer facilitation of generalization in a preschool classroom. *Journal of Abnormal Child Psychology, 6*, 203–209.

Stokes, T. F., Fowler, S. A., & Baer, D. M. (1978). Training preschool children to recruit natural communities of reinforcement. *Journal of Applied Behavior Analysis, 11*, 285–303.

Strain, P. S., Shores, R. E., & Timm, M. A. (1977). Effects of peer social initiations on the behavior of withdrawn preschool children. *Journal of Applied Behavior Analysis, 10*, 289–298.

Walker, H. M., Greenwood, C. R., Hops, H., & Todd, N. M. (1979). Differential effects of reinforcing topographic components of social interaction: Analysis and direct replication. *Behavior Modification, 3*, 291–321.

Whitman, T. L., Zakaras, M., & Chardos, S. (1971). Effects of reinforcement and guidance procedures on instruction-following behavior of severely retarded children. *Journal of Applied Behavior Analysis, 4*, 282–290.

Williams, J. A., & Stokes, T. F. (1982). Some parameters of correspondence training and generalized verbal control. *Child and Family Behavior Therapy, 4*, 11–32.

INDEX

A

Abused children, coercive behavior and, 51, 76

Academic achievement
social skills training and, 376, 395
sociometrics and, 254–256

ACTH, social development and, 30

Adaptability, coercive behavior and, 59

Adaptation, social development and, 10
infancy, 30
interpersonal influences, 34
interpersonal stages, 29
social inertia, 39

Adaptive behavior, social competence assessment and, 146, 147

Adolescence
coercive behavior, 50
criminal parents, 55–57
genetic differences, 58
matching process, 79–83
generalization programming, 415, 416, 420, 421, 423
preventive mental health skills, 290, 291, 321
prosocial behavior modification
intervention, 352, 353
reinforcement, 341
social development
interpersonal bias, 36
ontogeny, 19–21
social inertia, 38–40
social network, 44
stages, 13, 28
social skills training, 374
sociometrics, 221, 236, 244

Adoption, preventive mental health skills and, 317

Age, social development stages and, 11–13

Aggression, *see* Aggressiveness

Aggressiveness
coercive behavior and, 49, 50
abused children, 53
coercion training, 62, 63, 65
delinquent adolescents, 57
genetic differences, 58
inconsistency training, 65
matching process, 76
modeling, 60–62
parental punishment, 53–55
generalization programming and, 408, 410, 411, 415, 428
naturalistic observations and, 202, 203, 205
development, 204
qualitative measures, 188, 193–195
rate of interaction, 185
sex differences, 204
peer relations and, 108
preventive mental health skills and, 289–291, 294, 296
contingent reinforcement, 308–310
fantasy, 299, 301
intervention, 316, 319–321
IQ, 295
modeling, 305
parent training, 311
prosocial behavior modification and, 331, 332, 334
assessment, 365
behavioral rehearsal, 337, 338
intervention, 352
picture-cue training, 347
pragmatic aspects, 357
reinforcement, 339